ANTHROPOLOGICAL PAPERS

MUSEUM OF ANTHROPOLOGY, UNIVERSITY OF MICHIGAN

NO. 59

AN ANALYSIS OF EFFIGY MOUND COMPLEXES IN WISCONSIN

BY
WILLIAM M. HURLEY

ANN ARBOR, MICHIGAN
1975

ISBN (print): 978-1-949098-02-0
ISBN (ebook): 978-1-951519-12-4

Browse all of our books at
sites.lsa.umich.edu/archaeology-books.

Order our books from the University of Michigan
Press at www.press.umich.edu.

For permissions, questions, or manuscript queries,
contact Museum publications by email at umma-
pubs@umich.edu or visit the Museum website at
lsa.umich.edu/ummaa.

This book is dedicated

to the memory of

Margaret P. Hurley

CONTENTS

Figures v
Tables vii
Plates ix

Acknowledgments xi

I. Introduction 1

II. Previous Effigy Mound Research 11
1836-1919 12
1919-1956 18

III. Bigelow Site 47-Pt-29-1, 47-Pt-29-2:
Location, Description, and Excavation Procedure 39

IV. Bigelow Site Material Culture 83

V. Bigelow Site Analyses 115
Analytical Procedures 118
Internal Comparisons 129

VI. Sanders Sites 47-Wp-26, 47-Wp-69, 47-Wp-70:
Location, Description, and Excavation Procedure 167

VII. Material Culture From the Sanders Sites 213

VIII. Sanders Sites Analyses 289

IX. The Effigy Mound Tradition 353
Early Effigy Mound (A.D. 300 to A.D. 700) 355
Middle Effigy Mound (A.D. 700 to A.D. 1100) 365
Late Effigy Mound (A.D. 1100 to A.D. 1642) 390

Bibliography 401

Plates 415

FIGURES

1. Some sites and locations mentioned in the text 2
2. Map of Wisconsin showing the Tension Zone and site locations 12
3. 47-Pt-29; hydrology 38
4. Plan view of 47-Pt-29-1 and 47-Pt-29-2 41
5. Plan view of 47-Pt-29-2 43
6. Mound N profiles 47
7. Mound L profiles 50
8. Area P profile 53
9. Mound S profiles 55
10. Mound B profiles 57
11. Mound B Burials 58
12. Mound A profiles (Sec. 1) 63
13. Mound A profiles (Sec. 1), cont. 63
14. Mound A profiles (Sec. 2) 65
15. Mound A Burials 66
16. Mound Q profiles 67
17a. 47-Pt-29-2 soil distributions (A.D. 670-1850). 71
17b. 47-Pt-29-2 soil distributions (A.D. 1850-1966). 71
18. Mound 13 excavation plan 73
19. Mound 13 profile 74
20. 47-Pt-29-1 plan view 76
21. Mound 4 profiles 78
22. Mound 9 profile and Burial 3 80
23. Mound 9, Burials 3 and 4 81
24. $z\begin{smallmatrix}s\\s\end{smallmatrix}$; $s\begin{smallmatrix}z\\z\end{smallmatrix}$; $Z\begin{smallmatrix}s & \begin{smallmatrix}z\\z\end{smallmatrix}\\ s & \begin{smallmatrix}z\\z\end{smallmatrix}\end{smallmatrix}$ and $S\begin{smallmatrix}z & \begin{smallmatrix}s\\s\end{smallmatrix}\\ z & \begin{smallmatrix}s\\s\end{smallmatrix}\end{smallmatrix}$ cords. 87
25. $Z\begin{smallmatrix}s\\s\\s\end{smallmatrix}$; $Z\begin{smallmatrix}s & \begin{smallmatrix}z\\z\end{smallmatrix}\\ s & \begin{smallmatrix}z\\z\end{smallmatrix}\end{smallmatrix}$/ss; $Z\begin{smallmatrix}\begin{smallmatrix}s\\s\end{smallmatrix}\\ \begin{smallmatrix}z\\z\end{smallmatrix}\end{smallmatrix}$ and $S\begin{smallmatrix}z & \begin{smallmatrix}s\\s\end{smallmatrix}\\ z & \begin{smallmatrix}s\\s\end{smallmatrix}\end{smallmatrix}$/zz cords 89
26. $Z\begin{smallmatrix}s & \begin{smallmatrix}z\\z\end{smallmatrix}\\ s & \begin{smallmatrix}z\\z\end{smallmatrix}\end{smallmatrix}$ multiple stick cord-wrapped stick 90
27. $Z\begin{smallmatrix}s & \begin{smallmatrix}z\\z\end{smallmatrix}\\ s & \begin{smallmatrix}s\\s\end{smallmatrix}\end{smallmatrix}$; $Z\begin{smallmatrix}S\begin{smallmatrix}z & \begin{smallmatrix}s\\s\end{smallmatrix}\\ z & \begin{smallmatrix}s\\s\end{smallmatrix}\end{smallmatrix}\\ S\begin{smallmatrix}z & \begin{smallmatrix}s\\s\end{smallmatrix}\\ z & \begin{smallmatrix}s\\s\end{smallmatrix}\end{smallmatrix}\end{smallmatrix}$; cord over wood and cord over cord 91
28. Bigelow Site C-14 dates 117
29. Histogram of traits used in computer analysis of Bigelow ceramics . . 124
30. Scattergram of principal component analysis of Bigelow ceramics . . . 128
31. Plan view of 47-Wp-26 169
32. Mound 11 and Mound 12 profiles 173
33. Mound 4 profiles 176
34. Mound 1 profiles 177
35. Mound 3 profiles 179
36. Area between Mound 2 and Mound 3 profiles 180
37. Bisequal profile 182
38. Mound 19 profile 184
39. Mound 23 profile 186

40. Mound 28 profiles 188
41. Plan of "House 1" 190
42. Plan of House 2 and House 3 195
43. Cross-sections of House 2 and House 3 201
44. 47-Wp-26 soil distribution 203
45. 47-Wp-70 plan view 206
46. 47-Wp-70 plan view at two feet below surface 209
47. 47-Wp-70, House 1 211
48. Double oblique twining 232
49. Double twining; Spaced weft-twining with simple linked warps; Paired spaced weft-twining with fixed knotted loop warps; and Spaced weft-twining with spaced warps. 233
50. Spaced weft-twining with spaced warps; Spaced weft-twining with paired spaced warps; and Spaced weft-twining with tripled spaced warps. 234
51. Spaced weft-twining with spaced warps; Spaced weft-twining with paired spaced warps; Paired spaced weft-twining with spaced warps; and Paired spaced weft-twining with paired spaced warps. 235
52. Spaced weft-twining with spaced warps and accessory cords 236
53. Spaced weft-twining with paired spaced warps and accessory cords; and Spaced oblique weft-twining with spaced warps 237
54. Spaced oblique weft-twining with spaced warps and accessory cords; and Spaced horizontal and oblique weft-twining with spaced warps. . . 239
55. Spaced horizontal and oblique weft-twining with spaced warps; and Spaced horizontal and oblique weft-twining with paired spaced warps . 241
56. Spaced horizontal and oblique weft-twining with spaced warps and fixed knotted loops; and Spaced horizontal and oblique weft-twining with spaced warps and accessory cords 242
57. Spaced warp-twining on single spaced weft; Spaced warp-twining with suspended cords; Spaced warp-twining with fixed cords; and Spaced warp-twining with single spaced wefts and fixed cords. 243
58. Spaced horizontal and oblique weft-twining with spaced warps and fixed knotted loops. 257
59. Sanders Site 1 C-14 dates 291
60. Sanders Site 3 C-14 dates 292
61. Histogram of traits used in computer analysis of Sanders ceramics . . . 293
62. Scattergram of principal component analysis of Sanders ceramics . . . 295
63. Scattergram of principal component analysis of Bigelow and Sanders ceramics 373

TABLES

1. First principal component analysis of Bigelow ceramics 125
2. Second principal component analysis of Bigelow ceramics, in ranked order 126
3. Distribution of ceramics, lithic and Historic artifacts in Mound A . . . 130
4. Distribution of ceramics, lithic and Historic artifacts in Mound S . . . 131
5. Distribution of ceramics, lithic and Historic artifacts in Mound L . . . 132
6. Distribution of ceramics, lithic and Historic artifacts in Mound 4 . . . 135
7. Distribution of ceramics, lithic and Historic artifacts in Mound B . . . 137
8. Distribution of ceramics, lithic and Historic artifacts in Mound R . . . 139
9. Distribution of ceramics, lithic and Historic artifacts in Mound 13 . . 145
10. Distribution of ceramics, lithic and Historic artifacts in Mound M . . . 147

11. Distribution of ceramics, lithic and Historic artifacts in Area K 149
12. Distribution of ceramics, lithic and Historic artifacts in forest area . . 151
13. Distribution of ceramics, lithic and Historic artifacts in grass area . . . 152
14. Distribution of ceramics according to soil horizons and cords . . . 154-155
15. Distribution of s $\frac{z}{z}$ and z $\frac{s}{s}$ cord-marked body sherds according to natural soils horizons 156
16. Frequency of rims and associated body sherds from 47-Pt-29 157
17. Rim sherds, decorated body sherds, and body sherds according to chronological order and Mound or non-Mound distributions 158
18. Lithic artifacts according to chronological order and Mound or non-Mound distributions 161
19. Dimensions of projectile points from 47-Wp-26 and 47-Wp-70 (in mm) 269
20. Principal component analysis of Sanders ceramics 294
21. Distribution of ceramic and lithic artifacts from Mound 28 296
22. Distribution of ceramic and lithic artifacts from Mound 25 298
23. Distribution of ceramic and lithic artifacts from Mound 23 299
24. Distribution of ceramic and lithic artifacts from Mound 19 301
25. Distribution of ceramic and lithic artifacts from Mound 17 302
26. Distribution of ceramic and lithic artifacts from Mound 3 304
27. Distribution of ceramic and lithic artifacts from Mound 2 305
28. Distribution of ceramic and lithic artifacts from Mound 1 307
29. Distribution of ceramic and lithic artifacts from Mound 4 309
30. Distribution of ceramic and lithic artifacts from Mound 11 310
31. Distribution of ceramic and lithic artifacts from Mound 12 311
32. Distribution of ceramic and lithic artifacts from Mound 13 312
33. Distribution of ceramic and lithic artifacts from Area 9 314
34. Distribution of ceramic and lithic artifacts in soil body $\frac{1}{A}$ 317
35. Distribution of ceramic and lithic artifacts in soil body $\frac{4}{A}$ 320-321
36. Distribution of ceramics: Houses (47-Wp-26) 325
37. Distribution of lithic and copper artifacts: Houses (47-Wp-26) 326
38. Distribution of ceramic artifacts: 47-Wp-70 (by levels) 335
39. Distribution of ceramic and lithic artifacts: 47-Wp-70 (by features) . . 336
40. Distribution of lithic artifacts: 47-Wp-70 (by levels) 338
41. Distribution of s $\frac{z}{z}$ and z $\frac{s}{s}$ cord-marked body sherds according to natural soils horizons: 47-Wp-26 340
42. Rim sherds, decorated body sherds, and body sherds in chronological order 342
43. Lithic and copper artifacts: 47-Wp-26 and 47-Wp-70, in chronological order 343
44. Frequency of rims and associated body sherds from 47-Wp-26 and 47-Wp-70 346
45. Principal component analysis: 47-Wp-29 and 47-Wp-26 (539 specimens). 372
46. Multivariate analysis of variance: ceramics from 47-Pt-29 and 47-Wp-26 373
47. Multiple group discriminant analysis 374
48. Radiocarbon dates of Hopewellian, Effigy Mound, and Mississippian manifestations in the Effigy Mound region 379-384

PLATES

1. Mound B, Burial 7
2. Mound A, Section 1, North and East walls
3. Mound R, Burial 1
4. Madison Cord Impressed; Madison Folded Lip; and Madison Fabric Impressed
5. Madison Cord Impressed; Madison Folded Lip; and Madison Fabric Impressed
6. Madison Fabric Impressed and Madison Cord Impressed
7. Reconstructed Madison Cord Impressed vessel
8. Madison Plain
9. Reconstructed Madison Plain vessel
10. Madison Punctated; Madison Fabric Impressed; and Madison Cord Impressed
11. Aztalan Collared; Hahn Cord Impressed; and Point Sauble Collared
12. Unclassified rim sherd; Madison Fabric Impressed, trailed and incised sherds
13. Sanders Triangular, Triangular, and Corner Notched projectile points; End scrapers; conventional gunflint, and blade core
14. Sanders Triangular and Triangular projectile points; and drill
15. Deer antler flaker; cut bone; polishing stone; pecked stone; and pecked hammerstone
16. Sisters Creek Punctated; Rocker Stamped, Dane Incised, interior cord rolled, and interior brushed ceramics
17. Dane Incised rim and body sherds
18. Dane Incised rim sherds
19. Dane Incised rim and body sherds
20. Shorewood Cord Roughened rim sherds; Dane Incised variety fingernail impressed rim and body sherds
21. Dane Incised variety fingernail impressed and Shorewood Cord Roughened rim sherds
22. Madison Cord Impressed and Madison Fabric Impressed rim sherds
23. Madison Cord Impressed and Madison Fabric Impressed rim sherds
24. Madison Cord Impressed and Madison Fabric Impressed rim sherds
25. Madison Folded Lip rim sherds
26. Madison Cord Impressed, Madison Fabric Impressed, and Madison Folded Lip rim sherds
27. Madison Plain and Madison Plain variety punctated rim sherds
28. Reconstructed Madison Plain vessel
29. Madison Punctated rim and body sherds
30. Shorewood Cord Roughened and Madison Punctated rim sherds
31. Partially reconstructed Madison Punctated vessel
32. Leland Cord-marked rim sherds
33. Leland Cord-marked, Grand River Trailed, and Grand River Plain sherds
34. Aztalan Collared, Hahn Cord Impressed, and Point Sauble Collared rim sherds
35. Point Sauble Collared rim sherd
36. Heins Creek Corded Stamped rim and body sherds; Leland Cord-marked rim sherds; child's pot; elbow pipe
37. Grand River Trailed rim and body sherds; and Grand River Plain rim sherds
38. Partially reconstructed Leland Cord-marked and Grand River Plain vessels

39. Side Notched and Corner Notched, Waubesa Contracting Stem, and Durst Stemmed projectile points
40. Durst Stemmed, Sanders Triangular, and Triangular projectile points; and scrapers
41. Waubesa Contracting Stem, Madison Side Notched, and Triangular projectile points; diminutive scraper; and worked burin spall
42. Diminutive scrapers; drills; and graver
43. Celt, gorget; and adzes
44. Ceramic bead and copper artifacts
45. Windrow Cord Impressed

ACKNOWLEDGMENTS

The field and laboratory research conducted on the Wisconsin Effigy Mound tradition was supported by a University of Wisconsin School of Graduate Studies grant and by the National Science Foundation, Social Sciences Division, grant GS-1141 which were both awarded to Dr. David A. Baerreis of the University of Wisconsin. I am particularly indebted to Dr. Baerreis, of the Department of Anthropology, who has served as my adviser, project director, and chairman of my doctoral committee. He was unstinting in his encouragement during all phases of the Effigy Mound research and he provided constructive criticism of the dissertation.

The typing of the original thesis was supported by a Humanities and Social Sciences Grant from the University of Toronto. This edited version was supported by a grant from the Canada Council (S72-0274). This book has been published with the help of a grant from the Social Science Research Council of Canada, using funds provided by the Canada Council. I wish to acknowledge their awards and express my sincere gratitude for their financial aid.

The success of any archaeological excavation depends on the preliminary survey and testing operations and I wish to express my gratitude to the 1965 crew of Knut Helskog and Peter Storck and for the assistance of Guy Gibbon at the Sanders site. The 1966 field crew was supervised by Lynn Berry, Brad Hertel, and my wife Mary Hurley. My assistant field director was Frederick Lange who had worked for me in 1964 in the Kickapoo River Valley. Fred has a remarkably warm outlook on life and archaeology and he transmitted this feeling to me and the crew and he made contact with *Toxicodendron radicans* more bearable. His gift of friendship, unstinting work, and scientific insights cannot be properly acknowledged. The crew during the 1966 field season rendered valuable assistance in the field and, more importantly, in the field laboratory at nights and on weekends. I am most grateful to my fellow crew members, Terry and Virginia Prewitt, James Stokes, Robert Hockmayr, Linda James, Chad Phinney, Richard Rhay, Jonathan Porter, Allen Wigren, and Ronald Sanders. Mary Fergoda had the crucial position of cook and in this capacity she did a most admirable job. Lois Lippold conducted ethnozoological and botanical research during the 1966 field season and the results of her work are incorporated in a separate report.

The wealth of material recovered from the excavations brought together an excellent laboratory crew who worked during 1966 and 1967 to bring order to the many thousands of artifacts. David Trapp and Knut Helskog cleaned the charcoal samples which have placed the Bigelow and Sanders sites so firmly in time. Josephine Teitel and Josaphene Oyama sorted, glued, and counted sherds. The majority of the lithic drawings in this report were done by James Stokes; the soil profiles by Chad Phinney; the ceramic drawings by Richard Rhay; and the fabrics by Marta Black of Toronto. The quality of this report would suffer if these illustrations were not included. Ronald Argelander assisted in the initial photography, John Glover of the University of Toronto produced the photographs used in this report. Nancy Jex aided me in the distribution tables and the terrestrial gastropod identifications included for the Sanders site were done by Dr. David A. Baerreis.

The field soils map included in the analysis of the Sanders site was done by John Cook, Anne (Shinkwin) Powers, Lathel Duffield, and William Workman. They spent many hours and weekends commuting from Madison to document what was only imperfectly known.

We wish to thank Mr. Joseph Hartz of Stevens Point, Wisconsin who was the owner of the Bigelow site. He allowed excavations to be conducted even as plans were being put into operation to turn the site into a subdivision for summer cottages. Mr. Walter Sanders and his three sons Ronald, Dennis, and James gave us considerable aid at the site and provided us with living accommodations when none could be obtained nearby. The constant coming and going through their farmyard must have been a bit bothersome and yet the Sanders family was always most helpful and concerned about our well-being. I wish to thank

Ronald Sanders who gave us valuable help in the field and served us most capably as an operator of power equipment.

During the work on this report I had the benefit of a great deal of co-operation from my fellow students at the University of Wisconsin and am particularly indebted to Guy Gibbon, Dale R. Henning, and Peter Storck. I also wish to thank Mrs. Barbara MacSporran whose typewriter spells better than mine and who had the arduous task of typing the thesis. Mrs. Catharine Aird who typed this report and I wish to acknowledge her assistance.

Throughout all phases of the Effigy Mound research, my wife Mary assisted me with her optimism that the work would come out well. I hope this monograph is a partial reward for her optimism.

I should like to also acknowledge my debt to the members of my doctoral committee: David A. Baerreis (chairman), Donald Thompson, Catharine McClellan and James Stoltman of the Department of Anthropology, and Gehard Lee of the Department of Soils.

It was a very great pleasure to have been introduced to active field research in Wisconsin at the site of Aztalan by the late Dr. Stephan F. Borhegyi, the former director of the Milwaukee Public Museum. Dr. Borhegyi allowed this novice anthropology student to roam his museum storerooms and archaeological laboratory; made him publish his museum and field activities; provided many evenings of stimulating conversation after exotic meals; and allowed him to develop his interests at the museum. He was a valued friend who will be missed.

Finally I should like to acknowledge the very able editorial assistance of both Barbara Bluestone and Mary Coombs of the Museum of Anthropology, University of Michigan.

I

INTRODUCTION

THE Wisconsin Effigy Mound tradition is a distinctive prehistoric cultural manifestation characterized by effigy and non-effigy shaped mounds, and camp, rockshelter, cave, and village sites. The culture's geographic center is in Wisconsin, although limited representation exists in the adjacent states of Illinois, Iowa, and Minnesota (Fig. 1; Thomas, 1894:531 and Rowe, 1956:10-11). Extensive exploration of the sites associated with this culture has allowed archaeologists to suggest that the tradition began after A.D. 100 and declined by A.D. 1400 (Gibbon, 1969; Griffin, 1960*b*:826, 1967:77; Hurley, 1966; Keslin, 1958:266; Quimby, 1960:87; Rowe, 1956:83 and 91; Willey, 1966:281; and Wittry, 1959*c*:259, 261). The Effigy Mound culture is thought to have been carried by peoples who were mainly food gatherers and hunters, whose generalized ceramics are difficult to place in meaningful typological categories (Rowe, 1956:52, 59), whose culture was in a state of gradual decline from the more dynamic Hopewell (Griffin, 1960*a*:26) and consisted of a reduced, specialized, and geographically distinct version of the Woodland tradition (Willey, 1966:281).

Rowe (1956) assessed the Effigy Mound culture by concentrating on burial practices and the ethnographic present without quantifying or specifying the associated material culture. Many of the deficiencies in Effigy Mound culture research prior to and subsequent to Rowe's assessment can be directly tied to: (1) limited cultural material from mounds, campsites, rockshelters or caves; (2) uncertainty as to whether rockshelter occupations form a component part of the seasonal life of the Effigy Mound

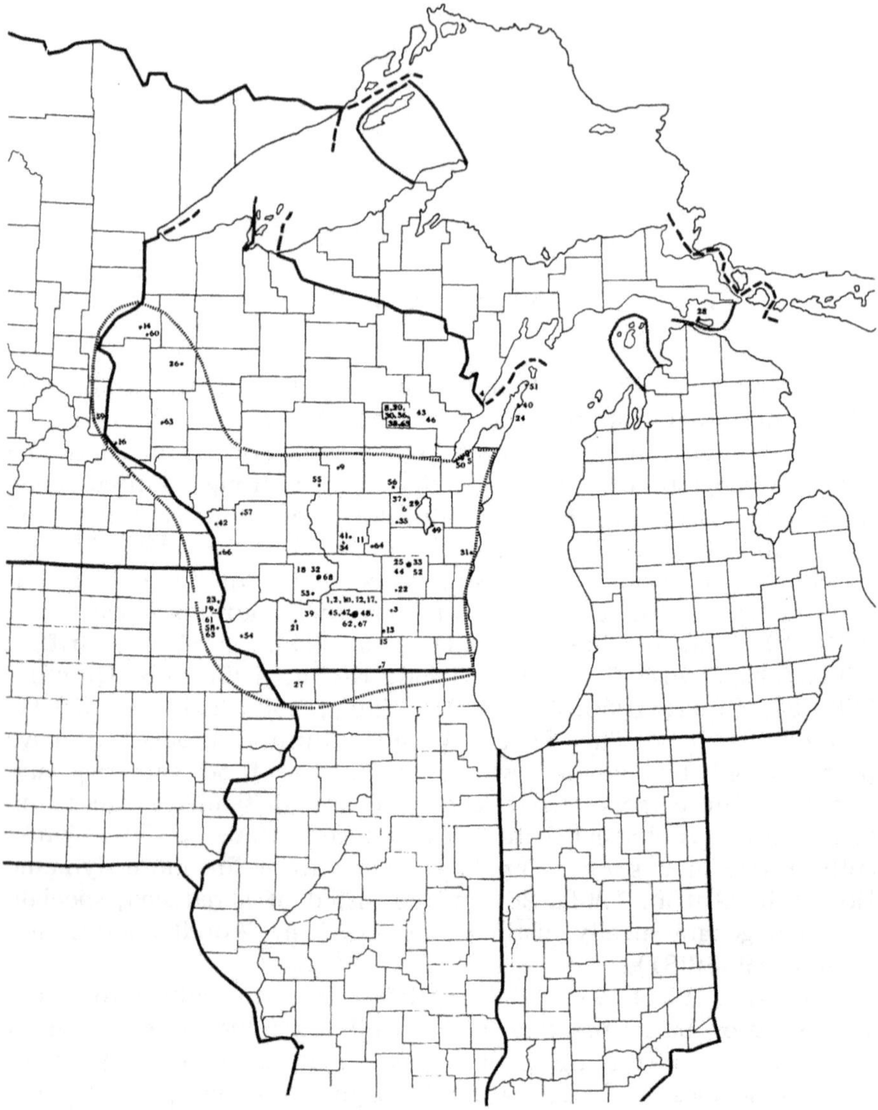

FIG. 1. Some sites and locations mentioned in the text.

KEY TO FIGURE 1*

1. AIRPORT
2. ARBORETUM
3. AZTALAN
4. BACKLUND
5. BEAUMIER
6. BELL
7. BELOIT
8. BIG EDDY
9. BIGELOW
10. BLACKHAWK
11. BORNICK
12. BURTON
13. CARCAJOU
14. CLAM LAKE
15. COOPER'S SHORE
16. DIAMOND BLUFF
17. DIETZ
18. DURST
19. EFFIGY MOUNDS NATIONAL MONUMENT
20. FIVE ISLANDS
21. GOV. DODGE
22. HAHN (1 and 2)
23. HARPERS FERRY
24. HEINS CREEK
25. HORICON
26. INDIAN MOUNDS
27. JO DAVIESS
28. JUNTUNEN
29. JAMES ISLAND
30. KAKWATCH
31. KLETZIEN
32. KNOOP
33. KOLTERMAN
34. KRATZ CREEK
35. KRISBAHER-LLEWELLYN
36. LA BELLE LAKE
37. LASLEY POINT
38. MAKIMITAS
39. MAYLAND
40. MERO
41. MC CLAUGHRY
42. MIDWAY
43. NAKUTI
44. NITSCHKE
45. OUTLET
46. PEWISIT
47. PICNIC GROVE
48. PICNIC POINT
49. PIPE
50. POINT SAUBLE
51. PORTE DES MORTS
52. PRAWATSCHKE
53. RADDATZ
54. RAISBECK
55. ROSS
56. SANDERS
57. SILVER CREEK
58. SNY-MAGILL
59. SORG
60. SPENCER LAKE
61. SPIKE HOLLOW
62. UNIVERSITY RIDGE
63. WAKANDA PARK
64. WALKER-HOOPER
65. WATASA LAKE
66. WHITE
67. WILLOW DRIVE
68. ZECH

*DASHED LINE IN MINNESOTA, IOWA, ILLINOIS AND WISCONSIN INDICATES EFFIGY MOUND CONFINES ACCORDING TO THOMAS (1894:527, 531).

peoples and whether excavated campsites are a part of the sedentary aspects of this culture; (3) the lack of clear chronological sequences and ceramic types for rockshelters and campsites, and methods of validating these sequences and types in themselves, and in their spatial and temporal position in the Effigy Mound culture; (4) the lack of a synchronic and diachronic link between mounds, mound sites, and campsites; and (5) the inability, in some instances, to separate or associate intentional mound inclusions from earlier artifacts incorporated in the mound fill or sub-mound artifacts and to recognize contiguous cultural components earlier or later than the mounds.

This study examines and assesses previous research conducted at Effigy Mound culture sites and at those of other prehistoric cultures which interacted with this tradition. Effigy Mound research spans 134 years and the data recovered suggest that the Effigy Mound culture was an in situ cultural tradition, a "... culture pattern persisting through time...." (Willey, 1966:249). The Effigy Mound tradition appears to represent one of the major indigenous prehistoric Wisconsin manifestations, beginning in about A.D. 300 and lasting until A.D. 1642. During this 1,300 year period the Effigy Mound peoples appear to have interacted with Middle Woodland, Late Woodland, and Mississippian peoples while retaining their own cultural identity. Because most summary statements about the Effigy Mound tradition failed to produce a "culture core" from which this tradition could be assessed, any attempted tradition reconstruction has so far lacked the needed thread of continuity. The mounds themselves had been utilized, but their shapes, included burials, and absence of sufficient artifactual data negated any meaningful assessment.

Excavations conducted at two Effigy Mound culture sites (Fig. 2) dating from the middle of this tradition yielded valuable information concerning the longevity of site occupation, the possible rate of mound construction, the cultural utilization of a location over a controlled time period, burial customs, settlement patterns, and the nature and extent of the associated material culture. The Bigelow site (47-Pt-29) and the Sanders site (47-Wp-26 and Wp-70) yielded a total of 55,414 artifacts from sites containing 56 mounds, three houses, 91 features, and 10 prehistoric burials. The analyses of these phenomena were greatly facilitated by 31 radiocarbon assessments, natural and man-made stratigraphy, and such ceramic decorative attributes as trailing or cord and fabric impressed designs. With two distinct sites that date from the middle of this tradition yielding unprecedented amounts of information, the early and late phases of this tradition could be re-assessed. The "culture core" utilized in this re-assessment is the material culture with constituent parts that themselves have long traditions. Artifacts previously proposed as belonging to this tradition form an important part of the material culture and additional ceramic and lithic types are proposed which help to complete the cultural inventory of Effigy Mound tradition. Excavations conducted at the Bigelow site (47-Pt-29) indicated that 28 conical, linear, and effigy mounds were constructed by Effigy Mound peoples between A.D. 670 and A.D. 1120. These peoples continued to use the site as a camping area until A.D. 1370. Analysis of the artifacts recovered from the sub-mound, mound, and non-mound areas of the site indicates a cyclic temporal pattern of residence quite similar to the proposed "Central-Based Wandering" community pattern (Meggers, 1956:138). The central base purpose of the Bigelow site was not habitation but rather the construction of effigy and non-effigy mounds. Bird, bear, and turtle-shaped mounds plus linear and conical forms were added to the site and a limited number of artifacts were intentionally placed within the mounds as grave goods or in separate pits. The elimination of any possible earlier component and the isolation of a later component (Lange, 1969) allowed for the association of all mound forms with the Effigy Mound culture and the association of camping remains as well as mound fill artifacts with the material culture associated with the Effigy Mound tradition.

The Effigy Mound culture ceramic artifact types from the Bigelow site are placed into an expanded Madison Ware category, including Madison Cord Impressed, Madison Fabric Impressed, Madison Folded Lip, Madison Plain, Madison Punctated, Leland Cord-marked, Aztalan Collared, Hahn Cord Impressed, and Point Sauble Collared. The diagnostic lithic and bone artifacts associated with the Effigy Mound component at the Bigelow site include the proposed Sanders Triangular projectile point type; Triangular and corner notched forms; drills; scrapers; cores; worked flakes; pecked stones; polishing stones; and an antler tine flaker. Madison Cord Impressed, Madison Fabric Impressed, Madison Plain, and Madison Punctated types and the Sanders Triangular and Triangular points are present at the site as early as A.D. 670. The Madison Folded Lip, Leland Cord-marked, Aztalan Collared, Hahn Cord Impressed, and the Point Sauble Collared types are present by A.D. 810. Most of these types continue until the last effigy-shaped mound was constructed at circa A.D. 1120, with the Aztalan Collared type remaining until circa A.D. 1370. The Bigelow site is used as the mound type site for the Middle Effigy Mound period (A.D. 700 to A.D. 1100) and the Sanders site (47-Wp-26 and Wp-70) is used as the village type site for this period.

The Sanders site (47-Wp-26 and Wp-70) is a multi-functional site having panther, bird, and bear effigy-shaped mounds, conical, linear, oval, and indeterminate shaped mounds, plus an associated village. The 12 excavated mounds, 63 features, three houses, four burials, and approximately 45,000 artifacts are associated with the Effigy Mound component. Middle Woodland peoples also utilized this site at circa A.D. 290 and the few artifacts associated with their limited occupation of the area include Sister Creeks Punctated, Shorewood Cord Roughened and rocker stamped ceramics. The material culture associated with the mounds, features, and houses belonging to the Effigy Mound component included types and their varieties similar to those recovered from the Bigelow site. The Madison Ware types from the Sanders site are: Madison Cord Impressed, Madison Fabric Impressed, Madison Folded Lip, Madison Plain, Madison Plain variety punctated, Madison Plain variety jar, Madison Punctated, Leland Cord-marked, Aztalan Collared, Hahn Cord Impressed, and Point Sauble Collared. In addition to these types associated with the Effigy Mound component, there are ceramics generally thought to be earlier (Dane Incised) or belonging to a different Late Woodland manifestation (Heins Creek Corded Stamped). A detailed analysis of the Sanders site demonstrated that Dane Incised and its proposed variety, Dane Incised variety fingernail impressed, are important to the Effigy Mound material culture and form an important link to other Wisconsin sites. The Heins Creek Corded Stamped ceramics are included at the Sanders site as part of the expanded Madison Ware category; however, future research in northern Wisconsin may bring about the removal of this type from this Effigy Mound ware category. The lithic and copper categories found to be a part of this rich cultural assemblage include Waubesa Contracting Stem, Madison Side Notched, Durst Stemmed, Sanders Triangular, and Triangular projectile points; drills; diminutive scrapers; scrapers; knives; cores; gravers; burins; burin spalls; blades; worked and utilized flakes; a shaft polisher; adzes; celts; a gorget; polished stone; a grinding stone; hammerstones; copper beads, knife, pendant, conical point and awls; and an elbow pipe.

Of the total of 21 radiocarbon assessments for this Effigy Mound site, only four could not be associated with the Effigy Mound component. One date is much too early, one dates the Middle Woodland component, and two are too recent. The remaining dates are clustered between A.D. 670 and A.D. 1060 and indicate an occupation of considerable duration. The artifacts recovered from the Sanders site number only a possible 10 percent of the total, as it is estimated that the village area still contains between half a million and a million artifacts. One of the most important aspects of the Sanders research is the recovery of 266 Oneota sherds representing 35 vessels associated with the Grand River Focus. The specimens represent the earliest dated examples of Oneota (if not Middle Mississippian) ceramics in Wisconsin; their dates, by four separate radiocarbon assessments, range from A.D. 670 to A.D. 860. These vessels do not represent the earliest evidence of an Effigy Mound metamorphic transformation into an emerging Oneota tradition as suggested by Gibbon (1972), but trade vessels from an as yet unknown early Oneota site. The total number of mounds, features, and artifacts suggests that the Sanders site was either a major center of a Central-Based Wandering community or a Semi-Permanent Sedentary village (Meggers, 1956). The Sanders and Bigelow sites in turn are suggested as a part of a larger settlement pattern network which has not been fully clarified for the Effigy Mound tradition.

With the Bigelow and Sanders sites yielding such an impressive amount of controlled data the proposed Effigy Mound tradition can be re-examined. This tradition is seen as having three chronological phases or periods: Early Effigy Mound (A.D. 300 to A.D. 700), Middle Effigy Mound (A.D. 700 to A.D. 1100), and Late Effigy Mound (A.D. 1100 to A.D. 1642). Many of the sites previously reported lack radiocarbon dates or have one or two dates and limited material remains. Other Effigy Mound sites or sites related to the Effigy Mound tradition have artifacts which can be re-assessed in the light of the Bigelow and Sanders analyses.

The Early Effigy Mound period sites are grouped into five main categories: mound group, camp, village, rockshelter or cave site, with rockshelter sites common for this period. Sites dating from this time may also extend into other periods; because chronological lines have had to be drawn on the basis of a date or two and a group of additional factors, decisions of temporal placement are somewhat arbitrary. The Early Effigy Mound sites are generally restricted to northern

Illinois, southern Wisconsin, and eastern Iowa. This appears to be the area of origin of the Effigy Mound tradition; radiocarbon dates, ceramic design elements, and site associations suggest that the Early Effigy Mound peoples were interacting with indigenous and intrusive Middle Woodland cultures even as the Middle Woodland progenitor of the Effigy Mound tradition was being replaced. Not all artifact types or categories are present at each site during this time but the individual site assemblages combine into an extensive list of material culture items associated with the Effigy Mound tradition.

The Middle Effigy Mound (A.D. 700-1100) period is the portion of the tradition which is best known because the most extensive manifestations of mounds and camp or village sites occurred at this time. The southern half of Wisconsin was extensively utilized during this period, and there were trade and site-unit intrusions into northern Wisconsin. Rockshelter or cave sites diminish during this period and the village sites may be found adjacent to mound groups. The northern areas may have been the loci of such other Late Woodland cultures as the Keshena, Clam River, or the Heins Creek Complex, as well as the origin area of the indigenous Oneota tradition. Although evidence of culture change from the Effigy Mound tradition to the Oneota tradition was lacking at the Sanders site, there are strong indications that a Late Woodland to Oneota culture change occurred in northern Wisconsin. The contact between Effigy Mound and Oneota peoples did not bring about an attenuation of the Effigy Mound tradition; its viable character is attested to by the number of sites presently known from the Late Effigy Mound period. Sites which may be placed in the Early Effigy Mound period (Silver Creek I and V), the Middle Effigy Mound period (Heins Creek), or the Late Effigy Mound period (Clam Lake) have produced proposed artifact types which may have a longevity beyond the estimated age or dates recorded for the site. The Silver Creek (Hurley, 1966) types from southwestern Wisconsin include the proposed Angelo Punctated and Windrow Cord Impressed ceramics and McCoy Corner Notched points. The Clam River Focus of northwestern Wisconsin has produced two ceramic candidates (McKern, 1963), Burnett Stamped conoidal and Clam River wrapped-stamped globoid. The Heins Creek Complex of northeastern Wisconsin includes the following Heins Creek types (R. Mason, 1966): Heins Creek Cord-marked, Heins Creek Corded Stamped, and Heins Creek

Cord-wrapped stick. Subsequent excavations in these three regions of Wisconsin will clarify the nature and extent of these types.

The Late Effigy Mound period is one of site expansion into northern Wisconsin as well as continued occupancy of southern Wisconsin. The artifact types recorded for the two earlier periods continue to be found at mound and camp or village locations and the Effigy Mound peoples continued to interact with the Late Woodland and Mississippian cultures present in the state. The most impressive site of this time is the "hybrid culture" site of Aztalan which was occupied by Middle Mississippian and Effigy Mound peoples prior to A.D. 1000. The major utilization of this site appears to have occurred at circa A.D. 1100 to A.D. 1300 with the Effigy Mound peoples constructing both effigy and non-effigy mounds on the eastern and western margins of a stockaded village containing truncated pyramidal mounds. The Effigy Mound people may also have been the cause of the ultimate burning and abandonment of this complex site. In northeastern Wisconsin at the Mero site, the Heins Creek component was interacting with the Effigy Mound tradition while setting the cultural base which was necessary for the unique in situ development of the Oneota Mero Complexes, which appear to conform to McKern's (1945) proposed Green Bay Focus. In nearby Menominee County was a series of camp, village, and mound locations which were utilized from the Middle through the Late Effigy Mound periods and these manifestations have been grouped into the proposed Keshena culture. This culture appears to have fully exploited the southern part of the county, with only limited intrusions into the northern part. The data from the excavations of Barrett and Skinner (1932) suggest that the Effigy Mound occupation of this region continued up to the historic period.

In Dunn County to the west, the Wakanda Park Mound Group (Wittry, 1959*b*) yielded Effigy Mound artifacts dated at A.D. 1200 ± 200 (M-814) and excellent evidence of Middle Mississippian intrusion into northwest Wisconsin. This "migration" of Middle Mississippian peoples is also evident at the Diamond Bluff site, where an effigy-shaped mound yielded Effigy Mound, Middle Mississippian, and Oneota artifacts. The use of combined Middle Mississippian and Oneota ceramic elements suggested to Maxwell (1950) culture contact and a late date (circa A.D. 1200 to A.D. 1400?) for this site. Farther to the northwest is Indian Mounds Park at Rice Lake where one "double round" mound was excavated. This mound produced prehistoric and historic artifacts suggesting that mounds were constructed by Dakota Sioux (or Effigy Mound) peoples during the seventeenth century. The artifacts recovered, i.e., an elbow pipe, Triangular points, antler tine flaker, and Madison Cord Impressed ceramics, suggest the Effigy Mound culture as the author of the mound; however, some Blackduck ceramics indicated to Cooper (1959) that the Dakota Sioux constructed this mound.

The proposed tradition pattern of the Effigy Mound culture still remains somewhat open-ended. Its beinnings can be reasonably documented and its subsequent growth and development are recorded from many localities. Many facets of this cultural tradition still need to be explored. The present analysis of the Effigy Mound tradition was brought about by an apparent lack of associated artifacts securely placed as the material culture of this tradition. It is somewhat of a paradox that the bulk of this report is a descriptive and an analytic presentation of one of the largest prehistoric artifact collections excavated from Wisconsin sites.

II

PREVIOUS EFFIGY MOUND RESEARCH

DESPITE the fact that an investigative base has been established and a broad prehistoric chronological outline has emerged for Wisconsin (see Wittry, 1959*c*:143-155 for summary), there remains today a paramount need to define and appraise the nature, character, and extent of each prehistoric cultural manifestation. Such an assessment has been lacking partly because of the inadequacy of knowledge concerning the range of cultural activity represented at different types of sites and an actual or believed paucity of diagnostic artifacts. A recent attempt to evaluate Wisconsin prehistory dealt with the Effigy Mound culture (Rowe, 1956). But even Rowe's conclusions need to be re-examined as a result of recent research presented in this report and to be placed in perspective by reviewing major scientific reports concerned with the Effigy Mound culture prior to his report.

To survey Effigy Mound research, it is useful to divide historical treatments of the subject into three major time periods: (1) 1836 to 1919—initial effigy mound recognition and systematic survey; (2) 1919 to 1956—continued mound survey, systematic mound excavation, and the recognition of effigy mound habitation sites; (3) 1956 to 1972—continued survey, mound excavation, and habitation site excavation. The latter division will be presented in the final chapter as this period is marked by the application of precise dating techniques and a greater range in the types of sites excavated and artifacts recovered.

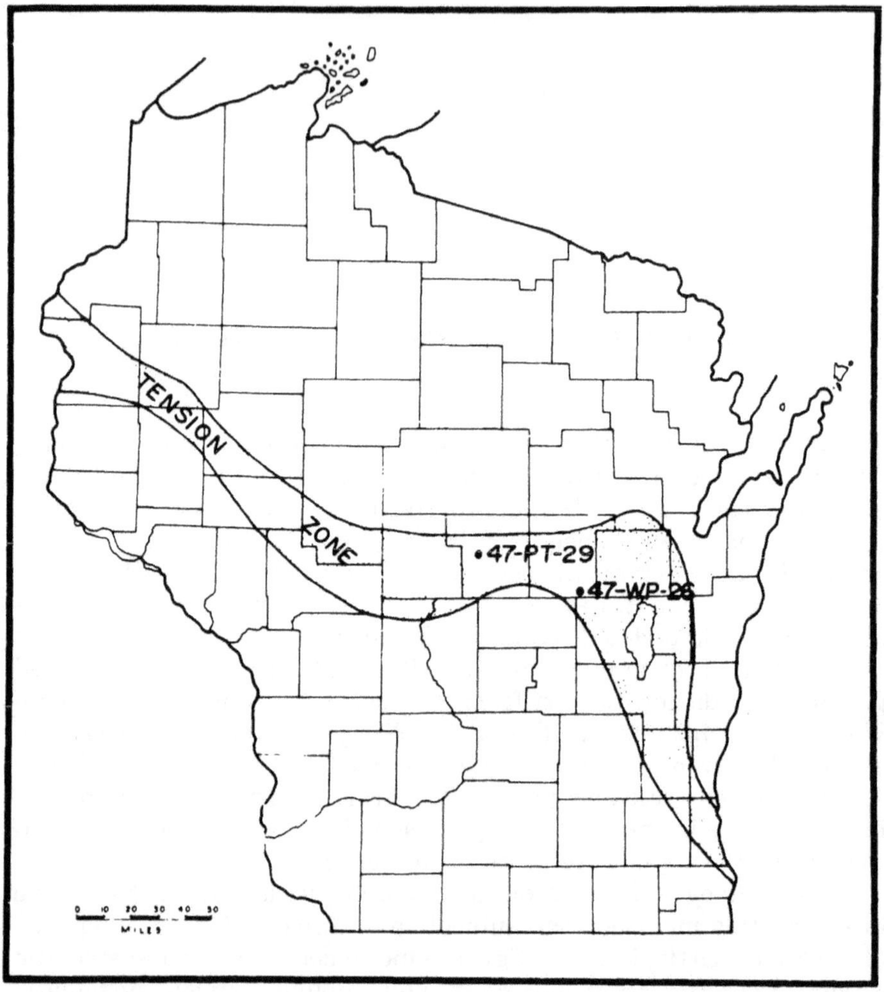

FIG. 2. Map of Wisconsin showing the Tension Zone and site locations.

(1) 1836 to 1919

The first published article (1836) and the first national scientific treatise (1855) marking the beginnings of archaeological research in Wisconsin were concerned primarily with effigy mounds. I. A. Lapham's 1836 account of a turtle effigy mound was carried by the "newspapers of the day" (Lapham, 1855:vi) and from this report until 1855, Lapham, on behalf of the

American Antiquarian Society, conducted research on aboriginal earthworks which ultimately resulted in the publication of his prominent *Antiquities of Wisconsin*. While this report is now mainly utilized for its survey information and for data on leveled earthworks, it should be stressed that Lapham also conducted excavations in the mounds for the express purpose of clarifying the nature and degree of their antiquity (1855:27-30). While it was not the main objective of Lapham's monograph, he did delineate the character of archaeological research that would be conducted in Wisconsin for the next half century. This research was primarily concerned with the additions, corrections, and faithful recording of earthworks rapidly being obliterated by increasing urban and rural expansion.

Mound excavation during the latter half of the nineteenth century became the favored activity of the antiquarian or "local authority" who excavated for precious ceremonial items which could be sequestered in the home after an account of the ancient monument excavation was serialized for the local newspaper. This unrestrained looting of mounds was not restricted to any local area but rather it effloresced from the Plains to the eastern seaboard. The aim of many of these excavators was to establish once and for all the prehistoric existence of a vanished race of mysterious mound builders who built these structures for religious or sacrificial purposes. There were also at this time scientists who believed that extensive and careful surveys, limited excavation, and the thoughtful presentation of empirical data would quell or at least partially suppress some of the fanciful misconceptions concerning the authorship of these earthworks. One such early model of accuracy and careful interpretation is the impressive monograph by Cyrus Thomas for the Bureau of American Ethnology in 1894. Thomas was a member of that generation of scientists (Powell, Dorsey, and Holmes) working for the Bureau of American Ethnology who were seeking to answer "big questions" in American history and prehistory and they focused their attention on the problems surrounding languages, artifacts, and earthworks.

Thomas and his associates made a close, careful, and systematic examination of mounds and other ancient monuments which were believed to be typical or representative of each archaeological district east of the Rocky Mountains. The origin of the mounds was considered to be the important pivot on which all other problems would be pursued and resolved. Thus, the most important question to be settled by Thomas was: "Were the mounds built by the Indians?" Thomas' solutions to some of the pressing problems of his day were based on the survey and description of hundreds of mound groups and the exploration of over 2,000 mounds (*ibid.*:19-21). As is now obvious, Thomas was dealing with a complicated array of then diachronically unrelatable surface phenomena which were being ranked, graded, and chronologically ordered according to their size, shape or number. The fact that his area of investigation was east of the Rocky Mountains was not happenstance for, as his map of the mound distribution ably illustrates (Plate XX), a great portion of the Eastern United States had earthworks of one form or another. As there were as many views of their origin, purpose, historic affiliations, and spatial significance as there were mound groups, it was the broad overview which seemed to offer Thomas a means of resolving these broad problems. Thomas' regional or district investigations served as a vehicle, and in specific instances as an integral part, contributing to the ultimate demise of the multifarious ideas then prevalent.

In Wisconsin, his explorations were confined mainly to the southwestern portion of the state where he sought out unreported mound groups. He and his associates excavated numerous mounds (*ibid.*: 51, 59, 64-91, 93-98) and these excavations were incorporated into his ultimate interpretation of Eastern United States earthworks. Thomas was the first to systematically excavate conical, linear, and effigy mounds in Wisconsin. While he did not attempt to establish a local or regional prehistoric chronology, he did document the fact that items of historic manufacture were being recovered from Wisconsin mounds (*ibid.*:51, 73, 78, 80), although he did not suggest that these mounds were constructed during historic times, i.e. after 1634. Thomas proposed that a large portion of the Wisconsin effigy mounds were situated along the principal rivers and lakes in the southern half of the state, and he then described the known confines of the effigy mound area (*ibid.*:527, 531) which have not been subsequently modified to any great degree (Rowe, 1956:10-11).

It had been suggested by early excavators that mound stratification or its absence was a result of and an indicator of temporal differences attributable to different prehistoric groups. Thomas was able to show that these differences could be found within a single mound group (*ibid.*:709). When a tree ring growth—tree circumference index was favored as a means of dating mounds, Thomas again pointed out the inconsistencies of the technique and showed that it was considerably overrated (*ibid.*:627-630). Thomas lists the more important conclusions of his monograph as an outline (*ibid.*:17-18) establishing that the Indians constructed the mounds without any known influence from the American Southwest or Mesoamerican areas. Thomas surely believed that he had laid many of the then popular theories to rest; however, as is the case with many monumental works, they are as easy to ignore as are the less well-known publications. For at least another decade the question concerning the Indian authorship of the earthworks in Wisconsin was still open to debate (West, 1907:169-186).

In 1907, George A. West believed that there still remained a considerable need to give ". . . accurate information on the subject of the authorship of our state's antiquities . . . upon which present accepted theories are based" (*ibid.*:167). Even though Thomas' extensive monograph on the subject of mounds should have resolved many of the ideas concerning their construction, West saw that:

> . . . there are yet among our citizens many for whom the favorite theory of a mysterious, lost race of "Mound Builders" has a fascination not readily dispersed. The antiquated publications of misguided authors, frequent fanciful newspaper articles and contributions to popular periodicals, and the exaggerated statements of lecturers, of relic hunters and others possessing a smattering of archeological knowledge are responsible for such ridiculous and erroneous beliefs (*ibid.*:167).

West's extensive account of Wisconsin earthworks begins with many statements by researchers in the United States and Canada which give accurate accounts of mound research, and while most are quite conservative, there was one who was:

> . . . in favor of the contention that the mounds were built by just plain Indians. I do not mean Indians of the plain, but just common Indians. There are many reasons for arriving at this conclusion; one is that since European contact, travellers have seen Indians at work in the erection of these earthworks. Another reason is that we have not yet found anything in these mounds indicating a higher condition of development than we find among the Indians themselves or than we find in places of sepulchre or other earthworks. It is of course very sad to think that this theory or belief is calculated to demolish utterly the long and pleasantly entertained idea that the mound-builders were a happy and cultivated people, given to agriculture, and horticulture, keeping immense herds of buffalo cows and generally conducting themselves like people who go to church nowadays, but who were driven off or cruelly massacred by the blood thirsty and malevolent beings whom we now call Indians (*ibid.*: 173-174).

West cites a few of the available records of mounds built by historic Indians (*ibid.*:178-186) and he, like many of the anthropologists since his time, bemoans the failure of the early missionaries and explorers to record either the presence of effigy mounds or any instance of historic utilization of these mounds for intrusive burials. While Thomas suggested that effigy mounds and burial mounds (conicals?) were attributable to the same people (1894:709), West suggested that as a class effigy mounds did not appear to be primarily intended for burials; however, he noted that many original interments were reported (1907:202). West suggested that the building of "... both burial and imitative mounds must have proceeded simultaneously for a long period of time" (*ibid.*: 206) and yet the time interval was difficult to establish according to the relative dating techniques then available (*ibid.*:208-219).

Concerning the authorship of the effigy mounds, West was among the many then current and later researchers who postulated that the Winnebago Indian tribe were the authors of the effigy mounds (*ibid.*:244). West cites numerous ethnological authorities plus Winnebago traditions and legends to support his view that the effigy shapes represented clan totems or emblems (*ibid.*:244-253). It was West and A. B. Stout (see below) who were the first Wisconsin representatives to encourage this view and to ultimately contribute to Paul Radin's hypothesis concerning Winnebago-effigy mound relationships (Radin, 1911:518, 532).

A. B. Stout in his "Prehistoric Earthworks in Wisconsin" (1911) intended to clarify the nature and relationships of earthen enclosures, conical, linear, and effigy mounds from the data compiled by Wisconsin survey work. What is important for our consideration here is that he concluded that: (a) linear mounds were actually effigy mounds (*ibid.*:22); (b) there were, by his estimates, at least 20,000 conical, linear, and effigy mounds in Wisconsin (*ibid.*:24); and (c) effigy mounds were built as clan totems (*ibid.*:26). It was Paul Radin (1911, 1923), however, who fully elaborated upon the latter conclusion of Stout and who "... demonstrated beyond any doubt that the effigy mounds were the work of the Winnebago alone" (1911:521). Radin accomplished this by concluding that the Central Algonkian tribes were intruders into Siouan areas and as the Algonkian tribes did not build mounds they could be eliminated from consideration (*ibid.*: 521-522). Using Thomas' map of the effigy mound distribution he contended that the various habitats of the Winnebago coincided with the effigy mound distribution. He also offered the "fact" that effigy mounds were clan property marks (*ibid.*:524-525). Radin considered that archaeologists' attempts to clarify tribal relationships were a "pseudo-archaeological problem" (*ibid.*:538) and that the archaeologists made the ". . . cardinal error in all their attempts . . . [with] the assumption that the mounds were necessarily of great antiquity" (1923:79), i.e., ". . . three centuries previous to the discovery of America by Columbus" (West, 1907:252). In order to diminish the believed antiquity and to settle the question concerning effigy mound origins, Radin (1911:524-527) relied upon Winnebago traditions and legends to support his conclusion that ". . . the effigy mounds are unquestionably supposed to represent the eponymous clan animals of the Winnebago . . ." (1923:80). Radin's interpretations remained unchallenged until W. C. McKern (1928, 1929*a*, and 1930) pointed out serious flaws in Radin's arguments. Finally, concerning Stout's proposal that linear mounds were actually effigy mounds, Radin considered linear mound origins, purpose, and associations as an enigma (1911:528; 1923:81-82); the mounds were, according to Stout, ". . . constructed for the purpose of symbolizing inanimate things and consequently as really conventionalized effigies" (Radin, 1911:529). However, as the Winnebago did not practice conventionalized art, Radin proposed the alternative view that linear mounds were possibly defensive works or remnants of earth lodges (*ibid.*:531-532).

The last contribution during this period of effigy mound research is Barrett and Hawkes' report of "The Kratz Creek Mound Group" (1919). Excavations at this mound group were intended as an initial step by the Milwaukee Public Museum toward the development of a systematic series of Wisconsin excavations (1919:10). As this was the first archaeological research by the Museum, Barrett and Hawkes considered it necessary to state that excavators of mounds should not conduct their work with preconceived ideas concerning the origin, construction, or purpose of the mounds but, rather, that the site should tell its own story. Furthermore, Barrett and Hawkes noted that mound form is not necessarily equated with use; that is, conical mounds are not necessarily burial mounds nor simply piles of heaped up earth (*ibid.*:11). This latter view prompted them to record mound stratification which had been generally overlooked. They proposed that single strata mounds might represent the primary stage of mound construction and that a conical mound ". . . may have been employed as a delineator in building larger mounds" (*ibid.*:16-17). Barrett and Hawkes were able to demonstrate that conical, linear, and effigy mounds contained a wide variety of burial forms—flexed, bundle, cremated, etc.—which were incorporated into the sub-mound area or mound during construction as contrasted to those burials placed into the mounds by later peoples (*ibid.*:23-29). Barrett and Hawkes excavated 36 mounds and they suggested that complex mound stratigraphy plus the degree of skeletal preservation might be useful criteria for temporal ranking of the mounds. These two variables plus the differences observed (but not presented) between the mound artifacts and the nearby surface artifacts, prompted them to conclude that there were two cultures responsible for the 51 mounds of the Kratz Creek mound group (*ibid.*:30-33, 99-100).

The first division of effigy mound research was the period of effigy mound recognition, mound survey, and the repudiation of the erroneous view that these mounds were constructed by a uniform race of mound builders. Statements concerning origin, purpose, and tribal associations were offered with only cursory efforts to compare mound to non-mound artifacts. The next period of effigy mound research opened, therefore, with major hypotheses that remained unresolved and many questions unasked.

(2) 1919 to 1956

During this second period of effigy mound research, mound survey was continued, mound excavation increased, and sites were suggested as being habitation localities associated with the mound builders. In 1925, W. C. McKern, as the curator of the Department of Anthropology of the Milwaukee Public Museum, sought to design a research program of mound investigations in order to solve ". . . the principal archeological problems in this district" (1928:225; 1930:426). He proposed east to west excavations across the center of Wisconsin, crossing different water courses and drainage basins which would yield the greatest amount of cultural diversity as represented by prehistoric trade and migration. Mound excavations imposed restrictions on McKern's results as they led to sampling only one aspect of cultural behavior, a limited number and range of material objects, and almost total exclusion of habitation areas. Thus, the questions still remained: who, why, how, and when, with the focus almost totally on mound construction research (1928:226). Certain patterns were beginning to emerge concerning excavation techniques, mound shapes, dimensions, arrangements, orientation, and mound source material, all of which led to greater detail in burial, feature, and mound descriptions (1928:227-257, 261-265, 288-367; 1930:434-456,

478-523). However, there are two aspects beyond these field techniques which deserve discussion here. The first is concerned with the age and authorship of the mounds. McKern dismissed Radin's age estimates for the effigy mounds by citing the absence of European artifacts and the almost total absence of cradle board deformation which argued for a prehistoric age for the mounds (1928:276; 1930:457, 461-462). McKern then effectively questions Radin's arguments for Winnebago authorship of the mounds by demonstrating that: (a) the Winnebago did not construct mounds after European contact; (b) Algonkian Indians were known to have constructed mounds; (c) Radin's Winnebago distribution did not coincide with the distribution of effigy mounds; (d) there were many effigy mound forms which did not resemble Winnebago clan animals; and (e) Radin was somewhat naive to accept *in toto* Winnebago claims that their ancestors built the mounds (1928:267-288; 1929*a*:562-564; 1930:462-463).

The second aspect of McKern's reports is that he now refers to the *Effigy Mound culture* and *Effigy Mound pottery* (1929*a*: 564; 1930:463-478). McKern proposed that all the effigy and non-effigy mounds excavated at the Kletzien and Nitschke sites (65 out of a possible 96) were a product of the Effigy Mound culture. By 1930, archaeologists at the Milwaukee Public Museum had excavated a total of 171 mounds (Barrett and Hawkes, 1919; McKern, 1928, 1930). On the basis of these excavations McKern proposed his effigy mound pottery which included grit-tempered, cord-marked ceramics which were incised, rouletted, fluted (trailed), noded, collared, cord impressed, punctated, and fingernail impressed (1928:266-268; 1930:463-467). These effigy mound ceramics were incorporated into a sub-type of his proposed Lake Michigan Ware which was suggested as being Algonkian pottery "... specifically those who lived in the pottery-making Woodlands area" (1930:468-496). This pottery is suggested as being similar to that recovered from Menomini and Potawatomi campsites. The Lake Michigan Ware is contrasted to his Type II ceramics (1928:268-270) which are a part of his proposed Upper Mississippi ceramics or those which are characterized as being shell-tempered, incised with geometric patterns, and found at Winnebago campsites (1930:469-470, 473-477). McKern concludes his discussion of ceramics by stating:

> ... judging from the occurrence and distribution, the local Algonkians were the authors of the Lake Michigan type of pottery. The conclusion follows that the effigy mounds are the products of people possessing the Algonkian pottery culture, whereas the Winnebago, who have laid claim

> to the authorship of the effigy mounds, according to all available evidence, made a markedly different type of pottery, an important sub-type of Upper Mississippi ware" (*ibid.* 1930:477).

McKern qualitatively lumped into his Lake Michigan Ware several types of ceramics without regard to possible differential temporal placement and nowhere does McKern offer any quantitative data. Most of the ceramics that he illustrates have been subsequently grouped into formal ceramic types and as time goes on more and more of the types are suggested as having effigy mound affiliations (R. Mason, 1966:151). The importance of McKern's research at this time is the evidence offered to refute the Winnebago claim of authorship of the mounds and to suggest that the ceramic aspects of this prehistoric culture were a part of a somewhat synchronous development found throughout the Middle West.

In 1932, S. A. Barrett and A. Skinner reported on "Certain Mounds and Village Sites of Shawano and Oconto Counties, Wisconsin." These counties are northeast of the previous Effigy Mound research area and they are in an area historically claimed by the Menomini. The mounds explored consisted of conicals, linears, and effigy forms, i.e., "catfish" and one bird effigy. The fact that Barrett and Skinner investigated both mounds and habitation sites represents a departure from the exclusive mound excavations. In addition, they report on mounds considered as effigies beyond the known northern range of the effigy mound distribution. They recovered artifacts which generally conform to McKern's Lake Michigan and Upper Mississippi wares (1932:415) with the suggestion that some habitation sites were occupied by Effigy Mound peoples. While their ceramics are not quantitatively presented, we are again offered a range of Lake Michigan (Woodland) ceramics (without rouletted representatives) which are believed to be associated with the Effigy Mound culture.

One important aspect of mound research at this time was that another mound building culture was recognized in Wisconsin (McKern, 1929*b*:307-312) and in 1931 McKern published his study "A Wisconsin Variant of the Hopewell Culture." Diagnostic Hopewell ceramics, such as rouletted specimens, were removed from the effigy mound assemblage and it soon became apparent that numerous Wisconsin conical mounds had to be included within the Hopewell manifestation. McKern's report on the Hopewell mounds in Wisconsin was followed in 1933 by Philleo Nash's report on his excavations at the Ross Mound Group I in Wood County. Eight mounds were excavated at this effigy mound site and Nash classified the ceramics as belonging within the general Lake Michigan type (1933:26-27). In 1965 I conducted limited testing and a survey for Ross Mound Group II. This work failed to produce any evidence of the mound group or any indication that further excavations at Mound Group I would be productive. In addition, a mound group (47-Wo-14) containing one bear effigy, one linear, and 10 conical mounds was tested and this mound group, two miles northwest of the Ross group, was so unproductive that it is excluded from this report.

One archaeological publication at this time which will stand as a monument to research is Barrett's "Ancient Aztalan" (1933). His monograph represents several years of field and laboratory research at this large Middle Mississippian stockaded village site and it is of particular importance to effigy mound research because numerous conical, linear, and effigy mounds outside the stockaded village were recorded and excavated (1933:227-255). A portion of the ceramics recovered from the excavations within the village included both Lake Michigan and Barrett's Woodland ware (*ibid.*:301). The latter term was applied to angular mouth collared specimens. Barrett suggested that these ". . . two types of grit-tempered ware are in reality but one, differing in the form of the opening" (*ibid.*:302), but this attribute was subsequently shown to be of low value (Baerreis and Freeman, 1958). Barrett presented a variety of grit-tempered ceramics under his two ware groupings and similar specimens were later formally grouped into Madison Plain, Madison Cord Impressed, and Aztalan Collared. The first two types are presently recognized as Effigy Mound ceramics, and R. Mason (1966:151) has proposed that Aztalan Collared be included within this group (Madison Ware). Of major concern here, however, is the occurrence of various effigy and non-effigy mounds adjacent to the village and the well-documented evidence that Lake Michigan (Effigy Mound) ceramics are associated with the Middle Mississippian ceramics throughout the village site (Barrett, 1933:302; and Hurley, n.d.).

The cultural aspects of the Effigy Mound culture in relationship to the other prehistoric cultures in Wisconsin had been up to this time somewhat uncertain and its temporal relationship to the Mississippian and Hopewell manifestations awaited additional data. In 1942, McKern in his publication "The First Settlers of Wisconsin" reviewed the state of research up to that time and presented a simplified classification of these cultures. Their order from the oldest to youngest was: Old Copper; Hopewellian; Lake Michigan (Effigy Mound); Middle Mississippian; and Upper Mississippian (Oneota). The Lake Michigan Phase—Effigy Mound Aspect was considered by McKern to belong to a Woodland Pattern. McKern considered this Woodland (post-Hopewellian) manifestation as the golden age of forest-dwelling hunters (1942:163). The Effigy Mound Aspect:

> . . . did not come into the state as such; it was entirely a local development, a true product of Wisconsin. There is some evidence that the culture began to assume specific character in *northwestern Wisconsin,* where the peculiarities of many small mounds and their contents, apparently erected during an earlier period, are significantly prophetic of Effigy Mound characteristics (*ibid.*:164) [emphasis mine].

This reference to northwestern Wisconsin as a possible source area for the Effigy Mound culture contradicts his age estimates for the only known Focus in that area, i.e. the Clam River Focus, a variety of mound builders within the Woodland Pattern found in Burnett County, which he considered were of a rather recent origin (*ibid.*:157; 1963). The cultural origins referred to by McKern remain as much an enigma as does the answer to what or who caused the decline or departure of the Effigy Mound people (*ibid.*:164). McKern suggested that a change in burial customs, termination of the building of mounds with effigy shapes, or possible attacks by invading enemies, i.e. Upper Mississippians, might have been the reasons for their loss of cultural identity. Finally, McKern also recognized a pre-Hopewellian Woodland Pattern in Wisconsin. He considered this earlier Woodland Pattern as being derived from some culture whose origin was in Asia and whose ultimate center of development was within the region of Minnesota and Wisconsin (*ibid.*:167).

Within the southern edge of the effigy mound distribution, W. B. Nickerson and members of the Department of Anthropology of The University of Chicago, conducted extensive mound and village surveys of Jo Daviess County, Illinois (Bennett, 1945). A total of 655 mounds were recorded of which ". . . 73% were conicals, 25% linears, and a total of seven (ca. 1%) effigies . . ." (1945:5). Bennett proposed that linears and effigies shared several construction features and that there were a number of traits linking small conicals and Hopewell mounds to his linear-effigy complex (ibid.:6, 12). Lake Michigan ceramics were considered by Bennett as affiliated with the Wisconsin Effigy Mound ceramics and as he contrasts these with the recovered Hopewellian ceramics, Bennett states: ". . . in Jo Daviess . . . there is strong indication that Hopewellian and Effigy Mound were contemporaneous . . ." (*ibid.*: 80-81). His cord impressed ceramics (Madison Cord Impressed) were suggested as being similar to those recovered from the McClaughry Group (McKern, 1928), Kletzien and Nitschke Groups (McKern, 1930), and Woodland specimens from Aztalan (Barrett, 1933); however, he viewed the Jo Daviess effigy mound manifestations as slightly later than the Wisconsin representatives (1945:82). The evidence from the mounds and the ceramics prompted Bennett to propose that the Lake Michigan (Effigy Mound) and Hopewellian peoples in Jo Daviess County might have been contemporary (ibid.:108-112).

If the Jo Daviess Hopewellian represents a late northern survival of this culture and if the Jo Daviess effigy mounds are later than the Wisconsin groups, then the question is how long did the Hopewell survive in this area? On the other hand, if the Effigy Mound culture is similar in time in Wisconsin and Illinois, and if the Hopewellian associations are valid, then northwest Illinois, northeast Iowa, and southwest Wisconsin might be considered as the actual source area of the Effigy Mound culture and not, as McKern suggested, northwestern Wisconsin. The possible association of Hopewellian and Effigy Mound ceramics had been illustrated by McKern (1928:Plate LIV). On the basis of work conducted at the Outlet site in Dane County (Whiteford, 1952; Bakken, 1950) it was reported that Lake Michigan (Effigy Mound culture) cord impressed (Madison Cord Impressed) and incised over cord ceramics were mixed in the mound fill with Hopewellian ceramics (Bakken, 1950:48-49, 52-53). The nearby Frost Woods Mound Group (47-Da-3) site, where a burial and a Triangular projectile point were excavated, was suggested as being affiliated with the Effigy Mound aspect (Baerreis, 1954:47). There may be multiple components at the Outlet site which were mixed together by later Effigy Mound peoples; however, the occurrence of incised over cord ceramics with effigy mounds had also been illustrated by McKern (1930:Pl. LXX-LXXVIII).

It was perhaps timely, after 30 years of effigy mound excavations (1919 to 1949), that a trait list of artifacts associated with the Effigy Mound culture was published (McKern and Ritzenthaler, 1949). The authors noted that although the Effigy Mound cultures participated in the Woodland Pattern they also ". . . developed some specific and distinctive elements of their own such as artifact types and burial in mounds in the shape of birds and animals" (1949:39). The trait list was based primarily on excavations at nine effigy mound sites. In addition to some of the obvious characteristics already presented, the list also included the following traits (*ibid.*:40-48):

(a) Community life: Semi-sedentary small villages.

(b) Economic life: Hunting, fishing, and the gathering of wild foods.

(c) Mound groups consisting of effigy, conical, and linear forms.

(d) Lithic artifacts: stemmed and notched points; scrapers; drills; grooved and fluted axes (not found in mounds); handled celts; and gorgets.

(e) Bone, shell and copper: awls, bone harpoon points; bone cup and pin games; *Anculosa sp.* shell beads; antler flakers; and copper celts and awls.

(f) Ceramic artifacts: grit-tempered cord-marked pottery having the following decorations: cord wrapped stick; punctated; cord impressed; incised (not in mounds); noded; stamped; or occasionally with thick outer lip margins or collar-like folds; and pottery elbow pipes.

The utility of such a trait list was questioned by Baerreis. His main arguments were that these traits should be grouped into clusters forming specific complexes; that the trait lists, as composed of variables, must be quantifiable; and that these lists tended to obscure differences (1949:65-73). In his reply to Baerreis' comments, McKern pointed out that these lists are restricted by the existing limited knowledge and while he agreed that quantitatively arranged data is justifiable he also noted that it is again dependent on existing data (McKern, 1950:71-76). The majority of today's archaeological monographs present traits in a quantified manner; certainly even in 1949, the utility of McKern's list, which did bring together data on the Effigy Mound culture for the first time, would have been enhanced and clarified through quantification.

Possibly the prime example of the need for the presentation of qualitative and quantitative data is reflected in Moreau Maxwell's article "A Change in the Interpretation of Wisconsin's Prehistory" (1950). This article is a popularized preliminary report on the excavations of the Diamond Bluff Mound Group in western Wisconsin. This mound group may have contained as many as 200 mounds prior to plowing; the mounds remaining consisted of 46 conical and long oval mounds, and one panther effigy. Artifacts from the adjacent fields were Upper Mississippian, Oneota, Orr

Focus specimens, and, therefore, temporally later than the mound group. During the field season of 1948, three conical mounds, one oval mound, and the one panther effigy were excavated. Only two of these mounds are worth nothing here—Conical Mound No. 4, and the panther effigy, Mound 26. Conical Mound 4 yielded 200 sherds, two projectile points, and a broken celt or axe. The sherds were composed of two-thirds grit-tempered Woodland examples and one-third shell-tempered. The fact that 66 or so sherds were shell-tempered might not be of great significance; however, enough fragments were recovered to reconstruct a small jar with two loop handles and a black polished bowl. The latter specimen is thought to be more similar to the Aztalan (Middle Mississippian) stage and the jar, Upper Mississippian. As these sherds were incorporated in the fill it was suggested that the mound was built at a time when the Effigy Mound culture and Oneota were contemporary, or else that mound 4 was built by Middle Mississippian peoples (Maxwell, 1950:438-440).

Panther Mound 26 contained the most enigmatic assemblage thus far recorded for an effigy mound. These inclusive artifacts include: a side notched projectile point; a triangular projectile point; shell-tempered sherds from an angular shouldered jar (Middle Mississippian?); a shell-tempered jar with small loop handles (Oneota); a larger shell-tempered, loop handled jar with Middle Mississippi design elements; and a shell-tempered bowl fragment with a rolled lip and angular shoulder. Maxwell concludes from the data derived from this effigy mound:

> . . . since there is no reason to doubt that the effigy mound complex is early in Wisconsin, we must assume either that the idea of the animal-shaped burial mound persisted until late times in some areas, or that Upper Mississippi culture begins in Wisconsin much earlier than we had previously supposed. In all probability the true picture is a compromise between the two suggestions.
>
> Secondly, the combination of Upper Mississippi and Middle Mississippi pottery traits, even the combination of traditions on the same clay vessel, must mean that in this area the two phases are contemporaneous and mutually influencing, or that the Upper Mississippi Phase is here in the process of developing out of an earlier Middle Mississippi culture base (1950:442-443).

Needless to say, this mound group is constantly cited as evidence for all sorts of combinations of cultural associations. However, the scientific value of this mound group will remain unknown as no descriptive report followed this popular version, nor has any additional work been done in the rest of the mounds or the adjacent village sites.

One of the first attempts to refine the broad descriptive categories of Woodland ceramics appeared in Robert Hall's "A Style Analysis of Wisconsin Woodland Pottery" (1950), a publication that is not well known and almost totally ignored. Using the Wisconsin ceramics as a departure point, Hall discussed the Lake Michigan category (McKern, 1930) in order to refine and clarify this large ceramic group. The Lake Michigan pottery included as a sub-variety Effigy Mound pottery; however, with subsequent investigations, the Lake Michigan pottery was expanded into a ware group including related pottery which was not necessarily associated with the Effigy Mound culture (Hall, 1950:5). By 1950 the Algonkian associations with this ware were more tenuous and difficult to demonstrate; therefore, Hall preferred to treat the Lake Michigan ware as a prehistoric Woodland manifestation and to chronologically order the ceramics through a stylistic analysis.

Hall proposed three basic groups or principal styles within the Woodland tradition in Wisconsin: a Northern Decorative Tradition; an Incised Over Cord Marked Style; and a Cord Decorated Style. The Northern Decorative Tradition included "pseudo-cord" and dentate-like (*Laurel*?) ceramics which had Hopewellian and Northeastern (New York) connections. As these ceramics appeared to be confined to a northern area (Minnesota, Wisconsin, and Michigan) and as their ". . . strongest affiliation [was] with eastern Woodland ceramics," (*ibid.*:14) Hall saw them as being chronologically related to the earliest New York sequences (Vinette and Point Peninsula). By indicating the distinction of these Lake Michigan ceramics plus their eastern relationships, Hall isolated ceramics whose far reaching distributions were later to be more fully documented and elaborated upon (Wright, 1967).

The Incised Over Cord Marked Style had also been included within the Lake Michigan ware-Effigy Mound pottery (McKern and Ritzenthaler, 1949) and was seen by Hall as a style distinct from both the Northern Decorative Tradition and the Cord Decorated Style. Hall viewed this style as chronologically pre-Hopewellian, despite its recorded associations with effigy mounds, basing his interpretations on the decorative similarities with the pre-Hopewellian Black Sand Incised type of Illinois (1950:20). He also suggested that as incised over cord ceramics had been recovered from mound fill and the adjacent Outlet village site, they would, therefore, pre-date the period of mound construction (*ibid.*:30-31). Interjected into these observations, Hall proposed the possibility that there may be two types of incised over cord: a bossed (noded) group similar to Black Sand Incised and a punched (punctated) group which remained undefined.

The Cord Decorated Style ceramics were believed to have the strongest relationships with effigy mounds and yet "... it is also found beyond the distribution of the effigy mound ... cord decoration may have survived into the historic period ... and the antecedents of the cord style have not been satisfactorily identified in a Wisconsin ceramic horizon earlier than Effigy Mound...." (*ibid.*:29-30). Hall attempted to reconstruct the types of cords utilized for decoration, providing one of the first attempts to understand this ceramic attribute; however, his reconstructions lacked precision, an aspect that will be more fully commented upon later in this report.

It was apparent to Hall that cultural and chronological relationships were being obscured by the term "Lake Michigan type" which did not allow for the separation of the early Northern Decorative Tradition or the early Incised Over Cord Marked Style or the later Cord Decorated Style (*ibid.*:30-35). Hall's explicit temporal ranking and cultural associations presented a sequence which has persisted in the archaeological literature until the present time.

In what must be considered the foremost archaeological publication of the decade, *Archeology of Eastern United States* (Griffin, 1952*a*), the article by Bennett on "The Prehistory of the Northern Mississippi Valley" represents a major effort to bring together a wide range of information in a cohesive manner. While Bennett's article is a chronological overview, eight of the 12 topics are devoted to outlining the then current knowledge concerning Woodland in this region. Bennett recognized three generalized Middle Woodland ceramic groupings which graded into one another: Middle Woodland, Hopewellian, and Lake Michigan. Included within the first group was the Laurel Focus material from Minnesota and effigy mound ceramics. Effigy Mound was seen as "... one of the Middle Woodland cultures in Wisconsin with suggestive Early Woodland antecedents, but [one that] persists throughout the period in which Hopewellian developments were present ..." (1952*a*:114). The first group was considered by Bennett to represent a generalized Middle Woodland which he contrasted to the sophisticated ceramics generally associated with Hopewellian manifestations in the Upper Mississippi Valley. The Lake Michigan pottery was placed by Bennett into a Transitional Woodland post-Hopewellian classification which he considered to be best represented by the Blackduck ceramics from Minnesota and the Woodland (Lake Michigan) ceramics from Aztalan (*ibid.*: 115-119). The other reported northern Wisconsin ceramics composed the last stages of Wisconsin Woodland which were believed to be linked ethno-historically with such known tribes as the Clam River culture ceramics ("pseudo-cord" according to Hall, 1950), and the Keshena culture ceramics from northeastern Wisconsin (Lake Michigan; Barrett and Skinner, 1932) (Bennett, 1952*a*: 121-122). Bennett's article was written in January 1948, at the time of the first radiocarbon dates. Griffin (1952*a*:369) best expressed the thinking of the time by stating:

> One of the major surprises in eastern radiocarbon dating has been the antiquity indicated for the Hopewellian period. In 1940 most of the eastern archeologists estimated Hopewell to be around A.D. 1200 to A.D. 1400. By 1949 some of them were willing to consider a beginning date of A.D. 500 and a longer time span for Hopewell up to around A.D. 800 to A.D. 900. The initial runs [radio-carbon] on Ohio and Illinois Hopewell at the University of Chicago gave the former a date of roughly 2,100 years ago and the latter some 2,300 years ago.

Placing the Effigy Mound culture within the same temporal period as Hopewell did not necessarily mean to the Upper Mississippi Valley archaeologists a beginning date of ca. 2,000 years ago; rather, most stressed that the northern manifestations of Hopewell might be marginal survivals co-existing with developing Effigy Mound. The gradual movement of Effigy Mound out of the Middle Woodland period (by archaeologists) was to occur in the years following 1952. The ceramic ordering by Bennett has not been too drastically revised and the nature and extent of the Clam River and Keshena cultures still need further documentation (Ritzenthaler, 1966:219-220). The Hopewellian-Effigy Mound relationships continued, however, to pose problems to archaeologists in the Middle West, as we shall see below.

Possible Hopewellian-Effigy Mound relationships were the central focus in Beaubien's 1953 article, "Cultural Variation Within Two Woodland Mound Groups of Northeastern Iowa." The extension of effigy mounds into Iowa had been recognized by Cyrus Thomas (1894), although the word extension may be a misnomer since this area was also an "origin area" as suggested by the contemporaneity of Hopewell and Effigy Mound (Bennett, 1945:108-112). The use of the term extension for Iowa and concentration for Wisconsin follows the idea that ". . . northeastern Iowa is *clearly marginal* to the primary growth of both cultures [Hopewell-Ohio and Illinois; Effigy Mound-Wisconsin], and it is not evident that a 'pure' complex of either has been strongly developed in the area . . ." (Beaubien 1953*b*:56; emphasis mine). However, Beaubien also stated that ". . . mounds in close proximity yielded dissimilar remains which, in their entirety, reflect a long transitional period between predominantly Hopewellian and predominantly Late Woodland cultures" (*ibid.*:65). Just what are these remains? Beaubien excavated at both the Sny-Magill mound group and at Effigy Mounds National Monument. The Sny-Magill group consisted of five effigies, six linears, and 85 conicals. Three conicals and one bird effigy were excavated. From Conical Mound 24 he recovered vessel fragments exhibiting combinations of Hopewellian zoned rocker dentate stamping and a series with Effigy Mound style cord impressions which Beaubien considered a reflection of a ". . . blending of cultural influences" (*ibid.*:60). Bird Effigy Mound 27 was void of artifacts; however, Conical Mound 24 yielded cord impressed vessel fragments (Madison Cord Impressed) plus one vessel fragment bearing rocker dentate decoration and yet Beaubien uses only this latter fragment to suggest that it ". . . implied a Hopewellian origin for mound 24" (*ibid.*:62). The last mound excavated at Sny-Magill was Conical Mound 7 and it produced three small triangular projectile points which were considered to be post-Hopewellian.

Beaubien then reported on his work at the National Monument where there were 45 conical, 10 linear, four effigy, and three conicals connected by linear embankments. Most of the mounds investigated were void of artifacts; however, Bear Effigy Mound 30 produced charcoal which was dated at A.D. 930 ± 300 (M-41) and Conical Mound 55, which produced Hopewellian artifacts (bear canines and large blades), yielded charcoal radiocarbon dated at A.D. 900 ± 300 (M-40). These dates led Beaubien to comment ". . . that the two groups were occupying the same territory concurrently. On the other hand, this might suggest that a fusion of these cultures was already in progress . . ." (*ibid.*:65). The date for the bear mound is currently within the accepted range for effigy mounds, but ". . . the date of 900 years ago is at variance with the previously obtained [Hopewell] dates" (Griffin, 1952*a*: 369). The variance in the date for this Hopewell mound is as unexpected as the variance found in decorative combinations utilized on the ceramics from Bird Effigy Mound 27 and Conical Mound 24 of the Sny-Magill mound group.

Hopewellian-Effigy Mound associations next appear in Wisconsin at the Blackhawk Village Site (Da5), Dane County,

Wisconsin (Baerreis, 1953*a*). The Blackhawk site was excavated under salvage conditions as the area was to be leveled prior to subdivision construction. Although the recovered cultural material was limited, the artifacts were diagnostic of material which had been previously illustrated as associated with the Effigy Mound culture. The Blackhawk site was excavated in 1950 and on the basis of the majority of diagnostic artifacts Baerreis proposed the first Wisconsin projectile point type, Monona Stemmed (1953*a*:10), and the first ceramic type, Madison Cord Impressed (*ibid.:*12-15). At a 1952 Wisconsin Archaeological Survey meeting held at the University of Wisconsin, Baerreis also proposed the following ceramic types: Dane Incised (Keslin, 1958:203-205); Kegonsa Stamped (Hurley, 1966:54-55); and Shorewood Cord Roughened (*ibid.:* 57-60). The descriptions for these four ceramic types were based on a much larger sample than had been excavated in Wisconsin and included similar material which had been either illustrated or recovered from surface collections (Baerreis, 1953*a*:6, 12). The Madison Cord Impressed type represented a ceramic category which was more restrictive than either of the broader Lake Michigan or Effigy Mound wares; moreover, ". . . there is no reason to doubt that the basic cultural affiliation is still with the Effigy Mound culture . . ." (*ibid.:*19). Associated with the Madison Cord Impressed ceramics were four Hopewellian specimens which ". . . serve to fix the time period . . . [and] on the basis of [these] trade sherds, it is evident that we are dealing with Effigy Mound culture during the Middle Woodland period . . ." (*ibid.:*19).

The Blackhawk site represents the first *specific* habitation site in Wisconsin, Illinois, or Iowa reported as being associated with the Effigy Mound culture. Although there were no mounds directly on the site, mounds were noted by the excavator in an area adjacent to the site (Baerreis, personal communication). Adding to the distinctiveness of the conclusions drawn from this site is the fact that an expanded stem point form, Monona Stemmed, is suggested as being a part of the material culture of Effigy Mound. At this time, small Triangular projectile points were considered as being associated with the later Mississippian cultures (Maxwell, 1950; Logan, 1953; Baerreis, 1953*a*, 1954); however, with subsequent investigations it was shown that Triangular projectile points were also associated with the Effigy Mound culture (Keslin, 1958:264-267). With the establishment of formal types for Wisconsin the nature of archaeological reporting took an important step forward toward greater explication and specification. Qualitative and quantitative presentations of artifactual material up to this point in time had been broadly categorized.

The use of typological nomenclature and techniques quickly spread to Iowa where they were utilized by Logan (1953) for his report on the "Archaeological Investigation of Spike Hollow Rock Shelter, Allamakee County, Iowa". Logan's report represented the first report of a rockshelter which was inhabited by Effigy Mound peoples. The Spike Hollow rockshelter had been previously excavated by members of the Iowa Archaeological Society and the range of the artifacts suggested to Logan that this shelter might contain stratified deposits representing a considerable temporal range (1953:4). The unexcavated portions of the rockshelter were quite limited and the much hoped for stratigraphy did not materialize. The range of artifacts was considerable, however, and Logan, working with the superposition of the artifacts, was able to derive a considerable amount of information (*ibid.*:4-11). The material cultural remains included: Side-notched, Corner-notched, Contracting-stemmed, Basal-notched, Straight Stemmed, and Triangular projectile points; Incised Over Cord Marked, Cord-marked (Cord Impressed), Stamped, and Oneota (Upper Mississippian) pottery.

Chronologically, but not quantitatively, Logan ordered his material into the following periods: Archaic/Early Woodland; Hopewell; Middle Woodland; Late Woodland; and Oneota. His projectile point sequence seems currently valid; therefore, only his ceramic sequence will be considered. The Incised Over Cord Marked pottery is equated by Logan with the pre-Hopewell Black Sand Incised pottery of Illinois (see also Hall, 1950; Baerreis, 1953*b*) and he follows Hall's interpretation that this variety of pottery is the earliest at the Outlet site (Logan, 1953:16). The ceramic representatives of Hopewell consist of 24 zoned (Hopewell Zone Stamped) and rockered-dentate stamped sherds, of which four were found in a feature (Feature 1) in direct association with three cord-decorated sherds (*ibid.*:12, 19).

The cord-decorated ceramics occurred with the highest frequency. Three types were recognized by Logan: Madison Cord Impressed, Land Farm Cord Impressed, and Lane Farm Stamped. Lane Farm Cord Impressed is a regional variety similar to Madison Cord Impressed, dissimilar only in ". . . handling of the ground on which the decoration is placed and some difference in decoration itself . . ." (*ibid.*:18). Lane Farm Stamped was slightly thicker than these two types and lacked complexity in cord decoration—the type specimens had single impressions widely separated on the lip, rim, or rim interior. However, the distinguishing characteristics of the two Lane Farm types could be viewed as a local variation of the Madison Cord Impressed type. Logan assigned these three ceramic types to his Middle Woodland Period and associated them with the Hopewellian specimens because they were seen as contemporary and temporally extending beyond Hopewell (*ibid.*:21). The Late Woodland, Lake Michigan Ware ceramics were few in number and were considered to be related to the Woodland pottery from Aztalan while the Upper Mississippian Oneota material was considered to be more representative of the local Orr Focus material. The sequence proposed by Logan and the associated ceramics again demonstrates the frequency of their relationships throughout the Middle West while supporting a view that Hopewell/Middle Woodland and Madison Cord Impressed/Effigy Mound could be considered contemporaneous.

The suggestion by Hall (1950) and Logan (1953) that Incised Over Cord Marked pottery from Iowa and Wisconsin belonged to a pre-Hopewellian temporal period was further supported by Baerreis (1953*b*) in his report on the Airport Village site in Dane County, Wisconsin. This site was distinctive in that lithic materials typologically belonged to an Early through Late Archaic period; they included Madison Side Notched and Waubesa Contracting Stem projectile points associated with finely-made lanceolate forms, gravers, scrapers, and knives (Baerreis, 1953*b*:153-158). This lithic assemblage represented the earliest excavated artifacts reported for Wisconsin which could be readily related to forms belonging to an Archaic stage in Illinois (*ibid.*:161-163). Lithic material was associated with ceramics also similar to Illinois material (Black Sand Incised) of the Early Woodland period. The Black Sand Incised pottery from the Airport site consisted of only two specimens which showed some divergence from the Illinois type specimens (*ibid.*:159) and these were later included in Baerreis' type description of Dane Incised ". . . which probably begins in the Early Woodland but may well continue into the Early Middle Woodland period" (Keslin, 1958:205).

The chronology of the types proposed thus far, in both the lithic and ceramic categories, appears to become more assured in temporal placement and to be found under conditions suggesting sequential order and assemblage associations. The artifact types suggested as belonging to the Effigy Mound culture became more restricted in number and in geographic distribution, and what was still to come was greater accuracy in chronometric dating. This aspect had its beginnings with the one date by Beaubien for the Bear Effigy Mound–A.D. 930 ± 300 (M-41)–which was followed by an additional radiocarbon date for an effigy mound in Wisconsin.

In 1955, Wittry and Bruder reported on their "Salvage Operations at the Kolterman Mound Group" located in Dodge County, Wisconsin. Four otter effigy mounds, one linear mound, and one conical mound were destroyed by road building operations. These six mounds represent only a portion of the original 22 mounds in this group. Two otter effigy mounds were excavated and, from a feature in Mound 18, Wittry and Bruder report the recovery of two Madison Cord Impressed vessel fragments, two Triangular projectile points, cremation fragments, and a charcoal sample which yielded a date of A.D. 776 ± 250 (M-398) (Wittry, 1956:133-134). The second excavated otter effigy mound, Number 17, also contained a burial feature composed of badly decomposed skeletal fragments. The recovered skull exhibited occipital deformation similar to only one other reported by McKern from an effigy mound (1930:452). The excellent association of the Madison Cord Impressed vessel fragments and the Triangular projectile points with an effigy mound dated at A.D. 776 ± 250 finally documented beyond any doubt the association of the Madison Cord Impressed type with the Effigy Mound culture and suggested that Triangular points were not exclusively associated with the Mississippian cultures. The two reported dates for effigy mounds with their plus or minus figures were also in agreement.

The second phase of effigy mound research generated problems of cultural associations, material culture assignments, and statements concerning chronological position. There was, therefore, a timely need for a summing up or for a definitive statement on this culture which had undergone over 100 years of investigations. Rowe's "The Effigy Mound Culture of Wisconsin" (1956) was aimed at compiling ". . . all the known data concerning the Wisconsin Effigy Mound culture . . . the time is at hand for re-examination of data, for new syntheses, and for possible establishment of concrete conclusions" (1956:9). Rowe proposed to synthesize the published data and to present information on the Raisbeck Mound Group which had been previously excavated by McKern.

Rowe begins by dealing with effigy mound research previous to 1915, allowing him to state: "... the only published data which report excavations and analysis of sites of this culture are the work of the archaeologists of the Milwaukee Public Museum .... no reports ... have been forthcoming from ... Illinois, Iowa, or Minnesota" (*ibid.*:10-12). However, Rowe's bibliography includes Baerreis, 1952; Bennett, 1945; Bennett, 1952; and Maxwell, 1950. Rowe also included within his assessment information from 483 mounds, of which 193 were excavated effigy, low-domed conical, and linear mounds (1956:14-17). Primary to his analysis is his report on the Raisbeck Mound Group which was considered a "... typical site of the culture under consideration" (*ibid.*:18).

The Raisbeck Mound Group consisted of 38 conical, 14 linear, 13 bird, 11 canine, and three oval mounds and one problematical mound, of which 13 conical, two linear, three bird, one canine, and one oval mound were excavated. A total of 80 individuals were removed from these mounds. Beyond the types of burials represented, no information is given concerning this population. Of the 445 ceramic fragments recovered, only 18 were rim sherds. The assemblage was grouped into Cord-wrapped paddle, Smooth-over CWP, Plain Surface (all Madison Plain?), Single Cord Impressions (Madison Cord Impressed?), and Rocked-Dentate Stamp, the latter recovered from the mound fill (*ibid.*:44-46). Descriptions of pipes, stone objects, projectile points, perforators, and bone objects from this site are covered in one short page.

From this typical site and its material culture, Rowe then presents a "General Description of the Effigy Mound Culture of Wisconsin." His discussion of community life can best be summed up by saying that he saw no evidence of permanent habitation, that is, villages and the data from campsites were considered as tenuous at best. It follows, therefore, that Rowe could support his premise that "... Effigy Mound peoples were mainly food gatherers and hunters" (*ibid.*:51-52). Rowe's treatment of stone, bone and antler, shell, and metal objects, pottery, and pipes is in the same vein. Effigy Mound pottery is "exceedingly generalized" so Rowe, after McKern, places it within the Lake Michigan ware, Effigy Mound type, and ignores Baerreis' Madison Cord Impressed type (*ibid.*:51, 59-62). Rowe does list the techniques of decoration: imprinting with single cords; punctating; puncturing or piercing; embossing; indentation (including rocked-dentate stamped); and incising. All of these decoration forms were extensively studied by Hall (1950) and ignored by Rowe. Under the heading of "Ceremonial Life," Rowe states that it ". . . becomes more and more apparent that the Mounds of Wisconsin which have given the Effigy Mound culture its name were built primarily as burial tumuli" (*ibid.*:66).

With this paucity of data Rowe had no alternative but to turn to mound form cultural affiliations, chronological position, and historic identification as topics which would ". . . stimulate research to bring to light additional information . . ." (*ibid.*:17). Rowe's comments on mound form are generally a restatement of what previous researchers had said concerning mound group locations, arrangements, orientations, numbers, and types. Rowe excludes "man mounds"; he believed that they were ". . . poor representations of swallow-tailed birds", an interpretation uniquely Rowe's. Rowe then discusses pits, altars, and cists, and offers a trait list for effigy mound which adds nothing of importance to the list recorded by McKern and Ritzenthaler (1949). The affiliative aspects of the Effigy Mound culture were supported by trait lists and consist of Hopewell, Illinois Central Basin, Red Ochre, Mille Lacs, Adena, and Hamilton (*ibid.*:77-82). The only local relationships are with the Clam River Focus (McKern, 1963) which were considered by Rowe to be related to the Minnesota Mille Lacs Aspect (1956:81). This relationship is important: Rowe concurred with McKern in suggesting that it originated or assumed its specific character somewhere in northwestern Wisconsin (*ibid.*: 77).

The chronological position of the Effigy Mound culture was considered by Rowe to be of considerable antiquity based on the large number of mounds found in a limited area and the generally poor skeletal preservation. He suggested that the Effigy Mound culture began in Hopewellian times and continued until Mississippian times. Proto-Effigy Mound was seen to be in the northwest Wisconsin area, an area without effigy mounds and ". . . this implies that the earliest manifestations of the Effigy Mound culture was limited to conical and linear forms and that the effigy mounds came in somewhat later" (*ibid.*:82-83).

Rowe's major contribution to effigy mound research was probably his discussion of historic tribal identification. Winnebago-Effigy Mound relationships had been shown to be invalid by McKern (1928:277-279); however, the idea still persisted that the mound effigy shapes represented totem or clan symbols which ". . . we cannot determine . . . archaeologically . . ." (Rowe,

1956:84). Rowe presented lists of eight tribes known to have inhabited Wisconsin (Menomini, Chippewa, Chiwere Sioux, Fox, Sauk, Winnebago, Mascouten, and Kickapoo) with their respective clans. He combined these various clans under effigy mound categories—i.e., eagle, pigeon, owl, etc.= Bird—in order to relate types of clans and types of mounds to tribes. Rowe concluded that "... the clan theory of the mound purpose can be discarded ... [and] ... none of the historic Woodland clan systems tie in very well with the effigy mound shapes, nor have any of these groups built mounds of this type during the historic period" (*ibid.*:88). The fact that the effigy shape of these mounds does not correlate well with clan or totem symbols of historic Wisconsin Indian tribes does not necessarily preclude the fact that the mounds may not have been built in the form of clan or totem symbols and that their shapes were for a purpose unknown to us either archaeologically or historically. With this view, seven of the contenders (excluding the Winnebago) may eventually be eliminated one by one until direct historic connections on the basis of material culture can be demonstrated.

With the above synthesis of Rowe's attempts to present a re-examination of data, a new synthesis, and concrete conclusions of the most dynamic and largest indigenous culture in Wisconsin, it can be seen that his assessment presents few new valid scientific observations—only impressions and speculations gathered from secondary sources. These secondary sources were the archaeologists who provided Rowe with a plethora of data that were most amenable to scientific enquiry. He grossly categorized or ignored, prompting one reviewer to object to his interpretations (Baerreis, 1958); yet McKern (1958) vehemently defended Rowe's interpretations as the only appropriate ones until confirming evidence was produced. Perhaps it is appropriate here to review some of the problems generated during the second phase of effigy mound research and to see how many Rowe effectively dealt with and how many remained to be resolved during this third and continuing phase of effigy mound research.

Early in the second phase McKern demonstrated a prehistoric age for the mounds (1928:276; 1930:457, 461-462) and determined that Radin's claims for Winnebago authorship of the mounds were erroneous (1928:267-288; 1929*a*:562-564; 1930:462-463). McKern also proposed the terms Effigy Mound culture, Effigy Mound pottery, and Lake Michigan Ware which gave some semblance of order to the cultural manifestation being investigated. The Hopewell manifestation along with the Mississippian manifestations were recognized (McKern, 1931, 1945; Barrett, 1933) and the broad ceramic grouping was culturally and temporally ordered. Habitation sites were reported by Barrett and Skinner (1932) and Baerreis (1953*a*) and Hopewellian-Effigy Mound-Mississippian contacts were demonstrated by McKern (1928), Barrett (1933), Bennett (1945, 1952), Maxwell (1950), Beaubien (1953*a*), Baerreis (1953*a*), and Logan (1953). Effigy mound sites were being excavated outside of Wisconsin (Bennett, 1945; Beaubien, 1953*b*; and Logan, 1953), and ceramic and lithic typology was introduced as a means of clarifying Effigy Mound material culture problems (Baerreis, 1953*a*; Beaubien 1953*a*; and Logan, 1953). Hall's 1950 style analysis set the stage for broad ordering and affiliations in a more exacting manner than broad categories of Lake Michigan ware or Effigy Mound type could hope to accomplish. Rowe could have resolved a wealth of problems—the actual relationships of effigy, conical, and linear mounds; the possible source or origin areas; the nature of habitation sites and rockshelter utilization; effigy mound characteristics outside of the Wisconsin "core" area; synthesis and explication of the material culture associated with Effigy Mound; clarification of his "food gatherers and hunters" concept; and the nature and character of the Effigy Mound-Hopewell, Effigy Mound-Middle Mississippian, and Effigy Mound-Upper Mississippian relationships. The data that could have been derived from an analysis of the Woodland (Effigy Mound) ceramics at the Aztalan site would have enhanced and contributed greatly to his report. As it is, Rowe's report only serves as a partial indicator of over 100 years of effigy mound research. The period following Rowe's report is a period of numerous archaeological advances in the understanding of Effigy Mound prehistory by archaeologists attempting to answer some of the questions Rowe perhaps considered unimportant.

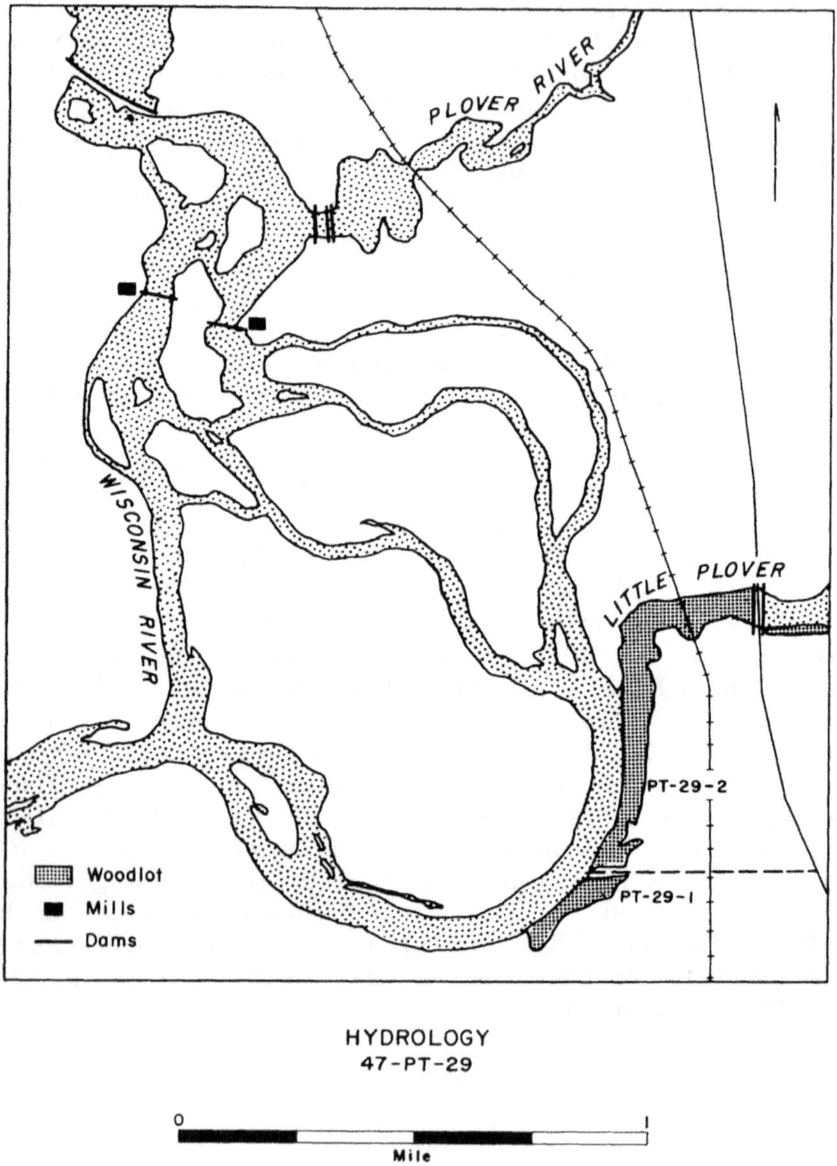

FIG. 3 Hydrology of 47-Pt-29.

III

BIGELOW SITE (47-Pt-29-1 AND 47-Pt-29-2): LOCATION, DESCRIPTION, AND EXCAVATION PROCEDURE

THE Bigelow site (47-Pt-29-1 and Pt-29-2) was located on an outwash plain and stream terrace of the east side of the Wisconsin River. The outwash plain is some two miles west of a glacial end moraine (Wisconsin Stage, Woodfordian Substage, former Tazewell and Cary) which dates from approximately 22,000 to 12,500 years ago (Frye, Willman, and Black, 1965:55). The site was in the northeast quarter of Section 21 T23N, R8E, Plover Township, Portage County, Wisconsin, latitude North 44°28′ and longitude West 89°33′. The site was in a woodlot next to the river bluff which has a 50 to 58 percent slope to the water level. The river channel below the site is an oxbow of the Wisconsin which bends from the south to west-southwest. Separating this 300-foot wide channel and the main river channel are a series of nine islands, of which the largest is 1 1/8 miles long and 5/8 of a mile wide (see Fig. 3).

The site was first reported by Lewis in 1890 and at that time he excavated one effigy mound from which he recovered bone, charcoal and a copper awl (1890:5, Brown, 1906:366). Collie and Becker reported the mound group as the Bigelow Group (1912:50-51) and they compiled a list of nine conical mounds, a bear effigy, and a bird effigy. At the time of their survey they recorded the undergrowth around the conical mounds (47-Pt-29-1) as scrub oak and they mentioned that the eastern wing of the bird effigy (Mound L) extended into a cultivated field, which would imply that the mound was in a woodlot.

In 1956 Dixon, Blake, and Scribner conducted a survey of the mound group (1956:65-72) in order to redefine the Collie and Becker report of 1912. Their survey produced 12 additional mounds consisting of seven linear, two effigy, and four conical mounds. The vegetation at the time of the 1956 report consisted of a weedy field which contained a "... dense concentration of scrub pine east of the mound grouping" (*ibid.*:67). In 1957, Blake excavated conical Mound G which yielded four burials, ceramics, and lithic material which he assigned to a Late Middle Woodland to Late Woodland temporal period (1961:57-76). An air photograph taken during Blake's excavation shows a gallery-like woodlot adjacent to the riverbank, the extent of the Town of Plover's dumping grounds, and to the south of Mound G a small cluster of jack pine.

In July 1965 I resurveyed and tested the Bigelow site and added to the number and types of mounds by recording four additional mounds. At that time I was informed that the property was owned by Mr. Joseph Hartz of Stevens Point, and after conferring with Mr. Hartz I learned that the mound group was destined for destruction because of a planned subdivision development.

After the 1966 excavations had begun, the original Collie and Becker conical mound group was relocated. Bear effigy Mound 13 was located 500 feet south of Mound N and the conical cluster of 13 mounds was 500 feet south of Mound 13 (Fig. 4). It was decided in the field to arbitrarily divide the conical cluster and the bear mound and to designate them numerically. The original Collie and Becker group (less Mound L) was codified as 47-Pt-29-1 (labeled G.L. 6 on plate) and the Bigelow group as 47-Pt-29-2 (labeled G.L. 7 on plate), although both groups are presented here as a unit according to our sequence of excavation.

An overview of the Bigelow site from the south to north is as follows: 47-Pt-29-1 is totally within a woodlot in Government Lot 6 (Fig. 4) and the woodlot ranges from 300 to 370 feet east to west and approximately 445 feet north to south. Within the woodlot we located and mapped 13 conical mounds oriented in an east to west arrangement. The bear effigy, Mound 13, is in the northern end of this woodlot. Mound 13 is oriented in a north-south direction with the feet pointing to the east. Between this mound and 47-Pt-29-2 is Government Lot 7. 47-Pt-29-2 is partially within a woodlot which ranges from 150 to 50 feet east to west and approximately 1,000 feet north to south. The field

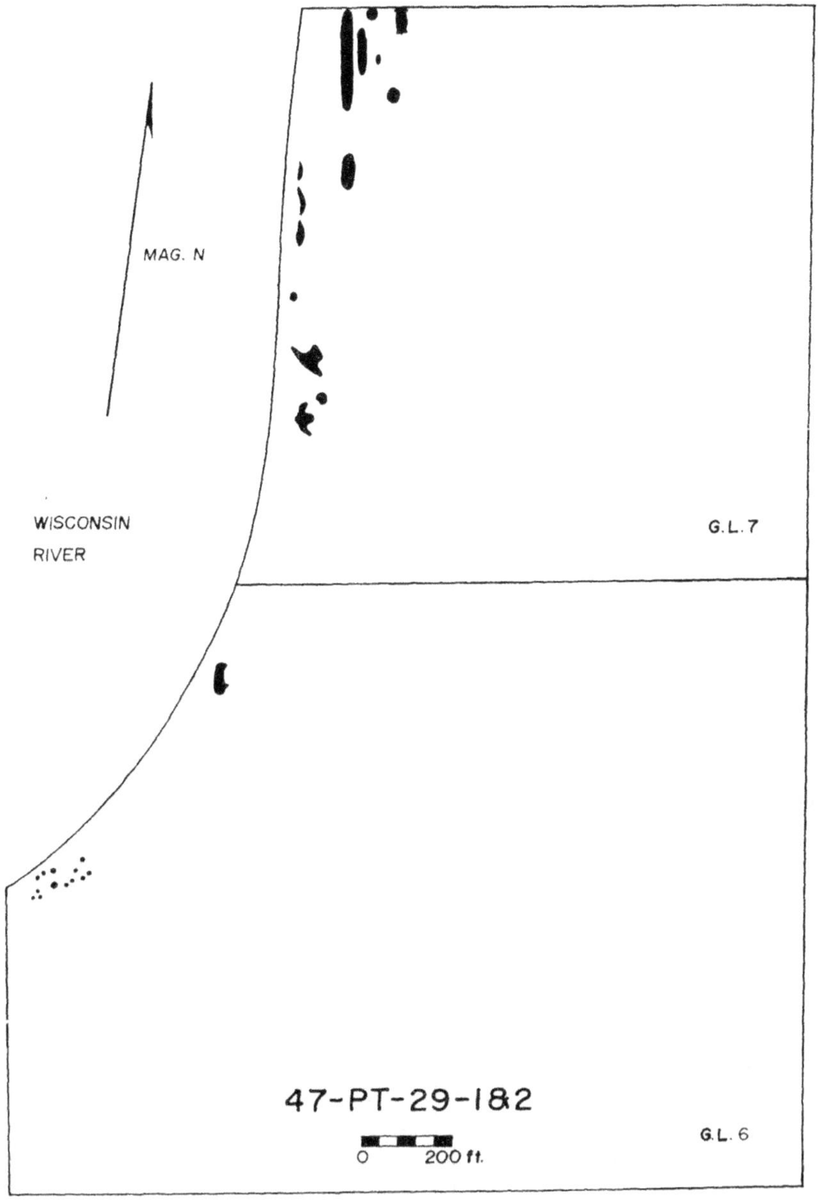

FIG. 4. Plan view of 47-Pt-29-1 and Pt-29-2.

east of the woodlot contained mounds and limited habitation material and is approximately 750 feet east to west and 1,000 feet north to south. Both Government Lots 6 and 7 have been recently platted for the subdivision.

47-Pt-29-2

Testing operations at 47-Pt-29-2 were begun on July 14, 1965, and terminated on August 2, 1965. During this time mounds A, B, L, and P were tested and one surface aquare (S5L40) was excavated. On the basis of our testing operations and the fact that the site had still not been located and would be destroyed, it was recommended that full exploration be conducted in the mounds and the possible habitation areas.

On June 13, 1966, excavations were begun at the Bigelow site and they were terminated on July 23, 1966. At 47-Pt-29-2 the underbrush and small saplings were cleared from the woodlot and an initial 50-foot grid system was established. Our limited testing in 1965 had indicated that there was habitation material within the woodlot and the 50-foot grid system was selected so that 2.5-foot by 2.5-foot test squares could be placed throughout the woodlot as an aid in defining the areas of habitation. With the grid system established, the test squares were staked out and the southwest corner of each square was used as the key stake for square designation. Efforts were made to correlate the test levels to natural soil horizons. All levels were initially hand trowelled but as our work progressed, trowelling was combined with soil screening. Soil profiles were drawn of each excavated square and a soil description of the profile was made from at least one representative wall. The cataloguing and marking system utilized identified each markable artifact by site codification number (i.e., 47-Pt-29-1) (Hurley, 1965*b*), the square number, level number, and artifact number. Thus, a sherd from 47-Pt-29-1, square N10W80, level 2, and catalogue number one, would be marked and recorded as 47-Pt-29-1/N10W80-2-1.

During the first week of excavations it became apparent that the woodlot had not been subjected to historic cultivation and that the greatest concentration of non-mound prehistoric artifacts was to be found in the woodlot south of grid line N200 (Fig. 5). Those squares which yielded the most artifacts were expanded in the direction of high yield. In addition, we began to recover a previously unreported aboriginal and historic artifact mixture

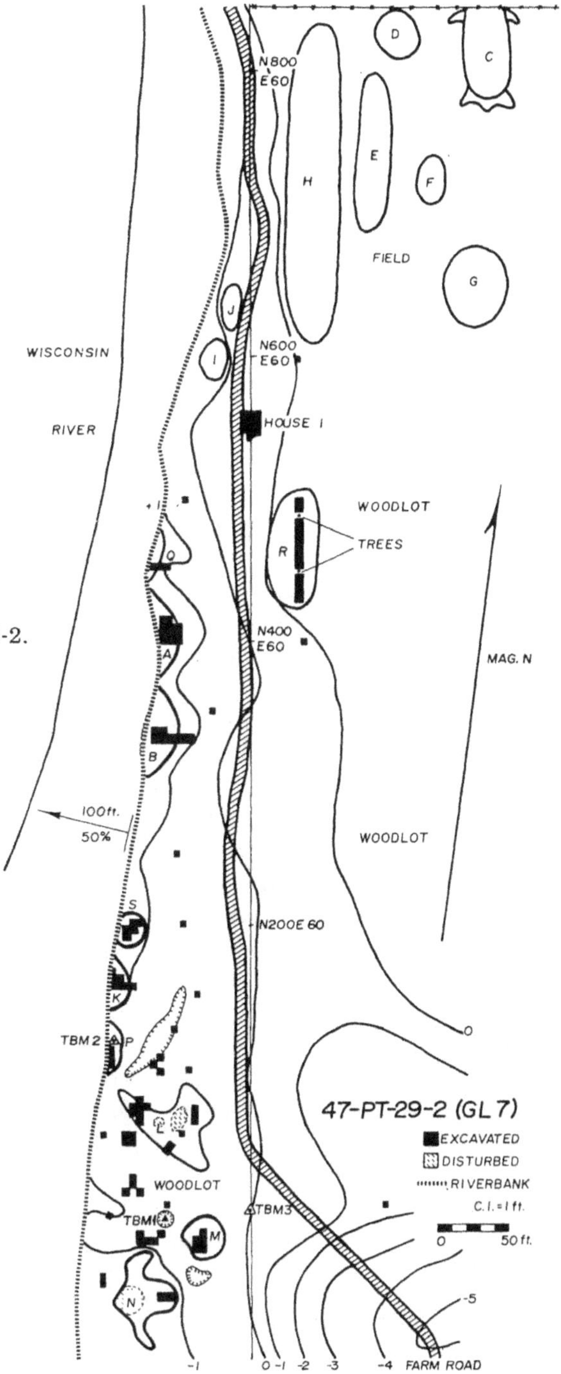

FIG. 5. Plan view of 47-Pt-29-2.

within and adjacent to the woodlot from grid localities N200 to N700. This mixture corresponded, in the woodlot, to those areas with present surface vegetation of mainly short to medium grasses. Continued exploration in this area produced additional evidence of Late Historic material (circa 1850 to 1890) and one historic structure (House 1, Fig. 5). While the nature and extent of this Historic component were not fully explored, their contribution toward understanding the Historic aboriginal manifestations in Central Wisconsin is recorded in the report by Lange (1969). Brief commentaries will be made on those historic manifestations which directly affected surface or mound interpretations.

Excavation at 47-Pt-29-2 proceeded from south to north and those mounds or surface areas which seemed to be most productive were intensively explored. Rather than presenting a description of each mound, its excavation, and its soil characteristics, selected examples with detailed profile descriptions will be presented and those which have similar profiles eliminated.

One auxiliary line of field research at both the Bigelow site and the Sanders site was soils. Previous effigy mound excavations had reported buried soils below the mounds, and these preserved soils (paleosols) or buried soil profiles (solums)—i.e. A and B horizons—reflect former climate and vegetation, while the present-day soil profiles reflect present climate and vegetation. It was thought that the similarity or contrast in soil profiles would serve as an important indicator of the surroundings in which the Effigy Mound peoples lived (Hurley, 1971).

The utility of a soils approach to archaeological excavations is illustrated in the following mound and surface square soil descriptions, which also present conclusions concerning the soils horizons. However, these conclusions are based exclusively on field morphological and classificational interpretations and they are subject to revision when the final report is submitted by the Soils Department of the University of Wisconsin. The identification and nomenclature designating the soils horizons were derived from the conventions described in the *Soil Survey Manual* (1951) and the supplement to that manual which was issued in 1962. The following descriptions of master horizons, layers, and symbols are from the supplement and these horizon designations plus additional field symbols were utilized at the Bigelow site:

01 "Organic horizons in which essentially the original form of most vegetative matter is visible to the naked eye."

Ap "The symbol p is used as a suffix with A to indicate disturbance by cultivation or pasturing."

A11 "Mineral horizons, formed or forming at or adjacent to the surface, in which the feature emphasized is the accumulation of humified organic matter intimately associated with the mineral fraction."

A12 A subdivision of the A1 horizon.

A1b A buried A1 soil horizon (b).

A1b2 A second A1 horizon which is buried (b).

A1b3 A third A1 horizon which is buried (b).

A/B A soil horizon composed of both A and B but which is the result of subsurface man-made mixture. This designation is recommended for archaeologists and it is not to be found in the supplement.

A/Bb A buried A/B horizon (b).

A/Bb2 A second A/B horizon which is buried (b).

A/Birb An A/B horizon, buried (b), which has an "accumulation of illuvial iron [ir] as coatings on sand or silt particles or as pellets of silt size. . . ."

Bir11 "A transitional horizon between B and A1 or between B and A2 in which the horizon is dominated by properties of the underlying B2 but has some subordinate properties of an overlying A1 or A2."

Bir12 A subdivision of the Bir1 horizon.

Bir2 "That part of the B horizon where the properties on which the B is based [with] clearly expressed subordinate characteristics indicating that the horizon is transitional to an adjacent overlying A or an adjacent underlying C or R."

B21irb A buried (b) B2 horizon which has been subdivided.

B22irb A buried (b) B2 horizon which has been subdivided.

Bir3 "A transitional horizon between C or R in which the properties diagnostic of an overlying B2 are clearly expressed but are associated with clearly expressed properties characteristic of C or R."

B3irb A buried (b) B3 horizon.

C "A mineral horizon or layer, excluding bedrock, that is either like or unlike the material from which the solum is presumed to have formed, relatively little affected by pedogenic processes, and lacking properties diagnostic of A or B. . . ."

C12 A subdivision of the C horizon.

Cb A buried (b) C horizon.

Mounds at 47-Pt-29-2

For the great majority of mounds or mound groups recorded in the eastern United States there has been little difficulty in recognizing aboriginal earthen constructions from tree falls, surface midden accumulation, sand dunes, small levees and other natural surface additions. There is that instance in sand barrens or outwash terraces where natural rises compete with man-made rises, and at

47-Pt-29-2 we have such instances. Resolving a situation such as this can be accomplished with extensive testing or, more easily, with the use of a soil probe. However, this site locality is somewhat unique in that there are not only natural and man-made rises but also four prehistoric earthen mounds which had been buried by aeolian deposition.

In addition, we were also hampered by the common occurrence of reported mounds being levelled by historic cultivation. Nineteen (A to S) natural or man-made tumuli had been put forth for candidacy as earthen manifestations of prehistoric cultural behavior at 47-Pt-29-2. Because of the many factors involved in mound identification at this locality, each mound and non-mound (referred to hereafter as "area") will be discussed according to the extent to which each was either excavated or examined in the field. Furthermore, the mounds will be presented from south to north (Fig. 5) which is somewhat at variance with the order of excavation, numerical feature designations, and burial designations. In the introductory remarks to this chapter it was mentioned that Collie and Becker (1912) recognized one mound (Mound L); Dixon, Blake, and Scribner (1956) added 13 mounds; and I contributed five more mounds to 47-Pt-29-2 during the 1965 survey. These mounds were given alphabetical designations from A to S; however, areas I, J, K, O, and P (see below) are natural rises. Thus, the 14 remaining mounds at 47-Pt-29-2 are of three types: three effigy mounds (C, L, and N); eight conical (A, B, D, F, G, M, Q, and S); and three linear (E, H, and R) (Fig. 5).

Mound N (Fig. 6)

Mound N was a "flying" bird effigy with a body 44 feet long, 28 feet wide, and three feet high. The total wing length was 71 feet, the maximum wing width was 13 feet, and the wing height was two feet. The wings had the appearance of being folded backward as if in a diving posture. A 10-by-16-foot disturbance was present in the head to the heart region, giving the head a tuning-fork appearance. This excavation extended below the base of the mound and the removed mound fill was piled around the excavation. From what we observed in this mound and from the description of Lewis' excavation in 1890, it would appear that this was the mound from which he recovered bone, charcoal, and copper awl (Lewis, 1890:5; Brown, 1906:366). During the 1965 testing of this mound one five-foot square was excavated (S60R0) in the undisturbed proximal tail area; during the 1966 excavations two additional squares were excavated to and across the distal portion of the tail. The mound was excavated according to the discernible soils horizons within the mound and to those preserved as paleosols below the mound (Fig. 6). The 1965 square (S60R0), as well as all others discussed or illustrated, will be placed within parentheses to distinguish them from the 1966 grid system. The mound profile consisted of an A11 horizon formed under a mixed forest cover approximating a mixture of scrub oak barrens and a pine barren (Curtis, 1959:326, 338-339). Below this A11 horizon was a developing A12 which averaged .4 feet in thickness. The mound fill was designated as an A/B horizon (Fig. 6) and interstratified within this fill was an A1b horizon which did not fully extend across the north and south walls. This horizon indicated a primary stage in construction and below it there was a second A/B horizon or an A/Bb. Below the A/Bb was the A1b2 horizon which is a preserved buried surface soil. This horizon was

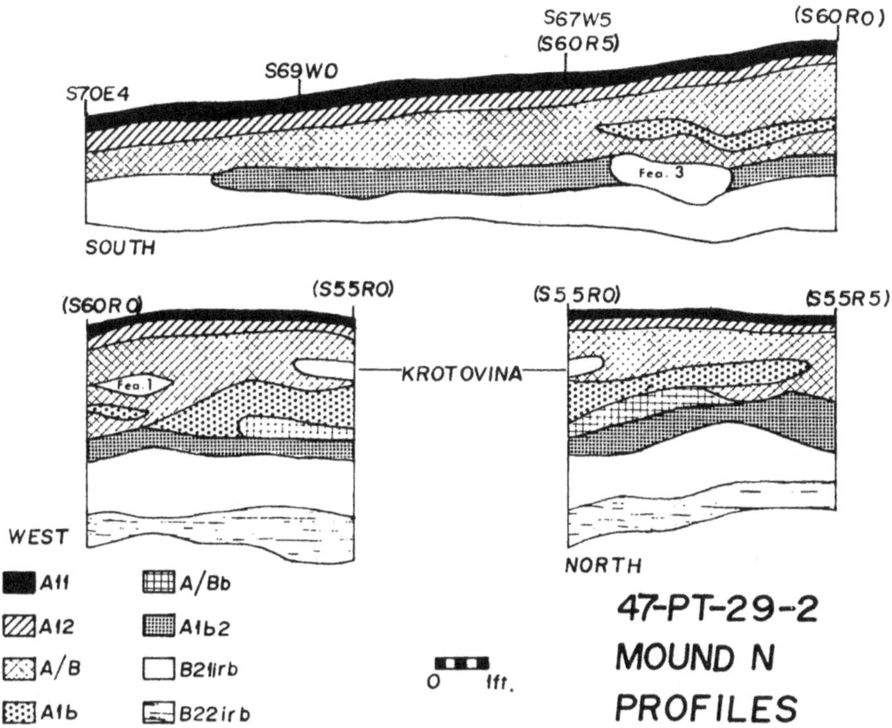

FIG. 6. Mound N profiles.

also considered to have been formed under a mixed forest cover. The lower part of the paleosol solum (Fig. 6) consisted of a B21irb and a B22irb which were above (not illustrated) a B2irb, a C1, and a C2 which completed the paleosol profile.

In the 1965 excavations of Mound N three subsurface features were defined and excavated; during the 1966 excavations one additional feature was removed. The vertical and horizontal placement and a description will be presented here along with a brief listing of the artifacts.

Feature 1 (1965) extended into the west wall of square (S60L5) and was only partially excavated. Its orifice originated at 1.1 feet below the surface (A/B horizon) and it extended to a depth of 1.5 feet. Feature 1 appeared to be basin-shaped in cross section (Fig. 6) and its charcoal-concentrated fill was void of artifacts.

Feature 2 (1965) was irregular in outline and flat basin-shaped in cross section. Its orifice originated at 1.7 feet below the surface (A1b horizon) and it extended to a depth of 2.7 feet (B21irb horizon). The sandy fill of Feature 2 contained one grit-tempered, cord-marked body sherd, one quartzite flake, one chert flake, nine stone fragments, and charcoal.

Feature 3 (1965) extended into the north wall of square (S65R0) and approximately two-thirds of the feature was excavated. It was irregular in outline, 3.7 by 2.0 feet, and flat basin-shaped in cross section, and was confined to the A1b2 soil horizon. This subsurface pit appears to have been utilized prior to mound construction. The sandy fill contained one ground stone, one grit-tempered, cord-marked body sherd, one quartz flake, one stone fragment, and charcoal. Charcoal samples submitted to the Radiocarbon Dating Laboratory of the Center for Climatic Research of the University of Wisconsin were dated A.D. 1120 ± 70 (WIS-168).

Feature 1 (1966) was an area which apparently served as a fireplace. A small charred log .8 foot long and .1 foot wide was uncovered in its darkened matrix at a depth of 1.5 to 1.7 feet below the surface in the A1b2 horizon of square S65W5.

It would appear that the order of features either below the mound or incorporated within the mound would be as follows: Feature 1 (1966) was on the original (A1b2) surface and Feature 3 (1965) intruded into the original surface prior to mound construction. From the evidence from this 5-by-15-foot trench it would appear that the body of the bird effigy was constructed first, as is indicated by the interstratified A1b and A/Bb soil horizons. At this time Feature 2 (1965) was intruded into this A1b surface down to the B12irb horizon. The second and probably final stage of construction occurred with the further addition of soil to the body region above the A1b and the extension or addition of soil beyond the body region. During this final addition, a portion of the A/B horizon served as a fireplace area for Feature 1 (1966).

Mound M (see Fig. 5)

Mound M was a conical mound measuring 28 feet north-south, 30.5 feet east-west, and 1.5 feet high. The mound had been subjected to Historic cultivation which had modified approximately 10 feet of the eastern edge. Excavations were begun with square S30E20 which was eventually expanded into an area covered by five five-foot squares.

In the center of square S30E25 in the B21irb horizon, at a depth of 2.1 feet, a small concentration of burned bone was uncovered. It was designated in the field as *Burial 2* and the preliminary analysis by Martin Q. Peterson, of the University of Nebraska, indicates that the bone was highly fragmented long bone shafts which may or may not be human. The bone was a secondary deposition which seemed to have occurred prior to the construction of Mound M as there was an absence of pit outline and charcoal. During the excavation of Mound M two additional subsurface features (5 and 8) were defined and excavated.

Feature 5 was defined at a depth of 2.5 feet in the B21irb horizon; it was roughly oval and approximately 5.5 feet long and 3.0 feet wide. The feature was .4 foot deep and its dark sandy loam fill was surrounded by light colored C1 sands. In cross section the pit was basin-shaped and the fill yielded one rim sherd, one quartzite Triangular projectile point, 13 grit-tempered, cord-marked body sherds, six bone fragments, and one quartzite flake.

Feature 8 was first recognized in the A/B horizon in the east wall of square S20E25. As this square was excavated it was noted that the disturbed soil extended into the B21irb horizon and that it was void of artifacts. The presence of recent organic matter and the mixture of soil indicated that this subsurface pit was in reality a recent rodent burrow (krotovina).

The undisturbed mound profile did not have a developed solum and the present A11 surface horizon was similar to the

A1b2, indicating that both were formed under a similar mixed forest cover.

Mound L (Fig. 7)

Mound L was a "flying" bird effigy with a body 41 feet long, 25 feet wide, and 3.0 feet high. The total wing length was 80 feet, the maximum wing width was 12 feet, and the wing height was 2.0 feet. An estimated 25 feet of the distal portion of the eastern wing had been levelled by plowing. Excavations in 1965 were confined to the head region extending northeastward into the body region. In 1966 a portion of the tail region, one square in the body region adjacent to a recent disturbance (N50E10), and a series of squares in the distal portion of the western wing were excavated.

On the tail of Mound L there was a thin layer of vegetative matter (01 horizon) over the A11 horizon. The A/B horizon was quite thick (Fig. 7) and there were no apparent subdivisions within this horizon, which was highly disturbed by tree roots.

A total of four subsurface features were excavated in Mound L. Two of these (Features 2 and 3) were in the tail region and two (Features 13 and 18) were under the distal portion of the western wing.

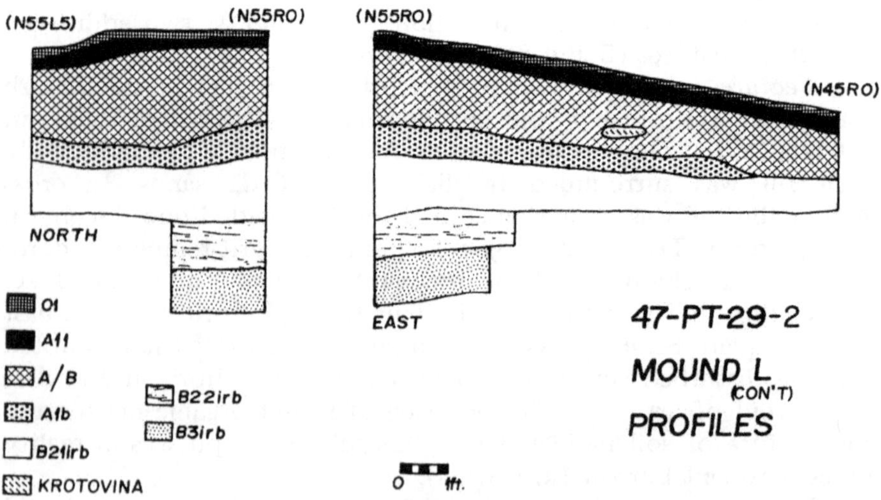

FIG. 7. Mound L profiles.

Feature 2 was totally confined to the A1b horizon in which it was defined at depth of 2.4 feet and it extended to a depth of 2.7 feet. This feature was circular (2.1 feet in diameter) and shallow basin-shaped in cross section. The matrix of the feature was a sandy loam which yielded 711 Madison Cord Impressed sherds, four quartzite flakes, and one stone fragment.

Feature 3 was recognized and defined in the B21irb soil horizon at a depth of 1.7 feet below the surface. The feature was a small circular pit, 1.0 foot in diameter, which extended to a depth of 1.9 feet. The only object recovered was a portion of a dog skull.

Feature 13 was initially noted at a depth of .6 foot below the surface in the A/Bb horizon and the soils immediately above and adjacent to the feature were mixed A1b soils interspersed with sands similar to those of the B22irb horizon. At a depth of 1.4 feet in the B22irb horizon, a circular outline, 4.5 feet in diameter, was clearly discernible. Feature 13 was a deep basin-shaped pit beginning at .6 foot and extending to a depth of 3.0 feet. Feature 13 contained 320 vessel fragments of which 317 belong to the reconstructed Madison Cord Impressed vessel shown in Plate 7. In addition to the ceramic fragments, Feature 13 also yielded a fragment of a quartzite Sanders Triangular projectile point, four quartzite flakes, one quartz flake, and seven stone fragments. The charcoal recovered yielded a date of A.D. 810 ± 50 (WIS-200).

Feature 18 was located in square N65W25 slightly above and west of Feature 13. The pit was slightly oval in outline, 1.9 feet by 2.4 feet and was defined at a depth of 1.3 feet in the A/Bb soils horizon. Feature 18 was a shallow basin-shaped cooking or fire pit. Sandy fill from the pit yielded charcoal flecks, four large flat stones, 14 smaller stones, one grit-tempered cord-marked body sherd, and shell fragments.

Seven five-foot squares were excavated in the distal portion of the western wing of Mound L in the area which contained Features 13 and 18. Both Features 13 and 18 were associated with the construction stage of the western wing as both were utilized while the mound fill (A/Bb) was being added. Feature 2 was totally within the A1b horizon, sealed in with the construction of Mound L. Feature 3, with its dog skull fragments, was below Mound L in the B21irb horizon. The A1b horizon below Mound L was a thick horizon which appeared to have been formed under grass vegetation.

Areas O and P (Figs. 5 and 8)

In 1965 I recorded two rises adjacent to the river bank and designated them as possible prehistoric mounds. Area O was thought to be a large conical mound upon which a linear mound, Area P, had been built. During the 1966 field season soil probing showed that the area designated as Area O was in reality a localized rise of aeolian sand deposition. Area P had all the characteristics of a linear mound: it was 24 feet long, 5.6 feet wide, and 1.5 feet high.

As a trench in Area P was excavated and the profile walls exposed, it was noted that there were sequential AC profiles horizontally stratified above a paleosol (A1b3—B21irb; Fig. 8). The C horizons were uniform in their lack of pedogenic development, indicating that Area P was a natural rise produced by a series of horizontal lenticular aeolian sand depositions (C horizons), each having a subsequent surface horizon (A1b2, A1b, and A1). A charcoal sample was removed from a cup-shaped fired area confined to the top of the A1b3 (Fig. 8) and yielded a radiocarbon date of A.D. 1610 ± 65 (WIS-157). This date and the artifacts recovered will be discussed in the following chapters; however, it should be mentioned that historic artifacts were found to be well mixed throughout the profile illustrated. Although Area P gives excellent evidence of natural stratigraphy, the area involved and the truncated nature of the horizons are such that Area P is of secondary importance in stratigraphic and artifact interpretations.

Area K (Fig. 5)

Area K was first reported by Dixon, Blake, and Scribner in 1956 as ". . . the last of the linear mounds . . . south of mound 'B'. Mound 'K' is 29 feet long and 19 feet wide and measured 16 inches from the summit to ground level . . ." (1956:69). I excavated one test square directly east of the eastern edge of Area K. This square was considered productive and it was expanded into an 18-foot trench. As this trench was extended to the west we could again see sequential AC profiles and the absence of a mixed A/B mound fill. This form of aeolian deposition resulted in natural stratigraphy subsequent to the prehistoric utilization of the site.

Four subsurface features were uncovered and excavated in Area K and their order from earliest to latest is as follows:

Feature 12 was uncovered at a depth of 2.5 feet at .2 foot below the top of the B21irb horizon. Feature 12 was circular, 1.4

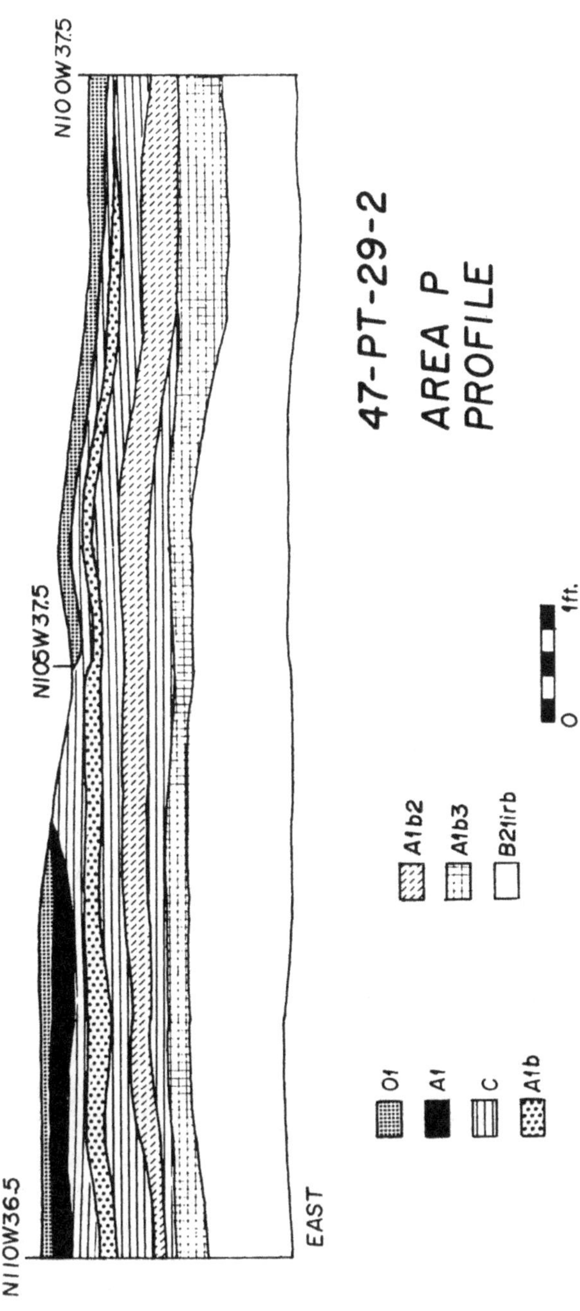

FIG. 8. Area P profile.

feet in diameter, basin-shaped in cross section, and it extended into the B21irb horizon to a depth of 3.05 feet. The fill of Feature 12 was a sandy loam containing charcoal flecks, one grit-tempered cord-marked body sherd, one sherd fragment, and one quartz fragment.

Feature 6 was located at a depth of 2.2 feet and it extended to a depth of 3.2 feet, or well into the B21irb horizon. The orifice outline and confines of Feature 6 could be readily ascertained and the sandy loam fill contained one grit-tempered smooth surface body sherd, a quartz flake, and five fulgurite fragments. We had recovered fulgurite in the A/Bb horizon and it was thought that lightning (which produced the fulgurite) may have produced the charcoal subsequently recovered in Feature 6. However, the presence of artifacts, the fact that the B21irb sands below Feature 6 were not altered by intense heat, nor their color changed from the normal 7.5YR4/4 (moist) recorded for this horizon, and the size of the feature suggest that the date from Feature 6 was not a result of lightning. The charcoal recovered from this feature yielded a date of A.D. 1370 ± 65 (WIS-187).

Feature 11 was located at a depth of 1.9 feet. The sandy loam fill was quite distinct from the surrounding A/Bb soil. The feature was circular in outline with a diameter of 1.8 feet; in cross section it was shallow basin-shaped extending to a depth of 2.4 feet. The fill from Feature 11 yielded only three stone fragments.

Feature 15 was located in square N165W40 at a depth of 1.9 feet and although the sandy loam fill contained charcoal flecks it was void of artifacts. Feature 15 began in the A/Bb horizon and extended into the B21irb horizon. Feature 15 was circular in outline with a diameter of 2.0 feet.

It appears that the area nearest to the present river bank was subjected to the earliest aeolian deposition, i.e., the A1b2 and the A/Bb horizons. The former surface or the A11b horizon appears to conform to the generally undulating topography of the site and it is this surface which seems to have served as the major prehistoric living surface. From the location and depth of the four features uncovered and excavated in this area it appears that the regions closest to the bank were favored as occupation zones which have been sealed in and undisturbed since their utilization.

Mound S (Fig. 9)

The area of Mound S was one of the last to be excavated at this site because it was thought to be a natural rise similar to Areas

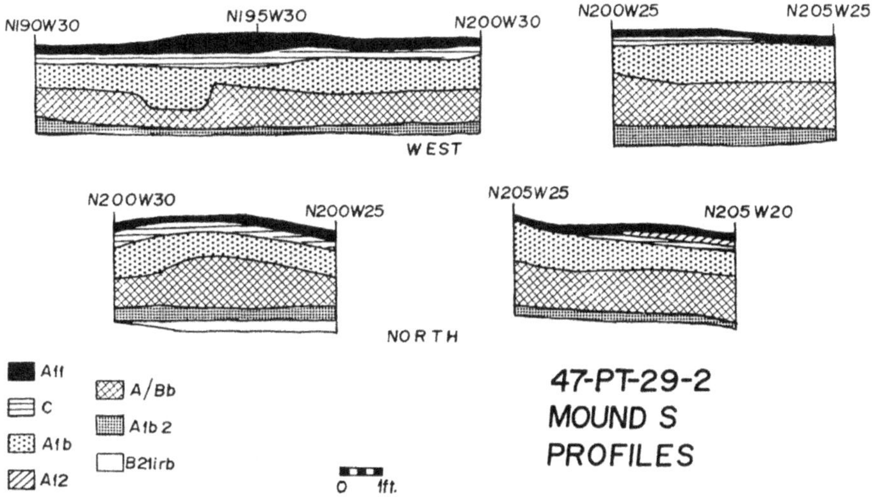

FIG. 9. Mound S profiles.

P and K and because of its nearness to the Historic component (Lange, 1969). A test square was placed near the river bank and indicated a soil profile quite different from that of Area K. The immediate area was cleared and the center of the rise was excavated. It became clear that this was a mound which had been *buried* by aeolian deposition (Fig. 9).

Five five-foot squares were excavated in Mound S and a large, roughly rectangular subsurface pit was uncovered at the top of the A1b2 horizon at a depth of 2.1 feet. The pit was oriented from the SW to the NE and it was 7.7 feet long and 4.0 feet wide. The pit and its contents, designated as *Burial 8*, consisted of a compact mixture of burned bones and charcoal. Martin Q. Peterson, of the Department of Anthropology, University of Nebraska, in a preliminary analysis stated that there were non-human bones present and that there was a lack of diagnostic human remains. Most of the fragments were less than 2.5 cm^2 and he suggested that it was *possible* that most of the bone was human—but not demonstrable.

The southwestern half of the pit contained most of the bone and charcoal and the northeastern half had been disturbed by recent rodent activity. The pit extended to a depth of 2.6 feet. The charcoal yielded a date of A.D. 800 ± 55 (WIS-202). The sequence of vegetation in the Mound S area appears to be mixed forest (A1b2), short grass (A1b), and then mixed forest (A11).

Mound B (Fig. 10)

Mound B was first recognized and reported by Dixon, Blake, and Scribner as a "... linear mound which runs north and south [and] is 53 feet long and 51 feet wide and measures three and one-half feet from the summit to ground level ..." (1956:67). It is now difficult to state the actual dimensions of Mound B as it was a buried mound which was only partially excavated. The rise designated as Mound B measured 65 feet long, 22.5 feet wide, and 3.2 feet above the present surface. Mound B was tested in 1965 by placing a six-foot wide cut along the face eroded at the bank and extending this cut to a depth of over seven feet. During the 1966 field season a five-foot, east-west trench was excavated from the eastern feather-edge of the mound, removing each soil horizon as we progressed toward the 1965 profile exposure. The first 10 feet of this 30-foot trench consisted of excavations through aeolian deposition which had been utilized and altered by both the prehistoric and Historic components. This aeolian deposition was not restricted to the eastern edge of the mound, however, and it varied in thickness from east to west and from south to north (Fig. 10).

Although only eight five-foot squares were excavated in the rise containing Mound B, the natural topography and aeolian deposition suggest that Mound B was a somewhat truncated conical mound rather than a linear mound, as suggested by Dixon, Blake, and Scribner. The surface covered by the mound appears to have had a localized aeolian dune (A/Birb) along the western edge of our excavations (Fig. 10) which was utilized prior to mound construction. The original surface (A1b2) which was preserved as a paleosol was judged in the field to have been formed under grass vegetation and it yielded only prehistoric artifacts. The mound surface horizon (A1b) did not appear to have served as a living surface for the Historic component at 47-Pt-29-2; as the cross section and profile illustrated for Burial 11 (Fig. 10, west wall) indicate, the burial pit orginated in the A/B horizon and intruded through the A1b horizon. In addition, a fireplace with galena cubes was found above the pit of Historic Burial 11 and well above the A1b.

A total of five features (Feature 1, 1965; and Features 20-22 and 24) and six burials (4, 6, 7, 9, 11, and 12) (Fig. 11) were excavated in Mound B.

Feature 1 (1965) was exposed in the vertical face cut in 1965. The pit was basin-shaped in cross section and its orifice

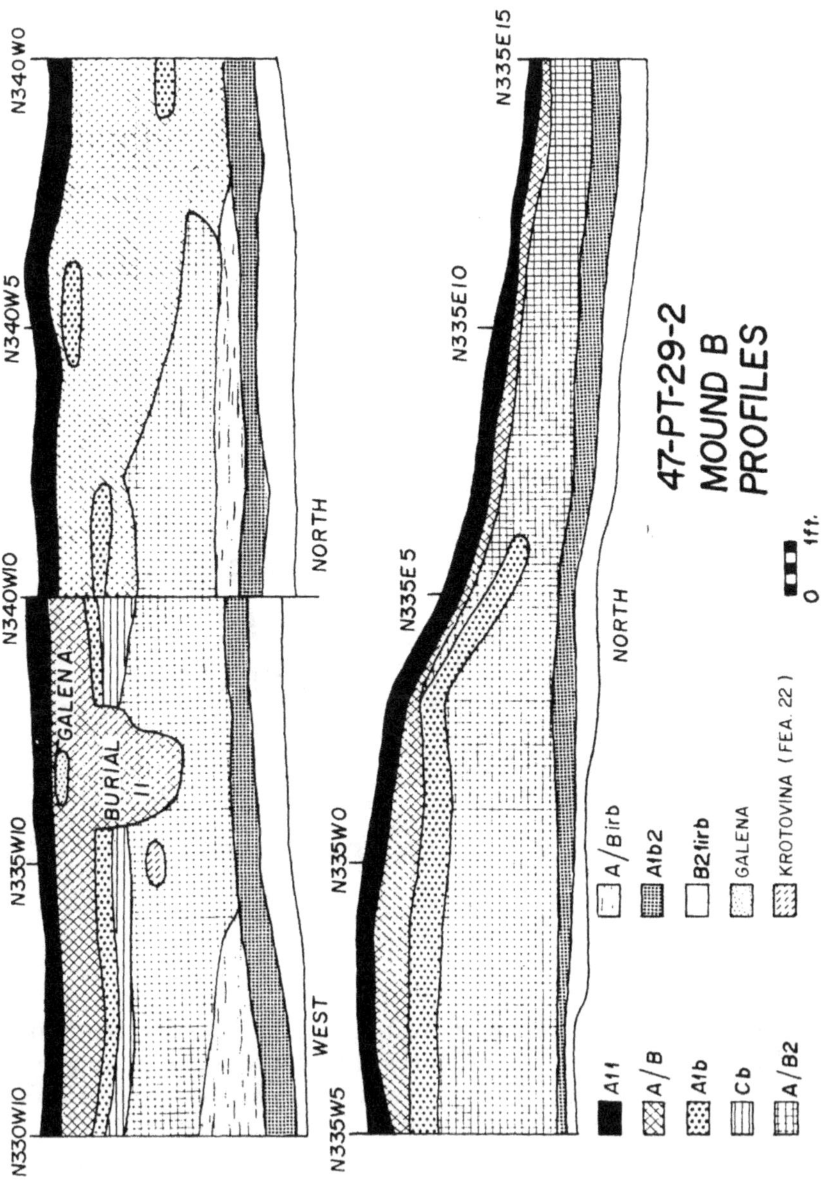

FIG. 10. Mound B profiles.

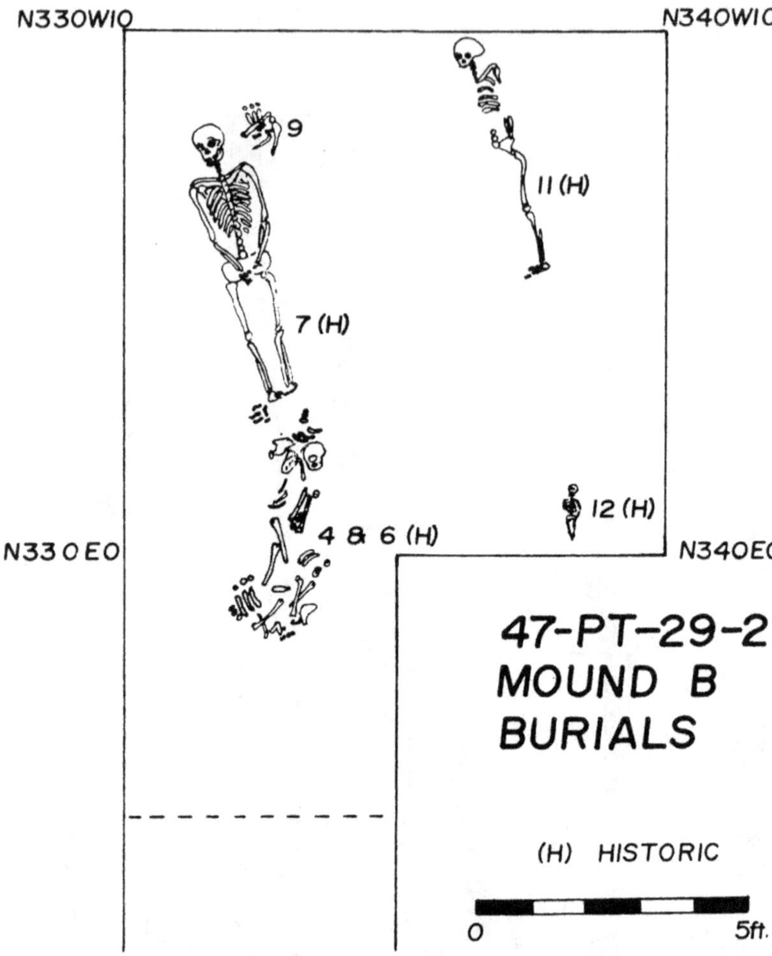

FIG. 11. Mound B burials.

began at 1.7 feet (the A/B2 horizon). It extended to a depth of 3.2 feet to the top of the A1b2 horizon and it was approximately 2.3 feet north to south. The pit was not excavated in 1965; however, one shell fragment, two quartz flakes, one quartzite flake, and a small amount of charcoal were recovered from the sandy fill. During the interval between field seasons the face of the profile was badly eroded and the remainder of Feature 1 was lost. Charcoal from this pit and the A1b2 horizon directly below it yielded a date of A.D. 930 ± 70 (WIS-242).

Feature 20 was a shallow basin-shaped pit totally confined to the A1b2 horizon originating at 3.4 feet and extending to 3.7 feet. It was oval shaped in outline, 2.4 feet north-south, and 1.5 feet east-west. The fill was sand which yielded one grit-tempered cord-marked body sherd and charcoal fragments.

Feature 21 was located at a depth of 4.5 feet and it was found to be an extension (rodent?) of the A/Birb horizon.

Feature 22 was located at a depth of 2.4 feet and totally confined to the A/B2 horizon. This feature is actually a krotovina or rodent burrow at the left of Burial 11 in the west wall. When this darkened area was uncovered it was found to contain the decomposing remains of a freshwater decapod crustacean which had entered the face of the 1965 profile cut and intruded laterally into the A/B2 horizon.

Feature 24 was a shallow basin-shaped pit which was uncovered in the A/B2 horizon at a depth of 3.2 feet. The dark sandy pit fill was void of any artifacts.

A total of six burials were uncovered and removed from Mound B and it would appear (with the possible exception of Burial 9) that each had been intruded into Mound B by the members of the historic component at 47-Pt-29-2 (Lange, 1969). These burial pit intrusions disturbed the soil horizons sealing in the mound and the buried mound itself and they were numbered as they were uncovered in the field.

Burial 4 was in a rectangular burial pit which was 7.0 feet long and 2.5 feet wide. The pit had intruded into the A/B2 mound fill. The burial was located between 1.4 and 2.2 feet below the surface. Wood fragments and 32 iron nails were found adjacent to and within the burial. The burial was originally extended, but had been greatly disturbed and its position was somewhat telescoped. In association were one gunflint, a metal coffin handle, approximately 100 white seed or compound beads, slit hollow brass beads, and fragments of human hair. The seed beads were clustered around the feet and are possibly moccasin beads, and the brass beads were scattered across the clavicles. In addition, there were three large stone fragments at the feet and two above the head area. A field skeletal inventory indicated that the skull and mandible were missing and that extra thoracic ribs and a right cuneiform were present from Burial 6, which may account for the disturbance of Burial 4.

Burial 6 was discovered when a skeletal inventory had been completed for Burial 4. The extra thoracic ribs and right cuneiform were separated from those of Burial 4 after the cleaning, inventory, and marking had been completed in the field laboratory (Fig. 11).

Burial 7 (Fig. 11 and Pl. 1). The burial pit was approximately 6.5 by 2.0 feet and it intruded into the A/B2 mound fill. The burial was at a depth of 2.1 to 2.5 feet in a supine fully extended position. The feet were turned inward as if bound prior to burial and from the feet to the tenth thoracic vertebra were approximately 500 white seed or compound beads. The head, hands, and pelvis were wrapped with birch-bark; placed laterally around the body were 13 iron nails and wood fragments which seemed to have held down a shroud of cloth or birch-bark. On the side of the sternum at the clavicle articulation there was a small brass coat button. Continuing toward the feet, at approximately the tenth thoracic, there was a woven belt. The hands were folded over the pelvic region; around the left wrist there were four brass buttons. On the left innominate lay a pipe stem, a white clay pipe, and an iron knife with a wooden handle which was in a sewn birch-bark case. Under the knife handle was a fragment of hematite and a small mirror. On the right innominate was a woven bag or pouch with red ocher and cowrie shells and a small silver pin.

Burial 9 was located at a depth of 3.3 feet. Its orifice was in the A/Birb soil horizon and it extended into the B21irb soil horizon (Fig. 11). The burial pit was circular and within this pit were fragments of burned bone which had the appearance of human cremations recorded elsewhere at the site. However, the bone, according to Martin Peterson of the University of Nebraska, unfortunately lacks any diagnostic human features.

Burial 11 (Figs. 10 and 11) was located at a depth of 2.4 feet. The orifice of the burial pit originated in the A/B horizon and the pit intruded into the A/B2 mound fill. Burial 11 was extended on its right side facing south and portions of the right side of the cranium were missing, as well as some of the vertebrae and ribs. Historic artifacts associated with Burial 11 were as follows: approximately 250 glass seed beads or composite white beads, which were scattered along the legs; on the sternum were one brass circular pin, one gunflint, and one coffin handle with preserved fabric adhering to the surface. Approximately one foot above the burial pit was a small charcoal concentration (Fig. 10) which contained two galena cubes and it seemed that this fireplace was in association with the burial.

Burial 12 was uncovered at a depth of .9 to 1.1 feet in the A1b soil horizon (Figs. 10 and 11). When these bones were uncovered they were thought to be an articulated rodent and it was not until they were cleaned in the field laboratory that they were identified as approximately 12 infant fragments. Although there were no Historic artifacts in association with the burial, the soil consistency was similar to that of the other Historic burials and it was assumed that Burial 12 also belonged to the Historic component.

Eight five-foot squares which crossed this buried mound yielded considerable evidence of mound stratigraphy which served to clarify the nature and extent of the Historic utilization of this area. Mound B was built upon a localized sand deposit and upon a thick surface soil (A1b2) which appeared to have been formed under grass vegetation. Features 1 (1965), 20, and 24 seem to be associated with the construction stages of this mound; Feature 22 and the burials (except Burial 9) appear to have occurred subsequent to mound construction. While historic artifacts were found within and above the A1b horizon and associated with the historic burial intrusions, all evidence indicates that Mound B during historic times was favored only as a burial area, while the area to the east of the mound was utilized for historic habitation.

Mound A (Pl. 2, Figs. 12-15)

Mound A (Fig. 5) was reported by Dixon, Blake, and Scribner (1956:67) as the "... first of the series, runs north to south and is centrally located. This mound is the most prominent of the group and is outstanding when viewed from a distance....... Mound 'A' is 110 feet long and 55 feet wide and measures four feet from the summit to ground level. Mound 'A' lies on the very edge of the river bank." Although this mound was tested in 1965 and remeasured, both Dixon's and the 1965 measurements were of an aeolian rise which actually contained a buried mound but of smaller dimensions. Severe erosion had modified the east-west dimensions and with the separation of contiguous Mound Q in 1966 the north-south measurements were diminished. The rise containing Mound A was 67.5 feet north-south and 42.0 feet east-west, and 4.0 feet high from the 1966 surface.

During the 1965 testing operations a 5.5-foot wide by 7.8-foot deep cut was made into the bank to expose a profile of the rise. Preliminary soil probing indicated that the rise might be a modern sand dune and excavations were started with the idea of removing this overburden. At approximately 3.0 feet below the surface on the east wall, historic glazed ceramics, cut animal bone, and wood fragments (all of which were designated as Feature 7) were uncovered. It is suggested that the Historic component dates at circa A.D. 1850 ± 25 and the artifacts provide good evidence that the last major aeolian deposition at 47-Pt-29-2 occurred within the last 100 years. At this point we had no indication of a mound profile and with the removal of the A1b2 horizon we uncovered a sterile C aeolian sand horizon which sealed in an A1b3 horizon containing prehistoric artifacts. This natural stratigraphy of the buried A horizons was considered an asset to the interpretation of the site and we expanded our excavations to include the area delineated as section 1 (see Pl. 2).

With the removal of this section (section 1) the profile revealed a buried mound. The sequence of soils horizons illustrated in Figures 12 and 13 was essentially retained throughout the excavations of sections 1 through 3 of the Mound A area. The thin A1b2 contained historic artifacts *only* in that portion profiled in Figure 12. This horizon appeared to merge with the A1b2 surface horizon of buried Mound A. However, no historic artifacts were recovered at the point at which this horizon was part of the mound profile. Only the north and northeastern mound margins were unexcavated and with the numerous wall profiles and the determined and projected mound walls, there is enough data to suggest that Mound A was a conical mound 19 feet north-south, approximately 20 feet east-west, and approximately three feet high (Fig. 15 and Pl. 2).

The area of Mound A produced six features (7, 10, 23, 25, 26, and 27) and three burials (3, 5, and 10).

Feature 7 extended from a depth of 3.0 to 3.2 feet, or entirely within the A1b2 horizon (Fig. 12 and Pl. 2). Feature 7 was not a subsurface pit, but rather a 10 by 10-foot concentration of Historic glazed ceramics, cut animal bone, and wood fragments which were sealed in by aeolian deposition and which were separated from the lower prehistoric artifacts by a half-foot thick layer of aeolian sands.

Feature 10 was located at a depth of 4.4 to 6.0 feet. The orifice of Feature 10 began in the A1b3 horizon directly beneath Mound A and this deep basin-shaped pit extended into the B2hirb horizon. Feature 10 was roughly circular in outline, measuring 3.3 by 3.8 feet; the sandy fill yielded 22 grit-tempered cord-marked body sherds, seven quartzite flakes, two quartz flakes, and two stone fragments. With the intrusion of the pit through the former

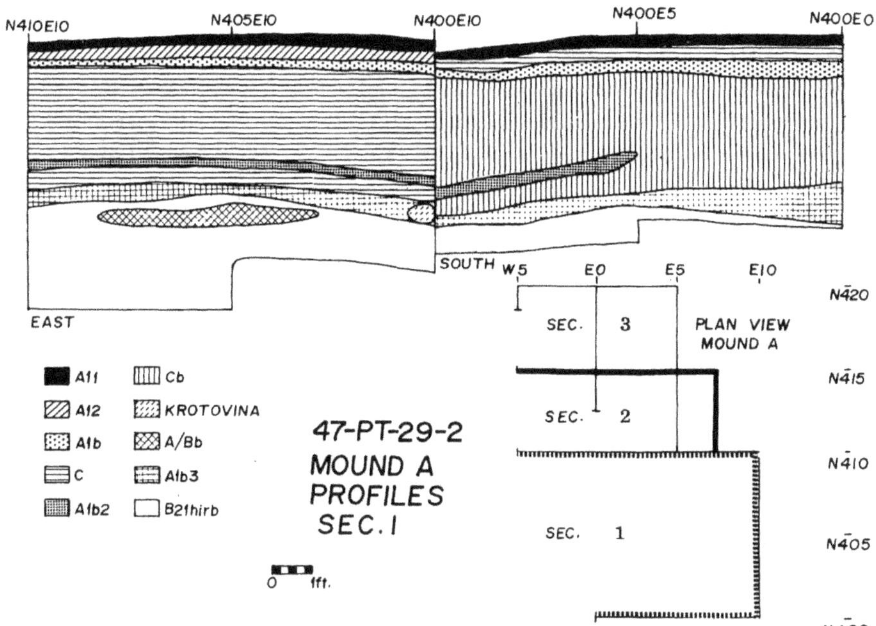

FIG. 12. Mound A, profiles (Sec. 1).

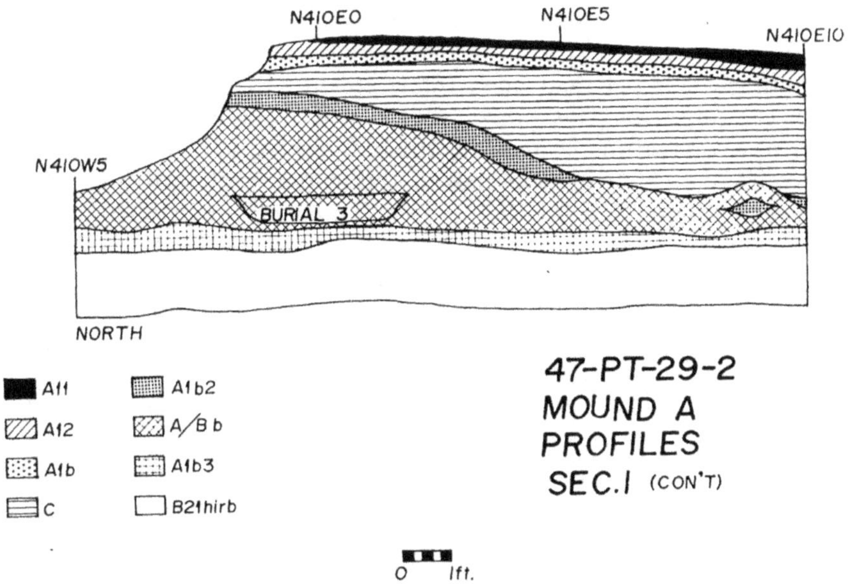

FIG. 13. Mound A profiles (Sec. 1, con't.).

surface A1b3 soils horizon, there is evidence that Feature 10 was utilized prior to mound construction and that it was probably associated with the mound building activity.

Feature 23 was a pit containing charcoal, circular in outline, 1.2 by 1.2 feet, and basin-shaped in cross section. Feature 23 began at a depth of 4.8 feet in the B21hirb horizon and it extended to a depth of 5.4 feet. This feature was void of artifacts.

Feature 25 consisted of a one-foot square concentration of 36 non-human bone fragments contained in the A1b3 and B21hirb horizons at a depth of 4.1 to 4.6 feet. This concentration was under Mound A and it lacked associated artifacts.

Feature 26 was in the mound surface A1b horizon at a depth of 1.9 to 2.4 feet and it consisted of a charred log which was incorporated into the mound during the final stages of construction. The charcoal from this log, which was about one inch thick, yielded a date of A.D. 670 ± 55 (WIS-197).

Feature 27 was located at a depth of 3.9 to 4.3 feet in the A1b2 horizon beneath Mound A. This feature consisted of a small area of non-human burned bone and charcoal concentrated in a .6 by .6 foot area within the former surface horizon. This feature was void of artifacts.

Burial 3 (Fig. 15) was uncovered at a depth of 3.1 feet in the A/Bb mound fill. It was an articulated burial of a child of six to nine years of age which had on its chest an iron knife on top of a small fabric fragment. The burial was supine and fully extended in a rectangular pit which had been intruded into the western or bank edge of the mound. The pelvic region was accidentally removed during our excavations; however, the remainder of the burial was in place. Associated in the burial pit were nine grit-tempered cord-marked body sherds, six quartz flakes, 19 quartzite flakes, and three stone fragments, all of which may have been added to this historic burial from the mound fill.

Burial 5. The orifice of the burial pit began in the A1b3 horizon at a depth of 3.8 feet. In plan view, the outline of the pit was roughly oval, approximately three feet long and two feet wide. In the upper levels of the pit were recovered disarticulated, unburned human bones consisting of a mandible, a right scapula, a fragment of a right innominate, and a long bone fragment. In addition, the pit fill yielded an unburned, worked deer antler tine which is perforated for the insertion of a beaver incisor, a beaver incisor, a fragment from a soft-shell turtle, fish scales, fish vertebrae, and shell fragments. The pit fill also contained a very large number of human and non-human cremated bones as well as

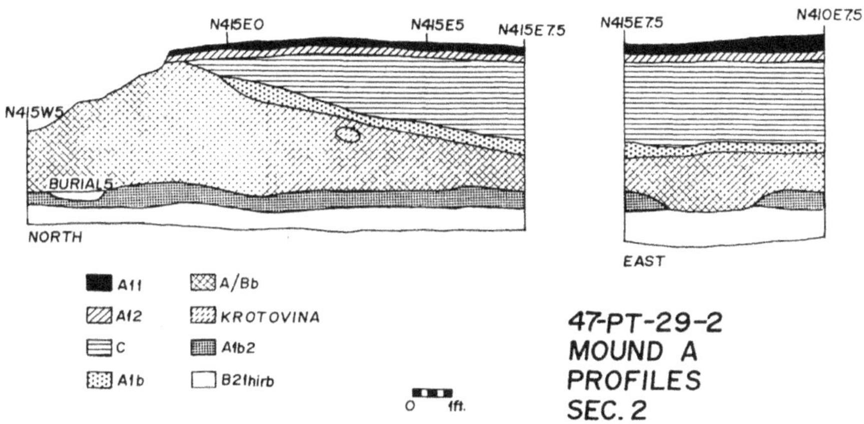

FIG. 14. Mound A profiles (Sec. 2).

eight cord-marked sherds, 13 quartzite flakes, and one quartz flake. In addition, one Triangular quartzite projectile point was recovered from the pit. The pit was contained totally in the A1b3 and extended to a depth of 4.2 feet (Fig. 14). It was associated with the construction of the mound.

Burial 10 (Fig. 15) was located in the A/Bb horizon at a depth of 2.6 feet. Burial 10 consisted of articulated human hand bones and from its depth and location it did not appear to be associated with Burial 5. No pit outline could be ascertained and there were no associated artifacts.

Excavations of the rise containing Mound A suggest that this buried conical mound was built upon a paleosol which was formed under grass vegetation. This horizon was utilized prior to mound construction as indicated by the presence of Features 7, 10, and 25, and it was penetrated by the central burial pit, Burial 5. Within the mound fill and during construction of the mound, a human hand was deposited (Burial 10) and a charred log was sealed in beneath the mound surface. Above the mound surface horizon was the first series of sterile aeolian sands which were in turn sealed in by an A1b2 which contained Historic artifacts. Subsequent to the Historic utilization of this area, another greater or more prolonged aeolian deposition occurred, but not before a burial of a child (Burial 3) was intruded into the mound. The soil sequences represented in the Mound A area are similar to sequences which are found at other mound locations and habitation areas at 47-Pt-29-2.

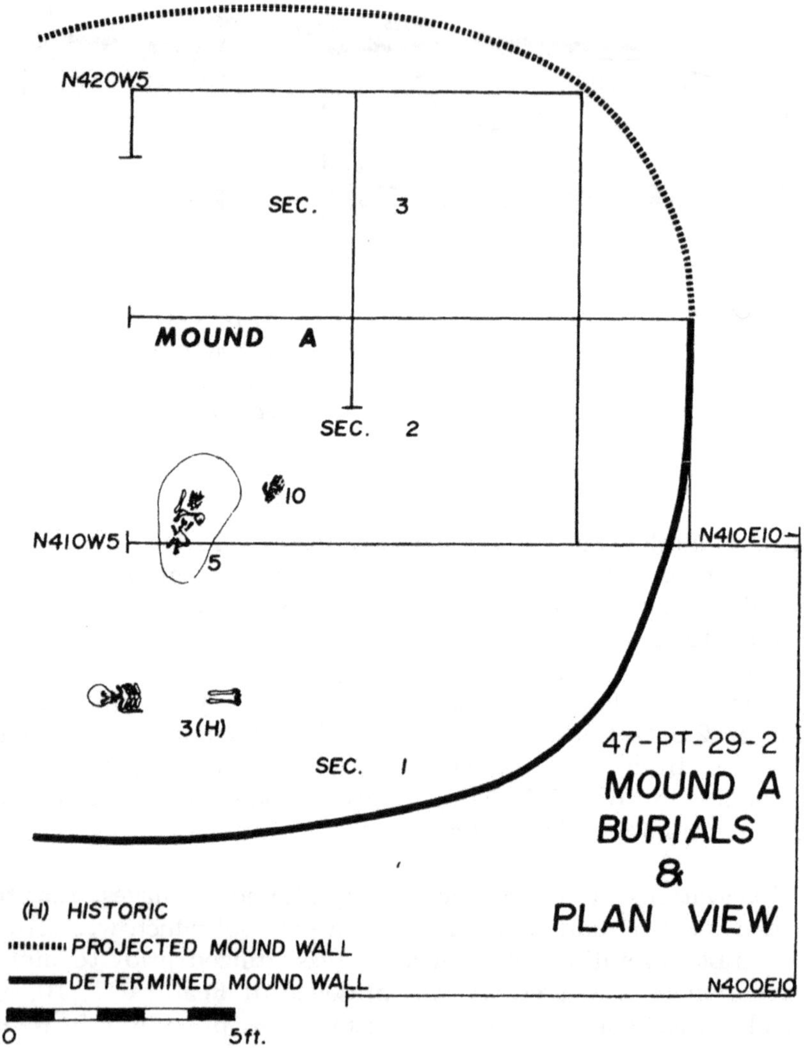

FIG. 15. Mound A burials.

Mound Q (Fig. 16)

The rise designated as Mound Q was 47 feet long north-south, 22 feet wide east-west, and three feet high. Mound Q was thought to be a part of Mound A by Dixon, Blake, and Scribner (1956:67). Due to a lack of time and the rediscovery of Pt-29-1, Mound Q was neither excavated nor tested. On August 6, 1966, a front-end loader began leveling the mounds, and as it was using Mound Q to fill in our excavations of Mound A, Lange (the assistant field director) cut a trench into the mound from which he extracted Burial 13, the contents of Feature 28, and artifacts within the mound fill. He observed that Mound Q was indeed a buried mound and that the depth of aeolian deposition was less than that for Mound A.

Feature 28 (Fig. 16) was located at a depth of 2.5 feet in the A/Bb mound fill. This darkened area contained five sherd fragments, charred bone, and one quartz flake. The pit was shallow basin-shaped and extended to a depth of 2.9 feet.

Burial 13 was located in the northwest corner of the trench in a sandy burial pit which began in the A1b3 horizon and extended to a depth of approximately 6.0 feet (Fig. 16). The burial was in a tightly flexed position with an east-west orientation. The skull was not in situ, having been lifted out by the front-end loader. The lack of Historic artifacts, the flexed and the vertical positions suggest that Burial 13 was a part of the mound building activities at 47-Pt-29-2.

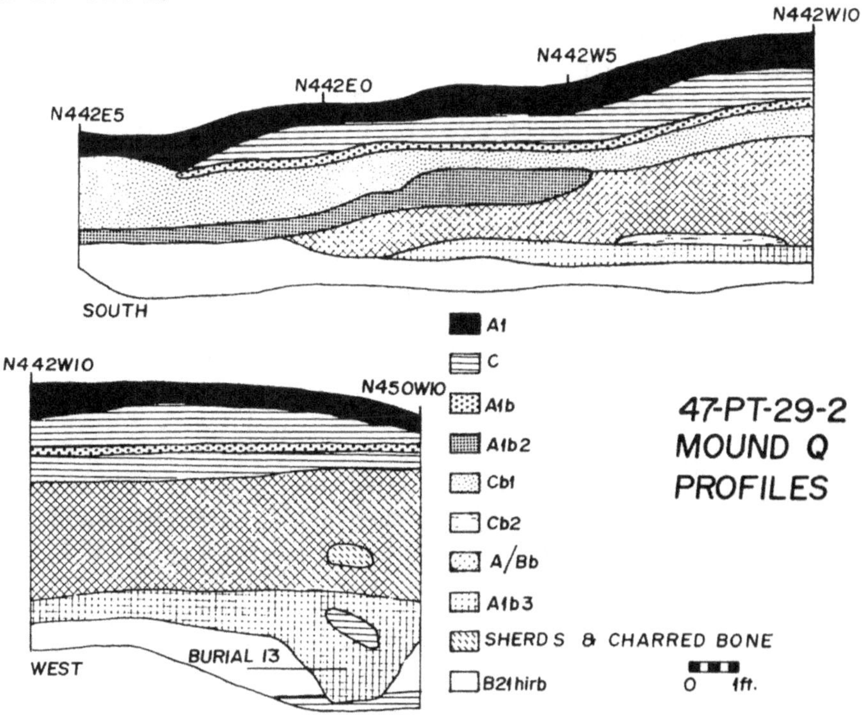

FIG. 16. Mound Q profiles.

Areas J and I (Fig. 5 and Dixon, Blake, and Scribner, 1956:66-69)

The rises designated as mounds J and I by Dixon were soil probed and a face was cut along the bank to view the profile. Instead of the expected mound profiles, these two rises were seen to be the result of aeolian deposition and modern sand dunes which sealed in the paleosol.

Mound R (Fig. 5 and Pl. 3)

Mound R was discovered during the 1966 field season. In the first week of excavations I traversed the site and soil probed throughout the woodlot and field. In the Mound R area the subdivision engineer had made soil borings and a soil percolation test. At this location I saw bleached human skull fragments on the surface which had been brought up by the boring operation. The area immediately adjacent to this stake was excavated by trowel and mixed soil with bone fragments continued below the surface. Burial 1 was excavated, the limits of Mound R were delineated, and a grid system was extended across the mound. Mound R was the only known excavatable linear mound at 47-Pt-29-2 and it was almost completely trenched from north to south. This 60-foot by 5-foot discontinuous trench exposed the longest simplified mound profile at this locality.

Mound R yielded four features (14, 16-17, and 19) and one burial (Burial 1).

Feature 14 was located in the A1b horizon. It was oval in outline, 1.5 by 1.2 feet, and shallow basin-shaped in cross section. The pit extended from 1.7 to 2.3 feet into the B21irb horizon. The pit fill was sand flecked with charcoal and void of artifacts.

Feature 16. The orifice of this pit may have have been in the bottom of the A/B horizon as the A1b soil above the pit was either very thin or non-existent. The pit was circular in outline, 2.0 feet in diameter, and deep basin-shaped in cross section. The fill of Feature 16 yielded 167 Madison Plain sherds (four rims and 163 body sherds), one quartz flake, and 10 stone fragments. In the reconstruction of the Madison Plain vessel (Pl. 9) it was discovered that the level above Feature 16 also contained 355 sherds of the vessel from Feature 16. Charcoal from level 2 (.4 to 1.5 feet) of the same square yielded a date of A.D. 990 ± 60 (WIS-226).

Feature 17 was a small circular pit in the same square and level as Feature 16; however, the outline of the pit was not delineated until the B21irb horizon had been removed and a definite A1b horizon could be seen over the pit. The pit was probably dug sometime prior to mound construction and cannot be associated with the mound building. No cultural material was recovered.

Feature 19 was assigned to an area in the A1b horizon. Upon excavation it was found to lack any aspects of a feature and was removed along with the rest of the level in this square.

Burial 1 (Pl. 3) had no associated artifacts. The lack of prehistoric primary burials (at the time) led me to believe in the possibility of Historic burial intrusion into Mound R. With the excavation of Mound Q and the recovery of Burial 13 we had evidence from our field season that burials other than prehistoric cremations were occurring in the mounds. In addition, Blake (1961) reported that his Burials Nos. 2 and 4 in Mound G at this locality were primary flexed burials. Burial 1 of Mound R was in a rectangular pit 3.3 feet north-south and 1.7 feet east-west. The burial was on its right side in a tightly flexed position and facing east.

Prior to the construction of Mound R, one feature, 17, was utilized. At the time of construction, features 14 and 16 and possibly Burial 1 were intruded through the original mixed forest surface and the mound was then constructed. The mound profile indicates that pedogenic modification has taken place only in the present-day mound surface horizon. Historic artifacts were recovered from the extreme southern edge of the mound.

Mounds C through H (Fig. 5)

These mounds were reported by Dixon, Blake, and Scribner in 1956 and by Blake in 1961, and at the time of the 1966 excavations the mounds were barely discernible. Extensive soil probing demonstrated that the plowing had almost obliterated the mounds.

Non-Mound Soils and Habitations at 47-Pt-29-2

Mound and sub-mound stratigraphy in this area presented unique comparative data on paleosols, buried mounds, and mound profile developments which yielded an excellent setting for artifact analysis. The data ultimately derived, however, would give a distorted view of the degree and extent of the prehistoric and Historic utilization of the site as a whole and therefore the non-mound areas must be turned to in order to clarify and fill in those gaps which would arise from only mound analysis. Surface square excavations at 47-Pt-29-2 were primarily designed to discover the nature and extent of the prehistoric occupation, and, as we later found, the degree of horizontal and vertical separation between the historic and prehistoric components. Since surface square excavations were conducted according to natural soil stratigraphy, it is necessary to give an overall view of these soil bodies and their profiles and to compare these profiles to both mound and sub-mound profiles prior to artifact analysis.

With the excavation of 105 five-foot squares (2,625 square feet) in mound and non-mound areas at 47-Pt-29-2 and countless soil probings, we were able to plat the soil bodies and their boundaries with a good degree of accuracy. Trenches and squares leading into the mounds added to the information derived from surface square excavations and both allowed us to draw a soils map of 47-Pt-29-2 (Figs. 17*a* and *b*). Profiles from the historically uncultivated woodlot showed that in areas where mound fill borrowing did not occur, there was a developed mixed forest profile which had not been subjected to aeolian deposition. This profile had A11 and A12 horizons and a developed series of B horizons (Bir11 to Bir3) which were repeated throughout the woodlot south of Mound L (Soil Body No. 4, Fig. 17*a*). The majority of artifacts were recovered from the A12, Bir11, Bir12, and Bir2 horizons. These artifacts belonged to the prehistoric component and were not mixed with the historic artifacts. East to the E50 line from S100 to N850 was a large area (Soil Body No. 2, Fig. 17*a*) subjected to plowing until 1956-1958. The recent addition of pine trees resulted in a very thin A11 horizon over the Ap (plow zone) from N100 to N600 and from E250 to E125 (Soil Body No. 1, Fig. 17*a*).

Along the river bank, in Areas P and K, and Mounds S, B, and A, the present surface soil was formed under a mixed forest cover over both the mounds and the areas of aeolian deposition. Only in the Mound Q area did we have evidence that the present-day grass vegetation cover or surface A horizon replaced the mixed forest cover which was sealed in by aeolian deposition (Soil Body No. 3, Fig. 17*a*). North of Mound Q the A horizons indicating a mixed forest cover were again repeated. Between the areas delineated as mixed forest and plow was a narrow band (Soil Body No. 5, Fig. 17*b*) of grass vegetation and thick (over 7 inches) surface A horizons. It was in this region that the greatest number

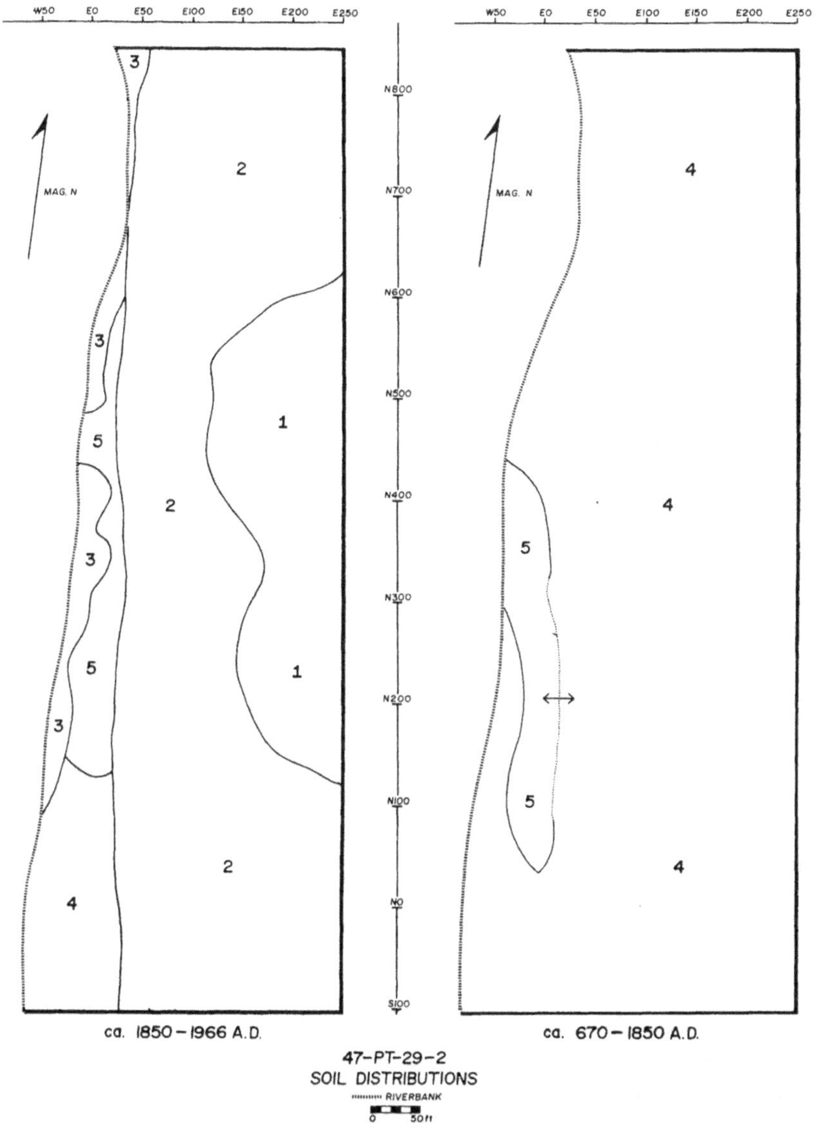

FIG. 17a. 47-Pt-29-2 soil distributions (A.D. 670-1850).

FIG. 17b. 47-Pt-29-2 soil distributions (A.D. 1850-1966).

of historic artifacts were found, which indicates that this soil and/or vegetation was preferred and somewhat stable since the historic occupancy, circa A.D. 1850 ± 25 (Hurley, 1971).

Only two features (4 and 9) were located outside of mound or aeolian deposition areas. These two features were between Mounds L and N in the woodlot.

Feature 4 was oval in outline, 2.5 by 2.9 feet. This shallow basin-shaped pit began in the A12 horizon and extended into the Bir2 horizon. The sandy fill of Feature 4 yielded one rim sherd, two cord-marked body sherds, and one quartz flake.

Feature 9 was circular with a diameter of 1.7 feet and the orifice began in the Bir11 horizon. Feature 9 was shallow basin-shaped in cross section. The sandy fill of Feature 9 yielded three grit-tempered cord-marked body sherds, 11 quartzite flakes, and five quartz flakes.

47-Pt-29-1

This locality conforms to the original Bigelow Mound Group as proposed by Collie and Becker (1912:50-51). During the 1966 excavations the mound group was relocated and numerical designations were given to 13 conical mounds and one bear effigy mound.

Mound 13 (Figs. 18 and 19)

Mound 13 was bear effigy mound 70 feet long, north-south, two feet high, and 30 feet wide. The head was to the south and the feet to the east. The mound was badly potted and at the time of our relocation of this mound it was thought to be so badly disturbed that the remaining portions would lack inclusive features, burials, and artifacts. A separate grid system, similar to the one used at Pt-29-2, was set up (Fig. 18).

Approximately 25 five-foot squares (625 square feet) were excavated in the Mound 13 area. Mound 13 in its construction buried a paleosol and the mound fill had not developed a B horizon; its mixture (Fig. 19) was quite distinct from the A1b and A12 horizons. The A12 soil horizon extended across the mound to the east and west and it was this horizon which seemed to have been the major zone of prehistoric utilization. The A11 horizon was a forest horizon.

Four features (Nos. 6 to 9) were uncovered and excavated in the Mound 13 area.

Feature 6 was found in the head region in the A/B mound fill. Feature 6 was oval in outline, 2.3 by 1.9 feet, and shallow

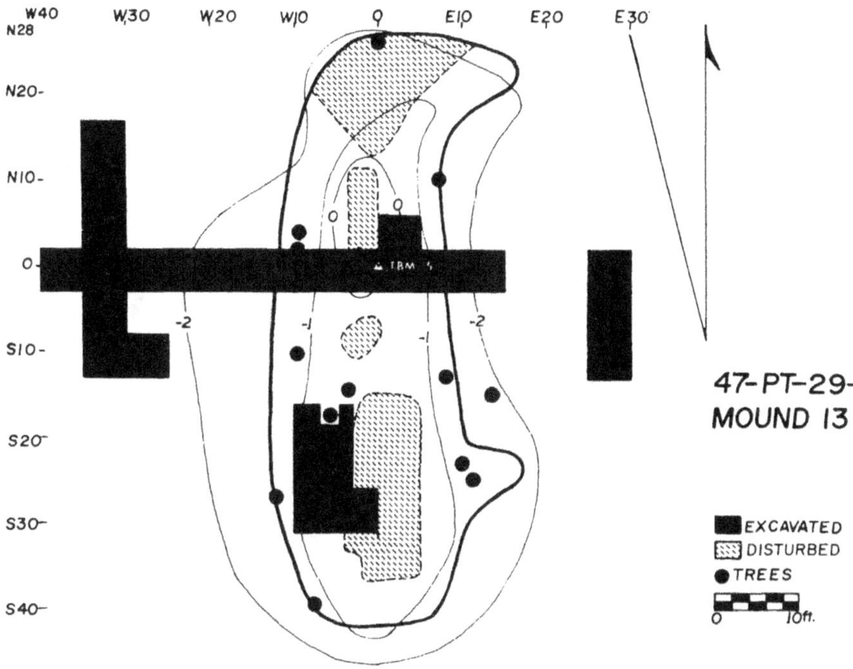

FIG. 18. Mound 13 excavation plan.

basin-shaped in cross section. The feature extended into the B21irb horizon. The sandy fill yielded charcoal flecks, three grit-tempered cord-marked body sherds, one bone fragment, 10 quartzite flakes, four quartz flakes, and two stone fragments.

Feature 7 was located directly west of Mound 13. This circular pit, 1.2 feet in diameter, began at the bottom of the A12 horizon and it extended into the B21ir horizon. The feature contained only charcoal which yielded a modern date (WIS-227).

Feature 8 was located in the head region of Mound 13. The orifice of this bowl-shaped pit originated at the base of the A1b and extended into the B21irb. In outline Feature 8 was roughly rectangular, 1.0 by 1.3 feet, and the sandy fill yielded two cord-marked grit-tempered rim sherds, 10 cord-marked grit-tempered body sherds, and three quartz fragments.

Feature 9 was located in the mid-section of Mound 13. The pit began in the A1b horizon and extended slightly into the B21irb horizon. This circular pit, one foot in diameter, was void of artifacts and contained only charcoal fragments.

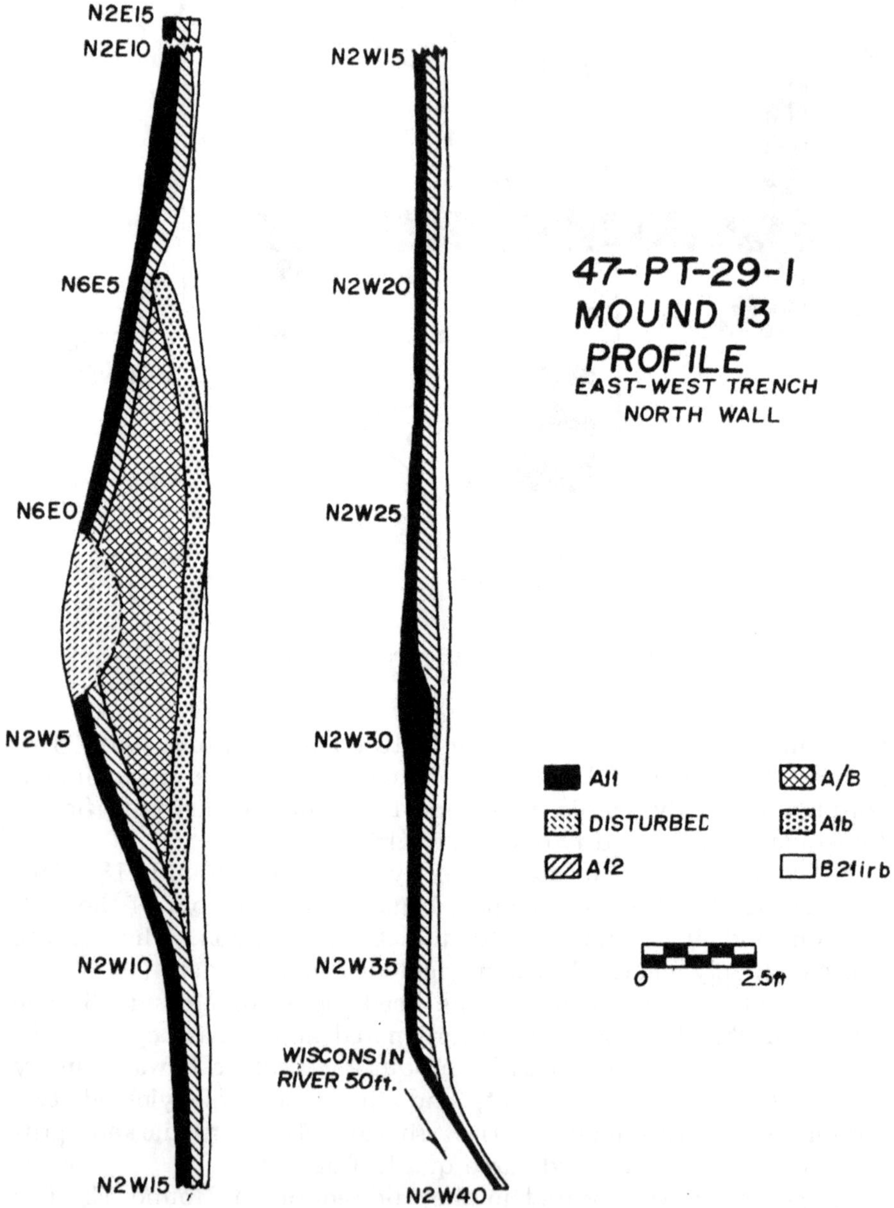

FIG. 19. Mound 13 profile.

It would appear that, prior to the construction of Mound 13, two features (Nos. 8 and 9) were intruded through the surface. During the initial stages of mound construction, a third feature, Feature 6, was also intruded through the A1b and the A/B horizons. At some unknown time, post-dating mound construction, Feature 7 was utilized by the historic inhabitants of this area.

The planimetric view of the conical mound cluster at 47-Pt-29-1 (Fig. 20) is a modification of the original Collie and Becker survey (1912). Because of the limited height of mounds above the surface it is understandable why they missed some mounds and why I did not see them in my survey. In addition, one mound (No. 14) was not noted until after the mound area had been cleared and the numbers assigned. A grid system similar to those used at 47-Pt-29-2 and Mound 13 area was established. Both Mounds 5 and 10 (Fig. 20) had large trees growing on the surface and in Mound 5 some pot-hunting had occurred. These mounds were not excavated and in the case of Mounds 8 and 12 (Fig. 20) the squares were off-center because of the above mentioned factors. Of 13 conical mounds in this cluster, 11 were excavated. The mounds trended east-west; the largest concentration lay close to the river bank and there three 2.5 by 2.5-foot test squares were excavated. The woodlot has been cut several times; however, the forest canopy appeared to be more closed than the one at 47-Pt-29-2. There was no evidence of historic cultivation; indeed, had there been long-term plowing, most of these mounds would have been levelled.

Mound 1 (Fig. 20)

Mound 1 was a conical mound measuring 17.5 feet east-west and 18 feet north-south. The mound was 1.4 feet high and our excavations consisted of two five-foot squares and one 2.5 by 5.0 foot extension into the center of the mound. The soil profiles of these mounds are relatively simple and no descriptions other than the illustrated profiles will be presented. These illustrations will be limited to the more significant mounds in the cluster. Mound 1 was void of both features and burials.

Mound 2 (Fig. 20)

Mound 2 was a small conical mound 16 feet north-south by 18 feet east-west. It was only one foot high and, on the basis

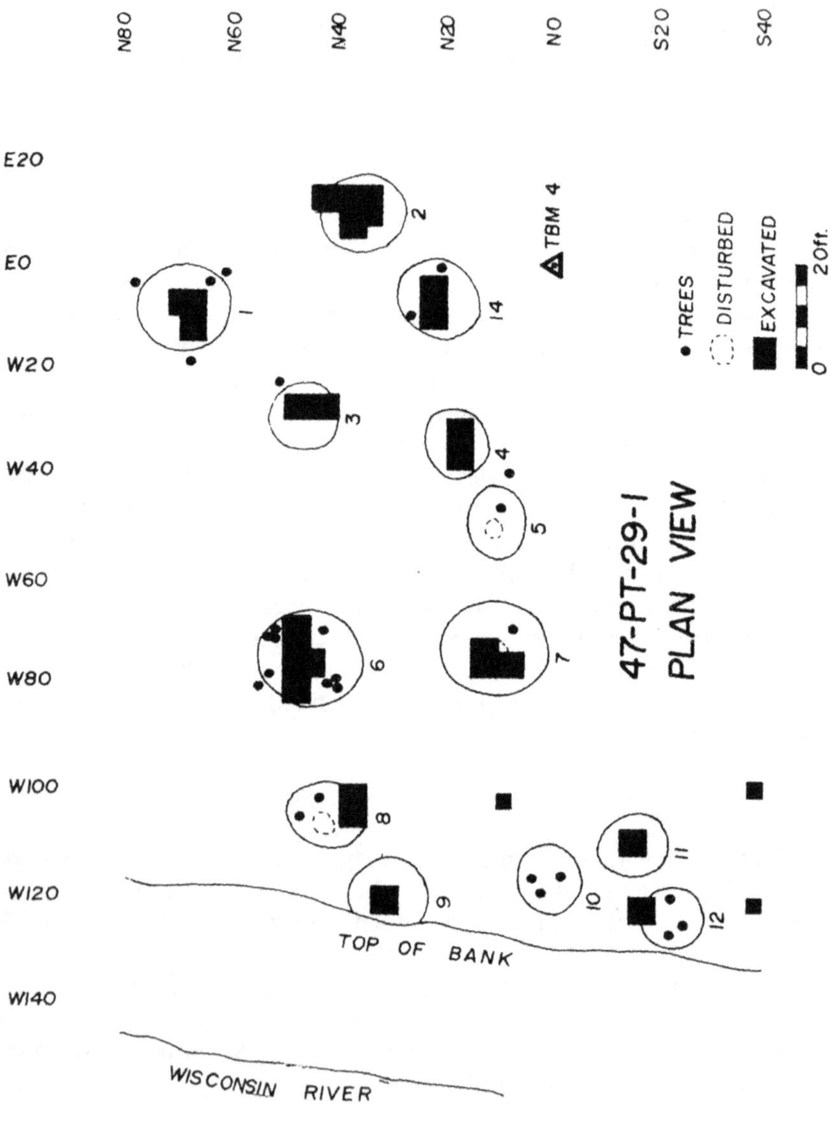

FIG. 20. 47-Pt-29-1 plan view.

of our excavations, which consisted of approximately three five-foot squares, it appeared as if only the central portion of the mound buried a paleosol. One feature, Feature 5, was uncovered.

Feature 5 was in the A1b horizon and the pit extended into the B21irb horizon. This shallow basin-shaped pit was void of artifacts and contained only charcoal flecks. Feature 5 appeared to have been intruded into the A1b prior to mound construction. No other features or burials were found in this mound.

Mound 3 (Fig. 20)

Mound 3 was a small conical mound 13 feet in diameter and .8 foot high. Two five-foot squares were excavated near the center of this mound and it was found to be greatly disturbed by rodent activity. Mound 3 was void of any features or burials.

Mound 14 (Fig. 20)

Mound 14 was a small conical mound 17.5 feet north-south and 18 feet east-west and it was approximately one foot high. Excavations of two five-foot squares produced two features (3 and 4) and Burial 2.

Feature 3. The orifice of the pit began at the top of the A1b horizon and extended to the top of the B21irb horizon. The feature was shallow basin-shaped and circular in outline. The sandy fill contained only flecks of charcoal.

Feature 4. This area was rectangular in outline and upon excavation it was found to be caused by roots or rodent activity. The disturbed area was void of artifacts.

Burial 2 was a secondary cremation scattered in an area of about three feet square in the A1b horizon. No pit outline could be seen and the burial was void of artifacts.

Prior to the construction of Mound 14, both Feature 3 and Burial 2 were intruded into the A1b and the mound covered them and preserved a paleosol profile.

Mound 4 (Figs. 20 and 21)

Mound 4 was a small circular conical mound 14 feet in diameter and approximately 1.5 feet high (Fig. 21). Two five-foot squares excavated in the center of the mound encountered two features (1 and 2) and Burial 1.

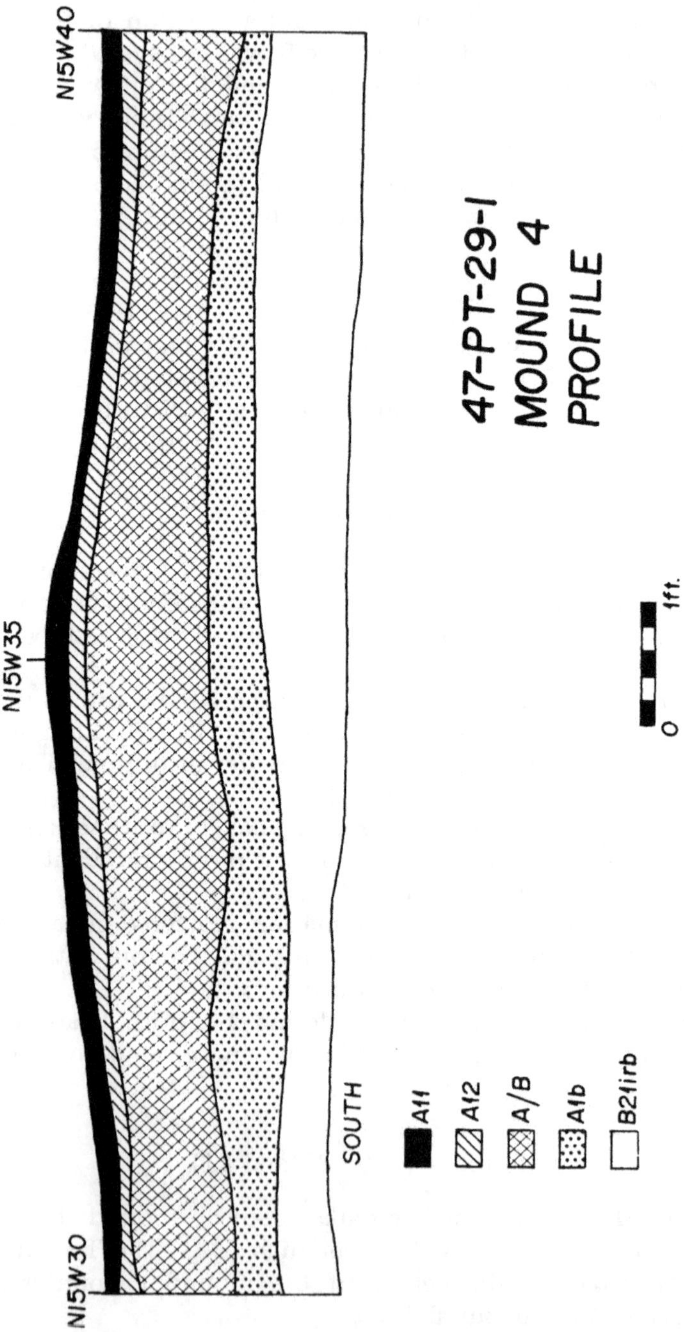

FIG. 21. Mound 4 profiles.

Feature 1 was a pit filled with charcoal. The feature was void of artifacts and the charcoal yielded a date of A.D. 830 ± 65 (WIS-192).

Feature 2 consisted of a charcoal-flecked area in the B21irb horizon. Feature 2 was circular in outline and was void of artifacts.

Burial 1 was located in the A1b horizon and extended into the B21irb horizon. Burial 1 was a secondary cremation lacking associated artifacts.

The features and the burial beneath Mound 4 appear to predate the mound construction which sealed in the paleosol profile.

Mound 5 (Fig. 20)

Mound 5 was a small conical mound measuring 14 feet east-west and 11 feet north-south. The mound was less than one foot high. Because of a large tree near the center and evidence of pot-hunting activities in the center, it was felt that the remaining portions of the mound would not be very productive; thus, Mound 5, like Mound 10, was not excavated.

Mound 6 (Fig. 20)

Mound 6 was one of the largest mounds within this group. It was 20 feet north-south and 19 feet east-west, and approximately 1.2 feet high. A 17 by 5 foot trench was excavated from east to west through the center of the mound with one 2.5 by 5 foot extension in the center of the mound. The excavation in Mound 6 was found to be void of both features and burials.

Mound 7 (Fig. 20)

Mound 7 had dimensions and a profile similar to that of Mound 6. Two five-foot squares with a 2.5 by 5 foot extension into the center of the mound were excavated with very limited results. Mound 7, which had been disturbed in its center, was void of features and burials.

Mound 8 (Fig. 20)

Mound 8 was one of a cluster of five mounds which were constructed close to the river bank. This mound had been extensively potted and our excavations were confined to two five-foot squares at the southern edge of the mound. Mound 8 was 13 to 14 feet in diameter and approximately one foot high. Our excavations failed to produce any features or burials.

Mound 9 (Figs. 20, 22, and 23)

Mound 9 was 15 feet long from north to south and approximately 13 feet east to west. Mound 9 had a maximum height of 1.4 feet above the surface. Erosion of the river bank had removed approximately one-quarter of the western edge of this conical mound. Two burials (3 and 4) were uncovered.

Burial 3. The burial pit and a portion of the cremated human bones appeared in the lower portion of the A/B horizon with the major concentration in the center of the burial pit (Fig. 22). This pit was rectangular in outline and oval in cross section. The cremation appeared to be a secondary deposit which contained very little charcoal. In direct association with this cremation were nine burned and broken quartzite Sanders Triangular and Triangular projectile points (Pl. 14).

Burial 4 (Fig. 23) was directly southwest of Burial 3. This highly fragmented, undiagnostic, cremated bone concentration was in the lower portion of the A/B mound fill and the pit intruded into the A1b horizon. A pit outline could not be established in the field due to the similarity in color and consistency of the pit fill and the A1b horizon. One small grit-tempered sherd was found with this cremation.

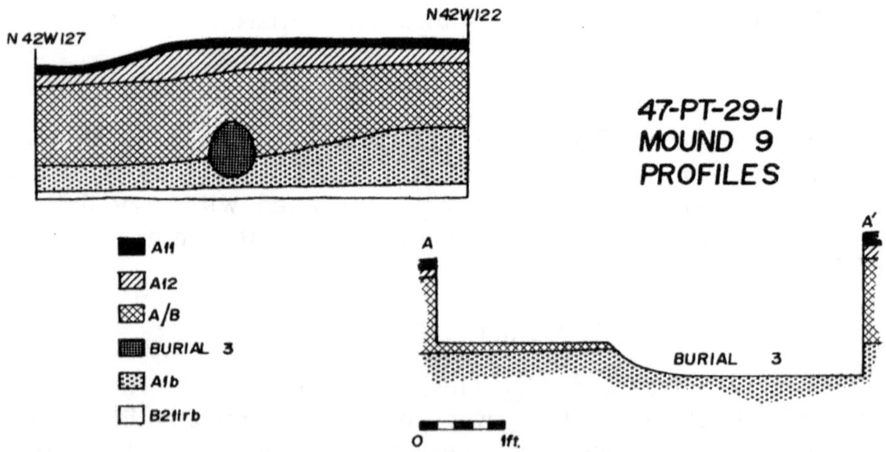

FIG. 22. Mound 9 profile and Burial 3.

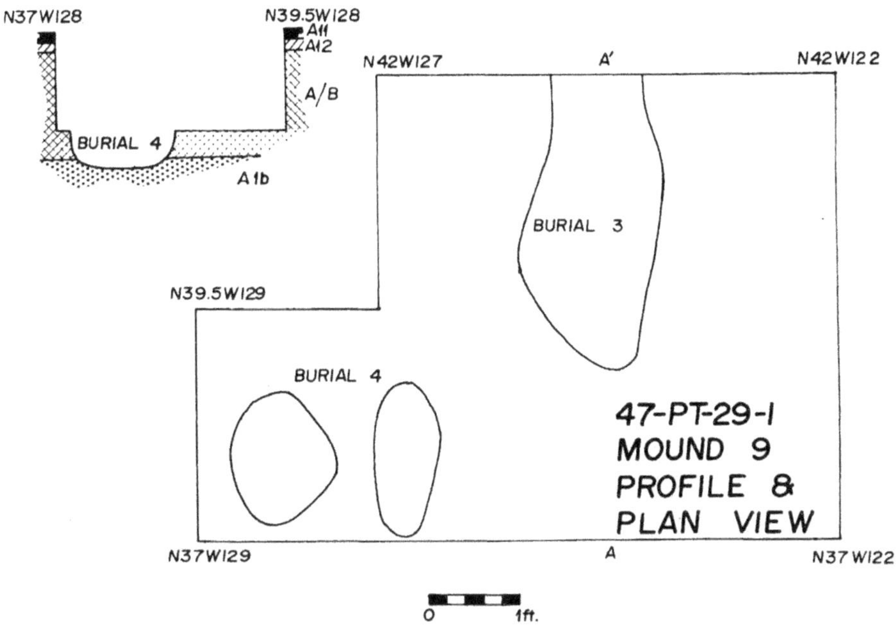

FIG. 23. Mound 9, burials 3 and 4.

Both Burial 3 and Burial 4 appear to have been intruded through the paleosol horizon prior to and during the initial stages of mound construction. The cremations were located in the center of the mound and, except for Burials 1 and 2, which were found in Mounds 4 and 14 respectively, no other cremations were uncovered in the other eight excavated mounds.

Mound 10 (Fig. 20)

Mound 10 was a small conical mound approximately 12 to 14 feet in diameter and one foot high. Three large trees in the center of the mound prohibited any excavation into this mound.

Mound 11 (Fig. 20)

Mound 11 was a small conical mound 13 feet in diameter and approximately one foot high. One five-foot square was excavated in the center of this mound and it was found to be void of features and burials.

Mound 12 (Fig. 20)

Mound 12 was one of the last mounds excavated in this mound group and the large trees in the central portion of the mound allowed excavation of only one five-foot square in the northern portion of the mound. This small conical mound was 12 feet in diameter and approximately 1.2 feet high. Mound 12 was void of features and burials.

Non-Mound Soils at 47-Pt-29-1

The excavation of 1,190 square feet at 47-Pt-29-1 was undertaken during the end of our allotted time at the Bigelow site and with the paucity of artifacts in the conical mound cluster, it was believed that a limited number of 2.5 by 2.5 foot test squares should be excavated along the river bank and, if the amount of recovered artifacts warranted further work, we would expand our test squares. These test squares yielded only one grit-tempered body sherd.

Sub-Mound Soils at 47-Pt-29-1

In every case of mound excavation extending below the mound fill of the conical cluster and the bear effigy mound, the paleosol profile exhibited characteristics that indicated it had been formed under a mixed forest vegetation. The present-day mound and non-mound surface soils are also mixed forest horizons and this vegetation appears to have been somewhat stable since this area was utilized for mound construction (at least for the last 1,100 years as the date of Mound 4 indicates [WIS-192, A.D. 830]). While field impressions need to be validated or proved by laboratory analysis, the mound fill of the conical cluster (A/B horizon) seemed to be in the process of developing toward a Bir horizon. Pt-29-1 appears to have been almost totally forest during mound construction; the soil body reconstruction for Pt-29-2 (Fig. 17*b*) indicates that a large percentage of its area was also under forest vegetation. The soils data derived from our excavations of the two areas at the Bigelow site suggest that a forest vegetation was preferred by the prehistoric peoples at the Bigelow site and that any clearing that was done was in the area intended for mound construction only.

IV

BIGELOW SITE MATERIAL CULTURE

THE analyses of the material culture remains from Effigy Mound sites have ranged from the broad lumping of such items as ceramics into Lake Michigan categories, effigy mound categories, and Effigy Mound ceramic types grouped into wares. Lithic types associated with the Effigy Mound culture have included Waubesa Contracting Stem, Monona Stemmed and Triangular points (Baerreis, 1966:101-131) plus the Kolterman Indented Base knives (Wittry, 1959*c*:185). Various items such as pipes, pecked, ground and polished stone, copper, shell, and bone artifacts (Rowe, 1956:52-56) have also been suggested as part of effigy mound assemblages. Additional artifact types and categories will also be proposed here and in subsequent archaeological reports. These additional types may only expand the range of artifact styles associated with this long viable tradition. What is also needed are indications of their temporal, spatial or cultural ties with other objects of similar manufacture and their gradual stylistic changes through time. Thus, a ceramic type such as Madison Cord Impressed cannot be used as a horizon marker narrowly bracketed in time since the cord impressed *style* spanned more than a millennium, with as yet undocumented micro- and macro-motif changes.

Statistical techniques utilized to demonstrate the probability of associations are designed to quantify type or class relationships, and yet their applicability to effigy mound material objects can only be justified when we can demonstrate that the objects under consideration—for example, Madison Cord Impressed ceramics—are from the same temporal period *or* from cultures interacting within a tradition. Utilization of the Bigelow or Sanders sites by Effigy Mound peoples *could have* spanned 700 years for the former and 400 years for the latter. Both temporal ranges are of considerable importance in culture change interpretations: many prehistoric cultures in the eastern North America known to have used ceramics were only in existence for 400-700 years. Any constant or periodic utilization of a site over 400-700 years, by the same cultural tradition, should provide evidence of change in the form of remaining material artifacts, since cultures and cultural traditions are viable and continually changing. It is, therefore, the obligation of the archaeologist to pick up the clues of such internal change and trace them through time and space.

In the preceding chapter, soils techniques were applied to the mound, sub-mound, and village areas. This form of analysis supplements pollen and floral and faunal studies which are in turn dependent upon the core of archaeological research, i.e., the material culture. One method of material culture analysis presented in this chapter is based on the fact that the predominant styles of Woodland ceramic decoration were cord-marking, cord-impressing, and fabric-impressing. Effigy Mound ceramics exhibit one or more of these techniques and an analysis of these styles should demonstrate continuity of each ceramic type through time and its relationship to each of the other proposed Effigy Mound ceramic types. This form of style analysis treats several classes of cord attributes which were also combined into distinct cord or fabric motifs. These formerly unrecoverable cords and fabrics of the Effigy Mound culture will allow us to more fully expand our knowledge and appreciation of utilitarian and artistic manifestations of great complexity which have until now received little attention. The method of analysis presented below is only a supplement to the major techniques and proved methods of ceramic research and as such it is meant to clarify an important class of attributes associated with ceramics.

CORD TWIST: ANALYSIS AND NOTATION

The cord research to be presented for the Bigelow and Sanders sites is a direct outgrowth of the analysis of the ceramic from the Silver Creek sites (47-Mo-1 to Mo-5), a complex of five prehistoric sites in Monroe County, Wisconsin, whose ceramics belonged to both the Havana Hopewell tradition and the Madison

Ware-Effigy Mound tradition (Hurley, 1966). Approximately 30 percent (609) of the vessel fragments from the Silver Creek sites exhibited cord-marking or cord-impressing as the only surface treatment or decoration present or associated with separate distinct decorative motifs. What was sought was a method of ceramic analysis of these cord-marked or cord-impressed fragments which went beyond a description of temper, texture, color, or direction and type of decoration. Several analyses (Hall, 1950; MacNeish, 1958; Wray and MacNeish, 1961; and Coe, 1961) included the twist of the cord. Rarely did these treatments include discussions, such as Hall's, dealing with the form, construction, and spatial-temporal significance of the cord-marking.

At this point three concepts involved in a cord twist analysis should be clarified. First, the description of the direction and manner of twist, derived from viewing the surface of the vessel fragment, can yield erroneous comparative information concerning cultural behavior. That is, a description of this sort, such as used by Japanese archaeologists for Jomon ceramics (Yamanouchi, 1964), is based on the end result of pressing cord into plastic vessel clay and does not accurately describe the direction and twist of the cord. The cord impression on a sherd or vessel is the mirror image of the cord and, therefore, opposite of the cord itself; the impression derived from plasticine impressed into a sherd represents the actual cord which is/was a cultural reality. Therefore, it is suggested that the description of the cord twist should be from the plasticine positive to avoid misleading interpretations and conclusions.

Secondly, in the description of cord-marking or cord-impressing, as seen from the plasticine positive, the angle of each segment or bar, whether it proceeds from the upper right to lower left (z to Z) or from upper left to lower right (s to S), will again be a description of the end result of manipulative techniques. These techniques are implied in the Z or S designations but they are not descriptions of the actual steps or twists from which this end product is derived. Finally, such descriptive terms as clockwise or counter-clockwise twist, used by MacNeish (1958), are descriptions of the end result of two or more cords twisted together. These terms do not explain the initial manipulative steps necessary to arrive at this end result.

Duplication of the cords represented on the positive impressions of the vessel fragments might justifiably represent only a low level of significance, unless the following initial steps can be accomplished: (1) each form and variety found on the positive impressions can be duplicated as accurately as possible; (2) the manipulative steps involved in each cord twist can be presented in such a manner that the cords can be reduplicated: and (3) each category can demonstrate relationships to either simpler or more complex forms in order that the logical stages of manufacture can be completely understood. What must be achieved, therefore, are cords with individual segments nearly identical to those found on the positive impressions; cords that will hold their form and shape indefinitely; and cords whose length would only be restricted by the length of the material used. A single cord held at one end and twisted on the other end has a strong tendency to unravel. What was found to be utilized on Wisconsin ceramics are cords twisted in such a manner that opposing forces hold them together (Fig. 24). In other words, two cords are twisted individually in a clockwise direction (s cord, right [r] twist) and combined together by twisting in a counter-clockwise direction (z cord, left [L] twist) to make a cord that has the appearance of a counter-clockwise twisted cord, i.e., $z\,{}^{s}_{s}$ cord with an $L\,{}^{r}_{r}$ twist. This cord will hold its twist indefinitely and can be made to any desired length.

Another basic concept in cord twisting must be clarified here. Two cords twisted individually in a clockwise direction (to the right or r) can only be combined together in a counter-clockwise direction (L) to arrive at an $L\,{}^{r}_{r}$ twisted cord which is designated here as a $z\,{}^{s}_{s}$ cord (Fig. 24). Two small $z\,{}^{s}_{s}$ cords cannot be combined to make a large Z cord because cords twisted and combined in this fashion will unravel and cannot be combined. Thus, two s cords (r twist) are combined together to make a $z\,{}^{s}_{s}$ cord and two $s\,{}^{z}_{z}$ cords are combined together to make a $Z\,{}^{s\,{}^{z}_{z}}_{s\,{}^{z}_{z}}$ cord (Fig. 24). The designation Z and S simply means the cord segments are oriented from upper right to lower left, as is the slanted line of an S. Analysis of the Silver Creek vessel fragments subsequently disclosed that four basic cord combinations were being utilized by the occupants of these sites: $z\,{}^{s}_{s}$, $s\,{}^{z}_{z}$, $Z\,{}^{s\,{}^{z}_{z}}_{s\,{}^{z}_{z}}$, and $S\,{}^{z\,{}^{s}_{s}}_{z\,{}^{s}_{s}}$ (Fig. 24). These four basic cord combinations were found to have a degree of mutual exclusiveness in their positions on the

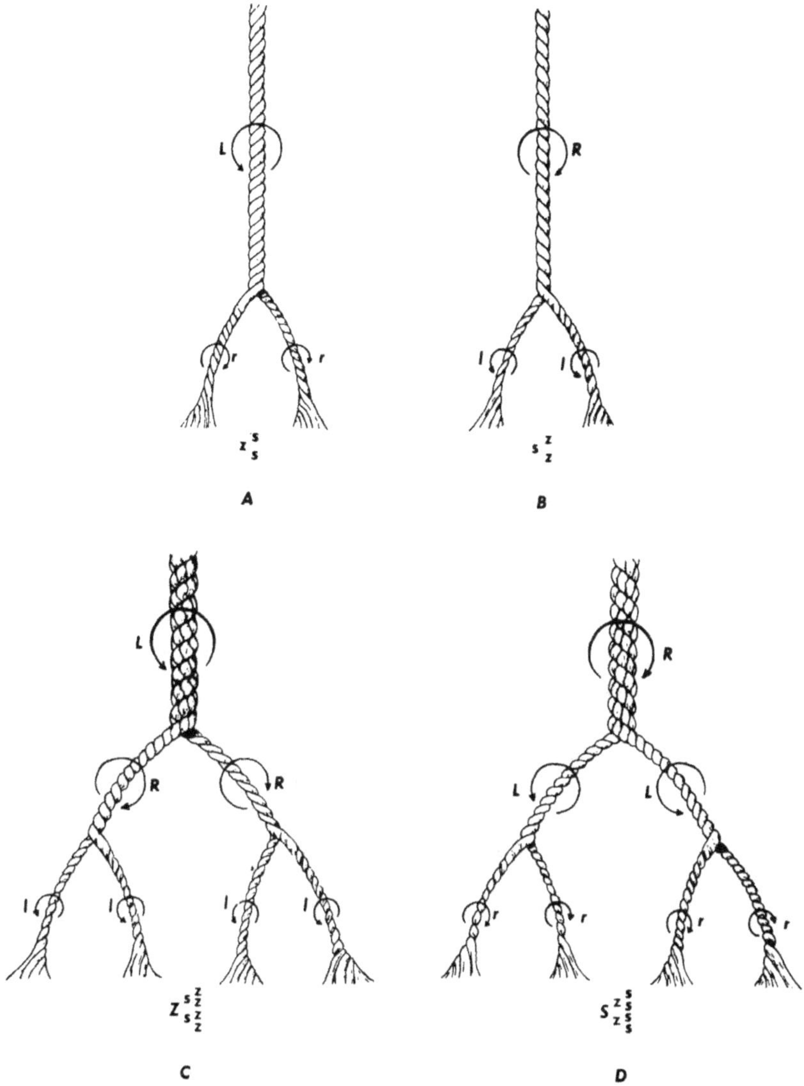

FIG. 24. (A) $z\,{}^{S}_{S}$; (B) $s\,{}^{Z}_{Z}$; (C) $Z\,{}^{S\,{}^{Z}_{Z}}_{S\,{}^{Z}_{Z}}$; and (D) $S\,{}^{Z\,{}^{S}_{S}}_{Z\,{}^{S}_{S}}$ cords.

vessel fragments: $S\,{}^{Z\,{}^{S}_{S}}_{Z\,{}^{S}_{S}}$ and $Z\,{}^{S\,{}^{Z}_{Z}}_{S\,{}^{Z}_{Z}}$ cord impressions were found, as Hall suggested (1950:32), to be used on the area above the vessel shoulder. The $s\,{}^{Z}_{Z}$ and $z\,{}^{S}_{S}$ cords were used on the body as cord-marking, as well as for cord impressions or cord-wrapped-stick impressions on the rims. The fragments from the Silver Creek sites, which are cord-decorated on the rim and which are cord-marked farther down the vessel wall, have cord-marking of $s\substack{Z\\Z}$ cord with the cord decorations of $s\substack{Z\\Z}$ or $Z\,{}^{s\substack{Z\\Z}}_{s\substack{Z\\Z}}$ cord (which is made from $s\substack{Z\\Z}$ cords). Where the cord-marking is $z\substack{S\\S}$ cord, the cord decoration was always of the $z\substack{S\\S}$ or $S\,{}^{z\substack{S\\S}}_{z\substack{S\\S}}$ cord. In no instance were these two sets of combinations mixed or combined. Had this mixing occurred, as it did at the Bigelow and Sanders sites, a different and opposite set of cords for decoration and cord-marking or the use of fabrics for decorations would have been required. Cord twist analysis makes it possible to associate rim sherds with body sherds on the basis of these characteristics. When these characteristics are combined with temper, texture, color, hardness, and provenience, our ceramic categories become more meaningful.

Designating these four cord combinations as basic cords implies that cords which are complex combinations of alternate cord twists are begun with these four combinations (see Fig. 25). Elaborations beyond these basic cord twists require complete comprehension of the concept of opposing forces needed to produce these four cords. The Silver Creek ceramics, therefore, did not represent the full range of cord decoration found on Woodland ceramics. Inspection of cord-marked and cord-decorated ceramics from the Blackhawk, Horicon, Hahn, Durst Rockshelter, Outlet, Bigelow, and Sanders sites indicates the great range and diversity of cord-impressed decorations found on prehistoric Wisconsin ceramics. Attempts to duplicate the cords utilized on these ceramics proved to be easier after the principles involved in the four basic cord twist combinations were understood. A total of 78 cord combinations for the S and Z cords have been listed (Hurley, 1966). The maximum number of cord combinations was not attempted because there appeared to be culturally limited possibilities, self-imposed limits beyond which cord manipulations were not attempted, but these limits cannot yet be established. Thirty-two potential cord combinations were identified, mainly from the analysis of the Durst specimens (Hurley, 1966:318); from inspection of the Bigelow and Sanders fragments, the total number of combinations exceeds 78.

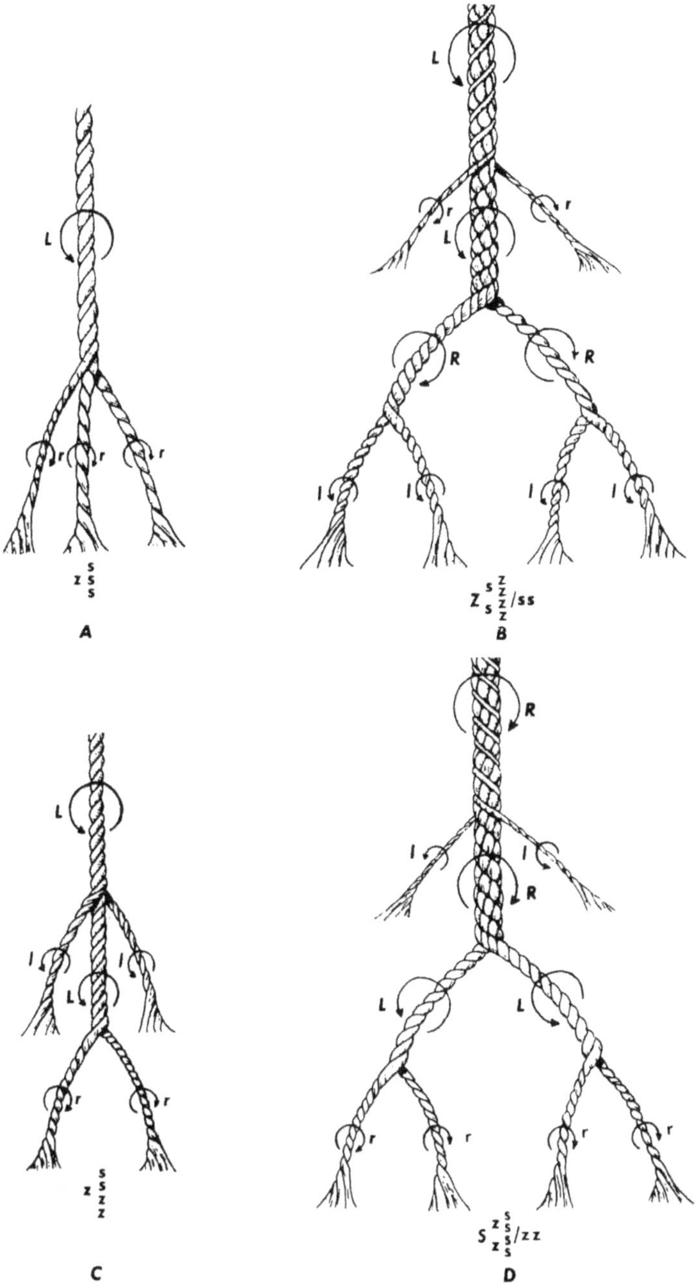

FIG. 25. (A) z $\substack{s\\s\\s}$; (B) Z $\substack{s\\ \\s}\substack{z\\z\\z\\z}$/ss; (C) Z $\substack{s\\s\\z\\z}$; (D) S $\substack{z\\ \\z}\substack{s\\s\\s\\s}$/zz cords.

Analysis of one ceramic decoration present on vessel fragments from Silver Creek Site 5 (Hurley, 1966: Figs. 44-45) was so complicated that no matter how complex the cord, the combination would still lack the necessary elements present in one unit of decoration. Believing that multiple cord-wrapped sticks were involved I began with $Z\,{}^{S\,{}^{Z}_{Z}}_{S\,{}^{Z}_{Z}}$ cords and multiple sticks until, using five sticks, I could closely approximate the decoration. It took two hours to produce a cord 14 inches long. The cord was then wrapped around five sticks in three steps which are repeated (Fig. 26). It was found that any consecutive set of three of these cord-wrapped sticks, for example, 1-2-3 or 2-3-4, would result in a very close approximation of the original implement utilized for the horizontally impressed decoration (Pl. 45). This implement represents a composite complex tool which appears to have been specifically produced for ceramic decoration and was probably a part of a potter's tool kit.

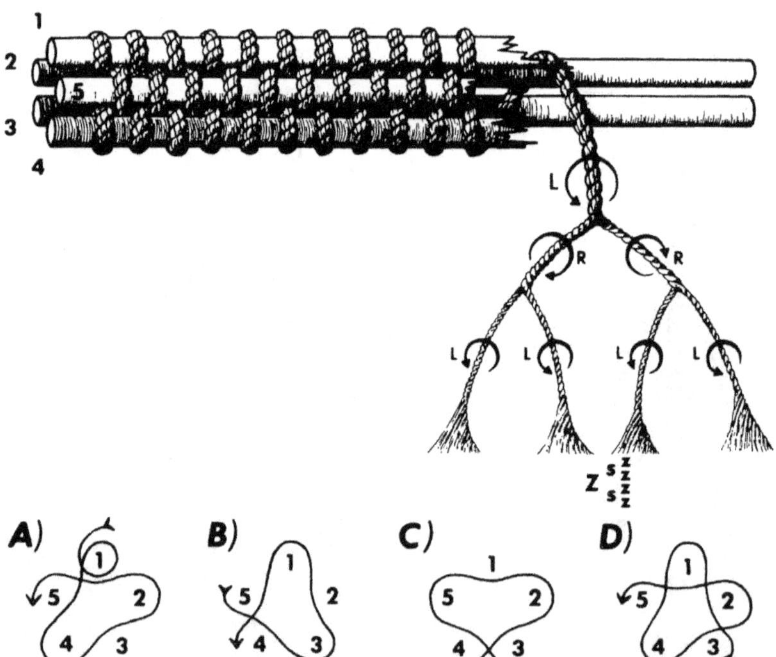

FIG. 26. $Z\,{}^{S\,{}^{Z}_{Z}}_{S\,{}^{Z}_{Z}}$ Multiple stick cord-wrapped stick.

As a term, cord-marking has several pitfalls in addition to those to be presented in this report. There are at least two forms of cord-marking: one which is functional and one which is decorative. The functional method of cord-marking was used to make the clay more compact. A paddle is wrapped with cord because the plastic clay does not stick as readily to the covered paddle as it would to an unwrapped paddle. In the decorative form, a vessel is modeled or molded into shape and a cord is wrapped over cord or a round wood or bone fragment (Fig. 27: C-D). The cords are rolled over the vessel *after* it is shaped and formed and prior to firing. Cord rolling, the predominant cord-

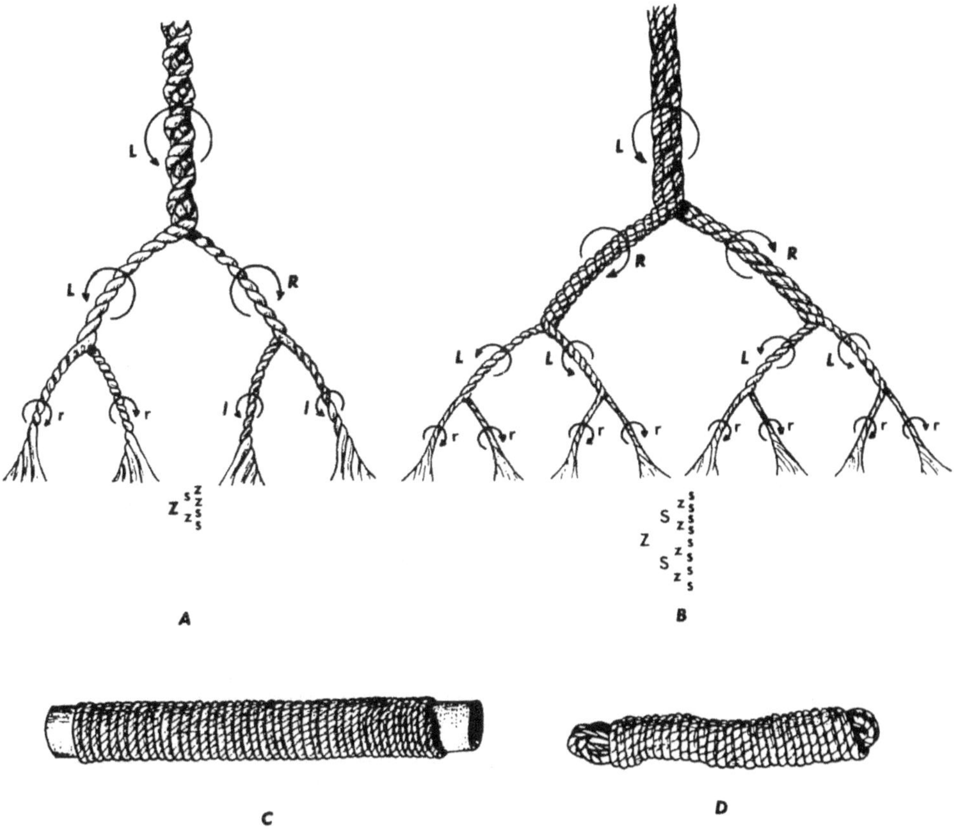

FIG. 27. (A) $Z\,{}^{S\,{}^{Z}_{Z}}_{Z\,{}^{S}_{S}}$; (B) $Z\,{}^{S\,{}^{Z\,{}^{S}_{S}}_{Z\,{}^{S}_{S}}}_{S\,{}^{Z\,{}^{S}_{S}}_{Z\,{}^{S}_{S}}}$; (C) cord over wood; (D) cord over cord.

marking method utilized on Jomon ceramics in Japan, was used on vessel fragments from Silver Creek V (Hurley, 1966:Figs. 44, 45). Cord rolling as a form of decoration is not restricted to the vessel body; it may also be utilized on the upper rim. Cord rolling is also found on the interior of rim sherds and body sherds and in many instances it is the direct result or by-product of interior rim decoration.

The fact that cord rolling is present on the interior of vessels suggests that the idea that the impressions on the interior rim of four of the Aztalan Collared rim sherds (Baerreis and Freeman, 1958:Table 2) and four of the Point Sauble Collared rim sherds (*ibid.*: Figs. 6-7: a) are textile impressions should be re-examined. Mason (1966:134-135), examining his Point Sauble specimens for textile impressions, states that:

> . . . these impressions in their frequent but not universal occurrence, appear on the interior surface below any decoration of any kind, but it [sic.] seems to be a relic of the manufacturing processes. In all the sherds that I have examined from the Door Peninsula this feature is confined to the Point Sauble Collared, and it occurs with surprising regularity on such sherds. It may be, with but one known possible exception, unique to the type. . . .

Mason comes close to one possible solution to this problem: that the decoration is a relic or a by-product of the manufacturing processes. As the cord or cord-wrapped stick was impressed into the clay and moved by rolling to the next location of decoration, the cords passed over the lower undecorated interior rim and left a band or remnant of cord rolling. I have examined 36 Point Sauble Collared type specimens and found that on the interior, 29 were cord impressed, two had cord rolling, and three were fabric impressed. In addition, an examination of the exterior surfaces of these type specimens revealed that 28 had the expected cord impressions; however, eight were fabric impressed.

Being confident of the data derived from the Silver Creek analysis on the types of cord twists utilized for cord marking and cord impressions, I was somewhat surprised to note the variety of cords used on Wisconsin specimens, especially the Madison Ware ceramics at the Durst site (Hurley, 1966:318). After the 1966 field season I was in possession of a large body of cord-marked, cord-impressed, cord-wrapped stick, and cord-rolled ceramics. During the preliminary analysis of the Bigelow ceramics it soon became obvious that the use of combinations of twisted cords to decorate a vessel would have required the use of multiple sets of cords to produce the decorations. The patterned behavior had been logically consistent and these inconsistent occurrences were significant enough to seek an alternative solution to my opposite sets of cords hypothesis. With the publication in 1966 of Emery's definitive work, *The Primary Structures of Fabrics*, these inconsistent occurrences became logical because cords of opposing twists may be used in fabric construction (Emery, 1966:196). Some fabric reconstructions will be presented in this chapter and an elaboration of the fabric types will be presented in Chapter VII along with the larger ceramic sample from the Sanders site.

Two further statements concerning cord twist analysis should be made here. One concerns the Japanese and New World methods of cord analysis and the second concerns a possible means of eliminating errors in cord twist notation. Yamanouchi (1964), who has been examining Jomon ceramics since the 1930's, has been able to determine finer ceramic divisions through the reconstruction of cords applied to temporally restricted, local Jomon ceramic types. In *Nihon Genshi Bijutsu* (Primitive Arts of Japan) (1964, I:218-220) Yamanouchi illustrated 33 plasticine impressions taken from Jomon vessels. For comparative purposes it is important to stress that Yamanouchi, like other Japanese archaeologists, preferred to describe the cords as viewed from a vessel or as seen from a sherd fragment. Thus, their $z\,{}^{\mathrm{S}}_{\mathrm{S}}$ cord is actually an $s\,{}^{\mathrm{Z}}_{\mathrm{Z}}$ cord as suggested here. The form of analysis of the cord twist suggested here essentially follows the tradition utilized by anthropologists in the New World (Emery, 1952, 1966; Osborne and Osborne, 1954), a tradition which should be continued so that one set of cord designations can be applied to cord-marked or cord-impressed vessels, the individual warp and weft in netting or textiles, or the recovered cordage itself.

Finally, such terms as counter-clockwise, clockwise to the left, to the right, or z-Z or s-S are not satisfactory in themselves. What is needed, and what has been proposed by Emery, Osborne and Osborne, Yamanouchi, and myself, is a set of symbols such as the Z and S to designate the twist. A single z designation does not adequately describe a $z\,{}^{\mathrm{S}}_{\mathrm{S}}$ cord with an $L\,{}^{\mathrm{r}}_{\mathrm{r}}$ twist. Emery (1966:10-14) used such terms as two-ply, S-spun, Z-plied; Z-spun, S-plied yarns; plying, doubling, re-plying, and re-doubling. She also proposed that cords be enumerated as z-S, s-s-Z, s-z-s-Z, with the final letter in the series designating the final twist. The 78 cord twist combinations identified by Hurley (1966), presented both the cord—$S \begin{smallmatrix} z \begin{smallmatrix} s \\ s \end{smallmatrix} \\ z \begin{smallmatrix} s \\ s \end{smallmatrix} \end{smallmatrix}$—and the twist—$R \begin{smallmatrix} l \begin{smallmatrix} r \\ r \end{smallmatrix} \\ l \begin{smallmatrix} r \\ r \end{smallmatrix} \end{smallmatrix}$—to provide a visual presentation of both the cord and the twist so that no matter how complex they became, their components or constituent parts would be readily apparent. I propose that this system be retained (as it will be throughout this book) and that a consecutive number be given to each cord twist for those who find these combinations unwieldy.

UNCOLLARED CERAMICS

Of a total of 10,043 ceramic fragments recovered from the Bigelow site, 163 are rim sherds with 1,262 associated body sherds; 25 are decorated body sherds; and 8,593 are undecorated body sherds. The rim sherds and their associated body sherds fall into six Wisconsin pottery types: three proposed types—Madison Punctated, Madison Fabric Impressed, and Madison Folded Lip—and three descriptive categories. The decorated body sherds which cannot be associated with the rim sherd categories are placed into three descriptive categories. The undecorated body sherds (less the small sherdlets and eroded body sherds) are grouped into four categories on the basis of surface treatment.

Madison Ware

Archaeologists who have dealt with various aspects of the Effigy Mound tradition have proposed several ceramic types for this tradition. Wittry (1959*c*:218) proposed that Madison Cord Impressed and Madison Plain be included in the Madison Ware category. Keslin (1958:23) added Hahn Cord Impressed and Mason (1966:151) suggested the addition of Aztalan Collared and Point Sauble Collared to this Effigy Mound ware grouping. Mason added, however, that:

> not all of these types are fully contemporaneous, of course, nor do they occupy exactly the same geographic range. But they all seem to partake of a common *cultural tradition* best expressed between Lake Michigan and the Mississippi Valley and spanning in time a good part of the Late Woodland period [emphasis mine].

At the Bigelow site limited samples of these five types were recovered, as well as examples of Leland Cord-marked and three proposed ceramic types—Madison Fabric Impressed, Madison Folded Lip, and Madison Punctated. On the basis of the evidence to be presented in the following pages and from the analysis of the ceramics from the Sanders site, it is recommended that these four additional ceramic types be added to the five types already proposed for the Madison Ware ceramic category.

Madison Ware is represented at the Bigelow site by 1,410 sherds from approximately 141 vessels. Madison Ware specimens from this site are characterized by medium to granule size temper (1/4 to 4 mm in diameter) of angular quartz and granitic fragments in a paste that is compact, slightly contorted or slightly laminated. Surface hardness ranges from 1.5 to 4.0, with the average 2.0. Interior, exterior, and paste core colors range from tan, red brown, to dark brown, with the average a medium brown. Exterior surface finishes, less decorations, exhibit characteristic cord-wrapped paddle cord-marking from the base to the lip or collar, some specimens having smoothed-over-cord or smooth areas. Exterior cord marking ranges from fine to pronounced vertical imprints which do not show a high degree of paddle overlapping; however, five specimens have exterior cord-rolled surfaces. Only the Madison Fabric Impressed specimens have fabric impressed bodies below the area of decoration and these fabric impressions do not exhibit the twined variations of complexity of the decorated areas.

Lips are flattened, rounded, slightly thickened, beveled to the exterior or interior, or slightly rolled. Lip thickness ranges from 2 to 11 mm, with the average 5.3 mm. Rims are insloping, vertical, or slightly outflaring, and the rim thickness ranges from 3 to 9 mm with the average 5.6 mm. Twenty-one vessels had discernible rim diameters and they ranged from 7 to 40 cm, with the average 27.2 cm.

Madison Cord Impressed

The Madison Cord Impressed ceramics from the Bigelow site consist of 13 rim sections, 28 associated decorated body sherds and two vessels consisting of 1,025 fragments (Pl.7), representing at least 12 vessels. The following subdivisions are based on the type of cord twist utilized in the decoration of these specimens. On the Madison Cord Impressed ceramics from 47-Pt-29 (and from 47-Wp-26 and Wp-70), combinations beyond the four basic twists described earlier (s $\begin{smallmatrix} z \\ z \end{smallmatrix}$; Z $\begin{smallmatrix} & z \\ s & z \\ s & z \\ & z \end{smallmatrix}$; z $\begin{smallmatrix} s \\ s \end{smallmatrix}$; and S $\begin{smallmatrix} & s \\ z & s \\ z & s \\ & s \end{smallmatrix}$) were utilized. The subdivisions suggested below permit us to see the range of these combinations. They are broader than those in the original work (Hurley, 1966) where individual sherds or clusters of sherds were described by the twist of the cord, location and measurements of the decoration, number of twists per centimeter of cord, and direction of decoration. Since this data is now on record, the larger groupings will adequately present the range and variation within each type. The frequency and associations of these attributes will be presented in the next chapter where the cultural activity associated with this site will be examined.

$s\frac{Z}{Z}$-$Z\begin{smallmatrix}s\frac{Z}{Z}\\ s\frac{Z}{Z}\end{smallmatrix}$ *or* $Z\begin{smallmatrix}s\frac{Z}{Z}\\ s\frac{Z}{Z}\\ s\frac{Z}{Z}\end{smallmatrix}$ *twisted cord.* Nine rimsherds and 12 associated body sherds have decorations incorporating cords with $s\frac{Z}{Z}$, $Z\begin{smallmatrix}s\frac{Z}{Z}\\ s\frac{Z}{Z}\end{smallmatrix}$, or $Z\begin{smallmatrix}s\frac{Z}{Z}\\ s\frac{Z}{Z}\\ s\frac{Z}{Z}\end{smallmatrix}$ twists (Pls. 4, 5:A, and 6:F). One specimen has interior cord-wrapped stick impressions and eight have $s\frac{Z}{Z}$ cord-marked surfaces. In addition, one specimen has parallel rows of reed punctations.

$z\frac{S}{S}$ *or* $S\begin{smallmatrix}z\frac{S}{S}\\ z\frac{S}{S}\end{smallmatrix}$ *twisted cord.* Three rim sherds and 726 associated body sherds have impressed decorations of $z\frac{S}{S}$ or $S\begin{smallmatrix}z\frac{S}{S}\\ z\frac{S}{S}\end{smallmatrix}$ twisted cords (Pls. 4:E, G; and 6:B-C, E).

$s\frac{Z}{Z}$ *and* $S\begin{smallmatrix}z\frac{S}{S}\\ z\frac{S}{S}\end{smallmatrix}$ *twisted cord combined.* One reconstructed vessel (Pl. 7) consisting of 317 fragments has exterior and interior $S\begin{smallmatrix}z\frac{S}{S}\\ z\frac{S}{S}\end{smallmatrix}$ cord impressions and $s\frac{Z}{Z}$ exterior and interior cord rolling. The interior cord rolling is not a by-product of the decoration.

Madison Fabric Impressed

The fabric-impressed ceramics included within this proposed type represent only seven rim sections and 22 decorated body sherds representing 23 separate vessels, the only specimens from the Bigelow site with fabric impressions. Any statement concerning the range and variation of Effigy Mound Madison Fabric Impressed ceramics must wait until the larger samples from the Sanders site are presented. However, the vessels in this category form the second largest vessel count from 47-Pt-29 and one which could only have been attained through fabric analysis. Furthermore, specimens exhibiting surface decorations similar to these ceramics have been placed into the Madison Cord Impressed category in the past. Without a detailed analysis of every sample of Madison Cord Impressed ceramics from each reported site containing this Effigy Mound material, it would be unwise to consider the Madison Cord Impressed or Madison Fabric Impressed sample from 47-Pt-29 as inordinately small. The validity of this type and its fabric varieties does not, therefore, rest only upon the Bigelow sample. The patterned behavior exhibited in cord construction continues into fabrics and greater elaborations than those presented in this chapter will be seen in the examples from 47-Wp-26.

There are 10 different fabric-impressed sub-categories represented by the plasticine positives and by the fabric reconstructions from these positives. The sub-categories presented below are based primarily upon the fabric utilized and secondarily upon the cords of the fabric's structure. A separate drawing has been made from each sherd and, along with the analysis cards and the ceramics, they are grouped into divisions. (The drawings, cards, and sherds will remain, as will the Sanders specimens, at the Archaeological Laboratory of the University of Wisconsin for those who wish to refer to the type specimens.) The sub-categories presented below are not on the order of type-varieties.

Oblique Twining

(1) Double oblique twining. Double oblique twining ". . . can be described as double when the elements consistently function in pairs and twine continuously on both diagonals" (Emery, 1966:65). Three examples of double oblique twining occur at 47-Pt-29:

(a) One body sherd has double oblique twining fabric impressions of $z \substack{s \\ s}$ cords (Fig. 48:A)

(b) Two body sherds have double oblique twining of $Z \begin{smallmatrix} s & z \\ & z \\ s & z \\ & z \\ s & z \\ & z \end{smallmatrix}$ and $s \substack{z \\ z}$ cords; one has accessory $S \begin{smallmatrix} & s \\ z & s \\ z & s \\ & s \end{smallmatrix}$ cords added to the $s \substack{z \\ z}$ cords.

(2) Double twining. "To twine: to enclose one or more elements in the twisting of two (or more) others" (Emery, 1966:64).

(a) One body sherd has a double-twined fabric-impressed surface where the weft (the transverse set) is of $Z\begin{smallmatrix} s\frac{z}{z} \\ s\frac{z}{z} \\ s\frac{z}{z}\end{smallmatrix}$ cords and the warp (the longitudinal set) is of $Z\begin{smallmatrix} s\frac{z}{z} \\ s\frac{z}{z}\end{smallmatrix}$ cords (Fig. 49:A).

Weft-Twining

(1) Spaced weft-twining with simple linked warps (Fig. 49:B). "In *simple linking* . . . successive rows of running 'open loops' are formed by a stitch like that known in sewing as *overcasting* or whipping" (Emery, 1966:30).

(a) One body sherd has spaced $z\frac{s}{s}$ weft-twining with a simple linked $z\frac{s}{s}$ warp.

(b) One body sherd has spaced $Z\begin{smallmatrix} s\frac{z}{z} \\ s\frac{z}{z}\end{smallmatrix}$ weft-twining with simple linked $z\frac{s}{s}$ warps and accessory $Z\begin{smallmatrix} s\frac{z}{z} \\ s\frac{z}{z}\end{smallmatrix}$ cords.

(2) Spaced weft-twining with fixed knotted spaced warps. ". . . fixed knots . . . are those in which both the pendant loop and the active portion of the element are engaged in the knotting action" (Emery, 1966:37).

(a) One rim sherd has a fabric-impressed surface of spaced $s\frac{z}{z}$ weft-twining with fixed $Z\begin{smallmatrix} s\frac{z}{z} \\ s\frac{z}{z}\end{smallmatrix}$ knots and spaced $s\frac{z}{z}$ warps. On the interior upper rim there are also $Z\begin{smallmatrix} s\frac{z}{z} \\ s\frac{z}{z}\end{smallmatrix}$ cord impressions.

(3) Paired spaced weft-twining with fixed knotted loop warps. Five specimens exist of which two are rim sherds and two are associated body sherds from the same vessel, and one is a body sherd, all of which have fabric impressions of paired spaced $z\frac{s}{s}$ weft-twining with fixed knotted loops of $z\frac{s}{s}$ warps. The rim sherds have interior $z\frac{s}{s}$ cord impressions from the lip (Fig. 49:C).

(4) Spaced weft-twining with spaced warps (Fig. 50:B).

(a) Two fabric-impressed body sherds have spaced $Z\begin{smallmatrix} s\frac{z}{z} \\ s\frac{z}{z} \\ s\frac{z}{z}\end{smallmatrix}$ weft-twining with spaced $s\frac{z}{z}$ warps (Fig. 50:B).

(b) One body sherd was impressed with a fabric made of spaced $\mathrm{Z}^{\mathrm{s}\genfrac{}{}{0pt}{}{\mathrm{z}}{\mathrm{z}}}_{\mathrm{s}\genfrac{}{}{0pt}{}{\mathrm{z}}{\mathrm{z}}}$ weft-twining with spaced $\mathrm{s}\genfrac{}{}{0pt}{}{\mathrm{z}}{\mathrm{z}}$ warps.

(c) One fabric-impressed body sherd has spaced $\mathrm{Z}^{\mathrm{s}\genfrac{}{}{0pt}{}{\mathrm{z}}{\mathrm{z}}}_{\mathrm{s}\genfrac{}{}{0pt}{}{\mathrm{z}}{\mathrm{z}}}$ weft-twining with spaced untwisted warps.

(5) Spaced weft-twining with spaced warps and accessory cords or knots. Emery defines accessory structures as ". . . those that are worked into or attached to fabrics—after, rather than during, the process of fabrication" (1966:229). The accessory cords and knots recorded for the fabric-impressed ceramics at both the Bigelow and the Sanders sites appear to be additions or personal variations or elaborations added to the weft fabrication and removal from the fabric, by cutting or other such means, would not greatly alter the weft-warp structure.

(a) One fabric-impressed rim sherd and one body sherd have spaced $\mathrm{S}^{\mathrm{z}\genfrac{}{}{0pt}{}{\mathrm{s}}{\mathrm{s}}}_{\mathrm{z}\genfrac{}{}{0pt}{}{\mathrm{s}}{\mathrm{s}}}$ weft-twining with spaced $\mathrm{z}\genfrac{}{}{0pt}{}{\mathrm{s}}{\mathrm{s}}$ warps and $\mathrm{S}^{\mathrm{z}\genfrac{}{}{0pt}{}{\mathrm{s}}{\mathrm{s}}}_{\mathrm{z}\genfrac{}{}{0pt}{}{\mathrm{s}}{\mathrm{s}}}$ cords (Fig. 52:B, C). On the interior upper rim of one specimen there are $\mathrm{S}^{\mathrm{z}\genfrac{}{}{0pt}{}{\mathrm{s}}{\mathrm{s}}}_{\mathrm{z}\genfrac{}{}{0pt}{}{\mathrm{s}}{\mathrm{s}}}$ cord impressions.

(b) One body sherd has spaced $\mathrm{S}^{\mathrm{z}\genfrac{}{}{0pt}{}{\mathrm{s}}{\mathrm{s}}}_{\mathrm{z}\genfrac{}{}{0pt}{}{\mathrm{s}}{\mathrm{s}}}$ weft-twining with spaced $\mathrm{s}\genfrac{}{}{0pt}{}{\mathrm{z}}{\mathrm{z}}$ warps and accessory knots.

(6) Spaced weft-twining with paired spaced warps and accessory cords.

(a) Two fabric-impressed rim sherds and three body sherds have spaced $\mathrm{Z}^{\mathrm{s}\genfrac{}{}{0pt}{}{\mathrm{z}}{\mathrm{z}}}_{\mathrm{s}\genfrac{}{}{0pt}{}{\mathrm{z}}{\mathrm{z}}}$ weft-twining with paired spaced $\mathrm{s}\genfrac{}{}{0pt}{}{\mathrm{z}}{\mathrm{z}}$ warps and accessory $\mathrm{Z}^{\mathrm{s}\genfrac{}{}{0pt}{}{\mathrm{z}}{\mathrm{z}}}_{\mathrm{s}\genfrac{}{}{0pt}{}{\mathrm{z}}{\mathrm{z}}}$ cords. One rimsherd has interior cord-wrapped stick impressions and below this decoration is cord rolling of unknown cord.

(b) One rim sherd has a fabric impression of spaced $\mathrm{Z}\begin{matrix}\mathrm{s}\genfrac{}{}{0pt}{}{\mathrm{z}}{\mathrm{z}}\\ \mathrm{s}\genfrac{}{}{0pt}{}{\mathrm{z}}{\mathrm{z}}\\ \mathrm{s}\genfrac{}{}{0pt}{}{\mathrm{z}}{\mathrm{z}}\end{matrix}$ weft-twining with paired spaced $\mathrm{s}\genfrac{}{}{0pt}{}{\mathrm{z}}{\mathrm{z}}$ warps and accessory $\mathrm{Z}\begin{matrix}\mathrm{s}\genfrac{}{}{0pt}{}{\mathrm{z}}{\mathrm{z}}\\ \mathrm{s}\genfrac{}{}{0pt}{}{\mathrm{z}}{\mathrm{z}}\\ \mathrm{s}\genfrac{}{}{0pt}{}{\mathrm{z}}{\mathrm{z}}\end{matrix}$

cords. On the interior there are also $Z^{s}_{s}\begin{smallmatrix}z\\z\\z\\z\end{smallmatrix}$ cord impressions (Fig. 53:A).

(c) One body sherd has a fabric impression of spaced $Z^{s}_{s}\begin{smallmatrix}z\\z\\z\\z\end{smallmatrix}$ weft-twining with paired untwisted warps and accessory $Z^{s}_{s}\begin{smallmatrix}z\\z\\z\\z\end{smallmatrix}$ cords.

(7) Spaced horizontal and oblique weft-twining with spaced warps. One fabric-impressed body sherd has spaced horizontal and oblique $Z\begin{smallmatrix}s\\s\\s\end{smallmatrix}\begin{smallmatrix}z\\z\\z\\z\\z\\z\end{smallmatrix}$ weft-twining with spaced untwisted warps.

Incomplete fabrics. Two fabric-impressed body sherds were recovered with suspended $Z^{s}_{s}\begin{smallmatrix}z\\z\\z\\z\end{smallmatrix}$ knots and $z\begin{smallmatrix}s\\s\end{smallmatrix}$ warps. Emery defines suspended knots as those hung over a passive element (warp in this case) and which are "... to a certain extent movable" (1966:34).

Madison Folded Lip (Pls. 4 and 5B)

There is only one example from the Bigelow site of this proposed type and reference should be made to the description of Madison Folded Lip ceramics from the Sanders site. The Bigelow rim sherd has an insloping rim 8 mm thick and 32 cm in diameter. The characteristic attribute of this proposed type is the rounded lip which is folded over on the interior and/or exterior as a result of lip decoration—cord, fabric, or cord-wrapped stick decorations. It is suggested that this folding over may mark the beginnings of collaring and that it is related to the collared types associated with the Effigy Mound tradition.

Madison Plain (Pls. 9 and 10)

The Madison Plain sample from the Bigelow site consists of 103 rim sections and 168 body sherds representing approximately 74 vessels. The exteriors exhibit the characteristic undecorated surfaces except for the cord markings and none yielded evidence of exterior cord rolling or fabric impressions. However, as fabric analysis of ceramics becomes more refined, it is likely that a large number of Madison Plain ceramics will be shifted into the Madison Fabric Impressed categories.

The subdivisions of the Madison Plain rim sherds, to be found below, are based on the presence or absence of lip and interior rim decoration and on the type of cord utilized for the decoration or for cord-marking the surfaces. The subdivisions should *not* be considered as formal type-variety designations.

$s{}^{Z}_{Z}$, $Z\begin{matrix}s{}^{Z}_{Z}\\ s{}^{Z}_{Z}\end{matrix}$, *or* $Z\begin{matrix}s{}^{Z}_{Z}\\ s{}^{Z}_{Z}\\ s{}^{Z}_{Z}\end{matrix}$ *cord twist.* Seventeen sherds lack interior decoration; however, their exterior surfaces are $s{}^{Z}_{Z}$ cord-marked.

Nine $s{}^{Z}_{Z}$ cord-marked rim sherds and 10 rim sherds were found with smoothed-over cord surfaces which have the following interior decorations: (a) one rim sherd has interior cord rolling which is *not* a by-product of other interior decoration; (b) one rim sherd has interior cord-wrapped stick decoration; (c) 16 rim sherds have interior cord impressions, one with interior cord rolling as a by-product of decoration; and (d) one partially reconstructed vessel consisting of 170 fragments has interior cord impressions. Directly below this decoration, as a by-product of the cord impressing, is a band of cord rolling (Pl. 9).

$z{}^{S}_{S}$ *cord twist.* Five Madison Plain rim sherds lack interior decoration; however, their surfaces are $z{}^{S}_{S}$ cord-marked.

Five $z{}^{S}_{S}$ cord-marked rim sherds and five rim sherds with smoothed-over cord surfaces have the following interior decorations: (a) one rim sherd (Pl. 8:I) has cord-marking on the lip; (b) five rim sherds have interior cord impressions; (c) three rim sherds have interior rows of cord-wrapped stick impressions; and (d) one rim sherd has interior cord-rolling which is *not* associated with other interior decorations.

$z{}^{S}_{S}$ *and* $Z\begin{matrix}s{}^{Z}_{Z}\\ s{}^{Z}_{Z}\\ s{}^{Z}_{Z}\end{matrix}$ *cord twist.* One Madison Plain rim sherd (Pl. 8L) represents the only instance, for this sample, of a $z{}^{S}_{S}$ cord-marked exterior surface with an interior decoration composed of $s{}^{Z}_{Z}$

elements. The decoration is cord impressing of $Z \begin{matrix} s\frac{Z}{Z} \\ s\frac{Z}{Z} \\ s\frac{Z}{Z} \end{matrix}$ cord. Two different sets of cords were, therefore, used on this vessel.

No discernible cord twist. Thirty-seven lack interior decoration and their exterior surfaces have light to moderate smoothed-over cord-marking. Twelve have cord-wrapped stick impressions of unknown cord on the interior rim, lip, or lip and interior rim.

The remaining two Madison Plain rim sherds have either cord impressions of x-shaped knots, or fingernail impressions on the lip.

Madison Punctated (Pl. 10:A, E)

The proposed ceramic type, Madison Punctated, consists of cord-marked vessel fragments similar in almost all respects to the Madison Plain ceramics except that it exhibits exterior stick- or reed-punctated decorations which would exclude these sherds from the Madison Plain category. In order to more fully appreciate the range and variety of the ceramics belonging to the Effigy Mound tradition, it has been suggested by Mason (1966:151) and myself that the Madison Ware category be expanded. Expansion should not at the present be on the order of a type-variety because this type, and the others proposed, is characterized by decorations or attributes (such as folded lips) which are as distinctive as those associated with the Madison Cord Impressed ceramics. Madison Punctated appears to have developed out of the Effigy Mound ceramic continuum which must have had a greater diversity than has been proposed thus far. Mason has proposed a ceramic type, Becker Punctated (1966:208), which conceivably fills a partial spatial and temporal hiatus between Middle and Late Woodland cultural manifestations as they are now, incompletely, known for central and northern Wisconsin. Becker Punctated does not increase the types of ceramic associated with the Effigy Mound culture, however, since it developed from a Middle Woodland base (North Bay culture), preceded Madison Ware (1966:208), and was not associated with the Effigy Mound culture.

The Madison Punctated ceramics from 47-Pt-29 consist of six rim sections and four associated body sherds which represent at least eight separate vessels. Exterior surfaces are smooth (4) or cord-marked (6), four having $s\frac{z}{z}$ cord-marking and two having $z\frac{s}{s}$ cord-marking. The exterior punctations, which have *no* raised interior nodes, were placed in parallel horizontal rows around the upper rim after the vessel had been cord-marked. The rows of stick or reed punctations are located between 3 and 23 mm below the exterior lip with one to three rows which are 3.5 to 7 mm apart. The punctations are rectangular or circular and average 3.4 mm in length, 2.6 mm in width, and 4.1 mm in distance apart. Only three rim sherds have interior decoration, one of which has $z\,{}^{S}_{S}$ cord impressions and a band of cord rolling below the lip which is a by-product of the decoration. The second rim sherd has interior $z\,{}^{S}_{S}$ cord-wrapped stick impressions and a band of cord rolling below this decoration which is a by-product of the decoration. The third rim sherd has a series of fine open crossed trailed lines from the interior lip.

Leland Cord-marked (not illustrated)

The Leland Cord-marked (Wittry, 1959*c*:207-209) sample from 47-Pt-29 consists of six rim sections and 13 associated body sherds representing 10 separate vessels. These ceramics are very similar to the Madison Plain, Madison Cord Impressed and Madison Punctated ceramics, except that their exterior upper rim has shallow cord-wrapped stick impressions over a cord-marked (9) or smoothed-over cord (10) surface. Three of the cord-marked specimens have exterior surfaces of cord rolling produced by a cord-wrapped cord. The cord-wrapped stick decorations on the exterior rim are confined to the upper 30 mm. On the interior, the cord-wrapped stick decoration is from the lip and the cord utilized in the decoration is of $Z\begin{matrix} s\,{}^{Z}_{Z} \\ s\,{}^{Z}_{Z} \\ s\,{}^{Z}_{Z} \end{matrix}$ cord (1), $s\,{}^{Z}_{Z}$ cord (4), or $z\,{}^{S}_{S}$ (1) cord while of the cord-marked surfaces, three have $s\,{}^{Z}_{Z}$ and five have $z\,{}^{S}_{S}$ cord-marking.

COLLARED CERAMICS

At the present time three established ceramic types represent the known Wisconsin collared ceramics. These ceramic types—Hahn Cord Impressed (Keslin, 1958:221-224); Aztalan Collared (Baerreis and Freeman, 1958:35-61), and Point Sauble Collared (Freeman, 1956:21-23; Baerreis and Freeman, 1958:35-61) appear to represent the range and variation of collaring as it is now known for Late Woodland. Keslin suggested that Hahn Cord Impressed belonged with the Effigy Mound cultural manifestation (1958:221, 223, 270); Mason (1966:151, 193) suggested that Hahn Cord Impressed, Point Sauble Collared, and Aztalan Collared be included within the Madison Ware "ceramic family." Neither Baerreis nor Freeman proposed the inclusion of Aztalan Collared or Point Sauble Collared within this grouping, although Mason (1966:151) saw them as part of a "common cultural tradition." The ceramic manifestations of the Effigy Mound tradition appear to have derived, I would suggest, from such local Early and Middle Woodland ceramics as Shorewood Cord Roughened, Kegonsa Stamped, and Dane Incised; the early Madison Ware ceramics had their beginnings circa A.D. 300; and with the addition of several new types, this ware lasted until A.D. 1400-1700. It remains to be demonstrated just when these types made their appearance and what were the differences and similarities between the ceramics of this "common cultural tradition."

The separation of Aztalan Collared and Point Sauble Collared as types seems quite apparent. Mason has suggested, however, that ". . . several pottery types have been subsumed in Keslin's proposed type [Hahn Cord Impressed] . . ." and that many of these sherds ". . . more properly belong in the type Point Sauble Collared . . ." (1966:140-141). Since Mason concurred with the establishment of both Aztalan Collared and Point Sauble Collared as ceramic types (1966:133-137), it was thought that for the analysis of the Bigelow collared specimens the detailed class and trait analysis conducted by Baerreis and Freeman (1958) could be profitably utilized. However, it became apparent that there were no means of ascertaining which decorative technique or combinations of techniques were located on any given specific area of a vessel (1958:41-42; 55-56). As these are mutually exclusive attributes, each location and decoration will be presented individually and independently in order that more significant comparisons can be made between collared types in the following chapter.

Aztalan Collared (Pl. 11:A-C)

The Bigelow sample consists of 11 rim sections representing at least 10 separate vessels. Collars are secondary additions of clay;

the result of intentional thickening; or a by-product of the decoration. The collars are straight or convex and increasing in thickness; straight or convex and uniform in thickness; or concavo-convex toward the lip. Lips are squared; rounded; beveled to the exterior; or beveled to the interior. The height of the collar ranges from 7 to 18 mm, with the average 10.1 mm. The thickness of the collar ranges from 5 to 11 mm, with the average 7.2 mm. The thickness of the lip ranges from 4 to 8 mm, with the average 5.8 mm and the thickness of the neck ranges from 4 to 7 mm, with the average 5.4 mm. Only two rim sherds had sections complete enough to measure orifice diameters, which were 22 cm and 30 cm respectively.

The decorations on these specimens can be grouped together either by location on the vessel or on the basis of all locations for each specimen. As the sample of Aztalan Collared from the Bigelow site is small the sherds will be grouped together wherever possible in an order of increasing complexity. Interior decorations consist of cord-wrapped stick impressions or $s\frac{Z}{Z}$ cord or $Z^{s\frac{Z}{Z}}_{s\frac{Z}{Z}}$ cord-impressed. Lip decoration is present on two specimens and consists of cord-marking or cord-impressing of unknown cords. Collar decoration represents relatively simple motifs of cord-marking, cord-wrapped stick impressions, cord impressions, or fingernail impressions.

The area below the collar or the lower margin of the collar is either undecorated or has punctations, cord impressions, or cord-marking. The neck region is undecorated, cord-marked, or punctated. Overall, this sample displays simple decoration; a large number lack decoration on the collar, lower margin of collar, neck, and body areas. Cord-wrapped stick decorations and cord impressions are mainly confined to the collar and interior rim (five cord-impressed and six cord-wrapped stick). $Z^{s\frac{Z}{Z}}_{s\frac{Z}{Z}}$ cords were used on four areas and $s\frac{Z}{Z}$ cords were utilized in three instances. The only tentative inferences to be drawn from this sample are the preference for $s\frac{Z}{Z}$ or $Z^{s\frac{Z}{Z}}_{s\frac{Z}{Z}}$ cords and the relative paucity of sub-collar decoration.

Hahn Cord Impressed (Pl. 11:D)

One rim section has been identified as Hahn Cord Impressed. This specimen is collared as a by-product of cord-wrapped stick decoration with a concave face increasing in thickness. The lip is rounded and 4 mm thick. The collar height is 16 mm, its thickness 10 mm, while the neck is 5 mm thick. The interior rim is undecorated; the lip, collar, and lower margin of the collar are cord-wrapped stick impressed with an $s\genfrac{}{}{0pt}{}{Z}{Z}$ cord. The neck, which is also cord-wrapped stick impressed, is decorated with a $Z\begin{array}{l} s\genfrac{}{}{0pt}{}{Z}{Z} \\ s\genfrac{}{}{0pt}{}{Z}{Z} \\ s\genfrac{}{}{0pt}{}{Z}{Z} \end{array}$ cord.

Point Sauble Collared (Pl. 11:E, F)

Two rim sections, representing two vessels recovered from the Bigelow site, have collars which are the result of the addition of secondary clay to the upper rim. Both are straight or convex with uniform thickness or increasing in thickness. One rim sherd has a lip which is beveled to the interior and 4 mm thick. The collar is 17 mm high and 10 mm thick; the neck is 6 mm thick and the orifice diameter is 30 cm. This specimen has cord impressions on the lip, collar, and lower margin of the collar: the lip is impressed with a $z\genfrac{}{}{0pt}{}{S}{S}$ cord; the collar and lower margin of the collar are impressed with a $Z\begin{array}{l} s\genfrac{}{}{0pt}{}{Z}{Z} \\ s\genfrac{}{}{0pt}{}{Z}{Z} \\ s\genfrac{}{}{0pt}{}{Z}{Z} \end{array}$ cord. The neck area was cord-rolled with an $s\genfrac{}{}{0pt}{}{Z}{Z}$ cord. The second rim section has a squared lip which is 5 mm thick and a collar which is 11 mm high and 6 mm thick. The neck is 5 mm thick and the estimated orifice diameter is 26 cm. The interior rim has cord impressions of $S\begin{array}{l} z\genfrac{}{}{0pt}{}{S}{S} \\ z\genfrac{}{}{0pt}{}{S}{S} \end{array}$ cords and two rows of parallel rectangular punctations beginning 10 mm below the interior lip which do *not* raise exterior nodes. The lip has $S\begin{array}{l} z\genfrac{}{}{0pt}{}{S}{S} \\ z\genfrac{}{}{0pt}{}{S}{S} \end{array}$ cord impressions; the collar has $z\genfrac{}{}{0pt}{}{S}{S}$ cord impressions. The lower margin of the collar has two parallel rows of rectangular punctations which duplicate the interior punctations; however, the rows and the individual punctations are in alternate, rather than overlapping, locations. The neck region has cord impressions of $S\ \substack{z\,\substack{s\\s}\\ z\,\substack{s\\s}\\ z\,\substack{s\\s}}$ cord.

Unclassified Rimsherds

(1) One rim sherd and two associated body sherds (Fig. 40:A), with the rim sherd having a vertical rim with a diameter of 32 cm and a thickness of 9 mm. The lip is flattened and irregular, 12 mm thick, and has $z\,\substack{s\\s}$ cord-wrapped stick impressions. Over this lip decoration is a row of impressed $z\,\substack{s\\s}$ cord. The upper exterior rim has two rows of $z\,\substack{s\\s}$ cord-wrapped stick impressions. The surface is $z\,\substack{s\\s}$ cord-marked.

(2) This rim sherd (Pl. 12:C) has an insloping rim 6 mm thick and a flattened lip 5 mm thick. Its temper is medium grit 1/2 to 1/4 mm in diameter and the paste is compact. The hardness is 2.0 and the surface colors are brown with a black paste core. The lip has wedge-shaped punctations. On the exterior rim and lip there are shallow trailed lines.

(3) Eleven rim sherds have eroded exterior surfaces; 10 have interior cord-wrapped stick decoration (six with $s\,\substack{z\\z}$ cord) and one has interior $S\ \substack{z\,\substack{s\\s}\\ z\,\substack{s\\s}}$ cord impressions.

BODY SHERDS

Decorated Body Sherds

(1) Eleven body sherds, of which nine have interior cord rolling of $z\,\substack{s\\s}$ cord (6); $s\,\substack{z\\z}$ cord (1); and one with both $z\,\substack{s\\s}$ and $s\,\substack{z\\z}$ cord rolled on the interior. This latter specimen also has a $Z\ \substack{s\,\substack{z\\z}\\ s\,\substack{z\\z}}$ cord-marked exterior surface. Two specimens from Mound L are neck fragments which have exterior $s\,\substack{z\\z}$ cord-rolling and they may be associated with the Point Sauble Collared rim sherd recovered from this mound (Pl. 11:F). The interior cord-rolling does not appear to be associated with any other interior decoration.

(2) Eleven body sherds (Pl. 12:D-F) are incised or have broad shallow trailing. The incised specimens have incisions which were placed over a cord-marked surface. Two of the trailed specimens (Pl. 12:F) have very shallow trailed lines over a cord-marked surface and these parallel horizontal lines could be the result of passing the fingers around the cord-marked vessel prior to firing. The remaining five trailed specimens are intentionally decorated by trailing or trailing combined with stick punctations. One specimen has a shallow curvilinear trailed line over a smooth surface.

(3) Four body sherds which have: interior brushing; $z\frac{S}{s}$ cord-rolled over $z\frac{S}{s}$ cord; a repair hole 5 mm in diameter; and one specimen which could be a handle fragment.

Undecorated Body Sherds

A total of 9,295 undecorated body sherds were recovered from the 1965 and 1966 excavations at the Bigelow site. Of this total, 7,989 (85.9 percent) were recovered from Pt-29-2 and 1,306 (14.0 percent) were recovered from Pt-29-1. Of the total number of body sherds, 7,776 (83.6 percent) are small sherdlets or have eroded surfaces. The remaining 1,519 (16.3 percent) are grouped into four categories on the basis of surface treatment: cord-marked, smoothed-over cord, smooth surface grit-tempered, and smooth surface shell-tempered. The cord marked category is further subdivided into $s\frac{Z}{z}$ cord marked and $z\frac{S}{s}$ cord marked.

Category 1—Cord-marked body sherds. There are 897 (59.0 percent) cord-marked grit-tempered body sherds in this category, representing many vessels. These sherds have tempering ranging in size from fine to granular, with a diameter from 1/4 to 4 mm. In texture the sherds are compact, contorted, or laminated. The paste cores range in color from tan to black and the surfaces are light tan to dark brown. The hardness ranges from 1.5 to 3.0 with the average 2.0. Of the sherds, 553 (61.6 percent) have $s\frac{Z}{z}$ cord-marked surfaces while 344 (38.3 percent) have $z\frac{S}{s}$ cord-marked surfaces.

Category 2—Smoothed-over cord body sherds. There are 441 (29.0 percent) body sherds which have been smoothed intentionally or by use subsequent to cord-marking.

Category 3—Smooth body sherds, grit-tempered. These sherds (167 or 11.0 percent) represent specimens which did not have any evidence of previous cord-marking and they may represent the lower portions of the vessels.

Category 4—Smooth surface, shell-tempered body sherds. These 13 (.8 percent) shell-tempered body sherds are all from a square and level which also contained eight grit-tempered sherds, and two historic copper (22 caliber) expended cartridges. The sherds are light tan to gray in surface color; highly polished; between 2 to 3 mm in thickness, and have a hardness of 1.5.

Lithic Artifacts

Compared with the ceramic artifacts from the Bigelow site, the classifiable lithic artifacts, modified stone fragments, and waste flakes are relatively few in number. Only 158 artifacts or modified stone fragments were recovered and of this total, 10 or 6.3 percent are proximal or distal portions of projectile points. The remaining artifacts are grouped below into one proposed projectile point type (Sanders Triangular); three projectile point categories (Triangular (A), Triangular (B), and Corner Notched); drill; core; worked flakes; pecked; polishing stone; or modified stone categories. In addition to these items, 3,901 unworked flakes were recovered. The following proposed point type and lithic categories are suggested as belonging to the prehistoric Effigy Mound culture component at the Bigelow site.

Projectile Points

A total of 43 projectile points were recovered from the Bigelow site. Of this number, 42 (97.7 percent) are Triangular points and one (2.3 percent) is a corner notched point. The Triangular points are subdivided below on the basis of unifacial workmanship with limited edge retouch (Sanders Triangular) or according to bifacial workmanship with serrated lateral blade edge retouch versus non-serrated edges.

Sanders Triangular (Pl. 13:A, C-F, H; Pl. 14:C, E, H, J). The distinguishing attributes of this proposed type are that the combinations of the retouch are confined to one face (the convex face) and to the lateral and basal edges. Only rarely is edge retouch found on the opposite or plano face. The characteristics of these points, together with their relationships to other Triangular points, will be amplified in the discussion of Sanders Triangular points from 47-Wp-26. However, the Sanders Triangular points are considered to give formal recognition to distinctive projectile points which are normally grouped under the broad classification of Madison Points (Scully, 1951) or the category Triangular points. The proposed Sanders Triangular points are contemporary with the other two point categories presented below and their temporal range will be discussed in the following chapter.

Projectile points included within this proposed type category number 17 (40.5 percent) and they are either isosceles (6 or 35.3 percent) or equilateral (11 or 64.7 percent) in outline. Two of the points are of cream or gray chert and the remaining 15 points are of tan, cream, or gray fine-grained quartzite. Of the total number, 16 are plano-convex and one is flat lenticular in cross section. The Sanders Triangular points from 47-Pt-29-2 and Pt-29-1 have medium to steep lateral blade edge serrations on two of the equilateral and three of the isosceles points. The range in length for these specimens is between 17 and 28 mm, with the average 20.7 mm. In width they measure between 12.5 and 20 mm, with the average 16.2 mm; in thickness the range is between 2 and 5 mm, with the average 3.0 mm. The basal measurements normally are between 1 and 2 mm, less than the overall thickness of these points.

(1) Triangular. Included within this category are 11 projectile points (26.2 percent), of which six (54.5 percent) are isosceles and five (45.4 percent) are equilateral in outline. All of these Triangular points are bifacially worked and they are biconvex in cross section. One of the points is of a cream chert and the remaining points are either tan, pink, cream, or gray quartzite. The distinguishing attribute of this Triangular subdivision is the presence of fine to deep edge retouch, resulting in lateral blade edge serration extending from the base to the tip of the points (Pl. 13:B; Pl. 14:A-B, D, G, I). The bases are either unworked or thinned to 1 or 2 mm less than the blade thickness. These points range in thickness from 3 to 4.5 mm with the average 3.8 mm; in length from 13 to 34 mm with the average 21.6 mm; and in width from 9 to 22 mm with the average 16.6 mm.

(2) Triangular. Within this category are 14 projectile points (33.3 percent), of which nine are isosceles (64.3 percent) and five (35.7 percent) are equilateral in outline. Two of these Triangular points are of cream chert; two are of clear quartz; and 10 are of tan, cream, or gray quartzite. All of the points are lenticular in cross section and, although they lack lateral blade serration, they do exhibit fine to steep blade edge retouch (Pl. 13:G, I-K; Pl.

14:F). These specimens also have basal thinning 1 to 2 mm less than the blade thickness. The points range in thickness from 2.5 to 6 mm, with the average 3.7 mm; in length from 12 to 34 mm with the average 21.1 mm; and in width from 11 to 21 mm with the average 16.4 mm. Combining the three categories of Triangular points, the average thickness is 3.5 mm; the average length is 21.3 mm; and the average width is 17.0 mm.

(3) Corner notched (Pl. 13:L). This point is of a fine grained gray quartzite with unifacial chipping and it is plano-convex in cross section. The blade edges and proximal end are finely retouched. The point is 3 mm thick, 21 mm long, and 18.5 mm wide. The stem is 2 mm thick, 8.5 mm long, and 14 mm wide. The base is 1 mm thick, 3 mm long, and 14 mm wide. The minimum width between notches is 10.5 mm.

(4) Drills. Four specimens fall into this category, one of which is a reworked triangular projectile point (Pl. 14:K). This latter drill is of a fine grained tan quartzite and is 21.5 mm long, 14 mm wide, 4.5 mm thick, and flat lenticular in cross section. Two specimens are flakes, of which a portion has been worked into drill shafts 14 mm long. The specimens are of quartz or quartzite and irregular in outline. The fourth specimen is of chert and represents the distal portion of a drill shaft. It is 45 mm long, 16 mm wide, 8 mm thick, and somewhat plano-convex in cross section.

(5) End scrapers. Included within this lithic category are two end scrapers with steep distal and lateral edge retouch. Both end scrapers are of tan quartzite and plano-convex in cross section. One scraper (Pl. 13:M) is 21 mm long, 23 mm wide, and 8 mm thick. The second scraper (Pl. 13:N) is 33 mm long, 20 mm wide, and 11 mm thick.

(6) Cores. (Pl. 13:P) There are 17 specimens, 16 of which are classified as cores which have been "exhausted" by flake removal. The cores are irregular in outline and cross section and in general their shape is somewhat amorphous. Eight of these cores are of quartz, five are of quartzite, and three are of chert. They range in length from 11 to 41 mm, in width from 11 to 41 mm, and in thickness from 7 to 31 mm. The cores do not exhibit subsequent modification into scrapers or cutting implements, nor do they have secondary edge battering. Included within this core category is one blade core (Pl. 13:P) of mottled chert, 37.5 mm long, 23 mm wide, and 10 mm thick. This blade core appears to be a portion or face of a large core and has retained a portion of the striking

platform. The obverse face has had six very thin blades less than .5 mm in thickness pressed off from the distal platform end and two blades pressed off from the proximal end. The blades removed were 2 to 4 mm wide, and 12 to 18 mm long. With detachment of these fragments from the primary core, the reverse face was retouched along one lateral edge and used as a scraping or cutting tool.

(7) Flakes. In this category there are 3,910 flakes, of which nine (.2 percent) are worked flakes. The non-worked and non-utilized waste flakes consist of 85 (2.2 percent) chert flakes, 1,732 (44.4 percent) quartz flakes, 2,075 (53.2 percent) quartzite flakes, and nine (.2 percent) basalt flakes. The large number of quartz and quartzite flakes strongly indicates that as a source material both were highly preferred. This is further supported by the high number of quartzite and quartz artifacts. The nine worked flakes are single edge flake side scrapers of which five are of quartzite, three of chert, and one of quartz. These worked flakes are all plano-convex in cross section and irregular in outline. Six of the specimens retain their striking platforms and the bulbar surface is generally flat and smooth. The convex dorsal surfaces do not exhibit any secondary chipping on the face; however, one lateral, dorsal, or ventral edge has fine steep retouch. In length these worked flakes range from 18 to 44 mm, with the average 27.1 mm; in width from 11 to 26 mm, with the average 18.8 mm; and in thickness from 4 to 9 mm, with the average 6.9 mm.

(8) Pecked stones. Of the two basalt stones in this category, one has been used as a hammer stone (Pl. 15:E) and is 85 mm long, 62 mm wide, 38 mm thick, with lateral edge battering. In the center of this hammer stone, on both faces, there are pecked circular depressions 20 mm in diameter and 2 mm deep. The other basalt stone (Pl. 15:D) has a pecked circular depression on the dorsal surface which is 24 mm in diameter and 9 mm deep. The function of this stone and its depression is uncertain; however, the orifice shows polishing and ware. This pecked stone is 47 mm long, 40 mm wide, and 25 mm thick.

(9) Polishing stones. Nineteen specimens are suggested for this category. The oval outline and cross section (except that illustrated in Pl. 15:C), the smooth and polished surfaces, and the overall size suggest that they were used as smoothing implements. These specimens range in length from 22 to 49 mm, with the average 32.0 mm; in width from 20 to 38 mm with the average 26.4 mm; and in thickness from 6 to 25 mm with the average 15.0 mm.

(10) Modified stone and stone fragments. In the excavations of test and surface squares at the Bigelow site it was noticed that there was an absence of water rolled or water worn pebbles larger than 4 mm in diameter and that as the site was on a lacustrine outwash terrace, just two miles west of a glacial end moraine (Black, 1964:174), the absence of glacial till was to be expected. However, in our excavations 54 stone fragments were recovered which had some battering on the edges, polishing, or a moderate amount of grinding. These stones were mainly confined to mounds (41 or 75.9 percent), as opposed to surface squares (13 or 24.1 percent). They are oval or irregular in outline and oval or lenticular in cross section. They are of fine grained basalt or quartz and range in thickness from 3 to 68 mm, in length from 18 to 168 mm, and in width from 13 to 115 mm. Their function could have been grinding, polishing, or for stone boiling.

WORKED BONE

Only two worked bone fragments were recovered from the Bigelow site and both were associated with Burial 5 in Mound A (Pl. 15:A, B). The first specimen is a deer antler tine which has been worked into a flaker. Associated with this artifact was a beaver incisor which fits into the cut hole in the dorsal surface. The flaker is 177 mm long, 23 mm high, and 18 mm wide. The oval hole is 12 mm long and 6 mm wide. The one proximal side which is present has a parallel series of incised lines 22 mm long and 2 mm wide. Two of these lines extend to the distal end. The second specimen (Pl. 15:B) is a bone fragment which does not appear to belong to the flaker. This specimen has a parallel series of cut notches at its apex which are 2 mm long and 2 mm apart. The fragment is 36 mm long, 6 mm high, and 9 mm wide. At its distal end, which is cut, there appears to be wear polishing.

COPPER

Only one copper fragment was found at the Bigelow site and it appears to belong to the prehistoric component. This fragment, recovered from Mound B, N330W10-3-10, is a small irregular-shaped fragment of flattened copper 12 mm long, 7 mm wide, and 2 mm thick. No copper artifacts were recorded by Blake (1961:57-76) and none were recovered during the 1965 or 1966 excavations.

HISTORIC ARTIFACTS

A description of these artifacts has been included in separate reports on the Historic component at 47-Pt-29-2 (Lange, 1969; Hurley, 1970). As this component gives every indication of having occurred after A.D. 1850 it is believed to have had little, if any effect on the prehistoric occupation except in the case of mound intrusions for burial purposes.

V

BIGELOW SITE ANALYSES

THE distribution, chronology, and relationships of artifacts recovered from sites with both effigy and non-effigy mounds have yet to be elaborated upon in any detail. Sub-mound, mound inclusions and intrusions, and adjacent camp or village refuse relationships have not been demonstrated because of the paucity of diagnostic artifacts, the absence of sub-mound or habitation material, and the lack of good chronological control. In the previous chapters several lines of investigation have been introduced and they will now be brought to bear on the problem of associations. The soils analysis clarified the points of separation between natural and man-made stratigraphy. The vertical and horizontal soil sequences will be coupled with the analysis of mound, non-mound, and feature sequences. The use of the typological method of material culture analysis has allowed for the ordering of a large quantity of artifacts. These artifacts were subjected to detailed attribute analysis in the case of cord- and fabric-impressed ceramics and this line of investigation should reflect cultural preferences and micro-stylistic change. The soils and material culture analyses are strongly aided by a series of radiocarbon dates which allow for greater precision in the chronological ordering of these phenomena as they were recorded for the Bigelow site.

A chronology by itself offers little more than a scheme of internal order. Proposals for internal and external chronological order for the Effigy Mound culture have so far been based on vague artifact associations (A.D. 300 to A.D. 1000 [Rowe, 1965:83]) or on a series of effigy mound sites in a restricted geographic area ordered on the basis of limited remains (Baerreis, 1966). Effigy mounds have been assumed to be prehistoric, with a moderate degree of longevity. Individual radiocarbon dates on Effigy Mounds in Wisconsin (Wittry, 1956, 1959*b*; Bastian, 1958, 1962) have tended to support both assumptions. However, the Bigelow site is unique: it is the first Wisconsin Effigy Mound site to have yielded a series of 10 radiocarbon dates. Eight of these dates indicate that the occupation and mound construction activity at this location could have begun as early as A.D. 560 (WIS-197) and terminated as late as A.D. 1500 (WIS-187), covering almost 1,000 years of proposed Effigy Mound cultural activity. A narrower view is illustrated in Figure 28, which shows that the radiocarbon dates for the Bigelow site tend to cluster between A.D. 700 and A.D. 1250, a period of about 550 years.

The Bigelow site radiocarbon dates are also the first series of dates to indicate that an effigy mound location was intermittently re-occupied over a considerable span of time. The mounds appear to have been built at this location over several centuries and the culture that built these mounds had a tradition of successive reoccupation during which artifacts were intentionally or unintentionally left behind. The artifacts themselves should reflect both stability and change at this site. That is to say, mounds were not built and artifacts left behind at the Bigelow site over a short (50-year) period of time, a situation which would allow for the assessment of a brief segment of the Effigy Mound cultural continuum. The view of an Effigy Mound band moving to one location and building a cluster of mounds representing a completed site does not agree with the information from the Bigelow site. A band belonging to the Effigy Mound cultural tradition might, however, have moved on a regular basis to a large series of sites, adding a mound or two and completing a site over a period of several hundred years. The internal time depth implied by the radiocarbon dates for the Bigelow site allows us to evaluate the appearance and development of mounds, features, burial and material cultural items by providing us with unprecedented control over the time factor.

In the analysis of artifacts, reliance is placed on their horizontal and vertical distribution as they occurred in particular soils horizons, mounds, and features, as well as on the associated radiocarbon dates. Each mound is a separate and distinct entity having sub-mound, mound fill or mound surface features, burials, and artifacts. The natural and man-made stratigraphy, combined

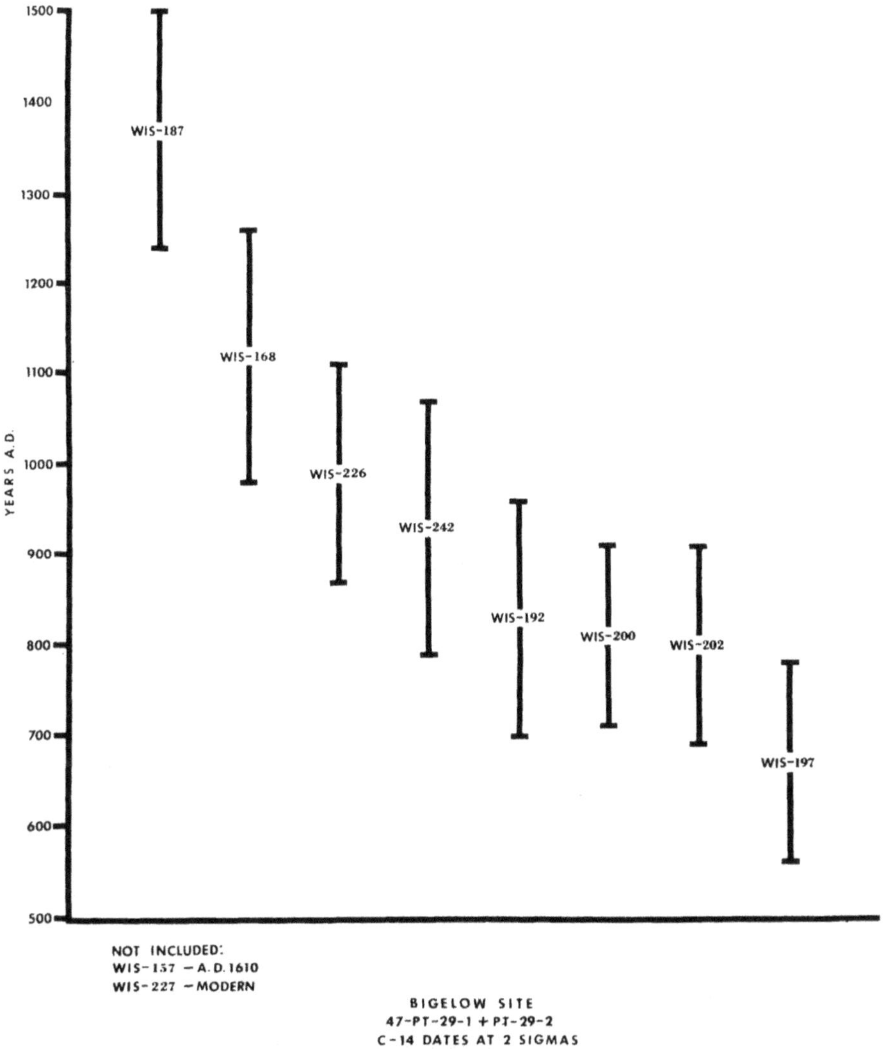

FIG. 28. Bigelow Site C-14 dates.

with the radiocarbon dates, therefore should allow for greater precision in the process of associating and ordering mounds and artifacts. Furthermore, with the exclusion of the intrusive Historic burials and artifacts, the Bigelow site should prove to be a single component site (in its broadest sense) belonging to the Effigy Mound tradition. In order to test these assumptions, I propose to examine each mound (sub-mound, fill, features, burials, and surface) and determine the associations in a chronological order so that sequences can be demonstrated.

ANALYTICAL PROCEDURES

The most difficult task confronting an archaeologist today is resolving which form of analytical methodology he will use to assure that his artifact categories, reconstructions, associations, and sequences become as accurate as possible. During the first third of this century most New World archaeologists described specimens as representative or unique without quantifying or qualifying the site assemblage. During the late 1930's and 1940's large quantities of data were synthesized via mode and attribute analyses or typological methods, and these techniques were offered as the key to understanding prehistoric culture patterning (Krieger, 1944; Rouse, 1939). With the advent of dam, pipeline, and highway salvage programs the former technique of site sampling (generally related to limited budgets) yielded to larger excavations and increased numbers of recovered artifacts. Thousands of specimens needed washing, cataloguing and marking prior to the protracted laboratory time required to describe and analyze the greater variety of artifacts. During the second third of this century the ordering and categorization of artifacts into recognizable, formally named types became the archaeologist's methodological core, from which cultural reconstructions, relative chronologies, trade patterns, and prehistoric market places were described. Sequences became more complex and the temporal and spatial connections between cultural manifestations increased in degree and detail.

The temporal aspects of sites were not generally controlled except in those areas where tree-ring (dendro-chronological) dating techniques could be applied. The McKern or Midwest Taxonomic Method ordered prehistoric culture manifestations according to a relative ranking system in the absence of reliable methods of dating such phenomena. Such methodological constructs were greatly dependent upon establishing the existence of related classes of artifacts which were ordered and ranked according to an ever greater range and variation of attributes which were then used to describe the category or the proposed types. Subsequent controls which were placed on a type, such as quantification and qualification of micro- and macro-attributes, provenience associations, spatial ranges and temporal ordering according to chronometric determinatives aided in the establishment of local and regional sequences, cultural chronologies, and prehistoric culture areas. The plethora of formal artifact types and sub-varieties has now reached a point where the archaeologist has difficulty controlling all the data from a sub-continental area. With the increase of the number of artifact types, such as the ceramic types, the archaeologists have grouped many types together under a more inclusive hierarchical heading called the ware group (for example, Madison Ware which includes Madison Plain and Madison Cord Impressed type), associated more ceramic types with a prehistoric culture, or rejected the technique of naming sub-varieties and shifted into attribute analysis for category groupings. In the latter technique a type is generally not given a formal designation but is ordered into a particular category with the diagnostic attributes (color, decoration, shape, size) listed and quantified, with the totals of the percentages recorded. This method sets one category off from another while demonstrating shared common or specific attributes.

There are numerous archaeological reports in which attribute analyses have formed the major research method. As one researcher (Wright, 1967:3) has stated:

> The advantage of attribute analysis lies in its reduction of the data to their simplest denominator thereby allowing ready comparison with later data. It also permits the individual testing of attributes to determine their relative worth as time and space indicators. The disadvantage of the technique lies in the overwhelming mass of descriptive data involved which inhibits communication, especially to those not directly involved in the specific problems . . .

Central to the ceramic analysis presented in the previous chapter is the listing of attributes under each type and of their contribution to the definition or clarification of the ceramics from the Bigelow site. According to Krieger, ". . . the purpose of a type in archaeology must be to provide an organizational tool which will enable the investigator to group specimens into bodies which have *demonstrable historical meaning in terms of behaviour patterns* . . . and thus serve as tools for the retracing of cultural developments and interactions" (1944:272). The final classification of various types is ". . . a process of discovery of combinations of attributes favoured by the makers of the artifacts, not an arbitrary procedure of the classifier" (Spaulding, 1953:305). The distinction between type and attribute analysis lies not in the point that attributes do not form types but rather in the researcher's feeling that his information is not sufficiently complete to proceed from meticulously comparing attributes to formally proposing types

(Wright, 1967:3). Baerreis (1968:145) holds that both techniques can be combined:

> . . . typology is a powerful and indeed an essential research tool of sound archaeological and anthropological investigation. . . . While it is evident that many types . . . could be improved, archaeologists are caught in a dilemma in that in order to attain comparability with published data, older but inadequate types are often retained. Perhaps we should be more willing to restudy earlier collections to update inadequate descriptions though this is a difficult decision when so much recent work is entirely undescribed.

In the earlier report on the Bigelow site (Hurley, 1970*b*) the ceramic artifacts were examined according to their diagnostic attributes, grouped into types and categories, and examined according to their internal spatial and temporal relationships. The typological methods used were basically sound but the statistical methods were limited to only quantity and percentage, and they may have failed to give convincing support to the conclusions drawn. In order to test those conclusions, it is necessary to amplify the quantitative data according to procedures which should clarify the original interpretations. Subjecting my own typological data to impersonal statistical techniques will hopefully improve inadequate and rudely presented relationships. Although many statistical techniques are currently being used by archaeologists—chi-square, "t" tests, coefficients of similarity, or association analysis (Loy, 1968; Whallon, 1972). One technique which has been considered as being too laborious for normal typing purposes is the Principal Component method (Rao, 1964). It is this procedure, plus others, which will be used to clarify the full range of the artifact associations.

During the original analysis various crude codes were developed to order the wide range of attributes present on collared ceramics, including the code devised for the analysis of the Aztalan Collared and Point Sauble Collared ceramics (Baerreis and Freeman, 1958). However, the time expénded seemed inordinate for a sample of fewer than 20 specimens. With continued examination of the decorative techniques of cord and fabric impressions (Hurley, 1970*b*) or incising versus trailing (Chapter VII; Hurley, 1970) it became apparent that the discontinuous attributes of decoration and location of decoration seemed to be the major criteria used to define Effigy Mound pottery types. Prehistoric decisions seemed to have been made according to predetermined cultural patterns when the location and type of decoration were being considered by the artisan. Decorative attributes seemed to be shared between several types and stylistic analyses were ultimately envisioned. Micro-attribute analysis (type of cord twist, not just the presence of cord impressions) increased the descriptive detail given to individual or related specimens so that the typological method seemed to revert to descriptions of single specimens.

Further complications in the ceramic analyses arose when it was realized that a pottery type lasted for several hundred to over a thousand years while still recognizable as a member of an established type. Changes must have taken place through time and space, although they were generally not noticed when a type was used or viewed within a temporal reconstruction. For example, site Y dated at A.D. 900 with type 1 ceramics may be compared to site Z which also had type 1 specimens which were undated, but belonged to a period of A.D. 400 to A.D. 500. The attribute changes of one type and their effects on related types may not have been immediately synchronic either at a site or even within the prehistoric culture area.

A selective analytical code was devised which included provenience data, radiocarbon date, proposed type and decoration information. The code was not an exhaustive descriptive code; the variables of site, time, space, and decoration appeared to be the maximum detail that I could hope to control with the limited means then at my disposal. The code covered two cards and consisted of the following:

CARD A

Columns	
1 — 4	New reference number
5	Card designation
6 — 8	Site number
9 — 16	Horizontal grid location
17 — 18	Level
19 — 21	Specific artifact number
22	Soils horizon (mound, sub-mound, non-mound)
23 — 24	Mound number
25	Type of mound (5 types): effigy, conical, linear, oval, natural
26 — 27	Feature number
28 — 29	Burial number
30 — 35	Radiocarbon date
36 — 37	Ceramic type
38	Rim or body sherd
39	House number
40	House level

CARD B

Columns	
1 — 4	New reference number
5	Card designation
6 — 7	Location of decoration (1 st of series): 12 possible locations

8	Type of decoration (1st location): 9 possible types
9 — 10	Type of fabric (1 maximum—1st location): 19 possible types
11 — 12	Type of cord (1st location—1st of 3 possible) 83 possible types
13 — 14	Type of cord (1st location—2nd of 3 possible)
15 — 16	Type of cord (1st location—3rd of 3 possible)
17 — 18	Location of decoration (2nd of 6 possible)
19	Type of decoration (2nd location)
20 — 21	Type of fabric (2nd location—1 maximum)
22 — 23	Type of cord (2nd location—1st of 3 possible)
24 — 25	Type of cord (2nd location—2nd of 3 possible)
26 — 27	Type of cord (2nd location—3rd of 3 possible)
28 — 29	Location of decoration (3rd of 6 possible)
30	Type of decoration (3rd location)
31 — 32	Type of fabric (3rd location—1 maximum)
33 — 34	Type of cord (3rd location—1st of 3 possible)
35 — 36	Type of cord (3rd location—2nd of 3 possible)
37 — 38	Type of cord (3rd location—3rd of 3 possible)
39 — 40	Location of decoration (4th of 6 possible)
41	Type of decoration (4th location)
42 — 43	Type of fabric (4th location—1 maximum)
44 — 45	Type of cord (4th location—1st of 3 possible)
46 — 47	Type of cord (4th location—2nd or 3 possible)
48 — 49	Type of cord (4th location—3rd of 3 possible)
50 — 51	Location of decoration (5th of 6 possible)
52	Type of decoration (5th location)
53 — 54	Type of fabric (5th location—1 maximum)
55 — 56	Type of cord (5th location—1st of 3 possible)
57 — 58	Type of cord (5th location—2nd of 3 possible)
59 — 60	Type of cord (5th location—3rd of 3 possible)
61 — 62	Location of decoration (6th of 6 possible)
63	Type of decoration (6th location)
64 — 65	Type of fabric (6th location—1 maximum)
66 — 67	Type of cord (6th location—1st of 3 possible)
68 — 69	Type of cord (6th location—2nd of 3 possible)
70 — 71	Type of cord (6th location—3rd of 3 possible)
72 — 80	*Blank*

All of the rim sherds and decorated body sherds (258) from 47-Pt-29-2 and Pt-29-1 were coded (excluding pieces from a single vessel which were counted as one specimen). Advice was sought from Norman Wagner of Sir Wilfred Laurier University whose preliminary reports on "Computer Studies of Ontario Iroquois Ceramics" (1971*a*; 1971*b*) indicated that he had begun to critically evaluate the merits and limitations of coding ceramics. We agreed that an equal size sample would be coded from 47-Wp-26 even though the Bigelow sample represented the total diagnostic ceramics. The Bigèlow sample was then printed out according to specimen number, card number, location of decoration, type of decoration, type of fabric, and type of cord. Histograms of location and type of decoration were then plotted. Only location of decoration, type of decoration, type of cord, location of second decoration, and type of decoration at second location were significant in their numerical distributions. These five variables with their frequency counts are presented in Figure 29.

These variables were then subjected to a principal component analysis the purpose of which is to simplify data relationships by reducing the number of variables:

> When a large number of measurements are available, it is natural to enquire whether they could be replaced by a fewer number of the measurements of their functions, *without loss of much information*, for convenience in the analysis and in the interpretation of data. Principal components, which are linear functions of the measurements . . . provide a reduction of the data without much loss of *information we are seeking from the data* (Rao, 1964:329).

Principal component analysis is somewhat similar to factor analysis as the ". . . former is the first step of factor analysis but the aim of each approach is quite different" (Wagner, 1971*b*:18). To paraphrase Clarke (1968:563-564), a principal component analysis commences with a complete table of intercorrelations among the data, expressed as a matrix of correlation coefficients varying in value from -1 to +1, according to the degree of correlation among the variables concerned. This variation in value is measured by the variance or square of the standard deviations of the variables in the matrix. A principal component table of intercorrelations among the Bigelow specimens was plotted according to a matrix of correlation coefficients in a numerical specimen sequence and a portion of this run is reproduced in Table 1.

Principal component analysis assumes a correlation between the values of some of the variables, the common variance, which is then expressed by a smaller number of factors in order to summarize the common variance of the many variables. To achieve this correlation, a similarity coefficient, a coefficient of linear correlation (r), is computed. To do this, pairs of units—measurements, counts, or ratios—are given definite numerical values and compared:

> . . . the coefficient *r* is essentially an indicator of how close the best possible straight line comes to passing through all the points [then shown in a scattergram]. A value of *r* close to plus 1 means that the points almost lie on a straight line sloping up to the right, while an *r* close to minus 1 means that the points are close to a straight line sloping down to the right. In either case, a simple straight-line equation will enable one to predict the value of one variable quite accurately from knowledge of the other variables value in a specific case (Cowgill, 1968:371).

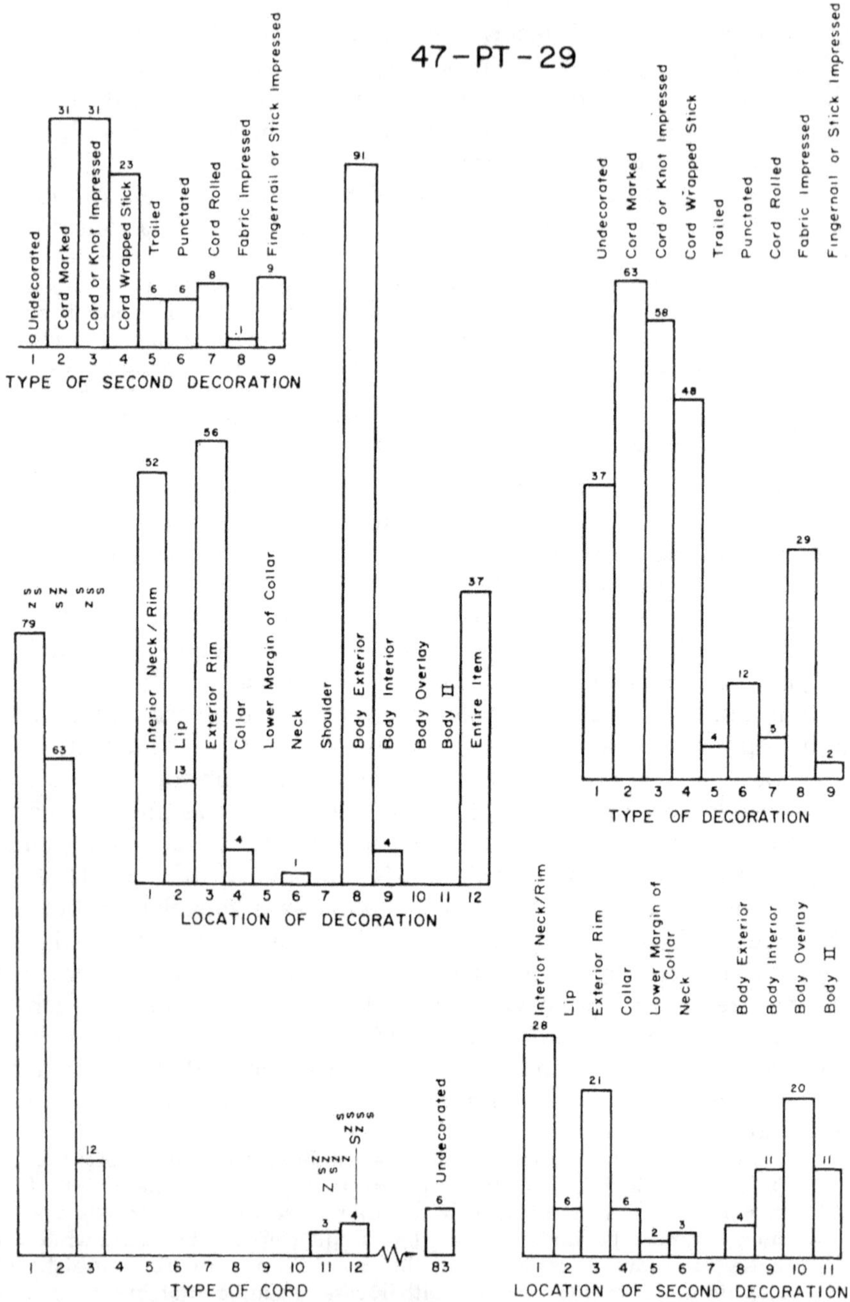

FIG. 29. Histogram of traits used in computer analysis of Bigelow ceramics.

TABLE 1

PRINCIPAL COMPONENT ANALYSIS: 47-PT-29
(258 Specimens; 5 Variables of Decoration)

	Decoration 1	Decoration 2	Decoration 3	Decoration 4	Decoration 5
Eigenvalues	1.71176	1.25183	0.92378	0.79860	0.31402
Cumulative Percentage of Eigenvalues	0.34235	0.59272	0.77747	0.93719	0.99999
Eigenvectors					
Vector 1	-0.04142	-0.11323	0.35233	0.65151	0.66095
Vector 2	0.74094	-0.63236	0.00591	0.12505	-0.18831
Vector 3	-0.25019	-0.29636	0.83906	-0.33388	-0.18461
Vector 4	0.51907	0.70302	0.41422	0.14399	-0.20979
Vector 5	0.34244	0.07238	0.01497	-0.65398	0.67051

Item Number (of 258 specimens)	Principal Component No. 1	Principal Component No. 2	Principal Component No. 3
1	-0.50806	-0.25664	0.55784
2.	-0.50806	-0.25664	0.55784
3	-0.53978	0.51915	0.20286
4	1.01949	0.82639	-0.88209
5	-0.53978	0.51915	0.20286
6	-0.53978	0.51915	0.20286
7	0.30947	-0.52736	0.07617
8	1.12197	0.85329	-0.97941
9	0.96464	-0.78940	-0.34417
10	-0.52454	-0.25702	0.48513
11	0.90687	0.68382	-1.11415
12	0.09437	-0.73669	0.26909
13	0.75785	0.76206	-0.16610
14	1.00301	0.82601	-0.95480
15	1.01949	0.82639	-0.88209

Wagner, however, believes that this is contentious ground "... since some people will argue that the use of the linear coefficient of correlation (r) distorts the picture, since not all relationships are of a linear nature" (Wagner, 1971*b*:18). He suggests that we ignore this question for the time being for "... what we are after is a reduction in the number of variables ... without any loss of information" (*ibid.*).

The procedures outlined by Wagner (*ibid.*) were then utilized to reduce the number of variables. "By calculating the eigenvalues and eigenvectors [see below] of a matrix of correlation [Table 1] we arrive at a new set of variables which are linear combinations of the original variables and which are independent from one another." Table 1 shows that the first eigenvalue accounts for 34 percent of the total variance while the second brings the total to 59 percent. This means that the two new, uncorrelated values can account for 59 percent of the variance. If we were to consider the third, the percentage would rise to 78 percent. However, it must be remembered that these new variables are combinations of the original attribute classes.

For each of the 258 specimens, individual attributes were multiplied by each respective eigenvector to produce a ranked value known as the inner product. The results of this run were achieved by taking the first two eigenvalues and plotting them according to two vectors (Table 2). Clarke (1968:670) defines a vector as "a compound entity, having a definite number of components." Eigenvalues (λ_1 and λ_2) are also called latent roots or characteristic roots. Eigenvalues are quantities analogous to variances and they measure variability along the major and minor axes respectively:

TABLE 2

PRINCIPAL COMPONENT ANALYSIS: 47-PT-29
(258 Specimens; 5 Variables of Decoration)
According to Ranked Order

	Decoration 1	Decoration 2	Decoration 3	Decoration 4	Decoration 5
Eigenvalue	1.71176	1.25183	0.92378	0.79860	0.31402
Cumulative Percentage of Eigenvalues	0.34235	0.59272	0.77747	0.93719	0.99999

Item Number (of 258 specimens)	X	Y	K	L
233	0.75698	0.88867	103	100
183	0.71892	1.81962	104	77
45	0.70979	0.65378	104	105
46	0.70979	0.65378	104	105
47	0.70979	0.65378	104	105
231	3.36161	0.46448	202	132

X = principal component No. 1.
Y = principal component No. 2.
K = vertical location on scattergram.
L = horizontal location on scattergram.

> The technique of principal axes is important in multivariate analysis, where instead of ellipses we encounter clouds of observations describing hyperellipsoids in a multidimensional space. To simplify the description of these clouds of points, we calculate principal axes through the hyperellipsoids . . . the eigenvalues, which represent the variance along the principal axes, are always maximized, so that as we take successive principal axes . . . we are successively removing the greatest, second greatest, and successively smaller sources of variation (Sokal and Rohlf, 1969:532).

The results of Table 2 were then plotted by reducing the three vectors of Table 1 to two vectors, as illustrated in the scattergram in Figure 30. A third dimension could be added to this scattergram by using a vertical scale or different size dots.

Much of the rationale behind principal component analysis is a direct outgrowth of numerical taxonomy and Clarke (1968:Ch. 12) gives an excellent synthesis of this approach. He makes several important observations concerning its usefulness as an analytical tool for archaeologists. Numerical taxonomy has the capacity

> . . . for a more objective definition of our conceptual and actual archaeological entities. . . . [gives us] the ability to determine and express the degree to which different entities are similar or dissimilar using an explicit and repeatable procedure. . . . [and allows for the entities] to be ranked relative to one another in a hierarchy of increasing structural complexity. . . . (1968:518-519).

Repeatability and objectivity, then, allows groups to be ascertained by giving equal weight to all traits utilized which are then placed in a sorted matrix (Table 2). Traits are clustered according to two or three dimensions which produces clusters ". . . closely approaching our prevailing constellation of mind-models of archaeological relationships" (1968:543). However, these relationships are taxonomical and not typological.

Clarke argues that archaeological taxonomy should be "natural" in an empirical sense and should allow most propositions to be made about its constituent entities, that is, it should be the taxonomy with the best predictive capacity. As most archaeological entities are structured and can be ordered or clustered then they can be ranked in a hierarchy of propositions. Typology, he maintains, embraces the sequence of data on a seriation basis (time and space) which can be measured and expressed within limits (1968:517-519). The degree of similarity between the Bigelow ceramic specimens has been arranged into a matrix (Table 1), rearranged (Table 2), and then clustered according to positive and negative status (Figure 30). The traits considered are discontinuous and "subjective"—decoration and location—and not continuous and

47 - PT - 29

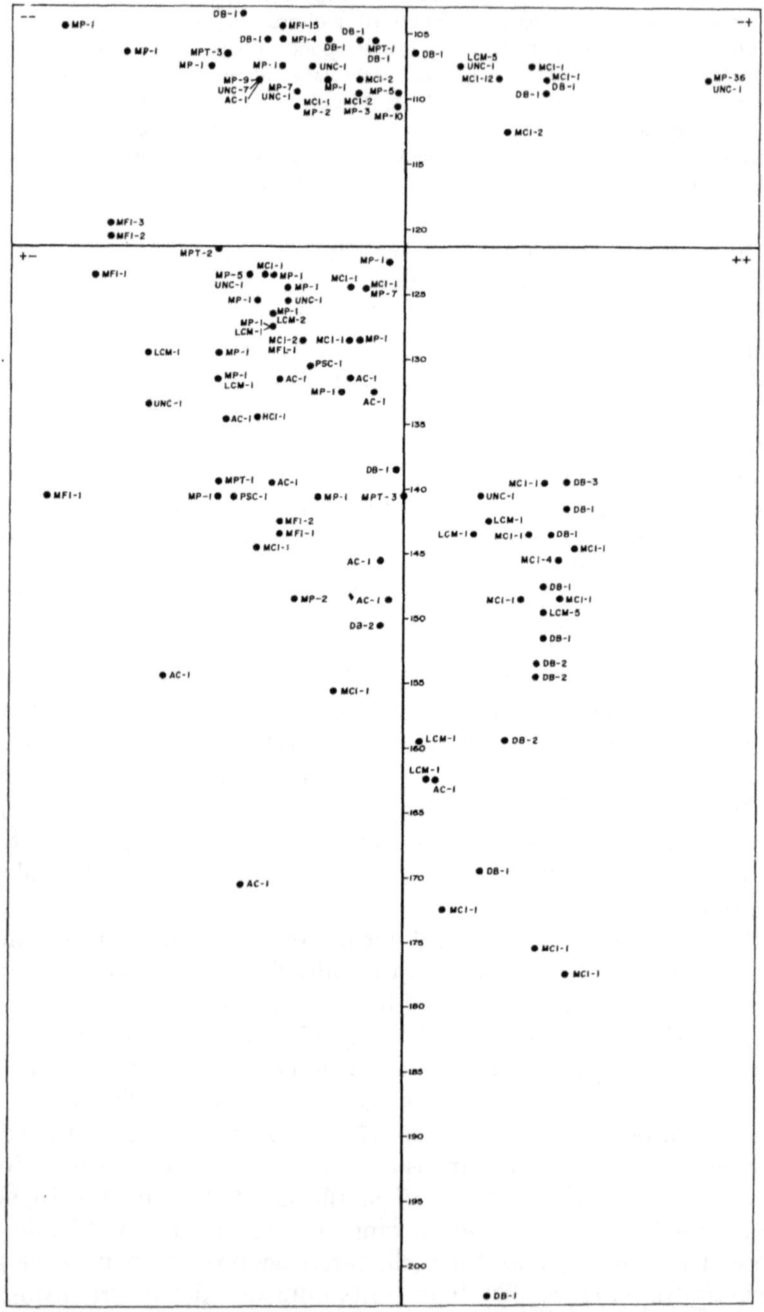

FIG. 30. Scattergram of principal component analysis of Bigelow ceramics.

"objective"—length, width, or thickness. Cowgill has pointed out that one can calculate a correlation coefficient for variables which can be measured *or counted* (1968:371). The decoration traits are considered here to be exceedingly important attributes which will yield results as accurate as those which are measured.

The groups and relative distances between the ceramic specimens from the Bigelow site are indicated, for example, by the type abbreviation (MP = Madison Plain) and the number of specimens at each location. Table 2 and Figure 30 show the item, the two vectors (X and Y), their minus or plus values plotted to five places and arranged according to minus/minus, minus/plus, plus/minus and plus/plus in the four quadrants according to vertical position (Lines 103 to 202) under K, and the horizontal position, if on the same line, under column L, In some instances specimens from widely differing areas of the site are considered so similar that they are plotted to one location, e.g., the 36 Madison Plain on line 108 (Fig. 30), or they are tightly grouped together, e.g., the Madison Ware specimens in the scattergram. Those specimens which clustered together (for example, between lines 103 and 115, 118 and 135, and 137 and 165), could be treated as three separate entities until all specimens are incorporated into one tight cluster. However, Cowgill (1968:370) has argued that pieces are then forced together even if they are not related in any meaningful way. We will leave these clusters without drawing lines around them until the scattergram from 47-Wp-26 (Chapter VIII) is combined with that from the Bigelow site (Chapter IX) and subjected to further statistical analysis. Clarke cautions that:

> It cannot be emphasized too strongly that these factors, like all the summarizing statistics of relationship, including correlation coefficients, these are all summarizing statistical relationships which may not be simply interpreted as archaeological relationships. The groups of artifact-types or attributes constituting the factors will be related in a statistical association—the exact archaeological relationships responsible for this statistical relationship may well be very subtle and complex (1968:563).

With this warning we shall now examine the results of both the principal component and the typological analyses.

INTERNAL COMPARISONS

The earliest dated mound at the Bigelow site is Mound A, a buried conical mound, which is dated A.D. 670 ± 55 (WIS-197). This radiocarbon date is from a charred log (Feature 26) which was in and directly below the buried A1b mound surface. Mound A is particularly significant because it contained the earliest prehistoric artifacts and burials both of which are directly associated with the mound building phase of Mound A.

Mound A yielded 16 ceramic fragments which could be placed within typological or other ceramic categories (Table 3); the lithic assemblage of Mound A is almost exclusively represented by Triangular points (Table 3). The locations of these points indicate that they were in use at the Bigelow site prior to A.D. 670 and during the time of mound construction. One core was included in the mound fill in the A/Bb horizon and three polishing stones were recovered from the non-mound A11 surface horizon.

At the A.D. 670 ± 55 base line the Bigelow site was occupied as a camp area with cooking locations (Features 23, 25, 27) and refuse pits (Feature 10) being utilized by Effigy Mound peoples. They had among their material culture inventory Madison Cord Impressed, Madison Fabric Impressed, Madison Plain and most probably Madison Punctated ceramics, as well as Sanders Triangular and Triangular projectile points. At this time conical Mound A was constructed and it contained the cremated remains of an unknown number of individuals (Burial 5) and animal bones which were capped

TABLE 3

DISTRIBUTION OF CERAMICS, LITHIC, AND HISTORIC ARTIFACTS: MOUND A

Soil Location	Madison Cord Impressed	Madison Fabric Impressed	Madison Plain	Madison Punctated	Unclassified (C)	Sanders Triangular	Triangular (A-B)	Cores	Polishing Stones	Historic Artifacts
A11 (non-mound)									3	4
A12 (non-mound										1
A1b (non-mound)										
C (non-mound)			1							4
A1b2 (non-mound)										
A1b2 (mound)			1							
A/Bb	1		3	2	2	2	1	1		
A1b2-3	1		2				1			
B21irb	2	1					1			
Total	4	1	7	2	2	2	3	1	3	9

by unburned human remains and animal bone artifacts. A human hand (Burial 10) was most probably omitted from the main burial pit. As the mound was capped, a fire was built, resulting in the presence of the charred log (Feature 26) from which the temporal base line was determined. Mound A remained undisturbed for over 700 years while other mounds were being added to this location by Effigy Mound peoples. There followed another hiatus of almost 500 years until historic Indians utilized this mound for the burial of a child (Burial 3) and its iron knife.

The next dated manifestation at the Bigelow site is conical Mound S. Prior to the construction of this mound the Effigy Mound peoples excavated a long rectangular pit into which a compact mixture of cremated animal and possible human bones was placed (Fig. 9). The pit containing these bones was designated as Burial 8 and, although it lacked associated artifacts, the charcoal yielded a radiocarbon date of A.D. 800 ± 55 (WIS-202). The diagnostic artifacts recovered from Mound S are listed in Table 4.

Mound S yielded a radiocarbon date and a possible human cremation similar to Burial 5 of Mound A. With the two sigma range illustrated for the radiocarbon dates from the Bigelow site (Fig. 28), Mound S, as well as Mound L and Mound 4 (to be examined next), temporally overlaps Mound A.

At approximately the same time as the construction of Mound S, the Effigy Mound peoples constructed a mound in the shape of a bird. Bird effigy Mound L has yielded charcoal from

TABLE 4

DISTRIBUTION OF CERAMICS, LITHIC, AND HISTORIC ARTIFACTS: MOUND S

Soil Location	Madison Plain	Sanders Triangular	Worked Flakes
A11		1	1
C			
A1b			
A12			
A/Bb	1		
A1b2			
B21irb			
Total	1	1	1

one of its pits (Feature 13) which has dated the mound at A.D. 810 ± 50 (WIS-200). The excavation of Mound L failed to produce human remains, and of the four features excavated only one produced identifiable animal bones. In this same area in the next highest horizon was Feature 2, a pit which contained over 700 ceramic fragments associated with a Madison Cord Impressed vessel. Feature 13, in the western wing, contained 320 vessel fragments, of which 317 belong to one Madison Cord Impressed vessel, and one Sanders Triangular projectile point. The charcoal recovered from this pit produced a radiocarbon date (Fig. 28) of A.D. 810 ± 50 (WIS-200).

The ceramic artifacts from the sub-mound and the mound fill horizons agree typologically with the ceramics recovered from Mounds A and S (Table 5). But there remains the century-old problem of what to do with items accidentally included in the mounds during their construction. The assumption is that artifacts may be incorporated in the soil as it is skimmed from adjacent areas or borrowed by excavations. If the borrow pits are deep and if there were occupations by earlier differing cultures, such as those associated with the Archaic, Early Woodland, or Middle

TABLE 5

DISTRIBUTION OF CERAMICS, LITHIC, AND HISTORIC ARTIFACTS: MOUND L

Soil Location	Madison Cord Impressed	Features 2, 13	Madison Fabric Impressed	Madison Folded Lip	Madison Plain	Madison Punctated	Leland Cord-marked	Aztalan Collared	Hahn Cord Impressed	Point Sauble Collared	Unclassified Ceramics	Drills	Cores	Polishing Stones
A11														
AB														
A/B	3		3	1	3	1	1	1	1	1	2		1	1
A1b			2		2						1	1		
B21irb					1								1	1
B22irb														
B3irb														
Total	3	2	5	1	6	1	1	1	1	1	3	1	2	2

Woodland peoples, then artifacts associated with these peoples could be unintentionally included in the mound. Sub-mound and adjacent non-mound excavations can be of great aid in resolving the nature and character of artifacts recovered from the fill. The cultural and/or chronological position of these artifacts can then be ascertained and the mound, less radiocarbon dates, can then be dated relatively as having been built subsequent to those earlier occupations.

If the mound fill artifacts are typologically similar to those recovered from inclusive features or burial pits, then some contemporaneity can be assumed. Moreover, if excavations fail to produce evidence of occupations by earlier and differing cultures then the contemporaneity factor is assumed to be strengthened. With the exclusion of all later intrusions (prehistoric or Historic), then the mound fill artifacts appear to take on an aura of respectability even though they cannot be used in any fine vertical analysis. The horizontal provenience analysis, i.e., that the artifacts were originally in the immediate area, appeared to be supported as Parsons (1962:23) demonstrated that the builders of effigy and non-effigy mounds in northeastern Iowa did not go much beyond 50 feet for their borrow. However, Lange (1968:116) has recently shown that greater distances were exploited and particular soils were being utilized. Thus, the artifacts in the fill may not have been used in the area adjacent to the mound. To carry this investigation further, if we assume the Effigy Mound peoples were the only peoples using the Bigelow site in prehistoric times, we then must consider the evidence that an extended temporal range of several centuries was involved at this location. We cannot, therefore, assume sychronous use and accidental re-use of these artifacts. We then return to the original view that the artifacts are no younger than the (radiocarbon) age of the mound. We can then utilize a series of chronological sequences as well as internal stylistic change or stability within a type at one locality on the basis of its sub-mound or mound position. This brings us to the diagnostic artifacts recovered from the fill of bird effigy Mound L (and all other mounds described in this report).

Five additional Madison Ware types were incorporated into the A/B mound fill of Mound L. Each type is represented by one specimen, and they are the proposed type Madison Punctated, and the established types of Leland Cord-marked, Aztalan Collared, Hahn Cord Impressed, and Point Sauble Collared. The occurrence of these Madison Ware types marks their initial or earliest dated context and I would contend that the temporal range for these types, as well as for the other four associated Madison Ware types, at the Bigelow site *now* lies somewhere between the earliest range of sample WIS-197 (A.D. 560) and the latest range of sample WIS-200 (A.D. 910) (Fig. 28). This range represents the first dated context for the proposed Madison Folded Lip and Madison Punctated types and the earliest dated context for collared ceramics in Wisconsin—Aztalan Collared, Hahn Cord Impressed, and Point Sauble Collared. While Baerreis and Bryson considered the site of Aztalan to have been occupied from A.D. 1100 to A.D. 1300 (1965:206-209) and, by extension, dated the Aztalan Collared ceramics from the type site, neither they nor Baerreis and Freeman (1958) give a temporal range for the type. No temporal range exists either for Hahn Cord Impressed (Keslin, 1958) or Point Sauble Collared (Freeman, 1956). At a minimum, the radiocarbon date for Mound L indicates that the three collared types came into existence at least 300 years earlier than had been proposed. Leland Cord-marked ceramics were considered by Wittry to belong to a Middle Woodland chronological position at the Durst site (1959*c*:209, 220) and these ceramics were suggested as resembling the Weaver Ware ceramics of Illinois. As the Durst specimens were also associated with Madison Ware ceramics it may be suggested that they may extend into Late Woodland times. The initial, median, or terminal range for the sample WIS-200 from Mound L would uphold this view. In any event, Mound L also supports the proposal that all of these types are contemporary, even though each had its own temporal range. Furthermore, their associations in this analysis indicate that the expansion of Madison Ware proposed by Mason (1966) is also correct for the ceramic types presented thus far.

The lithic artifacts from the Mound L area consist of one drill, two cores, and two pecked stones. The drill is the earliest specimen in this category recorded for the Bigelow site (Table 5) and it represents one-quarter of the total sample recovered. The pecked stones are of two varieties, a hammerstone (Pl. 15:E) and a basalt stone with a pecked circular depression (Pl. 15:D). Together they comprise the total sample of excavated pecked stones from the Bigelow site.

The artifacts recovered from the sub-mound horizons, mound fill, and mound features of bird effigy Mound L have been sorted and presented according to their relationship to this effigy mound both prior to and during its construction. With the exception of

Madison Folded Lip, Leland Cord-marked, Aztalan Collared, Hahn Cord Impressed, and Point Sauble Collared ceramics, and the drill and pecked stones, all other artifacts were in use at the Bigelow site prior to the construction of Mound L. Two assumptions can be made concerning the artifacts listed above: the five ceramic types plus the two lithic categories were not in use at the Bigelow site prior to A.D. 800, or they were in use but not in the areas of Mounds A and S. As the difference between the median dates for Mounds A and L is 140 years (WIS-197, 200; Fig. 44), I would favor the second assumption. In addition, two of these ceramic types (Leland Cord-marked and Aztalan Collared) were subsequently in use at this locality. Of major importance is the fact that, with the exception of corner-notched points and end scrapers, effigy Mound L has associated with it *all* major ceramic and lithic types or categories recorded for the Bigelow site. The implication appears to be that at circa A.D. 800 a peak in the number of diversified artifacts was reached and from this point onward there was a diminution in the major varieties of artifact types utilized at this site.

At Bigelow site 1 (47-Pt-29-1) in the area of the conical mound cluster (Fig. 20) was Mound 4, a small conical mound containing two features and one burial. Feature 1 of Mound 4 was a shallow pit in the A1b horizon with an accumulation of charcoal and no artifacts. As this pit appeared to have been utilized just prior to the construction of Mound 4, the charcoal was submitted for radiocarbon dating, which yielded a date of A.D. 830 ± 65 (WIS-192).

The artifact yield from Mound 4 is somewhat limited as only three diagnostic specimens were recovered (Table 6).

The first four radiocarbon assessments (WIS-197; 202; 200; 192) for mounds A, S, L, and 4 appear to represent a possible initial phase of occupancy by Effigy Mound peoples at the Bigelow

TABLE 6

DISTRIBUTION OF CERAMICS, LITHIC, AND HISTORIC ARTIFACTS: MOUND 4

Soil Location	Madison Cord Impressed	Madison Plain
A1		
A/B		
A1b	1	2
Total	1	2

site. Let us now, therefore, assess those mounds containing artifacts which lack associated radiocarbon dates. Three conical mounds belonging to the cluster at 47-Pt-29-1 have such a limited number of diagnostic artifacts that they could date anytime between A.D. 670 and A.D. 1370. These mounds (2, 12, and 5) will be presented and discussed before proceeding to the next dated mound.

Mound 2 was a small conical mound containing one sub-mound pit (Feature 5) which extended into sub-mound soil horizons prior to the construction of the mound. Feature 5 lacked associated artifacts, and, in fact, the only diagnostic artifact recovered from Mound 2 was an oval basalt polishing stone from the A/B mound fill. Mound 12, a small conical mound, was void of features and burials. The A1 horizon of Mound 12 did yield a cord-marked rim sherd with a slightly eroded surface (Category C) which has a cord-wrapped stick impressed interior. Mound 5, a conical mound, was not excavated due to previous pot-hunting activities. The back dirt of a central pit did yield one Madison Plain rim sherd.

Mounds 2, 12, and 5 from 47-Pt-29-1 could have been constructed at any time during the occupancy of the Bigelow site by Effigy Mound peoples. Mound 2, with its developing B horizon, suggests construction between A.D. 800 and A.D. 1000 (Hurley, 1971). The sub-mound pit (Feature 5) does fit a pattern for the site as it did contain flecks of charcoal, suggesting cooking or ceremonial activity prior to mound construction. Mound 12, with its low artifact yield, does tell us that cord-wrapped sticks were in use at 47-Pt-29-1. Finally, unexcavated conical Mound 5 produced from the back dirt a Madison Plain rim sherd which connects this mound with Mound 4 of the same conical cluster and, in turn, this cluster with 47-Pt-29-2.

Returning now to the dated mounds at the Bigelow site, 47-Pt-29-2, Mound B, a large buried conical mound, had a fairly complex stratigraphy (Fig. 10) which was further complicated by Historic feature and burial intrusions. Five features and six burials were uncovered and excavated. Excluding the Historic intrusions, the features and burials from Mound B are almost totally void of diagnostic artifacts. Feature 1 (1965) produced a date of A.D. 930 ± 70 (WIS-242). The date indicates that both the pit and the mound were constructed approximately 260 years later than Mound A, which was directly adjacent to and almost touching the northern edge of Mound B (Fig. 5). Feature 20 of Mound B yielded one body sherd and charcoal fragments; Feature 24 was void of artifacts. All three features were within 15 feet of one another and it would appear that the more functional view of cooking prior to (Feature 20) and during mound construction (Features 1 and 24) was one habitation pattern utilized at this site.

Burial 9 is the only burial excavated at Mound B which lacked associated Historic artifacts and was not a primary interment. The other burials (4, 6, 7, 11, and 12) are considered to belong to the Historic component at 47-Pt-29-2.

The artifacts recovered from the sub-mound, mound, and non-mound horizons are listed in Table 7.

Buried conical Mound B produced few surprises; it yielded data consistent with the patterns thus far ascertained for the Bigelow site. Just prior to and during mound construction, pits were dug and used for cooking and near these pits was a possible burial pit containing either the partial remains of one of the mound builders or the remains of a non-human meal (the evidence fails to offer any conclusive proof that these mound builders practiced cannibalism). In fact there is no evidence from the Bigelow site or the Sanders site which suggests that Effigy Mound

TABLE 7

DISTRIBUTION OF CERAMICS, LITHIC, AND HISTORIC ARTIFACTS: MOUND B

Soil Location	Madison Cord Impressed	Madison Fabric Impressed	Madison Plain	Madison Punctated	Leland Cord-marked	Aztalan Collared	Unclassified Ceramics (C)	Sanders Triangular	Triangular	Cores	Worked Flakes	Historic Artifacts
A11	1											7
A12			4	1			3					12
A/B			1				1					
A1b											1	4
Cb												
A/Bb	4	1	7		1	1		2	1	2		5
A1b2			2						2			
A/Birb												
B21irb												
Total	5	1	14	1	1	1	4	2	3	2	1	28

peoples followed the custom of cannibalism. The sub-mound and mound position of these features and "burial pit" suggests a more mundane and functional interpretation of cooking.

The artifacts recovered from the sub-mound A1b2 and the mound fill A/Bb horizons consisted of the Madison Cord Impressed, Madison Fabric Impressed, Madison Plain, Leland Cord-marked, and Aztalan Collared ceramics, The diagnostic lithic artifacts associated with these horizons are Sanders Triangular points, Triangular points, cores, and a worked flake. From the time of the construction of Mounds A and B or circa 260 years, Madison Cord Impressed, Madison Fabric Impressed, Madison Plain, Madison Punctated, $s\frac{z}{z}$ and $z\frac{s}{s}$ cord-marking, Sanders Triangular, and Triangular points, and cores were in use by Effigy Mound peoples and they were re-introduced or used as each mound was constructed. The interpretation that the artifacts from the A/Bb fill or Mound B were already in the area and were left by the builders of adjacent Mound A might be acceptable, but it is not the only possible interpretation—the evidence from Mounds S, L, 4, R, and N indicates a considerable longevity for these artifact types. In addition, the data provided by both Mounds L and B indicate that Leland Cord-marked and Aztalan Collared ceramics have a minimum cultural duration of 120 years. The use of radiocarbon determinations and the treatment of each mound as a separate entity have allowed for limited estimates of mound building rates and material culture temporal ranges at one Effigy Mound culture site. Such estimates could not have been attempted with any success without these dates. As we consider the evidence from dated Mounds R and N, the dated Area K, and the non-radiocarbon dated mounds at the Bigelow site, we shall see further extensions and diminutions of the temporal ranges of the mound and artifact cultural manifestations.

Linear Mound R was the only linear mound excavated at the Bigelow site, as the other possible linear mounds (Mounds E and H) were badly disturbed by plowing. A north-south 60 foot by five foot trench was excavated in Mound R, an unburied mound which had one of the least complicated mound profiles and soil horizon sequences. Mound R had four areas which were designated as features (14, 16, 17, and 19) and one burial (Burial 1); however, one feature (19) was only a soil discoloration. Feature 14 was an oval pit void of artifacts. Feature 16 was a circular basin-shaped pit. Ceramics from this pit, and from the level above, belonged to the same Madison Plain vessel (Pl. 9), which was broken into 522 fragments. The level containing a portion of the vessel was dated at A.D. 990 ± 60 (WIS-226). Feature 17 was in the same square and level as Feature 16 and its fill lacked any cultural material.

Burial 1 (Pl. 3) was a primary, tightly flexed burial located in a large rectangular pit which was probably dug just prior to the construction of linear Mound R. The pit lacked any associated diagnostic artifacts. Linear Mound R appears to have the same feature and burial pit sub-mound pattern as that presented thus far for the Bigelow site, and Features 14 and 16 (possibly 17), and Burial 1 appear to have been utilized before Mound R was constructed. The artifacts recovered from Mound R are listed in Table 8.

As Mound L marked a point of numerical variety of artifact types, Mound R appears to date some significant trends at the Bigelow site. From a broad point of view, Mound R is the last dated mound containing Madison Cord Impressed ceramics; it represents a high point in the popularity of Madison Fabric Impressed and Leland Cord-marked ceramic types and the beginning of the recorded decline for Madison Plain ceramics at 47-Pt-29. The date A.D. 990 ± 60 (WIS-226) also appears to date the discontinuance of Sanders Triangular, Triangular, and corner notched points; end scrapers and polishing stones are also discontinued at this time, and the cores appear to be on the decline.

TABLE 8

DISTRIBUTION OF CERAMICS, LITHIC, AND HISTORIC ARTIFACTS: MOUND R

Soil Location	Madison Cord Impressed	Madison Fabric Impressed	Madison Plain	Leland Cord-marked	Unclassified Ceramics	Sanders Triangular	Triangular	Corner-notched	End Scrapers	Cores	Polishing Stones	Historic Artifacts
A11	4	1	1	3	1	1		1		1		12
A12												1
A/B	3	7	6	5					1	1	1	9
A1b	1		5	1			1			1		1
B21irb										1		
Total	8	8	12	9	1	1	1	1	1	4	1	23

Cords and fabrics composed of basic s $\frac{z}{z}$ cord twist appear to be numerically most popular for cord-marking and decoration. A Triangular point appeared earlier in the Mound R locality than the Sanders Triangular and corner notched points. This mound contained or buried one-third of all the cores recovered from the Bigelow site.

Linear Mound R is an important mound from many viewpoints. It was not buried by aeolian sand deposition and the stratigraphy was undisturbed. Mound R contained a primary burial which lacked grave goods; however, the burial form is relatable to those forms from Mounds Q and G. Mound R contained almost all the lithic artifact categories (except drills and worked flakes), and all the ceramic types from the Bigelow site except Madison Folded Lip, Madison Punctated, Aztalan Collared, Hahn Cord Impressed, and Point Sauble Collared. The remaining ceramic types were present beneath or within the fill of Mound R. This linear mound contained, therefore, over 50 percent of the Madison Ware types and the diagnostic lithic types and categories as recorded for the Bigelow site. Furthermore, Mound R, as a linear mound, is the first to be associated with effigy and conical forms at this site and offers evidence that Effigy Mound peoples built linear mounds. Therefore, although linear Mounds E and H were not excavated, we can assume that they were constructed by peoples belonging to the same cultural tradition as those who constructed linear Mound R.

Before proceeding to dated Mound N, we shall consider those undated mounds which may have been added to the Bigelow site between the time of Mound 4 (circa A.D. 830) and Mound R (circa A.D. 990). This 160-year time interval is not overly long and yet on the basis of the associated artifacts it would appear that mounds Q, G, 1, 6, and 9 were constructed during this time. Mound Q was not subjected to the same excavation procedures as were the majority of the mounds at the Bigelow site as it was used by the landowner as fill for the Mound A area once excavations had been terminated at the site. Mound Q was a buried conical mound which was originally considered part of Mound A (Dixon, Blake, and Scribner, 1956:67); however, the excavation of Mound A showed that these two mounds were separate. One feature and one burial (Burial 13) were excavated in Mound Q.

An Aztalan Collared rim sherd was recovered from Mound Q along with 15 cord-marked body sherds, and according to the present radiocarbon assessments it should date between A.D. 810 and A.D. 1120 (Mound N) (Table 17). Buried Mound Q also yielded one worked flake and the dated occurrence of these artifacts at the Bigelow site tends to support this chronological position for Mound Q.

Conical Mound G was excavated in 1957 by Blake (1961:57-76) and as the material is not available for analysis I shall try to place his work and interpretations into the framework presented in this chapter. Conical Mound G was not a buried mound, as it was in the field east of the extensive aeolian deposition (Fig. 5). This large conical mound did seal in a former surface horizon and from the data presented four features occurred in the mound fill, each containing grit-tempered ceramics, charred bone, unworked flakes, shell, or copper. Feature 4 was reported as containing several fragments of Madison Plain ceramics (1961:60).

Mound G contained a large number of prehistoric burials: two infant burials were located in the mound fill and one child and one adult female burial were located on the floor of the mound or directly above the A1b horizon. Each of these burials was partially flexed and lacked associated grave goods. The absence of Historic items and the fragmentary and poor condition of the burials indicate that they are not associated with the Historic component at 47-Pt-29-2. Burial 4, an adult female of 56 to 70 years of age, was the most complete burial; its partially flexed position is similar to that recorded for the prehistoric burials from Mounds R and Q.

The artifacts recovered from the excavation of Mound G are quite informative regarding the range and possible date for the construction of the mound. Blake reported that there appeared to be "... no correlation between pottery types and their respective locations within the mound fill" (*ibid.*:67). A total of 1,012 sherds were recovered, 499 of which were too small for classification. Forty-eight rim sherds were classified as Madison Plain ceramics. One exhibited interior incised lines and three had interior cord-wrapped stick decorations. Thirty-two rim sherds were classed as Madison Cord Impressed; only 10 had exterior cord impressions, while the remaining 22 "... possessed a single horizontal row of stick impressions one-half to one inch below the lip of the rim" (*ibid.*:70). These rim sherds might actually belong within the Leland Cord-marked ceramic type. One category reported by Blake is Denzer Stamped, of which there were 13 fragments, each with cord-wrapped stick impressions extending from the exterior lip and some evidence of exterior reed punctations below this decoration. I would question the identification, however; none of the specimens excavated in 1965 or 1966 should be placed in the Denzer Stamped category. The chronological placement of this type has been suggested as Middle Woodland (Wittry, 1959*c*:209) and the specimens from the Durst Rockshelter resemble the Havana ware ceramics of Illinois. The illustrated specimens from the Bigelow site appear to closely resemble the ceramics described under rim sherd Category A and also Mason's proposed type Heins Creek Corded Stamped (1966:203-204).

The lithic artifacts from Mound G are also consistent with the forms thus far reported for the Bigelow site. Of the 19 points recovered, 17 were classed as small Triangular points, one as a small side notched point, and one as a stemmed point. In addition to these artifacts, Blake (1961:74) listed two chert awls, one quartzite scraper, 350 quartz flakes, 54 shell fragments, two copper fragments, two granitic hammer stones, and one grit-tempered, smoothed-surfaced pipe stem. None of these artifacts is inconsistent with the material expected to be associated with a site belonging to the Effigy Mound tradition.

If we modify Blake's temporal estimate of Late Middle to Late Woodland (which is not far from the actual time of occupation), we can see that Mound G was most probably constructed before A.D. 1120, for this is the last dated occurrence of Triangular points at the site. Its early temporal limit would be before A.D. 990, since adjacent Mound R contained the last dated Madison Cord Impressed ceramics. Burials 1 and 3 (an infant and the child) were interpreted as secondary interments and Burials 2 and 4 (an infant and the adult female) were flexed primary burials. As Mound R is the only other dated mound with a primary flexed burial it would seem that the age of Mound G can be placed at circa A.D. 990 to A.D. 1120 without unduly stretching the information supplied in Blake's excellent report. The question of identification of his Denzer Stamped will remain an open one until the ceramics are re-examined. The remaining artifacts are well within the types expected and the sub-mound burials fit the primary burial pattern. The major exceptions appear to be the features which were located in the mound fill; however, their contents suggest that they are associated with the Effigy Mound culture and not with the Historic component. The two intruded secondary burials could well be intrusions during historic times and since they lack associated artifacts, their temporal placement must remain in doubt.

Returning to 47-Pt-29-1 where there are three conical mounds, mounds 1, 6, and 9 (which appear to have been constructed at this time), interpretations are based on the artifacts recovered from the excavations of these mounds, as the mounds lack radiocarbon assessments. Mound 1, a conical mound, was void of features or burials, but the mound fill yielded one Madison Plain rim sherd, one z $\frac{S}{S}$ cord-marked body sherd, and one Sanders Triangular projectile point (Fig. 42:J). Mound 6 was also a conical mound with no features or burials, but the mound fill and the A1 mound surface horizons did yield one Madison Cord Impressed body sherd, one Madison Plain rim sherd, five cord-marked body sherds, and one polishing stone.

The third mound, conical Mound 9, is by far the most interesting of this conical cluster. Erosion had removed over one-quarter of the mound (Fig. 20); however, two burial pits remained in the undisturbed portion. Burial 3 consisted of cremated human remains with nine burned and broken quartzite projectile points representing three forms of Triangular points: three Sanders Triangular points (Pl. 14:C, E, H); five serrated Triangular points (Pl. 14:A, B, D, G, I); and one Triangular projectile point (Pl. 14:F). Burial 3 lacked sufficient charcoal for dating purposes. Burial 4 (Fig. 23) was directly southwest of Burial 3 and, like Burial 3, it intruded into the former surface. This secondary cremation was highly fragmented and could not be identified as human. Only one small grit-tempered sherd was associated with Burial 4. The sub-mound and mound horizons of Mound 9 yielded two Madison Plain rim sherds and three cord-marked body sherds.

Examining Mounds 1 and 6, several patterns emerge: both were constructed over the former surface and the builders continued the pattern of neither clearing nor making any obvious preparation of the surface prior to construction. Although the mounds lacked sub-mound or mound features or burials, they did contain artifacts linking them to the other mounds in this cluster and to the mounds at 47-Pt-29-2. The Madison Plain rim sherd and Sanders Triangular point found in Mound 1 indicate that it was constructed at circa A.D. 1000—the last dated Sanders Triangular point at the Bigelow site is from Mound R which dates to this time. Mound 6 contained both Madison Cord Impressed and Madison Plain specimens; the former ceramic type also terminated here at circa A.D. 1000. Therefore, at this time two Madison Ware ceramic types, one proposed projectile point type, and two forms of cord twist are present in two conical mounds which are suggested as belonging to the Effigy Mound component at the Bigelow site.

Mound 9 also sealed in a former surface during its construction, but prior to completion of the mound, two burial pits were dug and secondary cremations added to the pits. The artifacts in undisputed association with Burial 3 show that at the same time isosceles, equilateral, unifacial (Sanders Triangular) serrated and non-serrated Triangular projectile points were used and included as grave goods. The presence of these points links this mound to the others at 47-Pt-29-1 and Pt-29-2. The secondary cremation plus the burial pits conform to one of the two forms of interment recorded for the Bigelow site. If our termination dates are correct, Triangular points decreased in popularity at this site at circa A.D. 1000.

Before proceeding to dated bird effigy Mound N, we will examine the only effigy mound assigned to 47-Pt-29-1, bear effigy Mound 13. Bear effigy Mound 13 was a large mound which had been badly potted during the spring of 1965. The backdirt from this activity was screened and on the basis of the artifact yield a series of trenches and squares were excavated in and adjacent to this mound (Fig. 18). In spite of the non-professional digging, the area of Mound 13 produced four features and a large quantity of artifacts. Feature 6 was located in the head region of Mound 13 and yielded charcoal flecks, three body sherds, one bone fragment, 10 quartzite flakes, four quartz flakes, and two stones. Feature 7 contained only charcoal which proved to be modern (WIS-227). Feature 8 contained two Madison Plain rim sherds, 10 body sherds, and three quartz fragments. The last feature, Feature 9, contained only charcoal flecks and was void of artifacts.

The sub-mound, mound, adjacent occupation areas, and the backfill contained numerous artifacts associated with Mound 13 (Table 9).

The sub-mound, mound fill, and adjacent regions of Mound 13 contained representatives of ceramic types belonging to the proposed expanded Madison Ware category: Madison Plain, Madison Punctated, and Aztalan Collared ceramics occur in the sub-mound A1b and Madison Plain ceramics are the most numerous. Madison Cord Impressed ceramics are also present in the A/B mound fill and from the adjacent area and the backfill both a Madison Fabric Impressed and a Leland Cord-marked representative

TABLE 9
DISTRIBUTION OF CERAMICS, LITHIC, AND HISTORIC ARTIFACTS: MOUND 13

Soil Location	Madison Cord Impressed	Madison Fabric Impressed	Madison Plain	Madison Punctated	Leland Cord-marked	Aztalan Collared	Unclassified Ceramics	Sanders Triangular	Triangular	Drills	Polishing Stones	Historic Artifacts
B. F.	3		6		1	1		1	1			
A11 (NM)[1]	4	1	2					1	1		5	4
A11			2			1			1		2	
A12 (NM)												
A12												
A/B	3		13	2			3	1	1		3	1
A1b			4	1		1			2			
B21irb (NM)										1		
B21irb												
Total	10	1	27	3	1	3	3	3	6	1	10	5

[1]NM=Non-mound soils horizon.

were recovered. The repeated associations of these artifacts are apparently not affected by the fact that some are from the backfill or the adjacent areas of Mound 13 because all types, except the Madison Fabric Impressed and the Leland Cord-marked specimens, are present in the mound. The Aztalan Collared specimens from Mound 13 constitute more than one-quarter of the total excavated at the Bigelow site and their presence in a bear effigy mound helps to strengthen the proposal that the collared specimens recovered from Mound L, a bird effigy, were not accidental intrusions. Aztalan Collared ceramics also link Mounds 13, L, and N: they are all effigy shaped mounds and contain similar artifacts. Within the area excavated around Mound 13 it is difficult to exclude the Madison Fabric Impressed and the Leland Cord-marked specimens from the activity associated with the building of Mound 13 because there is no obvious evidence of other forms of activity which would have brought them to the immediate area.

The lithic artifacts from Mound 13 strongly link this mound with those to the north (Pt-29-2) and with the conical cluster to the south. The presence of almost one-third of all the excavated

Triangular points (9 out of 30), three of them Sanders Triangular points, again associates this mound with the others described thus far. The projectile points also served as a possible time-marker, since none is recorded at the Bigelow site after A.D. 900 (Mound R). However, an evaluation of the ceramic and lithic categories present in the Mound 13 area suggests that a relative age estimate for Mound 13 would be circa A.D. 1000 ± 100 years.

The last dated mound at the Bigelow site is bird effigy Mound N. This mound was as badly disturbed as Mound 13 and its record of excavation goes back to 1890 (Lewis, 1890:5). As the excavations in 1965 and 1966 were limited to the undisturbed tail region, a full range of cultural activity at this location cannot be reconstructed through excavation. Even so, a total of four features were excavated and exhibited the following important characteristics: Feature 1 (1965) was void of artifacts; Feature 2 (1965) contained only one body sherd, two flakes, and nine stone fragments; Feature 3 (1965) contained only a ground stone, one body sherd, one flake, and one stone fragment, and enough charcoal to warrant a radiocarbon assessment in light of its stratigraphic position. The resulting date is A.D. 1120 ± 70 (WIS-168). The last feature excavated in Mound N was Feature 1 (1966) which was assigned to an area believed to be a fireplace, as a charred log was exposed in situ.

The non-feature artifacts from Mound N are somewhat limited. The earliest specimen is an Aztalan Collared rim sherd from the A1b horizon. The mound surface A11 horizon yielded one Madison Plain rim sherd. Eight cord-marked body sherds were excavated from the A1b2 and A1Bb soil horizons. What does associate this mound with the other mounds is its bird effigy shape and the presence of Aztalan Collared and Madison Plain ceramics. While only one specimen of each type was excavated, they serve to link Mound N to the other mounds and help to date the decline of Aztalan Collared ceramics and the possible construction of bear effigy Mound 13. The Historic artifacts from the mound fill are believed to have been intruded by two separate and different sources: the Historic component at the site and Lewis' excavations.

Directly north of bird effigy Mound N, and between it and bird effigy Mound L, was conical Mound M (Fig. 5). Mound M was constructed over the unmodified mixed forest surface (A1b) which was then sealed in until our excavations. One burial and two feature numbers were assigned to pits in Mound M. A secondary deposition of fragmented cremated bones was designated as Burial

2 and laboratory analyses could not indicate if they were definitely human. The first feature excavated, Feature 5, produced one Madison Punctated rim sherd, one non-serrated Triangular point, 13 grit-tempered body sherds, six bone fragments, and one quartzite flake. An area in the A/B mound fill was recognized as having been disturbed and a feature number (Feature 8) was assigned to it, but it turned out to be recent rodent burrow.

Mound M did contain a fairly rich variety of ceramic artifacts, as can be seen from Table 10.

The Madison Fabric Impressed ceramics from Mound M appear to be from three different vessels, based on the differences observed in the exterior fabric impressions or on the interior upper rim decorations. The association of Madison Fabric Impressed, Madison Plain, Aztalan Collared, and Point Sauble Collared ceramics at Mound M was similar to the association previously recorded for Mound L. For Madison Fabric Impressed, Madison Plain, and Aztalan Collared types, the record of association has been recorded in mounds L, B, and 13. The Point Sauble Collared rim sherd with its cord decoration and rectangular punctations appears to be unique.

The contents of Feature 5—the Madison Punctated rim sherd, the Triangular projectile point, and the Madison Ware specimens, and the Sanders Triangular point from Mound M, suggest that this mound was constructed later than A.D. 810. It is after this date

TABLE 10

DISTRIBUTION OF CERAMICS, LITHIC, AND HISTORIC ARTIFACTS: MOUND M

Soil Location	Madison Fabric Impressed	Madison Plain	Aztalan Collared	Point Sauble Collared	Scrapers	Drills	Hammerstones
A11		1					1
A12	1						
Ap2							
A/B	2			1	1	1	
A1b	1		1				
A1b2							
B21irb							
Total	4	1	1	1	1	1	1

that Aztalan Collared and Point Sauble Collared ceramics are found in Mound L, and on the basis of the terminal date for Sanders Triangular points (A.D. 990) from Mound R, it would seem that Mound M dates somewhere within this 200-year period. It is important to point out that a Madison Punctated specimen and a Triangular point were intentionally included in Feature 5 of this mound and that the proposed Madison Ware types—Madison Fabric Impressed, Madison Plain, Aztalan Collared, and Point Sauble Collared—plus the proposed Sanders Triangular projectile point, all of which are suggested as belonging to the material culture associated with the Effigy Mound tradition, are also found in a conical mound or a non-effigy shaped mound.

In 1956 Dixon, Blake, and Scribner assigned the letter K to one area which looked like a linear mound just south of Mound B (1956:69). Excavations of this location in 1966 revealed that this area had undergone aeolian deposition which had built up sequential AC profiles sealing in the former prehistoric occupation. Four features were uncovered in the Area K location. From earliest to latest they are: Feature 12, which yielded two body sherds and one quartz fragment; Feature 6, which yielded a body sherd, a quartz flake, five fulgurite fragments, and charcoal (the charcoal was submitted for dating and produced a date of A.D. 1370 ± 65 [WIS-187]); Feature 11 which yielded only three stone fragments; and Feature 15, which contained only charcoal flecks.

Each of these features appears to have served the function of cooking pits if the presence of charcoal is any indicator of cooking activity. The area next to the river bank would seem to be a natural location for such activity and based on the radiocarbon assessment from Feature 6, this activity took place well into the fourteenth century (A.D. 1370 ± 65). The date from Feature 6 most probably represents the end of the utilization of this locality by Effigy Mound peoples. Area P dates even later, but I consider the date from Area K (WIS-187) as representing the prehistoric termination date (although the date is within the two-sigma range of Mound N) and even at that it dates approximately 250 years after the last dated mound (Mound N, A.D. 1120).

Although the features from Area K did not contain diagnostic artifacts, this stratified deposit did yield some important artifacts all of which are earlier than the beginning of the AC series of aeolian deposition (Table 11).

The artifacts excavated from stratified Area K were sealed in and undisturbed from the time of Feature 6 (A.D. 1370 ± 65)

TABLE 11
DISTRIBUTION OF CERAMICS, LITHIC, AND HISTORIC ARTIFACTS: AREA K

Soil Location	Madison Fabric Impressed	Madison Plain	Madison Punctated	Leland Cord-marked	Drills	Cores
A1/C						
A1b				1		1
A/Bb	4	2		1		1
A1b2		3	1		1	1
B21irb						
Total	4	5	1	2	1	3

until the time of the beginning of aeolian deposition. It would now appear that one established Madison Ware type, Madison Plain, and three proposed Madison Ware types—Madison Fabric Impressed, Madison Punctated, and Leland Cord-marked—were in use until the fourteenth century by peoples belonging to the Effigy Mound tradition. The information derived from Area K indicates that limited amounts of material were left in regions adjacent to the mounds and that some pits were dug outside of the immediate mound and its construction area. Furthermore, the four ceramic types present in this area seem to be the longest lasting ceramic types at the Bigelow site; the others appeared later or disappeared earlier according to the radiocarbon sequence presented in Figure 28.

The remaining mounds and non-mounds at the Bigelow site will now be briefly considered as they are important for the total picture of cultural activity at this site. Mounds C, D, E, F, and H were located in the same field as excavated Mound G. These mounds were reported by Dixon, Blake, and Scribner in 1956 and since that time extensive plowing has almost obliterated the mounds. Mound C was described as a turtle effigy 63 feet long, 27 feet wide, and 16 inches high (1956:Fig. 1). Mound D was described as a conical mound 43 feet long, 33 feet wide, and 16 inches high. Mound E, a linear mound, measured 100 feet long, 27 feet wide, and also 16 inches high. Mound F was a conical mound 40 feet long, 34 feet wide, and 20 inches high. Finally, Mound H was described as a linear mound 286 feet long, 34 feet wide, and 16 inches high. With the exception of Mound G, which was excavated by Blake (1961), all were leveled by the time of our excavations. With the exception of the turtle shape none of these shapes is inconsistent with those reported for this site and there is no reason, therefore, to exclude them from the Effigy Mound component at this site.

The final group of undescribed mounds are those located in the conical cluster at 47-Pt-29-1. These mounds (numbers 3, 7, 8, 10, 11, and 14) were all excavated, the exception being Mound 10 which had large trees on its center. Mound 3 (Fig. 20) was a small conical mound constructed over a forest horizon and thus it preserved a paleosol. Mound 3 lacked features or burial pits and its fill yielded only two smoothed-over cord-marked body sherds. Mound 7, a conical mound, had been disturbed in its center and excavation of two five-foot squares failed to produce any features, burials or artifacts. Conical Mound 8 had also been extensively disturbed and two five-foot squares excavated along its southern edge failed to yield mound or sub-mound pits, burials, or artifacts. One five-foot square was excavated in the center of conical Mound 11 which was void of features, burials, or artifacts. Finally, in Mound 14 of this group, also a conical mound which sealed in a forest horizon (A1b), the excavation of two five-foot squares produced two features and one burial. Feature 3 of Mound 14 was considered to be the result of a natural disturbance and it was void of artifacts. The area designated as Burial 2 was a secondary deposition of highly fragmented cremated bones lacking diagnostic human characteristics and lacking associated artifacts. The limited information from Mound 14 (which lacked artifacts from the sub-mound or mound horizons) still indicates that cooking pits (Feature 3) and possibly a secondary human cremation were added to the former surface prior to mound construction—a practice which conforms to the pattern observed so far.

There are four non-mound areas remaining which received alphabetical designations from Dixon, Blake, and Scribner (1956) or myself in 1965. Areas I and J were originally described as linear mounds next to the river bank at 47-Pt-29-2: Area I measured 35 feet long, 14 feet wide, and 15 inches high; J measured 19 feet long, 10 feet wide, and 16 inches high (1956:68-69). Profile cuts were made at the river bank in 1966 and in both cases these rises were found to be aeolian depositions and no excavations were undertaken. Areas O and P were noted in 1965 as possible mounds located adjacent to the river bank at 47-Pt-29-2. Area O was found to be a localized rise caused by aeolian deposition and no excavations were attempted. Area P, however, had the surface characteristics of a small linear mound and subsequent trenching in 1966 of this rise exposed sequential AC profiles horizontally stratified above a paleosol solum. The evidence indicated that Area P had undergone repeated aeolian deposition. The artifacts—a Madison Plain rim sherd and a core—found in this rise were well mixed with recent Historic materials and are not considered reliable for stratigraphic context. In 1965 a cup-shaped fire pit was excavated from the A1b3 horizon and charcoal contained in the fill was submitted for dating. The resulting date is A.D. 1610 ± 65 (WIS-157). I would suggest that this date does not chronologically place the prehistoric component and that this assessment and the one of A.D. 1600 ± 55 (WIS-215) from 47-Wp-26 most probably date a forest fire (such as the Peshtigo, Wisconsin fire of October 8, 1871, which claimed over 800 lives) which was widespread enough to occur at both localities.

The final excavated areas to be discussed are those surface areas designated as forest or grass or soil bodies No. 4 and No. 5 (Figs. 17*a* and *b*). In the area delineated as forest soil body No. 4, non-mound excavations were conducted which produced the artifacts listed in Table 12.

TABLE 12

DISTRIBUTION OF CERAMIC, LITHIC, AND HISTORIC ARTIFACTS: FOREST AREA

Soil Location	Madison Cord Impressed	Madison Fabric Impressed	Madison Folded Lip	Madison Plain	Madison Punctated	Leland Cord-marked	Aztalan Collared	Sanders Triangular	Triangular	Cores	Worked Flakes	Polishing Stones	Hammerstones
A11		4		1		1	1	1	2		3	1	5
A12	6			7	1	3	2	1		2			2
Bir11		1	1	2						2			
Bir12				1		1							
Bir2													
Bir3													
Total	6	5	1	11	1	5	3	2	2	4	3	1	7

The artifacts excavated from the grass soil body (No. 5; Figs 17*a* and *b*) are more restricted in variety and number (Table 13).

In addition to the obvious facts that Madison Plain, Madison Fabric Impressed, and Leland Cord-marked are the earliest ceramic types in the forest soils and that Madison Plain is the only Madison Ware type in the grass soils, it should be noted that Madison Cord Impressed and Madison Punctated ceramics, and Sanders Triangular projectile points are present at the earliest time levels at this site. This temporal priority is also true for the Triangular points and the Aztalan Collared ceramics which follow shortly thereafter.

The ceramics from both 47-Pt-29-1 and Pt-29-2 were ordered according to type, soil horizon (non-mound or mound), and decoration, and were then subjected to a principal component analysis. Examination of the Madison Cord Impressed sequence presented in Table 14 shows that for the non-mound soils both of the major forms of cords begin at the same time, but z^{S}_{S} cords appear to be numerically superior. For the mound soils cords used in decoration and composed of s^{Z}_{Z} elements appear earlier and are more numerous than those with z^{S}_{S} elements. The Madison Cord Impressed ceramics from the features tend to blend these differences and suggest an almost equal representation, the z^{S}_{S} cords being represented by six more examples and the features also containing two examples of combined cords of opposing twists.

TABLE 13

DISTRIBUTION OF CERAMICS, LITHIC, AND HISTORIC ARTIFACTS: GRASS AREA

Soil Location	Madison Plain	Unclassified Ceramics (B)	Triangular	End Scrapers	Worked Flakes	Polishing Stones	Hammerstones
A11		1		1		1	14
A12			1		1		18
Bir12	3				1		27
Bir2	1		1				17
Bir3							2
C							1
Total	4	1	2	1	2	1	79

The Madison Fabric Impressed ceramics from the non-mound soils horizons have equal numbers of decorations composed of $s\,^{Z}_{Z}$, $z\,^{S}_{S}$, and combined cords; however, the latter appear to be earlier. In the mound soils the fabrics composed of $s\,^{Z}_{Z}$ cords outnumber those of $z\,^{S}_{S}$ by 2 to 1 and they occur earlier while the combined cords are the same for both non-mound and mound soils. Little can be said concerning the combined cords on the single Madison Folded Lip specimen except that these cords certainly link it to both sequences and this example appears to have occurred early in the overall sequence. The Madison Plain ceramics from the Bigelow site's non-mound soils appear to have the earliest and longest sequence, with $s\,^{Z}_{Z}$ cords being preferred over $z\,^{S}_{S}$ cords. In the mound soil horizons the same numerical superiority occurs, even in the feature representatives, but the one specimen from the A1b2 is not sufficient for determining priority. In one Madison Plain specimen combined cords are used for interior decoration.

The Madison Punctated ceramics are less complex than the Madison Plain—only one $z\,^{S}_{S}$ cord-decorated sherd was from the non-mound soils. In the mound soils, however, the sherds are decorated with $s\,^{Z}_{Z}$ cords, with the exception of three $S\,{}^{z\,{}^{S}_{S}}_{z\,{}^{S}_{S}}$ specimens from the mound features.

Leland Cord-marked ceramics from the Bigelow site non-mound soil horizons begin in the Bir12 horizon and are limited to $s\,^{Z}_{Z}$ cord-decorated ceramics. In the mound and sub-mound soil horizons diversification of cords on the Leland Cord-marked ceramics is limited to the $s\,^{Z}_{Z}$ and $z\,^{S}_{S}$ element combinations, the $z\,^{S}_{S}$ cords having been utilized earliest. The totals of both non-mound and mound horizons indicate that both forms of cords were used equally on this Madison Ware ceramic type. The diagnostic collared ceramics are not as easy to deal with as their decorations would suggest. The Aztalan Collared ceramics from non-mound soil horizons seem to appear late in the stratigraphic sequence and to be represented by one specimen only for the $s\,^{Z}_{Z}$, $z\,^{S}_{S}$, and the combination of $s\,^{Z}_{Z}$ and $z\,^{S}_{S}$ cord decorations. In the mound soil horizons, the Aztalan Collared ceramics with discernible cord decorations occur earlier but there is almost equal distribution

TABLE 14

DISTRIBUTION OF CERAMICS ACCORDING TO SOILS HORIZONS AND CORDS

	Madison Cord Impressed					Madison Fabric Impressed				Madison Folded Lip	Madison Plai			
	s	Z	z	S	s+z	Z	z	S	s+z	s+z	s	Z	z	s
Non-Mound														
A11		3	1			2	2		1					
A12		1	5								3			
A1b														
A1b2											2			
Bir11									1		1		1	
Bir12													1	
Bir2														
B21ir														
C											1			
Sub-Total		4	6			2	2		2		7		2	
Mound														
A11	1	2	3					1			3			
A12						1						3		
A/B	2	3	4			9	1		2	1	7		7	
A/Bb	3	1		1			4	1			3		1	
A/B2														
A1b		1	1			3					4		4	
A1b2		1									1			
A1b2 (MS)[1]														
A1b2-3														
B21irb		2				1								
Features	51		62		2						48			
Sub-Total	57	10	70	1	2	14	5	2	2	1	66	3	12	
TOTAL	57	14	76	1	2	16	7	2	4	1	73	3	14	

[1]MS=mound surface.

among cord forms. This inconclusive observation can be made about the remaining two collared types and the unclassified ceramics listed in Table 14.

Table 15 lists the same non-mound and mound (plus sub-mound) horizons; however, the cord distribution is restricted to those body sherds with $s\frac{z}{Z}$ or $z\frac{S}{s}$ cord-marking. The 697 body sherds with these forms of cord-marking have some proportional differences: in the non-mound horizons the $s\frac{z}{Z}$ cord-marked body sherds are present in almost a 2 to 1 ratio over the $z\frac{S}{s}$ cord-marked

Madison Punctated			Leland Cord-marked			Aztalan Collared			Hahn Cord Impressed	Point Sauble Collared	Unclassified		
s	z	S	s	Z	z	s	z	s+z	s	s+z	s	S	s+z
			1				1						
			1			1		1					
	1												
			1										
	1		3			1	1	1					
					2	1					1		
											2		
3			1	2	3				1	2	1	2	1
											2		
1					1	1	1					1	
		3											
4		3	1	2	6	2	1		1	2	6	3	1
4	1	3	4	2	6	3	2	1	1	2	6	3	1

body sherds. The 2 or more to 1 proportion of s $\frac{Z}{Z}$ cord-marked body sherds is consistent from the Bir2 horizon to the A12 horizon where there is a diminishing shift. Even though s $\frac{Z}{Z}$ cord-marked sherds appear earlier in the B21ir horizon, there is no real priority of one form over the other.

In the mound horizons the overall impression is of equal distribution except for the A1b and A/B2 horizons, where there is a numerical shift for the s $\frac{Z}{Z}$ cord-marked specimens. At only one

TABLE 15

DISTRIBUTION OF s^{z}_{z} AND z^{s}_{s} CORD-MARKED BODY SHERDS ACCORDING TO NATURAL SOILS HORIZONS

	s^{z}_{z}	z^{s}_{s}
Non-Mound		
A11	21	10
A12	41	34
A1b	8	
A1b2	5	3
Bir11	31	10
Bir12	6	3
Bir2	5	2
B21ir	3	
C		
Sub-Total	120	62
Mound		
A11	13	24
A12	4	2
A/B	105	95
A/Bb	19	17
A/B2	30	6
A1b	108	35
A1b2	9	6
A1b2 (MS)[1]	6	6
A1b2-3	11	7
B21irb	12	
Sub-Total	317	198
TOTAL	437	260

[1] MS=mound surface.

time, the A11 horizon, do the z^{S}_{S} cord-marked body sherds number more than s^{Z}_{Z} cord-marked body sherds. The totals for the mound and non-mound horizon distribution of these cord-marked sherds indicate that both forms of cord twist were present at almost the same time and the frequency of s^{Z}_{Z} cord twisting for cord-marking suggests a cultural preference for this cord by the Effigy Mound peoples who utilized this locality.

The distribution of s^{Z}_{Z} and z^{S}_{S} cord-marked body sherds from a chronological view (Table 17) indicates that both forms are present at Mound A, or from circa A.D. 670. The data in Table 17

TABLE 16
FREQUENCY OF RIMS AND ASSOCIATED BODY SHERDS FROM 47-Pt-29

	Rim Sherds		Body Sherds		Combined Rims and Body		Estimated Number Vessels	
	No.	%	No.	%	No.	%	No.	%
Madison Cord Impressed	13	7.9	1053	83.4	1066	74.8	12	8.3
Madison Fabric Impressed	7	4.2	22	1.7	29	2.0	23	16.0
Madison Folded Lip	1	.6			1	.07	1	.6
Madison Plain	103	63.1	168	13.3	271	19.0	74	51.7
Madison Punctated	6	3.6	4	.3	10	.7	8	5.5
Leland Cord-marked	6	3.6	13	1.3	19	1.3	10	6.9
Aztalan Collared	11	6.7			11	.7	10	6.9
Hahn Cord Impressed	1	.6			1	.07	1	.6
Point Sauble Collared	2	1.2			2	.1	2	1.3
Unclassified A	1	.6	2	.1	3	.2	1	.6
Unclassified B	1	.6			1	.07	1	.6
Unclassified C	11	6.7			11	.7	?	
Madison Ware Total	150	92.0	1260	99.84	1410	98.94	141	98.60
TOTAL	163	99.4	1262	100.10	1425	99.99	143	99.00

suggest shifts in preference through time: s $\frac{Z}{Z}$ and z $\frac{S}{S}$ cords seem to be almost equal from A.D. 670 until A.D. 810, when z $\frac{S}{S}$ cord-marked body sherds outnumber the s $\frac{Z}{Z}$ examples. This trend continues until A.D. 930, when the preference is reversed until A.D. 1120 (Mound N). The limited examples at this time suggest slight shifts until A.D. 1370. I would propose that the 2 to 1 preference (261 to 130) for s $\frac{Z}{Z}$ cords for cord-marking is probably valid, but that the figures given at each chronological interval are not as valid as the smoother trends seem in Table 15.

The sharp shifts seen in the cord frequencies presented in Table 17 appear to be blunted for the typed ceramics as illustrated in Table 16. On the basis of the eight dates, the introduction, longevity, and decline of certain ceramic types can be postulated. For example, Madison Cord Impressed, Madison Fabric Impressed, Madison Plain, and Madison Punctated are the earliest dated Madison Ware ceramics at the Bigelow site. The Madison Cord Impressed ceramic type appears to have had a 300-year period of utilization by Effigy Mound peoples at this site. There is only a slight indication that its popularity increased through time. I do not view the suggested hiatus at the time of the construction of

TABLE 17

RIM SHERDS, DECORATED BODY SHERDS, AND BODY SHERDS: CHRONOLOGICAL ORDER AND MOUND OR NON-MOUND DISTRIBUTIONS

Mound or Area	Madison Cord Impressed	Madison Fabric Impressed	Madison Folded Lip	Madison Plain	Madison Punctated	Leland Cord-marked	Aztalan Collared	Hahn Cord Impressed	Point Sauble Collared	A Unclassified	B Unclassified	C Unclassified	a Decorated Body Sherds	b Decorated Body Sherds	c Decorated Body Sherds	s^z_z body sherds	z^s_s body sherds	Total
A:A.D. 670	4	1		7	2							2				31	25	72
S:A.D. 800				1												1		2
L:A.D. 810	3	5	1	6	1	1	1	1	1	3			2		1	53	63	142
4:A.D. 830	1			2													6	9
B:A.D. 930	5	1		14	1	1	1					4	3	1		43	12	86
R:A.D. 990	8	8		12		9						1				125	16	179
N:A.D. 1120				1			1						1			2	6	11
K:A.D. 1370		4		5	1	2							1			6	2	21
TOTAL	21	19	1	48	5	13	3	1	1	3		7	7	1	1	261	130	522
Effigies[1]	13	6	1	34	4	2	5	1	1	0	0	3	3	0	1	114	106	294
Conicals	10	7	0	32	3	1	3	0	1	3	0	7	3	1	1	140	88	300
Linear	8	8	0	12	0	9	0	0	0	0	0	1	0	1	0	160	58	257
Surface	6	9	0	21	2	7	3	0	0	0	1	0	3	1	0	124	88	265
TOTAL	37	30	1	99	9	19	11	1	2	3	1	11	9	3	2	538	340	1116

[1]Associated vessel sherds not included.

Mound S as conclusive, because shortly thereafter Mound L contained the types omitted from Mound S. At the bottom of Table 17 the Madison Cord Impressed distribution is ordered according to mound form and surface squares excavated. The frequency is highest in the effigy mounds which constitute only about 14 percent of the total at the Bigelow site and the three excavated in 1965 and 1966 represent only 10 percent of the total. The now obvious fact that these ceramics are found in all three mound forms at the Bigelow site will be elaborated upon below.

The Madison Fabric Impressed ceramic type, while not as numerous as the Madison Cord Impressed ceramics, continued to be used at the Bigelow site throughout its occupancy. If we omit the plus and minus factors illustrated in Figure 28, the Madison Fabric Impressed ceramic type had a 700-year history at the Bigelow site. The time of maximum popularity of Madison Fabric Impressed, like Madison Cord Impressed, appears to have been around A.D. 1000. Madison Fabric Impressed rim sherds were not present in the conical cluster of 47-Pt-29-1, perhaps explaining its absence from Mound 4 at A.D. 830. However, one Madison Fabric Impressed specimen was recovered from the Mound 13 area. The almost equal frequency of this type in conical, linear and effigy shaped mounds and the surface squares suggests that the builders of these mounds had access to ceramics with fabric impressions during the prehistoric utilization of the Bigelow site. The one Madison Folded Lip rim sherd from the wing of bird effigy Mound L only indicates its association with this form of mound and its very restricted use at this site.

The Madison Plain specimens have the only unbroken distribution from Mound A at A.D. 670 to Area K at A.D. 1370 and, like the Madison Fabric Impressed ceramics, the duration of this type at the Bigelow site is 700 years. While the type was not strongly represented at Mound 4 it was present in mounds 5, 6, 9, and 13. Its period of maximum utilization appears to have been from A.D. 930 to A.D. 990 and it is almost as popular at the termination date as it was at the initial date. Madison Plain ceramics are almost equally distributed between the effigy and conical mounds, the lowest distribution being from Mound R. However, at Mound R Madison Plain ceramics are the most numerous, so the figure of 12 specimens may be a result of the fact that only one linear mound was excavated. In addition, Madison Plain is the most numerous type found in the excavation of surface squares. On the basis of these figures, Madison Plain ceramics seem to have been the most utilized ceramics at the Bigelow site, indicating that it was more a utilitarian than a ceremonial ware of the Effigy Mound peoples.

The frequency and distribution of the proposed Madison Punctated ceramic type are somewhat sporadic: examples of this type were absent from mounds S, 4, R, and N. Its 700-year longevity is attested to by its occurrence in Mound A and at Area K; thus Madison Punctated, Madison Plain, and Madison Fabric Impressed ceramics are companion wares during the entire prehistoric utilization of the Bigelow site. The site distribution of Madison Punctated appears to be almost totally confined to

47-Pt-29-2, with only three examples recovered from bear effigy Mound 13. Madison Punctated ceramics are almost equally distributed between effigy and conical mounds and their absence from linear Mound R cannot be attributed to time, as one example of the type was recovered from Area K. It would seem from Tables 16 and 17 that both Madison Folded Lip and Madison Punctated were among the least utilized wares at the Bigelow site. This observation appears to apply also to Hahn Cord Impressed and Point Sauble Collared ceramics.

Beginning with the Leland Cord-marked ceramics the dated beginnings of the remaining typed ceramics at the Bigelow site appear to be circa A.D. 810. In fact, Leland Cord-marked, Aztalan Collared, Hahn Cord Impressed, and Point Sauble Collared ceramics all appear with the construction of bird effigy Mound L. Both Hahn Cord Impressed and Point Sauble Collared lack any other dated context and the latter type was found in only one other mound form, conical mound M. The Leland Cord-marked ceramics appear to have a longer time span (560 years) and greater distribution than Aztalan Collared ceramics. The Aztalan Collared ceramic type has a dated sequence of 310 years and was not present in linear Mound R. In the order of their percentage within the Madison Ware total for the Bigelow site, both Aztalan Collared and Leland Cord-marked are equal (6.9 percent); then Point Sauble Collared and Hahn Cord Impressed appear with lower frequency. From a distributional point of view all four types were absent at the conical cluster at 47-Pt-29-1 and only Leland Cord-marked and Aztalan Collared ceramics were present in the Mound 13 area.

Of the unclassified rim sherds (Categories A, B, and C), the specimens of Category A from Mound L with cord-wrapped stick decorations seem to be diagnostic of the prehistoric component at this site. The exterior decoration on these sherds suggests similarities to Mason's proposed Heins Creek Corded Stamped ceramics from the Door Peninsula (1966:16-18, 202-204). One rim sherd of Category C is totally inconsistent in paste, hardness, surface finish, and decoration with the other ceramics from 47-Pt-29-2 and I would suggest that a date of 1860 for an aboriginal sherd seems unlikely. The 11 eroded specimens from Category C and the decorated body sherds (Categories a, b, and c) are unclassified ceramics which will be excluded from this analysis. The totals presented for each dated mound and mound form or surface square offer two sets of information. At circa A.D. 670, or the dated beginning of prehistoric occupation, the ceramic representation seems diverse and vigorous and there is a doubling of ceramic artifacts between A.D. 800 and A.D. 830. The growth and utilization climax appears to have been between A.D. 930 and A.D. 990, when a total of 260 dated ceramic artifacts are recorded. From circa A.D. 1000 to A.D. 1370 there appears to be a decline in the number of dated artifacts. These observations are dependent on seven dated mounds and one dated area and the figures are only rough indicators of the time of maximum occupation. The four totals listed below the dated totals of Table 17 are almost equal and they seem to indicate site uniformity and the lack of differences between mound form and surface areas, as if only one prehistoric component had utilized this site.

The lithic artifacts presented in Table 18 are also presented according to chronological order and mound or non-mound distribution. The proposed Sanders Triangular projectile point type

TABLE 18

LITHIC ARTIFACTS ACCORDING TO CHRONOLOGICAL ORDER AND MOUND OR NON-MOUND DISTRIBUTIONS

Mound or Area	Sanders Triangular	Triangulars (A-B)	Corner notched	Drills	End Scrapers	Cores	Worked Flakes	Pecked Stones	Polishing Stones[1]	Total
A:A.D. 670	2	4				1			3	10
S:A.D. 800	1						1			2
L:A.D. 810	1			1		2		2		6
4:A.D. 830										0
B:A.D. 930	2	3				2	1			8
R:A.D. 990	1	1	1		1	4			1	9
N:A.D. 1120										0
K:A.D. 1370				1		3				4
TOTAL	7	8	1	2	1	12	2	2	4	39
Effigies	4	5		2		2		2	10	25
Conicals	10	3		1		3	3		5	25
Linears	1	1	1		1	4			1	9
Surface	2	4		1	1	8	5		2	23
TOTAL	17	13	1	4	2	17	8	2	18	82

[1]Historic artifacts not included.

is present at circa A.D. 670 and it continued as a preferred point form until circa A.D. 990, or for approximately 320 years (Table 18). Sanders Triangular points were not present at dated Mound 4 of 47-Pt-29-1, but they were found in mounds 1, 9, and 13. In Mound 9 three Sanders Triangular and six other Triangular points were in direct association with Burial 3. Of the 17 Sanders Triangular points listed at the bottom of Table 18 it appears that more than half were associated with the conical mounds, one-quarter with the effigy mounds, and the remainder with linear Mound R and the surface areas. In contrast, the 13 serrated and non-serrated Triangular points listed are most numerous in the effigy mounds, then the surface squares, the conical mounds, and then linear Mound R. However, the conical figure of three would change if the 17 points from Blake's excavation of Mound G were added to these totals. The temporal range for these Triangular points seem to be the same as that for the Sanders Triangular (320 years). The hiatus illustrated in Table 18 between A.D. 670 and A.D. 930 appears to be valid and seems to be more than just chance, and yet, these points are present in equal numbers at both A.D. 670 and A.D. 930-990.

The corner notched point from Mound R is dated at A.D. 990 and perhaps it and the small side notched point from Mound G were introduced into this area at this time. Our knowledge concerning the types, space and time ranges, and cultural associations of the numerous projectile point forms found in Wisconsin is very limited despite Ritzenthaler's publication (1967) on the local types. At best we can say that both point forms were present at the Bigelow site at circa A.D. 1000. The drills are not of any significant form to be considered diagnostic beyond their possible function. Only one drill fits a pattern already established for this site and it was made from a Triangular projectile point from the Mound 13 area.

Only two scrapers were recovered from the Bigelow site; one was from linear Mound R and the other from surface excavations. Very little can be said concerning this class of artifact except on the basis of negative evidence. The paucity of scraping and cutting tools at this site suggests that their production and activities associated with them took place elsewhere. In fact, the total of 158 artifacts and 3,901 unworked flakes suggests the site was not a major workshop locality for the production of finished tools. The scraper/Triangular point index of 2/30 is very low, much lower than that recorded for the Mero site (Mason, 1966:186). It is somewhat incongruous that one of the categories of lithic artifacts with strong representation (17) is the class described as cores. These "exhausted" cores span the full dated range of prehistoric utilization of the Bigelow site and are found in all mound forms. As is to be expected, more than half were located in the non-mound surface areas. Stone working at this site appears limited; the majority of the lithic objects were recovered from 47-Pt-29-2.

The nine worked flakes described in Chapter IV represent .2 percent of the total of 3,910 excavated flakes. The worked flakes are all single edge flake side scrapers, their associations restricted to 47-Pt-29-2 and to the conical form of mound. The two dated specimens from Mounds S and B date from A.D. 800 and A.D. 930 respectively. The pecked stones (Fig. 43:D, E) are recorded for only bird effigy Mound L, dated at A.D. 810. The polishing stones from the Bigelow site had a greater temporal range (320 years) and they were associated with all mound forms and surface areas. As the second most numerous class of lithic artifacts, it is important to note that more than half were associated with the effigy mounds.

In the overall totals of the ceramic artifacts some trends are apparent which are not evident in every respect from the lithic totals. The temporal period around A.D. 930 to A.D. 990 appears to agree with the estimated time of maximum site utilization, but the time of A.D. 670 is also well represented. The spread of gross artifact numbers between effigy mounds, conical mounds, and surface squares is almost identical to the ceramic distribution; however, only nine diagnostic lithic artifacts are associated with linear Mound R.

On the basis of all the evidence presented for the Bigelow site in this and the previous two chapters, we can now consider the site in its total prehistoric configuration. At 47-Pt-29-2 there were three effigy mounds (C, L, and N), eight conical mounds (A, B, D, F, G, M, Q, and S), and three linear mounds (E, H, and R). These 14 mounds comprise 21.4 percent effigy mounds, 21.4 percent linear mounds, and 57.1 percent conical mounds. With the addition of bear effigy Mound 13 and the other 13 conical mounds from 47-Pt-29-1, the total number of mounds at the Bigelow site is raised to 28. This number is divided between four effigy mounds (14.3 percent), three linear mounds (10.7 percent), and 21 conical mounds (75.0 percent). The radiocarbon assessments give us several possible alternative means of interpreting the rate of mound construction. If the lower range of sample WIS-187 is considered as A.D. 1500 (Fig. 28), then the range is 940 years, and if a mound were added one at a time at a regular rate the interval would be 33.5 years. Continuing through the possible interpretations, if the mean of these samples was considered—A.D. 670 (WIS-197) and A.D. 1370 (WIS-187)—the span would be 700 years, a mound being added every 25 years. If the cluster of dates illustrated in Figure 28 is interpreted as ranging from A.D. 700 to A.D. 1250, or 550 years of site utilization, then the possible separation could be 19.6 years per mound addition. If only mounds are considered, and we exclude the date from Area K, then the range would be A.D. 670 to A.D. 1120, or 450 years, with the possible interval being 16.1 years per mound addition.

I see no reason to exclude any of these possible ranges until more Effigy Mound tradition sites are dated, but I favor the interpretation of A.D. 670 to A.D. 1370, with the period of utilization being 700 years. The rate of mound construction might be interpreted as one mound every 25 years, but there are other factors to be considered. The interval between mounds A and S is 130 years while the interval between mounds S, L, and 4 is only 30 years. One hundred years may separate mounds 4 and B, whereas the apparent separation between mounds B and R is only 60 years, and between Mound R and Mound N a total of 130 years.

Another way of considering these dates is by mound form and location. Conical mounds A and B were close together in space but separated by 260 years. Bird effigy mounds L and N were also quite close together, but they are separated by 310 years. As there are more mounds than dates, I would favor the interpretation of approximately 25 years per mound *if* the rate of mound addition were a regular cyclic event regulated by the Effigy Mound peoples. In any event, the Bigelow site dates and interpretations suggest information which has heretofore been lacking for a site belonging to this cultural tradition. At a minimum the site was utilized for 450 years and at a maximum for 940 years. Mounds were added at *a possible regular interval of 25 years* and not constructed over a short 50- to 100-year period. This locality was known by Effigy Mound peoples for a minimum of a half-millennium and they returned to camp briefly while another conical, effigy, or linear mound was constructed. A few of these mounds covered a primary flexed burial (3) or a secondary cremation (9). These peoples built all three forms of mounds and there is very limited information from Mound N that it may have been a conical mound with the head, tail, and wings added during a second phase of mound construction.

The sub-mound, mound, and surface areas (with the exception of the unrelated Historic component) yielded artifacts which belonged exclusively to the Effigy Mound peoples as a portion of their material culture. The diagnostic ceramics are all considered as belonging to the Madison Ware category and these ceramic types—Madison Cord Impressed, Madison Fabric Impressed, Madison Folded Lip, Madison Plain, Madison Punctated, Leland Cord-marked, Aztalan Collared, Hahn Cord Impressed, and Point Sauble Collared—serve as links between mound forms and the surface areas. The ceramics had their own popularity frequency and duration at the Bigelow site and they all overlap one another as companion wares. On the basis of the estimated number of vessels present at the Bigelow site (Table 16) it would appear that the simple Madison Plain ceramics (51.7 percent of the total) had the longest duration and the most numerous representatives (74). The second most common ceramic type was represented by 23 vessels and these Madison Fabric Impressed vessels were a companion ware of the Madison Plain ceramics during the full range of site utilization. The remaining Madison Ware types are estimated as having the following percentages: Madison Cord Impressed (8.3 percent); Leland Cord-marked and Aztalan Collared (6.9 percent each); Madison Punctated (5.5 percent); Point Sauble Collared (1.3 percent); and Madison Folded Lip and Hahn Cord Impressed (.6 percent each).

The diagnostic lithic artifacts associated with the prehistoric Effigy Mound component are the proposed Sanders Triangular projectile points, Triangular projectile points and corner and possibly side notched projectile points. The remaining lithic artifact classes could have been recovered from any prehistoric component in Wisconsin, with the exception of the reworked Triangular point made into a drill.

Although all of the ceramic and lithic artifacts listed above are suggested as belonging to the Effigy Mound peoples who utilized this site, we can see that the total number of artifacts, if spread over even a half-millennium, does not suggest intensive village or campsite occupation. The absence of a large number of cooking and refuse pits, houses or settlement pattern data, working areas, and extensive midden deposits suggests that the Bigelow site was utilized for the primary purpose of constructing mounds. As conical and linear mounds are common at most sites belonging to the Effigy Mound tradition, we can only assume that the bird, bear, and possibly the turtle effigy shapes were purposely added to this site. In view of the absence of preceding Middle Woodland Hopewell or later Mississippian influences, with the exception of 13 shell-tempered body sherds which were in a mixed deposit (body sherd category 4), we can exclude other cultural influences. The presence of a high frequency of simple Madison Plain ceramics and the lower frequency of more elaborately decorated ceramics suggests that elaborate goods (grave goods?) were not being brought to this site. There is some suggestion of a preference for cords and fabrics composed of s $\frac{Z}{Z}$ elements over z $\frac{S}{S}$ elements but there is no indication that there were two different Effigy Mound bands having different cord and fabric techniques, one having replaced the other, or that both bands used the site at the same time. It appears that one group utilized two sets of cord twists and the frequency of the different cord twists does not allow for temporal ranking of the site according to intra-site analysis.

The absence of pipes, articles of personal adornment, or ceremonial objects, and the presence of only two decorated bone artifacts (Pl. 15:A, B) suggest that the only major ceremonial activity was mound construction. The decorations on their vessels and the complexity of the fabrics impressed into vessels suggest that these people were not completely lacking stylistic expression. The absence of horticultural implements and the absence of preserved by-products of farming or hunting, fishing or gathering again support the view that the site was occupied for short time intervals by a very few families (30 individuals?) at a time for the purpose of mound construction. The possible presence of cremated non-human remains in sub-mound pits and in association with cremated burials, for example, Burial 5 of Mound A, suggests both normal cooking activities and ceremonial activities.

If the addition of mounds to this site was a cyclic event it may have been repeated at other nearby sites and thus part of a larger geographic and temporal cyclic pattern would be represented at the Bigelow site. I would suggest that this pattern is similar to the proposed "central-based wandering" community pattern (Meggers, 1956:138-140) with the central-based aspect of the concept linked to mound construction, and not subsistence, at the Bigelow site. It is possible that the Effigy Mound peoples who constructed these mounds at the Bigelow site lived at a more permanent center or a "semi-permanent sedentary" site (Meggers, 1956:141-143) such as the Sanders Site 1 (47-Wp-26) which will be examined next.

VI

SANDERS SITES (47-Wp-26 and 47-Wp-70): LOCATION, DESCRIPTION, AND EXCAVATION PROCEDURE

SANDERS SITE 1: 47-Wp-26

SANDERS site 47-Wp-26 is located in the southeast quarter of the southeast quarter of Section 24, 21N. R13E., Fremont Township, Waupaca County, Wisconsin. On the Weyauwega Quadrangle the site is at latitude 44°16′ and longitude 88°51′. Only one three-line reference to the site has been published: "Group of effigy and other mounds on the bank of the Wolf River, N.E. 1/4 Sec. 25 and S.E. 1/4 Sec. 24. Camp site in adjoining field" (Brown, 1925:131).

The site is within the Central Plain, a physiographic province composed of weak Cambrian sandstone which has a surface elevation ranging from 1,242 to 685 feet above mean sea level (Martin, 1965:319-320). The area was at one time covered by the Late Wisconsin Cary and Valders ice and during Valders time, the ice of the Green Bay lobe inundated the area, with the glacial runoff flowing generally southwest. The sedimentary history of Waupaca County is very complicated—the Valders ice picked up till and lacustrine deposits of Cary and Two Creek age and re-distributed and re-deposited them (Horn, 1960:84, 91).

There is probably a hiatus of an indeterminate number of years between the onset of soil formation on Valders till, or the parent material, and the onset of soil formation in Later Lake Oshkosh lacustrine sediments (*ibid.*:192). The parent material of clay and sand at the Sanders site is considered to be of a lacustrine origin. These sediments were apparently deposited by Later Lake

Oshkosh, a proglacial lake dammed up against the retreating Valders ice, which at its maximum covered most of the lowland areas associated with the present Wolf River and its tributaries. The maximum recorded elevation for Later Lake Oshkosh is 750 to 780 feet above mean sea level (*ibid.*:29, 140, 192) which is greater than the elevation of the Sanders site (750 feet). The Sanders site is on a terrace escarpment, the lacustrine sediments of which were presumably cut by the Wolf River when it was about 30 feet higher than it is today. The beginnings of soil formation of the present soils did not start until after the Wolf River reached its maximum height.

The site is located within and adjacent to a woodlot which is approximately 2,000 feet north-south and 200 to 500 feet east-west. The woodlot is on the first terrace, between 15 and 30 feet above, south, and east of the Wolf River. The slope of face of this west-facing escarpment ranges from 22 to 24 percent on the north to 14 percent on the southwest (Fig. 31). The Wolf River now flows about 15 to 30 feet north of 47-Wp-26 and up to one-quarter of a mile west of the escarpment, where it empties into Partridge Lake.

The woodlot containing 47-Wp-26 once extended one-quarter of a mile farther east (county Trunk H) and Mr. Walter Sanders, whose family has lived here since the late 1850's, informed me that this area was logged and cleared of mature pine trees in 1910 and that maple and elm trees were cleared in the 1920's. The present woodlot was also selectively cut in 1940 and 1962. During the 1940 cuttings, only those trees which were 200 years or older were selected. During the 1843 and 1852 land surveys, the area west of the present woodlot consisted of second rate land with extensive marsh which supported poplar, white oak, black oak, elm, sugar maple, alder, and willow. South of the woodlot the surface was rolling and considered second rate, and the timber was white and black oak, elm, pine, ash, maple, and prickly ash. In the woodlot the surveys recorded sugar maple, white and black oak, alder, willow, poplar, white birch, pine, and hazel on the level land, which they considered second rate. The present stand consists of mature oak, maple, elm, shagbark hickory, pine, aspen, ironwood, and prickly ash, with a very dense undergrowth of red raspberry, blackberry, nettles, and saplings of up to four inches in diameter at breast height. The fields to the east and south of the woodlot have been cultivated since 1910 and 1920 respectively and

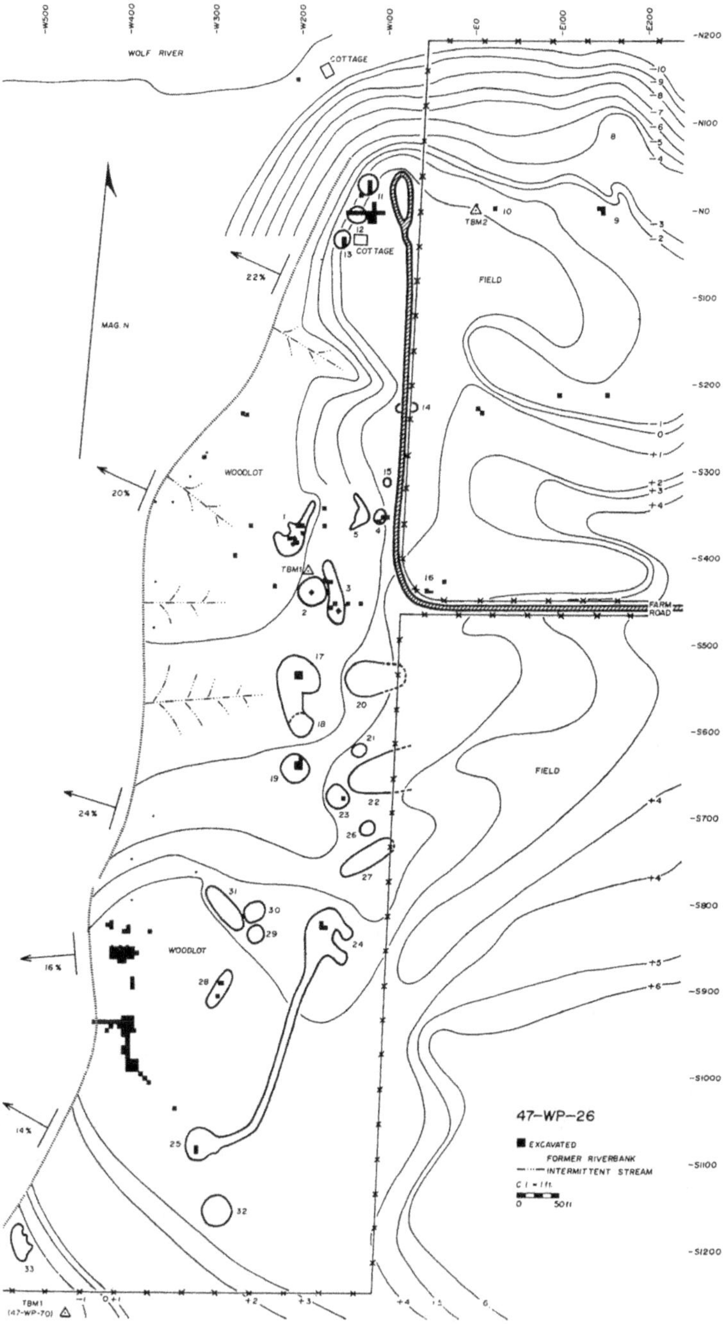

FIG. 31. Plan view of 47-Wp-26.

from these fields the Sanders family have collected a large number of surface finds.

Excavation Procedures

Testing operations at Sanders site 1 (47-Wp-26) were begun on August 10, 1965. At that time, the mounds within the woodlot and immediately adjacent to the woodlot were assigned consecutive numerical designations. As our testing operations were within the center of the woodlot, three mounds (Nos. 1, 2, and 3) were recorded, and these mounds reported to be in the then unharvested field and densely overgrown woodlot were assigned numbers from north to south. As the subsequent excavations of 1966 were conducted and the woodlot was cleared, the 25 consecutively numbered mounds were revised to consist of 28 actual mounds—1-6; 11-15; 17-33. During 1965 an area was cleared of underbrush and mounds 1-3 were tested and one surface square (S25E10) excavated. At that time the site was recommended for full exploration and 18 mounds were considered as worth testing and/or excavating. As with 47-Pt-29, the testing operations conducted during the 1965 season will be incorporated into this report. Again, as with 47-Pt-29, the 1965 square designations will be retained for these three mounds and for the test square between mounds 2 and 3. Feature and burial numbers assigned during 1965 will also be retained in this report.

During the 1966 field season, which began on July 25 and extended to September 1, it was believed that it was best to begin our excavations at 47-Wp-26 at the northern end of the woodlot and to divide the site into thirds in order to have greater horizontal control of the large woodlot. In excavating these units by extending the western grid lines into the woodlot only at mound locations and in moving through the woodlot in a southerly direction, it was believed that greater control of the mound and/or habitation areas would be possible before arriving in the southern one-half of the site with its greater concentration of mounds. TBM No. 2 (Fig. 31) was set up on the top of Area 10. The excavation procedures followed at Sanders site 1 are quite similar to those used at the Bigelow site: natural soils horizons were followed, similar field square and level numerical designations, and a similar field cataloguing system, were utilized.

Mounds at 47-Wp-26

The descriptions of the mounds at Sanders site 1 follow the excavations, as they were conducted during the 1966 field season and incorporate Mounds 1-3 of the 1965 season, as we proceed from north to south. Our initial excavations in 1966 were conducted in the field east of the woodlot and in the Mound 11-13 area. As we moved southward the excavations in the field diminished while the surface squares in the woodlot increased. These surface squares will be incorporated with the mound descriptions.

Mound 6

Mound 6 was a large conical mound adjacent to the summer cottages at Red Banks. Mr. Sanders reported that this mound had been trenched but he was uncertain as to what was recovered. As this mound seemed to be in a good state of preservation it was decided to concentrate on the mounds on the Sanders property and to leave this mound for subsequent excavation.

Areas 7 and 8

Areas 7 and 8 were in reality rises which project to the north and are a result of the topography. These two areas were not tested.

Area 9 (Fig. 31)

Area 9 was another case of a natural rise which appeared to have a mound outline and cross section. Three five-foot squares were excavated into the rise. At a depth of 2.6 feet a disturbed area was uncovered which produced ceramics, charcoal, stone, and flakes and it was at this time that the first five-foot square was expanded. With this expansion Feature 1 was uncovered.

Feature 1 was a large basin-shaped pit, irregular in outline. The orifice of this feature was at a depth of 2.6 feet or 1.9 feet below the plow zone; however, there were no soils indications that this pit was cut through the Ap or lower soils horizons. This feature yielded one Point Sauble Collared rim sherd; one Madison Cord Impressed rim sherd; one grit-tempered, cord-marked sherd; 11 grit-tempered sherd fragments; one quartz flake; one chert flake; and two stone fragments. The charcoal recovered from Feature 1 yielded a date of A.D. 1010 ± 60 (WIS-207).

Area 10 (Fig. 31)

The area designated as Area 10 was the last of four rises in this portion of the field which were thought to be mounds. Subsurface testing indicated this rise to have limited numbers of artifacts.

Mound 11 (Figs. 31, 32)

Mound 11 was a small conical mound 25.5 feet north-south, 24 feet east-west, and 1.2 feet high. Three five-foot squares were excavated in the center of the mound. Mound 11 is composed of soil belonging to soil bodies numbered as $\frac{1}{\text{D-1}}$ and $\frac{1}{\text{A-0}}$ on the soil distribution map (Fig. 44) for Wp-26. This soil had a thin A1 forest horizon; an A2x horizon of fragic character which was medium to thick platy in structure; and a blocky to subangular blocky red clay B22t (t is standard designation for clay) horizon (Fig. 32). The fragic designation is defined as follows: "...the symbol x is used as a suffix with horizon designations to indicate genetically developed properties of firmness, brittleness, high density, and characteristic distribution of clay that are diagnostic of fragipans" (*Soil Survey Manual* Supplement, 1960:183). The mound had a thin A11 forest horizon and the mound fill was a mixed redeposited A2x horizon which was designated as an A2x/A2x to show it was a result of man-made disturbance, like the A/B horizons for the Bigelow site. Beneath the mound fill of Mound 11 were the original A2xb and B22b horizons. The original A11 horizon could not be ascertained and with the contractions and expansions of the A2x horizons the original A11 was no longer present. Mound 11, like the other mounds constructed of this soil, must have been constructed in the moist spring or fall seasons—when the A2x horizon is dry it cannot be easily utilized as borrow for mound fill.

Mound 11 did not contain any features or burials and the artifacts recovered from the mound fill will be presented in the following chapters.

Mounds 12 and 13 (Figs. 31, 32)

Mound 12 was a small conical mound 22 feet north-south, 24 feet east-west, and 1.0 feet high. Mound 13 was a more circular conical mound 19 feet north-south, 18 feet east-west and 1.2 feet

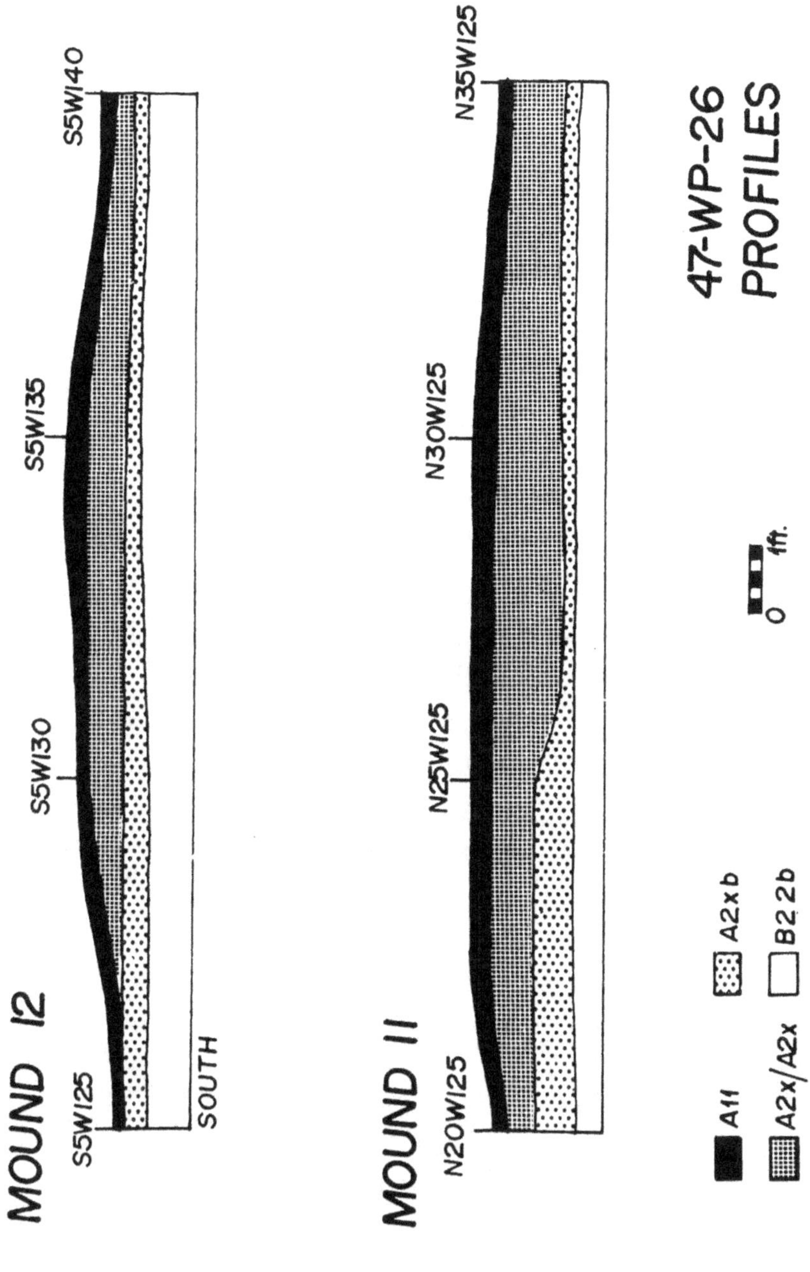

FIG. 32. Profiles of Mound 11 and Mound 12.

high. Mounds 12 and 13 had profiles similar to Mound 11. Two five-foot squares were excavated in the approximate center of Mound 13, and one 15-foot trench was excavated in Mound 12 totalling five five-foot squares. Beacuse Mound 12 produced the most artifacts of the three mounds in this area, an additional 10 five-foot squares were excavated. One square in this mound area uncovered an area that appeared to be a pit.

Feature 4 was uncovered at a depth of .7 feet. It was irregular in outline. The fill contained only charcoal flecks.

Feature 2 was circular in outline with a diameter of 1.2 feet. In cross section it was basin-shaped and extended from 1.5 to 2.4 feet below the surface. The artifacts recovered from this feature consisted of one sherd fragment, one quartzite flake, one chert flake, one basalt flake, seven stone fragments, and charcoal flecks scattered throughout the silty sand fill.

Mound 14 (Fig. 31)

Mound 14 was a short oval mound 25 feet long east-west, 12 feet wide north-south, and approximately 1.5 feet high. This mound had been cut through by the farm lane and fill had been removed. As the mound had been badly disturbed and as the surface was covered with poison ivy, this mound was not excavated.

Mound 15 (Fig. 31)

Mound 15 was a conical mound directly adjacent to and west of the farm land. Since this mound had been partially destroyed when soil was borrowed for the lane and had several large trees growing in its center, it was not excavated.

Area 16 (Fig. 31)

Area 16 was reported by Mr. Sanders to have been a mound so substantial that large portions of it had to be removed in order to construct the farm lane. Its present dimensions are approximately 70 feet in diameter and only one foot above the present surface. Two five-foot squares and one 2.5 by 5-foot extension were excavated. This large area proved to be a natural rise built up of soil accumulation resulting from a bisequal profile of a Brown Podzolic soil over an A′2x-B′t sequem which is similar to the profile illustrated for square S456W150 (Fig. 37) which was directly west of this area. (A profile which exhibits two sequa, one overlying the other in a vertical sequence, is designated by horizon followed by prime accent, e.g., A'2x). One feature was uncovered directly below the plow zone and it was designated Feature 3.

Feature 3 was a circular pit and basin-shaped in cross section. It contained six grit-tempered body sherds, one bone fragment, one quartz flake, three chert flakes, and 10 stone fragments. The loamy sand fill lacked charcoal.

Mound 4 (Figs. 31, 33)

Mound 4 was a small conical mound 14 feet in diameter and 1.0 feet high. In the center of this mound there was a maple tree which was estimated to be 50 to 80 years old. The eastern edge of this mound was excavated first; one additional five-foot square excavated on the southern edge of the mound produced one feature. The soil profile of Mound 4 contrasts sharply with those mounds constructed of the fragic soils or soil bodies No. 1 (Fig. 44). Mound 4 was constructed of fine to medium sands (Soil Body No. $\frac{2}{\text{A-0}}$, Fig. 31) which were present as a paleosol beneath the mound. Mound 4 had a forest A11 horizon and an A/B mound fill which have sealed in a paleosol profile consisting of a thin A11 forest surface horizon, a B21irb horizon, and a B22b sub-mound horizon (Fig. 33). Prior to the construction of the mound, Feature 9 was utilized.

Feature 9 was oval in outline and basin-shaped in cross section. The pit, whose orifice was in the A1b horizon, could not be outlined until the top of the B21irb horizon had been reached. The artifacts associated with Feature 9 are: two grit-tempered, cord-marked body sherds; one knife; one chert flake; and seven stone fragments.

Mound 5 (Fig. 31)

Mound 5 was a bird effigy mound 41 feet long north-south, 17 feet wide in the center of the body area, and 11 feet wide in the wing areas. It was approximately three feet high in the center and it supported several large maple trees. It was decided in the field that Mound 5 would not be tested unless our surface testing for habitation material proved fruitless. Mound 5, and nine other mounds, were not tested or excavated during the 1966 field season.

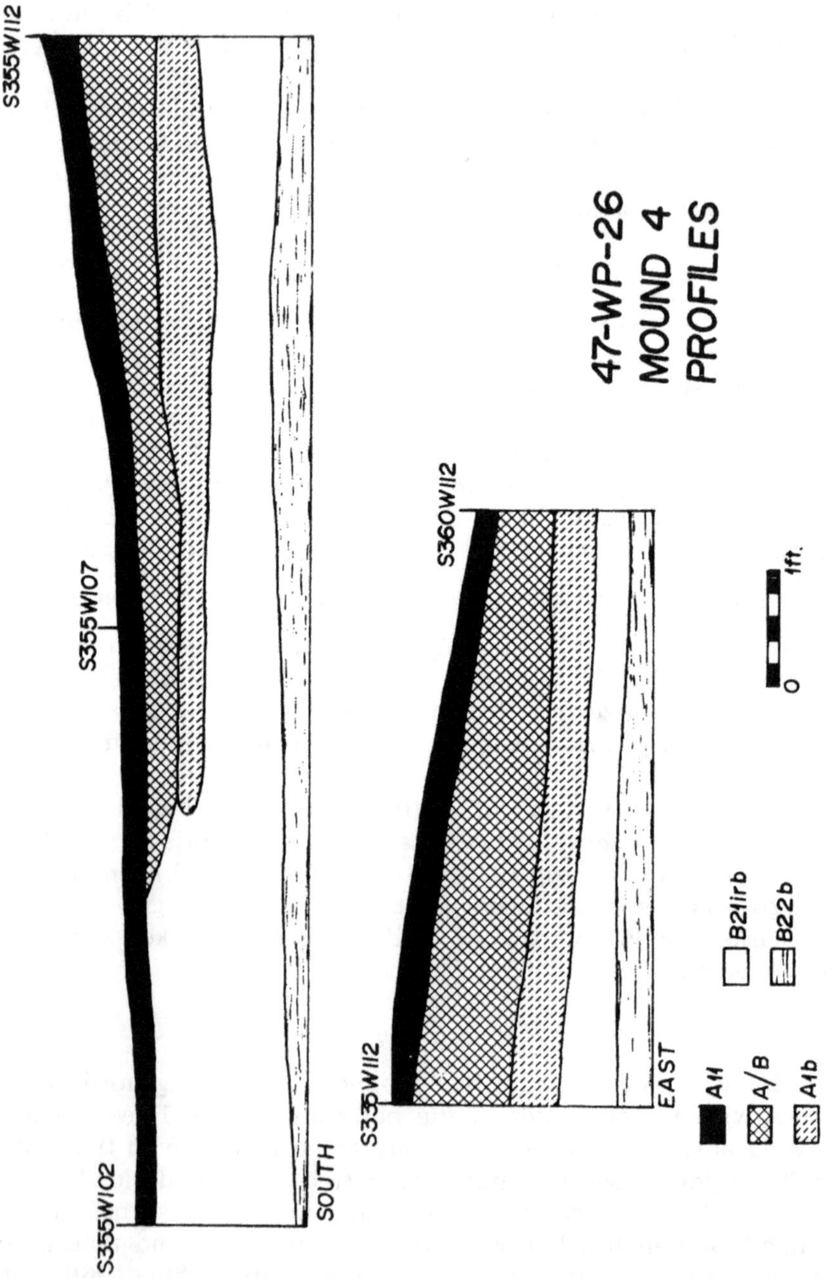

FIG. 33. Mound 4 profiles.

Mound 1 (Fig. 31, 34)

This panther effigy mound was 71 feet long with a maximum width of 34 feet and a maximum height of 2.5 feet. During the 1965 testing operations two five-foot squares were excavated in the head region. During the 1966 field season five additional five-foot squares were excavated. Mound 1 consistently exhibited rodent burrows (krotovinas) in all profile walls of the mound fill and the sub-mound profile was further distorted by the presence of the boundary line between two soil bodies or pedons (Soil Survey Staff 1960:2-4) which, on the Soil Distribution map (Fig. 44), are soil bodies $\frac{1}{\text{A-0}}$ and $\frac{2}{\text{A-0}}$. Two features were uncovered and excavated during the 1965 field season and their square numbers with the parentheses, as shown in Figure 34 for example, are meant to call attention to the 1965 grid locations.

Feature 1 (1965) was circular in outline and basin-shaped in cross section. Its orifice was in the A12 horizon and extended into the A1b horizon. The following objects were recovered from the fill of this feature: two grit-tempered cord-marked body sherds; one grit-tempered sherd fragment; one woodchuck calvarium; one chert flake; three fired sandstone fragments; and six stone fragments.

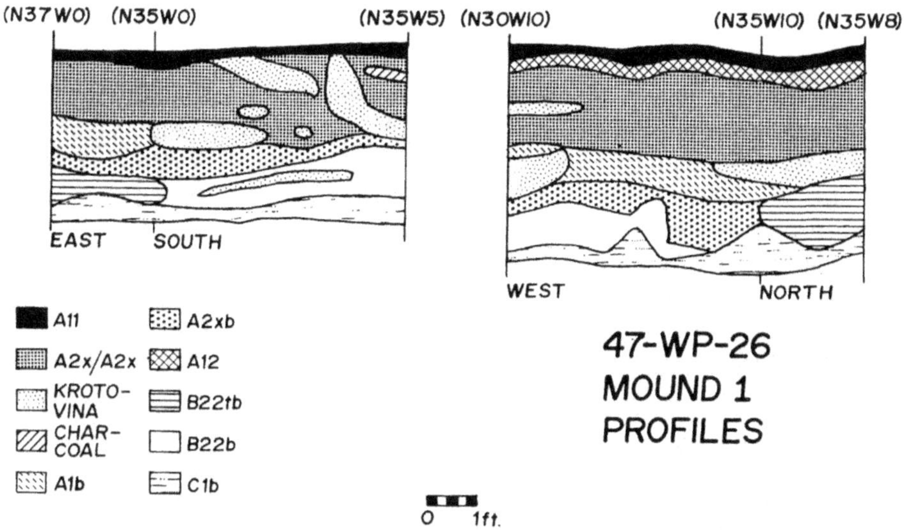

FIG. 34. Mound 1 profiles.

Feature 2 (1965). Feature 2 was roughly circular in outline and it was irregular basin-shaped in cross section. Its orifice originated in the A2x/A2x mound fill horizon and extended into the A2xb horizon. The fill of Feature 2 yielded 28 grit-tempered, cord-marked body sherds; 110 grit-tempered sherd fragments, and two chert flakes.

Mound 2 (Fig. 31)

Mound 2 was a conical mound 33 feet in diameter and approximately 2.5 feet high. One five-foot square was excavated (S30W5) during the 1965 field season. This square was placed in the center of the mound and from the artifacts produced it was decided in 1966 to forego any further excavations.

Feature 1 (1965) of Mound 2 was ovate in outline and basin-shaped in cross section. The orifice of this feature originated in the A2xb horizon and extended into the B21b horizon. One partially reconstructed Madison Punctated vessel (Pl. 31), consisting of 261 fragments, and one Madison Fabric Impressed decorated body sherd, which is not a portion of the vessel, were recovered from this feature. Charcoal found underneath the vessel yielded a date of A.D. 880 ± 70 (WIS-171). The vertical location of Feature 1 of Mound 2 indicates that the pit was dug into the old surface soil which was sealed in by the subsequent construction of the mound.

Mound 3 (Figs. 31, 35)

Mound 3 was a linear mound 75 feet long north-south with a maximum width of 20 feet and a height of two feet (Fig. 35). One five-foot test square was placed in the southern portion of this mound and three additional five-foot squares were excavated in the southern and northern portions of the mound.

Burial 1. During the 1965 excavations, Burial 1 of Mound 3 was found. The bone fragments were found between the A2x/A2x and A2xb horizons. Mr. Robert Meier, of the Department of Anthropology, Indiana University, made the following observations:

Burial 1 (1965) of Mound 3:

A. Description:
1. Human mandible fragment (area of root sockets to left 1st permanent molar?)
2. Six fragments (undiagnostic)
3. Human left parietal and frontal fragment

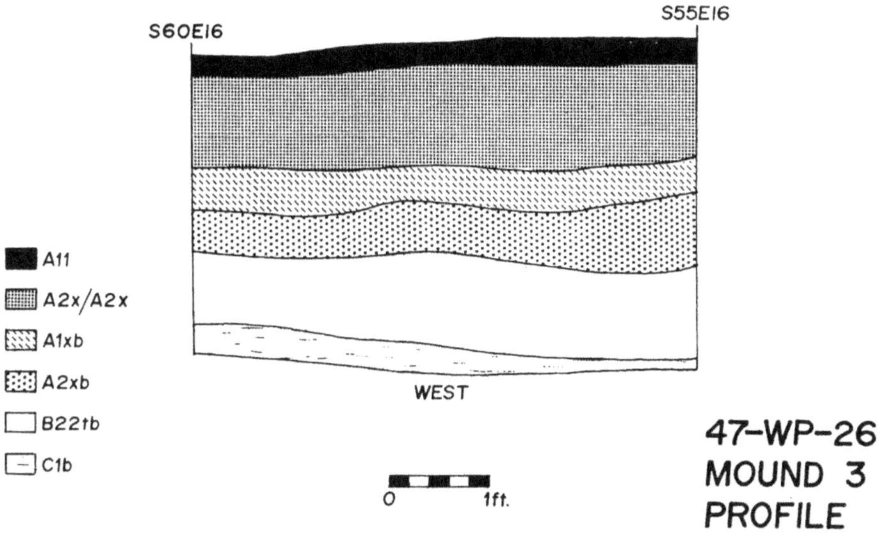

FIG. 35. Mound 3 profiles.

4. Human left parietal and right parietal fragment
5. Human left temporal fragment
6. Human terminal phalanx (right digit 1)
7. Human long bone shaft fragment (femur?)
8. Several smaller shaft fragments (to above?)
9. Three bone fragments (undiagnostic)
10. Spongy bone fragment
11. Brain case compact bone fragment (fired)
12. Three bone fragments (fired)
13. Human right calcaneum fragment

B. Comments: Much of the human cranial material was found nearly contact association in level 3. For this reason, and with no evidence to judge otherwise, these fragments are presumed to belong to the same skeleton. Furthermore, all the human material might well represent the remains of only one individual, because no duplicate bones were found and none of the fragments is distinct enough to indicate more than one skeleton. The fragments themselves are in rather poor condition as shown by the marked erosion of the surfaces. However, pieces of the cranium do permit certain qualitative determinations. First of all, the rather small mastoid process present of the temporal bone fragment would be representative of the female sex. In addition, cresting above the meatus and mastoid process is not present. It is unlikely that this temporal bone is from a young individual since the extent of suture closure on the vault fragments is quite advanced. The amount of suture closure indicates that age of death was in the adult stage, perhaps in the middle adult range (36-55 years).

A charcoal sample from this square from the same level as the burial yielded a date of A.D. 880 ± 70 (WIS-177).

In level 2 of Mound 3 a circular pit was outlined at .25 feet below the surface which had a diameter of 1.0 feet. This pit was shallow basin-shaped in cross section. It contained a secondary human cremation designated as Burial 2. In this same square and level there was a circular charcoal concentration and a grit-tempered elbow pipe.

During 1965, a test square was excavated between the conical mound (Mound 2) and the linear mound (Mound 3) for the purpose of finding the north-south feather edges of these mounds and to ascertain if there was a break in the east-west soil profile which would indicate that these mounds were built at different times.

The soil horizons did not show a break between Mounds 2 and 3 (Fig. 36) and it would seem that the A1b absent in the north wall was most probably removed for mound fill. The soils evidence from this five-foot square indicated that these two mounds were built at the same time. Subsequently two charcoal samples were submitted from Mounds 2 and 3 (WIS-171 and WIS-177) and they both produced a date of A.D. 880 ± 70.

Prior to clearing the underbrush and excavating the mounds to the south of Mound 3 it was decided that a series of five-foot

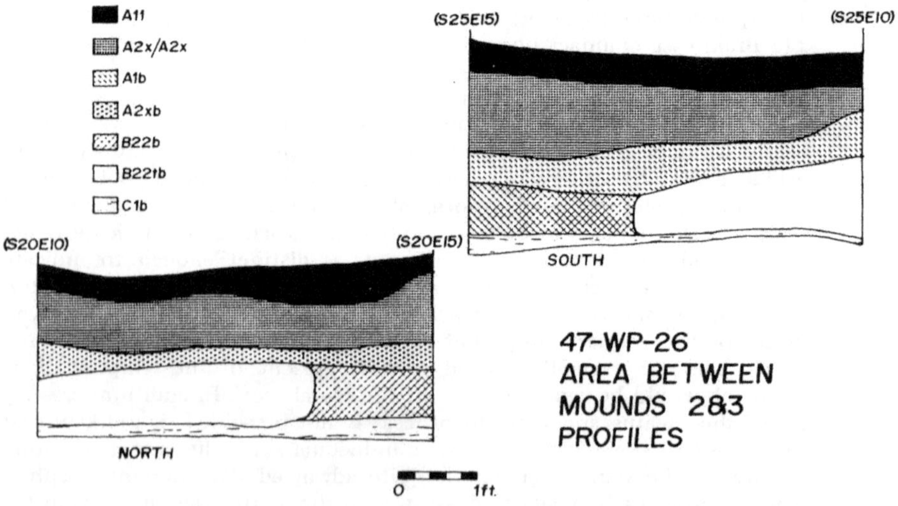

FIG. 36. Area between Mound 2 and Mound 3 profiles.

squares placed around Mounds 1 to 3 would aid us in seeking out possible habitation locations. Seven five-foot squares were excavated and while these squares were generally unproductive, one feature was uncovered:

Feature 5 was defined in and below the fragic A2x horizon. It was circular in outline and basin-shaped in cross section. The silty fill contained charcoal flecks, burned bone fragments, one stone fragment, and two grit-tempered sherd fragments.

East of Mound 3 in square S456W150 (Fig. 37) our third soil type, $\frac{3}{\text{A-0}}$, was exposed (Fig. 44). The profile of this square and of the soil body has the characteristics of a bisequal soil profile or a profile which exhibits two sequa, one overlying the other in a vertical sequence. The bisequal soil is believed to have been formed by genetic processes and lacks an A1 horizon (in the lower sequa) which would otherwise make it a buried soil profile or a paleosol. The bisequal profile at 47-Wp-26 appears to reflect changes in climate and vegetation: a Brown Podzolic (A1 and Bir horizons) over the lower sequa, which is a Gray Brown Podzolic. The Brown Podzolic reflects temperate to cool temperature, semi-arid to arid precipitation, and short grass vegetation; the Gray Brown Podzolic reflects temperate temperature, humid precipitation, and deciduous forest vegetation.

Mounds 17 and 18 (Fig. 31)

These two mounds appeared to be conjoined oval mounds with a connecting area 30 feet north-south, 14 feet east-west, and 1.5 feet high. Mound 18 is 26 feet east-west, 31 feet north-south, and two feet high at its center. In the center of this mound was a very large maple tree, approximately six feet in diameter, which prompted us to forego any excavations in this mound. Mound 17 was 50 feet long from east to west, 40 feet wide from north to south, and approximately two feet high. A 10 by 10 foot excavation was placed in the center of this mound and extended to a depth of 3.5 feet. Two features were uncovered and excavated in Mound 17.

Feature 6 was roughly rectangular in outline. It yielded 143 fragments of a Point Sauble Collared vessel, a proximal portion of a Durst Stemmed projectile point, one quartzite flake, two quartz flakes, four stone fragments, and charcoal. The vertical position of the charcoal so close to the surface and its association with the

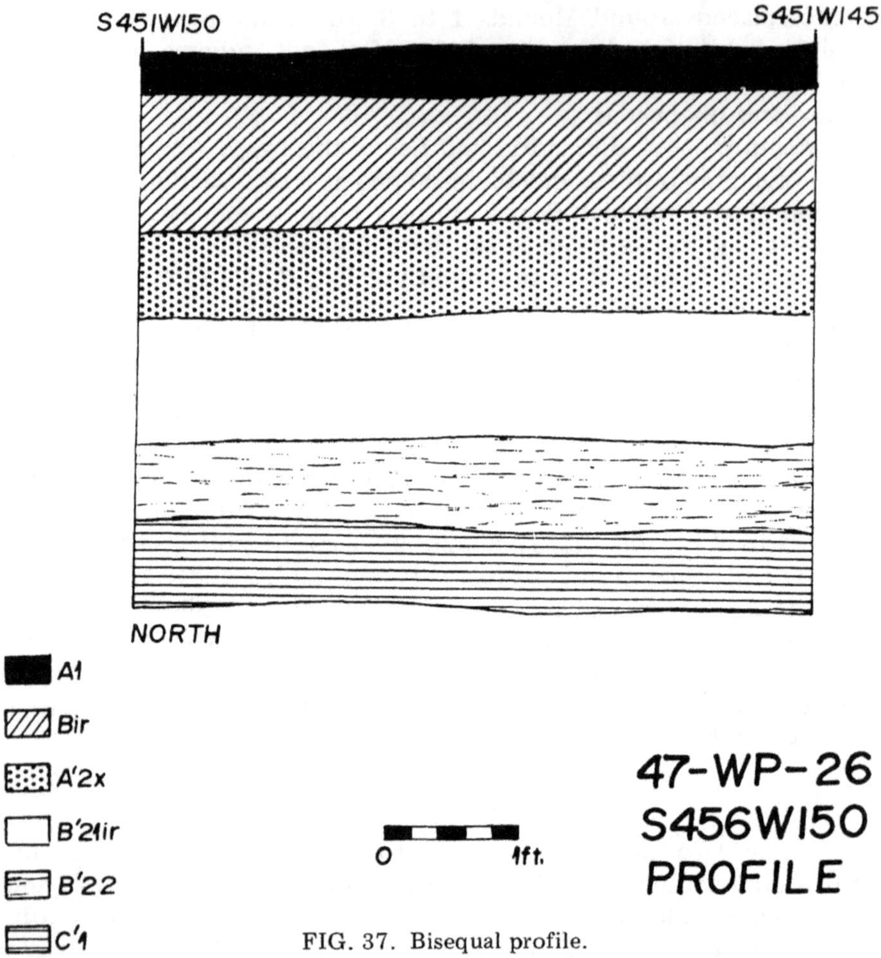

FIG. 37. Bisequal profile.

vessel fragments meant that great care had to be exercised to ascertain that the charcoal was not intruded through the mound surface. This sample was submitted along with the charcoal from Feature 8 of this mound in the hope that the rate of horizonation of the A2x/A2x mound fill could be ascertained; however, the charcoal yielded a modern date (WIS-205).

Feature 8 was circular in outline. The orifice of Feature 8 began in the A1b horizon and its steep straight walls extended through the A2xb. The sandy fill of this feature produced two grit-tempered, cord-marked body sherds and charcoal which yielded a date of A.D. 900 ± 70 (WIS-204).

Mound 19 (Fig. 31, 38)

Mound 19 was an oval mound 28 feet east to west, 36 feet north to south, and approximately 2.7 feet above the surrounding surface. Five five-foot squares were excavated in the approximate center of this mound through the sub-mound A2xb horizon, and one strata pit two feet wide by three feet deep was excavated below the A2xb horizon (Fig. 38). Two features were discovered and excavated in Mound 19.

Feature 7 was uncovered in the A2x/A2x mound fill horizon. This feature was irregular in outline and basin-shaped in cross section. It yielded two grit-tempered cord-marked body sherds; one knife; three charred bone fragments; eight chert flakes; eight grit-tempered sherd fragments; and two stone fragments.

Feature 10 was a small shallow basin of irregular outline. The pit was totally contained in the mound fill of the A2x/A2x and its fill yielded two rim sherds, two decorated body sherds, 34 grit-tempered body sherds, and one chert flake.

It would appear that both features 7 and 10 of Mound 19 were placed in the mound fill during construction.

Mound 20 (Fig. 31)

Mound 20 was a large oval mound whose maximum width is 40 feet north to south and 68 feet east to west. In the undisturbed portion of this mound, it was approximately 2.5 feet above the surrounding surface. The eastern 20 feet of Mound 20 have been nearly levelled for the clearing of a lane adjacent to the woodlot. Mound 20 was not excavated.

Mound 21 (Fig. 31)

Mound 21 was severely disturbed by the construction of the abandoned farm lane. Our measurements indicated that it was a small conical mound 18 feet in diameter and over 1.0 feet high. No attempt was made to test or excavate this mound.

Mound 22 (Fig. 31)

Mound 22 was disturbed by both the farm lane and over 50 years of cultivation, which has levelled the eastern portion of this mound. Mound 22 may have been a large oval mound. The remaining western portion has a maximum width of 44 feet and a maximum length of 47 feet. No testing or excavations were conducted.

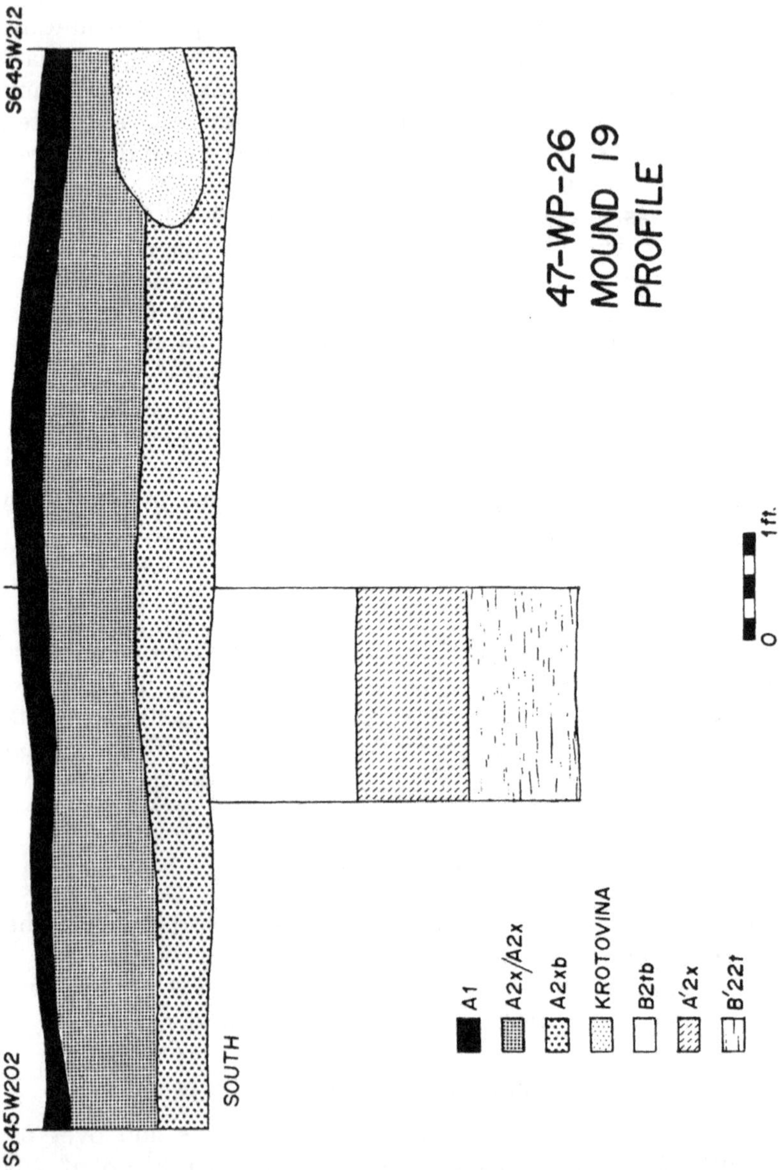

FIG. 38. Mound 19 profile.

Mound 23 (Figs. 31, 39)

Mound 23 was a conical mound 26 feet in diameter and 1.8 feet high. In the center of this mound there are several trees, of which one elm tree was estimated to be approximately 150 years old. One five-foot square was excavated and when a portion of Burial 3 was reached the square was expanded. Burial 3, a primary human cremation, intruded into the A1b and A2xb horizons (Fig. 39) and with the charcoal found in the pit and the A1b it is assumed that this burial was a partial or primary reason for the construction of this conical mound. While Burial 3 contained no cultural material, the charcoal from the pit and the A1b horizon yielded a date of A.D. 720 ± 55 (WIS-221).

Mounds 26 and 27 (Fig. 31)

These two mounds were in the area of the former farm lane and a great deal of their fill was removed and used to level the lane. Mound 26 was a conical mound 20 feet in diameter and approximately 1.0 feet high. Mound 27 has also been severely disturbed and while its length (72 feet) and width (24 feet) could be ascertained, its height could not be estimated. Neither conical Mound 26 nor linear Mound 27 was tested or excavated.

Mounds 24 and 25 (Fig. 31)

Mounds 24 and 25 presented unique problems to us during the field season. Mound 24 had a planimetric outline which does not lend itself to an effigy interpretation and in subsequent excavation of this mound it was found to be badly disturbed by Historic logging activities. Mound 25 appeared to be a conical mound; however, between and connecting these two mounds was a rise 250 feet long, three to five feet wide, and 1.5 to three feet high, which had a buried paleosol beneath it and which did not in any way appear to be a levee or embankment of a former stream or of a defensive earthwork. This rise was soil probed over its entire length and it showed strong evidence of containing artifacts in its A/B horizon as well as on the surface. An overall view of these two connected mounds prompts all sorts of mythological or problematical guesses as to its effigy shape, though none will be attempted here.

Mound 24 showed a high degree of disturbance as a result of removing a large tree plus a portion of its stump (a large portion remains) and rodent activity; Historic iron objects (plus a large logging

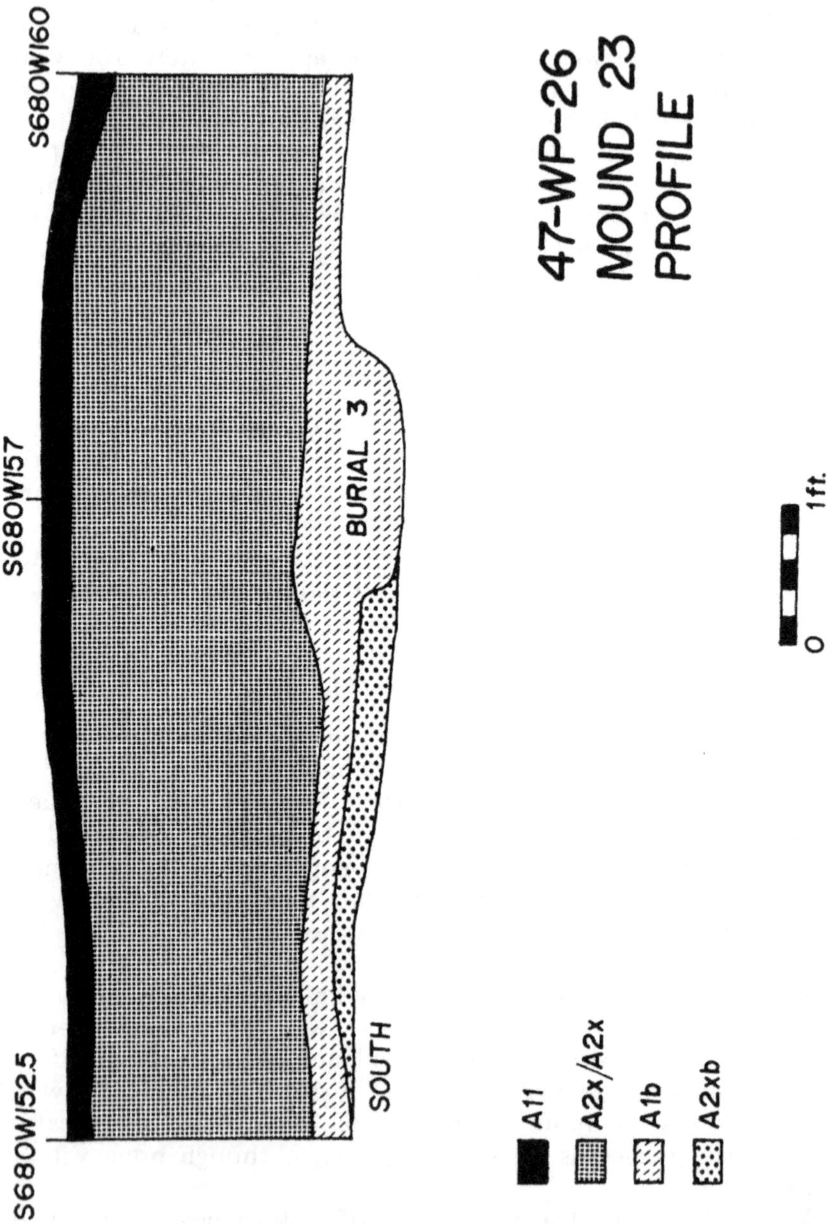

FIG. 39. Mound 23 profile.

chain) were recovered down to a depth of 2.7 feet below the surface. While numerous prehistoric objects were recovered, they will not be used in stratigraphic interpretations.

Mound 25 was oval in outline and it measured 37 feet north to south, 25 feet east to west, and approximately 1.7 feet above the surrounding surface. Three five-foot squares were excavated close to the approximate center. Mound 25 was attached to the rise extending southwest from Mound 24. Only one feature was uncovered in Mound 25.

Feature 13 was an oval, basin-shaped pit which had its orifice in the A1b horizon. Feature 13 was void of artifacts.

Mound 28 (Figs. 31, 40)

Mound 28 was the last mound excavated during the 1966 field season and it was considered to be the most productive mound because the mound fill and sub-mound soil horizons yeilded a large number of artifacts. It was a linear mound 46 feet long, 21 feet wide, and approximately 1.1 feet above the surrounding surface. Two features were uncovered and excavated in Mound 28.

Feature 26 was a small basin-shaped pit whose orifice began at the top of the B21irb horizon. The loamy sand fill contained charcoal flecks and one sandstone fragment.

Feature 38 was an oval-shaped pit. Feature 38 began below the A1b horizon and extended as a deep basin through the B21irb horizon. The black sandy fill and the 32 fire-cracked rocks recovered suggest that this pit was used as a fire pit prior to mound construction and it may antedate the mound. The fill of Feature 38 also yielded one charred bone fragment; one quartzite flake; two chert flakes; one grit-tempered, cord-marked body sherd; and nine *Helicodiscus parallelus* (Say) snails, (UWA-175).

Mound 29 (Fig. 31)

Mound 29 was a small conical mound 21 feet in diameter and approximately 1.5 feet high. Mound 29 was not tested or excavated.

Mound 30 (Fig. 31)

Mound 30 was an oval mound 28 feet long, 21 feet wide, and 1.5 feet high. It was not tested or excavated.

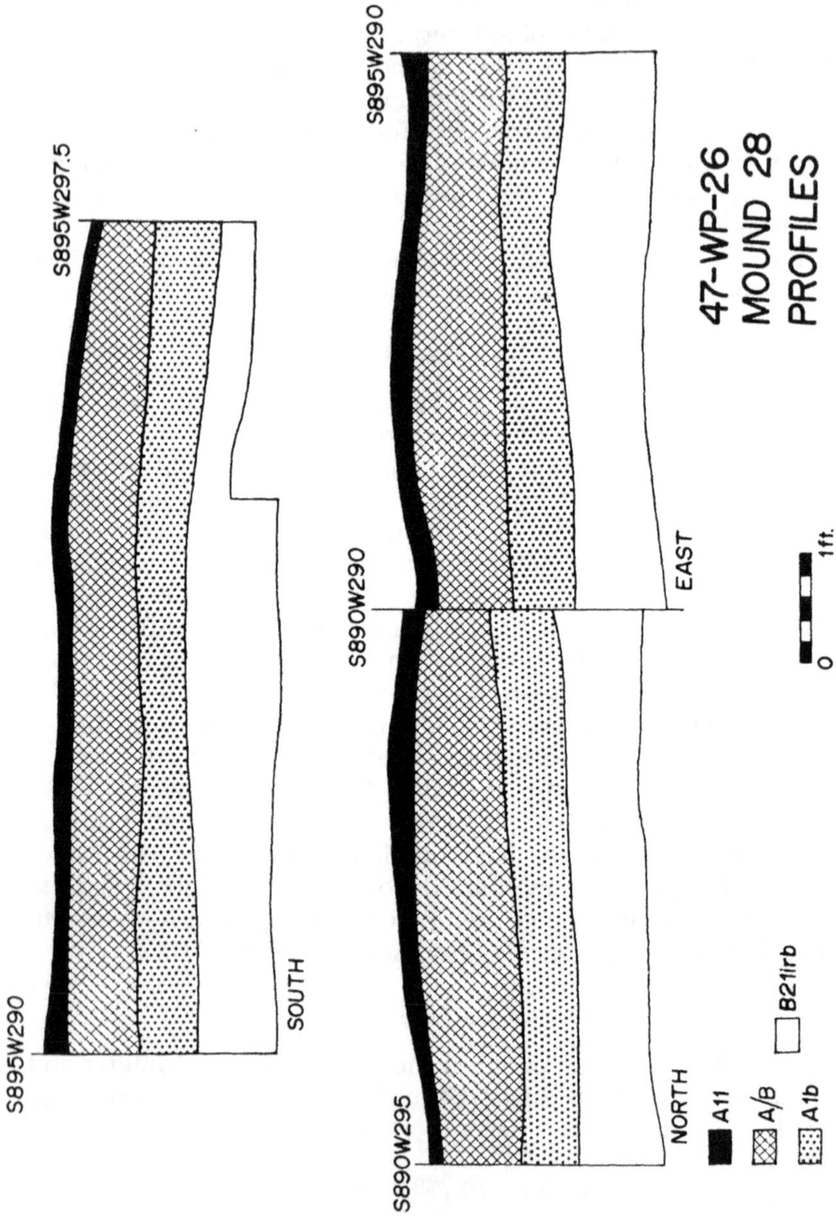

FIG. 40. Mound 28 profiles.

Mound 31 (Fig. 31)

Mound 31 was a linear mound 57 feet long, 22 feet wide, and 1.5 feet high. It was not tested or excavated.

Mound 32 (Fig. 31)

Mound 32 was an oval mound 39 feet long, 32 feet wide, and approximately 1.5 feet high. Mound 32 has been greatly disturbed by the landowners as they used the mound fill as a base subsoil during the construction of one of their silos. This mound was not excavated.

Mound 33 (Fig. 31)

Mound 33 appeared to be an effigy mound, possibly a bird or bear outline. Its maximum length was 46 feet and its maximum width was 21 feet. Mound 33 was over 1.5 feet high and was not tested or excavated.

The Village Area at 47-Wp-26

It was not until August 11, 1966, that we found our fourth soil body within the woodlot and one that exhibited characteristics of a buried grass solum sealed in by a Brown Forest or forest surface soil—the A11 had bleached sand grains and was only .3 foot thick. Below this A11 horizon was a buried A1bhir horizon .8 foot thick which was over a B21irb horizon. At the time of our testing it was thought that at one time there was a grass vegetation which was subsequently sealed in by a forest surface soil as a result of a change in climate and vegetation. However, it is possible that this large area composed of soil bodies $\frac{4}{\text{A-0}}$, $\frac{4}{\text{D-1}}$, and $\frac{4\text{A}}{\text{D-1}}$ was actually a village area which was cleared of forest vegetation and which had been overgrown with extended occupation grasses, the forest vegetation returning after the village was abandoned. Thus, the grass horizon which is now buried may have been maintained and possibly preferred by the prehistoric occupants of this village.

Our first excavated square, S995W395, produced two sherds from the surface A11 horizon and over 150 sherds plus lithic artifacts from the A1bhir horizon. Level 3, or the B21irb horizon, lacked artifacts. As additional squares were excavated (Fig. 41) we realized that we had reached the main habitation area of the site and that most of our efforts during our last three weeks would

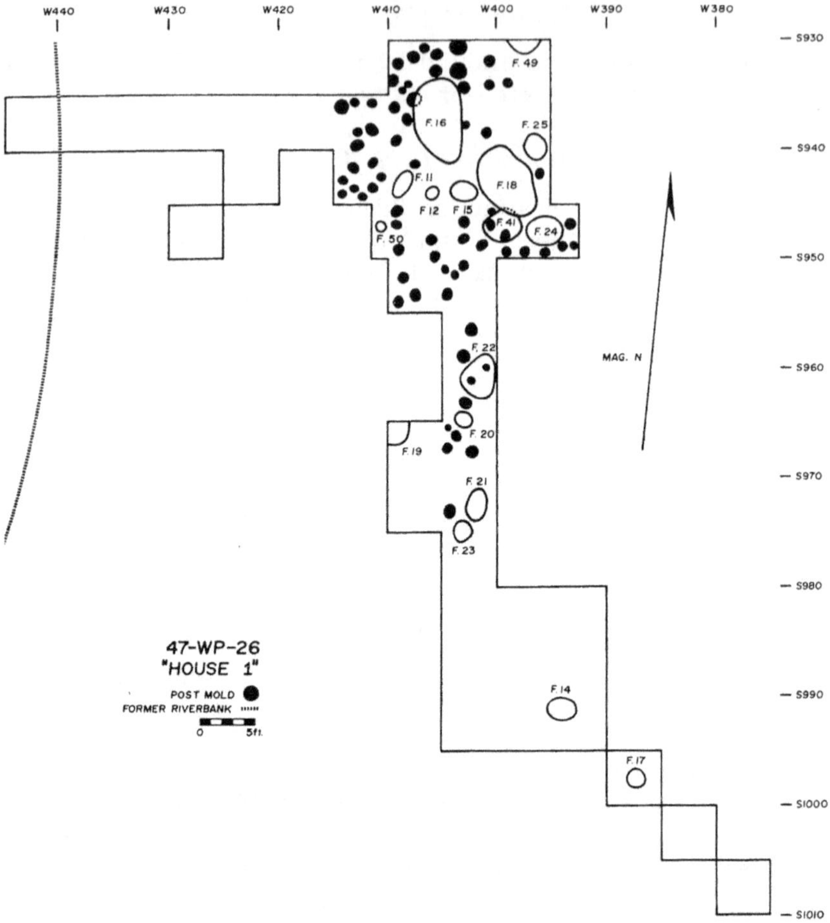

FIG. 41. Plan of "House 1."

have to be concentrated in this area. From a square adjacent to our initial square in the A1bhir horizon from .3 to .6 foot below the surface, there was a concentration of charcoal which appeared to be non-intrusive from the surface and which would perhaps yield information concerning the time of abandonment of the area and the subsequent natural reforestation. However, this sample yielded a late date, A.D. 1600 ± 70 (WIS-215). We then expanded our excavations in all four directions and as our excavations progressed numerous features and post-molds were defined. In order to place these post-molds and features in their proper context they will be presented out of numerical sequence and according to their south to north location as illustrated in Figures 41 and 42.

In a series of squares set off in a checker board toward Mound 25 the yield in the number of artifacts decreased from an average of 250 to a range between 75 and 100. In the first of these squares in the B21irb horizon, one sherd concentration was encountered which was designated as Feature 17.

Feature 17 consisted of the fragments of a Leland Cord-marked vessel which had been placed, orifice down, in a soils horizon which lacked other artifacts. A total of 128 vessel fragments were recovered and partially reconstructed (Pl. 38).

Feature 14 was an oval-shaped pit which began in the A1bhir horizon and was basin-shaped in cross section. Feature 14 yielded one rim sherd, five grit-tempered body sherds, two chert flakes, and two quartzite flakes.

The area between Feature 14 and Feature 23, while highly productive of artifacts, lacked both post-molds and features. Features and post-molds appeared to increase in intensity as squares were opened to the north. The post-molds outlined in Figure 41, designated "House 1," appear to defy any house or structural outline or pattern. A total of 71 post-molds were outlined in this area and they appeared to originate at a depth of 1.0 to 1.3 feet below the surface or below the buried A1bhir horizon. It is unfortunate that all of these post-molds were not excavated; it was only on the last day of operation that 21 post-molds were excavated. The planimetric view of these 71 post-molds yields little of interpretive value other than the fact that more than one structure existed at this location. This interpretation might have been drastically altered had the depth of each post been ascertained and then plotted to see if any patterns would emerge. Of the 21 posts excavated only 15 posts had their lowest depth recorded; two went to a depth of 1.8 feet; nine between 2.1 and 2.6 feet; and two between 2.9 and 3.1 feet. Thus, the majority appear to have extended below the A1bhir for a depth of between .7 and 1.3 feet, and as they may have originated at the top of the A1bhir or within the A1bhir, these posts could have been placed as deep as 1.5 to 2.1 feet. In two instances, Features 22 and 41, posts did superimpose the features, extending to a depth of 2.1 feet and 2.3 feet respectively.

Our excavations probably reached the western limits of these post-molds, as can be seen from the 30-foot trench extending beyond the former river bank. One reason for this distribution may be that to the west the buried B horizon was similar to the hard red clay found beneath the fragic A2x horizon in the rest of the woodlot. The post-molds from just north of Feature 22 and extending southward may represent a portion of a separate house structure and not a part of the main post-mold concentration. However, any reconstruction of this area which is designated as "House 1" must await further excavations expanding to the north and east from our squares.

Feature 23 (Fig. 41) was a circular pit which extended from the base of the A1bhir horizon into the B21irb horizon. The sandy fill of Feature 23 yielded two rim sherds, 17 grit-tempered sherds, 36 sherdlets, 11 chert flakes, two quartzite flakes, one basalt flake, and one stone fragment.

Feature 21 (Fig. 41) was an oval pit and its irregular cross section extended well into the B21irb horizon. Feature 21 yielded one rim sherd, three grit-tempered body sherds, one quartz flake, three chert flakes, and six stone fragments.

Feature 19 (Fig. 41). The orifice of Feature 19 was below the top of the B21irb horizon. This feature was only partially excavated and in outline it appeared to be circular. This shallow basin-shaped pit yielded one bone fragment, one quartzite flake, four chert flakes, and one stone fragment.

Feature 20 (Fig. 41) was totally confined to the B21irb horizon. This shallow, basin-shaped pit contained only snail fragments.

Feature 22 (Fig. 41). Feature 22 was a large pit oval in outline and shallow basin-shaped in cross section. The sandy fill of Feature 22 yielded one rim sherd, three grit-tempered body sherds, three decorated body sherds, one projectile point fragment, 45 sherd fragments, one basalt flake, three quartz flakes, one quartzite flake, 20 chert flakes, two stone fragments, and five *Helicodiscus parallelus* (Say) snails (UWA-173).

The following 10 features, barring Feature 12 which was a post-mold, appear to have been associated with the major concentration of post-molds comprising the structure or structures designated as "House 1." Each of the features was defined at a depth of 1.0 to 1.4 feet below the surface, in the B21irb horizon which in this 20 by 15 foot square was the only area to yield an abundant number of artifacts.

Feature 11 (Fig. 41) was rectangular in outline and had a shallow basin-shaped cross section. The sandy fill of Feature 11 yielded one grit-tempered, cord-marked body sherd, two charred bone fragments, three rim sherds, one decorated body sherd, two basalt flakes, two chert flakes, two quartz flakes, six sherds, and eight stone fragments.

Feature 12 (Fig. 41) turned out to be a post-mold which contained one grit-tempered body sherd, one chert flake, and one stone fragment.

Feature 15 (Fig. 41) was a shallow basin-shaped pit. The sandy fill yielded three grit-tempered body sherds, one basalt flake, one quartz flake, two chert flakes, 16 sherdlets, and four stone fragments.

Feature 16 (Fig. 41) was a large oval-shaped pit with a deep basin-shaped cross section. In its original construction or excavation it cut through and superimposed one post-mold which extended beyond the basal depth of Feature 16, i.e., 2.1 feet below the surface. Feature 16 contained one copper awl, charred bone fragments, 10 rim sherds, two decorated body sherds, 46 grit-tempered, cord-marked body sherds, 223 sherd fragments, 120 stone fragments, 47 chert flakes, nine quartzite flakes, 31 quartz flakes, two *Helicodiscus parallelus* (Say) snails, and one *Discus cronkhitei* (Newcomb) snail (UWA-170).

Feature 18 (Fig. 41) was a large oval-shaped pit. Feature 18 partially superimposed Feature 41; however, due to the differences in the pit fill of each feature the excavations were accomplished with little mixing of the two. The sandy fill of Feature 18 yielded one copper knife, one copper awl, one utilized quartz fragment, two quartz scrapers, one chert implement fragment, one chert scraper, 56 grit-tempered, cord-marked body sherds, five rim sherds, charred bone, 212 sherd fragments, 27 quartz flakes, 13 quartzite flakes, 38 chert flakes, charcoal flecks, 68 stone fragments, and one *Helicodiscus parallelus* (Say) snail (UWA-169).

Feature 41 (Fig. 41) was superimposed on its northern edge by approximately .5 foot of Feature 18. Feature 41 was a fire pit which was oval in outline. It had a distinctive black fired sandy fill which contained 93 fire-cracked rocks, five chert flakes, four quartz flakes, and one quartzite flake.

Feature 24 (Fig. 41) was an oval-shaped pit. The sandy fill of Feature 24 yielded one rim sherd, three grit-tempered body sherds, 20 sherd fragments, two quartz flakes, two quartzite flakes, 11 chert flakes, and 10 stone fragments.

Feature 25 (Fig. 41) was an oval-shaped pit and in cross section it was basin-shaped. The sandy fill of Feature 25 yielded one rim sherd, five body sherds, 64 sherd fragments, eight chert flakes, one quartzite flake, six quartz flakes, bone fragments, and six stone fragments.

Feature 49 (Fig. 41) was defined at 1.3 feet below the surface, but it remained unexcavated.

Feature 50 (Fig. 41) was a concentration of one reconstructable vessel consisting of 153 fragments recovered from .3 to 1.3 feet below the surface.

In the area of "House 1" several squares were excavated below the B21irb horizon to determine the depth of the artifact deposit, the existence of stratigraphy other than that of the buried grass type soil, and the location of features below this horizon. The artifact yield from these buried B horizons was very limited and of the same variety as those recovered from the A1bhir horizon and the fill of the features. Trenches were also extended to the west and in checker-board fashion to the east, and again our yield from the A1bhir diminished and the B21irb horizons were nearly void of artifacts. In soil probing to the north of House 1 for approximately 150 feet, the buried horizons were seen to continue and it was decided to continue our excavations in a northerly direction. While our excavations were confined to the area south of the S820 line (Fig. 42), we did excavate a series of test squares up to the S700 line which still produced a high number of artifacts from the A1bhir, and with subsequent soil mapping we were able to ascertain that the paleosol extended from the S700 to the S1300 line (Fig. 60).

The area designated as Houses 2 and 3 is almost exactly similar to the House 1 area in that there again was a thin (.3 foot) A11 forest soil at the surface which contained very few artifacts; a thick (.8 foot) horizon which was buried and which contained a large number of artifacts; and beneath this undisturbed horizon 13 features, two semi-subterranean houses, and six features in the floors of those houses were defined.

The features and houses in this area will be presented below as in the House 1 area, from south to north. It should be stressed that there remains a considerable area to be excavated around and between both the House 1 area and the area of Houses 2 and 3.

Feature 28 (Fig. 42) was a shallow basin-shaped pit which had its orifice at the top of the B21irb horizon. In outline the feature was circular, and the fill was a very fine loamy sand. At the base of the feature there were two rodent burrows which did not appear to extend upward through the pit fill. Feature 28 contained bone fragments, one basalt flake, one quartz flake, and one chert flake.

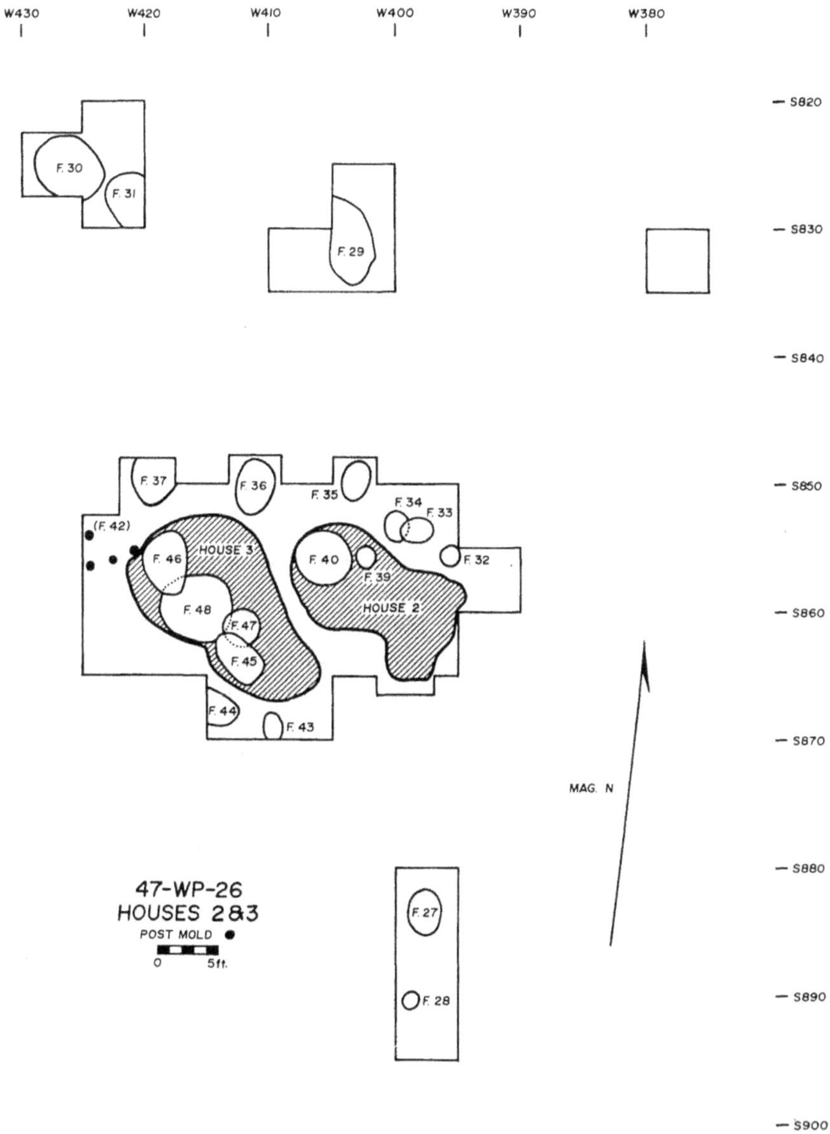

FIG. 42. Plans of House 2 and House 3.

Feature 27 (Fig. 42) was a deep basin-shaped pit beginning at the base of the A1bhir horizon, circular in outline. The sandy fill of Feature 27 yielded bone fragments, two quartzite scrapers, two quartzite flakes, three basalt flakes, 29 quartz flakes, 44 chert flakes, 92 sherd fragments, and 12 stone fragments.

Directly north of Houses 2 and 3 there was a series of six features (Nos. 32-37) which trended in an east to west direction and which are believed to be associated with the house structures. The orifices of these features were directly below the A1bhir horizon and all were less than four feet in diameter, most of them less than two feet in diameter.

Feature 32 was a small circular pit with a shallow basin shape. The loamy sand fill of Feature 32 contained one Triangular projectile point, nine shell-tempered body sherds, one quartz flake, three chert flakes, charcoal flecks, and five stone fragments.

Feature 33 (Fig. 42) was a small oval-shaped pit which superimposed Feature 34. In cross section this feature gave the impression that it was a post-mold because it extended from 1.2 to 3.7 feet below the surface. When it was excavated the orifice measured 1.8 feet in width; the width of its base narrowed to .5 foot. However, Features 33 and 34 could be (and were) separated according to their outline and cross section. The sandy fill of Feature 33 yielded bone fragments, two rim sherds, one copper fragment, one decorated body sherd, 14 shell-tempered body sherds, 10 grit-tempered, cord-marked body sherds, one modified stone fragment, three quartzite flakes, one basalt flake, 11 chert flakes, 99 grit-tempered sherdlets, seven stone fragments, and charcoal which yielded a date of A.D. 860 ± 55 (WIS-219).

Feature 34 (Fig. 42) was a circular pit which began at the top of the B21irb horizon. Although Feature 34 was superimposed by Feature 33, the sandy fill was of a firmer consistency than that of Feature 33, which allowed for easy separation of the artifacts. The fill of Feature 34 yielded bone fragments, one Triangular chert projectile point, four decorated body sherds, two rim sherds, 13 grit-tempered, cord-marked body sherds, 17 chert flakes, five quartzite flakes, eight quartz flakes, 107 grit-tempered sherd fragments, 20 stone fragments, and a small amount of charcoal.

Feature 35 (Fig. 42) was an oval-shaped pit which was defined just below the A1bhir horizon. The loamy sand fill of Feature 35 yielded bone fragments, a copper awl, a worked chert flake, four rim sherds, two decorated body sherds, five grit-tempered body sherds, one quartzite flake, 10 quartz flakes, 20 chert flakes, 64 grit-tempered sherd fragments, and charcoal flecks.

Feature 36 (Fig. 42) was an oval pit which was defined at the bottom of the A1bhir horizon. The sandy loam fill of Feature 36 yielded the following artifacts: one decorated body sherd, one quartzite end scraper, two shell-tempered body sherds, 13 grit-tempered body sherds, bone fragments, two quartzite flakes, nine chert flakes, 16 quartz flakes, 20 stone fragments, 143 grit-tempered sherd fragments, three shell-tempered body sherd fragments, and charcoal flecks.

Feature 37 (Fig. 42) was located in two squares and only one-half of the feature was excavated. From the planimetric outline of the portion excavated Feature 37 appeared to be a circular pit approximately 3.5 feet in diameter. The outline of Feature 37 was defined at the base of the A1bhir horizon. The sandy fill yielded bone fragments, four rim sherds, one decorated body sherd, 35 grit-tempered body sherds, 51 grit-tempered sherd fragments, 38 chert flakes, 12 quartzite flakes, 39 quartz flakes, and 54 stone fragments.

Feature 42 was actually a post-mold which had a larger outline at the top (the base of the A1bhir) and it was only with the removal of .2 foot that its actual outline was ascertained. The post-hole was .6 foot in diameter and extended with straight side walls from .8 foot to 2.5 feet below the surface. The fill of this post-hole yielded four grit-tempered, cord-marked body sherds, three chert flakes, one quartz flake, one quartzite flake, 15 grit-tempered sherd fragments, and four stone fragments.

The three other post-molds south of Feature 42 and west of House 3 were not excavated; however, they were soil probed and they did contain a dark brown fill which extended to a depth of 2.5 feet below the surface. The purpose of these posts is unknown for there is not a sufficient number to ascertain if they represent a portion of another house. It is quite possible that these post-molds were at one time posts that provided a screen to the northwest winds; however, no real entrance could be found leading into House 3 at this area. The use of a screened opening has been recorded for House 2 at Aztalan (Wittry and Baerreis, 1958:67-69); however, any comparisons with Aztalan with the idea that it may be a wind screen rest on very limited information.

Feature 43 (Fig. 42) was a small oval pit south of House 3. The orifice of Feature 43 was at the base of the A1bhir horizon. The fine-grained loamy sand of Feature 43 contained no artifacts.

Feature 44 (Fig. 42) was defined in the immediate area of Houses 2 and 3. Feature 44 was an oval-shaped pit, of which approximately two-thirds was excavated due to the extent of backfill covering the unexcavated portion. It was shallow basin-shaped in cross section. The loamy sand fill yielded two grit-tempered sherd fragments, three quartz flakes, five chert flakes, and four stone fragments.

House 2 (Fig. 42). The area designated as House 2 was first noticed in clearing and defining features 32 to 36. At that time the northern edge was defined and it was noted that its size did not conform to the pattern established for the previous 37 features at the site. We removed a total of 13 five-foot squares and the full outline, and part of House 3, was drawn in. The area was designated as House 2 prior to excavation. The sandy loam fill of House 2 was excavated from a depth of 1.0 to 1.9 feet below the surface. During this excavation the walls on all four sides slanted inward until we reached a depth of 1.9 feet where the soil was quite firm and compact. Believing that this might be the house floor, we defined two features, one of which was above the floor (.3 foot) and dug into the slanting north wall. The artifacts from this upper house fill were bagged and catalogued separately and they consisted of bone fragments, land snails (one *Triodopsis albolabris* [Say], five *Anguispira alternata* [Say] [UWA-184]), one copper bead, 25 rim sherds, five decorated body sherds, 40 grit-tempered, cord-marked body sherds, three shell-tempered body sherds, two clay fragments, 59 stone fragments, 131 chert flakes, 71 quartz flakes, 18 quartzite flakes, four basalt flakes, 583 grit-tempered sherdlets, one iron concretion, and charcoal, which because of its small quantity was combined with the charcoal beneath the house floor. This charcoal sample yielded a date of A.D. 775 ± 55 (WIS-224). Prior to the excavation of the house floor and the remainder of the house fill, Features 39 and 40 were excavated and kept separate from the rest of the house artifacts.

Feature 39 was a circular, shallow basin-shaped pit. The outline and fill were quite distinct in consistency and color from that of the house fill. The feature yielded bone fragments, one chert flake, seven grit-tempered sherds, and one stone fragment.

Feature 40 (Fig. 42) was a very large circular pit. This deep straight-sided pit had a loamy sand fill which could be easily separated from the sub-floor house fill. The fill of Feature 40 yielded the following artifacts: charred and uncharred bone fragments, one copper pendant, 11 rim sherds, two worked chert flakes, one worked quartz flake, 37 grit-tempered, cord-marked body sherds, 313 grit-tempered sherd fragments, 99 stone fragments, 20 quartzite flakes, 39 quartz flakes, 100 chert flakes, and a charcoal sample which yielded a date of A.D. 930 ± 55 (WIS-203).

With the excavation of Features 39 and 40 the house floor and the remainder of the house fill were removed to a depth of 2.4 feet below the surface. The house walls continued to slope gently toward the house basin. The final overall dimensions of House 2 were: 14.2 feet long, 8.3 feet wide, and 1.4 feet deep (see Fig. 43). The fill from this floor and lower sub-floor yielded two bone fragments, land snails (62 living *Helicodiscus parallelus* [Say], and one *Zonitoides arboreus* [Say] [UWA-190]), 15 rim sherds, three decorated body sherds, two chert scrapers, 37 grit-tempered, cord-marked body sherds, three basalt flakes, 57 chert flakes, 22 quartz flakes, 18 quartzite flakes, 133 sherd fragments, and 20 stone fragments. Along the northeastern edge of House 2 there appeared to be an extension which was thought to be an entrance way. During the excavation it was noted that this projection had fill which was similar to that of the house and that once the house floor had been reached, this projection or entrance way did not extend any deeper.

House 3 (Fig. 42) was recognized in the field as a possible semi-subterranean house basin prior to excavation and it was designated as House 3 and excavated in a manner similar to that of House 2. The upper house fill extended from 1.1 to 1.8 feet below the surface. The fill was screened and the artifacts were kept separate from the floor and sub-floor fill. The house walls of this basin, as with House 2, again sloped inward to a compact living floor which was more dense than the fill above and in which four features were defined. The loamy sand fill above the floor yielded bone fragments, an animal canine tooth, 15 rim sherds, nine decorated body sherds, 193 grit-tempered, cord-marked body sherds, four shell-tempered body sherds, two clay fragments, one utilized stone, four implement fragments, one polished stone fragment, 11 worked chert flakes, two utilized quartz flakes, two utilized quartzite flakes, 471 grit-tempered sherd fragments, 246 stone fragments, 25 quartzite flakes, 18 basalt flakes, 111 chert flakes, and 55 quartz flakes. At the living floor of House 3 there were four features (Nos. 45 to 48) which had their orifice at this level and which were excavated and kept separate from the rest of the house fill.

Feature 45 (Fig. 42) was a large oval-shaped pit which was basin-shaped in cross section. Upon excavation it was noted that Feature 45 had been originally dug through and superimposed on Feature 47. The very fine-grained sandy loam fill yielded one quartz scraper, one worked chert flake, one chert spall, bone fragments, 10 quartz flakes, four quartzite flakes, 26 chert flakes, nine stone fragments, and a large quantity of charcoal. When the abundance of charcoal was noticed, each fragment was carefully removed and immediately placed in aluminum foil. The great care taken was prompted by the belief that this sample would aid in dating of the house floors and at least Features 45 and 47. However, this sample yielded a date of 5520 B.C. ± 90 (WIS-222).

Feature 46 (Fig. 42) was a large oval-shaped pit which intruded upon and partially superimposed Feature 48. Feature 46 was basin-shaped in cross section. The sandy loam fill had been recently disturbed by a rodent and from this disturbance, bones were removed belonging to the rodent. The following artifacts were recovered from Feature 46: three rim sherds, one quartzite projectile point base, one worked quartzite flake, 22 cord-marked, grit-tempered body sherds, 50 grit-tempered sherds, one quartzite flake, 10 quartz flakes, 12 chert flakes, 23 stone fragments, and a large quantity of charcoal which yielded a date of A.D. 770 ± 55 (WIS-223).

Feature 47 (Fig. 42) was superimposed by Feature 45 and in turn partially superimposed the eastern edge of Feature 48. Feature 47 was a circular pit which was defined slightly below the house floor level as its sandy loam fill was similar in color to the house floor. The fill of Feature 47 yielded one grit-tempered body sherd, one copper fragment, three chert flakes, and 12 stone fragments.

Feature 48 (Fig. 42) was partially superimposed on its eastern edge by Feature 47 and on its western edge by Feature 46. Feature 48 was a large oval pit which yielded one sherd, six chert flakes, four quartzite flakes, and bone fragments. It is most likely that some artifacts included within the sub-floor fill are actually from this feature.

The sub-floor fill of House 3 extended from 1.9 feet to an average depth of 2.9 feet below the surface; however, along the western edge of the house (Fig. 43) the original house basin was 3.65 feet below the surface. The sandy loam fill yielded the following: bone fragments, 17 rim sherds, one decorated body sherd, two clay fragments, two quartzite diminutive scrapers, one quartz end scraper, one chert drill, four worked chert flakes, one worked quartzite flake, 32 grit-tempered, cord-marked body sherds, 131 stone fragments, 112 grit-tempered sherd fragments, 157 chert flakes, 14 quartzite flakes, 56 quartz flakes, and charcoal which yielded a date of A.D. 290 ± 65 (WIS-218). Upon completion of

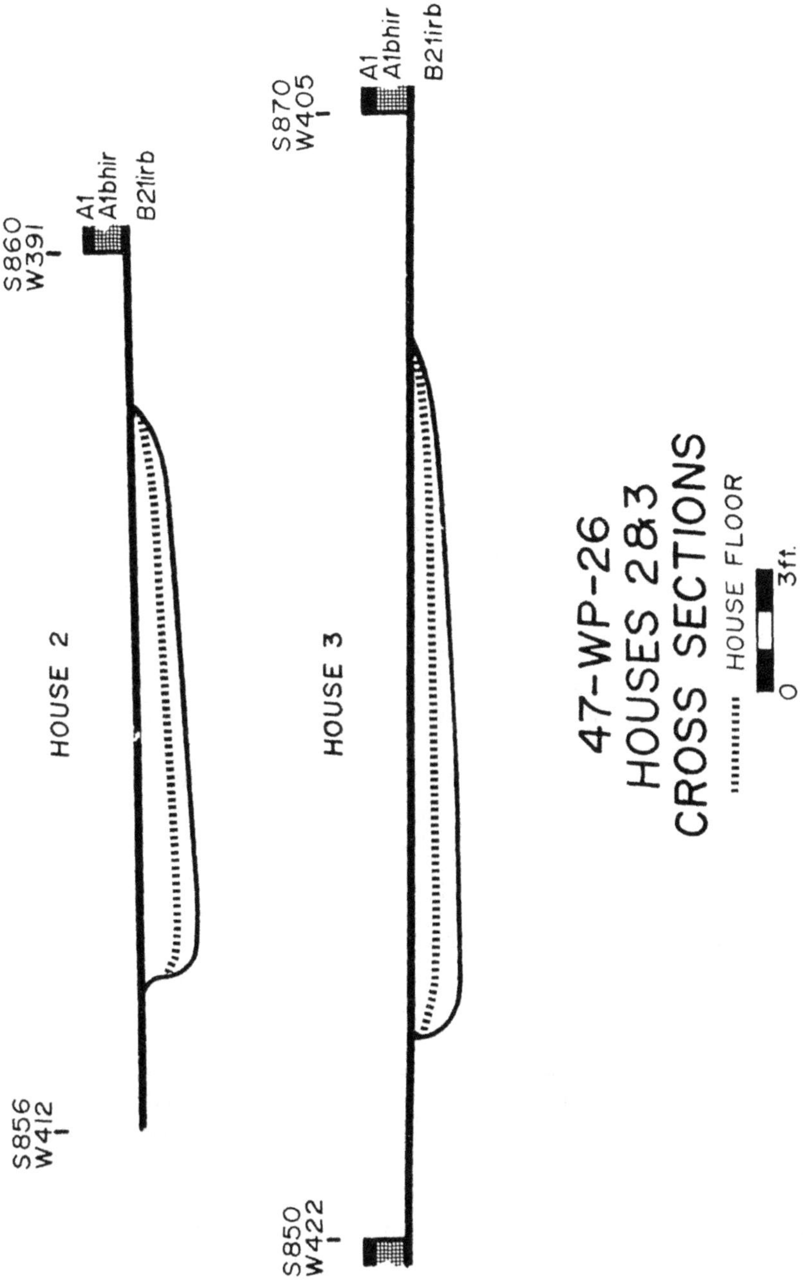

FIG. 43. Cross-sections of House 2 and House 3.

the excavation of House 3, its final overall dimensions were: 17.1 feet long and 10.9 feet wide. The average depth from orifice to basin was 1.8 feet; however, along its western edge it did extend to a depth of 2.55 feet.

To the north of the Houses 2 and 3 area we excavated seven five-foot squares (Fig. 42) which contained three features.

Feature 29. The northwest corner of this feature was not excavated due to a very large maple tree; however, more than four-fifths of this oval pit was removed. The pit was defined at the base of the A1bhir horizon. It was a straight walled pit with a flat bottom. The fill of Feature 29 yielded one land snail (*Triodopsis albolabris* [Say] [UWA-178]), bone fragments, 6 rim sherds, one chert Triangular projectile point, four decorated body sherds, one clay fragment, 35 grit-tempered, cord-marked body sherds, 14 stone fragments, one basalt flake, 53 quartz flakes, 14 quartzite flakes, 77 chert flakes, 167 grit-tempered sherdlets, and charcoal which yielded a date of A.D. 890 ± 60 (WIS-206).

Feature 30 (Fig. 42) was a large oval pit, basin-shaped in cross section. The sandy fill yielded bone and shell fragments, five rim sherds, 37 grit-tempered body sherds, 13 stone fragments, four basalt flakes, 49 chert flakes, 13 quartzite flakes, 44 quartz flakes, 106 sherd fragments, and charcoal which dated at A.D. 670 ± 75 (WIS-217).

Feature 31 (Fig. 42). Feature 31 was defined at the base of the A1bhir horizon and it was a basin-shaped pit. The sandy fill of Feature 31 yielded charred bone fragments, two rim sherds, four worked chert flakes, six grit-tempered body sherds, 30 grit-tempered sherd fragments, six quartz flakes, one quartzite flake, 13 chert flakes, and 27 stone fragments.

Soils at 47-Wp-26

There were four main soil series at 47-Wp-26 (Fig. 44): (1) a clayey soil with a fragic platy A2x horizon; (2) a soil with a Brown Podzolic over a Gray Brown Podzolic; (3) a sandy soil similar to the soil at the Bigelow site; and (4) a buried solum (A1bhir and B21irb horizons) sealed in by a forest surface soil (A11 horizon). The grass vegetation horizon (A1bhir) soil bodies marked the confines of a village whose occupants appeared to have cleared a portion of the forest, which allowed grasses to invade the area. When the village was abandoned, the forest vegetation returned. A series of charcoal samples from features, house fill, or house

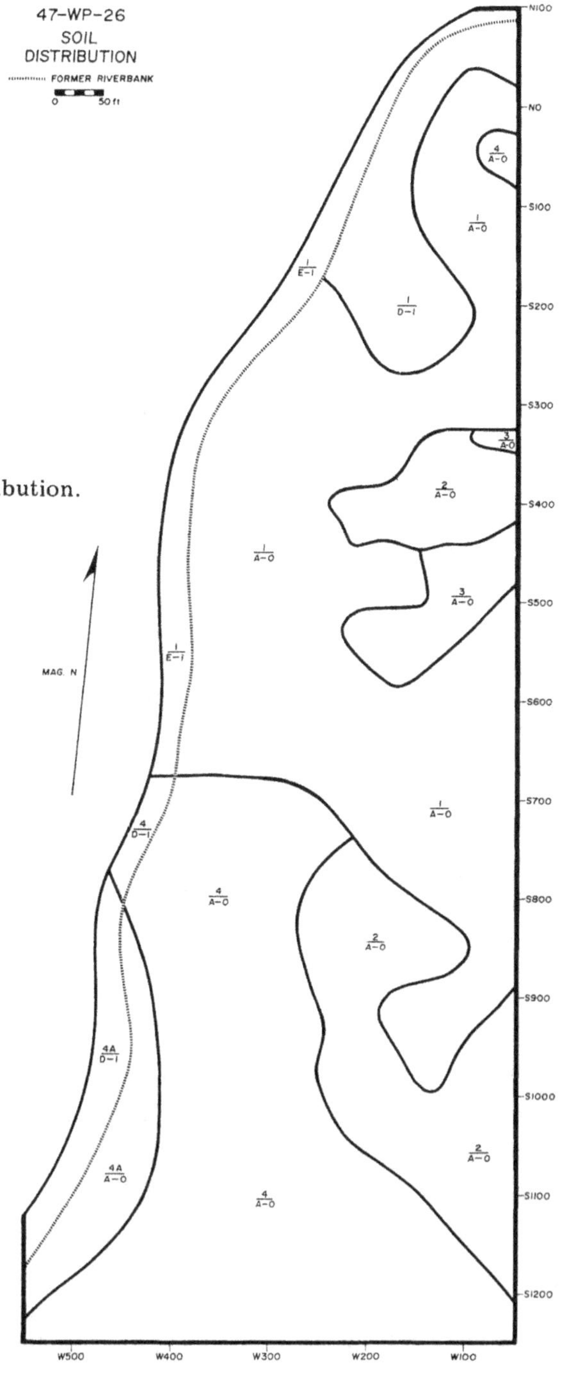

FIG. 44. 47-Wp-26 soil distribution.

features (all of which had their orifice at the bottom of the A1bhir horizon at one foot below the surface) yielded a series of seven C-14 dates (WIS-203; 204; 206; 219; 224; 223; and 217) which indicate that between A.D. 670 and A.D. 930, or circa 1,280 to 1,020 years ago, a grass surface horizon (A1bhir) developed. Subsequent to the village occupation, or within the last 1,020 years, a forest A11 horizon developed and sealed in the grass solum.

One natural rise at the Sanders site (Area 9) yielded temporal information concerning B horizon development. This horizon was of sands and it is a weakly developed B2ir horizon which occurred within approximately 940 years (WIS-207). Four mounds from this site have yielded an approximate range of between 1,230 and 1,050 years for the development of mound fill A2x/A2x and mound surface A11 horizons (WIS-171; 177; 204; and 221); non-mound village soils indicate that the present surface forest A11 horizon developed in approximately 1,020 years.

The 200-year difference in time for the B horizon development between the Bigelow and Sanders sites could well be due to morphology or to the degree of horizon development; that is, the B2ir horizon at Sanders was judged to be very weakly developed. There were no A2 horizons at the Bigelow site and no horizons having fragic characteristics; therefore, no comparisons can be made. However, the range of 1,230 to 1,050 years seems to be reasonable for the Sanders site. There is some disagreement in the terminal dates for the A12 and A11 forest horizons; if one natural rise (Area K) were to be omitted from the Bigelow range, the range would be 1,280 to 830 years. There is no reason, however, to omit this natural rise, as the aeolian activity occurred after the occupation of this area. Thus, the temporal range for the development of either an A12 or A11 forest horizon appears to be from 1,280 to 580 years. The aeolian activity with its A-C profiles is unique to the Bigelow site and the temporal period appears to be well established. Finally, there seems to be excellent agreement on the temporal range for the development of a grass surface horizon at these two sites.

At the time of Parsons' analysis there were only a limited number of radiocarbon dates to work with (1962: Table 1); however, there are several points of agreement concerning both of our results and there seems to be some expansion in temporal ranges. Both bodies of evidence indicate that color and textural B horizons may be formed in 1,000 years or less but that structural

B horizons need more than 1,000 years to form. The platy structure of A2 horizons becomes evident in 1,000 years; however, the fragic character of the A2x horizons at the Sanders site indicates that this character aids in the formation of medium to coarse platy structure expression throughout the horizon.

The *maximum* degree of expression of A11 and A12 horizons in 1,000 years (Parsons, 1962) tends to be supported by the Wisconsin data. Information from the Bigelow site (47-Pt-29) suggests that this horizonation can occur in a minimum range of 830 to 530 years and, with aeolian activity, in less than 100 years. The data from Wisconsin also indicate that A1 horizons of soils formed under a grass vegetation can occur between 1,280 to 1,020 years.

There appears, therefore, to be little in the line of disparities between the data from Wisconsin and Iowa except in the minimum time needed for the formation of an A12 or A11 horizon. Parsons based his mound chronology on soils data from both the field and laboratory phases of his study on horizon differentiation. The information derived from his study and this report gives every indication of *supporting* his mound chronology interpretations (Hurley, 1971).

SANDERS SITE 3: 47-Wp-70

The area designated as 47-Wp-70 is located in a cultivated field just south of 47-Wp-26. At the time of the 1965 survey, two rises were considered to be separate from the Effigy Mound component in the woodlot. Surface collections attributed to this area were considered to belong to an "Archaic" stage and they were codified separately. A new TBM (Stake 0.0 for 47-Wp-70 and grid locality S1275W475 within the 47-Wp-26 sequence) was set up in order that a cross-shaped grid would cross both rises (Fig. 45). Although all features, burials, houses, and artifacts were numbered consecutively and separately from those of 47-Wp-26, it soon became apparent that this location lacked an Archaic component and was in reality an extension of Sanders Site 1. The site code and catalogue numbers of 47-Wp-70 are being retained in order that the grid localities will not be confused between 47-Wp-26 and Wp-70. However, the prehistoric occupation at 47-Wp-70 belongs to the Effigy Mound component at 47-Wp-26.

As work was initiated on the west rise at Wp-70, one square was begun in the center of the east rise. At a depth of 1.1 to 1.6

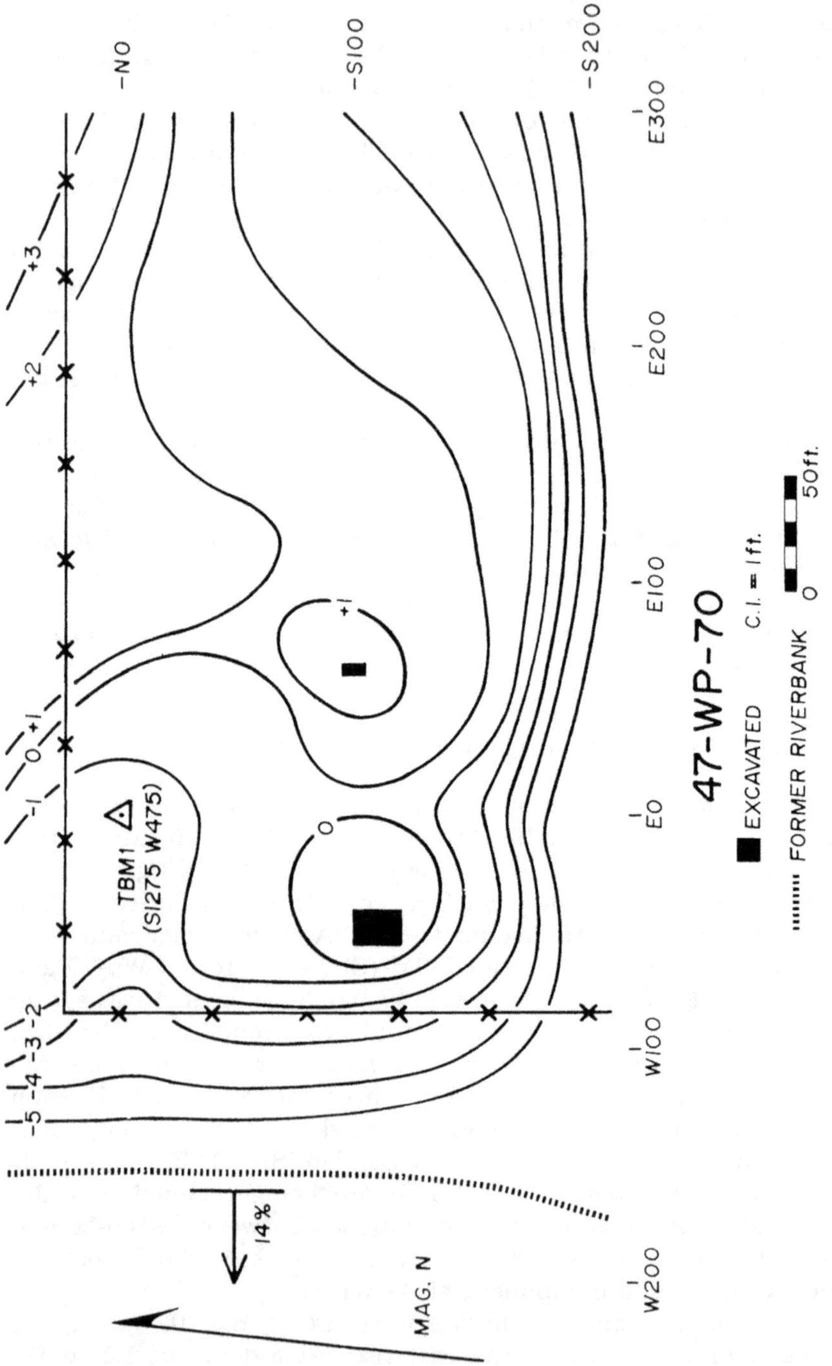

FIG. 45. 47-Wp-70 plan view.

feet a series of four large charred logs was uncovered. As they were located .3 foot below the plow zone, laid horizontally, and did not appear to be roots from a burned stump, they were designated as Feature 3.

Feature 3 consisted of four logs which were .2 to .6 foot in diameter and .5 to 1.5 feet long. They were laid horizontally in no apparent pattern between 1.1 and 1.6 feet below the surface. With the removal of these logs, and in their immediate area, the following objects were recovered: burned bone fragments, two decorated body sherds, one grit-tempered, cord-marked body sherd, 18 grit-tempered sherd fragments, one quartz flake, nine chert flakes, and 24 stone fragments. Although there was a large charcoal sample which could have been submitted for radiocarbon dating, as we subsequently realized from the contents of Feature 4, the sample would most likely have yielded a modern date.

Feature 4 was partially located in the same square as Feature 3 and from what we initially uncovered, it was thought that we were about to excavate an articulated elk, moose, or buffalo. These bones were well below the plow zone and in questioning the landowners, who have had this land in their family for over 100 years, we were fairly certain that it has been the custom to deposit their dead horses or cows in the woodlot ravines instead of burying them. Our excavations and clearing resulted in a well preserved adult horse with small hooves. The skeleton was lying on its right side, head facing east, with tightly flexed front and rear legs which indicate burial while the horse was relatively flexible. In its articulated state the horse was 7.3 feet long and the pit in which it was placed was from 1.0 to 2.3 feet below the surface. The burial pit itself seemed to have been shorter than what was needed as neck and head were on a slope and it was the head and front legs which were only 1.0 feet below the surface. A careful search failed to produce any horseshoes, iron nails, or historic objects of any kind. The objects recovered from the soil in and adjacent to the horse consisted of one utilized quartzite flake, one rim sherd, six decorated body sherds, two grit-tempered, cord-marked body sherds, 45 grit-tempered sherd fragments, nine chert flakes, one quartzite flake, and eight stone fragments. These artifacts may well have been redeposited after the horse was placed in the pit. The position, lack of historic objects, and the fact that most Wisconsin farmers do not normally bury their horses or cows suggest that this relatively small statured big girthed animal may be an Indian horse or pony.

As this horse burial had disturbed the east rise at Wp-70 to a great depth, and as we were finding features and artifacts in the west rise, we concentrated our efforts in the excavation of a 20 by 15 foot area in the west rise. In the area of excavation the soils below the Ap, or plow zone, from 1.0 to 2.8 feet consisted of loamy sand which was highly disturbed and mixed due to the prehistoric occupation. There were no apparent horizons in this 1.8 feet and the only change that could be noted was a shift in soil pH from 6.3 for this A/B zone to 6.7 for the plow zone. There was, however, a color, consistency, and shape change when features were encountered. A total of 13 features were defined and excavated in both the east and west rises, of which 11 were located in the west rise. As the west rise of Wp-70 offered a greater depth of occupation, our levels were divided as follows: Level 1 = the plow zone 0.0 to .8 foot; Level 2 = A/B, .8 to 1.2 feet; Level 3 = A/B, 1.2 to 1.8 feet; Level 4 = 1.8 to 2.8 feet; Level 5 = House floor, 2.8 to 3.4 feet. These vertical divisions were in many instances determined by the orifice of features or the house floor.

Feature 1 was located in level 2. It was oval-shaped in outline and shallow basin-shaped in cross section. The loamy sand fill yielded one quartz flake and one stone fragment.

Feature 2 was a charcoal concentration at 1.3 feet below the surface. The charcoal yielded a date of A.D. 930 ± 60 (WIS-230).

Feature 5 consisted of a very black lens of compact soil and charcoal which could be readily defined on the profile walls but in plan view its outline remained somewhat vague. Feature 5 extended from the base of the plow zone as a basin-shaped pit to a depth of 2.0 feet. The fill yielded six grit-tempered body sherds, 10 grit-tempered sherd fragments, two chert flakes, one quartzite flake, five stone fragments, and considerable charcoal which dated at A.D. 960 ± 75 (WIS-238).

Feature 6 was oval in outline and basin-shaped in cross section. In the center of the pit there was a cluster of six small stone fragments. The loamy sand fill yielded bone fragments, one grit-tempered, cord-marked body sherd, one basalt flake, one quartz flake, and two chert flakes.

Beginning at 1.9 to 2.0 feet below the surface the area of disturbed A/B soils became somewhat more confined and the features and small charcoal concentrations became more numerous. The pattern of features, charcoal, and the disturbed areas in conjunction with the believed area of occupation (Fig. 46) all

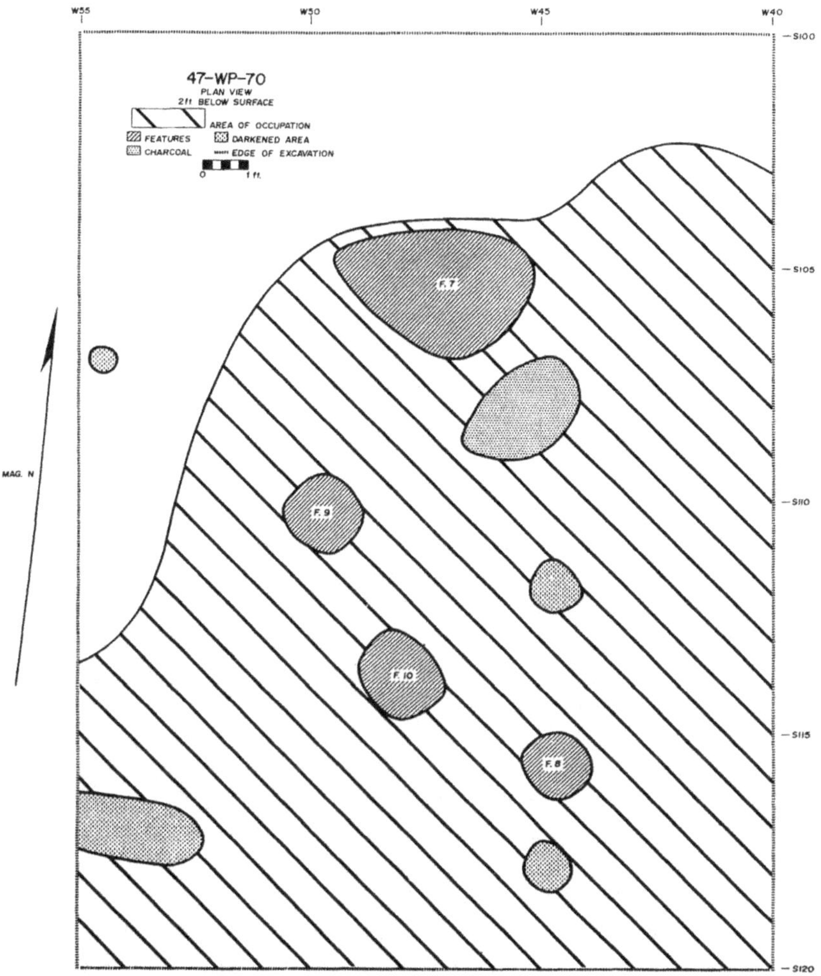

FIG. 46. 47-Wp-70 plan view at two feet below surface.

suggested that we were possibly within a structure similar to the semi-subterranean houses at 47-Wp-26, though no peripheral post-mold outline could be seen. The disturbed regions in the center of this area of occupation were considered as possible central support posts; however, they extended no deeper than 2.8 feet below the surface. Four features (Nos. 7-10) were defined and excavated in this area of occupation which continued to yield artifacts.

Feature 7 (Fig. 46) was an oval-shaped pit. The orifice of Feature 7 was in level 4 and this basin-shaped pit extended to a depth of 2.6 feet. The sandy loam fill yielded bone fragments, one decorated body sherd, two grit-tempered, cord-marked body sherds, two grit-tempered sherd fragments, one quartz flake, one quartzite flake, two chert flakes, five stone fragments, and charcoal which yielded a date of A.D. 1060 ± 65 (WIS-232).

Feature 8 (Fig. 46) was located in level 4. This roughly circular pit was basin-shaped in cross section. The sandy loam of Feature 8 yielded one body sherd, four grit-tempered sherdlets, one quartz flake, two chert flakes, and two stone fragments.

Feature 9 (Fig. 46) was located in level 4 and its outline was roughly irregular while having a basin-shaped cross section. Feature 9 yielded bone fragments, four grit-tempered body sherds, 21 grit-tempered sherd fragments, 11 chert flakes, two quartz flakes, and two stone fragments.

Feature 10 (Fig. 46) was located in level 4 and this circular pit had a cross section that was roughly cup-shaped. The sandy loam fill of Feature 10 yielded 23 fragments representing one Point Sauble Collared vessel, one rim sherd, two grit-tempered body sherds, one blade, 14 stone fragments, and one quartz flake.

Feature 11 consisted of fish scales, bone, and twigs which were found in a rodent burrow that was not recognized as such until it had been excavated.

The area of occupation outlined in Figure 46 was level 4 of the excavation from 1.9 to 2.7 feet below the surface. This level was relatively rich in artifacts, and charcoal recovered from square S105W45 at a depth of 2.7 feet gave a date of A.D. 940 ± 75 (WIS-235). At 2.8 feet, level 5 took on the pattern of a house floor which contained two features, a burial, and 12 post-molds which partially formed approximately one-half of an oval house more than 17.5 feet long and 12 feet wide (Fig. 47). This area was designated as House 1 of 47-Wp-70. It is of importance to note here that the area of occupation outlined in Figure 46 is totally within the post-molds and projected edge of the house in Figure 47. In only one instance is any feature from the area of occupation superimposed on a feature from the house floor, and that is Feature 10, which is over Feature 12 but does not seem to have disturbed it.

The projected edge of House 1 (Fig. 47) seems to have enclosed the area of occupation (Fig. 46). The material from this floor (2.7 to 2.8 feet) was kept separate from features 12, 13, and Burial 1 and the house basin was eventually excavated to a depth of 4.6 feet below the surface.

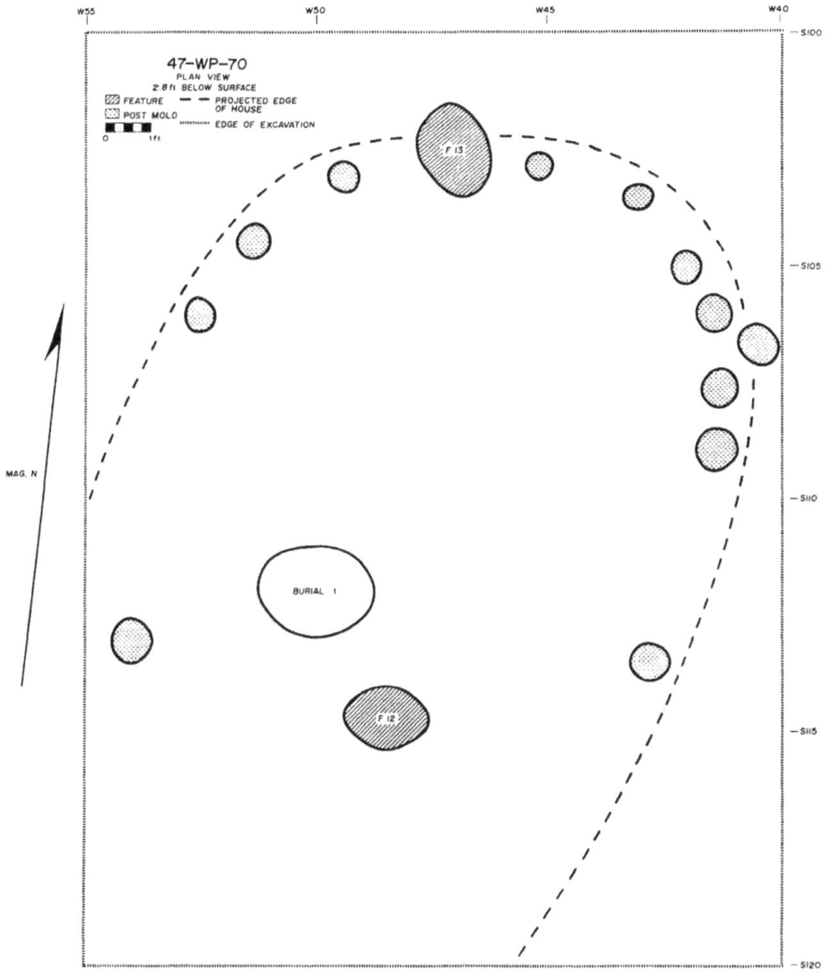

FIG. 47. 47-Wp-70, House 1.

Feature 12 (Fig. 47) was an oval-shaped pit, basin-shaped in cross section. The sandy loam fill contained bone fragments, one body sherd, one grit-tempered sherd fragment, three chert flakes, and 10 stone fragments.

Feature 13 (Fig. 47) was an oval-shaped pit, shallow basin-shaped in cross section. The sandy loam fill contained shell fragments, two stone fragments, and charcoal.

Burial 1 (Fig. 47) was located in an oval-shaped pit. The burial consisted of one human skull with seven *Anculosa* sp. shells

(UWA-189) on its forehead. The sandy loam fill also yielded one grit-tempered, cord-marked body sherd, four grit-tempered sherd fragments, two chert flakes, three stone fragments, and charcoal which was combined with charcoal from the house floor and yielded a date of A.D. 720 ± 60 (WIS-233).

The post-molds of House 1 extended from 2.7 to between 3.2 and 3.4 feet below the surface and contained a small number of flakes and stones. The projected edge of House 1, as illustrated in Figure 47, enclosed a very dark brown sandy loam in contrast to the yellow C horizon sands outside of this area. The house fill below the living floor of this semi-subterranean house was excavated to a depth of 4.6 feet below the surface. Thus, the house basin, which had gently sloping walls on all sides except the unexcavated southern portion, was 1.9 feet deep and similar to the house basins as recorded for 47-Wp-26. From the house fill the following were recovered: bone fragments, three rim sherds, two decorated body sherds, two chert end scrapers, three worked chert flakes, 13 grit-tempered, cord-marked body sherds, 176 grit-tempered sherd fragments, 11 quartzite flakes, 25 quartz flakes, 115 chert flakes, 63 stone fragments, and one snail (*Triodopsis albolabris* [Say] [UWA-180]).

VII

MATERIAL CULTURE FROM THE SANDERS SITE

THE excavated artifacts from 47-Wp-26 and 47-Wp-70 are combined in this chapter as preliminary field and laboratory analysis indicated little difference between the objects recovered from both locations. It had been thought that 47-Wp-70 might represent an earlier isolated component on the basis of the artifacts from the landowner's collection. Preliminary analysis of the excavated artifacts and the clustering of the radiocarbon dates from both Sanders site 1 and Sanders site 3 (Figs. 59 and 60, at end of chapter VII) indicate quite strongly that both localities were occupied at the same time.

The Sanders site is unique in many respects. Its outstanding characteristic is the number and diversity of artifacts recovered from a locality associated with effigy mounds. One very short testing operation and a six-week excavation of 47-Wp-26 and Wp-70 yielded 45,213 prehistoric artifacts. On the basis of an average of 250 artifacts per five-foot square in the village area of 47-Wp-26, there are over one million artifacts remaining in the unexcavated area of soil bodies $\frac{4}{\text{A-0}}$, $\frac{4}{\text{D-1}}$, and $\frac{4\text{A}}{\text{D-1}}$. Few excavated sites in Wisconsin have produced artifacts in such a magnitude. For a locality associated with the Effigy Mound tradition, this artifact wealth is a paradox when one considers the yield from the previously excavated sites. The analyzable number of artifacts is, in fact, considerably less than the total excavated: only 7,541 could be classified into categories other than waste flakes or sherdlets. This total is still impressive and the problems generated by the variety of decorations or manufacture are diverse when the full range of manipulative techniques is considered. As the major emphasis of this Effigy Mound research is the analysis of the material remains, there is a need for accurate description. The wealth of material from the Sanders site offers a broad view of the range and variety of objects associated with the Effigy Mound tradition.

Artifacts belonging to earlier or differing contemporary cultures are minimal at the Sanders site and they are viewed as trait-unit intrusions or trade items. Greater amplification will be given to cultural associations in the following chapter, which deals with the analysis of the Sanders site. The form of analysis to be followed in this chapter is similar to that used in the analysis of the Bigelow material culture.

CERAMICS

A total of 32,992 ceramic fragments were excavated from 47-Wp-26 and 47-Wp-70. Of this total, 25,958 (78.7 percent) are either very small sherdlets or their surfaces are too eroded to be utilized in the following analysis. The remaining 7,034 (21.3 percent) sherds belong to the following broad categories: rim sections, 1,017 (14.4 percent); associated decorated body sherds, 1,421 (20.2 percent); undecorated body sherds, 4,584 (65.1 percent); one ceramic elbow pipe; and one "child's" or seed pot.

The rim sherds and their associated body sherds are placed into the following categories: one Illinois ceramic type—Sister Creeks Punctated; 10 Wisconsin ceramic types—Shorewood Cord Roughened, Dane Incised, Madison Cord Impressed, Madison Plain, Leland Cord-marked, Aztalan Collared, Hahn Cord Impressed, Point Sauble Collared, Grand River Trailed, and Grand River Plain; four proposed ceramic types—Madison Fabric Impressed, Madison Folded Lip, Madison Punctated, and Heins Creek Corded Stamped; and three proposed type varieties—Dane Incised variety fingernail impressed, Madison Plain variety punctated, and Madison Plain variety jar. In addition, three decorated or associated body sherd categories are presented—rocker stamped, Grand River body sherds, and decorated body sherds—which are then followed by the undecorated body sherds which are grouped into categories on the basis of surface treatment. Vessel counts are made wherever possible by grouping rim sections and associated body sherds together or by grouping restorable vessel fragments together. At best, these vessel counts are considered only a close approximation and not as evenly accurate as the numbers may imply. The only category which may have a high degree of accuracy is the proposed Madison Fabric Impressed group, as their decorations lend themselves to fine sorting.

The ceramics recovered from the Sanders sites are ordered into three major and three minor classifications: Dane Incised ceramics, Madison Ware, and Grand River Ware for the major classifications; and Sister Creeks Punctated, rocker stamped, and Shorewood Cord Roughened for the minor classes. Excluding the undecorated body sherds, the Dane Incised group represents 13.8 percent of the sample (Table 16), the Madison Ware 74.7 percent, the Grand River Ware 10.9 percent, and the minor varieties .5 percent. However, vessel representation offers different percentages: Dane Incised 20.6 percent Madison Ware 75.3 percent, Grand River Ware 3.2 percent, and the minor varieties .9 percent. The difference is the Dane Incised-Grand River vessel percentage changes over the raw sherd counts.

Sister Creeks Punctated

This late Early to Middle Woodland Illinois ceramic type (Griffin, 1952*b*:100-101) is represented at the Sanders site by two rim sherds and six body sherds which belong to approximately six different vessels. Six of these specimens have smooth or smoothed over cord-marked surfaces, one has an $s\frac{z}{Z}$ and one has a $z\frac{s}{S}$ cord-marked surface. Sister Creeks Punctated ceramics have been illustrated or reported in eastern Wisconsin (Freeman, 1956:Fig. 10*e*; Mason, 1966:108); the total sample, however, consists of only four specimens. This type, like the rocker stamped specimen below, has distinctive decorative attributes which permit identification of these specimens according to Illinois types. The large hemiconical or annular bone or reed punctations, 4 to 14 mm in diameter for the Sanders specimens, are similar to those illustrated by Mason (1966:Pl. XVI, Fig. 2). The Sanders ceramics are 6 to 8 mm thick, the rim sherds having vertical rims 7 to 8 mm thick with flattened, or beveled to the exterior, lips. Hardness ranges between 2 and 3; the colors are dark brown or red brown. Texture is compact or contorted with medium to coarse grit tempering, ranging from 1/4 to 1 mm in diameter.

The punctated decorations were most probably produced by a hollow bone pressed at right angles to the surface of the vessel. The thickness of the impressions is between 1 and 3 mm and they are 1 to 2.5 mm deep. One specimen has an annular punctation 2.5 mm deep which has raised an interior node 1 mm high and 10 mm in diameter (Pl. 16:C). Another rim sherd has two parallel horizontal rows of vertical hemiconical punctations on the exterior and incomplete cord-wrapped stick impressions at the upper interior rim.

Rocker Stamped

One decorated body sherd was recovered. This smooth surfaced sherd has a parallel series of rocker stamped impressions 14 mm long, 2 mm wide and .5 mm deep (Pl. 16:D) It is a unique specimen from Sanders site 1 and may be an example of the Hopewell Rocker variety plain ceramic type as it is similar to the one illustrated by Griffin (1952*b*:118; Pl. XXXV:L).

Shorewood Cord Roughened

The Shorewood Cord Roughened ceramic type was proposed by Baerreis in 1952 and excavated examples of this type were reported from Silver Creek I (Hurley, 1966:57-65). The three rim sherds and one decorated body sherd (three vessels) from 47-Wp-26 are very similar to those described by Baerreis and those from 47-Mo-1 except for the fact that punctations on those from 47-Wp-26 are on the exterior and nodes on the interior. The location of the punctation, thickness, and surface treatment of these specimens are quite similar to those from 47-Mo-1 and to the proposed variety, Dane Incised, variety fingernail impressed and to the proposed type Madison Punctated, when the form of decoration is considered. The three rim sherds from 47-Wp-26 have insloping to vertical rims 10 to 11 mm in thickness with orifice diameters between 19 and 22 cm. The lips are flattened, rounded, or beveled to the exterior; hardness is 3 for these specimens. Textures are compact or contorted with medium to coarse (1/4 to 1 mm in diameter) grit temper; the surface colors range from tan to black. Two specimens have s $\frac{Z}{Z}$ cord-marked exteriors and two have s $\frac{Z}{Z}$ cord-rolled exterior surfaces (Pl. 20:B). Two rim sherds have exterior punctations at 25 or 27 mm below the lip which are 7 to 8 mm in diameter, 6 to 8 mm deep, and 10 mm apart. They have raised interior nodes 2 mm high and 7 mm in diameter (Pl. 20:A, B; Pl. 30:A). The third rim sherd has, 21 mm below the lip, a stick or finger punctation 15 mm long, 9 mm wide, and 9 mm deep which has raised an interior node 3 mm high and 10 mm in diameter (Pl. 21:B).

Dane Incised

The ceramic type Dane Incised was proposed and described by Baerreis (1952) and the type description was included in Keslin's report on Hahn Site I (1958:203-205); however, no totals were recorded for this type at Hahn Site I. R. Mason recovered Dane Incised ceramics from the Mero site (1966:94-99; Table III) where 32 specimens were recorded. The Sanders sites (47-Wp-26 and Wp-70) contained a total of 290 excavated Dane Incised ceramics consisting of 40 rim sections and 250 decorated body sherds representing approximately 185 vessels. This total sample exceeds the total thus far reported for Wisconsin. In the original type description (Baerreis, 1952; Keslin, 1958) the chronological position of this type was proposed as Early Woodland into early Middle Woodland. This position has been questioned by C. Mason (1964:158-159) and R. Mason (1966:97-99) and will be reconsidered here and in the following chapters with respect to its longevity, association with other ceramic types, and according to a reconsideration of the term incising.

The recognition of the techniques behind the production of ceramic decorations has long been considered of importance by archaeologists. Such terms as incised, trailed, grooved, scratched, scored, and engraved have often been the latter name in binomial ceramic type names. This usage suggests that line production is a cultural trait and a diagnostic ceramic attribute. There does not appear to be a consensus, however, as to what is involved in these various techniques, especially trailing and incising. Although the technique of decoration may not be detectable, both definitions and traits will be offered here and they are derived from experiments conducted by myself, Patricia Cummings, and Michael Mitchell at the archaeology laboratories of the University of Toronto.

Trailing is defined as "... to drag ... to be drawn along the ... surface ..." (Random House Dictionary, Unabridged Edition, 1966). Wedel (1959:89) considers a trailed line to be the outcome of drawing or trailing an instrument lightly across an area to produce a line as broad as, or broader than, deep. Trailing appears to be considered as very much like incising by Emerson (1968:10) He suggests that in trailing the same type of stylus used to produce a trailed line is drawn across the clay without cutting and that the resulting line is less sharp than an incised line and often evidences characteristic little edges of clay paralleling the line. Shepard (1968:195-196) does not use the term trailing and it is clear from her general description of incising that she would merge the two terms into one.

The idea of dragging, which is inherent in the usage of the word trailing, makes the trailing operation one of displacement rather than cutting. This distinction is fundamental when trailing and incising are being considered. Clay displacement can be effected by a variety of tools—bone, sticks or shell, or a sharp stylus such as a knife when it is held and moved in a certain manner. Central to the idea of trailing is that the tool employed be moved so that its leading edge, the effective part of the tool that makes initial contact with the clay, be a plane, dull or rounded rather than sharp or angular. The cord-marked Sanders ceramics yield information concerning the direction of trailing because the vessels were cord-marked and then trailed; the trailing pushed or distorted the vertical impressions as the implement moved across the surface. Displacement with a dull tool is possible only on a plastic surface. Experimentation shows that application of trailing techniques to a leather hard surface requires considerable pressure and produces a poor line. Therefore, in terms of this discussion, trailing is a technique limited to use in wet clay.

A trailed line has distinctive characteristics which are dependent upon the tool used and the plasticity of the clay. These characteristics occur in various combinations on different specimens and where post-trailing smoothing, scraping, brushing, or polishing has been intensive they may be absent. The clay displaced by trailing offers the main method of confirming the technique. The displaced clay forms parallel ridges of clay bordering the line and as the tool does not form shavings the clay will be pushed before the moving tool to form a fold-over of clay at the end of the line. Conversely, trailing operations on leather hard clay usually lack the parallel ridges of clay and the end fold-overs. The clay, in this instance, is depressed and displaced outwards to form a convex hump on either side of the line and the volume of this hump is equal to the depth of the depression. The ratio of line depth to breadth has often been used to distinguish trailing from incising (Wedel, 1959:89). Such relationships are not considered here to be valid as there is nothing intrinsic to the trailing technique that dictates that a trailed line should be broader than deep.

The term incising has been subject to the same loose usage as the term trailing. Shepard defines incising as "... freehand decoration by *pressing* or cutting into the paste" (1968:195 [emphasis mine]). Wedel is more accurate but she is dependent upon the depth to breadth ratio in order to reach her definition, which is in part quoted from Webster's New Collegiate Dictionary: " 'to cut into with a sharp instrument' ... a mark deeper than wide" (1958:88). Emerson states that an incised line is "... made with a stylus-like instrument ... which cuts a sharply defined line into the wet clay to produce the design element" (1968:10).

Incising involves cutting with a sharp tool such as a knife, blade, flake, stylus, or any naturally sharp object. It is the manner in which the tools are articulated with respect to the surface that makes the resultant line an incised rather than a trailed one. The incising tool is held so that the leading edge of the moving tool is the cutting one. Attempts to incise wet clay involve more displacement than cutting; for example, the fluid clay presents little resistance to the tool, so cutting cannot occur. As an end fold-over and parallel ridges form when a sharp tool is passed through wet clay, the result must be classed as a trailed line and, thus, incising is limited to leather hard and dry (pre-fired) clays and to fired clays.

Incising in leather hard clay is characterized by a clean sharp line, the formation of removable shavings, and the absence of ridging on either side of the decoration line. The small infilling ridges that trailing pushes into the section of crossed lines in a cross-hatched pattern are not in evidence in a pattern produced by incision. If an obsidian blade is used to produce incisions, as Shepard illustrates (1968:Fig. 15*e*), the edge of the trough opposite the hand of the tool user will bear small chips marking the side of the groove formed by the unbeveled end of the blade, a less efficient cutting edge.

Incision in dry clay is often marked by less depth than in leather hard clay and it manifests a string of minute chips in the vessel surface on either side of the incision. The bottom of the dry incision is porous and grainy in appearance, whereas the clay is sufficiently fluid in the leather hard incision and wet trailing to fill in the internal pores to produce a smooth surface. Henning

(1970:35) has observed that the major characteristic of post-fired incisions, which are deep enough, are that in cross-section the core of the vessel will be cut into and if it is of a "carbon core" the color change will be visible.

Such terms as scratched, scored, or grooved should be avoided in discussions of depressed linear decoration and lines produced by undetermined techniques should be referred to as linear depressions. Impressing and its variant forms of stamping provide an alternative means of creating depressed linear designs similar to incised or trailed designs. However, impressed lines are notable for their lack of continuous linear striations within the surface of the line (the outcome of tool movement), the absence of chipping, displacement ridges, and cross line infilling. Impressed troughs are matte in appearance, having a discontinuous texture varying with the material used to fashion the impressing tool.

Examination of the type name Dane Incised and the specimens from the Sanders site creates a slight "dilemma." The majority of the linear depressed decorations are the result of the trailing techniques described above and yet, despite the terminological inconsistency, these ceramics are suggested as belonging within the ceramic type Dane Incised. The Sanders linear depressed ceramics have, as we shall see below, ceramic attributes of this type—thickness, hardness, location of decorations, etc.—and they should not be placed into a new ceramic type. Type-variety designations (for instance, Dane Incised variety trailed) would not be terminologically correct, as the inconsistency would detract from the type name. Temporally there could be an early incised phase which was replaced by trailed phase. However, inspection of the Outlet site and Hahn Site I ceramics at the University of Wisconsin (both ends of the continuum?) showed that these ceramics were trailed and not incised. There is no technological or terminological problem as long as it is recognized that under the category Dane Incised, as it is reported for the Sanders site, the ceramics have trailed linear depressions unless otherwise stated.

Baerreis could propose that the name be changed to Dane Trailed; however, I would suggest that this decision be held in abeyance until more is known about the type. Both Hall and R. Mason have expressed the possibility that there may be two possible types of incised-over-cord ceramics: a bossed (noded) group similar to Black Sand Incised and a punched (punctated) group which Hall did not define (1950:30-31). R. Mason's view is:

> As originally defined by Baerreis (1952), there are good typological reasons for postulating Dane Incised as Early Woodland, at least in its

> initial development. Dane Incised, or a very close relative, has now been found at the Mero site in direct stratigraphic association with pottery of the North Bay Culture, a Middle Woodland manifestation. Similar pottery, but with Late Woodland style deeply notched rims, has been recovered from some sites of the Late Woodland Effigy Mound Culture, though as yet only in the mound fill. It thus seems likely that incised-over cord-marked pottery had a long career and that Dane Incised is one temporal variant rather than being co-extensive with the whole complex (1966:98).

As there are no deeply notched incised rim sherds from the Sanders site, the problem then reverts to the temporal longevity of Dane Incised, its Early Woodland status and Black Sand Incised relationships, and its possible associations continuing into the Late Woodland period and with ceramics belonging to the Effigy Mound tradition. These particular problems will be discussed in the following chapters after all the material culture items from the Sanders site have been presented. However, before the descriptive attributes of the Dane Incised ceramics from 47-Wp-26 and Wp-70 are presented, a type-variety of the type will be proposed and this type-variety, Dane Incised variety fingernail impressed, is viewed as a companion ware to the major type. In addition to the association of fingernail inpressing with trailing and punctation decorations, five of the 48 examples of this proposed variety (9.6 percent) have $s\,\frac{z}{z}$ or $z\,\frac{s}{s}$ cord-impressed lips while the more complex forms of cord twisting are absent from the type and its variety.

The Dane Incised ceramics from 47-Wp-26 and Wp-70 have medium to very coarse grit tempering (1/4 to 2 mm in diameter) with compact to contorted texture and surface colors ranging from tan to black. The rim and lip thickness range from 4 to 13 mm, averaging 7.3 and 7.2 mm respectively. Orifice diameters (six examples) range from 14 to 40 cm, the average being 22.3 cm. The body sherds have a thickness ranging from 3 to 14 mm, with the average 7.5 mm; the hardness range for 285 of the sherds was between 2 and 3, the average being 2.5. The major decoration, trailed linear impressions, was measured and the range and average calculated. Because almost all trailed impressions are horizontal or incomplete vertical lines, there are a few (five) length measurements. Their length ranges between 7 and 63 mm, with the average 27.2 mm. The width ranges between 1 and 8 mm, with the average 2.3 mm. The distance between these parallel horizontal, oblique, or vertical lines is between 1 and 13 mm, the average being 4.5 mm, and the depth ranges from 1 to 2 mm, the average being 1.1 mm.

The Dane Incised ceramics from the Sanders site are presented below according to their surface treatment.

s $\frac{Z}{Z}$ *cord twist.*

1. Nine rim sherds and 65 decorated body sherds have s $\frac{Z}{Z}$ cord-marked or s $\frac{Z}{Z}$ cord-rolled exterior surfaces. One of the more elaborate examples of the Dane Incised type from the Sanders site is illustrated in Pl. 17:A and Pl. 18:A. This rim sherd has, 20 mm below the lip, a series of parallel horizontal trailed lines which have been stroked from right to left and which have pulled or distorted the cord-marked surface. Other examples with stick punctations or distorted cord surfaces are illustrated in Pl. 17:C, D, E, L, N, O; Pl. 18:B, E, F; Pl. 19:D, F). The decorated body sherd in Pl. 17:O had the horizontal trailing executed over the s $\frac{Z}{Z}$ cord-marking and then horizontal rows of stick punctations were placed over the trailing so that clay is pushed over the lines.

z $\frac{S}{S}$ *cord twist.*

2. Eleven Dane Incised decorated body sherds have z $\frac{S}{S}$ cord-marked exterior surfaces and two body sherds have z $\frac{S}{S}$ cord-marked interior surfaces (Pl. 16:H). Four of these Dane Incised body sherds have exterior and/or interior cord-wrapped stick impressions.

s $\frac{Z}{Z}$ *and* z $\frac{S}{S}$ *cord twist.*

3. One body sherd has an exterior surface of s $\frac{Z}{Z}$ cord-wrapped stick impressions, a trailed line 6 mm wide, and then a z $\frac{S}{S}$ cord marked surface.

Distorted cord surface.

4. Two rim sherds and 50 decorated body sherds have horizontal, vertical, or oblique trailed lines over cord-marked surfaces which have pulled or distorted the fresh cord-marking so that the twist cannot now be ascertained. The direction of trailing on a sherd can be noted by the direction of the cord distortion (Pl. 17:I, J, M, P; Pl. 18:A; Pl. 19:G).

Smooth or smoothed-over cord-marked.

5. Eleven rim sherds and 93 decorated body sherds have smooth or smoothed-over cord-marked exterior surfaces and single or parallel horizontal, vertical, or oblique trailed decorations (Pl. 17:F, G, H, Q; Pl. 19:B, C). In addition these sherds also exhibit: (a) joined trailed lines (Pl. 19:I); (b) two parallel trailed-over cord-marked "zig-zag" lines (Pl. 19:H); (c) cord-wrapped stick decorations at the lip; or (d) exterior punctations.

Dane Incised—type variety fingernail impressed

The proposed fingernail impressed variety of the Dane Incised ceramic type has, as its variety name implies, the diagnostic decorative attribute of fingernail impressing. This impressing occurs on the upper interior rim, lip, or exterior rim or in all three locations. The decoration also occurs in conjunction with cord-marking, punctations, or trailing. One of the better examples of this proposed type variety is a specimen which has fingernail impressions, exterior stick punctations with interior nodes, and trailed horizontal lines (Pl. 20:C; Pl. 21:A). Two other ceramic types from Wisconsin have fingernail and/or incised or trailed lines: Marion Thick (C. Mason, 1964:159) which is an early Early Woodland type and to which the Dane Incised variety fingernail impressed appears to be related, and Tomah Fingernail Impressed, a proposed type from Silver Creek III (47-M0-3), which is placed at late Early Woodland to early Middle Woodland in west-central Wisconsin (Hurley, 1966:228-233). The Tomah Fingernail Impressed ceramics appear to have little relationship to the proposed Dane Incised variety because of the former's sandy texture, thinness, hardness, smoothed rims, and the presence of exterior nodes.

The Dane Incised variety fingernail impressed sample from 47-Wp-26 and Wp-70 consists of 18 rim sherds and 30 decorated body sherds, representing approximately 40 vessels. The hardness, color, texture, temper, measurements, and trailed decoration measurements have been described above under the type category; however, the fingernail decorations were not recorded. It would seem that there would be little in the way of range and variation in fingernail impressions due to the nature of the "tool" utilized, and yet the Sanders specimens show considerable range. The length of the fingernail impressions ranges from 3 to 11 mm, with the average length of the impression 7.1 mm. The width ranges from 1 to 8 mm, with the average 3.0 mm; the depth ranges from 1 to 3 mm, with the average 1.5 mm. The distance between individual impressions ranges from 1 to 11 mm, with the average 4.5 mm, and the distance between parallel rows of impressions is between 2 to 11 mm, with the average 5.1 mm.

s $\frac{Z}{Z}$ *cord twist.*

6. Seven rim sherds and 15 decorated body sherds have s $\frac{Z}{Z}$ cord-marked exterior surfaces (Pl. 20:I, F, H, D, J; Pl. 21:D, E, C). One rim sherd has, 15 mm below the exterior lip, a horizontal row of vertical fingernail impressions and a second row 30 mm below the lip which are *not* connected to those on the interior.

Smoothed or smoothed-over cord-marked.

7. Eleven rim sherds and 15 decorated Dane Incised variety fingernail impressed body sherds have smooth or smoothed-over cord-marked exterior surfaces over which fingernail impressions are located (Pl. 20:C, K, L, M; Pl. 21:A, F). Three rim sherds have s $\frac{Z}{Z}$ cord impressions on their lips and, in addition, one has exterior and interior fingernail impressions.

Madison Ware

In the analysis of the Bigelow ceramics several proposed ceramic types were suggested as belonging to the Madison Ware group: the original types are Madison Cord Impressed and Madison Plain (Wittry, 1959*c*:218); Keslin (1958:23) added Hahn Cord Impressed; Mason (1966:151) has recently proposed that Aztalan Collared and Point Sauble Collared be added; and I have suggested that the Madison Ware group be expanded to include Leland Cord-marked, Madison Fabric Impressed, Madison Folded Lip, and Madison Punctated. Excavations at the Sanders site have tended to confirm the associations of these ceramics. The larger range of recovered sherds allows for slightly greater refinement, adding two type varieties—variety punctated and variety jar—to the Madison Plain type.

I would also suggest that Mason's proposed Heins Creek Corded Stamped ceramic type be included within the ceramics associated with the Effigy Mound tradition—its possible inclusion into the Madison Ware group must await clarification of its space and time relationships. If these proposals are fully acceptable, then the Madison Ware ceramics (plus the Heins Creek Corded Stamped specimens) consist of 906 rim sections, 925 associated decorated body sherds (a total of 1,831 specimens), representing approximately 822 vessels. The range in hardness, texture, temper, color, and surface treatment will be described under each heading along with the size attributes.

Madison Cord Impressed. The Madison Cord Impressed ceramics from 47-Wp-26 and 47-Wp-70 consist of 67 rim sections and 126 decorated body sherds representing at least 96 vessels. These totals are somewhat small for an Effigy Mound culture village site; however, 108 fragments or 86 vessels have been excluded from this type and placed into the proposed Madison Fabric Impressed type and 32 additional specimens have been placed into the proposed Madison Folded Lip type.

The Madison Cord Impressed specimens from the Sanders site are grit-tempered with medium to granule size (1/4 to 4 mm in diameter) grit of quartz and granitic fragments in a compact to contorted paste. Surface hardness ranges from 1.5 to 4.0, with the average 2.0. Colors for exteriors, interiors, and paste cores range from tan to dark brown, with medium brown being the average. Exterior surfaces are cord-marked or smoothed-over cord with smooth areas confined to the upper rim regions. Exterior cord rolling below the rim is present on one specimen and a second specimen has a brushed surface over which cord impressions were added. The Madison Cord Impressed lips are flattened, slightly thickened, rounded, or beveled with the thickness ranging from 4 to 13 mm, the average being 6.8 mm. Rims are insloping, vertical, or slightly outflaring with a thickness which ranges from 4 to 10 mm, with the average 6.1 mm. Five vessels have discernible orifice diameters of 26 cm (2), 36 cm (2), and 40+cm (1), an average of 32.8 cm.

The subdivisions of these ceramics, to be found below, are the same as those used for the Bigelow sample and they are based on the type of cord twist utilized in the decoration. The following subdivisions are, therefore, only separation devices and are not of the order of type-variety categories.

$s\substack{Z\\Z}$—$Z\begin{smallmatrix}s\substack{Z\\Z}\\s\substack{Z\\Z}\end{smallmatrix}$ *or* $Z\begin{smallmatrix}s\substack{Z\\Z}\\s\substack{Z\\Z}\\s\substack{Z\\Z}\end{smallmatrix}$ *twisted cord.*

1. Eight rim sherds and 27 body sherds have parallel exterior impressions of $s\substack{Z\\Z}$ twisted cord (Pl. 22:B; Pl. 24:E). The exterior surfaces of six of these specimens have $s\substack{Z\\Z}$ cord marking, 28 have smoothed-over cord, and one has a brushed exterior surface.

2. Twenty-one rim sherds and 32 decorated body sherds have exterior impressions of $Z\begin{smallmatrix}s\substack{Z\\Z}\\s\substack{Z\\Z}\end{smallmatrix}$ cord (Pl. 22:E, F; Pl. 24:A; Pl. 26:A, C). Nine of these sherds have an $s\substack{Z\\Z}$ cord-marked surface and the remaining 44 have smoothed-over cord-marked surfaces.

3. Six rim sherds and nine body sherds have exterior impressions of $Z\begin{smallmatrix}s\substack{Z\\Z}\\s\substack{Z\\Z}\\s\substack{Z\\Z}\end{smallmatrix}$ twisted cord. All 15 specimens have smoothed-over cord-marked exterior surfaces.

$z\substack{S\\S}$; $S\begin{smallmatrix}z\substack{S\\S}\\z\substack{S\\S}\end{smallmatrix}$; *or* $S\begin{smallmatrix}z\substack{S\\S}\\z\substack{S\\S}\\z\substack{S\\S}\end{smallmatrix}$ *twisted cord.*

4. Nineteen rim sherds and 34 decorated body sherds have exterior impressions of $z\substack{S\\S}$ twisted cord. Fourteen specimens of this group have $z\substack{S\\S}$ cord-marked exteriors and the remaining 39 have smoothed-over cord-marked exterior surfaces.

5. Four rim sherds and 10 decorated body sherds have exterior cord impressions of $S\begin{smallmatrix}z\substack{S\\S}\\z\substack{S\\S}\end{smallmatrix}$ twisted cord. One decorated body sherd (Mound 17, S540W212-4-2) has a cord-rolled surface of $S\begin{smallmatrix}z\substack{S\\S}\\z\substack{S\\S}\end{smallmatrix}$ cords. Only one example from this group has a $z\substack{S\\S}$ cord-marked surface; the remaining 12 specimens have smoothed-over cord-marked surfaces.

6. Four rim sherds and five decorated body sherds have exterior cord-impressed decorations of $S\begin{smallmatrix}z\substack{S\\S}\\z\substack{S\\S}\\z\substack{S\\S}\end{smallmatrix}$ cord.

$s\,{}^{z}_{z}$ *and* $z\,{}^{s}_{s}$; $z\,{}^{s}_{s}$ *and* $Z \begin{matrix} s\,{}^{z}_{z} \\ s\,{}^{z}_{z} \end{matrix}$ *or* $Z \begin{matrix} s\,{}^{z}_{z} \\ s\,{}^{z}_{z} \\ s\,{}^{z}_{z} \end{matrix}$; *or* $s\,{}^{z}_{z}$ *and* $S \begin{matrix} z\,{}^{s}_{s} \\ z\,{}^{s}_{s} \end{matrix}$ *cord.*

7. Ceramics with the above cord decorations consist of: (a) One body sherd with $s\,{}^{z}_{z}$ cord impressions over a $z\,{}^{s}_{s}$ cord-marked surface; (b) one $z\,{}^{s}_{s}$ cord-impressed body sherd with an $s\,{}^{z}_{z}$ cord-marked surface; (c) three rim sherds exhibiting combinations of $z\,{}^{s}_{s}$ and $Z \begin{matrix} s\,{}^{z}_{z} \\ s\,{}^{z}_{z} \\ s\,{}^{z}_{z} \end{matrix}$ cord twist; and (d) one decorated body sherd with horizontal rows of $S \begin{matrix} z\,{}^{s}_{s} \\ z\,{}^{s}_{s} \end{matrix}$ cord impressions over an $s\,{}^{z}_{z}$ cord-marked surface.

Miscellaneous cord and knot impressed.

8. One rim sherd and six decorated body sherds have exterior cord or knot impressions of cords of unknown twists. Four specimens have smoothed-over cord-marked exterior surfaces and three have $s\,{}^{z}_{z}$ cord-marked exterior surfaces.

Fabric Impressed Ceramics

Analysis of cordage, basketry, and fabrics has a long history in New World anthropology. As aspects of material culture, their value has been demonstrated by numerous anthropologists who have described these complex cultural manifestations as they occur throughout this hemisphere. Much of this research was prompted by the early pioneering works of Holmes (1884, 1888, and 1896) who depicted varieties of New World aboriginal cordage, basketry, and fabrics. Greater clarification and elaboration of these preserved materials has been accomplished by anthropologists through continued descriptions of construction and design techniques and their cultural implications (Emery, 1966:260-306).

One aspect of fabric analysis, which Holmes (1884) was the first to notice, is the fact that fabric structures can be derived from vessels or vessel fragments. With clay impressions from these fragments, Holmes was able to demonstrate that fabrics were utilized as decorative devices. He reconstructed numerous construction techniques, illustrating that these reconstructed fabrics were similar to those constructed by historic Indians (1884:401-425). Holmes pointed out that fabrics have their own geometric systems and these systems influenced, by direct or indirect transmissions, other art styles. Herringbone and checker patterns were applied to vessels either as direct fabric impressions or as patterned copies found on incised vessels (1888:246). Vessels were also painted with decorative patterns derived from basketry and the accouterments of effigy vessels were often replicas of the original fabrics (*ibid.*:248-249). This sharing of design motifs from fabrics to vessels or to architectural facades has been so well documented for Meso- and South America that examples need not be presented here. Since the 1880's, there has been a multitude of publications dealing with preserved fabrics or basketry (Emery, 1966:260-306). However, since 1884, when Holmes presented his evidence concerning fabric impressed vessels, there has been very little in the way of explication of the nature and character of this cultural manifestation. This is especially striking in those areas in eastern North America where fabric impressed ceramics are recovered and where preserved fabrics are a rare occurrence.

The types of analyses that have been accomplished have been concerned with the terminologies of cordage and fabrics (Miner, 1936; Emery, 1952, 1966; Wilder, 1951; Osborne and Osborne, 1954), the recognition of fabric impressed ceramics (Douglass, 1946; Quimby, 1961), or with latex mold techniques for recording fabric impressions (Rachlin, 1955; McPherron, 1967). The phenomenon of the widespread occurrence of cord and fabric impressed ceramics has been the subject of only one short excellent paper (Hall, 1950). Detailed studies of important areas of New World prehistory have only skirted the problem. Evans (1955), stated that determination of the various fabric subdivisions of his fabric impressed ceramics was impossible and ". . . all fabric impressions were lumped together as a single type" (1955:36). Wood (1967), only differentiated between what he called S and Z twisted cord impressions. McPherron (1967) reported on 101,477 sherds, representing 1,688 vessels, of which over 1,000 vessels were cord-marked, cord-impressed, or fabric-impressed. McPherron illustrated only his latex mold techniques of recording these impressions and how cord was either cord rolled or used in knot impressions.

The above statements are not meant to imply that some forms of fabric-impressed ceramic analyses were not being used. Douglass (1946) reported on some varieties of fabrics present on Wisconsin ceramics. Evans did attempt to distinguish the types of fabrics impressed into the Virginia ceramics (1955:39-76). Lewis and Kneberg recorded 2,527 "textile-marked" sherds which exhibited four fabric construction techniques (1946:107-108), and they also illustrated these techniques (1946: Pl. 49). Wilder (1951) described the fabrics impressed into the Kincaid ceramics, although Emery has found several errors in the terms utilized by Wilder. Wilder also showed that fabrics were utilized by three different components at this site. However he did not quantify or qualify the similarities or differences; nor did he show whether fabric impressing crossed ceramic types.

We must ask why this important cultural and ceramic manifestation is ignored, grossly presented, or imperfectly understood. A great majority of ceramics in eastern North America are either cord-marked, cord-impressed, or fabric-impressed and yet no objective presentation of these attributes has been made in the archaeological literature. There are several factors involved here. The first is that reconstruction of these impressions requires the time to press plasticine into every sherd fragment exhibiting these features. Second, reconstructions may be hampered by the clarity or the subsequent erosion of the impression or the completeness of the decorative motif. Third, individual elaborations, or that little extra design added to a fabric, may add to the number and variety of possible subdivisions or may make fabric analysis appear more complex than it is in reality. Fourth, many of the basic foundations or warps are obscured as the thicker, more prominent wefts were pressed into the vessel. Fifth, separation of cord-impressed from fabric-impressed varieties requires the ability to determine connecting wefts, warps, cords, or knots which hold sets together, and this can only be done with a degree of accuracy after examining several hundred specimens. Finally, how does one designate these fabric impressions? With the publication of Emery's monograph, (1966), this last problem is temporarily resolved. Needless to say, as the archaeologists illustrate more complex fabrics, Emery's classifications may need to be expanded.

Despite these qualifications, it must be stressed that these cord and fabric reconstructions are, in many cases, the only remaining visible aspects of a portion of the material culture. These reconstructions may, however, represent only a small segment of the cords, nets, or fabrics utilized or they may give a disproportionate emphasis to behavior which may actually have played a very minor role in the culture. Archaeological emphasis, research designs, and methodology have changed and will continue to change as we modify and clarify those aspects of prehistory that we deem important. The reconstruction of the fabrics and the classification of fabrics serve only as departure points from which cultural patterns can be temporally postulated.

The utilization of fabrics as a decorative style at the Bigelow site was present only on the Madison Fabric Impressed ceramics. Fabric decoration was not employed as exterior or interior decorations on other ceramic types as was exterior and interior cord impressing and cord rolling. At the Sanders site (47-Wp-26 and Wp-70) fabric impressing, cord rolling, and cord impressing as exterior or interior decorations were utilized on several ceramic types separable on the basis of other distinctive attributes. Analysis of the fabrics utilized on the Sanders specimens was greatly facilitated by depending upon the excellent presentation and illustration of fabrics and their structures by Emery. For those who wish to undertake fabric analysis, the first concept that must be understood is as follows: "There is, however, no immutable relationship between the complexity of either the processes that precede fabric construction or the equipment used and the complexity of the fabric. Given sufficient time and skill, the most complex structures and designs can be produced with the simplest of equipment" (Emery, 1966:27). In order that the most complex fabric structures recorded for the Sanders material be understood, the different fabrics utilized will be presented from simple to complex and under three main headings: oblique twining, warp-twining, and weft-twining.

Of primary concern is the understanding of warp and weft: ". . . warp threads act as a basic structure which has been set in place before being interworked by the weft . . ." (*ibid.*:55). Oblique twining lacks warps and wefts as "pairs of elements moving on an oblique course enclose elements moving on the opposite diagonal as they twine about each other" (*ibid.*:64). Twining elements ". . . simply 'enclose' or 'clasp' the non-twining elements in their *twining interaction* with each other. Nor do the non-twining elements secure the twining itself . . .; they serve only to join successive groups or 'cords' of twined elements in a coherent fabric, and if they are removed the twined elements remain twined—but as separate cords, not as a fabric" (*ibid.*:196).

A critical cultural factor concerning twining is the fact that twining "... as a means of constructing a fabric does not lend itself to mechanization. It seems to have no counterpart in machine production, and its use in hand-weaving in the modern world has tended to become restricted to narrow bands, edge finishes and small areas of decorative detail" (*ibid.*:199). The illustrations to be presented support this view; however, these examples are prehistoric and not modern.

Weft-twining is the predominant form of fabric construction at both the Bigelow and Sanders sites. Emery states (*ibid.*:200) that:

> ... weft-twining was undoubtedly one of the very earliest methods of constructing fabrics with two different sets of elements. It remains one of the simplest methods, and one of those least amenable to implementation. It has served all over the world for a great variety of fabrications, from fish-weirs and wattled fences to fine and often elaborately patterned fabrics, in all types of fibers either spun or unspun that are suitable to fabric construction of any kind (*ibid.*).

The fabric analysis presented in the following pages will be arranged in order from simple oblique twining, simple to complex weft-twining, to warp-twining.

Madison Fabric Impressed. The ceramics included within this proposed type from 47-Wp-26 and 47-Wp-70 consist of 108 fragments, of which 31 are rim sections and 77 decorated body sherds, representing 86 vessels. Under each of the fabric headings in Hurley (1970:620-651), the impressions were further subdivided according to types of cord twist utilized: double oblique twining was divided into six categories, spaced weft-twining with spaced warps into 14 divisions. As these micro-attributes are tabulated and presented later, they will be omitted here. However, examples of the complexity of the cords used in fabric construction can be seen in Figures 48 to 58.

Double oblique twining (Fig. 48)

Four rim sherds and 10 body sherds have fabric impressions of double oblique twining composed of $\mathrm{z}\,\substack{\mathrm{S}\\\mathrm{S}}$, $\mathrm{S}\begin{array}{l}\mathrm{z}\,\substack{\mathrm{S}\\\mathrm{S}}\\\mathrm{z}\,\substack{\mathrm{S}\\\mathrm{S}}\\\mathrm{z}\,\substack{\mathrm{S}\\\mathrm{S}}\\\mathrm{z}\,\substack{\mathrm{S}\\\mathrm{S}}\end{array}$, $\mathrm{S}\begin{array}{l}\mathrm{z}\,\substack{\mathrm{S}\\\mathrm{S}}\\\mathrm{z}\,\substack{\mathrm{S}\\\mathrm{S}}\end{array}$, $\mathrm{s}\,\substack{\mathrm{Z}\\\mathrm{Z}}$, or $\mathrm{Z}\begin{array}{l}\mathrm{s}\,\substack{\mathrm{Z}\\\mathrm{Z}}\\\mathrm{s}\,\substack{\mathrm{Z}\\\mathrm{Z}}\\\mathrm{s}\,\substack{\mathrm{Z}\\\mathrm{Z}}\end{array}$ cords.

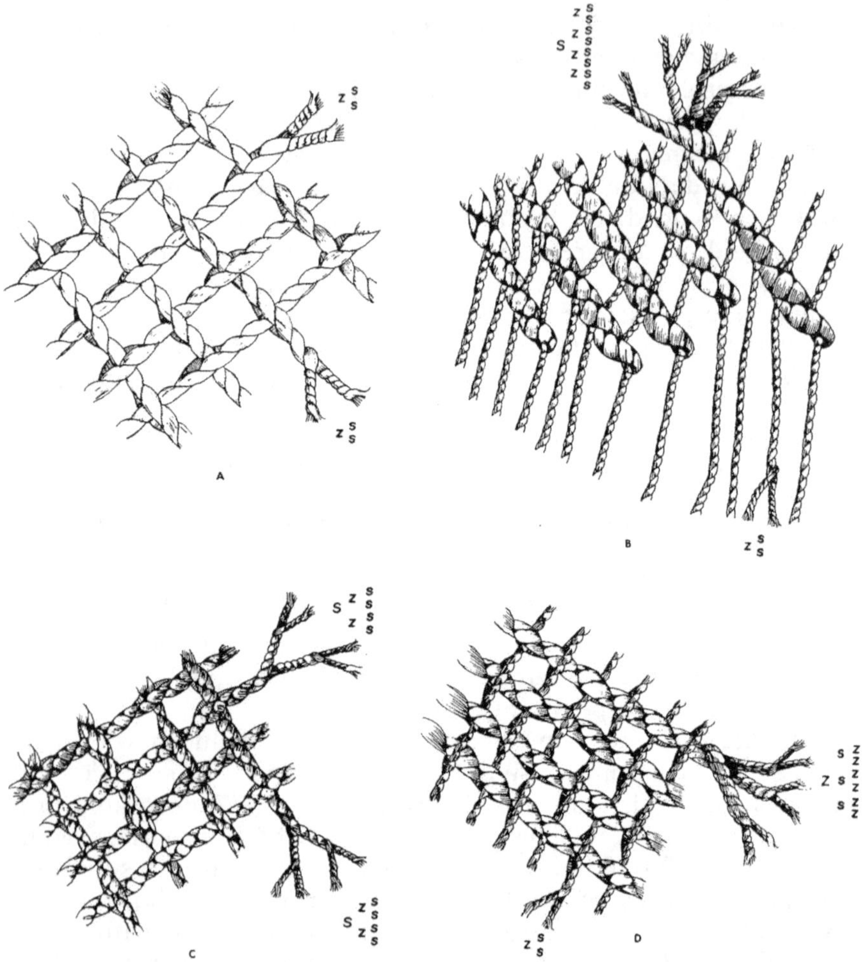

FIG. 48. Madison Fabric Impressed (a-c) and Madison Folded Lip (d) ceramics with double oblique twining: (a) 47-Pt-29-2, N50W25-1-2; (b) 47-Wp-26, S935W410-2-9; (c) 47-Wp-26, S945W415-2-53; (d) 47-Wp-26, S830W405-2-41.

Double twining (Fig. 49:A)

Three fabric impressed body sherds have fabric impressions of double twining composed of $Z\begin{smallmatrix} S\begin{smallmatrix}Z\\Z\end{smallmatrix} \\ S\begin{smallmatrix}Z\\Z\end{smallmatrix}\end{smallmatrix}$, $Z\begin{smallmatrix} S\begin{smallmatrix}Z\\Z\end{smallmatrix} \\ S\begin{smallmatrix}Z\\Z\end{smallmatrix} \\ S\begin{smallmatrix}Z\\Z\end{smallmatrix}\end{smallmatrix}$, or $Z\begin{smallmatrix} S\begin{smallmatrix}Z\\Z\end{smallmatrix} \\ S\begin{smallmatrix}Z\\Z\end{smallmatrix} \\ S\begin{smallmatrix}Z\\Z\end{smallmatrix} \\ S\begin{smallmatrix}Z\\Z\end{smallmatrix}\end{smallmatrix}$ cords.

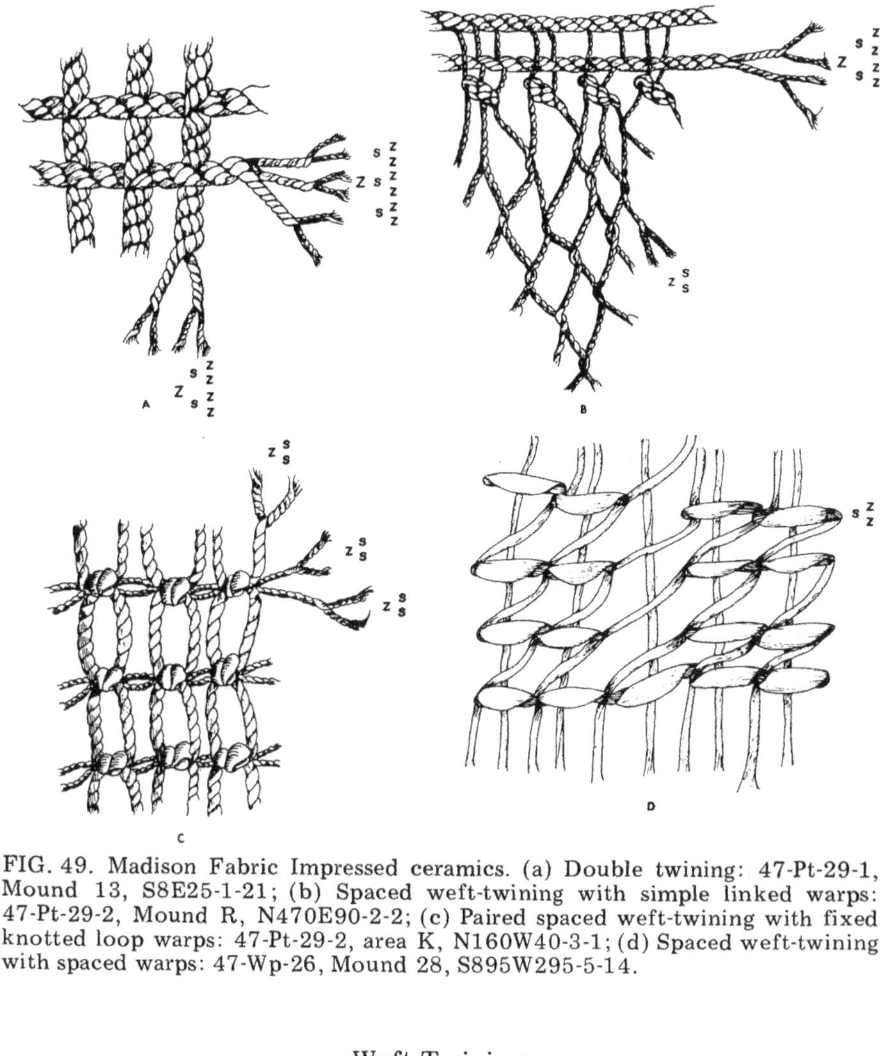

FIG. 49. Madison Fabric Impressed ceramics. (a) Double twining: 47-Pt-29-1, Mound 13, S8E25-1-21; (b) Spaced weft-twining with simple linked warps: 47-Pt-29-2, Mound R, N470E90-2-2; (c) Paired spaced weft-twining with fixed knotted loop warps: 47-Pt-29-2, area K, N160W40-3-1; (d) Spaced weft-twining with spaced warps: 47-Wp-26, Mound 28, S895W295-5-14.

Weft-Twining

Spaced weft-twining with spaced warps (Pl. 22:K, L, N; Pl. 24:B; Fig. 49:D; Fig. 50; Fig. 51:A)

Twelve rim sherds and 36 body sherds have fabric impressions of spaced weft-twining with spaced warps which contain cord elements of s $\begin{smallmatrix}Z\\Z\end{smallmatrix}$, Z $\begin{smallmatrix}s\begin{smallmatrix}Z\\Z\end{smallmatrix}\\ s\begin{smallmatrix}Z\\Z\end{smallmatrix}\end{smallmatrix}$, Z $\begin{smallmatrix}s\begin{smallmatrix}Z\\Z\end{smallmatrix}\\ s\begin{smallmatrix}Z\\Z\end{smallmatrix}\\ s\begin{smallmatrix}Z\\Z\end{smallmatrix}\end{smallmatrix}$, z $\begin{smallmatrix}S\\S\end{smallmatrix}$, S $\begin{smallmatrix}z\begin{smallmatrix}S\\S\end{smallmatrix}\\ z\begin{smallmatrix}S\\S\end{smallmatrix}\end{smallmatrix}$, or S $\begin{smallmatrix}Z\\Z\end{smallmatrix}$ twists. The rim sherd

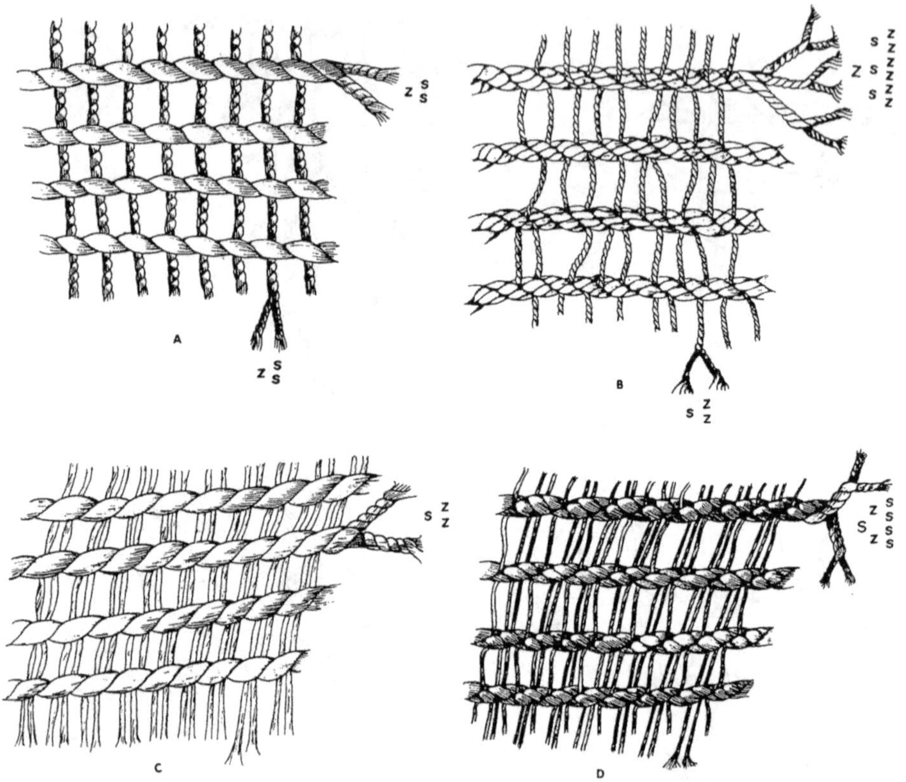

FIG. 50. Madison Fabric Impressed ceramics. Spaced weft-twining with spaced warps: (a) 47-Wp-26, Mound 12, S5W135-3-13; (b) 47-Pt-29-2, Mound R, N473E90-2-5; 2-9; with paired spaced warps: (c) 47-Wp-26, N0E0-2-1; with tripled spaced warps: (d) 47-Wp-26, S335W107-2-1.

interiors have cord, cord-wrapped stick, or fabric impressions of $z\substack{S\\S}$, $s\substack{Z\\Z}$, or $\begin{matrix} & s\substack{Z\\Z} \\ Z & s\substack{Z\\Z} \\ & s\substack{Z\\Z}\end{matrix}$ cords.

Spaced weft-twining with paired spaced warps (Fig. 51:B)

Two body sherds have fabric impressions of spaced weft-twining with paired spaced warps with cords of $s\substack{Z\\Z}$, $\begin{matrix} & s\substack{Z\\Z} \\ Z & s\substack{Z\\Z} \\ & s\substack{Z\\Z}\end{matrix}$, or $\begin{matrix} & z\substack{S\\S} \\ S & z\substack{S\\S} \\ & z\substack{S\\S}\end{matrix}$ twists.

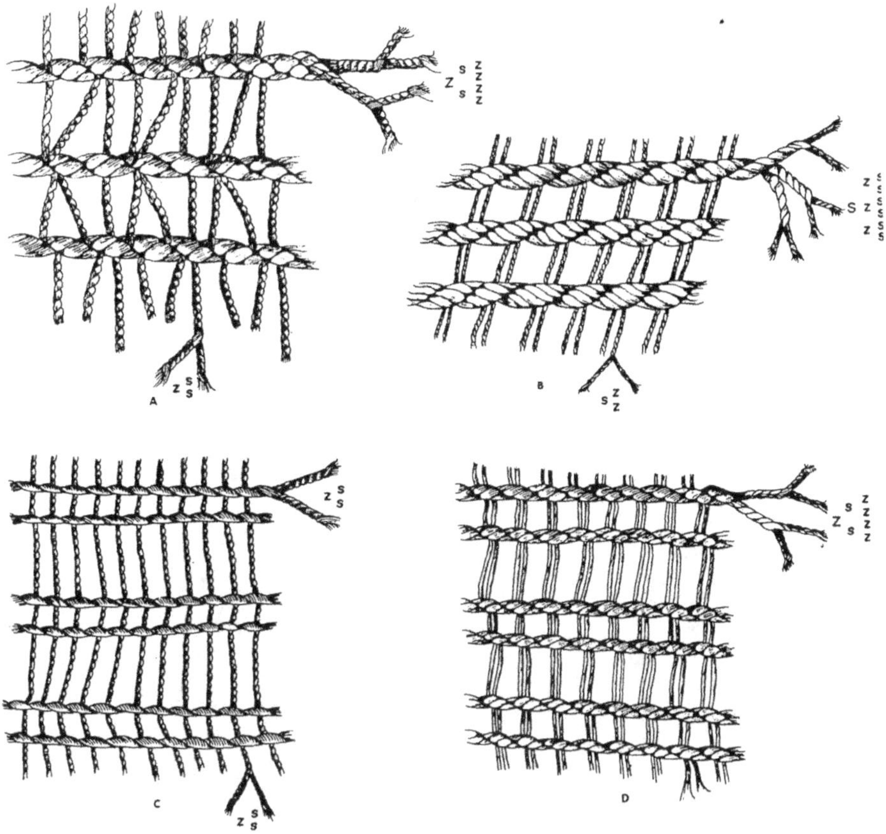

FIG. 51. Madison Fabric Impressed. Spaced weft-twining with spaced warps: (a) 47-Wp-70, S115W50-3-40; with paired spaced warps: (b) 47-Wp-26, feature 35-11; paired spaced weft-twining with spaced warps: (c) 47-Wp-26, area 9, N0E140-2-5; with paired spaced warps: (d) 47-Wp-26, S855W405-2-62.

Paired spaced weft-twining with spaced warps (Pl. 22:D; Fig. 51:C; Pl. 26:D)

One rim sherd and two body sherds have paired spaced weft-twining with spaced warps fabric impressions. The cords utilized had z $\begin{smallmatrix}S\\S\end{smallmatrix}$, S $\begin{smallmatrix}z & S\\ & S\\ z & S\\ & S\end{smallmatrix}$, or s $\begin{smallmatrix}Z\\Z\end{smallmatrix}$ twists.

Paired spaced weft-twining with paired spaced warps (Fig. 51:D)

Two body sherds have fabric impressions of spaced Z $\begin{smallmatrix} & Z\\ S & Z\\ & Z\\ S & Z\end{smallmatrix}$ weft-twining with paired, spaced, untwisted warps.

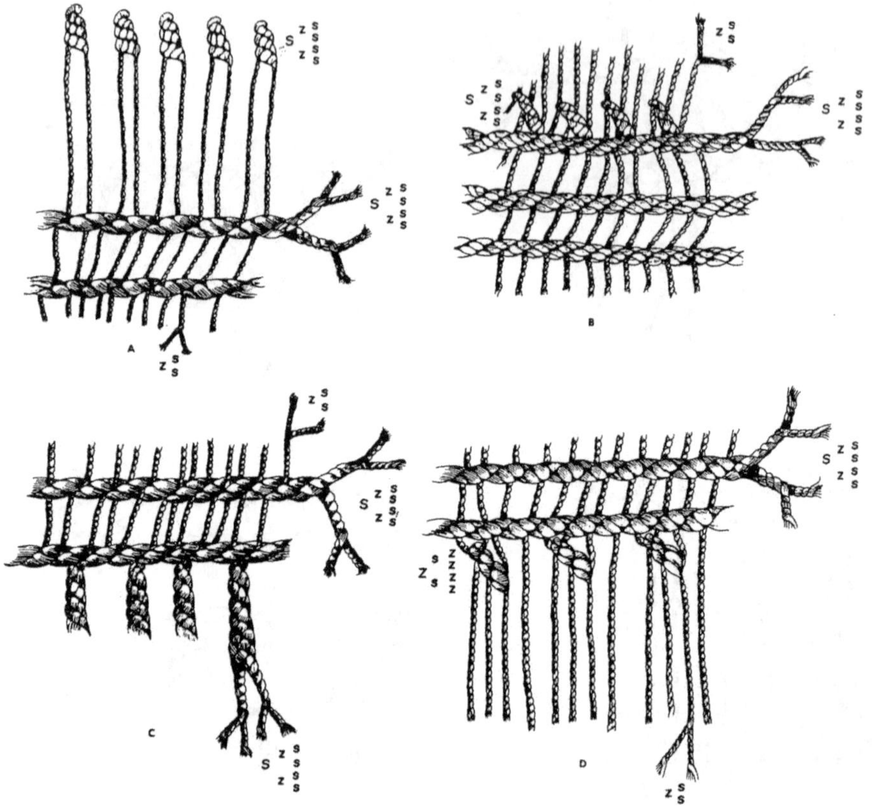

FIG. 52. Madison Fabric Impressed. Spaced weft-twining with spaced warps and accessory cords: (a) 47-Wp-26, S885W400-2-108; (b) 47-Pt-29-2, Mound R, N458E93-1-1; (c) 47-Pt-29-2, Mound B, N330W5-3-3; (d) 47-Wp-26, S870W415-2-4.

Spaced weft-twining with fixed knots and spaced warps

One body sherd has a fabric impression of spaced $Z\begin{matrix} s\,{}^{Z}_{Z} \\ s\,{}^{Z}_{Z} \\ s\,{}^{Z}_{Z}\end{matrix}$ weft-twining with fixed knots and spaced $s\,{}^{Z}_{Z}$ warps.

Spaced weft-twining with spaced warps and accessory cords (Fig. 52:A, B, C, D)

Three rim sherds and four body sherds have fabric impressions of spaced weft-twining with spaced warps and accessory cords

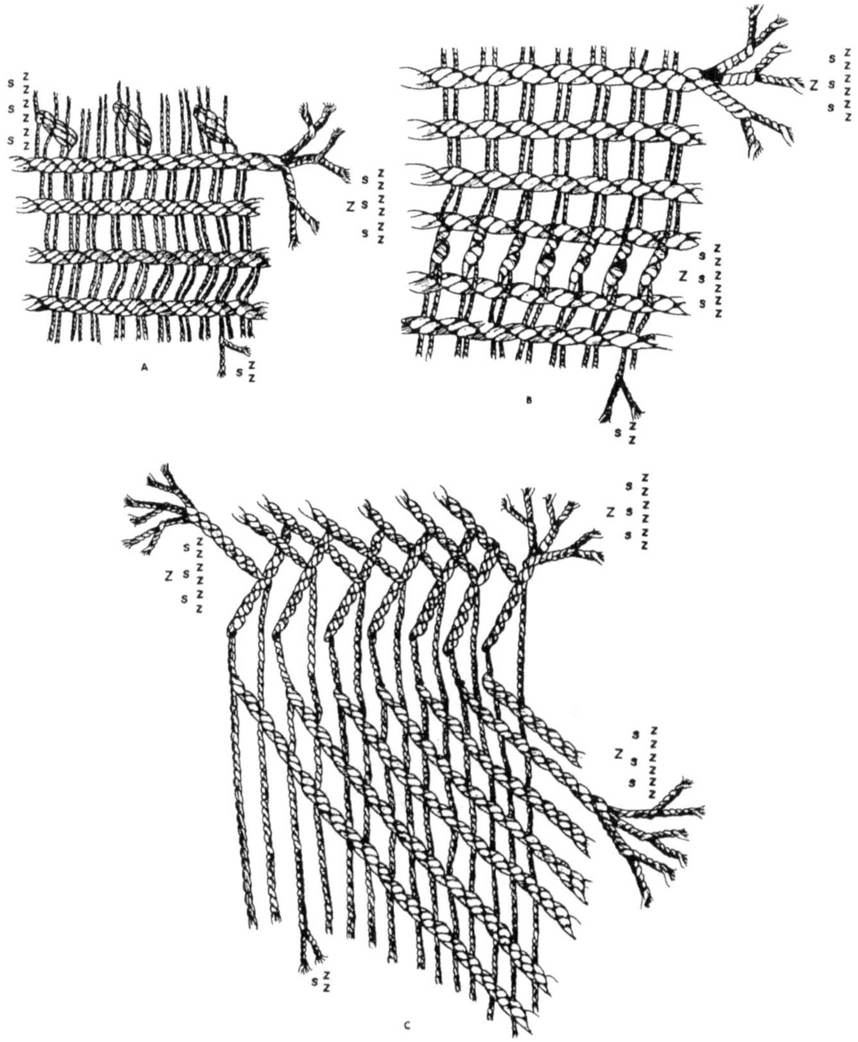

FIG. 53. Madison Fabric Impressed. Spaced weft-twining with paired spaced warps and accessory cords: (a) 47-Pt-29-2, Mound M, S25E25-3-1; (b) 47-Wp-26, S985W405-3-2; Spaced oblique weft-twining with spaced warps: (c) 47-Wp-26, S935W400-2-6.

composed of z $\begin{matrix}S\\S\end{matrix}$, S $\begin{matrix} & S\\ Z & S\\ Z & S\\ & S\end{matrix}$, s $\begin{matrix}Z\\Z\end{matrix}$, Z $\begin{matrix}S & Z\\ & Z\\ S & Z\\ & Z\end{matrix}$, or Z $\begin{matrix}s & Z\\ & Z\\ s & Z\\ & Z\\ s & Z\\ & Z\end{matrix}$ twists. On two of the rim sherds the fabric impressions extend onto the interior upper rim.

Spaced weft-twining with paired spaced warps and accessory cords (Pl. 22:M; Pl. 23:H; Fig. 53:A, B)

One rim sherd and three body sherds have fabric impressions of spaced $Z\begin{matrix} s\genfrac{}{}{0pt}{}{z}{z} \\ s\genfrac{}{}{0pt}{}{z}{z} \\ s\genfrac{}{}{0pt}{}{z}{z} \end{matrix}$ weft-twining with paired spaced $s\genfrac{}{}{0pt}{}{z}{z}$ warps and accessory $Z\begin{matrix} s\genfrac{}{}{0pt}{}{z}{z} \\ s\genfrac{}{}{0pt}{}{z}{z} \\ s\genfrac{}{}{0pt}{}{z}{z} \end{matrix}$ cords.

Spaced oblique weft-twining with spaced warps (Pl. 22:I; Pl. 24:C; Fig. 53:C)

One rim sherd has lip and interior impressions and one body sherd has exterior fabric impressions of spaced oblique weft-twining with spaced warp. These fabrics have $s\genfrac{}{}{0pt}{}{z}{z}$, $Z\begin{matrix} s\genfrac{}{}{0pt}{}{z}{z} \\ s\genfrac{}{}{0pt}{}{z}{z} \\ s\genfrac{}{}{0pt}{}{z}{z} \end{matrix}$, or $z\genfrac{}{}{0pt}{}{s}{s}$ cord elements.

Spaced oblique weft-twining with spaced warps and accessory cords (Fig. 54:A)

One body sherd has spaced $Z\begin{matrix} s\genfrac{}{}{0pt}{}{z}{z} \\ s\genfrac{}{}{0pt}{}{z}{z} \\ s\genfrac{}{}{0pt}{}{z}{z} \end{matrix}$ weft-twining with spaced $s\genfrac{}{}{0pt}{}{z}{z}$ warps and accessory $Z\begin{matrix} s\genfrac{}{}{0pt}{}{z}{z} \\ s\genfrac{}{}{0pt}{}{z}{z} \\ s\genfrac{}{}{0pt}{}{z}{z} \end{matrix}$ cords.

Spaced oblique weft-twining with spaced warps and suspended knots

One body sherd has fabric impressions of spaced oblique $z\genfrac{}{}{0pt}{}{s}{s}$ weft-twining with untwisted spaced warps and suspended knots.

Spaced horizontal and oblique weft-twining with spaced warps (Pl. 22:C, G, H; Pl. 23:D, E; Fig. 54:B; Fig. 55:A)

Five rim sherds and three body sherds have spaced horizontal and oblique weft-twining with spaced warps fabric impressions with

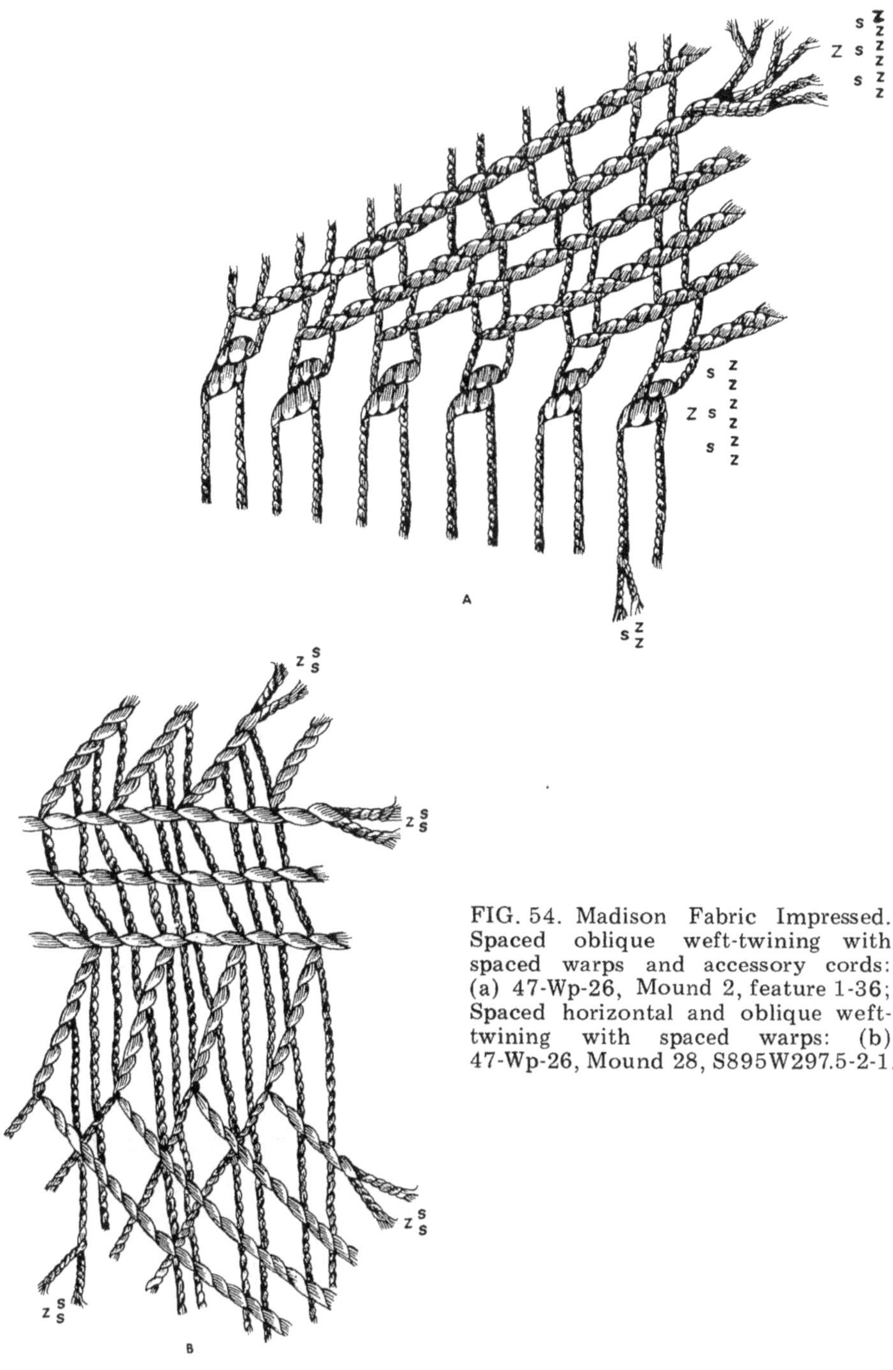

FIG. 54. Madison Fabric Impressed. Spaced oblique weft-twining with spaced warps and accessory cords: (a) 47-Wp-26, Mound 2, feature 1-36; Spaced horizontal and oblique weft-twining with spaced warps: (b) 47-Wp-26, Mound 28, S895W297.5-2-1.

the cord elements consisting of $z\substack{S\\S}$, $S\substack{z\substack{S\\S}\\z\substack{S\\S}\\z\substack{S\\S}}$, $S\substack{z\substack{S\\S}\\z\substack{S\\S}\\z\substack{S\\S}\\z\substack{S\\S}}$, $s\substack{Z\\Z}$, $Z\substack{s\substack{Z\\Z}\\s\substack{Z\\Z}}$, or $Z\substack{s\substack{Z\\Z}\\s\substack{Z\\Z}\\s\substack{Z\\Z}}$ twists. Three rim interiors are cord-wrapped stick impressed, cord-rolled, or cord-impressed with $z\substack{S\\S}$ or $S\substack{z\substack{S\\S}\\z\substack{S\\S}\\z\substack{S\\S}}$ cords.

Spaced horizontal and oblique weft-twining with paired, spaced warps (Pl. 23:F; Fig. 55:B)

One rim sherd has spaced horizontal and oblique $Z\substack{s\substack{Z\\Z}\\s\substack{Z\\Z}}$ weft-twining with paired, spaced $s\substack{Z\\Z}$ warps exterior fabric impressions. The interior rim is cord-wrapped stick impressed.

Spaced horizontal and oblique weft-twining with spaced warps and fixed knotted loops (Pl. 22:A; Pl. 24:D; Fig. 56:A)

One rim sherd has exterior, lip, and interior spaced horizontal and oblique $S\substack{z\substack{S\\S}\\z\substack{S\\S}\\z\substack{S\\S}}$ weft-twining with spaced $z\substack{S\\S}$ warps and fixed $S\substack{z\substack{S\\S}\\z\substack{S\\S}\\z\substack{S\\S}}$ knotted loops.

Warp-twining (Fig. 57:A)

One body sherd has interior spaced $z\substack{S\\S}$ warp-twining on single spaced untwisted weft passages. The exterior surface has $z\substack{S\\S}$ cord marking. The warp-twining on this specimen is similar to the example illustrated by Emery. Emery states that warp-twining is compact in comparison to weft-twining which can be compact or spaced (1966:196); however, the warp-twining illustrated in Figure 57 is spaced and not compact.

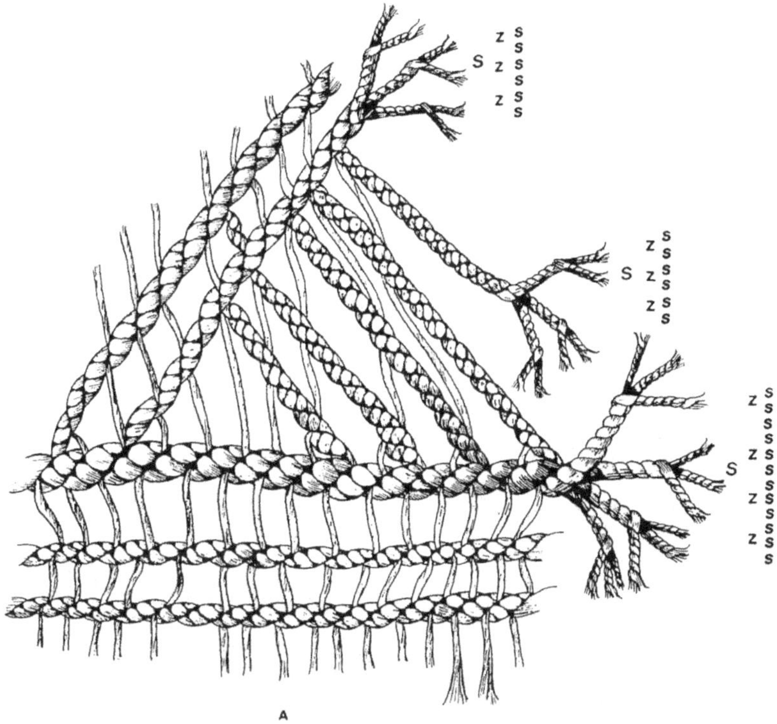

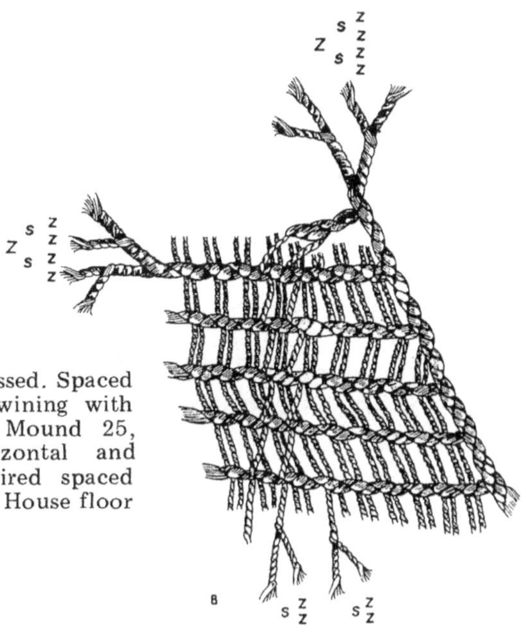

FIG. 55. Madison Fabric Impressed. Spaced horizontal and oblique weft-twining with spaced warps: (a) 47-Wp-26, Mound 25, S1088W325-5-2; Spaced horizontal and oblique weft-twining with paired spaced warps: (b) 47-Wp-26, House 3, House floor 1-18.

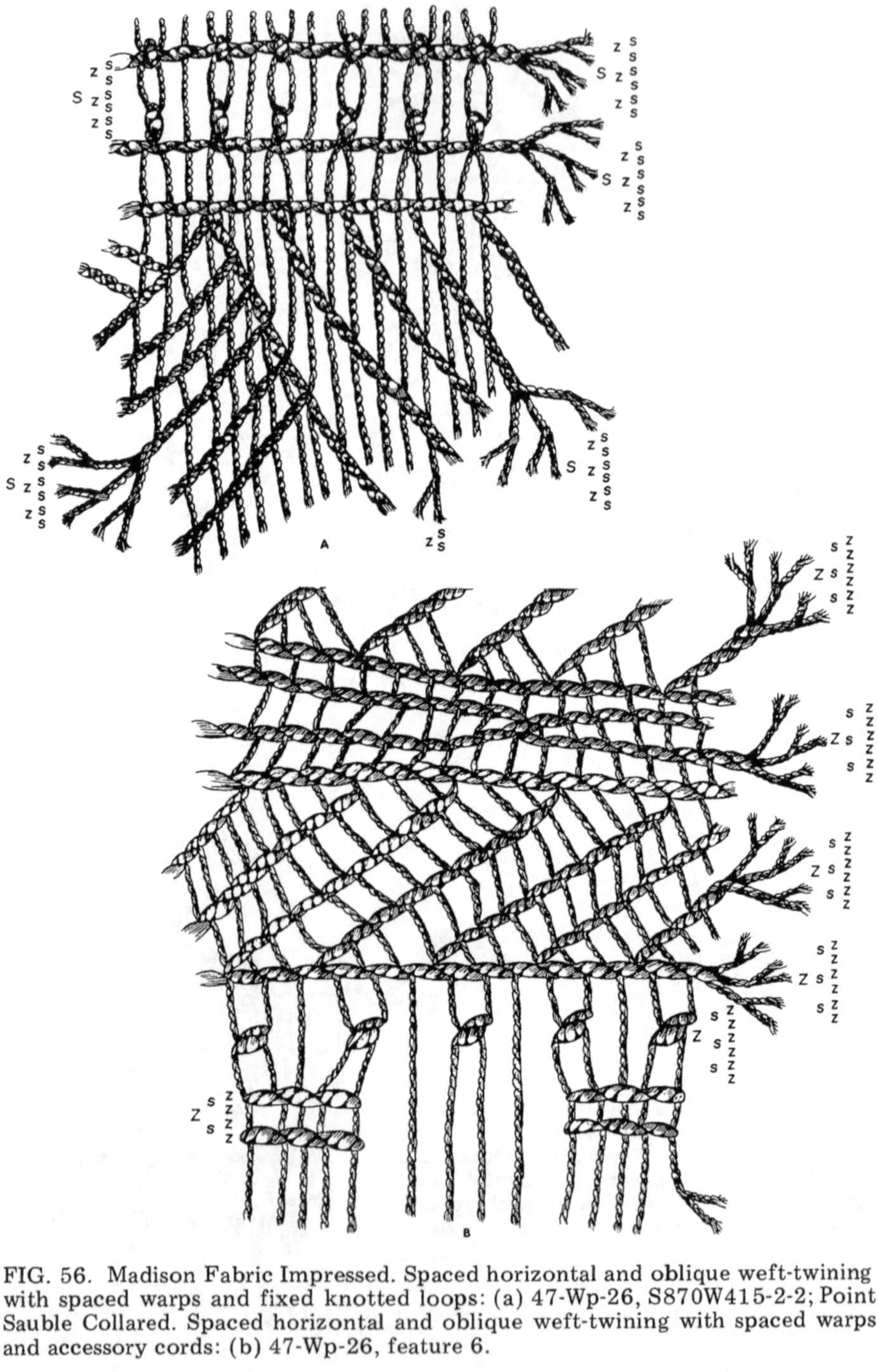

FIG. 56. Madison Fabric Impressed. Spaced horizontal and oblique weft-twining with spaced warps and fixed knotted loops: (a) 47-Wp-26, S870W415-2-2; Point Sauble Collared. Spaced horizontal and oblique weft-twining with spaced warps and accessory cords: (b) 47-Wp-26, feature 6.

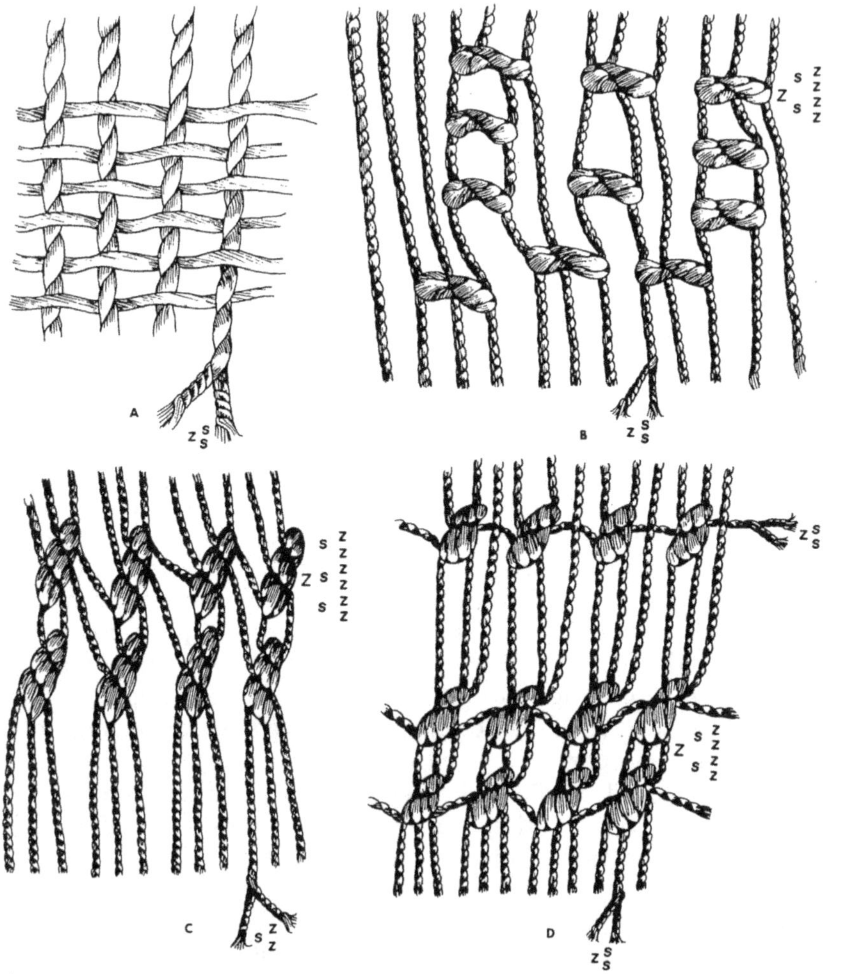

FIG. 57. Madison Fabric Impressed. Spaced warp-twining on single spaced weft: (a) 47-Wp-26, Mound 1, S385W209-2-11; Spaced warp-twining with suspended cords: (b) 47-Wp-26, S231W267-2-1; Spaced warp-twining with single spaced wefts and fixed cords: (d) 47-Wp-26, Mound 4, S360W117-3-1; Madison Folded Lip. Spaced warp-twining with fixed cords: (c) 47-Wp-26, S960W405-2-2.

Spaced warp-twining with suspended cords (Fig. 57:B)

One body sherd has exterior fabric impressions of spaced $z\,^{S}_{S}$ warp-twining with suspended $Z\ {}^{S}_{S}\ \begin{smallmatrix}Z\\Z\\Z\\Z\end{smallmatrix}$ cords.

Spaced warp-twining with single spaced wefts and fixed cords (Fig. 57:D)

Three rim sherds and four associated body sherds representing one vessel have exterior fabric impressions of spaced $z\genfrac{}{}{0pt}{}{S}{S}$ warp-twining with single spaced $z\genfrac{}{}{0pt}{}{S}{S}$ wefts and fixed $Z\,\genfrac{}{}{0pt}{}{S}{S}\begin{smallmatrix}Z\\Z\\Z\\Z\end{smallmatrix}$ cords. On the interior of the rim sherds there are oblique to the right $Z\,\genfrac{}{}{0pt}{}{S}{S}\begin{smallmatrix}Z\\Z\\Z\\Z\end{smallmatrix}$ cord impressions.

Madison Folded Lip

The Sanders sample of 32 rim sherds for this proposed type represents the largest site sample grouped under this heading. One example from the Bigelow site exhibited the same characteristic attributes as the Sanders specimens in that the lip has a high degree of exterior overlap. However, the lower margin of the folded lip does not, in all instances, meet or join the rim in the characteristic collared form and the lip may be quite rounded. It was suggested earlier that this folding of the lip may mark the beginning of collaring and this attribute alone suggests strong relationships to the collared types proposed as belonging to the Madison Ware category.

The proposed Madison Folded Lip ceramics may be viewed as a "transitional type": they, as other ceramics belonging to the Madison Ware category, have a major attribute—cord impressions, collar, or absence of exterior decoration—which allows for easy preliminary sorting. Only one type, Point Sauble Collared, has secondary cord decorations which aid in establishing its typological position. The proposed Madison Folded Lip ceramics have a cluster of secondary decoration attributes—cord, cord-wrapped stick or fabric impressions—which serve to link them with, or make them transitional to, other Madison Ware types. However, these secondary attributes become primary when the lip is absent, presenting problems in the proper placement of the decorated body sherds associated with these rim sherds: on the basis of the presence or absence of cord decorations such sherds might be included in one of several categories—Madison Cord Impressed, Madison Fabric Impressed, or Madison Plain. This problem also occurs when the lip and collar are absent from the Aztalan Collared, Point Sauble Collared, and Hahn Cord Impressed decorated body sherds. As a result, Madison Cord Impressed and

Madison Fabric Impressed categories are reported as having a large number of "associated" decorated body sherds. There are, of course, those undecorated body sherds which may be related to any of the Madison Ware types and whose associations are mainly based on cord twist. This negative aspect also has its positive side: it also demonstrates both the relatedness and the changing or transitional characteristics of the ceramic attributes within the Madison Ware category.

The 32 Madison Folded Lip rim sections from 47-Wp-26 and Wp-70 represent 20 vessels which have vertical to insloping rims that range in thickness from 3 to 7 mm, with the average 5.5 mm. The lips are rounded and thickened or folded with thickness ranging between 5 and 13 mm, the average being 8.8 mm. Vessel orifice diameter could be ascertained for only one rim sherd, which has a diameter of 30 cm. The proposed Madison Folded Lip specimens from the Sanders sites are ordered below according to cord or fabric surface treatment or decoration, and this ordering is not according to type-variety subdivisions.

$s\,{}^{Z}_{Z}$ or $Z \begin{matrix} s\,{}^{Z}_{Z} \\ s\,{}^{Z}_{Z} \\ s\,{}^{Z}_{Z} \end{matrix}$ cord twist

Nine Madison Folded Lip rim sherds have cord-wrapped stick or cord impressions of $s\,{}^{Z}_{Z}$ or $Z \begin{matrix} s\,{}^{Z}_{Z} \\ s\,{}^{Z}_{Z} \\ s\,{}^{Z}_{Z} \end{matrix}$ cord across the upper exterior rim or lip. Two specimens have stick or knot punctated lips and six have $s\,{}^{Z}_{Z}$ cord marked exterior surfaces (Pl. 25:F).

$z\,{}^{S}_{S}$ or $S \begin{matrix} z\,{}^{S}_{S} \\ z\,{}^{S}_{S} \end{matrix}$ cord twist

Seven Madison Folded Lip rim sherds have lip and interior $z\,{}^{S}_{S}$ cord-wrapped stick impressions (Pl. 25:I, K). In addition there is one rim sherd with exterior and lip $z\,{}^{S}_{S}$ cord impressions. All seven rim sherds have exterior $z\,{}^{S}_{S}$ cord-marked surfaces.

One Madison Folded Lip rim sherd has exterior, lip, and interior $S \begin{matrix} z\,{}^{S}_{S} \\ z\,{}^{S}_{S} \end{matrix}$ cord impressions.

No discernible cord twist

Four rim sherds have exterior smoothed-over cord-marked surfaces and cord-wrapped stick impressions or knot impressions across the lip and interior upper rims.

Fabric impressed

(a) *Double oblique twining.* Three Madison Folded Lip rim sherds represent one vessel (Pl. 25:A, D, E; Pl. 26:E) which has exterior double oblique twining of $Z\begin{matrix} s\frac{z}{z} \\ s\frac{z}{z} \\ s\frac{z}{z}\end{matrix}$ and $z\frac{s}{s}$ cords. The lip has deep cord-wrapped stick impressions of an unknown cord (Fig. 48:D).

(b) *Spaced weft-twining with spaced warps.* One rim sherd has spaced $Z^{s\frac{z}{z}}_{s\frac{z}{z}}$ weft-twining with a spaced untwisted warp. The lip and interior rim have $Z^{s\frac{z}{z}}_{s\frac{z}{z}}$ cord impressions.

(c) *Paired spaced weft-twining.* Two Madison Folded Lip rim sherds have exterior surface decorations of paired spaced $z\frac{s}{s}$ weft-twining over an open untwisted warp. The lip and interior upper rim have $S^{z\frac{s}{s}}_{z\frac{s}{s}}$ cord impressions (Pl. 25:B, C).

(d) *Spaced warp-twining with fixed cords.* Five Madison Folded Lip rim sherds represent one vessel with spaced $s\frac{z}{z}$ warp-twining with $Z\begin{matrix} s\frac{z}{z} \\ s\frac{z}{z} \\ s\frac{z}{z}\end{matrix}$ fixed cords (Fig. 57:C; Pl. 25:G, H, J; Pl. 26:B) on the exterior surface. The lip and interior rim has $s\frac{z}{z}$ cord-wrapped stick impressions.

Madison Plain (Pl. 27 and Pl. 28)

Specimens belonging to the Madison Plain ceramic type represent the largest number of rim sherds recovered from 47-Wp-26 and 47-Wp-70. A total of 645 rim sections and one partially restored vessel consisting of 142 sherds (Pl. 28) are derived from approximately 462 vessels. The rims are insloping to vertical and 608 have a range in thickness of 3 to 14 mm, the average measuring 5.5 mm. Lips are beveled to the exterior or to the interior, and flattened, rounded, or irregular. Range in thickness of 626 lips is between 2 and 13 mm, or 5.9 mm average. Fifteen rims have orifice diameters which range from 12 to 36 cm, with an average of 20.8 cm. The hardness for 632 rims ranges from 2 to 3, the average being 2.1.

According to the original type description (Keslin, 1958), Madison Plain vessels lack exterior decoration except for cord-marked or smoothed-over cord exterior surfaces. The Sanders sample represents the largest collection of excavated Madison Plain ceramics. The sherds exhibit attributes not recorded by Keslin. The lip or interior rim may have cord-wrapped stick impressions, cord impressions, fingernail or stick impressions, punctation on the lip, or it may have remained undecorated. Interior decorations relate Madison Plain ceramics to other types within the Madison Ware category: for example, exterior brushing and cord-wrapped stick impressions are attributes of Leland Cord-marked ceramics; rim punctations are found on Shorewood Cord Roughened and the proposed Madison Punctated ceramics; and cord impressions are found on both the interior and exterior of Madison Cord Impressed ceramics. As these Madison Plain ceramics, with their interior or lip decorations, have decoration links with the other Madison Ware types, they will be described below, as they may ultimately reflect spatial or temporal differences since they now appear to indicate cultural preferences.

The Madison Plain ceramics from 47-Wp-26 and Wp-70 are presented below according to the type of cord twist utilized and the presence or absence of lip or interior decoration. Those Madison Plain specimens with lip or interior rim cord-wrapped stick impressions have the following measurements: length—range 3 to 31 mm, average 10.3 mm (n = 200); width—range 2 to 10 mm, average 5.0 mm (n = 205); depth—range 1 to 5 mm, average 2.1 mm (n = 201); distance apart—range 2 to 10 mm, average 4.2 mm (n = 188). The other most popular decoration utilized on the Madison Plain specimens is lip or interior rim cord impressions, and they yielded the following measurements: length—range 4 to 23 mm, average 11.3 mm (n = 37); width—range 2 to 4 mm, average 2.4 mm (n = 37); depth of impression—range and average 2 mm (n = 37); distance apart—range 2 to 7 mm, average 3.7 mm (n = 35).

Not included in the general measurements recorded for this type (or in the decoration measurements) are two sub-categories which are presented as *type varieties*. These type-varieties (Madison

Plain, variety jar and Madison Plain, variety punctated) have distinctive attributes which are highly diagnostic. However, as both proposed type varieties are very limited in quantity, they are being suggested with this reservation in mind.

$\mathrm{s}\substack{\mathrm{Z}\\\mathrm{Z}}$, $\mathrm{Z}\substack{\mathrm{s}\substack{\mathrm{Z}\\\mathrm{Z}}\\\mathrm{s}\substack{\mathrm{Z}\\\mathrm{Z}}}$, *or* $\mathrm{Z}\substack{\mathrm{s}\substack{\mathrm{Z}\\\mathrm{Z}}\\\mathrm{s}\substack{\mathrm{Z}\\\mathrm{Z}}\\\mathrm{s}\substack{\mathrm{Z}\\\mathrm{Z}}}$ *cord twist*

One hundred and twenty-six Madison Plain rim sherds lack interior decoration; however, their exterior surfaces are cord-marked with an $\mathrm{s}\substack{\mathrm{Z}\\\mathrm{Z}}$ cord with an $\mathrm{R}\substack{\mathrm{l}\\\mathrm{l}}$ twist (Pl. 27:A). One hundred and fifty-nine rim sherds and one partially reconstructed vessel (Pl. 28) have $\mathrm{s}\substack{\mathrm{Z}\\\mathrm{Z}}$, $\mathrm{Z}\substack{\mathrm{s}\substack{\mathrm{Z}\\\mathrm{Z}}\\\mathrm{s}\substack{\mathrm{Z}\\\mathrm{Z}}}$, or $\mathrm{Z}\substack{\mathrm{s}\substack{\mathrm{Z}\\\mathrm{Z}}\\\mathrm{s}\substack{\mathrm{Z}\\\mathrm{Z}}\\\mathrm{s}\substack{\mathrm{Z}\\\mathrm{Z}}}$ cord-wrapped stick, cord-rolling or cord-impressed decorations on the lip or interior upper rim. Nine rim sherds have fingernail or stick impressions on the lip or interior rim that have no raised exterior nodes.

$\mathrm{z}\substack{\mathrm{S}\\\mathrm{S}}$, $\mathrm{S}\substack{\mathrm{z}\substack{\mathrm{S}\\\mathrm{S}}\\\mathrm{z}\substack{\mathrm{S}\\\mathrm{S}}}$, *or* $\mathrm{S}\substack{\mathrm{z}\substack{\mathrm{S}\\\mathrm{S}}\\\mathrm{z}\substack{\mathrm{S}\\\mathrm{S}}\\\mathrm{z}\substack{\mathrm{S}\\\mathrm{S}}}$ *cord twist*

Forty-two Madison Plain rim sherds lack interior decoration; however, their exterior surfaces are cord-marked with a $\mathrm{z}\substack{\mathrm{S}\\\mathrm{S}}$ cord with an $\mathrm{L}\substack{\mathrm{r}\\\mathrm{r}}$ twist. Sixty-eight $\mathrm{z}\substack{\mathrm{S}\\\mathrm{S}}$ cord-marked rim sherds and 22 rim sherds with an associated body sherd with smoothed-over cord exterior surfaces have $\mathrm{z}\substack{\mathrm{S}\\\mathrm{S}}$ or $\mathrm{S}\substack{\mathrm{z}\substack{\mathrm{S}\\\mathrm{S}}\\\mathrm{z}\substack{\mathrm{S}\\\mathrm{S}}}$ cord-wrapped stick, cord-marked, cord-impressed, or cord-rolled decorations on the lip or interior upper rim. Two rim sherds also have interior fingernail or stick impressions on the interior upper rim.

$\mathrm{s}\substack{\mathrm{Z}\\\mathrm{Z}}$ *and* $\mathrm{z}\substack{\mathrm{S}\\\mathrm{S}}$; $\mathrm{z}\substack{\mathrm{S}\\\mathrm{S}}$ *and* $\mathrm{Z}\substack{\mathrm{s}\substack{\mathrm{Z}\\\mathrm{Z}}\\\mathrm{s}\substack{\mathrm{Z}\\\mathrm{Z}}}$ *or* $\mathrm{Z}\substack{\mathrm{s}\substack{\mathrm{Z}\\\mathrm{Z}}\\\mathrm{s}\substack{\mathrm{Z}\\\mathrm{Z}}\\\mathrm{s}\substack{\mathrm{Z}\\\mathrm{Z}}}$; *or* $\mathrm{s}\substack{\mathrm{Z}\\\mathrm{Z}}$ *and* $\mathrm{S}\substack{\mathrm{z}\substack{\mathrm{S}\\\mathrm{S}}\\\mathrm{z}\substack{\mathrm{S}\\\mathrm{S}}}$

Seventeen Madison Plain rim sherds have $\mathrm{s}\substack{\mathrm{Z}\\\mathrm{Z}}$ cord-marked exterior surfaces or $z\begin{smallmatrix}S\\S\end{smallmatrix}$ cord-marked surfaces. In contrast to the exterior cord twist, they have interior or lip cord-wrapped stick or cord-impressed decorations composed of opposing $s\begin{smallmatrix}Z\\Z\end{smallmatrix}$, $z\begin{smallmatrix}S\\S\end{smallmatrix}$, $Z\,{}^{s}_{s}\begin{smallmatrix}Z\\Z\\Z\\Z\end{smallmatrix}$, $Z\begin{smallmatrix}s\\s\\s\end{smallmatrix}\begin{smallmatrix}Z\\Z\\Z\\Z\\Z\\Z\end{smallmatrix}$, or $S\,{}^{z}_{z}\begin{smallmatrix}S\\S\\S\\S\end{smallmatrix}$ cords.

No discernible cord twist

One hundred and eighty-four Madison Plain rim sherds with light to moderate smoothed-over cord-marked exterior surfaces lack interior or lip decorations (123), have cord-wrapped stick decorations of unknown cord (54), or have interior fingernail impressions (7).

Madison Plain—type varieties

The following two proposed type varieties have distinct attributes which allow for easy separation from other sherds of the Madison Plain type and from those types belonging to the Madison Ware category. Both varieties may eventually be elevated into formal types; however, they are being proposed here as varieties of the established type Madison Plain.

Madison Plain, variety punctated

There are nine rim sherds from 47-Wp-26 and 47-Wp-70 in this proposed variety and they have the following measurements: rim thickness—range 4 to 11 mm, average 7.1 mm; lip thickness—range 3 to 13 mm, average 8.5 mm; three examples with measurable orifice diameters ranging from 22 cm to 28 cm, with the average 24 cm; and hardness—range 2 to 3 mm, average 2.2. The diagnostic attribute of this proposed variety is the presence of deep circular punctations (2 mm in diameter) produced by a stick or reed on the center of the lip. These punctations form a single row and measure from 4 to 9 mm apart (Pl. 27:C, D). This particular attribute is *not* present at this vessel location on the other Madison Ware types and as a decorative attribute it suggests relationships to the Grand River ceramics as illustrated from the Walker-Hooper site (Griffin, 1966: Pl. CXLV, No. 34; McKern, 1945: Pl. 65, No. 8). The Sanders specimens lack interior decoration; however, this may alter as more examples are recorded. The exterior surfaces of these rim sherds are cord-marked: five examples have s $\frac{z}{z}$ cord-marking and three have z $\frac{s}{s}$ cord-marking.

Madison Plain, variety jar

Included within this proposed type variety are 16 rim sherds which have the following measurements: rim thickness—range 3 to 8 mm, average 4.9 mm; lip thickness—range 3 to 8 mm, average 4.6 mm; orifice diameter (one only) is 30 cm. The hardness of these rim sherds ranges from 2 to 3, average 2.1. As the variety name implies, the inward curving rim profile is of a container which may be a shallow jar; however, no profile was complete enough to determine the jar shape. The lip and rim measurements indicate that there is generally no real break in thickness from lip to rim except in those cases where the lip becomes somewhat pointed. Another major attribute of this proposed type variety is the fact that on these examples the exterior cord-marking is oblique to the left to the lip and this characteristic was noted on only two other rim sherds of the major Madison Plain specimens from the Sanders site.

One rim sherd has interior z $\frac{s}{s}$ cord-wrapped stick impressions from the lip. The exterior surface, in contrast, is cord-marked with an s $\frac{z}{z}$ cord. A second specimen has, 8 mm below the interior lip, a trailed triangle design 8 mm high, 11 mm wide at the base, with lines 2 mm wide. The exterior surfaces of these Madison Plain, variety jar examples were cord-marked with an s $\frac{z}{z}$ cord (8) or with a z $\frac{s}{s}$ cord (1).

Madison Punctated

The Sanders sample from both 47-Wp-26 and Wp-70 represents the largest collection of specimens from this proposed type. There are 24 rim sections, 50 decorated body sherds, and one partially reconstructed vessel (Pl. 31) consisting of approximately 200 fragments. These sherds represent approximately 60 vessels with insloping to vertical profile and a range in thickness from 4 to 8 mm, average 6.1 mm. The majority of the lips are flattened; however, a few are rounded or beveled to the exterior. Lip thickness ranges from 3 to 14 mm, average 6.1 mm, and orifice diameters, measured on five examples, show a range from 13 to 33 cm, average 26.8 cm.

The Madison Punctated collection from the Sanders site is similar to that from the Bigelow site in that this type category includes only ceramics which have exterior stick, reed, or bone punctations which rarely raise interior nodes. The punctations found on these specimens range in diameter from 1 to 7 mm, with the average 3.1 mm. The depth of the punctation ranges from 1 to 7 mm, but the average clusters nearer the lower range at 2.2 mm. Punctations within a row are separated by distances ranging from 1 to 12 mm, the average being 3.6 mm, and the separation between rows ranges from 2 to 16 mm, the average measuring 3.8 mm. Comparisons between the deep punctations and large nodes illustrated for a Shorewood Cord Roughened rim sherd (Pl. 30:A) and the Madison Punctated examples (Pl. 30:B-F) indicate the size differences. Ceramics which have exterior knot impressions belong in the Madison Cord Impressed or Madison Fabric Impressed categories and those with lip punctations only belong in the sub-type Madison Plain, variety punctated. The Madison Punctated ceramics from the Sanders site are ordered below according to cord twist.

$s\,{}^{Z}_{Z}$; $Z\,{}^{S}_{S}$; *or* $Z \begin{smallmatrix} s\,{}^{Z}_{Z} \\ s\,{}^{Z}_{Z} \\ s\,{}^{Z}_{Z} \end{smallmatrix}$ *cord twist.*

Eleven rim sherds and 17 decorated body sherds have exterior $s\,{}^{Z}_{Z}$ cord-marked surfaces over which single or parallel rows of bone, stick, or reed punctations have been placed (Pl. 29:A, C, G, J; Pl. 30:C, F). Twenty examples have cord-wrapped stick, cord-wrapped cord, cord-impressed, or cord-rolled decorations of $s\,{}^{Z}_{Z}$, $Z \begin{smallmatrix} s\,{}^{Z}_{Z} \\ s\,{}^{Z}_{Z} \end{smallmatrix}$, or $Z \begin{smallmatrix} s\,{}^{Z}_{Z} \\ s\,{}^{Z}_{Z} \\ s\,{}^{Z}_{Z} \end{smallmatrix}$ cords; two specimens have additional exterior $Z \begin{smallmatrix} s\,{}^{Z}_{Z} \\ s\,{}^{Z}_{Z} \end{smallmatrix}$ or $Z \begin{smallmatrix} s\,{}^{Z}_{Z} \\ s\,{}^{Z}_{Z} \\ s\,{}^{Z}_{Z} \end{smallmatrix}$ cord impressions. In addition two specimens have either fingernail impressions or interior punctations.

$z\,{}^{S}_{S}$ *cord twist*

Three rim sherds and 14 decorated body sherds have $z\,{}^{S}_{S}$ exterior cord-marked surfaces over which horizontal, vertical, or oblique rows of punctations have been placed (Pl. 29:I; Pl. 30:B).

s $\substack{z\\z}$ and z $\substack{s\\s}$; and z $\substack{s\\s}$ and Z $\begin{smallmatrix}s & z\\ & z\\ s & z\\ & z\end{smallmatrix}$ cord twist

One rim sherd and one decorated body sherd have exterior z $\substack{s\\s}$ cord-marked surfaces over which there are parallel rows of reed punctations and s $\substack{z\\z}$ cord impressions (Pl. 29:D).

One partially reconstructed Madison Punctated vessel (Pl. 31) consists of approximately 200 fragments. The rim is insloping, 7 mm thick and 33 cm in diameter; the flattened and punctated lip is 14 mm thick. The interior rim has Z $\begin{smallmatrix}s & z\\ & z\\ s & z\\ & z\end{smallmatrix}$ cord impressions. Across the lip, and not connected to the interior cord, are Z $\begin{smallmatrix}s & z\\ & z\\ s & z\\ & z\end{smallmatrix}$ cord impressions. The exterior upper rim has a smoothed-over cord-marked surface over which are parallel vertical sets of paired rows of hemiconical stick punctations. The globular body has a z $\substack{s\\s}$ cord-marked surface. The reconstructed height shown in Plate 31 is 28.1 cm.

Smooth or smoothed-over cord surface

Nine Madison Punctated rim sherds and 18 decorated body sherds have smooth or smoothed-over cord-marked surfaces. Over these exterior surfaces are rows of punctations which have raised slight interior nodes (Pl. 29:E, F, K). One rim sherd has stick punctations which have raised interior nodes. At the upper rim of this specimen are vertical stick punctations.

Leland Cord-marked

The Leland Cord-marked (Wittry, 1959*c*:207-209) sample from 47-Wp-26 and 47-Wp-70 consists of 48 rim sections, three associated body sherds, and one partially reconstructed vessel (Pl. 38:A) consisting of 128 fragments. These totals represent approximately 36 vessels, the largest collection of reported excavated ceramics belonging to this type. The rims are insloping to vertical or outflaring, with a range in thickness from 3 to 8 mm, the average being 5.8 mm. The lips are thickened, flattened, rounded, or beveled and they range in thickness from 4 to 10 mm, the average measuring 6.4 mm. On one specimen (Pl. 38:A) the orifice diameter measured 18 cm. The Sanders Leland Cord-marked specimens are grit-tempered, the tempering ranging from medium to very coarse crushed quartz and granitic pieces up to 4 mm in diameter. The texture is compact and slightly contorted; the hardness ranges from 2 to 3, average 2.5.

The Leland Cord-marked ceramics differ from both the Madison Plain and the Heins Creek Corded Stamped ceramics by the fact that the exterior cord-wrapped stick or the vertical incised decorations do extend beyond the bottom or lower margin of the lip and there are *no other decorations* farther down the exterior rim or neck. Nine of the Leland Cord-marked rim sherds have exterior incised lines and 13 have fine to medium brushed exterior surfaces. The dominant decoration is cord-wrapped stick impressions on the exterior upper rim and lip.

s $\frac{z}{z}$ *cord twist*

Fourteen rim sherds and one decorated body sherd have either s $\frac{z}{z}$ cord-marked exterior surfaces or s $\frac{z}{z}$ cord-wrapped stick impressions (Pl. 32:F, K, J; Pl. 33:A). Two rim sherds have vertical exterior and interior parallel incised lines which extend from the lip (Pl. 32:C).

z $\frac{s}{s}$ *cord twist*

Three Leland Cord-marked rim sherds and one decorated body sherd have z $\frac{s}{s}$ cord-marked surfaces or z $\frac{s}{s}$ cord-wrapped stick impressed decorations. One rim sherd has interior rows of z $\frac{s}{s}$ cord impressions.

Smooth, smoothed-over cord-marked, or brushed surface

Thirty Leland Cord-marked rim sherds, one body sherd, and one partially reconstructed vessel (Pl. 38:A), consisting of 128 fragments, have smooth, smoothed-over cord-marked, or brushed exterior surfaces. The exteriors are cord-wrapped stick impressed (Pl. 32:A, B, D; Pl. 36:F). One reconstructed vessel also has a band of horizontal brushing on the interior upper rim.

Aztalan Collared

Eleven Aztalan Collared rim sherds and one neck fragment representing 11 separate vessels were recovered from 47-Wp-26. Five rim sections have collars formed by the addition of secondary clay; four have intentional thickening of the upper rim to form the collar; and three are collared as a by-product of decoration. Three collars are straight or convex and increasing in thickness, seven are uniform in thickness, and one collar is concave and convex towards the lip. Four of these specimens have squared lips and six have rounded lips, the thickness of the lips ranging from 3 to 10 mm, with the average 7.0 mm. The height of the collars ranges from 4 to 23 mm, with the average 11.9 mm; the thickness of the collars is between 4 and 13 mm, with the average 7.6 mm. The necks of these Aztalan Collared sherds range in thickness from 3 to 7 mm, with the average 5.6 mm. Orifice diameters were recorded for only two rim sherds and they were 25 and 38 cm.

The 11 Aztalan Collared fragments have simple to complex decorations. These specimens have interior s $\frac{z}{z}$ or z $\frac{s}{s}$ cord-wrapped stick impressions or s $\frac{z}{z}$ or $Z\begin{matrix} s\frac{z}{z} \\ s\frac{z}{z} \\ s\frac{z}{z}\end{matrix}$ interior cord impressions. The lip, collar, and lower margin of the collar are s $\frac{z}{z}$ or z $\frac{s}{s}$ cord-marked, punctated, z $\frac{s}{s}$, s $\frac{z}{z}$, or $Z\begin{matrix} s\frac{z}{z} \\ s\frac{z}{z} \\ s\frac{z}{z}\end{matrix}$ cord-impressed or fabric-impressed with spaced $Z\begin{matrix} s\frac{z}{z} \\ s\frac{z}{z}\end{matrix}$ weft-twining over an untwisted warp (Pl. 34:F).

Hahn Cord Impressed

Only one Hahn Cord Impressed rim sherd was recovered from 47-Wp-26 and it has a convex collar which increases in thickness and which appears to be the result of the addition of secondary clay. The lip is beveled to the exterior and 6 mm thick; the collar is 14 mm high and 11 mm thick, while the neck is 5 mm thick. The interior rim has parallel vertical $Z\begin{matrix} s\frac{z}{z} \\ s\frac{z}{z}\end{matrix}$ cord impressions. This cord decoration is carried over onto the collar and the neck.

Point Sauble Collared

The Point Collared ceramics from the Sanders site consist of 15 rim sherds and two associated decorated body sherds, one partially restored vessel consisting of 143 fragments, and one vessel represented by 23 fragments, for a total of approximately 13 vessels. Six of the rim sherds have collars which were formed by the secondary addition of clay and 10 have collars formed by the intentional thickening of the upper rim. The collar height of these Point Sauble Collared examples ranges between 4 and 20 mm, with the average 13.3 mm. The thickness is between 7 and 11 mm, with the average 9.1 mm. The majority of the lips are rounded, one each squared or beveled, and in thickness the lips are limited to a range of 3 to 6 mm, with the average 4.6 mm. The necks below the collar are somewhat thicker than the lips, ranging between 4 and 8 mm, with the average 5.6 mm. Orifice diameters could be determined for five specimens and the recorded range is 16 to 34 cm, with the average 24.2 cm.

Of the recognized collared ceramic types in Wisconsin, the Point Sauble Collared vessels represent the most elaborate decorative expressions and baroque motifs. (The Aztalan Collared ceramics, on the other hand, are characterized by their lack of decoration expression, while the Hahn Cord Impressed ceramics fall within the mid-range.) As the Point Sauble Collared ceramics from 47-Wp-26 and from 47-Wp-70 exhibit these complex decorations, they will be grouped.

The interior decorations on these specimens consist of either interior channeling or cord impressions of $\mathrm{s}\begin{smallmatrix}\mathrm{Z}\\\mathrm{Z}\end{smallmatrix}$, $\mathrm{Z}\begin{smallmatrix}\mathrm{s}\begin{smallmatrix}\mathrm{Z}\\\mathrm{Z}\end{smallmatrix}\\\mathrm{s}\begin{smallmatrix}\mathrm{Z}\\\mathrm{Z}\end{smallmatrix}\end{smallmatrix}$, $\mathrm{Z}\begin{smallmatrix}\mathrm{s}\begin{smallmatrix}\mathrm{Z}\\\mathrm{Z}\end{smallmatrix}\\\mathrm{s}\begin{smallmatrix}\mathrm{Z}\\\mathrm{Z}\end{smallmatrix}\\\mathrm{s}\begin{smallmatrix}\mathrm{Z}\\\mathrm{Z}\end{smallmatrix}\\\mathrm{s}\begin{smallmatrix}\mathrm{Z}\\\mathrm{Z}\end{smallmatrix}\end{smallmatrix}$, or $\mathrm{S}\begin{smallmatrix}\mathrm{z}\begin{smallmatrix}\mathrm{S}\\\mathrm{S}\end{smallmatrix}\\\mathrm{z}\begin{smallmatrix}\mathrm{S}\\\mathrm{S}\end{smallmatrix}\\\mathrm{z}\begin{smallmatrix}\mathrm{S}\\\mathrm{S}\end{smallmatrix}\end{smallmatrix}$ twisted cord. The exteriors have combinations of decorations on the lip, collar, lower margin of collar or neck consisting of cord-marking, knot impressions, or cord impressions of $\mathrm{z}\begin{smallmatrix}\mathrm{S}\\\mathrm{S}\end{smallmatrix}$, $\mathrm{S}\begin{smallmatrix}\mathrm{z}\begin{smallmatrix}\mathrm{S}\\\mathrm{S}\end{smallmatrix}\\\mathrm{z}\begin{smallmatrix}\mathrm{S}\\\mathrm{S}\end{smallmatrix}\end{smallmatrix}$, $\mathrm{s}\begin{smallmatrix}\mathrm{Z}\\\mathrm{Z}\end{smallmatrix}$, $\mathrm{Z}\begin{smallmatrix}\mathrm{s}\begin{smallmatrix}\mathrm{Z}\\\mathrm{Z}\end{smallmatrix}\\\mathrm{s}\begin{smallmatrix}\mathrm{Z}\\\mathrm{Z}\end{smallmatrix}\end{smallmatrix}$, $\mathrm{Z}\begin{smallmatrix}\mathrm{s}\begin{smallmatrix}\mathrm{Z}\\\mathrm{Z}\end{smallmatrix}\\\mathrm{s}\begin{smallmatrix}\mathrm{Z}\\\mathrm{Z}\end{smallmatrix}\\\mathrm{s}\begin{smallmatrix}\mathrm{Z}\\\mathrm{Z}\end{smallmatrix}\end{smallmatrix}$, or $\mathrm{Z}\begin{smallmatrix}\mathrm{s}\begin{smallmatrix}\mathrm{Z}\\\mathrm{Z}\end{smallmatrix}\\\mathrm{s}\begin{smallmatrix}\mathrm{Z}\\\mathrm{Z}\end{smallmatrix}\\\mathrm{s}\begin{smallmatrix}\mathrm{Z}\\\mathrm{Z}\end{smallmatrix}\\\mathrm{s}\begin{smallmatrix}\mathrm{Z}\\\mathrm{Z}\end{smallmatrix}\end{smallmatrix}$ twisted cord (Pl.34:D, E).

Fabrics were also impressed upon the Point Sauble Collared vessels from the Sanders site and they range from the simple spaced $\mathrm{Z}\begin{smallmatrix}\mathrm{s}\begin{smallmatrix}\mathrm{Z}\\\mathrm{Z}\end{smallmatrix}\\\mathrm{s}\begin{smallmatrix}\mathrm{Z}\\\mathrm{Z}\end{smallmatrix}\\\mathrm{s}\begin{smallmatrix}\mathrm{Z}\\\mathrm{Z}\end{smallmatrix}\end{smallmatrix}$ weft-twining over $\mathrm{s}\begin{smallmatrix}\mathrm{Z}\\\mathrm{Z}\end{smallmatrix}$ warps with the upper weft having $\mathrm{Z}\begin{smallmatrix}\mathrm{s}\begin{smallmatrix}\mathrm{Z}\\\mathrm{Z}\end{smallmatrix}\\\mathrm{s}\begin{smallmatrix}\mathrm{Z}\\\mathrm{Z}\end{smallmatrix}\\\mathrm{s}\begin{smallmatrix}\mathrm{Z}\\\mathrm{Z}\end{smallmatrix}\end{smallmatrix}$ knots (Pl. 34:B) to the most complex prehistoric fabric recorded for Wisconsin. The first vessel, consisting of 143 fragments, has interior rim-to-neck spaced horizontal and oblique

$Z \begin{array}{l} s\,{}^{Z}_{Z} \\ s\,{}^{Z}_{Z} \\ s\,{}^{Z}_{Z} \end{array}$ weft-twining with spaced $s\,{}^{Z}_{Z}$ warps and accessory $Z \begin{array}{l} s\,{}^{Z}_{Z} \\ s\,{}^{Z}_{Z} \end{array}$ and $Z \begin{array}{l} s\,{}^{Z}_{Z} \\ s\,{}^{Z}_{Z} \\ s\,{}^{Z}_{Z} \end{array}$ twisted cords (Fig. 56:B; Pl. 35). The complex fabric was found to be impressed upon a second vessel, consisting of 23 fragments, from 47-Wp-70, Feature 10. This fabric was a spaced horizontal and oblique $S \begin{array}{l} z\,{}^{S}_{S} \\ z\,{}^{S}_{S} \end{array}$ weft-twined fabric with spaced $z\,{}^{S}_{S}$ warps and fixed knotted loops (Fig. 58; Pl. 34:A).

Collared fragments. A total of eight vessel fragments recovered from the Sanders site are portions of collared vessels. These seven rim sections and one body sherd are too small or eroded to be placed within any of the type categories listed above.

Heins Creek Corded Stamped

Of the three proposed ceramic types representing Mason's Heins Creek Ware category (1966:202-204), one type, Heins Creek Corded Stamped (1966:16-18) is present at 47-Wp-26 and 47-Wp-70. The Sanders examples of this proposed type *differ from all others* recovered in that they have exterior cord-wrapped cord or cord-wrapped stick impressions which are located at the upper rim and lip *and* on the rim and neck regions. The length of these impressions, for the Sanders specimens, ranges from 4 to 55 mm; however, the average is 12.9 mm, with only seven examples exceeding 15 mm; the width ranges from 2 to 7 mm, with the average 3.6 mm; the depth of the impression is between 1 and 2 mm, with the average 1.4 mm; and the distance between the impressions is from 1 to 12 mm, with the average 3.9 mm. These decoration measurements agree with Mason's measurements (1966:17), and the other vessel measurements—of rim thickness (5 to 10 mm, average 7 mm), lip thickness (3 to 14 mm, average 7.7 mm), and orifice diameter (20 to 40 cm, average 30.6 cm)—also agree with those suggested by Mason for the type.

Seven rim sherds and 30 decorated body sherds representing approximately 20 vessels were recovered from the Sanders site. It should be noted that this category contains a large percentage of decorated body sherds and this association appears to be valid as no other type recovered has exterior cord-wrapped cord or stick decorations below the upper rim. Just as the cord- and fabric-

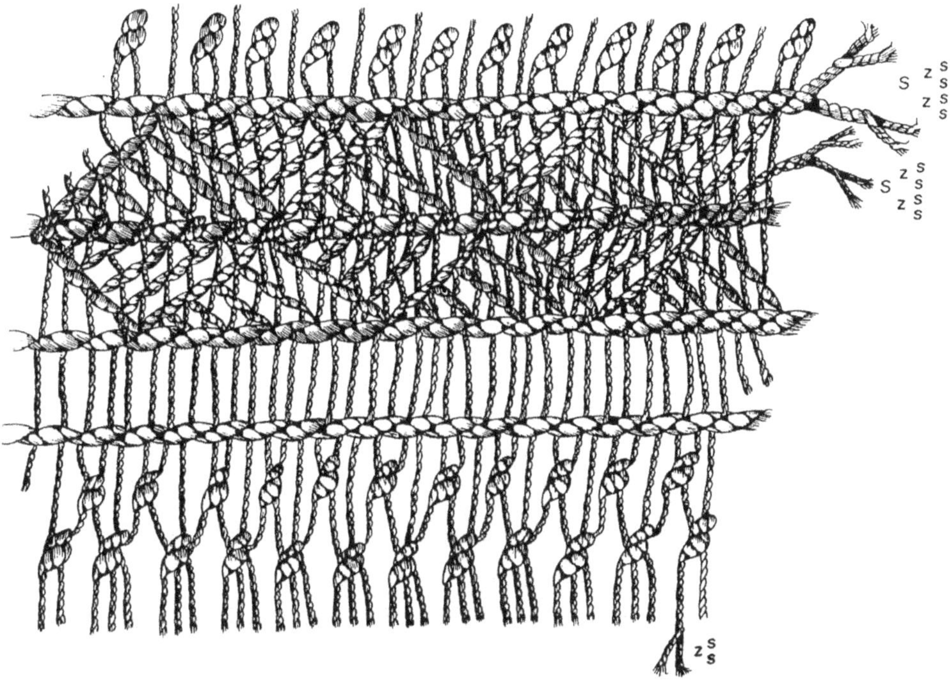

FIG. 58. Point Sauble Collared. Spaced horizontal and oblique weft-twining with spaced warps and fixed knotted loops: 47-Wp-70, feature 10.

impressed body sherds would be excluded from this category, so too, would those specimens with exclusive cord-wrapped cord or stick impressions be excluded from the cord- and fabric-impressed categories. Mason has suggested that Heins Creek ware ". . . is not a major variety of Effigy Mound pottery" (1966:145) and its numerical minority position at Sanders appears to support Mason's view. It may be that the proposed Heins Creek Corded Stamped and Heins Creek Cord-wrapped stick types bear strong relationships to the Kegonsa Stamped ceramic type proposed by Baerreis in 1952 (Hurley, 1966:54-57); however, the Sanders specimens also strongly resemble the Late Woodland Blackduck pottery of Minnesota and Canada (Evans, 1961) as Mason (1966:147) has suggested for his ware. Obviously, sites other than those on the Door Peninsula and the Sanders sites need to be excavated before the full temporal, spatial, and decoration range of these ceramics can be ascertained. The Heins Creek Corded Stamped ceramics from 47-Wp-26 and Wp-70 are ordered and presented below on the basis of the cord twist recorded for the exterior surface of the cord-wrapped cord or stick decorations.

s $\frac{z}{z}$ cord twist

Six rim sherds and 16 decorated body sherds utilize s $\frac{z}{z}$ cord for exterior cord-marking and/or exterior cord-wrapped stick decorations. These parallel decorations are placed on the lip and interior upper rim (Pl. 36:A, E) in addition to the exterior locations. Two decorated Heins Creek Corded Stamped body sherds have s $\frac{z}{z}$ cord-wrapped stick decorations which were impressed, rolled to the next location, and impressed again. Eleven specimens have smooth surfaces, two have smoothed-over cord-marked, and one has a brushed surface.

z $\frac{s}{s}$ cord twist

Six decorated Heins Creek Corded Stamped body sherds have z $\frac{s}{s}$ cord-marked exterior surfaces or utilize z $\frac{s}{s}$ cord in their exterior decorations (Pl. 36:C). One specimen has chevron-like cord-wrapped stick impressions (Pl. 36:D), and one body sherd has parallel horizontal z $\frac{s}{s}$ cord-wrapped stick impressions which have been rolled over the plastic clay to each new location.

s $\frac{z}{z}$ and z $\frac{s}{s}$ cord twist

One decorated Heins Creek Corded Stamped body sherd has two parallel vertical rows of horizontal s $\frac{z}{z}$ cord-wrapped stick impressions over a z $\frac{s}{s}$ cord-marked exterior surface.

Smooth and smoothed-over cord-marked

One rim sherd and seven decorated body sherds have smooth or smoothed-over cord-marked exterior surfaces and cord-wrapped stick or cord decorations in which the cord twist could not be ascertained. The rim sherd has cord-wrapped stick impressions on the lip and on the exterior rim (Pl. 36:B).

Grand River Ware

In 1927, Jeske reported on the Grand River mound group and camp site which actually consisted of four mound clusters of five conical mounds for Group No. 1; four conical mounds for Group

No. 2; eight conical mounds for Group No. 3; and five conicals and one bear effigy mound for Group No. 4. These mound groups plus the 14 "camp sites" (1927:Fig. 20) are located west of the Grand River in Green Lake County, Wisconsin. The ceramic artifacts recovered from the camp sites and the mounds, excluding the bear effigy which contained no artifacts, consisted of both shell- and grit-tempered ceramics, with shell tempering being the most popular variety. These ceramics were cord-marked, plain, or decorated with incised (trailed) decorations of the rim (Jeske, 1927:180-181) which could be somewhat elaborate (*ibid.*:Pl. XXXII). These Grand River sites (the Walker-Hooper sites) were briefly revisited by Towne Miller and George L. Pasco (Wisconsin Archaeologist, Vol. I, No. 1 and Vol. II, No. 3) and re-excavated by Gibbon in 1966 and 1967 (Gibbon, 1971). In addition, there are major reports dealing with the Grand River ceramics.

In 1945, McKern, using his "McKern" or Midwestern Taxonomic Method, placed the "Grand River culture" into the Grand River Focus which belongs in the Oneota Aspect of the Upper Phase of the Mississippi Pattern (1945:118). He saw this Upper Mississippi Oneota Grand River Focus as one of the three major variants (now four) or manifestations of this cultural tradition in Wisconsin and recognized the tentative status of other possible variants in Wisconsin (*ibid.*:27). The Grand River Focus ceramic type possesses ". . . certain fundamental characteristics [as Upper Mississippian pottery] which differentiate it from other wares known from the Wisconsin area . . ." (1945:143), i.e., light and flaky structure, predominantly shell temper, generally smooth surfaces with some tool marks, and generally gray to brown in color. The Grand River vessel decoration is simple in design and roughly executed and "a surprising majority of the vessels appear to have been undecorated" (*ibid.*:149). Notched or scalloped rims are rare and rim flare is less pronounced than on the other foci ceramics, for example Lake Winnebago and Orr foci. Loop handles are small and thick when present and in general the overall vessel size is medium, ca. 100 mm in diameter with restricted orifices. In summation, McKern characterized Grand River pottery as:

> . . . hard but carelessly finished ware; preponderance of drab surface coloring; complexity of shape notwithstanding a simplicity of rim shapes; scarcity of notched or scalloped rims; simplicity and scarcity of surface decoration; occasional use of paddle imprinting for purposes of surface decoration; apparent preponderance of small to medium-sized vessels (1945:152).

In his classification of the foci to be included within the Oneota Aspect, McKern saw the Upper Mississippi Phase as clearly distinct from the Middle Mississippi Phase and ". . . closer cultural similarity between the Grand River and Lake Winnebago foci than between either of these and the Orr Focus" (1945:152-163). While his differences were based on the relative abundance of chipped stone artifacts and the paucity of bone, antler, and shell artifacts for the Orr Focus sites, there are other cultural (Hall, 1962; Gibbon, 1966, 1971) and chronological differences between these foci. The chronological sequence continuum for Grand River ceramics, as represented by the published C-14 dates, suggests that the Koshkonong Focus apparently precedes the Grand River, which is an early contemporary of the Lake Winnebago, and which in turn is followed by the Orr Focus. The eastern Wisconsin location, intermediate chronological position, and the use of conical burial mounds suggests that Grand River-Effigy Mound relationships are highly probable. Thus, the Grand River Ware specimens from 47-Wp-26 take on an added significance.

Hall was the first to define the two Grand River types—Grand River Trailed and Grand River Plain (1962:65-70). Both ceramic types are considered to be diagnostic of the Grand River Focus and to occur as minor types in Hall's Koshkonong Focus. The cultural associations aside, Hall observed that these Grand River types reached ". . . their standardized form by about A.D.1000" (1962:109), which is at least 100 to 200 years earlier than the dated Grand River Focus sites.

Mason has also reported on Upper Mississippian ceramics from the Mero site where 8,628 classifiable shell- or grit-tempered sherds were recovered which represent the latest of the prehistoric manifestations at the site (1966:159). The majority of the Oneota ceramics were placed into the Mero Complex which was divided into Mero I and Mero II on the basis of grit- or shell-tempering, with the latter the latest component or phase (*ibid.*:160-161). Out of the 8,628 classified Oneota sherds from the Mero site (3,522 are Mero I and 5,106 are Mero II) only 146 or 1.7 percent are decorated and a high percentage (290 to 300 vessels out of the estimated 331) of the Oneota vessels are plain. Lip decoration did occur on over 391 rim sherds and the decoration consisted of scalloped, impressed, notched, punctated (rare), incised, or sinuous lips. Mason sees the Mero Complexes, especially Mero II, as having the lowest proportion of decorated ceramics of the thus far reported Oneota sites. A portion of these decorated ceramics (not quantified) belong to the Lake Winnebago Focus and they are either trade vessels or represent a separate later occupation (*ibid.*:162-182).

Hall (1962:64) included his type Carcajou Plain as "...a characteristic type of the Koshkonong and Grand River foci of the Oneota Aspect" and, along with the two Grand River types, it is found at Grand River sites. Carcajou Plain differs from Grand River Plain in that the former has notched lips. Lip notching is very high at Mero (75 percent) and an unquantified portion of the Mero I and II ceramics belongs to the type Carcajou Plain while the remainder (both grit- and shell-tempered) are either Grand River Plain or Grand River Trailed. However, the Grand River Trailed ceramic type is viewed as a rare type at the Mero site because of the scarcity of decorated ceramics (Mason, 1966:185-186). Mason concludes his analysis of the Mero Complexes by stating:

> It is proposed that the Mero I and II Complexes are best classified as sequential regional expressions of the widespread Grand River Focus. Adopting Hall's chronology of Oneota development (1962:Pl. 83), the Mero Complex should date some time between A.D. 1200 and 1400. (1966:186)

Outside the fact that Mason did not quantify his large sample into these Upper Mississippian Oneota ceramic types, I believe that his overall assessments are valid. However, as there is a scarcity of lip notching at 47-Wp-26, the two Oneota types present are Grand River Plain and Grand River Trailed and yet I wonder if Mason has not missed some nuances in his analysis of the Mero ceramics which were seen 20 years earlier. McKern made reference to two undefined foci, one around Lake Koshkonong (now the Koshkonong Focus) and one around Green Bay "... of which too little is known to warrant any present attempt at classification" (1945:127) or they "... may eventually be classed with one or more of these subdivisions, or may be found to rate separate classification" (1945:163). *If* there is another focus around Green Bay then Mason with his very large sample could have defined it. I assume that his classification of his ceramics into the Grand River Focus means that the unnamed focus around Green Bay does not exist and I will, therefore, follow Mason and consider the Upper Mississippian Oneota ceramics from Sanders site 1 as representative of the Grand River Focus whose age and relationships to the Effigy Mound tradition will be discussed in the following chapters.

Grand River Trailed

Included within this ceramic type are six rim sections and 14 decorated body sherds representing approximately 10 vessels. Four specimens have fine to medium grit tempering, eight have fine to medium shell tempering, and four are mixtures of both. The rims are insloping and they range in thickness from 3 to 8 mm, with the average 5.3 mm. Lips are rounded or flattened and they have the same thickness range and average as the rims, while the decorated body sherds range from 4 to 11 mm in thickness with an average of 6.6 mm. Textures are contorted or compact; the hardness is restricted to a range between 2 and 3, with the average 2.4. The surface colors vary from tan to dark brown and the exterior surfaces are generally lusterless with some evidence of tool marks on both surfaces. Some of the specimens included within this ceramic type have cord-wrapped stick, cord-impressed, or cord-rolled decorations and they are considered as decoration variations within the type at this site and not type varieties, as the sample is quite limited and these decorations have not been reported at other sites. It is suggested, therefore, that these decorations and the mixed tempering are indicators of local manufacture rather than of trade vessels. The ceramics presented below will be grouped according to cord twist plus decoration, or according to decoration alone.

s $\frac{Z}{Z}$ *cord twist*

Two rim sherds and three decorated body sherds utilize s $\frac{Z}{Z}$ cords in their decorations. One rim sherd has at the neck-rim junction a horizontal row of s $\frac{Z}{Z}$ cord impressions (Pl. 37:D). One rim sherd and one body sherd have parallel s $\frac{Z}{Z}$ cord-wrapped stick impressions. The remaining four specimens have s $\frac{Z}{Z}$ cord rolled exteriors or s $\frac{Z}{Z}$ cord marking.

z $\frac{S}{S}$ *cord twist*

One decorated rim sherd has exterior z $\frac{S}{S}$ cord impressions (Pl. 33:C; Pl. 37:C). Two body sherds in this category have z $\frac{S}{S}$ cord-marked exteriors.

Cord wrapped stick impressed, punctated, and trailed

(a) One rim sherd and one decorated body sherd have cord-wrapped stick impressions. On the rim sherd they are located at the upper interior and exterior rim. The body sherd has only an incomplete cord-wrapped stick impression. (b) One body sherd has one circular reed or bone punctation which has not raised an interior node, and one rim sherd has very shallow notches across the lip. (c) One rim sherd and six body sherds have trailed lines which join and form triangles (Pl. 33:F; Pl. 37:J, N).

Grand River Plain

In the Grand River Plain ceramic type category from 47-Wp-26 (Pl. 33:D, E; Pl. 37:A, B, E-I, K, M; Pl. 38:B), there are 42 rim sections and one associated body sherd representing approximately 25 vessels. They have the same texture and tempering as the Grand River Trailed ceramics and these specimens all have smooth exterior surfaces. Rims are insloping, vertical, or insloping and then vertical with a range in thickness between 3 and 8 mm, the average being 5.2 mm. Lips are rounded, flattened, beveled, or flattened with a slight exterior overhang or fold over of the clay. The lips range in thickness from 3 to 9 mm, with the average 4.9 mm. Surface hardness ranges between 2 and 3 with the specimens averaging 2.6, and the exterior surfaces exhibit both tool marks and brushing. Five of the Grand River Plain specimens have measurable orifice diameters and their range is between 9 and 40 cm, with the average 20.0 cm.

As the type name implies, these ceramics lack both lip and body decoration (Hall, 1962:68) and these examples conform to the type specimens. However, there are particular specimens which have individual attributes which need to be presented. One rim sherd, for example, has vertical brushing on its exterior surface and the point of "brush" and vessel contact can be seen below the exterior lip (Pl. 37:G). One partially reconstructed vessel has a pinched and thickened upper rim with slight exterior polish and horizontal brushing (Pl. 37:A, B; Pl. 38:B).

Grand River handle. One shell-tempered vessel fragment appears to be an effigy tail handle which was formed with the vessel, not subsequently attached. The handle extends at right angle 22 mm from the lip. It is triangular in outline, smooth surfaced, 6 mm thick, and 24 mm wide at the lip juncture.

Grand River body sherds. There are 203 body sherds included here which are a portion of the Oneota Grand River manifestation as it occurs at 47-Wp-26. These body sherds could be placed with either of the Grand River types as they are all smooth surfaced, lack decoration, and their hardness, texture, and colors are similar to those described above. Their thickness ranges from 2 to 9 mm, with the average 4.8 mm. Twenty-five of these specimens have mixed shell- and grit-tempering.

Eroded rim sherds

The large quantity of excavated ceramics from 47-Wp-26 and 47-Wp-70 included 193 rim sherds which could not be typologically ordered because of their eroded surfaces. These sherds do not conform to ceramics normally included under a heading of miscellaneous, trade, or aberrant. Their eroded surfaces preclude any positive identification other than the fact that they are grit-tempered and that they are rim sherds.

Decorated body sherds

Three decorated body sherds from 47-Wp-26 cannot be readily associated with any of the rim sherd categories listed above and yet their decorations are distinctive enough to be described. Two of the body sherds have s $\frac{z}{z}$ or z $\frac{s}{s}$ cord-marked exterior surfaces and interiors which are horizontally brushed in bands between 33 and 38 mm wide (Pl. 16:I, K). The third body sherd (Pl. 16:J) has an s $\frac{z}{z}$ cord-marked exterior, and interior parallel vertical rows of s $\frac{z}{z}$ cord-wrapped stick impressions. Below this decoration is a horizontal band of s $\frac{z}{z}$ cord rolling.

Child's vessel

The only whole or complete vessel excavated at the Sanders site was the "child's vessel" or "seed pot" found on the floor of House 1 at 47-Wp-70. This smooth surfaced vessel (Pl. 36:G) has a compact texture, medium grit temper, brown surface color, and black core, and a hardness of 2. The rim is outflaring and 3 mm thick, and the orifice measures 3.3 cm. The lip is rounded and 4 mm thick, and the overall height is 27 mm. The vessel bears no trace of food remains or evidence of use as a "paint pot."

Elbow pipe

One ceramic pipe (Pl. 36:H) was excavated at 47-Wp-26 and it was found in linear Mound 3. It has a smooth surface and the following dimensions: length: stem = 49 mm, bowl = 23 mm; width: stem = 17 mm, bowl = 30 mm for outer diameter and 21 mm for inner diameter; thickness: 3 mm for stem and 6 mm for bowl; stem outer diameter is 9 mm with its orifice diameter 4 mm. This pipe lacks decoration.

Clay fragments

Both fired and unfired clay fragments were recovered from mound, house, feature, and square areas. A total of 21 specimens were examined for molding, modeling, or decorations and they appear to be amorphous in shape and function.

Undecorated body sherds

The undecorated grit-tempered body sherds excavated at 47-Wp-26 and 47-Wp-70 represent the largest numerical category of sherds, totalling 20,215. More than three-quarters (15,631) of these sherds either were small sherdlets or their surfaces were too eroded to be included within the ceramic analysis. The remaining 4,584 body sherds are grouped below into two categories on the basis of surface treatment. The cord marked category is further subdivided into $s\frac{z}{z}$ cord marked and $z\frac{s}{s}$ cord marked.

Category 1. Cord-marked body sherds. Of the total 4,584 body sherds, 1,863 or 40.6 percent have exterior surfaces which have been cord marked. These sherds are grit-tempered, the temper size ranging from 1/4 to 4 mm, or from fine to granular temper in a paste texture which is either compact or contorted. The hardness ranges from 1.5 to 3.0, with the average 2.0, and the colors range through tan, red, brown, to black. These body sherds, along with those of Category 2, are associated with all but the Grand River Ware ceramics.

1a. $s\frac{z}{z}$ cord marked body sherds

Of the 1,863 cord-marked body sherds, 1,097 (58.9 percent) have $s\frac{z}{z}$ exterior cord marking and this number represents 23.9

percent of the total recorded in this undecorated body sherd category.

1b. z $\frac{S}{S}$ cord-marked body sherds

A total of 766 (41.1 percent) body sherds have z $\frac{S}{S}$ cord-marked exterior surfaces and of the total body sherds this represents 16.7 percent.

Category 2. Smoothed-over cord and smooth surface body sherds. There are 2,721 or 59.3 percent of the body sherds from the Sanders site which have exterior surfaces that have been smoothed prior to or subsequent to firing.

Ceramic Bead (Pl. 44:A)

One shell-tempered artifact is a circular bead 15 mm in diameter and 2 mm thick. The central hole appears to have been ground through with a pointed rotating object resulting in a hole 2 mm in diameter. There is no surface decoration and the surfaces are quite smooth.

LITHIC ARTIFACTS

The lithic artifacts excavated at the Sanders site consist of a total of 12,188 specimens: 476 (3.9 percent) are functional artifacts and the remaining 11,712 represent non-utilized waste flakes. Of the total 476 artifacts, more than one-third (188 or 39.4 percent) are grouped into the artifact categories of worked or utilized flakes. The lithic artifacts are few in number when compared to the ceramic artifacts from the Sanders site (there are 7,034 analyzable ceramic artifacts and only 476 lithic (6.3 percent) artifacts); however, both the total and percentage exceed those recorded for the Bigelow site.

Projectile Points

The projectile points are grouped below into the established types of Waubesa Contracting Stem, Madison Side Notched, and

Durst Stemmed and the proposed projectile point type of Sanders Triangular. In addition, the remaining points are grouped into four categories: corner notched, side notched, serrated Triangular and Triangular. The larger portion of the lithic artifacts is grouped below into the following descriptive categories: projectile point fragments, drills, diminutive scrapers, scrapers, knives, cores, gravers, burins, burin spalls, blades, worked flakes, utilized flakes, unworked flakes, shaft polisher, adzes, celt, gorget, polished stone fragments, grinding stone and hammer stones.

Waubesa Contracting Stem (Pl. 39:C, D; Pl. 41:A)

The projectile point type Waubesa Contracting Stem was first proposed by Baerreis (1953*b*:155) for points whose stems contracted gently towards the base. Points of this type were excavated at the Airport Village site along with Madison Side Notched points and ceramics which were later grouped under the typological heading of Dane Incised. The total assemblage from this site was placed by Baerreis into a Late Archaic component and an Early Woodland component (1953*b*:163-164). Waubesa Contracting Stem points were again reported by Baerreis for the Madison, Wisconsin area where five Waubesa Contracting Stem points were recovered from the mound fill of a bird effigy mound of the Willow Drive Mound group. The measurements recorded for these points are: length = 40, 48, and 63 mm; width = 27, 28, 29, and 33 mm; and thickness = 9, 9, 11, 11, and 12 mm (1966:108-109). In the same area, at the Picnic Grove Mound group, one linear mound yielded a Madison Side Notched point and a Waubesa Contracting Stem point, the latter measuring 27 mm in width and 8 mm in thickness. Baerreis considered these mounds and, by extension, possibly the points to date from circa A.D. 500 to A.D. 1100. However, in the publication "A Guide to Wisconsin Indian Projectile Point Types" (Ritzenthaler, 1967:27), the age and culture affiliation for the Waubesa Contracting Stem points is listed as Late Archaic through Middle Woodland, with the latter extending to A.D. 800 according to the cultural sequence presented for Wisconsin (1967:7).

Thirteen projectile points from 47-Wp-26 and Wp-70 are contracted stem specimens which are considered to be Waubesa Contracting Stem points. Their blades are equilateral or isosceles triangular in outline with convex blade edges that converge gradually or sharply towards the tip. The blades are plano-convex to biconvex in cross section and the shoulders are acute to slightly obtuse, although one specimen has one straight and one acute shoulder (Pl. 39:C). Surfaces have either fine flat bifacial workmanship with fine to medium edge retouch, or ruder workmanship which has left traces of the cortex. One specimen has almost unifacial workmanship with retouch confined to the blade edges. The stems are slight to pronounced in their contraction and in all instances the stems appear to have been produced by multiple blows from all angles. In three instances the stem was subsequently ground. The bases are straight or convex; three examples retain their striking platform and eight have been basally thinned. The measurements for these points can be found in Table 19.

Corner Notched (Pl. 39:B)

Six projectile points or point fragments from 47-Wp-26 and 47-Wp-70 are classed as corner notched points. These projectile points are tan quartzite or cream to gray chert. The blades are isosceles or equilateral in outline with convex blade edges converging gradually towards the tip. Blades are plano-convex to biconvex in cross section and the shoulders are straight to obtuse with slight to medium barbs. The corner notches are shallow to deeply set and form short to medium stems. The bases are concave to convex with slight grinding on one specimen and are thinned. The measurements for these points are listed in Table 19.

Side Notched (Pl. 39:A, B; Pl. 41:B)

Eight projectile points are included within this descriptive category: two are Madison Side Notched points (Baerreis, 1953*b*) and six are smaller, amorphous specimens. The Madison Side Notched points are gray or cream chert with blades that are isosceles in outline with convex edges that converge gradually towards the tip. There is medium to fine retouch along the blade edges with one specimen having slightly serrated edges. The shoulders are straight to acute with medium barbs and the side notching is shallow to medium in depth and placed into a short to medium stem. The remaining six side notched points are of mottled cream to gray chert with equilateral or isosceles blade outlines. The convex blade edges converge gradually toward the tip with the blades being biconvex in cross section and exhibiting medium lateral blade edge retouch. Shoulders are obtuse to acute with the notches shallow to medium, forming short to medium stems. Bases are straight or concave, basally thinned, and three specimens have

TABLE 19

DIMENSIONS OF PROJECTILE POINTS FROM 47-Wp-26 AND Wp-70
(in mm)

Type/ Category	Length	Maximum Width	Maximum Thickness	Minimum Width Between Notches	Stem Length	Stem Width	Stem Thickness	Base Length	Base Width	Base Thickness
Waubesa										
Contracting	R 33-48	20-32	5-10		9-15	12-18	4-9	2-2.5	7-13	2-6
Stem	$\bar{X}$ 41.2	24.2	7.9		12.0	14.8	6.3	2.2	11.0	3.1
Corner	R 28-46	19-28	4-8	9-18	3-5	9-19	3-6	2-5	11-18	1-2
Notched	$\bar{X}$ 36.5	21.2	5.8	13.7	4.0	13.7	4.5	3.4	14.3	1.6
Madison										
Side	R 35-48	19-26	6-8	14-16	4-5	17-21	6	4-5	17-19	1-2
Notched	$\bar{X}$ 41.5	22.5	7.0	15.0	4.5	19.0	6	4.5	18	1.5
Side	R 18-44	12-21	4-7	9-14	2-5	9-19	3-6	3-8	12-18	1-3
Notched	$\bar{X}$ 29.4	16.8	5.3	11.1	3.7	14.3	4.5	4.5	15.0	2.0
Durst	R 23-37	12-16	6-10		5-10	9-12	3-7	1-3	11-13	2
Stemmed	$\bar{X}$ 28.7	14.5	6.7		8.1	10.1	5.1	2.0	11.6	2
Sanders	R 17-30	12-20	2-6							1-6
Triangular	$\bar{X}$ 22.6	15.3	3.4							2.1
Serrated	R 19-30	14-21	3-5							1-3
Triangular	$\bar{X}$ 23.7	15.7	3.8							1.8
Triangular	R 14-30	9-19	3-6							1-2
	$\bar{X}$ 21.5	15.2	3.9							1.9

basal grinding. The measurements for the Madison Side Notched and these six side notched points are listed in Table 19.

Durst Stemmed (Pl. 39:D; Pl. 40:A)

Eight projectile points from 47-Wp-26 and Wp-70 are classed within the projectile point type Durst Stemmed (Wittry, 1959*c*:179-180). Three of these points are of clear to cream quartz, three are of tan or gray quartzite, and two are of gray or brown chert. The blades are biconvex in cross section and trianguloid in outline with the convex blade edges converging gradually to the tip. The lateral blade edges have slight to medium retouch which does not continue down onto the lateral stem edges. The stems were produced by multiple blows which have left acute shoulders on these specimens. The bases are convex or straight and they have been thinned. One characteristic of this type, which was noted for Durst Stemmed points from the Kickapoo River Valley in southwestern Wisconsin, was that the base was consistently 2 mm wider than the stem (Hurley, 1965*a*:92). The Durst Stemmed points from the Sanders site have bases which have measurements wider than the stem, with the range being between 1 to 3 mm more for the base. None of these points has basal grinding.

Triangular Projectile Points

The majority of projectile points recovered from the Bigelow site were Triangular points which were sorted according to the presence or absence of serrated lateral blade edge retouch. The Triangular specimens from the Sanders site can also be subdivided according to this attribute. There are 11 specimens, however, which have a distinctive cluster of attributes which appear to set them apart from the rest of the Sanders sample. Before we examine these specimens let us review how several archaeologists have classified Triangular points recovered from the Great Lakes area. The un-notched Triangular point is a rather innocuous technological and morphological projectile form which has received limited archaeological attention. As haft elements are most diagnostic in distinguishing variation between projectile point forms, the absence of these elements in Triangular points has led to a broad lumping of various sized points. Scully (1951:14) indicated that his Madison Points had a length range between 12 and 61 mm with an average of approximately 24 mm. In width these points range between 6 and 45 mm and, excluding the proposed sub-types, the points were suggested as being Middle Mississippian in cultural association. Ritchie (1961:33-34) states that the New York

Madison Points have a range of 19 to 38 mm for their length with the average being between 25 and 32 mm. Ritchie also considers these points to be associated with Middle Mississippian peoples but he extends the upper temporal range to early Historic times by including Upper Mississippian and Late Woodland associations. In the adjacent geographic area of Ontario, at the stratified Pic River site, three Triangular points from Stratum I have a length range between 27 and 30 mm and widths ranging from 16 to 20 mm, with an average width of 18.3 mm; four Triangular points from Stratum II have a length range from 24 to 35 mm, with an average of 29.0 mm, and a width range between 15 and 20 mm, with an average of 17.8 mm; and lower Stratum III produced 14 Triangular points with length ranges between 19 and 33 mm with an average of 25.5 mm, and a width from 11 to 24 mm with an average of 17.7 mm (Wright, 1966:66, 72, 82-83). Wright noted that one point from Stratum I was unifacial; two points from Stratum II were unifacial, with only lateral edge retouch; and from Stratum III "...four are unifacially retouched, and the remainder are predominantly retouched along the edges with little modification to the original flake surface on both faces" (*ibid*.:82). This multi-component site was occupied from A.D. 950 to Historic times by a single (Ojibwa?) ethnic group (*ibid*.:91).

At the stratified Michipicoten site on the north shore of Lake Superior, Wright (1968) recovered three Triangular points from Stratum II of which "... two are largely unaltered on both faces with chipping being restricted to the edges" (1968:17). The length measurements are 23 and 26 mm and the width measurements are between 13 and 16 mm. In Stratum III, 11 projectiles were un-notched Triangulars, of which six were largely worked on the edges only. Their length range is between 19 to 23 mm with an average of 20.3 mm, and the maximum width measurements were between 12 to 17 mm with the average being 15.4 mm (*ibid*.:27). In Stratum IV two Triangular points were recovered, one having unifacial retouch and the other having only edge retouch. The one complete specimen measured 16 mm in length; 15 and 14 mm were recorded as width measurements for these points (*ibid*.:33). The Michipicoten site was occupied from approximately A.D. 1100 until the Historic period. The Triangular points most probably date after A.D. 1400 and represent an indigenous Ojibwa culture history, and are relatable to the Pic River site (*ibid*.:49-51).

Closer to the effigy mound area is the Juntunen site on Bois Blanc Island in the Straits of Mackinac. This site produced a projectile point variety named "Juntunen Triangular," a proposed

Late Woodland form dating between A.D. 800 and A.D. 1400 (McPherron, 1967:148-153, Fig. 43). McPherron recovered points "... retouched on one face but with no retouch at all on the other, hence 'unifacial' artifacts, to points with both original surfaces of cleavage completely intact, the items having been brought to shape by edge-trim" (*ibid.*:149). Ninety-two points are considered as "Juntunen Triangular" specimens with a mean length of 27 mm and a mean width of 17 mm (*ibid.*:Table 18).

Within the effigy mound area at the site of Aztalan, Maher and Baerreis (1958) closely examined the un-notched Triangular points and compared their measurements with those from points recovered from other Wisconsin sites. The Triangular points from Aztalan were assumed to be Middle Mississippian in cultural affiliation (*ibid.*:5-6, 10). The Aztalan point maker showed "... a significant preference for a wider and longer point..." (*ibid.*:13) as 200 points were measured and the mean width was 18.75 and the mean length 25.82 mm. Moreover, of 341 Triangular points from Aztalan, 309 were straight based, 32 were concave based, and only six specimens had purposely produced lateral edge serrations (*ibid.*:8). Maher and Baerreis did find a similarity in form (triangular) between the Aztalan specimens and Upper Mississippian Phase points, the latter being narrower and shorter than the points from Aztalan (*ibid.*:Tables III-V). If the means are considered for all the sites included here in this discussion of Triangular points as well as those presented by Maher and Baerreis for five Upper Mississippian sites, we arrive at a figure of 24 mm for length and 16 mm for width, or a projectile point approximately one-third longer than wide. This ratio is held by all the sites except for the points from the Michipicoten site, which are more equilateral than those from the upper strata of the Pic River site and the Juntunen site.

To return to the central issue, there are Triangular points from 47-Wp-26 (and the Bigelow site) with distinctive attributes. Although these attributes have been noted for Triangular points from other sites, they were not used to propose a new point type. Wright (1966) described unifacial points with only lateral edge retouch and points having little surface modification at the Pic River site. At the Michipicoten site, these same characteristics were observed for the Triangular points from all strata as they had only edge retouch or unifacial retouch (Wright, 1968). The "Juntunen Points" from Bois Blanc Island include unifacial, edge retouched, and unretouched specimens and "... points were scattered in frequency fairly evenly through this range of variation . . ." (McPherron, 1967:149). This description fits both the proposed "Juntunen Triangular" and the "Juntunen Notched" points associated with the Mackinac, Bois Blanc, and Juntunen phases of occupation, or from circa A.D. 800 to A.D. 1400 (1967: 145, 257, 270). It was thought that some of the Triangular points from the Bigelow and Sanders sites were similar to the proposed "Juntunen Triangular" points. As the term Madison Points is so broad for points spread over considerable time, space, and cultural affiliations, it will not be used here, nor will the term "Juntunen Triangular" be applied as the particular attributes listed here were not quantified for these points and the term is, therefore, a local name for Madison Points. I will propose the type name of Sanders Triangular for those points listed and described below which have attributes allowing for easy separation from other Triangular points.

Sanders Triangular (Pl. 40:C, D)

Eleven projectile points recovered from the excavations at 47-Wp-26 are included within the proposed type Sanders Triangular. Ten are of cream to dark gray chert and one is of cream quartzite. Seven of these points are concavo-convex in cross section with the convex face exhibiting little or no surface modification. The remaining four points are plano-convex in cross section with the plane faces having random to medium edge retouch, while the obverse faces have medium to fine edge retouch leading in two instances to medium to steep serrated edges. The obverse faces also have medium to fine surface modification which heightens the unifacial aspects of the reverse faces. Three of the proposed Sanders Triangular points have equilateral outlines while the remaining eight points are isosceles in outline. Five bases have been thinned and one is unifacially retouched. Five bases are convex, five are straight, and one has a concavity of 2 mm. The measurements for this proposed type are listed in Table 19.

Serrated Triangular Projectile Points (Pl. 40:B, C, D)

Sanders Site 1 yielded 13 Triangular points with serrated lateral blade edges of which two also have serrated bases. Ten of these projectile points are of cream to gray quartzite and three are of gray chert. Ten of these points are isosceles and three are equilateral in outline. These points are biconvex in cross section with bifacial retouch across the faces. The serrated edges are medium to deep and one specimen has a blade edge beveled from the base to the tip (Fig. 99:B). The bases are retouched in nine examples and thinned in three and the base shape is almost equally divided between straight, concave, and convex. The measurements of these serrated Triangular points are listed in Table 19.

Triangular (Pl. 40:B, C, D; Pl. 41:C)

The remaining 33 befacial Triangular projectile points are grouped under this broad heading as they lack serrated edges. Twelve are a mottled cream, pink, or gray chert; two are of clear quartz; and 19 are of cream, tan, or brown quartzite. All of these points are biconvex in cross section with fine to medium flaking across each face and fine to medium retouch along the lateral blade edges. Twenty-one Triangular points have isosceles outlines and 12 are equilateral in outline. One specimen from Mound 24 has one lateral blade edge which is beveled. The bases are thinned on 18 specimens and retouched on the same number of points. Straight bases predominate with 18 examples, and then in decreasing order are 12 specimens with concave bases (between 1 to 2 mm in depth) and two with convex bases. Two specimens also have basal grinding and one Triangular point retains its striking platform as its base (Pl. 40:B). The measurements for these Triangular points can be found in Table 19.

Projectile Point Fragments. Fifty-six implement fragments are classed as projectile point fragments as their morphology excludes them from the drill, scraper, knife, or flake categories to be presented below. In addition, none of these fragments belongs to points classed as Triangular. Included within this category are 30 distal or tip fragments, 15 blade midsections, and eight stems and bases.

Drills (Pl. 42:D)

Eleven specimens from 47-Wp-26 and 47-Wp-70 are classed as drills or drill shafts. Ten of these specimens are of dark gray to cream chert and one is of brown quartzite. The complete examples, or those with haft elements, demonstrate a wide range of forms. For example: two are isosceles in outline but one has an irregular base and the other has a concave base (Pl. 42:D); one is also isosceles but 15 mm from the concave base it becomes pentagonal to the shaft; one specimen (Pl. 42:D) has a convex base which has been thinned and ground, and in outline it is semi-T shaped; two specimens (Pl. 42:D) are stemmed, the former being irregular and expanding and retaining its striking platform, and the latter sharply contracting so that it is a drill at both ends with an expanded mid-section. The remaining two drills are either reworked Waubesa Contracting Stem points with convex bases or straight stemmed specimens with irregular bases. The three drill shafts are narrow parallel sided (9 to 17 mm wide) with diamond-shaped cross sections and have fine to medium retouch. The drills themselves have diamond to thick lenticular cross sections and well defined shafts except where they have been reworked from a projectile point. All of the tips show complete grinding with the grinding extending away from the tip for distances up to 10 mm. As their shapes vary, only the maximum range of dimensions will be given: thickness = 5 to 12 mm; length = 32 to 58 mm; and width = stem: 14 to 26 mm and shaft: 7 to 14 mm.

Diminutive Scrapers (Pl. 41:D; Pl. 42:A, B, C)

Included within the tool category of diminutive scrapers are 71 specimens of which 45 are of chert (63.4 percent), 15 are of quartzite (21.1 percent), and 11 (15.5 percent) are of quartz. The colors range from clear, cream, tan, to black. In outline the diminutive scrapers are rectangular, square, triangular, oval, and irregular and in cross section they are plano-convex, flat lenticulate, and concave-convex. These scrapers are considered as diminutive because their length measurements range between 13 and 33 mm with the average 21.9 mm, in width between 10 and 32 mm with the average 19.5 mm, and in thickness between 2 and 13 mm with the average 7.2 mm. The method of manufacture appears to have been the utilization of a flake which was percussion flaked across the convex dorsal face and along the lateral and distal edges. The shaping of the ventral face is limited to secondary retouch after a few transverse flakes have been removed. The majority of the secondary retouch is steep pressure flaking across the distal end and lateral edges. One specimen (Pl. 42:B), for example, has a fine pressure flaked dorsal surface and steep lateral edge and convex distal edge flaking. At the juncture of the distal and lateral edge and at the opposite lateral and proximal juncture, are graver spurs. The proximal end is concave with steep pressure flaking. The ventral edges, which converge on the proximal end, have fine flat pressure flaking on both edges especially near the graver spur. This diminutive scraper lacks polishing on either the dorsal or ventral surfaces and only 6 or 8.4 percent of these scrapers give any evidence of use polish.

Graver spurs are generally located at the junction of an end and a lateral edge; however, some specimens have a central spur on the dorsal distal end. A total of 9 or 10.2 percent of these diminutive scrapers have graver spurs. The bulbar surface is generally the plano or concavo ventral surface and the unworked proximal end usually retains a striking platform. A few specimens have cortex remnants on their dorsal surface and a few also exhibit crushing or heavy usage along the distal or lateral working edges. One specimen (Pl. 42:B) has a convex dorsal edge with very steep pressure flaking, giving it a keeled cross section. The distribution of these scrapers indicates that one area of 47-Wp-26 was preferred for hide or wood working—the area adjacent to mounds 11-13, where 20 five-foot squares were excavated, yielded 24 diminutive scrapers, or 37.5 percent of those recovered from 47-Wp-26.

Scrapers (Pl. 40:E)

Included within this lithic category are five tools which have concentrations of secondary retouch confined to either the distal end and both lateral edges or to both lateral edges. One end scraper has non-convergent retouch (Movius, et al., 1968:11-14) across a straight edge with a steep to almost perpendicular edge produced by pressure retouch. The dorsal surface has extremely fine flat transverse parallel pressure flaking resulting in sinuous lateral edges. The edges expand to the distal end and they are worn by use. The ventral surface has one lateral edge with fine flat pressure flaking.

The two specimens illustrated in Plate 40:E are rectangular in outline and concave-convex in cross section. The first scraper is a primary decortation flake with cortex over the entire dorsal surface, except along the edges where there is very fine steep pressure flaking. The ventral surface is the bulbar surface and the proximal end has a retouched striking platform. The second example has a dorsal surface with fine longitudinal percussion flaking. The convex lateral blade edges converge to a graver spur tip and these edges have medium angled pressure flaking. The ventral surface is the bulbar surface and along the ventral lateral edges there are random usage flakes until a graver spur is reached where there is fine pressure flaking. The remaining side scrapers are large flakes (one is a decortation flake) with pressure flaked dorsal surfaces and medium angled pressure retouch along one lateral edge. Neither the proximal nor distal ends are worked and the ventral surface is the bulbar surface. None of these scrapers has polishing along its working edges and these scrapers were not included within the diminutive scraper tool class as their range and mean measurements are generally beyond that of the diminutive class. They have a length range between 36 and 50 mm with the average 45.6 mm; a width range of 31 to 42 mm with the average 34.2 mm; and a thickness range between 3 and 10 mm with the average 6.2 mm.

Knives

The tool category of knives includes 14 fairly amorphous bifacial implements classified as knives because their biconvex lateral blade edges are interpreted as having a cutting rather than a scraping function. Four of these knives are of cream to gray quartzite, four of green basalt, and the remainder are of cream to banded gray white chert. In outline they range from rectangular, triangular, ovate, asymmetrical to irregular, and in cross section they are biconvex to plano-convex. These knives are percussion flakes with now battered edges and they retain their striking platform. These specimens are not considered as wedges as the opposing edge lacks crushing or battering. One specimen is percussion flaked on both faces and along the lateral edges, and one lateral edge is convex and converges to the tip while the other is straight with a slight shoulder near the proximal end as if hafting was intended. Both lateral edges are sinuous and they are slightly worn through use. These knives have a length range from 41 to 83 mm with the average 59.2 mm; a width range from 25 to 67 mm with the average 42.7 mm; and a thickness range from 8 to 28 mm with the average 15.5 mm.

Cores

Three subdivisions are included within this category: tongue-shaped cores, polyhedral cores, and spent or exhausted cores. There is only one example of a tongue-shaped core on which two faces have been utilized for flake or blade removal. The top retains the striking platform and one lateral edge has some cortex. The core is of chert and is 30 mm long, 17 mm wide, and 10 mm thick.

Three specimens are classed as polyhedral cores. These cores had flakes removed from more than one face and the flakes were between 6 and 12 mm in width. One specimen from Mound 3 has a striking platform which appears to have been rejuvenated. The cores are between 30 and 45 mm in length, 24 and 35 mm in width, and 15 and 33 mm in thickness. Thirteen specimens (10 of chert and three of quartz) were probably polyhedral cores as almost all sides appear to have been utilized for flake removal and in some instances the striking platform is retained. Their amorphous outline is the result of the core being spent or exhausted resulting in a remnant or fragment of a larger core. Platforms were rejuvenated and some cores retain cortex; however, the remaining faces exhibit evidence of heavy percussion flake removal. These 13 specimens range in length from 16 to 35 mm with the average 23.2 mm; in width from 15 to 42 mm with the average 23.1 mm; and in thickness from 9 to 34 mm with the average 15.2 mm.

Gravers (Pl. 42:D)

Three chert examples of this tool class were recovered from the Sanders site and each will be described below. The first example is classed as a backed graver 23 mm long, 15 mm wide, and 2 mm thick. It is plano-convex in cross section and its blade is equilateral in outline. This specimen appears to have been hafted and the haft element is corner notched (Pl. 42:D) on a short stem. The edges show steep retouch and they gradually converge to the graver. The dorsal surface is percussion flaked while the ventral surface is not worked. The working end is heavily worn and thicker than the main body by about 1.5 mm. The second specimen is of gray chert, irregular in outline, and plano-convex in cross section. Its length is 22 mm, width 14 mm, and thickness 11 mm. It is a flake which has a small graver or punch 2 mm long, 2 mm wide, and 2 mm thick which has been carefully pressure flaked. The flake itself does not appear to be intentionally retouched or utilized. The third specimen is of cream chert, irregular in outline, and biconvex in cross section. Its dimensions are 24 mm long, 20 mm wide, and 6 mm thick. The flake is percussion flaked on both surfaces with a very carefully made graver or punch projection extending from one corner. The graver is 4 mm long, 6 mm wide, and 2 mm thick and there does not appear to be any flaking or usage indicated on the main flake.

Burins

Four lithic artifacts from 47-Wp-26 and 47-Wp-70 are interpreted as burins as they exhibit attributes of either Primary Burins or Secondary Burins (Hurley, 1965*a*:100). The Primary Burins are of cream chert, square to irregular in outline, and biconvex in cross section. They are 14 and 28 mm long, 12 and 33 mm wide, and 4 and 7 mm thick. By definition, the Primary Burins are those made on flakes or blades that are intended to be used only as burins and, therefore, technologically closest to the Old World specimens. The first example is bifacially percussion flaked with one lateral edge having had three burin spalls removed with the remaining facets at right angles to the main flake surface. Three hinge scars and one negative bulb of percussion remain. The direction of the blows was from the striking platform to the base where usage flaking occurs. There are no usage scars or wear evident elsewhere on the specimen. The second Primary Burin appears to be an exhausted core with remnants of the striking platform, and both surfaces exhibit numerous flake removals. At right angles to these surfaces, on one edge, are four burin facets, four hinge scars, and one negative bulb of percussion. There is no evidence of wear or usage. The proximal end has fine unifacial pressure retouch for 27 mm of its length.

The Secondary Burins or burins made on tools, whose original functions were later negated by burin utilization, are former corner notched and stemmed projectile points. The first specimen from 47-Wp-70 was a corner notched point with a convex blade edge which was broken lengthwise. It measures 36 mm long, 14 mm wide, and 11 mm thick. Five burin facets are located along the lateral edges with four hinge scars and two negative bulbs of percussion. One blow was delivered from the corner of the remaining acute shoulder towards the distal end. The remaining facets are from the distal end towards the proximal end. There is very little wear or usage evident.

The final Secondary Burin originally was a contracting stemmed projectile point 39 mm long, 18 mm wide, and 8 mm thick. The striking platform for burin spall removal was produced by removal of one lateral edge of the stem with the direction toward the distal end. The basal end was then retouched and two spalls were pressed off across the proximal basal end. There is one negative bulb of percussion and two hinge scars, and some evidence of use by the slight wear on the working edge. It is assumed that the *blade* of this Secondary Burin was hafted and served as the haft element as both lateral blade edges are ground.

Burin Spall Artifacts (Pl. 41:E)

Worked burin spalls have not been reported previously for Wisconsin and these four specimens are distinct enough to warrant separate descriptions. The first specimen from 47-Wp-26 is 22 mm long, 6 mm wide, and 4 mm thick. It is oblong in outline and flat lenticular in cross section. Indirect percussion removed this spall which has a diffuse bulb of percussion at its proximal ventral end. From the distal end, on one lateral side, there is one burin facet at right angles to the surfaces and it has a hinge fracture and a negative bulb of percussion. The opposing lateral edge has two facets with negative bulbs of percussion and hinge fractures. At the proximal end there is an additional facet with a negative bulb of percussion. Thus, this specimen has three hinge fractures, four negative bulbs of percussion and it appears to have been used at both ends. The second specimen was actually the first found at 47-Wp-26. It is 14 mm long, 4 mm wide, 4 mm thick, oblong in outline, and triangular in cross section (Pl. 41:E). Indirect percussion removed this spall whose ventral surface lacks a bulb of percussion due to its extensive utilization (at both ends) as a tool. The ventral lateral and dorsal lateral edges have fine steep retouch and the dorsal surface has had one spall removed from the distal end towards the proximal end where there is a hinge scar.

The third burin spall is 35 mm long, 7 mm wide, 9 mm thick, oblong in outline, and triangular in cross section. It was removed by indirect percussion and it has had a spall removed from the ventral surface leaving a negative bulb of percussion. Seven spalls were removed from one lateral edge leaving seven hinge scars and one negative bulb of percussion. The proximal end has been retouched and the distal end shows usage flaking and polishing along one lateral edge. The fourth example is 14 mm long, 3 mm wide, 2 mm thick, oblong in outline, and flat lenticular in cross section. This spall was detached by indirect percussion and the dorsal surface is faceted but apparently not for additional burins as no hinge scars remain and the distal end appears to have been used.

Blades

The eight specimens included in this category do not represent a viable blade industry at the Sanders site. These specimens are classed as blades as they are twice as long as they are wide, parallel sided, and have the outline of blades or blade-like flakes. Six of these specimens exhibit characteristics which are similar to "primary ridge flakes" (Sanger, 1968:197): they are triangular in cross section and have transverse flaking over both dorsal surfaces. These six specimens range in length from 25 to 49 mm with the average 35.8 mm; in width from 8 to 22 mm with the average 15.1 mm; and in thickness between 3 and 6 mm with the average 4.0 mm. Three are of basalt, two of chert, and one is of quartzite. They have all been pressure detached with a diffused bulb of percussion remaining at the ventral proximal end. The lateral edges appear to have been utilized with evidence of non-localized flake removal. The remaining two specimens are blades which lack transverse flaking and which are trapezoidal in cross section. Each specimen has a well defined longitudinal concave flute resulting from previous blade detachment. The striking platforms are at 90° angles to the dorsal face and there is no preparation on one while the other has a crushed end. One specimen appears to be a complete blade while the other is "proximally squared" (Sanger, 1968:195). These blades are 21 and 22 mm long, 9 and 11 mm wide, and 3 mm thick.

Worked Flakes

The tool category of worked flakes has been differentiated from utilized flakes by several authors: Nero (1948:23-28), Haag and Webb (1953:245-248), Bird (in Ford and Webb, 1956:85-87), and Deetz (1962:1-14). In the analysis of the flakes from Silver Creek I or 47-Mo-1 (Hurley, 1966:151-171) an attribute list was prepared for worked flakes and the most important observations were that: (a) conchoidal scars will extend from the scraping or cutting edge onto the obverse and/or reverse faces if the flake edges have been secondarily pressure or percussion retouched; (b) secondary retouch is minutely steep along one or more localized areas on the ventral and/or dorsal edges of worked flakes; and (c) worked and utilized flake side and end scraping implements are generally irregular in outline and plano to concavo-convex in cross section, whereas flake knives are longer than they are wide and are biconvex in cross section. The flakes from 47-Mo-1 were sorted according to descriptive functional categories and some of these categories will be used for the Sanders specimens.

Single Edge Flake Side Scrapers. Twenty-one specimens of cream to gray chert, three of clear quartz, and four of tan to pink quartzite are classed as Single Edge Flake Side Scrapers. These 28 specimens range in length from 10 to 51 mm with the average 21.5 mm; in width from 9 to 27 mm with the average 14.6 mm; and in thickness from 3 to 13 mm with the average 6.0 mm. These scrapers are irregular, semi-lunar, triangular, rectangular, and square in outline and in cross section they are plano-convex. The dorsal surface is generally percussion flaked with one lateral dorsal or ventral edge having fine regular steep pressure retouch. One specimen has dorsal pressure flaking over half the distance from the proximal end and the remaining one-half is pressure flaked distally along the ventral edge. The dorsal surface may retain cortex and the ventral surface is generally smooth with a prominent bulb of percussion.

Multiple Edge Flake Side Scrapers. Thirty-one worked flakes from 47-Wp-26 and Wp-70 are classed as Multiple Edge Flake Side Scrapers. Of this number 27 are of cream to gray chert, two are of clear quartz, and two are of red or cream quartzite. In length they range from 13 to 35 mm with the average 22.4 mm; in width they are between 13 and 29 mm with the average 17.6 mm; and in thickness they are between 3 and 11 mm with the average 6.0 mm. These scrapers range from rectangular to irregular in outline and in cross section they are concavo-convex or plano-convex. The dorsal surface is usually percussion flaked and the ventral surface is the bulbar surface. As their name implies, these worked flakes have two or more edges which have medium to fine pressure retouch. This retouch can be on alternating dorsal and ventral edges or, more usually, along the dorsal lateral edges. One specimen has five edges showing very fine pressure retouch. Only three of these worked flakes retain some cortex on their dorsal surfaces and seven examples have retained their striking platforms.

Flake End Scrapers. Seventeen Flake End Scrapers are of cream to gray chert, four are of clear quartz, and two are of cream quartzite. These worked flakes range in length from 12 to 33 mm with the average 20.0 mm; in width they range between 9 and 27 mm with the average 17.0 mm; and in thickness they range between 3 and 19 mm with the average 6.5 mm. They are rectangular to irregular in outline and plano-convex in cross section. The ventral or bulbar surface is generally smooth and the dorsal surfaces are transversely percussion flaked. The distal end is the working end of these scrapers and this end exhibits fine medium to steep pressure retouch and only one specimen has polishing. This Flake End Scraper has percussion flaked dorsal and ventral surfaces with the convex distal end exhibiting very heavy use and polishing which is carried over onto the ventral surface. A second scraper has on its dorsal face a straight proximal edge which has steep percussion flaking and ventrally the convex distal edge has steep pressure flaking; so this specimen could be considered a double ended alternate end scraper. Out of the total Flake End Scrapers, only two have some secondary retouch along one lateral edge.

Flake Knives. Included within this worked flake tool category are 25 tan, gray, red, orange, and cream chert examples; three of clear quartz; five of tan, cream, and pink quartzite; and one of red jasper. The Flake Knives range in length from 16 to 45 mm with the average length for the 34 specimens being 28.8 mm. In width they range from 12 to 30 mm with the average 22.6 mm, while the range in thickness for the Flake Knives is between 3 and 17 mm with the average 8.1 mm. The Flake Knives are longer than they are wide, biconvex in cross section, rectangular to irregular in outline, and have at least one bifacially secondary retouched lateral edge. This retouch may be fine flat pressure retouch or deep percussion flaking resulting in a sinuous cutting edge. One example has percussion flaked dorsal and ventral surfaces with straight lateral blade edges which exhibit deep bifacial pressure flaking resulting in a slightly sinuous edge. The cutting edge is worn through use and the distal end is broken. The proximal end retains both its cortex and its striking platform.

Utilized Flakes. The major attributes derived from the study of utilized flakes at Silver Creek I (47-Mo-1) were the following: (a) Unretouched flakes exhibit shallow to deep irregular hinge fractures restricted to the flake edge and on one face adjacent to the edge if the flake was used as a scraping implement. (b) Unretouched flakes used as cutting implements exhibit shallow to deep irregular flake scars on both the obverse and reverse edges which lose their sharpness with use. (c) Unretouched flakes used as cutting or scraping implements exhibit non-localized hinge fractures along the scraping or cutting edges. Under the heading of utilized flakes are three descriptive/functional categories which are described below for the specimens from 47-Wp-26 and 47-Wp-70.

Single Edge Utilized Flake Side Scrapers. Twenty-one specimens are of cream to dark gray chert, four are of clear quartz, and two are of tan quartzite. The Single Edge Utilized Flake Side Scrapers range in length from 15 to 44 mm with the average 24.9 mm; in width they range between 7 and 26 mm with the average 16.5 mm; and in thickness they are between 2 and 18 mm with the average 6.7 mm. The outlines of these scrapers are rectangular, semi-lunar, and irregular and in cross section they are plano-convex. Generally the flakes have percussion flaked dorsal surfaces with the ventral surface being the bulbar surface. One lateral edge will exhibit non-localized usage fractures. These small non-systematic use fractures do occur on the ventral lateral edge on two examples.

Multiple Edge Utilized Flake Side Scrapers. Included in this category are 25 chert flakes which are of banded cream and red, cream or gray color; three of quartz which are clear; and two of quartzite which are cream or tan. These utilized flakes range in length from 11 to 41 mm with the average 23.6 mm; in width from 10 to 30 mm with the average 18.5 mm; and in thickness they range from 2 to 14 mm with the average 6.0 mm. In outline these Multiple Edge Utilized Flake Side Scrapers are triangular, semi-lunar, rectangular, and irregular, and in cross section they are concavo-convex or plano-convex. These utilized flakes generally have two or more edges which exhibit non-localized usage flaking and this is normally confined to the dorsal lateral edges. There are, however, six out of the 30 specimens which have usage flaking along their ventral edges. The ventral surface is convex and it is generally the bulbar surface. In addition, 14 of these utilized flakes retain their striking platforms.

Utilized Flake End Scrapers. This utilized flake category consists of 15 specimens of which nine are of cream to gray chert, three are of clear quartz, and three are of tan quartzite. The length of these Utilized Flake End Scrapers ranges between 16 and 48 mm with the average 22.9 mm; their width is between 10 and 47 mm with the average 20.8 mm; and their thickness is between 2 and 10 mm with the average 5.4 mm. These utilized flakes are triangular, square, rectangular, or irregular in outline and plano-convex or concavo-convex in cross section. The dorsal surfaces are percussion flaked and the bulbar or ventral surface is generally smooth. The convex distal end has non-localized usage flaking which is usually on the dorsal surface except in four instances where it occurs on the ventral distal end. One specimen has cortex over its entire dorsal surface and two examples retain their striking platforms at the proximal end.

Unworked Flakes. The lithic artifacts are fewer in number than the ceramic representatives from the Sanders site and the number of worked flakes is also quite low in comparison to the number of flakes excavated. 47-Wp-26 and 47-Wp-70 yielded a total of 10,524 unworked flakes. A breakdown according to material and number is as follows: quartz:2,069; quartzite:1,359; chert:6,521; basalt:569; chalcedony:4; and Knife River Flint:2. It appears that the preferred order of source material was chert, quartz, quartzite, basalt, chalcedony and Knife River Flint. If the total number of worked and utilized flakes is added to the unworked total, or 116 worked flakes and 72 utilized flakes, the total would be 10,712. Of this total only 188, or 1.75 percent were worked or utilized.

Polished Stone Artifacts

Shaft Polisher. One brown chalcedony artifact has an irregular outline and a plano-convex cross section. This specimen is considered as a projectile shaft polisher as it has two semi-circular concave areas which are highly smooth and polished and they have vertical striations against the walls. These concavities are 13 and 15 mm in diameter and the overall dimensions of the polisher are 22 mm in length, 24 mm in width, and 13 mm in thickness.

Adzes (Pl. 43:C-E). The Sanders surface collection contained three adzes within a large lithic and ceramic collection gathered over several decades. One of these adzes is illustrated in Plate 43:E. Excavations at 47-Wp-26 and Wp-70 resulted in the recovery of two additional adzes which will be described here separately. The first specimen is of gray green basalt, 108 mm long, 29 mm wide, and 27 mm thick. In outline it is oblong and in cross section it is plano-convex. The adze has been chipped and ground into shape with percussion flakes removed from both lateral convex edges and both dorsal convex ends. The bit is concavo-convex in cross section and there is evidence of use polish on the distal bit end, the dorsal surface, and along the flat ventral surface. Usage flakes have been removed from both the lateral edges of the bit. The second specimen is also of gray green basalt and it is 101 mm long, 33 mm wide, and 29 mm thick. It is oblong in outline and plano-convex in cross section with percussion flakes removed from both lateral convex edges and the concave dorsal end. The bit is concave and concavo-convex in cross section and large usage flakes have been removed from the center of the bit. There is extensive use polish along one lateral distal end and all along the flat ventral surface.

Celts (Pl. 43:A). Two celts were excavated at 47-Wp-26 and one of green diorite is so battered and use modified that its original shape and length measurements are difficult to ascertain. At present it is rectangular in outline and biconvex in cross section. Its length is 72 mm, its width is 55 mm, and its thickness is 19 mm. The better preserved specimen is of gray green basalt, triangular in outline and rectangular in cross section. The overall dimensions are: length, 91 mm; width, 50 mm; and thickness, 19 mm, while the poll is 21 mm wide and 17 mm thick. This celt (Pl. 43:A) has been ground and partially polished and the sides appear to have been ground flat. The convex bit is still sharp and the poll appears to have been used for hammering.

Gorget (Pl. 43:B). One drilled gorget fragment was recovered from 47-Wp-26 and it is broken in half across the suspension hole (Pl. 43:B). This specimen is of dark green basalt, oblong in outline and rectangular in cross section. The sides are convex and it is now 46 mm wide and 12 mm thick. It is fully ground and polished with convex edges converging to the convex end. At 31 mm from this end is a drilled hole 8 mm in diameter on the surface and 4 mm across at the break. This hole is slightly off center, 20 mm from one edge and 25 mm from the other.

Polished Stone Fragments. Included in this category are 14 stone fragments from the Sanders site which appear to be portions of ground and polished artifacts and not artifacts which were used in their present form. They are of slate, basalt, quartzite, gneiss, and diorite. They are biconvex and have very irregular outlines except for the polished surfaces. The fact that one or more of their surfaces appears to have intentional polishing is the major attribute which called attention to otherwise ordinary stone fragments.

Ground Stone

Grinding Stone. One brown basalt stone was excavated from house floor number 1 of House 3 at 47-Wp-26 and this specimen appears to be a fragment of a larger grinding stone. The present portion is square in outline, rectangular in cross section, 120 mm long, 125 mm wide, and 35 mm thick. Only the dorsal surface appears to have been used and it is very smooth with the grinding trough 90 mm wide, 3 mm deep, and over 120 mm in length. Along one lateral dorsal edge is a raised ridge which is 3 mm high and 15 mm wide. The ventral surface, the ends, and the lateral edges are unmodified.

Hammer Stones. Two unretouched pebbles are of brown basalt and are considered hammer stones. They are 80 and 98 mm long, 62 and 67 mm wide, and 38 and 59 mm thick. Both specimens are oblong in outline and biconvex in cross section. These hammer stones appear to have been utilized on one end only or along a lateral edge as there is evidence of battering. The remaining surfaces are unmodified.

COPPER (PL. 44:B-L)

Eleven copper artifacts were recovered from the excavations at 47-Wp-26 and 47-Wp-70 and these artifacts can be grouped into five categories. The first category, *copper bead*, consists of one specimen which was a flattened copper strip that was then folded into a bead with a triangular orifice (Pl. 44:B). The bead is 8 mm in diameter, 5 mm thick, circular in outline, and biconvex in cross section. The second copper category, *copper knife*, is spatulate in outline and it has a pointed tang. The overall dimensions are: 68 mm long, 17 mm wide, and 3 mm thick, with the tang being 30 mm long and 5 mm wide. Prior to manufacture, the copper appears to have been a flat lenticular piece which was folded back on to the tang for over 16 mm. The blade orifice is 23 mm long and 7 mm wide. One *copper pendant*, the third category, is oblong in outline, rectangular in cross section, 26 mm long, 7 mm wide, and 6 mm thick. One end (Pl. 44:C) has a slight hook for suspension. A *copper conical point* is the fourth artifact category. The point is conical in outline and it appears to have been a flattened piece of copper which was folded around a shaft (Pl. 44:K). It is 29 mm long, 10 mm wide, and 6 mm thick.

The largest copper artifact category, *copper awls*, is represented by seven specimens (Pl. 44:E-J, L) which are bipointed or flattened at one end. They are rectangular to oblong in outline and circular to lenticular in cross section. One specimen (Pl. 44:J) has a flattened end which gives it an appearance of a nail. These awls range in length from 23 to 50 mm with an average of 38.8 mm; in width from 3 to 8 mm with the average 5.0 mm; and in thickness from 2 to 7 mm with the average 1.8 mm.

Copper Fragments

In addition to the copper artifacts, the Sanders site also yielded 20 copper fragments which are generally rectangular to irregular in shape and cross section. These fragments are all less than 25 mm in length and 7 mm in thickness. They do not appear to be portions of larger coppper artifacts.

GALENA

One galena cube was found and it is 9 mm long, 7 mm wide, and 5 mm thick. It does not appear to be worked.

IRON

One iron concretion was recovered. It is not considered as an artifact as it is very irregular in outline, 9 mm in diameter, and 7 mm thick.

HISTORIC ARTIFACTS

Outside of the normal Historic items one would expect to find on the surface of a farm woodlot, there were a very few Historic items actually excavated at 47-Wp-26. In the area of Mound 13 a total of 25 round nails were excavated from one square. One square nail and barbed wire fragments were recovered and one 22 caliber shell case was excavated. The remaining Historic metal fragments are all from disturbed Mound 24 and they are tin can fragments most probably associated with the logging activity noted for this mound, as a large logging chain was also recovered from a tree stump at a depth of 2.7 feet below the surface.

VIII

SANDERS SITES ANALYSES

IN THE analyses of the Bigelow site (47-Wp-29) the exclusion of the later Historic component from the main aboriginal occupation resulted in the isolation of one prehistoric component. This component was identified as belonging to the Effigy Mound tradition and the artifacts recovered were clearly bracketed in space, time, and cultural affiliation. The Bigelow non-mound, sub-mound, and mound artifacts strongly demonstrated that typological categories proposed by Baerreis, Keslin, Wittry, and Mason were in fact associated with this cultural tradition as represented at this locality. The resolution of this culture association problem at the Bigelow site enhances the probability that the culture context of these artifacts will continue to be considered as the material culture of the Effigy Mound peoples.

The spector of possible multiple prehistoric components at the Sanders sites (47-Wp-26 and Wp-70) needs to be critically examined: types of artifacts were recovered from the Sanders sites that differ from those described from the Bigelow site. Such typological ceramic categories as Sister Creeks Punctated, Shorewood Cord Roughened, and Dane Incised need to be evaluated and possibly assigned to an earlier Middle or Early Woodland component or considered as a part of the material culture of the Effigy Mound component at this locality. The recovered Grand River ceramics also suggest several possibilities: a later Oneota culture occupation of the area, contemporaneity of two separate cultural traditions having trade contacts, or the rapid transformation of the Effigy Mound cultural tradition into an emerging Oneota cultural tradition. The only relevant data to be considered are those from the Sanders sites since the Effigy Mound artifacts are the sole prehistoric representatives at the Bigelow site. If the cultural associations and context of the artifacts which are believed to be at both ends of the Effigy Mound cultural tradition are clarified, then the material from the Sanders sites will make a major contribution to our understanding of Wisconsin's prehistory.

Sanders site 1, 47-Wp-26, has conical, linear, and effigy-shaped mounds as does the Bigelow site, but, whereas the Bigelow site lacks good evidence of extensive occupation, the Sanders sites do not. The non-mound village context of artifacts recovered from pits and midden debris are quite rare for sites associated with the Effigy Mound tradition. The addition of houses from 47-Wp-26 and Wp-70 with their associated artifacts and the mounds from 47-Wp-26 presents us with a commanding perspective from which we can interpret function (ceremonial or utilitarian) and associations related to both mound and village activities. These diverse vantage points will yield a more rounded view of the life style of the Effigy Mound peoples from a unique location containing evidence of both everyday activity and special activity associated with contiguous mound construction.

In the analysis of the material culture from the Sanders sites (Chapter VII) the artifacts from 47-Wp-26 and Wp-70 were combined and presented together. In the analysis of the Bigelow site the artifacts, soils, and relative and chronometric dates were utilized for site reconstruction. The same three lines of investigation will form an integral part of the interpretation of the combined Sanders sites. Furthermore the number of radiocarbon dates for both 47-Wp-26 and Wp-70 (Figs. 59 and 60) are essential to site reconstruction as they provide very firm control over the rate and duration of cultural activity at the Sanders sites.

Although they are culturally related phenomena, the mound sequence and the village activity will be examined separately in order to eliminate the uneven movement from features, houses, and then to mounds. The mound construction sequence for 47-Wp-26 appears to be closely related to the village occupation: the sequence of mound construction is exactly the opposite of the sequence of excavation. The mound construction sequence appears to be from south to north or from mounds 33 to 6 (Fig. 31) instead of from mounds 6 to 33 as they were presented in Chapter VI. On the basis of four dated mounds (23, 17, 3, and 2) and Area 9 (Fig. 59), it would appear that mounds were first constructed to

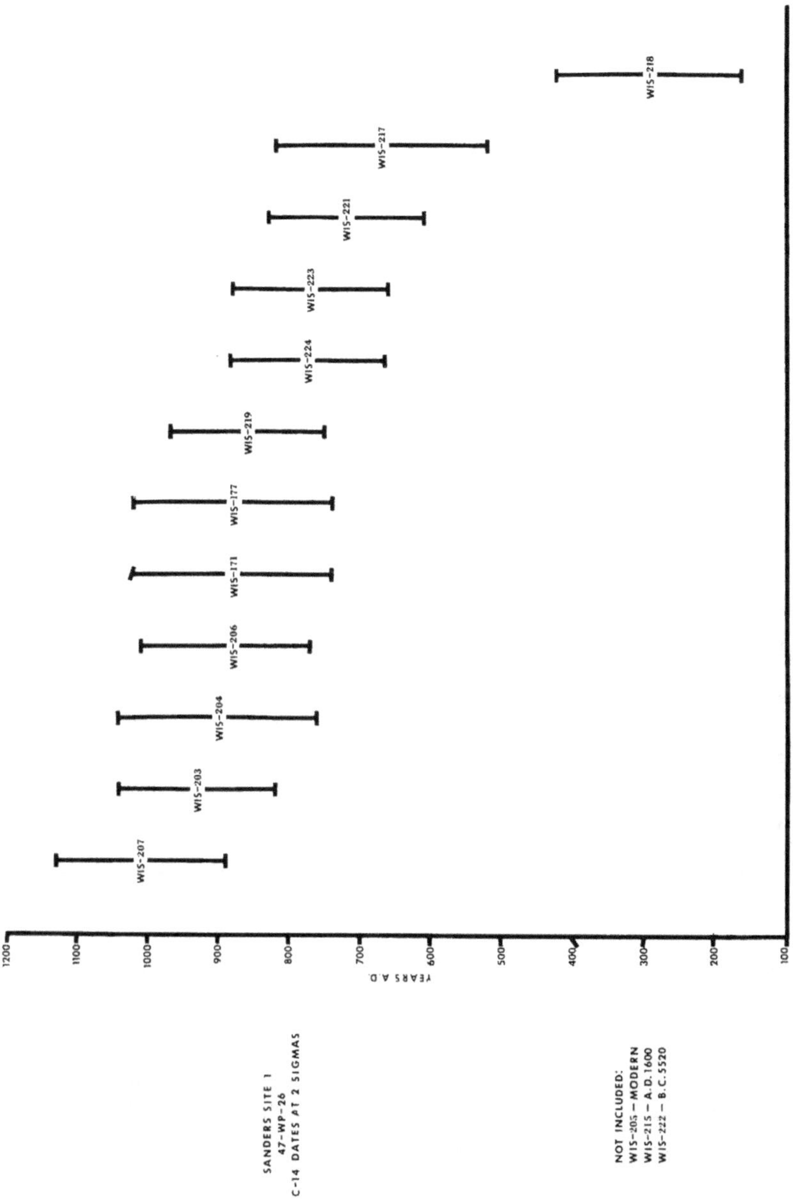

FIG. 59. Sanders Site 1 C-14 dates.

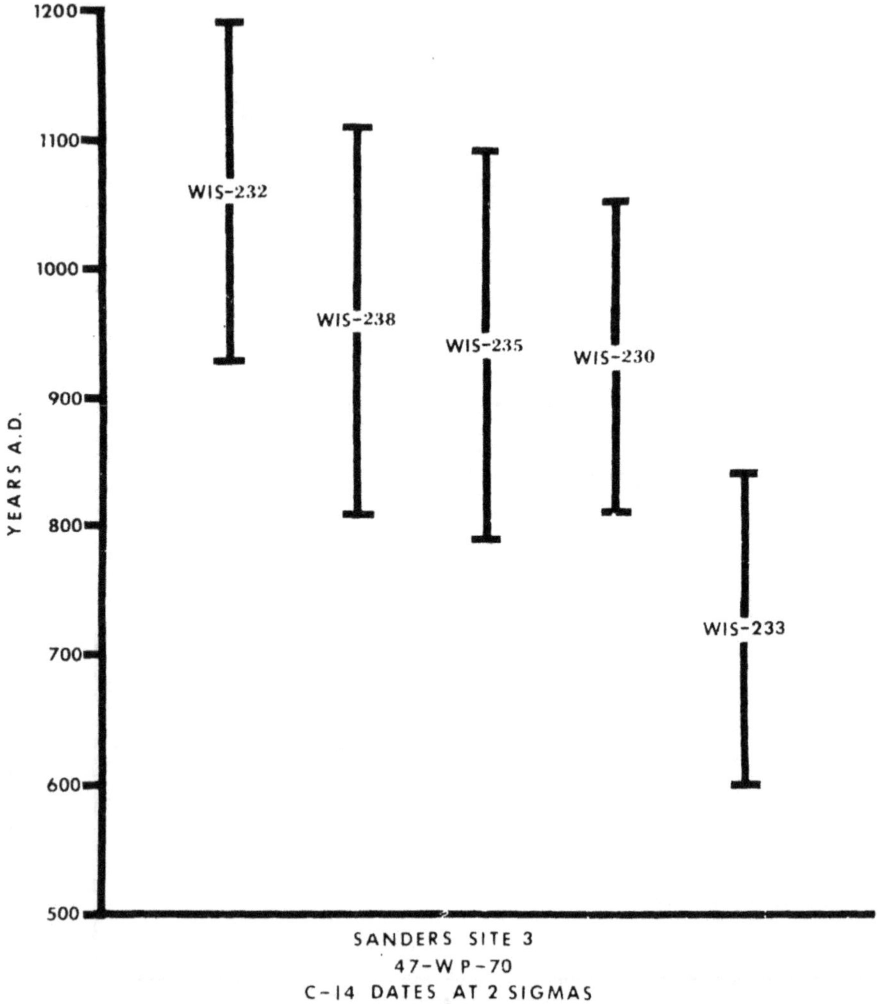

FIG. 60. Sanders Site 3 C-14 dates.

the south of the village (mounds 33, 32, and 25) and then to the east and north. It is in this order that they will be described.

The analyses to be presented in the following pages includes an edited version of a more detailed discussion (Hurley, 1970) with the addition of a principal component analysis similar to that used for the Bigelow site (Chapter V). The same procedures were used in the principal component analysis and the same five variables were examined both in histograph form (Fig. 61) and in an

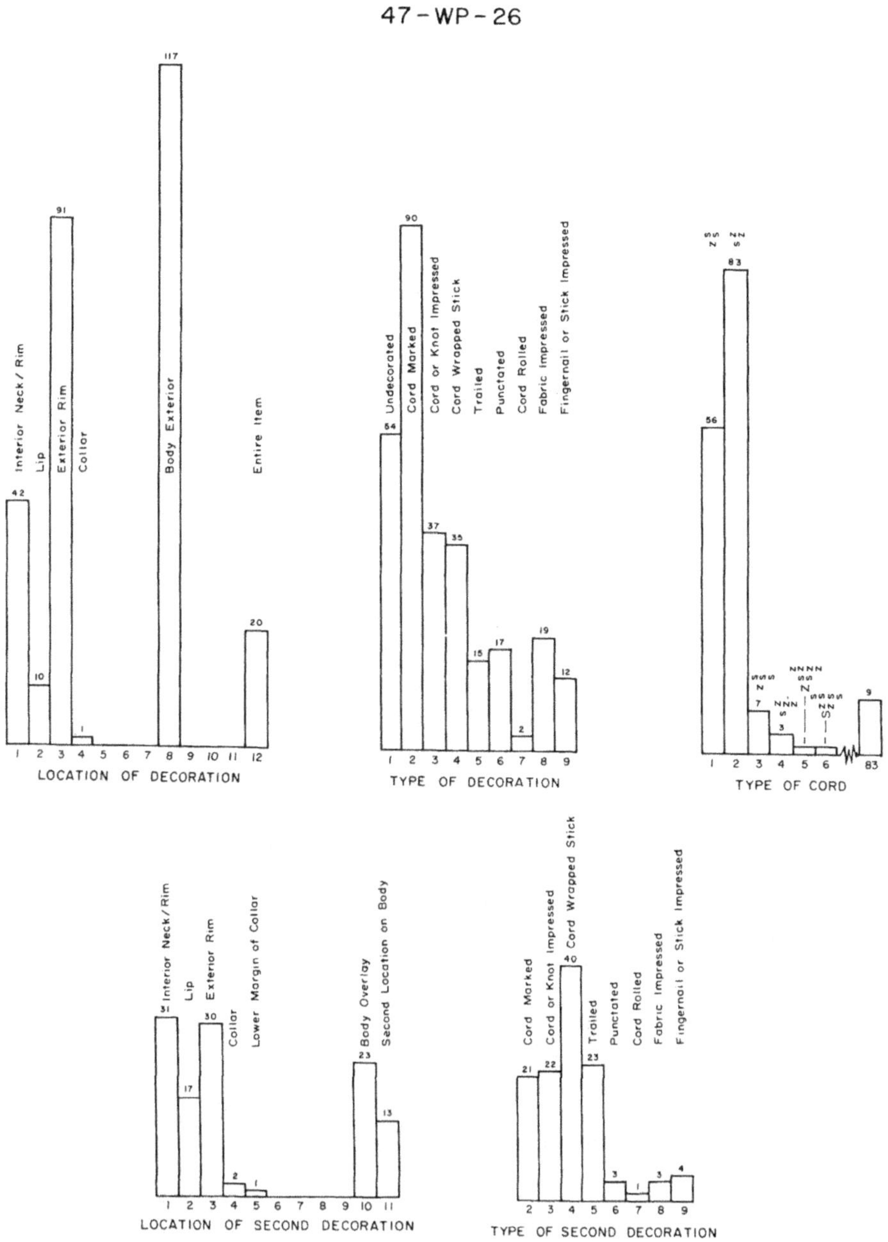

FIG. 61. Histogram of traits used in computer analysis of Sanders ceramics.

unsorted to a sorted correlation coefficient matrix which was ranked (Table 20) and then clustered into a scattergram (Fig. 62). Table 20 shows that the first eigenvalue accounts for 36 percent of the total variance, the first and second for 62 percent, and the first three for 80 percent. The first two eigenvalues were again plotted according to two vectors and to each location the pottery type (or category) plus frequency has been added (Fig. 62). As with the Bigelow scattergram, no attempt has been made to cluster the ceramics into smaller units or to draw lines around the "obvious" clusters until both sites have been compared, combined, and subjected to more refined statistical analyses (Chapter IX).

Mound 33 appeared to be an effigy-shaped mound having an outline similar to bear effigy Mound 13 of 47-Pt-29-1. This mound was not excavated, but the artifacts eroding from a nearby path indicate continuous village activity between this mound and the northern limits of soil body $\frac{4}{\text{A-0}}$. Oval Mound 32 was greatly disturbed by the landowners in their search for farm fill. It was reported that this mound contained a concentration of charcoal. Three other mounds adjacent to the village at 47-Wp-26, mounds 29 to 31, also remain unexcavated. Mound 29 is a small conical mound 21 feet in diameter, and Mound 30 is an oval mound 28 feet long and 21 feet wide. Linear Mound 31 is one of the five linear mounds recorded for 47-Wp-26. Mound 31 is 57 feet long and 22 feet wide, and although it was not tested in 1966 the amount of artifacts collected from the surface in the area of mounds 29 to 31 indicates that these mounds were constructed adjacent to an area of extensive occupation.

Mound 28 in a linear mound 46 feet long, 21 feet wide, and 1.1 feet above the surrounding surface. Two five-foot squares were excavated and a profile was exposed which indicated that Mound

TABLE 20

PRINCIPAL COMPONENT ANALYSIS: 47-WP-26
(281 Specimens; 5 Variables of Decoration)

	Decoration 1	Decoration 2	Decoration 3	Decoration 4	Decoration 5
Eigenvalue	1.82619	1.28757	0.92426	0.68274	0.27921
Cumulative Percentage of Eigenvalue	0.36524	0.62275	0.80760	0.94415	0.99999

47 - WP - 26

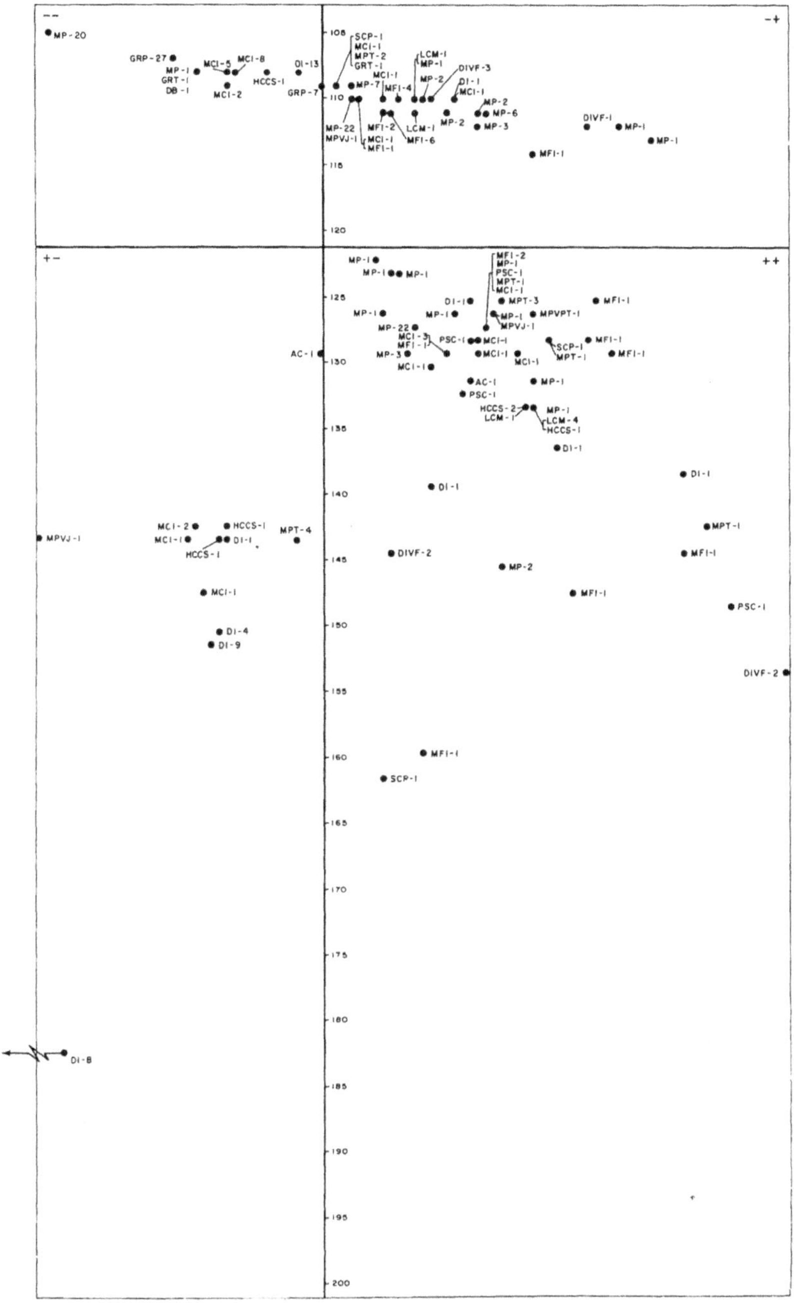

FIG. 62. Scattergram of principal component analysis of Sanders ceramics.

28 had sealed in a paleosol whose former surface was formed under grass vegetation. Two features were uncovered and excavated and both had orifices which began below the buried A1b horizon. Feature 26 contained charcoal flecks, one s$\frac{Z}{Z}$ cord-marked body sherd, one smoothed-over cord-marked body sherd, two diminutive scrapers, and one worked flake end scraper. Feature 38 had a black sandy fill which contained 32 fire-cracked rocks, a charred bone fragment, one quartzite flake, two chert flakes, and one grit-tempered cord-marked body sherd. From their location, it would appear that both features 26 and 38 antedate the construction of Mound 28 and that the function of Feature 38 was most probably that of a cooking pit.

The sub-mound and mound horizons of Mound 28 yielded the artifacts listed in Table 21.

The sub-mound and mound artifacts from Mound 28 can be treated as separate phenomena so that the sub-mound associations

TABLE 21

DISTRIBUTION OF CERAMIC AND LITHIC ARTIFACTS: MOUND 28

Soil Location	Shorewood Cord Roughened	Dane Incised	Dane Incised, v. fingernail impressed	Madison Cord Impressed	Madison Fabric Impressed	Madison Folded Lip	Madison Plain	s $\frac{Z}{Z}$	z $\frac{S}{S}$	Smoothed-over Cord-marked	Waubesa Contracting Stem	Triangular	Knives	Multiple Edge Flaked Side Scrapers	Flake Knives	Single Edge Utilized Flake Side Scrapers	Multiple Edge Utilized Flake Side Scrapers	Utilized Flake End Scraper	Polished Stones
A11							1			2						1			
A/B		7	2		1	2	3	22	7	31	1			1		1	1		
A1b	1	7	1	1		2	4	14	2	24		1			1				
B21irb	1	6	2		1	1	2	4		5			1			1		1	1
Total	2	20	5	1	2	5	10	40	9	62	1	1	1	1	1	3	1	1	1

can be considered as related to, and possibly not affected by, the artifacts included in the mound fill. In the lowest level, Shorewood Cord Roughened, Dane Incised, Dane Incised, variety fingernail impressed, Madison Fabric Impressed, Madison Folded Lip, Madison Plain, and $s\,\frac{z}{z}$ cord-marked sherds were recovered. Had the Madison Ware ceramics been restricted only to the A1b horizon, the associations could be considered the result of surface mixture of two components. However, the addition of a Madison Cord Impressed specimen and a serrated Triangular projectile point from the A1b horizon to the Effigy Mound assemblage only serves to strengthen the possible comtemporaneity of these artifacts. The Dane Incised, Dane Incised, variety fingernail impressed, Madison Fabric Impressed, Madison Folded Lip, Madison Plain, $s\,\frac{z}{z}$, $z\,\frac{s}{s}$, and smoothed-over cord-marked body sherds can be viewed as a mixture of mound borrow from a nearby multiple component midden. This may be a valid assumption based on the limited data from Mound 28 but it should be recognized that these associations are now recorded well below the base of Mound 28 and that they may be repeated at this site. As long as there is doubt concerning occupation of a mound area by Effigy Mound peoples prior to the actual construction of the mound, the only recourse is to present the sub-mound and mound artifacts separately.

Mounds 24 and 25 present unique problems to interpretation. If they and the connecting rise are viewed as a unit then the shape from its planimetric outline does not lend itself to any established and recognized effigy shape. The interconnecting rise is 250 feet long, 3 to 5 feet wide, and 1.5 to 3 feet high and it seals in a paleosol profile. The rise does not appear to be a levee, embankment, or defensive earthwork; however, only excavation of this rise will resolve its nature. Mound 24 had been badly disturbed by historic logging activity to a depth of 2.7 feet below the mound surface. Because of this disturbance, the artifacts recovered from the excavation of three five-foot squares are not included in the site interpretations.

Mound 25 is connected to the southern end of the 250 foot long rise and it is an oval mound 37 feet by 25 feet and 1.7 feet high. Three five-foot squares were excavated in the center of the mound and the profile exposed a buried paleosol profile formed under grass vegetation. One feature, Number 13, was exposed and it yielded one $s\,\frac{z}{z}$ cord-marked body sherd and charcoal flecks. The sub-mound and mound horizon contained the artifacts listed in Table 22.

The presence of Feature 13 and the Madison Fabric Impressed sherd in the B21irb horizon below the base of Mound 25 indicates that this area was utilized by Effigy Mound peoples prior to mound construction. The A1b horizon artifacts indicate that both s $\frac{z}{z}$ cords and those composed of z $\frac{s}{s}$ elements for the Madison Fabric Impressed rim sherd were present prior to the construction of the mound. The mound fill and mound surface horizons contained Dane Incised, Dane Incised, variety fingernail impressed, Madison Cord Impressed, Madison Fabric Impressed, Madison Plain, Madison Punctated, Heins Creek Corded Stamped, s $\frac{z}{z}$ cord-marked, z $\frac{s}{s}$ cord-marked, smoothed-over cord-marked ceramics, and the diagnostic Sanders Triangular projectile point. If we assume these artifacts represent midden debris, with the possibility that the Dane Incised ceramics are earlier, we can conclude that the Madison Ware, Heins Creek Corded Stamped, and Sanders Tri-

TABLE 22

DISTRIBUTION OF CERAMIC AND LITHIC ARTIFACTS: MOUND 25

Soil Location	Dane Incised	Dane Incised, v. fingernail impressed	Madison Cord Impressed	Madison Fabric Impressed	Madison Plain	Madison Punctated	Heins Creek Corded Stamped	s $\frac{z}{z}$	z $\frac{s}{s}$	Smoothed-over Cord-marked	Sanders Triangular	Triangular	Drills	Multiple Edge Flaked Side Scrapers	Flake End Scrapers	Flake Knives	Utilized Flake End Scrapers	Polished Stones
A1			1		2			2		5							1	
A/B	8	2	3	1	7	1	1	6	1	44	1		1	1	1	1		
A1b								3		10								1
B21irb										1								
Total	8	2	4	2	9	1	1	11	1	60	1		1	1	1	1	1	1

angular projectile point are contemporary and part of the Effigy Mound assemblage.

Mounds 26 and 27 were partially disturbed for fill for the farm lane. Mound 26 is a conical mound 20 feet in diameter and 1.0 feet high, while Mound 27 is believed to be a linear mound 72 feet long and 24 feet wide. Neither mound was tested or excavated in 1966. Mound 23, which is just northwest of these two mounds, is a conical mound 26 feet in diameter and 1.8 feet high. One five-foot square was excavated and a paleosol profile was exposed which showed that the former surface was formed under forest vegetation. This profile was penetrated by a pit containing a primary human cremation (Burial 3). This rectangular pit lacked artifacts but contained bone and charcoal. The latter yielded a date of A.D. 720 ± 55 (WIS-221). This date not only places the human cremation and the mound construction in chronological sequence but also confirms that Mound 23 is the earliest dated mound at Sanders site 1 (Fig. 59). The sub-mound and mound horizons contained the items listed in Table 23.

The human cremation contained in the A1b and A2xb horizons of Mound 23 (Fig. 39) represents one-third of the excavated burials at 47-Wp-26 and one-half the number of burials contained in mounds and of the type of burial recorded for this site. The radiocarbon assessment does tell us the time of the construction of this conical mound and that Mound 23 is almost as early as the first recorded village occupation (Fig. 59: WIS-217) at this site. It is unfortunate that Burial 3 lacked associated grave

TABLE 23

DISTRIBUTION OF CERAMIC AND LITHIC ARTIFACTS: MOUND 23

Soil Location	Dane Incised	Smoothed-over Cord-marked	Diminutive Scrapers	Single Edge Utilized Flake Side Scrapers	Cores
A11		1			
A2x/A2x	1	2	1	1	
A1b					
A2xb					1
Total	1	3	1	1	1

goods. As the celt was beneath Mound 23 and the Dane Incised, diminutive scraper, and single edge utilized flake side scraper artifacts were from the mound fill we can only observe that the artifacts were made prior to A.D. 720 ± 55 (WIS-221).

Mounds 20, 21, and 22 were not excavated during 1966, but on the basis of our underbrush clearing it would seem that sufficient mound area remains for excavation at each of these disturbed mounds. Mound 20 is a large oval mound 40 feet by 68 feet and 2.5 feet high. Mound 21 is a conical mound 18 feet in diameter and 1.0 feet high. Mound 22 may have been large and oval or linear in shape; the remaining portion measures 44 by 47 feet.

Mound 19 is a small oval mound 28 feet by 36 feet and 2.7 feet high. Five five-foot squares were excavated in the center of the mound and one profile indicated that Mound 19 had sealed in a soil sequa different from the surrounding $\frac{1}{\text{A-0}}$ soils (Fig. 38). Two features were excavated in Mound 19. Feature 7 yielded 10 sherd fragments, one knife, three charred bone fragments, eight chert flakes, and two stone fragments. Feature 10 contained one Madison Cord Impressed rim sherd, two Madison Fabric Impressed body sherds, four $z\frac{S}{S}$ cord-marked body sherds, five smoothed-over cord-marked body sherds, and one chert flake. The sub-mound and mound horizon artifacts are listed in Table 24.

The association of Madison Cord Impressed, Madison Fabric Impressed, and $z\frac{S}{S}$ cord-marked body sherds at Feature 10 of Mound 19 is also repeated in the mound horizons, with the exception that $z\frac{S}{S}$ cord-marked sherds are replaced by $s\frac{Z}{Z}$ cord-marked sherds. The location of Features 7 and 10 near the surface of this conical mound is a pattern not previously recorded for this site. The Madison Ware ceramics of Feature 10 may indicate intentionally included artifacts; however, they may also be considered as a part of the pit backfill which was replaced after the pit had served its function. The Madison Punctated sherd from the A1b horizon indicated that Madison Ware ceramics were in use in the Mound 19 area prior to mound construction. The remaining Madison Ware ceramics—Madison Cord Impressed, Madison Fabric Impressed, Madison Plain, the mound fill Madison Punctated, Leland Cord-marked, and Aztalan Collared examples—appear to be linked to both the sub-mound ceramics and to those from Feature

TABLE 24

DISTRIBUTION OF CERAMIC AND LITHIC ARTIFACTS: MOUND 19

Soil Location	Dane Incised	Madison Cord Impressed	Madison Fabric Impressed	Madison Folded Lip	Madison Plain	Madison Punctated	Leland Cord-marked	Aztalan Collared	s $\frac{Z}{Z}$	z $\frac{S}{S}$	Smoothed-over Cord-marked	Corner Notched	Diminutive Scrapers	Scrapers	Knives	Cores	Multiple Edge Utilized Flake Side Scrapers
A11		1			2						1						
A2x/A2x	1		1		4	6	1	2	2		18		1			1	1
A1b						1											
A2xb											4	1					
B2tb																	
Total	1	1	1		6	7	1	2	2		23	1	1			1	1

10. The single Dane Incised specimen, as those from mounds 28, 25, and 23, may have been in the area prior to the Effigy Mound occupation. This interpretation may also explain the presence of the corner notched projectile point in the A2xb horizon. The chronological and cultural affiliation problems of Dane Incised ceramics at 47-Wp-26 still need further clarification.

Mound 18 and Mound 17 appear to be joined by a 30 foot by 14 by 1.5 foot high rise. Mound 18 is a conical mound 26 by 31 feet and 2 feet high. A large maple tree prevented excavations in Mound 18 so work was centered on Mound 17. This oval mound is 50 feet long, 40 feet wide, and 2 feet high. A 10 by 10 foot square was excavated in the center of Mound 17 to a depth of 3.5 feet. Two features, 6 and 8, were excavated at Mound 17. Feature 6 contained 143 fragments of a Point Sauble Collared vessel, 56 s $\frac{Z}{Z}$ cord-marked, two z $\frac{S}{S}$ cord-marked, and 27 smoothed-over cord-marked body sherds, one Durst Stemmed (Pl. 40:A) projectile point, one quartzite flake, two quartz flakes, four stone fragments, and charcoal. The charcoal was submitted for dating but it yielded a modern assessment (WIS-205; Bender, Bryson, and Baerreis 1968*a*).

Feature 8 of Mound 17 produced one s $\frac{Z}{Z}$ cord-marked sherd, one sherdlet, and charcoal which yielded a date of A.D. 900 ± 70 (WIS-204). This date (Fig. 59) indicates that the Point Sauble Collared vessel and Durst Stemmed projectile point of Feature 6 date after the excavation and use of sub-mound Feature 8. The same observation made above may also hold true for the artifacts found beneath and within the fill of Mound 17 (see Table 25).

The sub-mound distribution of artifacts at Mound 17 documents the presence of Madison Ware ceramics—Madison Cord Impressed and Madison Plain vessels—prior to mound construction.

TABLE 25

DISTRIBUTION OF CERAMIC AND LITHIC ARTIFACTS: MOUND 17

Soil Location	Madison Cord Impressed	Madison Plain	Madison Punctuated	s $\frac{Z}{Z}$	z $\frac{S}{S}$	Diminutive Scraper	Side Scrapers	Knife	Single Edge Flaked Side Scrapers	Multiple Edge Flaked Side Scrapers	Single Edge Utilized Flaked Side Scrapers	Multiple Edge Utilized Flaked Side Scrapers	Utilized Flake End Scrapers	Adzes
A11			1	1						1	1			
A2x/A2x		5		5	8					1	1	1	1	
A1b	5	1		1	4									
A2xb	2	2		1	3	1	1	1	1					1
B2tb	1	1			1									
Total	8	9	1	8	16	1	1	1	1	2	2	1	1	1

The types of cords utilized for the Madison Cord Impressed ceramics suggest that three vessels were being utilized and at least two vessels of the Madison Plain ceramic type were also in use. It appears that z $\frac{S}{S}$ cord-marking had an earlier and more numerous distribution in the Mound 17 area before the mound was constructed. The most diagnostic artifacts from beneath Mound 17 are the diminutive scraper, knife, and adze. If the date from Feature 8 is acceptable then all of these artifacts date prior to or at A.D. 900 ± 70 (WIS-204). The mound fill horizons contained five Madison Plain rim sherds, one Madison Punctated body sherd, six s $\frac{Z}{Z}$ cord-marked and eight z $\frac{S}{S}$ cord-marked body sherds, plus the worked and utilized flakes. These artifacts are most probably a part of the sub-mound activity occurring at Mound 17 and date from the time of Feature 8, but the artifacts from Feature 6, i.e., the Point Sauble Collared vessel and the Durst Stemmed projectile point, could well have been intruded into this mound years after its construction.

Mounds 1, 2, and 3 were originally tested in 1965 and only mounds 1 and 3 were subjected to further exploration in 1966. Mound 3 is a linear mound 75 feet long, 20 feet wide, and 2 feet high. Four five-foot squares were excavated in this mound and two burials, Burials 1 and 2, and Feature 5 were uncovered and excavated in and adjacent to linear Mound 3. Burial 1 was excavated from the A2x/A2x mound fill and charcoal removed from this soil horizon was submitted for radiocarbon assessment and yielded a date of A.D. 880 ± 70 (WIS-177). Burial 1 of Mound 3 is believed to be more than just scattered bone; further excavation in this mound will probably demonstrate that rodents have greatly disturbed a primary burial. Just north of Burial 1 was a circular pit which contained a secondary human cremation designated Burial 2. A charcoal concentration and an elbow pipe (Pl. 36:H) found in the same level of this square are believed to be associated with Burial 2. Conical Mound 23 and linear Mound 3 contained the only identified human remains recorded for 47-Wp-26 and both types of burials seem similar to the forms recorded for the Bigelow site. The sub-mound and mound horizons yielded the artifacts listed in Table 26.

The radiocarbon assessment (WIS-177) from Burial 1 of A.D. 880 ± 70 suggests that Madison Cord Impressed ceramics, Madison Plain ceramics, and the Madison Side Notched projectile point from the sub-mound horizons at Mound 3 should date at or before

TABLE 26

DISTRIBUTION OF CERAMIC AND LITHIC ARTIFACTS: MOUND 3

Soil Location	Dane Incised, v. fingernail impressed	Madison Cord Impressed	Madison Plain	Madison Punctated	Leland Cord-marked	s $\frac{Z}{Z}$	z $\frac{S}{S}$	Smoothed-over Cord	Madison Side Notched	Triangular	Diminutive Scraper	Multiple Edge Flake Side Scraper	Single Edge Utilized Flake Side Scraper	Polished Stone
A11						1								
A2x/A2x	1			1	1	3	2	11		3	1	1		1
A1xb		1							1					
A2xb		1	1									1	1	
B22tb														
Total	1	2	1	1	1	4	2	11	1	3	1	2	1	1

the interment of Burial 1. The Madison Punctated and the Leland Cord-marked ceramics, plus the Triangular points, are a part of the material culture associated with the Effigy Mound tradition as it is manifested at this site at this time. The lone Dane Incised, variety fingernail impressed body sherd may antedate the construction of Mound 3. Both s $\frac{Z}{Z}$ and z $\frac{S}{S}$ cords were utilized at this time; however, the preference seems to have been for s $\frac{Z}{Z}$ cords on the Dane Incised, variety fingernail impressed and the Madison Ware sherds, except for the Madison Plain rim sherds from the A2xb horizon.

Feature 5 was located adjacent to Mound 3. It was defined at a depth of .2 foot in the A11 surface horizon and extended to a depth of .7 foot or into the A2x horizon. The fill of Feature 5 contained only charcoal flecks, burned bone fragments, one stone fragment, and two grit-tempered sherdlets.

Conical Mound 2 measured 33 feet in diameter and 2.5 feet high. One five-foot square was excavated in 1965. The one feature exposed was a basin-shaped pit utilized prior to, or at the time of, construction of this conical mound. The fill of Feature 1 (1965) yielded 200 fragments of a partially reconstructed Madison Punctated vessel (Pl. 31), a Madison Fabric Impressed body sherd (Fig. 54:A), 14 $z\frac{S}{S}$ cord-marked and 61 smoothed-over cord-marked body sherds, and charcoal. The charcoal was submitted for a radiocarbon assessment and produced a date of A.D. 880 ± 70 (WIS-171). The sub-mound and mound horizons of Mound 2 yielded the artifacts listed in Table 27.

If we assume that Feature 1 of conical Mound 2 was utilized as a cooking pit just prior to mound construction then we can state that at A.D. 880 ± 70 (WIS-171) Madison Punctated and Madison Fabric Impressed ceramics were being utilized in the Mound 2 area of Sanders site 1. Furthermore, the Dane Incised, variety fingernail impressed and Aztalan Collared rim sherds date at or before this time unless there was a considerable time lapse between the time of Feature 1 and the construction of Mound 2. I would propose that both the Madison Plain and the Aztalan Collared rim sherds from the mound fill also date at circa A.D. 880. As we are still reserving judgment on the temporal placement of

TABLE 27

DISTRIBUTION OF CERAMIC AND LITHIC ARTIFACTS: MOUND 2

Soil Location	Dane Incised, v. fingernail impressed	Madison Plain	Aztalan Collared	$S\frac{Z}{Z}$	$Z\frac{S}{S}$	Smoothed-over Cord	Celt
A11							
A2x/A2x		1	1		3	2	
A2xb	1		1	1	1	2	1
B21b							
B22tb						1	
Total	1	1	2	1	4	5	1

the Dane Incised ceramics, the specimens from Mound 2 and linear Mound 3 will be held in abeyance. However, with these two identical radiocarbon assessments (WIS-171 and 177) of A.D. 880 ± 70 I believe we can state at this point in the Sanders analysis that the sub-mound (especially those from beneath Mound 3) and most probably the mound artifacts and those from Feature 1 of Mound 2 date at this time. This date would include the Madison Ware ceramics of Madison Cord Impressed, Madison Plain, Madison Punctated, Leland Cord-marked, and Aztalan Collared ceramics and Madison Side Notched and Triangular projectile points. At Mound 17 there is evidence that Madison Cord Impressed, Madison Plain, and possibly Madison Punctated ceramics also date from this time (WIS-204; A.D. 900 ± 70).

Mound 1 is a panther effigy mound 71 feet long, 34 feet wide, and 2.5 feet high. Seven five-foot squares were excavated in this mound during the field seasons of 1965 and 1966. Two features were exposed and excavated in 1965. Feature 1 yielded three grit-tempered sherdlets, one woodchuck calvarium, one chert flake, three sandstone fragments, and six stone fragments. Feature 2 produced one s $\frac{Z}{Z}$ cord-marked body sherd, one smoothed-over cord-marked body sherd, 136 sherdlets, and two chert flakes. Both features 1 and 2 appear to have been utilized during mound construction and the absence of charcoal and burned stone suggests that they were not used for cooking. The woodchuck calvarium might suggest an intentional pit inclusion and its presence, coupled with the absence of other preserved animal bone, suggests that it was a ceremonial inclusion.

Numerous rodent burrows and two sub-mound soil bodies did not detract from the placement of artifacts into their proper sub-mound or mound soil horizon. Artifacts recovered from burrows were excluded from the distribution listed in Table 28.

The sub-mound A2xb horizon of Mound 1 and the mound fill and surface again indicate the presence of both Dane Incised ceramics and Madison Ware ceramics. The inclusion of an Aztalan Collared rim sherd in the mound fill aids in the dating of the remainder of the Madison Ware ceramics as there is only the date from Mound 2 of A.D. 880 ± 70 for Aztalan Collared from the Sanders sites. As only 11 such vessels were recovered from 47-Wp-26 and Wp-70 the specimens from Mound 2 serve as an important time marker. If we consider the radiocarbon assessments from mounds 17, 3, and 2 (WIS-204, 177, 171) and exclude the

TABLE 28

DISTRIBUTION OF CERAMIC AND LITHIC ARTIFACTS: MOUND 1

Soil Location	Dane Incised	Dane Incised, v. finernail impressed	Madison Cord Impressed	Madison Fabric Impressed	Madison Plain	Madison Plain, v. jar	Aztalan Collared	s $\frac{z}{z}$	z $\frac{s}{s}$	Smoothed-over Cord	Waubesa Contracting Stem	Triangular	Knife	Cores	Burin Spalls	Single Edge Flake Side Scrapers	Flake End Scrapers	Flake Knives	Single Edge Utilized Flake Side Scrapers
A11				1	3	1		2	2	5		1				1			1
A12		2						3	1	4			1		1		1	2	
A2x/A2x	1	4	2	4	5		1	7		26	2	1		1					
A1b								1		2									
A2xb	1				1					7									
B22tb																			
B22b																			
C1b																			
Total	2	6	2	5	9	1	1	13	3	44	2	2	1	1	1	1	1	2	1

Dane Incised ceramics, we can state that the following artifact types were in use at specific mound locations at the Sanders sites at this time: Madison Cord Impressed, Madison Fabric Impressed, Madison Plain, Madison Plain, variety jar, Madison Punctated, Leland Cord-marked, and Aztalan Collared, plus Waubesa Contracting Stem, Madison Side Notched, and Triangular projectile points and the adze from Mound 17. It should be added that at Mound 1 there was an apparent preference for cord and fabrics composed of s $\frac{z}{z}$ twisted elements and this also seems true for conical Mound 2 and linear Mound 3. Both s $\frac{z}{z}$ and z $\frac{s}{s}$ cords were used on ceramics for cord-marking, cord-impressing, and fabric construction.

If we temporarily exclude dated Mound 23 and only assess mounds 17-18, 3, 2, and 1 or three conicals, one linear, and one panther effigy mound located within 300 feet of one another, we seem to have at least four, and possibly five, mounds that were constructed at almost the same time. The Aztalan Collared rim sherd from panther effigy Mound 1 links it to conical Mound 2 and linear Mound 3; the sub-mound and mound assemblages from mounds 2 and 3 tie them to mounds 1 and 17-18. We have excellent evidence that these three mound forms were constructed by the same people, at circa A.D. 880-900 ± 70, people who utilized artifacts previously proposed as belonging to their culture. These diagnostic items were located adjacent to, beneath, and within the mounds and, with the possible exception of the Madison Punctated vessel from Feature 1 of Mound 2, none appears to be more than a utilitarian artifact. Had the excavations been limited to this area at Sanders site 1, we would have been able to say that with the inclusion of the Point Sauble Collared vessel from Feature 6 of Mound 17 we would have almost the same information as that derived from the excavation of the Bigelow site. In the case of Sanders site 1 we have added a panther effigy and conjoined mounds to the list of mound forms; Madison Side Notched, Durst Stemmed, and Waubesa Contracting Stem points plus an adze and celt to the list of associated artifacts and we have not recorded, thus far, Hahn Cord Impressed ceramics.

Mound 5 is a bird effigy mound 41 feet long, 17 feet wide, and 3 feet high. Due to a lack of time, Mound 5 was not tested or excavated in 1965 or 1966.

Mound 4 is a conical mound 14 feet in diameter and 1.0 feet high. Because of the large maple tree in the center, two five-foot squares were excavated on the edges of this mound. One feature, Feature 9, was excavated and the artifacts from this same square and level may belong to Feature 9. Those artifacts definitely associated with Feature 9 are two smoothed-over cord-marked body sherds, one knife, one chert flake, and seven stone fragments. The sub-mound and mound horizons of Mound 4 produced the artifacts listed in Table 29.

Feature 9 of Mound 4 appears to have been utilized prior to mound construction as it intruded into two sub-mound horizons. These soils horizons contained ceramic representatives of at least two Dane Incised vessels; one Dane Incised, variety fingernail impressed vessel; one Madison Fabric Impressed vessel; two Madison Plain vessels, and, as indicated by these vessel counts, ceramics impressed or cord-marked with either s $\frac{Z}{Z}$ or z $\frac{S}{S}$ cords.

TABLE 29

DISTRIBUTION OF CERAMIC AND LITHIC ARTIFACTS: MOUND 4

Soil Location	Dane Incised	Dane Incised, v. fingernail impressed	Madison Folded Lip	Madison Plain	$s\frac{z}{z}$	$z\frac{s}{s}$	Smoothed-over Cord	Flake End Scrapers	Flake Knives	Utilized Flake End Scrapers	Copper Artifacts
A11							1				
A/B				1	1	16	1		1		1
A1b	1		6	1			10	1			
B21irb	5	2	2	1	2	1	8			2	
B22b											
Total	6	2	8	3	3	17	20	1	1	2	1

Mound 4 contained a rim sherd from a separate Madison Plain vessel, a majority of $z\frac{s}{s}$ cord-marked body sherds, worked flakes in contrast to the sub-mound utilized flakes, and a copper awl. The sub-mound ceramics from Mound 4 again indicate the presence of both Dane Incised and Madison Ware ceramics at this site, although the provenience of the Dane Incised ceramics does not indicate that they were contemporary wares of the ceramics utilized by Effigy Mound peoples.

Area 16 was originally considered to be a conical mound 70 feet in diameter and six feet high, but testing operations indicated that this area was a natural rise. Two five-foot squares and one 2.5 by 5-foot extension were excavated. One feature, Feature 3, was exposed and it yielded one $s\frac{z}{z}$ cord-marked and five smoothed-over cord-marked body sherds, one bone fragment, one quartz flake, three chert flakes, and 10 stone fragments. The contents of this feature indicate only that some aboriginal activity took place at this area. Mound 15 is a conical mound north of Mound 4 and its fill had been used for borrow for the farm road. Testing or excavations were therefore not pursued. Mound 14 is a oval mound seriously disturbed by the farm road which cut through its center. Mound 14, like Mound 15, was neither tested nor excavated during 1965 or 1966.

Testing operations were conducted in the northeast field around TBM 2. To the south of this temporary bench mark was one test square where excavations exposed one feature, Feature 2. Feature 2 yielded one sherd fragment, one quartzite flake, one chert flake, one basalt flake, seven stone fragments, and charcoal flecks which indicated that this area, like Area 16, had been utilized for possible cooking activities.

Mounds 11, 12, and 13 (Fig. 31) form a small cluster of conical mounds at the extreme northwest portion of 47-Wp-26. Mound 11 did not contain any burials, but the sub-mound and mound fill horizons did yield diagnostic artifacts (Table 30).

The sub-mound Madison Fabric Impressed and Madison Plain and the cord-marked body sherds exhibiting $s\,{}^{Z}_{Z}$ cords or $Z\,{}^{s\,{}^{Z}_{Z}}_{s\,{}^{Z}_{Z}}$ cords suggest that at this location Madison Ware ceramics and $s\,{}^{Z}_{Z}$ cords were in use prior to the construction of conical Mound 11. At least three other Madison Plain vessels, as well as a Madison Cord Impressed and a Leland Cord-marked vessel, were in use before or at the time of construction. The combined cords used as

TABLE 30

DISTRIBUTION OF CERAMIC AND LITHIC ARTIFACTS: MOUND 11

Soil Location	Dane Incised	Madison Cord Impressed	Madison Fabric Impressed	Madison Plain	Leland Cord-marked	$s\,{}^{Z}_{Z}$	$Z\,{}^{S}_{S}$	Smoothed-over Cord	Triangular	Drills	Diminutive Scraper	Cores	Single Edge Flake Side Scrapers	Multiple Edge Flake Side Scrapers
A11				1				1				1		
A2x/A2x	1	1		4	1	2	3	14	1	1	2		2	1
A2xb			1			1		4						
B22b				1		1		5		1				
Total	1	1	1	6	1	4	3	24	1	2	2	1	2	1

decoration on the Madison Cord Impressed rim sherd are also represented, individually, on the recovered body sherds. The sub-mound and mound fill Madison Ware ceramic types and the Triangular projectile point are all part of the material culture associated with the Effigy Mound component at this site and we can now ascertain that this component is represented throughout 47-Wp-26. We are again confronted with a Dane Incised specimen from the mound fill which may belong to an earlier component and may have been accidentally included in Mound 11. The position of Dane Incised ceramics will be evaluated from a sub-mound and mound perspective after all the mounds and areas have been presented.

Mound 12 is a small conical mound 22 by 24 by 1.0 feet. A 15 by 5-foot west to east trench was excavated across the center of this mound and the yield was considered so productive that an additional 10 five-foot squares were excavated. Artifacts from the sub-mound and mound fill horizons of Mound 12 are listed in Table 31.

TABLE 31

DISTRIBUTION OF CERAMIC AND LITHIC ARTIFACTS: MOUND 12

Soil Location	Dane Incised	Madison Cord Impressed	Madison Folded Lip	Madison Plain	Madison Punctated	Leland Cord-marked	Z S Z	S Z S	Smoothed-over Cord	Waubesa Contracting Stem	Drills	Cores	Diminutive Scrapers	Single Edge Flake Side Scraper	Multiple Edge Flake Side Scraper	Flake End Scraper	Single Edge Utilized Flake Side Scraper	Multiple Edge Utilized Flake Side Scraper	Shaft Polisher	Copper
A11		1		2			1	2	3			2				1				
A2x/A2x	1	3	1	8	3		2	2	30		1		1							
A1b				1		1		1	25	1			1	1	1	1	1	1	1	1
A2xb				2			1		1											
B22b																				
Total	1	4	1	13	3	1	4	5	59	1	1	2	2	1	1	2	1	1	1	1

A brief review of the Mound 12 sub-mound soil horizon artifacts includes the Madison Ware, Madison Plain, and Leland Cord-marked specimens plus a Waubesa Contracting Stem projectile point, a diminutive scraper, worked and utilized flakes, and a copper fragment. The Madison Ware category from the mound itself includes Madison Cord Impressed, Madison Fabric Impressed, Madison Plain, and Madison Punctated ceramics, plus a drill, a diminutive scraper, cores, and a worked flake. The preferred cord appears to have been that of z $\frac{S}{S}$ elements for both decoration and cord-marking except for the sub-mound and mound Madison Plain specimens. Mound 12, like Mound 11 and Mound 13 below, also contained one Dane Incised example from the A2x/A2x mound fill.

Mound 13, the last mound in this conical cluster, is 19 by 18 by 1.2 feet; two five-foot squares were excavated in the center of this mound. The mound and sub-mound horizons yielded the artifacts listed in Table 32.

The sub-mound priority of Madison Ware ceramics (Madison Fabric Impressed and Madison Plain) and the use of z $\frac{S}{S}$ (Madison Fabric Impressed) or s $\frac{Z}{Z}$ (Madison Plain and a cord-marked body sherd) parallels the sub-mound record for Mound 11. The presence of other Madison Ware ceramics (Madison Cord Impressed, Madison

TABLE 32

DISTRIBUTION OF CERAMIC AND LITHIC ARTIFACTS: MOUND 13

Soil Location	Dane Incised	Madison Cord Impressed	Madison Fabric Impressed	Madison Plain	Madison Punctated	s $\frac{Z}{Z}$	z $\frac{S}{S}$	Smoothed-over Cord	Diminutive Scrapers	Single Edge Utilized Flake Side Scrapers
A11		1		5				21		1
A2x/A2x	1	1		4	1		1	10	1	
A1b			1	3		1		10		
A2xb										
B22b										
Total	1	2	1	12	1	1	1	41	1	1

Plain) in the mound fill, and Madison Punctated representatives has been documented for both Mound 12 and Mound 11. Mound 13 lacks the Waubesa Contracting Stem and Triangular points of these other two mounds, but shares the presence of diminutive scrapers and Dane Incised ceramics. If we again exclude the Dane Incised ceramics from our discussion, it would appear that the area of mounds 11, 12, and 13 was being extensively utilized by Effigy Mound peoples prior to the construction of these mounds. The presence of three different ceramic types belonging to the Effigy Mound Madison Ware category beneath these mounds and two additional types within the mounds, plus a Waubesa Contracting Stem point beneath Mound 12 and one Triangular point from the fill of Mound 11, strongly supports the view that Effigy Mound peoples constructed mounds 11, 12, and 13 and that they utilized this portion of Sanders site 1.

The Dane Incised ceramics indicate either that an earlier component not related to these people made these artifacts or that Dane Incised ceramics were part of the Effigy Mound material culture. The number of diminutive scrapers excavated from the 20 five-foot squares adjacent to mounds 11-13 was 24, or 37.5 percent of those recovered from 47-Wp-26. If the five specimens from mounds 11 and 12, the drills, cores, and worked and utilized flakes are included, this area seems to have been preferred as a workshop area for the manufacture of lithic tools or as an area for wood and hide working. These may have been male activities and they occurred as far from the village at 47-Wp-26 as possible. One feature, Feature 4, was uncovered and this irregular pit contained only charcoal flecks, so the limited evidence seems to suggest that little if any cooking was done in this area.

Area 10 is directly east of mounds 11-13 and TBM 2 and was considered a mound because its center is two feet higher than the surrounding topography (Fig. 31). Careful inspection of this area in 1966, plus testing operations, indicated that Area 10 is a natural rise. One five-foot square was excavated and it yielded one Madison Punctated body sherd, two smoothed-over cord-marked body sherds, one single edge flake side scraper, and one flake knife. Three other rises in this field, numbers 7, 8, and 9, were also suggested as mounds after the 1965 survey. This field was carefully examined in 1966 and all of these areas are now considered to be a part of the general rolling topography. However, the contour interval north of areas 9 and 10 strongly suggests that the Wolf River was at one time much closer to these areas than the approximate 250 foot distance of today.

Areas 7 and 8 were not tested, but excavations were conducted in Area 9 and three five-foot squares were excavated to a depth of 3.5 feet. One feature, Feature 1, was exposed at a depth of 2.6 feet or 1.9 feet below the plow zone and the artifacts from the pit fill were undisturbed. These artifacts include one Point Sauble Collared rim sherd; one Madison Cord Impressed rim sherd; and one s $\frac{Z}{Z}$ cord-marked body sherd, 11 sherd fragments, one quartz flake, one chert flake, two stone fragments, and charcoal. The charcoal was submitted for radiocarbon assessment and yielded a date of A.D. 1010 ± 60 (WIS-207). Before discussing this date and the associated artifacts we will examine the other artifacts from Area 9 which are listed in Table 33.

The date of A.D. 1010 ± 60 (WIS-207) for the two Madison Ware ceramic types—Madison Cord Impressed and Point Sauble Collared—from Feature 1 of Area 9 extends the dated range of Madison Cord Impressed ceramics thus far presented (Mound 3 at A.D. 880) approximately 300 years. It is also the only date for Point Sauble Collared ceramics at 47-Wp-26. Area 9 appears to have been subjected to alluvial deposition by the Wolf River and as the levels between the orifice of Feature 1 and the lower boundary of the Ap horizon contained very few artifacts—two Heins Creek Corded Stamped sherds and one utilized flake—it appears that there were two separate occupations of this area. The first occupation dates the typed artifacts contained in Feature 1 and

TABLE 33

DISTRIBUTION OF CERAMIC AND LITHIC ARTIFACTS: AREA 9

Soil Location	Madison Cord Impressed	Madison Folded Lip	Point Sauble Collared	Heins Creek Corded Stamped	z s s	Smoothed-over Cord	Diminutive Scrapers	Burin Spalls	Multiple Edge Flake Side Scrapers	Flake End Scrapers	Single Edge Utilized Flake Side Scrapers
Ap	1	1				3	1			1	
B1ir				2		3					1
B2ir		2	1		1	3					
B3ir	1	1		1		5	1	1	1		
Total	2	4	1	3	1	14	2	1	1	1	1

the Madison Cord Impressed, Madison Fabric Impressed, Point Sauble Collared, and Heins Creek Corded Stamped ceramics at A.D. 1010 ± 60. The later occupation could have occurred at A.D. 1010 to 1100 and would be represented by the types Madison Cord Impressed, Madison Fabric Impressed, and possibly the two Heins Creek Corded Stamped examples. The latter ceramic type was suggested in Chapter VII as a companion ware to the established Madison Ware types. All of the data from Area 9 suggest utilization by the Effigy Mound peoples who occupied 47-Wp-26.

Mound 6 is the last mound recorded during our survey and excavation seasons and this conical mound appears to be in good state of preservation. The mound is adjacent to a summer cottage at Red Banks and although it was not tested, Mr. Sanders has reported that it had been trenched.

If we temporarily view Sanders site 1 from the perspective presented thus far for the mound and area excavations we begin to see a pattern emerging for the distribution of the Dane Incised ceramics. Of the 12 mounds and three areas excavated, Dane Incised or Dane Incised, variety fingernail impressed ceramics were found beneath mounds 1, 2, 4, and 28 in association with Madison Ware ceramics. The Dane Incised ceramics included in the mound fill of mounds 1, 3, 11, 12, 13, 19, 23, 25, and 28 were in association with Madison Ware ceramics in all but Mound 23. Specimens which are considered to be Middle Woodland ceramics—Sister Creeks Punctated, Rocker Stamped, and Shorewood Cord Roughened—number only 10 vessels. On the basis of this figure, it can be assumed that the estimated 225 Dane Incised and Dane Incised, variety fingernail impressed ceramics represent a Middle Woodland component as widespread at 47-Wp-26 as the Effigy Mound component, *or* that these ceramics are a part of the material culture associated with the Effigy Mound cultural tradition. More emphasis and elaboration will be given this problem in the subsequent analyses of the various soil bodies and the village at 47-Wp-26 and Wp-70. At this time I suggest that the Dane Incised ceramics from both locations were made by Effigy Mound peoples.

In the analyses of the Bigelow site (Chapter V) it was suggested that if there had been a consistent and regular recognized rate at which mounds were added to a site the range might have been between 33.5 and 16.1 years, with the possible regular interval being 25 years per mound at 47-Pt-29. The four radiocarbon dated mounds at 47-Wp-26 suggest that they were constructed between A.D. 720 ± 55 (WIS-221) and A.D. 900 ± 70 (WIS-204). The maximum temporal range would be from A.D. 665 to A.D. 970, or 305 years, with the minimum temporal range between A.D. 775 to A.D. 830, or 55 years. However, the possible rates of mound construction at 47-Wp-26 are really spurious, as there is an associated village supporting a resident population capable of constructing a mound without a great deal of travel, unlike the cyclic revisiting of a site necessary at 47-Pt-29. Moreover, mounds 17-18 and Mound 2 or Mound 3 could have been constructed within 20 years of one another, while mounds 2 and 3 appear to have been built at the same time. Even if we accept the full range of dates presented in Figures 59 and 60 as applicable to the mounds—A.D. 670 ± 75 (WIS-217) to A.D. 1060 ± 65 (WIS-232)—we would still not have exceeded the temporal range recorded for the mounds at the Bigelow site and any of the four figures (33.5, 25, 19.6, or 16.1 years per mound) could apply *if* there were more dated mounds at 47-Wp-26.

Before examining the village at 47-Wp-26 and Wp-70, I will present a brief discussion of the artifacts recovered from excavations conducted in soil bodies $\frac{1}{A}$, $\frac{1}{D}$, and $\frac{\overline{3}}{A}$ (Fig. 44) which are separate from the village soils (soil bodies $\frac{4}{A}$ and $\frac{4}{D}$) and from the already presented mounds. In the Bigelow analyses and in the Sanders analyses thus far presented, the various cords or fabrics utilized to decorate the ceramics have been described. As the number of ceramic fragments excavated from these four soil bodies increases dramatically such a presentation would be meaningless in specific form unless each square and level were examined in detail. I will present these artifacts only according to their types or categories unless they have a feature or house context. Soil body $\frac{\overline{1}}{A}$ comprises half of the mapped soil bodies of 47-Wp-26 (Fig. 44) and these soil horizons yielded artifacts listed in Table 34.

The evidence from the excavation of this soil body suggests stability in the horizon representatives of both Dane Incised and Madison Ware ceramics. However, the lack of vertical depth as a result of a nearly impenetrable A2x fragipan horizon could have produced a telescoping of time and/or components into a relatively few inches. The number of Grand River ceramics from both

TABLE 34

DISTRIBUTION OF CERAMIC AND LITHIC ARTIFACTS: SOIL BODY $\frac{1}{A}$

Soil Location	Rocker Stamped	Dane Incised	Madison Cord Impressed	Madison Fabric Impressed	Madison Plain	Madison Plain, v. Jar	Leland Cord-marked	Aztalan Collared	Point Sauble Collared	Heins Creek Corded Stamped	Grand River Plain	Grand River Body Sherds	Z Z S	S S Z	Smoothed-over Cord	Waubesa Contracting Stem	Corner Notched	Triangular	Drills	Diminutive Scrapers	Scrapers	Knives	Cores	Burins	Blades	Single Edge Flake Side Scrapers	Multiple Edge Flake Side Scrapers	Flake Knives	Single Edge Utilized Flake Side Scrapers	Multiple Edge Utilized Flake Side Scrapers	Utilized Flake End Scrapers	Celts
A11		2	6	1	11	2			3			36	5	41				1		2	1	1						4	1	2	2	
A2x	1	2	5	1	12	2	2	1		1	4	17	7	54	3	1	1	1	1	13	2	2	1	1	1	2	1	1	2	2	1	1
Total	1	4	11	2	23	4	2	1	3	1	4	53	12	95	3	1	1	2	1	15	3	3	1	1	1	2	1	5	3	4	3	1

horizons (57) is unexpected outside of the main village area, as no Grand River specimens were recovered from our sub-mound or mound excavations. The number of Dane Incised examples, on the other hand, is relatively small as we have many examples from beneath or within mounds throughout 47-Wp-26. The lithic artifacts distribution indicates a clearer pattern—the area of soil body $\frac{1}{\text{A-0}}$ appears to have become less favored for activities associated with the manufacture or use of lithic artifacts. In Chapter VI it was reported that this soil body, with soil bodies $\frac{1}{\text{D-1}}$ and $\frac{1}{\text{E-1}}$, represented very difficult soils to excavate as even rock hammers had little effect on the fragic A2x horizon or the clayey B22t horizon. It is surprising, therefore, that whole or broken hoe or spade-like tools were not recovered because even under the most favorable moist conditions these soils would be difficult to use for mound borrow with just shell or bone tools. Excavated mounds 13, 12, 11, 1, 2, 3, 17, 19, and 23 and unexcavated mounds 20-22, 26, and 27 were constructed on and composed of these soils and the absence of lithic digging tools is paradoxical.

Soil body $\frac{1}{\text{D-1}}$ has no mounds on its surface nor were there any testing or excavation operations conducted. A surface survey of this area (Fig. 44) did produce one diminutive scraper from the A1 horizon. Soil body $\frac{3}{\text{A-0}}$ (Fig. 44) is the bisequal soil with a Brown Podzolic (A1 and Bir horizons) over a Gray Brown Podzolic (A′2x—B′t) sequem. Testing operations east of Mound 3 yielded one Grand River body sherd, one multiple edge flake side scraper, and one utilized flake end scraper from the Brown Podzolic Bir horizon.

Soil bodies $\frac{4}{\text{A-0}}$ and $\frac{\text{4-A}}{\text{A-0}}$ delimit the village at 47-Wp-26 and if the area between the southern edge of the woodlot and the area designated at 47-Wp-70 had not been plowed it is my belief that this soil body would have connected these two locations into one village. As excavations were not conducted between the S1100 grid line of 47-Wp-26 and House 1 of 47-Wp-70, we cannot estimate the number of houses, pits, or artifacts contained in this area. From the information to be considered below and the radiocarbon dates (Fig. 59) there is no reason in my mind to consider House 1 of 47-Wp-70 as separate from the village at 47-Wp-26. The soil bodies preserved at Sanders site 1 suggest that the village area was cleared, occupation took place, pits and houses were dug, grasses occupied a former forest area, and an organically and artifactually rich midden developed (the A1bhir horizon) which supported this vegetation. With the abandonment of the village at circa A.D. 1100, the present A11 horizon developed under a subsequent forest vegetation. The A11 horizon contained artifacts which are most probably a result of rodent activity, tree growth, and even excavation techniques. In any event, the A11 and the A1bhir horizons make up a one foot seal, undisturbed by plowing, which covered the intensive village occupation at Sanders site 1. The artifacts recovered from these soil bodies are listed in Table 35.

The occupation of the village (both 47-Wp-26 and Wp-70) began at A.D. 670 ± 75 (WIS-217) with the utilization of Feature 30 (Figs. 41 and 59) which yielded one Dane Incised, variety fingernail impressed rim sherd; three Madison Plain rim sherds; one Grand River Plain rim sherd; one Triangular projectile point; five Grand River body sherds; seven s $\frac{Z}{Z}$ cord-marked, seven z $\frac{S}{S}$ cord-marked, three smoothed-over cord-marked body sherds; 121 sherd fragments; bone and shell fragments; 13 stone fragments; four basalt flakes, 49 chert flakes, 13 quartzite flakes, and 44 quartz flakes. The charcoal from this feature yielded the date of A.D. 670 ± 75.

We are confronted with a two-fold interpretation dilemma: Dane Incised ceramics should not appear this late and Grand River ceramics from this feature may represent the earliest dated Oneota ceramics recorded for Wisconsin. Both wares are in association with Madison Plain ceramics and a Triangular projectile point which belong to the material culture of the Effigy Mound component. If the Dane Incised, variety fingernail impressed rim sherd was dug up and then replaced with the pit fill, then the Grand River ceramics are contemporary with the Madison Plain ceramics. If the Dane Incised, variety fingernail impressed and Madison Plain ceramics plus the Triangular projectile point are contemporary, then how did the Grand River ceramics come to be in the pit fill at this early date? Finally, are these three wares contemporary at this time? Let us examine six more features (numbers 11, 16, 22, 34-36).

TABLE 35

DISTRIBUTION OF CERAMIC AND LITHIC ARTIFACTS: SOIL BODY $\frac{4}{A}$

Soil Location	Sister Creeks Punctated	Shorewood Cord Roughened	Dane Incised	Dane Incised, v. fingernail impressed	Madison Cord Impressed	Madison Fabric Impressed	Madison Folded Lip	Madison Plain	Madison Plain, v. punctated	Madison Plain, v. jar	Madison Punctated	Leland Cord-marked	Aztalan Collared	Hahn Cord Impressed	Point Sauble Collared	Heins Creek Corded Stamped	Grand River Trailed	Grand River Plain	z s z	s z s	Smoothed-over Cord
A11			1		2	1		11			3							2	11	15	20
A1bhir	3	2	109	12	118	62	27	330	6	7	41	34	5	1	14	20	19	42	544	385	841
B1irb			4	1		4					2	1						1	6	2	25
Total	3	2	114	13	120	67	27	341	6	7	46	35	5	1	14	20	19	45	561	402	886

Soil Location	A11	A1bhir	B1irb	Total
Waubesa Contracting Stem		3		3
Corner Notched		3		3
Side Notched		3		3
Durst Stemmed		6		6
Sanders Triangular		9		9
Triangular	3	27		30
Drills		3		3
Diminutive Scrapers		12		12
Scrapers			1	1
Knives		3		3
Cores		5	2	7
Gravers		1		1
Burins		2		2
Burin Spalls			1	1
Blades		2	1	3
Single Edge Flake Side Scrapers		7	1	8
Multiple Edge Flake Side Scrapers		11		11
Flake End Scrapers		6		6
Flake Knives		13		13
Single Edge Utilized Flake Side Scrapers		7		7
Multiple Edge Utilized Flake Side Scrapers	2	3	2	7
Utilized Flake End Scrapers		2	1	3
Gorgets		1		1
Polished Stones		4		4
Copper Artifacts		9	1	10

Feature 11 (Fig. 41) yielded one Dane Incised body sherd; two Madison Plain rim sherds; one Grand River Plain rim sherd; one s $\frac{z}{z}$ cord-marked, one z $\frac{s}{s}$ cord-marked, and one smoothed-over cord-marked body sherd; six sherd fragments, two basalt flakes, two chert flakes, two quartz flakes, and eight stone fragments.

Feature 16 (Fig. 41) produced three Dane Incised specimens (Pl. 17:A, I; Pl. 18:A); one Madison Folded Lip rim sherd (Pl. 25:I); nine Madison Plain rim sherds; one Grand River Trailed body sherd; 10 s $\frac{z}{z}$ cord-marked, 14 z $\frac{s}{s}$ cord-marked, and 22 smoothed-over cord-marked body sherds; 223 sherd fragments; one copper awl or nail (Pl. 44:J); one knife; 47 chert, nine quartzite, and 31 quartz flakes; and charred bone fragments.

Feature 22 (Fig. 41) yielded two Dane Incised body sherds, one Dane Incised, variety fingernail impressed body sherd (Pl. 20:J); one Madison Plain rim sherd; one s $\frac{z}{z}$ cord-marked and two smoothed-over cord-marked body sherds; 45 sherd fragments; one projectile point fragment; one basalt, three quartz, one quartzite, and 20 chert flakes; and two stone fragments.

Feature 34 (Fig. 42) yielded one Dane Incised body sherd; two Madison Cord Impressed specimens; one Madison Fabric Impressed body sherd; one Madison Plain rim sherd; one Madison Punctated body sherd; five s $\frac{z}{z}$ cord-marked, two z $\frac{s}{s}$ cord-marked, and six smoothed-over cord-marked body sherds; 107 grit-tempered body sherds; one Triangular projectile point; 17 chert, five quartzite, and eight quartz flakes; 20 stone fragments; and charcoal flecks.

Feature 35 (Fig. 42) contained one Dane Incised body sherd; one Madison Cord Impressed rim sherd; one Madison Fabric Impressed body sherd (Fig. 51:B); three Madison Plain rim sherds; two z $\frac{s}{s}$ cord-marked and three smoothed-over cord-marked body sherds; 64 sherd fragments; one copper awl (Pl. 44:L); bone fragments; one single edge flake side scraper; one quartzite, 10 quartz, and 20 chert flakes; and charcoal flecks.

Feature 36 included one Dane Incised body sherd (Pl. 19:F); two Grand River body sherds; six s $\frac{z}{z}$ cord-marked, two z $\frac{s}{s}$ cord-marked, and five smoothed-over cord-marked body sherds; 143 grit-tempered sherd fragments, three shell-tempered sherd fragments; bone fragments; one diminutive scraper; one flake knife;

two quartzite, nine chert, and 16 quartz flakes; 20 stone fragments; and charcoal flecks.

Features 30, 11, 16, and 36 contained Dane Incised, Madison Ware, and Grand River ceramics plus the Triangular point of Feature 30. Features 22, 34, and 35 contained Dane Incised and Madison Ware ceramics, and a Triangular projectile point or copper awls were recovered from features 16, 34, and 35. The preferred cords appear to be s $\frac{z}{z}$ cords for features 30, 16, 22, 35, and 36, and z $\frac{s}{s}$ in Feature 34. Both types of cords or combinations for fabrics were recorded for Features 11 and 35. At this point in the analysis there appear to be seven features which have yielded Dane Incised and Madison Ware ceramics, four which also contained Dane Incised and Grand River ceramics (plus the Madison Ware examples), and two features containing Triangular projectile points in association with Dane Incised ceramics. Among the Effigy Mound Madison Ware ceramics, the individual types in association in these features with Dane Incised ceramics include Madison Cord Impressed, Madison Fabric Impressed, Madison Folded Lip, Madison Plain, and Madison Punctated ceramics. The Madison Ware types in association with the Grand River specimens include Madison Folded Lip and Madison Plain. If we assume the Effigy Mound component to be the major component of this locality then the evidence of Dane Incised-Madison Ware and now Grand River contemporaneity is much stronger.

The next segment of the occupation sequence includes the houses and associated house pits from 47-Wp-26 and Wp-70. House 1 at Sanders site 3 was defined at a depth of 2.7 feet below the surface and the living floor (Level 5) extended to 2.8 feet (Fig. 47). Two features and one burial were defined in the house floor and they were designated features 12 and 13 and Burial 1. The post-molds of House 1 were excavated and they extended to a depth of 3.4 feet below the surface and the fill of this semi-subterranean house continued to a depth of 4.6 feet. The house basin was 1.9 feet deep and the basin was subdivided into levels 6 and 7. Level 7 produced only one Dane Incised body sherd; Level 6 yielded one z $\frac{s}{s}$ body sherd, and the house floor, Level 5, and the post-molds were void of diagnostic artifacts. Burial 1 consisted of one skull with *Anculosa* shells on its forehead. The fill of this pit contained five body sherds, two chert flakes, three stone fragments, and charcoal. The charcoal from this pit and the house floor was combined and the radiocarbon assessment on this sample is A.D. 720 ± 60 (WIS-233). This assessment (Fig. 60) dates the initial construction of House 1 and its occupation, the time of the burial (a possible trophy skull), and the date of the utilization of features 12 and 13.

Feature 12 yielded one smoothed-over cord-marked body sherd, one sherd fragment, three chert flakes, 10 stone fragments, and bone fragments. Feature 13 contained only shell fragments, two stone fragments, and charcoal. From this information we can see that the house basin of House 1 contained one Dane Incised specimen which was sealed in beneath the house floor which is dated at A.D. 720 ± 60 or within the range of Feature 30 from 47-Wp-26 (WIS-217, A.D. 670 ± 75). As there appears to be a minimum hiatus of 90 years between the dated house floor and the subsequent levels of occupation (WIS-233 and WIS-230) we will hold the remaining analysis of this area in abeyance while we examine houses 1, 2, and 3 of Wp-26.

House 3 at Sanders site 1 was defined at 1.0 feet and this semi-subterranean house extended to a depth of 3.65 feet below the surface. The house fill was sorted into fill above the house floor (1.1 feet to 1.8 feet) and the floor and fill below (1.9 feet to 3.65 feet). The features which had their orifice at the house floor level include features 45 through 48 and they were excavated separately from the house material. The diagnostic material from House 3 is listed in Tables 36 and 37.

Feature 45 (Fig. 42) produced one z $\frac{S}{S}$ cord-marked body sherd; one diminutive scraper; one burin spall; one single edge flake side scraper; one polished stone; 10 quartz, four quartzite, and 26 chert flakes; nine stone fragments; and a large quantity of charcoal which yielded a date of 5520 B.C. ± 90 (WIS-222).

Feature 46 produced the following artifacts: two Madison Plain rim sherds; one Grand River Plain rim sherd (Pl. 37:I); seven s $\frac{Z}{Z}$ cord-marked, five z $\frac{S}{S}$ cord-marked, and 10 smoothed-over cord-marked body sherds; 50 sherdlets; one projectile point fragment; one graver; one multiple edge flake side scraper; one quartzite, 10 quartz, and 12 chert flakes; 23 stone fragments; and charcoal which was radiocarbon dated at A.D. 770 ± 55 (WIS-223).

Feature 47 (Fig. 42) yielded one body sherd, one copper fragment, three chert flakes, and 12 stone fragments. Feature 48 (Fig. 42) contained one sherd, six chert and four quartzite flakes, bone and shell fragments.

TABLE 36

DISTRIBUTION OF CERAMICS: HOUSES (47-Wp-26)

House 1		
Floor	Dane Incised	1
	Dane Incised, v. Fingernail Impressed	2
	Madison Fabric Impressed	1
	Madison Plain	2
	s^{z}_{z}	4
House 2		
Upper Fill	Dane Incised	1
	Madison Plain	26
	Madison Plain, v. Punctated	1
	Madison Punctated	1
	Leland Cord-marked	1
	Heins Creek Corded Stamped	1
	Grand River Plain	1
	Grand River Body Sherds	3
	s^{z}_{z}	19
	z^{s}_{s}	21
Floor and Lower Fill	Madison Cord Impressed	3
	Madison Plain	11
	Leland Cord-marked	1
	Heins Creek Corded Stamped	2
	Grand River Plain	1
	Grand River Body Sherds	2
	s^{z}_{z}	13
	z^{s}_{s}	5
House 3		
Upper Fill	Dane Incised	1
	Dane Incised, v. Fingernail Impressed	1
	Madison Fabric Impressed	1
	Madison Plain	11
	Aztalan Collared	1
	Grand River Trailed	1
	Grand River Plain	1
	Grand River Body Sherds	4
	s^{z}_{z}	2
Floor and Lower Fill	Dane Incised	1
	Madison Cord Impressed	2
	Madison Plain	31
	Madison Punctated	3
	Leland Cord-marked	2
	Heins Creek Corded Stamped	1
	Grand River Body Sherds	3
	s^{z}_{z}	1
	z^{s}_{s}	38

TABLE 37

DISTRIBUTION OF LITHIC AND COPPER ARTIFACTS: HOUSES (47-Wp-26)

House 1		
House Floor 1	Diminutive Scrapers	2
	Knife	1
	Blade	1
	Single Edge Flake Side Scrapers	2
	Flake End Scraper	1
	Multiple Edge Utilized Flake Side Scraper	1
	Copper	2
House 2		
House Fill 2	Triangular Point	1
	Diminutive Scrapers	2
	Copper	1
House 3		
House Fill 1	Drill	1
	Diminutive Scrapers	4
	Scraper	1
	Core	1
	Single Edge Flake Side Scrapers	3
	Multiple Edge Flake Side Scrapers	2
	Flake End Scrapers	2
	Flake Knife	1
	Single Edge Utilized Flake Side Scraper	1
	Multiple Edge Utilized Flake Side Scrapers	3
	Polished Stones	2
	Grinding Stone	1

The three radiocarbon dates from House 3 clearly indicate that the time of prehistoric activity in this area is not quite clear. The sample from Feature 45 (WIS-222) does not date this house or the feature at 5520 B.C. ± 90 and its association with the artifacts is questionable. The date may well be associated with a forest fire occurring after the maximum elevation of both Later Lake Oshkosh and the Wolf River (Horn, 1960:29, 140, 192). The charcoal from the sub-floor house fill dated at A.D. 290 ± 65 (WIS-218) is more difficult to explain. This sample may be associated with the Middle Woodland peoples who made such items at Sanders site 1 as the Sister Creeks Punctated and Rocker Stamped ceramics. Even though there is an earlier dated Middle Woodland semi-subterranean house (Hurley, 1966:186-190) dated at 200 B.C. ± 80 (WIS-153; Bender, Bryson, and Baerreis, 1967) and other Middle Woodland houses dated before or shortly after sample WIS-218 (Freeman, 1969; Bender, Bryson, and Baerreis,

1968*a*), the house at 47-Wp-26 is not considered to be a Middle Woodland house or an early Effigy Mound house. The sample from Feature 46 (WIS-223; A.D. 770 ± 55) is more in line with the other five dates from the area illustrated in Figure 42. These other dates are from House 2 (WIS-203 and 224); Features 30 (WIS-217), 33 (WIS-219), and 29 (WIS-206). If we include the mound dates and dates from 47-Wp-70 (Figs. 59 and 60) there are 15 radiocarbon assessments within the range of sample WIS-223. There is no evidence to suggest a prehistoric component dating at 5520 B.C. (WIS-222) at 47-Wp-26, while there is limited information suggesting a possible Middle Woodland component at A.D. 290 (WIS-218). As the question of the component identity of the Dane Incised ceramics is still open, the sample may also date these ceramics.

The date of A.D. 770 ± 55 from Feature 46 appears to be appropriate for the time of construction and use of House 3 and the associated fill and feature artifacts such as the upper fill Madison Fabric Impressed, Madison Plain, Aztalan Collared, and the Grand River ceramics as well as the Waubesa Contracting Stem projectile point. As Feature 46 intruded into the lower house fill, the Madison Cord Impressed, Madison Plain, Madison Punctated, Leland Cord-marked, Heins Creek Corded Stamped, and Grand River ceramics pre-date this feature. Feature 46 also had two Madison Plain rim sherds and a Grand River Plain rim sherd in association with the charcoal. The Dane Incised ceramics from the sub-floor house fill and the upper house fill are not a single problem, as the artifacts above the floor are dated after A.D. 770 ± 55 while those of the sub-floor fill are dated earlier. The information from House 3 again illustrates the association of Dane Incised and Madison Ware ceramics with the presence of apparently contemporary Grand River specimens from the house fill and from Feature 46. In this instance, the Grand River ceramics from House 3 and Feature 46 (as well as Feature 30) pre-date the earliest Upper Mississippian date recorded for Wisconsin, A.D. 890 ± 80 (WIS-77; Bender, Bryson, and Baerreis, 1966) for the Koshkonong Focus. The House 3 Grand River examples also represent another instance of the association of this Oneota ware with the material culture items attributable to Effigy Mound peoples. Finally, the data from House 3 support the proposal that the following Madison Ware ceramics are companion types: Madison Cord Impressed, Madison Fabric Impressed, Madison Plain, Madison Punctated, Leland Cord-marked, Aztalan Collared, and Heins Creek

Corded Stamped examples and the association of a Waubesa Contracting Stem projectile point, and thus supports the associations demonstrated for the mounds at 47-Wp-26.

House 2 of 47-Wp-26 is directly adjacent to House 3 (Fig. 42). The upper house fill extended from 1.0 to 1.9 feet below the surface. Its artifacts were kept separate from the lower fill, 1.9 feet to 2.4 feet below the surface, and the two features (numbers 39 and 40). The artifacts recovered from House 2 are listed in Tables 36 and 37.

Two features were located within House 2. Feature 39 yielded one body sherd, one chert flake, seven sherdlets, and one stone fragment. The second feature, Feature 40, contained one Dane Incised, variety fingernail impressed rim sherd (Pl. 22:J; Pl. 23:G); two Madison Fabric Impressed rim sherds (Pl. 22:M; Pl. 23:H); four Madison Plain rim sherds; one Madison Punctated body sherd; one Leland Cord-marked rim sherd (Pl. 32:C); six s $\frac{z}{z}$ cord-marked, eight z $\frac{s}{s}$ cord-marked, and 23 smoothed-over cord-marked body sherds; 313 sherdlets; one flake end scraper; one single edge utilized flake side scraper; one multiple edge utilized flake side scraper; one copper pendant (Pl. 44:C); 99 stone fragments; 20 quartzite, 39 quartz, and 100 chert flakes; and charcoal. The charcoal from Feature 40 was dated at A.D. 930 ± 55 (WIS-203; Fig. 59).

The upper fill of House 2 contained the ceramic type Dane Incised, Madison Plain, Madison Plain variety punctated, Madison Punctated, Leland Cord-marked, Heins Creek Corded Stamped, Grand River Plain, and Grand River body sherds. The house floor and sub-floor yielded Madison Cord Impressed, Madison Plain, Leland Cord-marked, Heins Creek Corded Stamped, Grand River Plain, and Grand River body sherds plus a Triangular projectile point. Charcoal from the upper and lower fill of House 2 dates these artifacts at A.D. 775 ± 55 (WIS-224). House 2, like House 3, has Dane Incised ceramics in association with Madison Ware and the Oneota Grand River specimens. The latter group is dated as early as the other examples from 47-Wp-26 and possibly earlier than any other Oneota ceramics from Wisconsin. The artifacts from Feature 40 include Dane Incised variety fingernail impressed, Madison Cord Impressed, Madison Fabric Impressed, Madison Plain, Madison Punctated, and Leland Cord-marked, or Madison Ware types in association once again with Dane Incised specimens. The date from the charcoal of Feature 40 of A.D. 930 ± 55 (WIS-203) suggests that House 2 was in use for 150 years. However, both WIS-224 and WIS-203 (Fig. 59) do overlap and indicate, as the other dates illustrated, that House 2 was constructed and used between A.D. 720 and A.D. 985. This temporal range is somewhat late for Dane Incised ceramics but well within the range of both Madison Ware and Grand River ceramics.

Excavation of a semi-subterranean house basin and its internal pits and associated external pits has been recorded for the Middle Woodland component at Silver Creek I (47-Mo-1) (Hurley, 1966) and the Millville site (Freeman, 1969). Their presence at an Effigy Mound locality at circa A.D. 700 to A.D. 1000 is not *now* unexpected; however, House 1 from 47-Wp-70 and Houses 2 and 3 from 47-Wp-26 represent *the only* excavated Effigy Mound houses to date. The site of Aztalan (47-Je-1), a Middle Mississippian site dating at circa A.D. 1100 to A.D. 1300, has produced 19 semi-subterranean or circular "figure-six" houses (Barrett, 1933:162-164, 175; Wittry and Baerreis, 1958:64-71; Ritzenthaler, 1961:139; and Schneider, 1964:5). Carcajou Point, an Upper Mississippian and early Historic site had three prehistoric dwellings, a wigwam, and two rectangular houses (Hall, 1962, I:17-21; II:6) dating after A.D. 890 ± 80 (WIS-77). The Bell site (47-Wn-9), an early Historic Fox village, had two house structures, a wigwam, and a rectangular house (Wittry, 1963:10-12). Finally, two "D-shaped" house structures were located at Kaukl Site 1 (47-Ve-11) (Hurley, 1965*a*:26-28), a site which is considered to belong within the Woodland cultural stage. It would seem that the semi-subterranean house form in Wisconsin continued from Middle Woodland through Middle Mississippian and Late Woodland times. The limited range of houses at 47-Wp-26 and 47-Wp-70 does not allow for statements concerning an Effigy Mound house type. Additional excavations at 47-Wp-26 and other Effigy Mound villages will no doubt reveal other house forms or variations as does "House 1" from Sanders site 1. Before we examine "House 1" we shall consider the location and contents of features 33 and 29.

Feature 33 (Fig. 42) was located north of House 2. The fill of Feature 33 yielded one Madison Cord Impressed body sherd; two Madison Plain rim sherds; 14 Grand River body sherds; one s $\frac{z}{z}$ cord-marked, three z $\frac{s}{s}$ cord-marked, and six smoothed-over cord-marked body sherds; 99 sherdlets; one copper fragment; bone fragments; polished stone; three quartzite, one basalt, and 11 chert flakes; seven stone fragments; and charcoal which yielded a date of A.D. 860 ± 55 (WIS-219). Feature 29 (Fig. 42) contained one Dane Incised body sherd; one Madison Fabric Impressed body sherd; two Madison Plain rim sherds; two Leland Cord-marked specimens (Pl. 32:F); eight s $\frac{Z}{Z}$ cord-marked, 13 z $\frac{S}{S}$ cord-marked, and 14 smoothed-over cord-marked body sherds; 167 sherdlets; one clay fragment; bone fragments; one serrated Triangular projectile point; 14 stone fragments; one basalt, 53 quartz, 14 quartzite, and 77 chert flakes; and charcoal dated at A.D. 890 ±60 (WIS-206).

Features 33 and 29 are the last two village phenomena at 47-Wp-26 which produced radiocarbon assessments. These dates are within the range of the dates from Feature 30 and Feature 46 of House 3 as well as the two dates from House 2 (WIS-217, 223, 224, and 203; Fig. 59) and the date for House 1 at 47-Wp-70 (WIS-233; Fig. 60). Feature 33 contained Madison Cord Impressed, Madison Plain, and Grand River ceramics, while Feature 29 yielded Dane Incised, Madison Fabric Impressed, Madison Plain, and Leland Cord-marked examples and a Triangular projectile point. The association of Dane Incised, Madison Ware, and Grand River ceramics between A.D. 860 and A.D. 890 represents continued evidence that Dane Incised and Madison Ware ceramics were made by Effigy Mound peoples. Features 11, 16, and 30 contained Dane Incised, Madison Ware, and Grand River specimens, as did the fill of Houses 2 and 3 at 47-Wp-26.

Dane Incised and Madison Ware examples were associated in features 22, 29, 34, 35, and Feature 40 of House 2, and Triangular points were recovered from Features 30, 34, 29, and House 2. Dane Incised and Grand River examples were in the fill of Feature 36; Madison Ware and Grand River specimens were removed from Feature 33. The only Dane Incised example found alone was the lone specimen from the lower fill of House 1 at Sanders site 3. Grand River ceramics were found without Madison Ware only in Feature 32, which is discussed below. The evidence presented thus far for sub-mound, mound, soil bodies, features, and houses strongly supports the view that Dane Incised and Dane Incised variety fingernail impressed belong within the Madison Ware category. It may well be that certain Effigy Mound peoples used only Dane Incised vessels at particular sites. However, the associations presented in Chapter II—for the Kletzien and Nitschke sites (McKern, 1928), Sanders site 1, and the Norwegian Bay site (G. Richard Peske, personal communication) a few miles south of

47-Wp-26—support the view that Dane Incised ceramics were made by Effigy Mound peoples. This type and its variety are considered here as a part of the material culture associated with the Effigy Mound tradition.

Grand River Trailed and Grand River Plain examples from the village at Sanders site 1 were not represented in the excavated mounds or at Sanders site 3. These ceramics exhibit a low frequency of decoration: 20 of 266 sherds were decorated, which represented only 10 of the estimated 35 Grand River vessels. The total number of vessels suggests that they were not a major utilized ware at Sanders site 1 and that they probably represent trade vessels from contemporary Oneota villages. The dated range at 47-Wp-26 for Grand River is between A.D. 670 to A.D. 860, which is earlier than the range for the Koshkonong, Grand River, Lake Winnebago, or Orr foci dates. Of major importance is the evidence of possibly 200 years of contact between Effigy Mound and Oneota peoples without any strong evidence of culture change by the former or assimilation by the latter. The data from the village at 47-Wp-26 suggest that these Oneota vessels represent a Type A1 culture contact situation. Type A1, or retention of culture identity with little trait change, is defined:

> In an area of more or less homogeneous culture, Culture A, a different culture, Culture B, appears as one or more site-units. Subsequently, the two cultures remain identifiable over a long period of time, but a few types of artifacts and design features characteristic of each culture are found in sites of the other (Lathrap, 1956:9).

If the thesis advanced here is correct, then Sanders sites 1 and 3 represent occupation by a single major cultural component, Effigy Mound, with very limited evidence that the area was utilized by possible Middle Woodland peoples at approximately A.D. 290 (WIS-218). The Effigy Mound village/mound complex at 47-Wp-26 and Wp-70 began at approximately A.D. 670 at a time when Emergent Oneota peoples traded their distinct material culture items to a vigorous and maturing Effigy Mound tradition. This contact was maintained for several hundred years with each tradition maintaining its own cultural identity. The prehistory of both traditions after circa A.D. 900 will form a part of the remaining analysis of the Sanders sites and a part of the concluding chapter, Chapter IX.

Feature 17 (Fig. 41) was a concentration of 128 vessel fragments which were partially reconstructed into a Leland Cord-marked vessel (Pl. 38:A). Feature 14 produced one Madison

Plain rim sherd; two s $\frac{Z}{Z}$ cord-marked and three smoothed-over cord-marked body sherds; and two chert and two quartzite flakes. Feature 23 yielded two Madison Plain rim sherds; two z $\frac{S}{S}$ cord-marked, and 11 smoothed-over cord-marked body sherds; 36 sherdlets; 11 chert, two quartzite, and one basalt flake; and one stone fragment. Feature 21 also contained a Madison Plain rim sherd; one s $\frac{Z}{Z}$ cord-marked and two smoothed-over cord-marked body sherds; one quartz and three chert flakes; and six stone fragments. Feature 19 contained only one bone fragment, one quartzite and four chert flakes, and one stone fragment. Feature 20 yielded only snail fragments. These features, which are located south of the main post-mold concentration, contained Madison Plain and Leland Cord-marked specimens and body sherds exhibiting a slight preference for s $\frac{Z}{Z}$ cords for cord-marking.

In the area of the post-mold and feature concentration (Fig. 41), Feature 24 was excavated and it yielded one Madison Plain variety jar rim sherd; two s $\frac{Z}{Z}$ cord-marked and one smoothed-over cord-marked body sherds; 20 sherdlets; two quartz, two quartzite, and 11 chert flakes; and 10 stone fragments. Feature 41 was penetrated by two post-molds and contained 93 fire-cracked rocks; and five chert, four quartz, and one quartzite flake. Feature 50 was a concentration of 153 sherds reconstructed into one Madison Plain vessel (Pl. 28). Feature 18 yielded one Madison Folded Lip rim sherd; three Madison Plain rim sherds; one Madison Plain variety jar rim sherd; 31 s $\frac{Z}{Z}$ cord-marked, four z $\frac{S}{S}$ cord-marked, and 21 smoothed-over cord-marked body sherds; and 212 sherdlets. The lithic and copper artifacts from the fill of Feature 18 include two diminutive scrapers; one single edge flake side scraper; one multiple edge flake side scraper; one flake end scraper; one copper knife, and one copper awl (Pl. 44:D, F); 27 quartz, 13 quartzite, and 38 chert flakes; and 68 stone fragments. Feature 15 yielded three smoothed-over cord-marked body sherds; 16 sherdlets; one basalt, one quartz, and two chert flakes; and four stone fragments. Feature 25 contained one Madison Fabric Impressed body sherd; three s $\frac{Z}{Z}$ cord-marked and two smoothed-over cord-marked body sherds; 64 sherdlets; eight chert, one quartzite, and six quartz flakes; bone fragments; and six stone fragments. The last feature in this area, Feature 49, was exposed but not excavated.

In this area of "House 1" the features previously examined, numbers 11 and 16, contained examples of Dane Incised, Madison Ware, and Grand River ceramics, while the features above contained the Madison Ware types Madison Fabric Impressed, Madison Folded Lip, Madison Plain, and Madison Plain variety jar; a copper awl and knife plus stone scrapers. Feature 41 appears to have been used as a cooking pit and the function of the remaining pits is as uncertain as is their relationship to the post-molds. The use of s $\frac{Z}{Z}$ cords continues as a preferred form but there is evidence of the use of z $\frac{S}{S}$ cords on the same vessel (Features 18 and 25) and the continued presence of z $\frac{S}{S}$ cords for decoration and cord-marking.

The undated features between "House 1" and houses 2 and 3 and Feature 31 beyond these houses (Fig. 42) are the remaining sub-surface pits at 47-Wp-26. Feature 28 contained one basalt, one chert, and one quartz flake, and bone fragments. Feature 27 yielded bone fragments; two diminutive scrapers; one flake end scraper; two quartzite, three basalt, 29 quartz, and 44 chert flakes; 92 sherdlets; and 12 stone fragments. Feature 43 (Fig. 42) contained no artifacts. Feature 44 yielded two sherdlets, three quartz and five chert flakes, and four stone fragments. Feature 42 was a post-mold which contained three s $\frac{Z}{Z}$ cord-marked body sherds; one smoothed-over cord-marked body sherd; three chert, one quartz, and one quartzite flakes, 15 sherdlets; and four stone fragments. Feature 37 yielded from its excavated portion one Madison Cord Impressed body sherd; four Madison Plain rim sherds; one Point Sauble Collared rim sherd with exterior cord-marking of unknown twist; 12 s $\frac{Z}{Z}$ cord-marked body sherds, two z $\frac{S}{S}$ cord-marked body sherds, and 21 smoothed-over cord-marked body sherds; 51 sherdlets; one single edge flake side scraper; 38 chert, 12 quartzite, and 39 quartz flakes; and 54 stone fragments. Feature 31 (Fig. 42) yielded two Madison Plain rim sherds; one z $\frac{S}{S}$ cord-marked body sherd and five smoothed-over cord-marked body sherds; 30 sherdlets; six quartz, one quartzite, and 13 chert flakes; and 27 stone fragments. The final feature, Feature 32, contained nine Grand River body sherds, one Triangular projectile point, one quartz and three chert flakes, charcoal flecks, and five stone fragments.

These remaining features contained the Madison Ware types Madison Cord Impressed, Madison Plain, and Point Sauble Collared along with the Grand River specimens associated with a Triangular projectile point. The preferred cord remains s $\frac{z}{z}$ for cord decoration and cord-marking but z $\frac{s}{s}$ cord continues to be present and associated with the s $\frac{z}{z}$ cord forms. An overview of these two areas shows some differences as the "House 1" area contains numerous sub-surface post-molds and pits while the House 2 and 3 area has clearly defined house structures with internal pits associated with house floors and eight pits immediately adjacent to these houses. With the exclusion of radiocarbon samples WIS-218 and 222 (Fig. 59) the range of occupation for the area is between A.D. 670 (WIS-217) and A.D. 890 (WIS-206). If we consider these two dates as a temporal bracket, then we may have a more realistic approach to the assessment of the cultural activity than a step by step reconstruction progressing from WIS-217 to WIS-224, WIS-203, WIS-219, and then to WIS-206. This view is of particular importance in our examination of the remaining 11 features and four radiocarbon dates from 47-Wp-70. The Sanders site 1 analyses were facilitated by the radiocarbon assessments in the sense that the period between circa A.D. 700 and A.D. 1000 delimits the time of mound construction and village activity which resulted in the association of a large sample of cultural items with the Effigy Mound tradition. On a smaller areal and temporal scale this same cultural activity, minus the mounds, took place at 47-Wp-70.

House 1 at Sanders site 3 is dated at A.D. 720 ± 60 (WIS-223) and, as mentioned earlier, the upper four excavation levels and 11 features may have occurred after a short hiatus as the re-occupation of this area (Feature 2) is dated at A.D. 930 ± 60 (WIS-230). The dates illustrated in Figure 60 indicate that a precise reconstruction of feature and level utilization would be meaningless because of the high degree of temporal overlap between samples WIS-230, 235, 238, and 232. The analysis of 47-Wp-70 will continue by working upward from House 1 through Level 4 to Level 1 and from Feature 11 to Feature 1.

Level 4 in the west rise of 47-Wp-70 (Fig. 45) was at a depth of 1.8 to 2.8 feet below the surface where the area of occupation was defined (Fig. 46) as being primarily within the limits of lower House 1 (Fig. 47). Features 7, 8, 9, 10, and 11 had their orifices in this level and charcoal at a depth of 2.7 feet gave a date of

A.D. 940 ± 75 (WIS-235; Fig. 60). The artifacts from Level 4 are listed in Tables 38 and 39.

Level 4 had in association, at A.D. 940 ± 75, Dane Incised and Dane Incised variety fingernail impressed, Madison Plain, Madison Plain variety punctated, and Leland Cord-marked ceramics with Waubesa Contracting Stem, Madison Side Notched, and Durst Stemmed projectile points plus copper artifacts. The relationship of these artifacts to House 1 is somewhat of a problem: there appears to be a temporal gap of at least 90 years between Level 4 and the House 1 date and there is no evidence of rebuilding of House 1. I suspect that Level 4, like the other upper levels, are stages of continued occupation as Figure 46 indicates utilization of the same area as defined by the post-molds of the house. An overlay of both planimetric views (Figs. 46 and 47) demonstrates that the features, charcoal, and darkened areas of Figure 46 *do not* superimpose any post-molds or features illustrated in Figure 47.

The features which originated in this level were features 7 through 11. As locations and measurements of these features have

TABLE 38

DISTRIBUTION OF CERAMIC ARTIFACTS: 47-Wp-70 (by levels)

Level	Sister Creeks Punctated	Dane Incised	Dane Incised, v. Fingernail Impressed	Madison Cord Impressed	Madison Fabric Impressed	Madison Folded Lip	Madison Plain	Madison Plain, v. Punctated	Madison Punctated	Leland Cord-marked	Heins Creek Corded Stamped	Z S Z	S Z S	Smoothed-over Cord	Total
1		4		2			3		2		2	6	9	14	42
2	4	26	3	10	2	1	10		2		2	26	44	51	181
3		15		2	3	1	6		3		1	20	18	49	118
4		5	3				4	1		1		6	11	24	55
5															
6													1		1
7		1													1

TABLE 39
DISTRIBUTION OF CERAMIC AND LITHIC ARTIFACTS:
47-Wp-70 (by features)

Feature	Sister Creeks Punctated	Dane Incised	Madison Plain, v. Punctated	Madison Punctated	Point Sauble Collared	Heins Creek Corded Stamped	s $\frac{z}{z}$	z $\frac{s}{s}$	Smoothed-over Cord	Blade	Total
1											
2											
3									1		1
4	1	1	1			3					6
5							1	1	4		6
6								1			1
7		1						2			3
8								1			1
9							1	2	1		4
10				1	23				2	1	27
11											
12									1		1
13											

been described in Chapter VI, only their contents will be considered here. Feature 7 contained one Dane Incised body sherd; two z $\frac{s}{s}$ cord-marked body sherds; two sherdlets; one quartz, one quartzite, and two chert flakes; five stone fragments; and charcoal which yielded a date (Fig. 60) of A.D. 1060 ± 65 (WIS-232). Feature 8 yielded one s $\frac{z}{z}$ cord-marked body sherd, four sherdlets, one quartz and two chert flakes, and two stone fragments. Feature 9 yielded bone fragments; one s $\frac{z}{z}$ cord-marked, two z $\frac{s}{s}$ cord-marked, and one smoothed-over cord-marked body sherds; 21 sherdlets; 11 chert and two quartz flakes; and two stone fragments. Feature 10 contained one Madison Punctated rim sherd; 23 sherds representing one Point Sauble Collared vessel (Fig. 58; Pl. 34:A); two smoothed-over cord-marked body sherds; one blade; one quartz flake; and 14 stone fragments. Feature 11 was a recent rodent burrow containing fish scales, bone, and twigs.

The features defined and excavated in Level 4 were not overly productive but they did yield significant types of artifacts. Features 8 and 9 contained sherds having both s $\frac{z}{z}$ and z $\frac{s}{s}$

cord-marking. Features 7 and 10 had their orifices at essentially the same depth below the surface (there is a one inch difference) and they extended to two inches *above* the house floor, i.e., 2.6 feet below the surface. Feature 7 had a Dane Incised body sherd in association with charcoal dated at A.D. 1060 ± 65. If this Dane Incised body sherd represents an artifact from an earlier component or occupation and this specimen was accidently included in the fill of Feature 7, then this component or occupation took place *after* House 1 was utilized. Feature 10 also dates from the tenth to the eleventh century A.D.; it yielded one Madison Punctated rim sherd and fragments of a Point Sauble Collared vessel impressed with a fabric which represents the most complex fabric recorded at an Effigy Mound site (Fig. 58). The artifacts from these features and Level 4 serve as a very strong cultural link with 47-Wp-26 and demonstrate the arbitrary nature of the decision to divide these two locations without testing 47-Wp-70.

Level 3 of 47-Wp-70 was 1.2 to 1.8 feet below the surface and the 12 squares excavated yielded the artifacts listed in Tables 38 and 40. Only one feature, Feature 2, was located in this level and it consisted of a charcoal concentration at 1.3 feet below the surface which yielded a date (Fig. 60) of A.D. 930 ± 60 (WIS-230).

The associated artifacts from Level 3, which is dated at A.D. 930 ± 60, include Dane Incised, Madison Cord Impressed, Madison Fabric Impressed, Madison Folded Lip, Madison Plain, Madison Punctated, and Heins Creek Corded Stamped ceramics as well as Waubesa Contracting Stem, Side Notched, and Triangular projectile points, scrapers, a burin, an adze, and copper artifacts. These items are all considered to be a part of the material culture associated with the Effigy Mound tradition and they, like the other artifacts at Sanders site 3, repeat the associations noted at 47-Wp-26.

Level 2 began below the plow zone (.8 foot) and extended to a depth of 1.2 feet. This level was by far the most productive as indicated by the artifacts listed in Tables 38 and 40. Three features are associated with Level 2 (Table 39) and, with the exception of features 3 and 4, which were in the eastern rise, these remaining features represent the final undisturbed prehistoric use of 47-Wp-70. Feature 6 had a cluster of six stone fragments in its fill which also yielded one z $\frac{s}{s}$ cord-marked body sherd; one basalt, one quartz, and two chert flakes. Feature 5 yielded one s $\frac{z}{z}$ cord-marked, one z $\frac{s}{s}$ cord-marked, and four smoothed-over cord-marked

TABLE 40
DISTRIBUTION OF LITHIC ARTIFACTS:
47-Wp-70 (by levels)

Level	Waubesa Contracting Stem	Corner Notched	Madison Side Notched	Side Notched	Durst Stemmed	Triangular	Drills	Diminutive Scrapers	Gravers	Burins	Burin Spalls	Single Edge Flake Side Scrapers	Multiple Edge Flake Side Scrapers	Flake End Scrapers	Flake Knives	Multiple Edge Utilized Flake Side Scrapers	Adzes	Polished Stones	Copper Artifacts
1				1				1						1					
2	1	1						2			1	1	2		3	3		1	3
3	1			2		1		4		1	1	1					1	1	4
4	1		1		1		1		1				1	1		1			3
5																			
6																			
7																			
Total	3	1	1	3	1	1	1	7	1	1	2	2	3	2	3	4	1	2	10

body sherds; 10 sherdlets; two chert and one quartzite flakes; five stone fragments; and charcoal dated A.D. 960 ± 75 (WIS-238). Feature 1, the final feature located in Level 2, yielded only one quartz flake and one stone fragment.

The date from Feature 5 of A.D. 960 ± 75 (WIS-238) is consistent with the range illustrated for the post-House 1 dates at 47-Wp-70 (Fig. 60). The continued association of Dane Incised, Dane Incised variety fingernail impressed, Madison Cord Impressed, Madison Fabric Impressed, Madison Folded Lip, Madison Plain, Madison Punctated, and Heins Creek Corded Stamped ceramics is no longer unexpected. The presence of four Sister Creeks Punctated examples is unexpected; however, they represent only 2 percent of the total (181) sherds recovered from this level. The lithic and copper artifacts are well represented and the Waubesa

Contracting Stem, Corner Notched, and copper conical points from the level indicate that projectile points and copper were in use throughout the occupation. In fact, the number and variety of lithic and copper artifacts listed suggest both manufacture and use in an area as restricted as the area around Mound 12 at 47-Wp-26.

Level 1 of this western rise at Sanders site 3 was the plow zone and all the artifacts are considered to be in a disturbed context; however, there are no unexpected items listed in either Table 38 or Table 40. The numbers recorded are only as valid as our excavation since the plow zone was quickly shoveled out to reach the undisturbed lower level and only a few artifacts were recovered. The disturbed context of these artifacts and those from the eastern rise requires that they be excluded from this analysis and that we turn instead to other observations that can be made concerning the Sanders sites.

The dates from Feature 7 at 47-Wp-70 of A.D. 1060 ± 65 (WIS-232) and from Feature 1 at Area 9 of A.D. 1010 ± 60 (WIS-207) most probably represent the termination of the Effigy Mound occupation. The one more recent assessment of A.D. 1600 ± 70 (WIS-215) from square S995W400, Level 2, or from the A1bhir horizon, has been mentioned in connection with the A.D. 1610 ± 65 date from Area P at 47-Pt-29 (WIS-157). Both of these dates are suggested as being connected with a possible forest fire as there is no evidence to suggest that either site was occupied at A.D. 1600.

The distribution of cord-marked body sherds according to non-mound and mound soil horizons at 47-Wp-26 is listed in Table 41. The z $\frac{s}{s}$ cords appear to begin slightly earlier in both categories, with s $\frac{z}{z}$ cords having a higher recorded frequency in the sub-mound and mound soils as well as from the A1bhir horizon. The only apparent shift occurs with the non-mound z $\frac{s}{s}$ cord-marked body sherds from the A2x and A11 horizons, where 100 are recorded compared to 23 with s $\frac{z}{z}$ cord-marking. The totals and percentages given for both non-mound and mound soil sequences suggest only a slight preference for s $\frac{z}{z}$ cords out of the 1,202 examples being considered. At 47-Wp-70 z $\frac{s}{s}$ cord-marked body sherds appear in Level 6 and they appear to be the preferred cord in all levels except Level 3. The totals of 58 examples with s $\frac{z}{z}$ and

TABLE 41
DISTRIBUTION OF $s\,^{z}_{z}$ AND $z\,^{s}_{s}$ CORD-MARKED BODY SHERDS ACCORDING TO NATURAL SOILS HORIZONS: 47-Wp-26

Non-Mound	$s\,^{z}_{z}$	$z\,^{s}_{s}$	Number
Ap			
A11	16	46	62
A2x	7	54	61
A1bhir	542	385	927
B1ir	2		2
B2ir			
B21irb	6		6
B2irb		3	3
B22t			
B22irb			
B3ir			
Sub-Total	573 (54.0%)	488 (46.0%)	1,061
Mound			
A11	7	4	11
A12	1	1	2
A/B	26	27	53
A2x/A2x	17	19	36
A1b	20	7	27
A1xb			
A2xb	2	4	6
B21irb	3	1	4
B21b	1		1
B2tb		1	1
B22tb			
B22b			
C1b			
Sub-Total	77 (54.6%)	64 (45.4%)	141
TOTAL (Percent)	650 (54.1%)	552 (45.9%)	1,202

83 with $z\,^{S}_{S}$ cord-marking indicate a preference for the latter cord form. Of the body sherds at 47-Wp-26, an overall percentage difference of 8.2 percent is not particularly meaningful nor are any decided shifts apparent in the typed ceramics presented above.

Local groups may have congregated at this site to construct mounds or to conduct trading activities, bringing their own ceramics or their own methods of decorating ceramics. The degree of cord heterogeneity on the ceramic types from the Sanders sites suggests that during the middle phase of the Effigy Mound tradition the cords become more complex and more than one cord form may be used on a vessel. Fabrics make their appearance at this time. Spaced weft-twining characterizes the majority of fabrics utilized in decorations and such elements as fixed knotted loops are incorporated into the more complex fabrics. Oblique twining, simple linking, fixed knotted loops, and warp-twining are secondary techniques used in the fabrics utilized for vessel decoration. An examination of all fabric-impressed examples from the Sanders sites produces a minimum of 55 different fabrics utilized for ceramic decoration. The cord and fabric analyses have also allowed for the separation of seemingly identical rim sherds and the linking of established and proposed types into an expanded ware category.

This stylistic analysis, to paraphrase Hall (1950:3), has allowed for the correlation of cord and fabric techniques, as utilized on specific pottery types, into a broader and yet more precise descriptive scheme. The possible temporal alignment of cords and fabrics in order to indicate the spread of cultural traits must await further analysis and tabulation of these attributes on other Madison Ware ceramics. In 1966 I suggested that there was a gradual shift through time from s $\frac{Z}{Z}$ cords to more complex cords and that by the time the Durst site was occupied (Wittry, 1959*c*) seven different cords were being utilized (Hurley, 1966:317-318). I considered the Silver Creek I ceramics as early in the Madison Ware sequence and the Durst site specimens would then fit between those from Silver Creek I and those from the Bigelow and Sanders sites or circa A.D. 500 ± 100. Further temporal ranking must wait until cord analyses are coupled with more radiocarbon assessments from sites yielding Madison Ware ceramics.

In the analyses of the Bigelow specimens the typed artifacts were examined from the view of appearance, time of maximum popularity, and the time of decline. This form of analysis had greater validity at the Bigelow site, where sub-mound and mound examples comprised the bulk of the specimens under examination. In this chapter the chronological implications of the artifacts and their context have been presented in an expanded form. To recapitulate by using only the totals presented in Tables 42 and 43 would not do justice to the body of this chapter. For example, Feature 30 with its Dane Incised, Madison Plain, Grand River, and Triangular point artifacts gives us an excellent early (A.D. 670) base line from which we could examine these and the other artifacts at the Sanders site. Feature 30 was also a part of the

TABLE 42

RIM SHERDS, DECORATED BODY SHERDS, AND BODY SHERDS
(47-Wp-26 AND Wp-70) (arranged chronologically)

Location	Sister Creeks Punctated	Rocker Stamped	Shorewood Cord Roughened	Dane Incised	Dane Incised, v. Fingernail Impressed	Madison Cord Impressed	Madison Fabric Impressed	Madison Folded Lip	Madison Plain	Madison Plain, v. Punctated	Madison Plain, v. Jar	Madison Punctated	Leland Cord-marked	Aztalan Collared	Hahn Cord Impressed	Point Sauble Collared	Heins Creek Corded Stamped	Grand River Trailed	Grand River Plain	Grand River Body Sherds	S Z Z	Z S S	Smoothed-over Cord
Fea. 30 A.D. 670				1					3										1	5	7	7	3
Md. 23 A.D. 720				1																			3
Wp-70, H1 A.D. 720																							4
H3, Fea. 46 A.D. 770									1										1		7	5	10
H2 A.D. 775				1	1	1			36	1		1	2				1		2	5	19	21	
Fea. 33 A.D. 860						1			2											14	1	3	6
Md. 3 A.D. 880					1	2			1			1	1								4	2	11
Md. 2 A.D. 880					1		1		1			1		2							1	4	5
Fea. 29 A.D. 890				1			1		5				2								8	13	14
Md. 17, F8 A.D. 900																					1		
H2, F40 A.D. 930							2		5			1									6	8	23
Wp-70, F2 A.D. 930																							
Wp-70 Level 4 A.D. 940				5	3				4	1			1								6	11	24
Wp-70, F5 A.D. 960																							
Area 9, F1 A.D. 1010						1										1					1		
Wp-70, F7 A.D. 1060				1																		2	
Total				10	6	5	4		58	2		4	6	2		1	1		4	24	61	76	103

TABLE 43

LITHIC AND COPPER ARTIFACTS: (47-Wp-26 AND 47-Wp-70)
(arranged chronologically)

Location	Waubesa Contracting Stem	Madison Side Notched	Durst Stemmed	Triangular	Drills	Diminutive Scrapers	Cores	Gravers	Burin Spalls	Multiple Edge Flake Side Scrapers	Flake End Scrapers	Single Edge Utilized Flake Side Scrapers	Multiple Edge Utilized Flake Side Scrapers	Celts	Polished Stones	Copper Artifacts
Fea. 30 A.D. 670				1												
Md. 23 A.D. 720						1						1		1		
Wp-70, H1 A.D. 720																
H3, Fea. 46 A.D. 770							1			1						
H2, A.D. 775				1		1										1
Fea. 33 A.D. 860															1	1
Md. 3 A.D. 880		1		3		1	1			2		1				
Md. 2 A.D. 880								1							1	
Fea. 29 A.D. 890				1												
Md. 17, F8 A.D. 900																
H2, F40 A.D. 930											1	1	1			1
Wp-70, F2 A.D. 930																
Wp-70 Lev. 4 A.D. 940	1	1	1		1			1		1	1		1			3
Wp-70, F5 A.D. 960																
Area 9, F1 A.D. 1010						2			1	1	1	1				
Wp-70, F7 A.D. 1060																
Total	1	2	1	6	1	5	2	2	1	5	3	4	2	1	2	6

cultural activity which took place in the area of houses 2 and 3, not an isolated phenomenon. Moreover, the contents of Feature 46 of House 3 at A.D. 770 do not reflect the total range of artifacts recovered from this house. Another example is the Aztalan Collared specimen from House 3 as its presence in the fill suggests that the two examples from Mound 2 at A.D. 880 are not the earliest at 47-Wp-26.

The Effigy Mound component at the Sanders sites existed for 300 to 400 years (circa A.D. 670 to A.D. 1060; WIS-217 to

WIS-232) without any apparent temporal break. Not all of the ceramic, lithic, or copper artifacts were in constant use; artifact replacement reflecting change is obvious from the number of excavated artifacts. The quantity and location of these Effigy Mound artifacts have served as a key in the attempt to derive a sequence while working within a prehistoric framework. The core of the Sanders data has been analyzed and assigned to the Effigy Mound component and the mounds, features, burials, and houses with their associated artifacts have been presented. Before attempting a brief overview of these data, it is of great importance to assess the possible multi-component aspects of the Sanders sites.

The possibility of a Middle Woodland occupation of the Sanders locality is suggested by the presence of Sister Creeks Punctated, Rocker Stamped, and Shorewood Cord Roughened ceramics (13 sherds representing 10 vessels) at approximately A.D. 290 ± 65 (WIS-218). The eight Sister Creeks Punctated examples were confined to the A1bhir horizon at 47-Wp-26 (three specimens), Feature 4 at Sanders site 3 (one specimen), and Level 2 of the same site (four specimens). The examples from Level 2 at 47-Wp-70 have been discussed above and the three from the A1bhir horizon at 47-Wp-26 could be the result of soil churning, rodent activity, tree root growth, or other factors. The one specimen from Feature 4 poses a context problem as it was associated with Dane Incised, Madison Plain variety punctated, and Heins Creek Corded Stamped ceramics which were *all* in the fill of the east rise containing the Indian horse. The single Rocker Stamped body sherd (Pl. 16:D) was located in the area of Mound 12 and its presence in that locality is not conclusive. The Shorewood Cord Roughened ceramics from Silver Creek I were thought to be earlier than House 1 from the site and that structure dated at 200 B.C. ± 80 (WIS-163; Bender, Bryson, and Baerreis, 1967). The four examples from 47-Wp-26 are divided between two examples from beneath Mound 28 and two from the non-mound A1bhir horizon. The two Shorewood Cord Roughened specimens from beneath Mound 28 are not conclusive as they were associated with Madison Ware ceramics. This type is most likely the antecedent type to both Madison Plain and Madison Punctated and as the full temporal range of Shorewood Cord Roughened ceramics is not known, the specimens from Sanders site 1 may be much more recent than those from 47-Mo-1.

Madison Side Notched, Durst Stemmed, and Waubesa Contracting Stem projectile points have been suggested as dating from

Late Archaic to Middle Woodland times (Ritzenthaler, 1967:25-27). Radiocarbon dates for these projectile points are quite rare and the dates from the Sanders sites do not agree with the estimated ages given by Ritzenthaler. The Madison Side Notched points are dated at A.D. 880 ± 70 (WIS-177) for Mound 3 and at A.D. 940 ± 75 (WIS-235) for Level 4 at 47-Wp-70. The date from Mound 3 is from the A2x/A2x mound fill while the Madison Side Notched projectile point is from the A1xb and it may or may not date from this time. A Durst Stemmed point was also recovered from Level 4 of 47-Wp-70 and in the analysis of that level it was stated that the evidence suggested that all the artifacts post-dated the construction of House 1 or after A.D. 720 ± 60 (WIS-233). Waubesa Contracting Stem projectile points were excavated from levels 4 to 2 at Wp-70 and they also post-date House 1. The only other dated context for the type is the single specimen from the fill of House 3 and the only acceptable date for this structure is A.D. 770 ± 55 (WIS-223) from Feature 46. The second radiocarbon assessment of A.D. 290 ± 65 (WIS-218) for the fill of the house does not date the fill but it may date this projectile point. It is quite possible that these point types continued beyond the Middle Woodland period and were utilized by Effigy Mound peoples or that one or more of these types, e.g., Waubesa Contracting Stem or Durst Stemmed, are Effigy Mound projectile points. At the present time their context is with an Effigy Mound component and until more is known concerning the longevity of these points, there is no reason to exclude them from this component.

The status and nature of the proposed Middle Woodland artifacts remain unanswered. Their number is quite limited and there were no other phenomena such as features, mounds, or burials which were associated with these artifacts. The early aspects of prehistoric utilization of the Sanders sites cannot be resolved by the data at hand. The other end of the "occupation continuum" is even more difficult to assess. The identity of Oneota tradition ceramics is more reliable: the Grand River Trailed and Grand River Plain types and their associated body sherds are quite distinct. Such copper artifacts as awls or such lithic artifacts as Triangular projectile points may also be associated with the Grand River Ware specimens. However, the only items we can ascribe to this tradition are the Grand River Ware examples which number 218 sherds representing an estimated 35 vessels or 3.1 percent of the total vessels from the Sanders sites (Table 44). The Grand River Ware

TABLE 44

FREQUENCY OF RIMS AND ASSOCIATED BODY SHERDS: 47-Wp-26 AND 47-Wp-70

	Rim Sherds		Body Sherds		Combined Rims & Body		Estimated Vessels	
	No.	%	No.	%	No.	%	No.	%
Sister Creeks Punctated	2	.2	6	.4	8	.3	6	.5
Rocker Stamped			1	.07	1	.04	1	.09
Shorewood Cord Roughened	3	.3	1	.07	4	.1	3	.3
Dane Incised	40	3.9	250	17.6	290	11.8	185	16.9
Dane Incised, v. Fingernail Impressed	18	1.8	30	2.1	48	2.0	40	3.7
Madison Cord Impressed	67	6.6	126	8.7	193	7.9	96	8.8
Madison Fabric Impressed	31	3.0	77	5.4	108	4.4	86	7.9
Madison Folded Lip	32	3.1			32	1.3	20	1.8
Madison Plain	645	63.4	142	10.0	787	32.1	462	42.3
Madison Plain, v. Punctated	9	.9			9	.4	5	.4
Madison Plain, v. Jar	16	1.6			16	.6	12	1.0
Madison Punctated	24	2.4	250	17.6	274	11.2	60	5.5
Leland Cord-marked	48	4.7	131	9.2	179	7.3	36	3.3
Aztalan Collared	11	1.0	1	.07	12	.5	11	1.0
Hahn Cord Impressed	1	.09			1	.04	1	.09
Point Sauble Collared	15	1.5	168	11.8	183	7.5	13	1.2
Heins Creek Corded Stamped	7	.7	30	2.1	37	1.5	20	1.8
Grand River Trailed	6	.6	14	.9	20	.8	10	.9
Grand River Plain	42	4.1	1	.07	43	1.7	25	2.2
Grand River Body Sherds			203	14.3	203	8.3		
TOTAL	1,017		1,421		2,448		1,092	

examples from 47-Wp-26 are not found outside the village area except for four Grand River Plain examples and 17 Grand River body sherds from soil body $\frac{1}{\text{A-0}}$. Grand River Ware specimens are also absent from 47-Wp-70 and it may be that their limited numbers precluded a wider distribution. The specimens excavated were recovered from excellent feature and house contexts and their associations with the four radiocarbon assessments have been presented; however, a brief review is necessary. Six examples are from Feature 30 which is dated at A.D. 670 ± 75 (WIS-217); one example is from Feature 46 of House 3 which is dated at A.D. 770 ± 55 (WIS-223); seven examples are from the upper and lower fill of House 2 which is dated at A.D. 775 ± 55 (WIS-224); and 14 specimens were recovered from Feature 33 which is dated at A.D. 860 ± 55 (WIS-219). In addition to these examples are other Grand River Ware specimens from Features 11, 32, and 36. These dates suggest a 200-year history of Oneota contact with the Effigy Mound component and they are the earliest Oneota dates for Wisconsin.

The status of the Grand River Ware ceramics from Sanders site 1 is critical to our understanding of Wisconsin prehistory because of their date, their context, and their function as an indicator of the viable tradition which subsequently develops. Their dates and context appear to be valid so the possible interpretations take on perhaps an exaggerated valence. The problem revolves around the hypothesis that the Oneota tradition developed from (or from a part of) the Effigy Mound tradition (Gibbon, 1972) or the hypothesis presented here that each continued to be a separate tradition after A.D. 1000 to A.D. 1100. In this analyses we will examine only the Sanders data to work from the known to the unknown; greater elaboration of these hypotheses will be included in Chapter IX.

There were 35 Grand River Ware vessels at Sanders site 1 and their presence could span a maximum period of 200 years or a minimum period of 60 years. The limited number of vessels suggests that they appeared as a result of trade into this village and not as a developing attempt to imitate or manufacture vessels according to a new and more difficult technique of production. Porter (1964:4-7) has presented evidence of how difficult it would be for the uninitiated to temper and fire shell-tempered vessels, concluding that the explosive results would produce a greater number of sherds. If the Effigy Mound peoples at the Sanders site were in transition between their mature tradition and a younger Oneota tradition, then more shell-tempered cord-marked and cord-decorated sherds would also be expected at this site. There are nine examples with cord-marking, cord impressions, or cord-wrapped stick decorations but these examples, even if they are early, do not equal the 3,522 grit-tempered specimens from Mason's Oneota Mero I Complex. Mason viewed the Mero I Complex as a developmental phase leading to the later Oneota Mero II Complex represented by 5,106 shell-tempered Oneota specimens (Mason, 1966:160-161).

It was stated earlier in this chapter that the Oneota vessels at 47-Wp-26 represent a Type A1 culture contact situation (Lathrap, 1956:9). The Oneota source village(s) would appear to belong to the Grand River Focus; however, we would have to exclude the Pipe, Walker-Hooper, and Bornick sites as they date from A.D. 1130 to A.D. 1290. The dates on the Sanders Grand River Ware ceramics suggest that the Grand River Focus began at circa A.D. 700 and lasted until A.D. 1290 ± 50 (WIS-228; Bender, Bryson, and Baerreis, 1969). The proposed 600 year-duration of the Grand River Focus is longer than the 500 years now recorded for the Lake Winnebago Focus. The earliest Grand River Focus sites for Emergent Oneota would date between A.D. 700 and A.D. 1000 and their location most likely would be in east-central Wisconsin near the Pipe, Walker-Hooper, Bornick, and Sanders sites. In the definition of a Type A1 culture contact situation the statement concerning shared traits is of importance: ". . . the two cultures remain identifiable over a long period of time, but a few types of artifacts and design features characteristic of each culture are found in sites of the other" (Lathrap, 1956:9). The types of artifacts referred to would be the Oneota Grand River Ware vessels found at the Sanders site while the design features can be recognized in two different ceramic situations. The first is cord-marking and cord decorations as found on the Sanders Grand River Trailed examples indicating that the Oneota potters were borrowing design features from the Effigy Mound peoples. The second design feature is the lip punctation of the proposed type variety Madison Plain variety punctated. This decoration is believed to have been borrowed from Oneota peoples as it is not present on the other Madison Ware types, while it is illustrated for ceramics from the Walker-Hooper site (Griffin, 1966:Pl. CXLV, No. 34; McKern, 1945:Pl. 65, No. 8). The only other example of possible change through contact is the smoothed and brushed exterior surfaces of the Leland Cord-marked ceramics from 47-Wp-26 which appear to approximate the smooth and lusterless surfaces of the Grand River Ware examples from the site. If we assume this culture contact situation continued as long as the Effigy Mound component occupied this locality, then the period of contact could be extended to A.D. 1000 or a period of 300 years. The evidence presented does not support an in situ Sanders site development of the Wisconsin Oneota tradition.

If we now turn to the Effigy Mound component we see a period of at least 300 years at the Sanders sites where there was a full, flowering, and apparently well adapted, mature Effigy Mound culture. The ceramic artifacts cover a wide spectrum of types and the design elements are almost baroque in style due in part to the cord and fabric improvisations exhibited in the decorations. In addition to cords and fabrics are the fingernail impressions, trailing, and punctations found on the Dane Incised and Dane Incised variety fingernail impressed examples. I consider this type and its variety as belonging within the Madison Ware category and they will play a very important role in future Effigy Mound tradition research as these ceramics are also found in the early phase of this tradition. I consider the Madison Ware types linked to other local types such as Kegonsa Stamped and Shorewood Cord Roughened and that the Madison Ware ceramics demonstrated the in situ development of this tradition out of the Middle Woodland stage. The Madison Ware category as envisioned here would be composed of the following types and type varieties: Dane Incised, Dane Incised variety fingernail impressed, Madison Cord Impressed, Madison Fabric Impressed, Madison Folded Lip, Madison Plain, Madison Plain variety punctated, Madison Plain variety jar, Madison Punctated, Leland Cord-marked, Aztalan Collared, Hahn Cord Impressed, Point Sauble Collared, and Heins Creek Corded Stamped. The lithic *types* belonging to the material culture associated with the Effigy Mound tradition include: Waubesa Contracting Stem, Madison Side Notched, Durst Stemmed, Monona Stemmed, Sanders Triangular, and Triangular projectile points plus the proposed Kolterman Indented Base knives (Wittry, 1959*c*:185). The fact that only one Hahn Cord Impressed example was recovered from both the Bigelow and the Sanders sites indicates that this type has a more southerly distribution and that it may be later than A.D. 1000. At the present time the proposed types Heins Creek Cord-marked and Heins Creek Cord-wrapped stick would be excluded from the Madison Ware category as their cultural affiliation has not as yet been demonstrated. The absence of Monona Stemmed projectile points from the Sanders and Bigelow sites could be due to the fact that these sites date from the end of the estimated temporal range of the type, A.D. 800 (Ritzenthaler, 1967:26). The absence of the proposed Kolterman Indented Base knives should not be due to age as the Kolterman site has been dated at A.D. 776 ± 250 (M-398); however, the knife type may be restricted to the Kolterman site and the immediate area.

Included as a part of the material culture associated with the Effigy Mound tradition are: drills, diminutive scrapers, scrapers, knives, gravers, burins, burin spalls, blades, worked and utilized flakes, shaft polishers, adzes, celts, gorgets, polished stones, grinding stones, hammer stones, copper awls, copper knives, copper conical points, worked animal bone flakers, pottery elbow pipes, a wide variety of cord forms, multiple stick cord-wrapped stick potters' tools, and at least 55 different fabric designs. If we exclude the estimated 10 vessels belonging to the Sister Creeks Punctated, Rocker Stamped, and Shorewood Cord Roughened categories and also the 35 Grand River Ware vessels, then 1,047 vessels from the Sanders sites and a remaining one-half to one million sherds are associated with the Effigy Mound component. If the 28 mounds, three houses, four burials, and over 50 cooking and refuse pits are added to the already extensive list then the Sanders sites represent the richest Effigy Mound locality excavated and one of the more productive sites in Wisconsin, ranking behind the site of Aztalan (47-Je-1) in artifact yield.

Unless the Effigy Mound culture at the Sanders sites had reached its cultural apogee and was entering a nova stage, there can be no other alternative than to consider this segment of the Effigy Mound tradition as its mature phase (middle phase) although it was a bit baroque in some of its ceramic designs and mound effigy forms. The archaeological site occupancy conundrum of 10 Indians for a 1,000 years versus 1,000 Indians for 10 years applies to the Sanders sites in that the occupants of the three excavated houses did not construct 28 mounds or leave all the artifacts. This riddle will only be solved by future excavations between Houses 2 and 3 at 47-Wp-26 and House 1 at 47-Wp-70. If the area is not a village but a location for trade and mound construction by a local dispersed population who returned on a regular basis, then this pattern can be ascertained by the negative evidence of the absence of houses as demonstrated by future excavations. I favor the view that the features and houses indicate a more permanent occupancy and that further excavations will expose additional house patterns. The present situation forces population estimates and community pattern statements to be based on material culture remains as there is an absence of extensive settlement pattern data and an absence of faunal or floral evidence favoring either a hunting and gathering or horticultural subsistence base. The evidence presented for the Sanders sites suggests a community pattern of Semi-Permanent Sedentary type which is defined as: "A community, which can be identified with a village, that establishes itself in successive locations, occupying each for a period of years. The population is stable and continuously sedentary, but able to be so only by moving the village periodically" (Meggers, 1956:140). The community characteristics listed are villages containing 500 to 1,000 individuals, each village being independent and self-sufficient. The Central-Based Wandering pattern proposed for the Bigelow site would also apply to the Sanders locality if the large number of artifacts were to be excluded. The Sanders locality differs significantly from all other reported Effigy Mound tradition sites in that an associated village was excavated along with the mounds. This is not to say that all Effigy Mound tradition sites have associated villages or that all camps or villages have associated mounds; the excavations at the Bigelow site showed that neither possibility occurred. The Sanders and Bigelow sites reflect extensive occupation and/or mound building in the northern edge of the recorded distribution of this culture. These sites are a part of a settlement pattern chain which includes rock-shelters, campsites, village sites, and mound sites which have been associated with this tradition by the distinctive artifacts and mounds left by these people. It is mainly the artifacts which will allow for the following brief assessment of this tradition.

IX

THE EFFIGY MOUND TRADITION

THE position that archaeologists should work within their discipline to construct their own theoretical models requires the judicious use of material remains to clarify the unknown. While inference and speculation are the prerogatives of every archaeologist, Julian Steward (1955:209) cautioned us that theories can only be replaced by better theories; they cannot be replaced by facts. A theory supported by objectively presented data has a soundness and a degree of validity. Inductively derived hypotheses may be as valid as those arrived at by deduction, but the former may yield a prehistoric model which can be tested by the data at hand.

The utilization of site data produced by other early archaeologists (Chapter II) and the analyses from the Bigelow and Sanders sites (Chapters III to VIII) to expand upon the prehistoric Effigy Mound culture tradition concept is not without its shortcomings. In this report stress has been placed on natural and man-made stratigraphy as ascertained by archaeological and pedological field techniques. Cord and fabric analyses have allowed for the proposal of a new Madison Ware type or for the separation of seemingly identical specimens for distribution studies. New types and type varieties have been proposed and only the analysis of all other sites containing Madison Ware ceramics would produce similar comparative data. The assumption that all Effigy Mound culture sites have effigy-shaped mounds and non-effigy shaped mounds is misleading: some Effigy Mound sites lack effigy-shaped mounds and not all sites of this tradition are mound sites. The nemesis of Effigy Mound tradition research was the lack of a "material culture core" for comparative purposes and this hiatus has been filled by previous researchers (Baerreis, 1953*a*, 1966; Keslin, 1958; Wittry, 1956, 1959*a*, 1959*c*; Mason, 1966) who have slowly reconstructed the tradition's material culture. The Bigelow and Sanders sites have yielded data which have permitted the extraction and elaboration of artifact nuances, the validation of proposed types on the basis of context, the proposing of new types, and the inclusion of types normally excluded from the Effigy Mound material culture. The present list of Effigy Mound marketplace items is not complete and additions or subtractions may occur as future research refines this re-assessment.

The ends of this tradition continuum remain research problems in their own right as they do not appear to be as "secure" as the proposed middle phase (A.D. 700 to A.D. 1100). However, we now have enough information from the middle of this tradition to attempt some reconstruction at both ends. The core of the following summary will be based on Effigy Mound research before and after 1956, reordered here to conform to a holistic re-evaluation of the Effigy Mound tradition. This shifting of the data should make the proposed prehistoric sequence more meaningful since we can use the more recent precise dating techniques as well as the comparative approach for those sites lacking radiocarbon assessments.

Chapter II of this report presented an historic division of early research related to the Effigy Mound culture. This chapter will present a division of the Effigy Mound tradition based on those previous archaeological reports, research conducted between 1956 and 1972, and the preceding analyses of the Bigelow and Sanders sites. Wherever possible the sites within each division have been assessed according to location, type of site, period or duration of occupation, mound or burial forms, trade or ceremonial items, settlement patterns, external relationships, and the floral and faunal remains. As some sites lack one or more of these cultural attributes, the thread of continuity used here will be the artifacts. The first division of this tradition, or Early Effigy Mound, is suggested as being the period between A.D. 300 and A.D. 700. The second division, Middle Effigy Mound, is suggested as dating from A.D. 700 to A.D. 1100. The third division, or Late Effigy Mound, would date from A.D. 1100 to A.D. 1642, or the time of historic contact.

EARLY EFFIGY MOUND (A.D. 300 TO A.D. 700)

The early phase of the Effigy Mound tradition appears to have developed out of a Middle Woodland base represented by an as yet undefined indigenous Middle Woodland culture characterized by such artifacts as Kegonsa Stamped, Shorewood Cord Roughened, Denzer Stamped, Baraboo Ware, Angelo Punctated, Tomah Fingernail Impressed, and Windrow Cord Impressed pottery types. Lithic types beginning at this time and continuing into the Effigy Mound tradition are Durst Stemmed, Madison Side Notched, Waubesa Contracting Stem, and Monona Stemmed projectile points. The actual beginnings of these artifact types are as yet unknown; however some continue beyond A.D. 300. This earlier culture, like the early phase of the Effigy Mound tradition, was centered in southern and southwestern Wisconsin, northwestern Illinois, and northeastern Iowa. This tri-state area was not the exclusive domain of the Effigy Mound culture as it, like its progenitor, interacted with the Middle Woodland Havana and Hopewellian phases (Struever, 1965) in the south and west, the Waukesha Focus (Salzer, 1967) in the east, and the North Bay (Mason, 1966) and Nakomis (Salzer, 1967) cultures of the north. The earliest radiocarbon dates for the Effigy Mound tradition are from Iowa and Wisconsin. In Iowa at the Harpers Ferry Valley Mound, which contained rocker stamped pottery and a cord-impressed vessel, there is the date of A.D. 220 ± 150 (M-743; Crane and Griffin, 1961:113). At the Effigy Mounds National Monument the construction of bear effigy Mound 1 is dated at A.D. 375 ± 100 (I-441) and the construction of bear effigy Mound 2 is dated at A.D. 625 ± 100 (I-412; Bastian, 1962). In southern Wisconsin at the Beloit College Mound Group, the excavation of two oval mounds produced a Triangular projectile point (Mound 4) and 213 Madison Cord Impressed sherds (Mound 6). The latter mound yielded a date of A.D. 490 ± 150 (M-871) and although Bastian was cautious about the nature of the association there is no reason to reject the date unless there is another earlier component (Bastian, 1958:155-173; 1962).

In Illinois, the Hopewellian Webber Mound (Melvin Fowler, personal communication) contained "classic Hopewell" inclusive artifacts and yet the fill and sub-mound horizons yielded the earliest and most complex cord impressed pottery I have seen from the Middle West. The report by Bennett on excavations conducted in Jo Daviess County, Illinois also suggests that Havana and Madison Ware (Madison Cord Impressed) types are contemporaneous (1945:80-81) and future research in northern Illinois should clarify the nature and extent of this relationship.

There are two mound locations in Iowa, two in Illinois, and one in Wisconsin which indicate the beginnings of the construction of effigy and non-effigy shaped mounds during this early phase of the Effigy Mound tradition. The artifacts from these mounds are Triangular projectile points and the type Madison Cord Impressed (or Lane Farm Cord Impressed?). Two additional mound groups, the Picnic Grove Mounds and the Willow Drive Mounds (Baerreis, 1966), from the Madison, Wisconsin area most probably date during this early phase of the Effigy Mound tradition. The Willow Drive Mounds consisted of both effigy and linear mounds which yielded flexed and disarticulated burials; a coyote mandible; a red fox; Madison Side Notched, Monona Stemmed, Waubesa Contracting Stem, and corner notched points; and Madison Cord Impressed and cord-wrapped stick impressed ceramics (1966:105-115). The Picnic Grove Mounds were two linear mounds which yielded a stemmed point, a knife, and Waubesa Contracting Stem, and Madison Side Notched projectile points (1966:117-118). Bird effigy and bear effigy, oval and linear mounds appear during this early phase and, while the Madison Ware ceramics appear to be restricted to Madison Cord Impressed examples, the lithic types include triangular, stemmed, corner and side notched varieties. Flexed and disarticulated burials appear to be the earliest burial forms from these mounds and both coyote and red fox were being hunted. I would also suggest that one additional mound site, the Outlet site (Whiteford, 1949; Bakken, 1950), be included. This multiple component location had such mound fill artifacts as cord impressed (Madison Cord Impressed), incised over cord (Dane Incised), and Hopewell ceramics and until surface and sub-mound excavations are conducted the association of these artifacts does not demonstrate an association of components. There is, however, an Effigy Mound component which needs to be clarified.

There are three open camp and village sites which are suggested as dating from Early Effigy Mound times. The first is the Airport Village site, a multi-component site, which yielded Madison Side Notched and Waubesa Contracting Stem points and Dane Incised ceramics in association with Archaic lithic artifacts (Baerreis, 1953*b*:1953-163). This site has not been previously considered as an Effigy Mound culture site; however, the artifacts suggest that one component is associated with this culture. The second village is the multi-component Silver Creek I (47-Mo-1) site from Monroe County.

In 1966 I reported on the excavation of five early Woodland to early Late Woodland sites in Monroe County in west central Wisconsin. These sites, Silver Creek I to V, were located adjacent to an inland drainage system and they were open sites, void of mounds and mortuary artifacts. The major locality was Silver Creek I at which 152 five-foot squares (3,800 square feet) were excavated to an average depth of 2.5 feet. This site had not been cultivated which aided in the preservation of 18 sub-surface features and one semi-subterranean house basin. The relatively undisturbed artifacts consisted of a total of 1,095 ceramic fragments of which 116 were rim sherds, 117 decorated body sherds, and 804 undecorated body sherds. The earliest ceramics recovered belonged to two Early Woodland to Middle Woodland types, Kegonsa Stamped and Shorewood Cord Roughened (Baerreis, 1952; Hall, 1962). The three Kegonsa Stamped vessels and 20 Shorewood Cord Roughened vessels were associated with a proposed pottery type, Angelo Punctated, which was represented by two vessels whose diagnostic characteristics included parallel horizontal incised lines zoning wedge-shaped punctations (Hurley, 1966:66-68).

In vertical association with these ceramics were vessels which exhibited decorative attributes similar to established Illinois Middle Woodland ceramics. At the time of analysis, these similarities appeared to be on the order of site-unit intrusions; however, I now view them as ". . . decorative devices, locally reinterpreted [which] alone attest to historical ties with the other localities" (Struever, 1964:104) or trait-unit intrusions (Type B3) with some dominance of the intruded ceramic attribute (Meggers, 1956:19-22). These ceramics were grouped into Illinois types consisting of five Sister Creeks Punctated vessels; two Steuben Punctated vessels; two Naples Stamped, Variety Dentate vessels; and three late Hopewellian Weaver Plain, Stamp Variety vessels. As the ceramic sample was listed, it was thought that shared decorative design elements would prove a valuable research lead. The Kegonsa Stamped, Shorewood Cord Roughened, Angelo Punctated, Sister Creeks Punctated and Steuben Punctated all shared exterior or interior punctations. Cord-wrapped stick impressions occurred on the upper exterior or interior rim and lip regions of Kegonsa Stamped, Shorewood Cord Roughened and Sister Creeks Punctated vessels. One ceramic attribute for both cord-wrapped stick impressions and cord marking was the twist of the cord utilized. An $s\,{}^{z}_{z}$ cord with an $R\,{}^{l}_{l}$ twist was the preferred form for all of the above types, Weaver Plain, Stamp Variety being the exception.

Based on the relative vertical sequence and a subsequent C-14 date, it was suggested that the final component at Silver Creek I began during late Middle Woodland times at circa A.D. 300. This component consisted of ceramic and lithic representatives of the Effigy Mound culture. The Madison Ware sample was restricted to nine Madison Cord Impressed vessels (38 sherds) which were placed into four temporary varieties on the basis of the cords utilized for decoration: $s\,{}^{z}_{z}$; $Z\begin{smallmatrix} & z\\ s & z\\ s & z\\ & z\end{smallmatrix}$; $z\,{}^{s}_{s}$; or $S\begin{smallmatrix} & s\\ z & s\\ z & s\\ & s\end{smallmatrix}$. The latter two forms of cord were utilized for decoration on approximately three-quarters of the Madison Cord Impressed ceramics. The $s\,{}^{z}_{z}$ form of cord twist, however, was the preferred cord for cord marking at Silver Creek I: it was found on 367 of 460 ceramic fragments or on 79.7 percent of those with recorded cord twist. The motif decorations on the Madison Cord Impressed vessels were relatively uncomplicated and the majority were parallel horizontal or parallel oblique impressions; only three vessels had chevron impressions of $Z\begin{smallmatrix} & z\\ s & z\\ s & z\\ & z\end{smallmatrix}$ cords.

The lithic assemblage from Silver Creek I (47-Mo-1) consisted of one Scottsbluff base and one Raddatz Side-notched point which were not associated with the ceramic components; three Madison Side Notched, six Monona Stemmed and three corner notched points (provisionally named McCoy Corner Notched) which were associated with the Late Early Woodland and the Middle Woodland occupations. Twelve Triangular points were suggested as being associated with the Effigy Mound component. Additional lithic artifacts included two drills, 20 scrapers, four knives, 43 worked flakes, and 63 utilized flakes.

Eighteen sub-surface features were excavated and they indicated the physical associations of Shorewood Cord Roughened, Madison Cord Impressed, Angelo Punctated, Sister Creeks Punctated, Steuben Punctated and Monona Stemmed artifacts. The vertical distribution of these features and their contents was in agreement with the vertical sequence of the artifacts recovered (Hurley, 1966:174-185). One semi-subterranean house was excavated and while it had no associated artifacts, the levels above the house contained a Steuben Punctated specimen, a dentate stamped sherd, and obsidian flakes. Charcoal from the house floor was subsequently dated at 200 B.C. ± 80 (WIS-163) (Bender, Bryson, and Baerreis, 1967:536).

The cultural activity at 47-Mo-1 indicated an initial utilization by late Early Woodland peoples using Kegonsa Stamped and Shorewood Cord Roughened ceramics. Between 400 B.C. and 200 B.C. Middle Woodland occupations began; by approximately A.D. 300 an early ceramic manifestation of the Effigy Mound tradition occurred; and by circa A.D. 500 the site became virtually unoccupied until historic times. Silver Creek I represented, therefore, a gradual development in place both of a northern manifestation of a Havana-related tradition and of an early portion of the Wisconsin Effigy Mound tradition. Shared decorative design elements, cord twist preferences, physical association of diagnostic artifacts, and the relative simplicity of the decorations of the Madison Cord Impressed ceramics indicated that the roots of the Effigy Mound tradition extended into Middle Woodland times and that the distinctive effigy shaped mounds were a later addition.

Silver Creek V was the easternmost site of the Silver Creek site complex. Thirty-six five-foot squares (900 square feet) were excavated to an average depth of 2.0 feet. This site had not undergone historic cultivation and the artifact inventory consisted of 152 ceramic fragments, of which eight were rim sherds, 16 were decorated body sherds, and 128 were body sherds. Sixty-eight of these vessel fragments were grouped into six type categories and two decorated categories. One proposed ceramic type, Windrow Cord Impressed (Pl. 45), had the following diagnostic attributes: horizontal multiple stick cord-wrapped stick impressions at the lip and at the vessel's point of maximum diameter which zoned a broad brushed rim; interior nodes placed below the lip and a body which was decorated by rolling a cord from the point of maximum diameter to the base (Hurley, 1966:275-283). In addition to the two Windrow Cord Impressed vessels there was one Naples Stamped, Variety Dentate vessel; one Sister Creeks Punctated vessel; one Naples Stamped, Variety Plain (Griffin, 1952:110) vessel; and one Angelo Punctated vessel. The lithic assemblage from this site included one corner notched point; three knives; nine worked flakes; and eight utilized flakes.

During Middle Woodland times at Silver Creek I, the shoulder and upper rim of the Naples Stamped, Variety Dentate specimens exhibited combinations of horizontal and vertical dentate stamped impressions. This form of decoration shifted to smooth rims with only the shoulder having a horizontal row of dentate impressions above a cord-marked body. Subsequently, this shoulder area with its smooth rim took the form of a decoration applied by a cord-wrapped stick. Specimens from both Silver Creek I and Silver Creek V show this gradual design development. The total assemblages from the Silver Creek area in themselves do not represent an impressive array when quantity is considered. However, as the western one-half of Wisconsin is still poorly known throughout the whole Woodland period, the indications derived from the Silver Creek data are of a nature to suggest tentative cultural events and some continuity. The ceramic specimens were provisionally assigned to Illinois ceramic types and to local types which differ stylistically from their Illinois counterparts. It is suggested that Shorewood Cord Roughened developed into a thinner ware which lacked nodes, i.e., Madison Plain. It is also suggested that the local Sister Creeks Punctated set the stage for the development of a type proposed in this report, Madison Punctated, which is associated with the Effigy Mound culture.

The camp and village information concerning Effigy Mound occupation is still quite limited for the early phase of this tradition and these camps and villages, like the later open sites, do not appear to be large habitation areas. Of the associated Effigy Mound material culture items, Windrow Cord Impressed may be one ceramic type which is not found in mounds at this time. The lithic types of Madison Side Notched, Waubesa Contracting Stem, Monona Stemmed, McCoy Corner Notched, and Triangular points include only one new form, the proposed McCoy Corner Notched type.

The early Effigy Mound period appears to be the time of maximum rockshelter utilization as five rockshelters in Iowa and Wisconsin have excellent evidence of Effigy Mound occupancy. The first report of rockshelter use by Effigy Mound peoples is at Spike Hollow Rockshelter in Iowa (Logan, 1953) where incised over cord-marked (Dane Incised), Madison Cord Impressed and the regional varieties of Madison Ware, Lane Farm Cord Impressed and Lane Farm Stamped were recovered. In one feature both cord impressed and rockered dentate stamped examples were found in association. The Lane Farm types have not been elaborated upon, but current research in northeast Iowa may show these types to have a wider distribution than Spike Hollow Rockshelter. In

Wisconsin, four rockshelters are suggested as having Effigy Mound components dating from this early phase of the Effigy Mound tradition. The Durst Rockshelter was excavated to a depth of 36 inches; however, only the first six zones (0 to 24 inches) produced artifacts. Seven features or pits were excavated (Zones 1 through 5) and they contained grit-tempered cord-marked, shell-tempered cord-marked, undecorated, and Madison Cord Impressed ceramics; a small notched projectile point; and Triangular points; however, these artifacts were not considered as necessarily in association (Wittry, 1959*c*:169) as they may have been a result of near-by surface or lower depth mixture. In his projectile point analysis of the Durst Rockshelter, Wittry proposed eight typological categories, of which Raddatz Side-notched, Durst Stemmed, and straight stemmed projectile points were associated primarily with the Archaic occupation (*ibid.*:173-180; 215-252); Monona Stemmed with the Hopewellian occupation (*ibid.*:255); and Small diagonal-notched, Side-notched Triangular, Large Triangular, and Small Triangular were associated with the Effigy Mound, Late Woodland, and Mississippi occupations of this rockshelter (*ibid.*: 260-261).

Ceramics recovered from Zone 6 were considered as intrusive and "... should be disregarded in the interpretation of the frequency tables and graphs" (*ibid.*:218). Therefore, only the upper 24 inches of deposit can be utilized in our assessment of his ceramic sequence. If Zone 6 is disregarded for his frequency illustrations in Table 8 and Figure 21, then it appears that Denzer Stamped has the highest frequency in Zone 5 but that Madison Cord Impressed, Leland Cord-marked, Baraboo Cord-marked, Baraboo Net-marked and dentate stamped ceramics are all *equally* represented in zones. Zone 4 shows an increase in Denzer Stamped; continued Madison Cord Impressed; the introduction of Madison Plain; *no* Leland Cord-marked; and a slight decrease in the Baraboo Ware and dentate stamped ceramics. In Zones 3 and 2 the Madison Ware, Leland Cord-marked, and Denzer Stamped ceramics constitute the major percentage of ceramics while the other three categories decline. These two illustrations show only trends and no clear-cut demarcations between the types, i.e., all appear contemporary; Denzer Stamped occurs earlier with a greater frequency; Baraboo Ware ceramics and Leland Cord-marked are coeval with Madison Ware; however, the former decline while the latter increase in frequency; and dentate stamped ceramics occur with greater frequency in Zones 4 and 3. As Zones 1 to 3 lacked natural stratification they were excavated in arbitrary four inch levels (1959*c*:217) and while the sequence for the lithic artifacts appears relatively secure, it would appear that the same cannot be said for the ceramic artifacts. It is most difficult, therefore, to understand how Wittry could be so positive in this proposed sequence of: (1) Denzer Stamped; (2) Leland Cord-marked and Baraboo Ware; and (3) Madison Ware (*ibid.*:218) and then state that "Zones 1-4 contain almost exclusively Middle Woodland materials . . ." (*ibid.*:220). The difficulties concerning this site can be resolved if one views this rockshelter as having evidence of a local Middle Woodland culture in transition into an Effigy Mound culture which then became distinctive at this locality at circa A.D. 300 to A.D. 500. Radiocarbon assessments will be of great interpretive aid for the Durst Rockshelter and the other three studied by Wittry.

The "culture in transition" concept is difficult to demonstrate; however, the transitional nature of two artifact types can be seen from an examination of 188 of the Madison Cord Impressed and Madison Plain ceramics from the Durst Rockshelter. These ceramics have the following cord twist breakdown: $z\,\substack{S\\S} = 134$ (71.3%); $S\,\substack{z\,\substack{S\\S}\\ z\,\substack{S\\S}} = 9$ (4.8%); $S\,\substack{z\,\substack{S\\S}\\ z\,\substack{S\\S}\\ z\,\substack{S\\S}} = 9$ (4.8%); $s\,\substack{Z\\Z} = 8$ (4.2%); $s\,\substack{Z\\Z} = 9$ (4.8%); $Z\,\substack{s\,\substack{Z\\Z}\\ s\,\substack{Z\\Z}} = 18$ (9.6%); and $Z\,\substack{s\,\substack{Z\\Z}\\ s\,\substack{Z\\Z}\\ s\,\substack{Z\\Z}} = 1$ (.5%). There were 152 (80.8 percent) examples with cord-marking or cord decoration composed of $z\,\substack{S\\S}$ cords versus 36 (19.1 percent) with $s\,\substack{Z\\Z}$ elements. There also appear to be differences in macro-decoration motifs in the Madison Cord Impressed type. The other three rockshelters produced information supporting a continuum from a Middle Woodland to Effigy Mound cultural development, as the Knoop Rockshelter (47-Sk-3) yielded Durst Stemmed, Monona Stemmed, and Triangular projectile points which were recovered with Dane Incised (?), Baraboo Net-marked, Denzer Stamped, and Madison Cord Impressed ceramics (Wittry, 1959*c*:223-227). The Zech Rockshelter (47-Sk-4) yielded Denzer Stamped, Baraboo Net-marked, and Madison Cord Impressed ceramics plus Monona Stemmed points (*ibid.*:238). Finally, the Gov. Dodge State Park Rockshelter (47-Ia-1), which now has a Middle Woodland date of A.D. 350 ± 55 (WIS-335), yielded the early Raddatz Side-Notched point type and Durst Stemmed points while the upper foot of the deposit produced Madison Cord Impressed sherds and 56 cord impressed dentate stamped sherds and an incised and punctated example (*ibid.*:243-245). If we exclude the Denzer Stamped, Baraboo Ware, and the Raddatz Side-notched forms, the remaining assemblage from these four rockshelters indicates a strong relationship to the Early Effigy Mound tradition. Even though these rockshelters were irregularly or seasonally occupied the evidence suggests that the gradual development of the Effigy Mound tradition from a Middle Woodland base is supported by the results of the excavation of these rockshelters. From the Durst site evidence Wittry positively stated that "... there is not now, and never has been any good evidence to indicate that Wisconsin Hopewellian and Effigy Mound ... were contemporary ... and whatever evidence exists ... is limited in its geographical distribution to the western border of the Effigy Mound area ..." (*ibid.*:256). I do not believe that the evidence offered for the Durst Rockshelter is that secure and a large portion of his Madison Ware ceramics need to be temporally placed within this ceramic tradition (Hurley, 1966:317-319).

The evidence for Hopewellian-Effigy Mound relationships in the western border of the Effigy Mound area was explained as the survival of some Hopewellian peoples after A.D. 500 in Jo Daviess County in Illinois. Rocker stamping as it is found associated with the Gov. Dodge State Park Rockshelter and the Iowa specimens represented a survival of a decorative technique and not a cultural tradition (*ibid.*:257-258). The Proto-Effigy Mound concept was suggested by McKern (1935:157) for mound groups in northwest Wisconsin and Wittry stated that these groups may represent marginal influence rather than a Proto-Effigy Mound state. He suggested that they might represent "... a dispersion of refugee groups from southeastern Wisconsin caused by the entrance of hostile early Mississippi peoples ... [and] ... may even actually post date the golden age of the Effigy Mound peoples ..." (1959*c*:258). Wittry had no other alternative than to suggest that the Effigy Mound culture developed after Hopewellian had disappeared from Wisconsin at circa A.D. 500-600 and that evidence for Effigy Mound-Mississippian relationships was much stronger because of the reported association of ceramics and small Triangular projectile points. He concluded this line of reasoning with the following statement:

> ... present evidence indicates a Late Middle Woodland origin for the Effigy Mound culture and a survival into the Late Woodland and

> Mississippi Period in the Wisconsin area. This interpretation is somewhat at variance with the current literature, but it seems justified by the available data (1959*c*:261).

Therefore, to answer the questions he proposed concerning Hopewellian-Effigy Mound relationships (*ibid.*:152) he suggested that the Effigy Mound culture developed after Hopewell had arrived and that Hopewell played a very little part in influencing this development. What is obviously needed is extensive excavation at the Gov. Dodge State Park Rockshelter and several radiocarbon dates from the Durst, Knoop, and Zech rockshelters.

The Early Effigy Mound tradition does not appear to be as weak as some authors would have us believe. Griffin (1960*a*:25) has suggested that the Effigy Mound culture was a gradual decline from Hopewell and the evidence presented here suggests that it was instead a gradual development in place from an indigenous population which interacted with both the Havana and Hopewell phases while it in turn gave rise to the Effigy Mound tradition.

The Early Effigy Mound period is bracketed by the Paleo-climatic Scandic episode, a warm climatic period estimated to date from A.D. 300 to A.D. 800-900 (Bryson and Wendland, 1967:280). The amelioration of climate was in contrast to the more severe Sub-Atlantic episode which preceded the Scandic and this favorable climatic period may have contributed to the wide distribution of mound, rockshelter, and open sites (Fig. 1). This early phase of the Effigy mound tradition established the types of settlements which are also found during the middle phase with the exception of the reduction of rockshelter sites. The campsite/village locations are not extensive and the community pattern evident at this time appears to be "Central-Based Wandering" or "A community that spends part of each year wandering and the rest at a settlement or 'central base' to which it may or may not consistently return in subsequent years" (Meggers, 1956:138). The central base at this time may have been the rockshelters with a shift toward open sites during the middle phase of the tradition. The mound groups include effigy, oval, conical, and linear forms with bear and bird effigies appearing early in the tradition. A hunting, fishing, and gathering economy based on the establishment of primary forest efficiency (Caldwell, 1958) appears to have offered abundant food resources and the stability need for the subsequent development of the tradition.

MIDDLE EFFIGY MOUND (A.D. 700 TO A.D. 1100)

The middle phase of the Effigy Mound tradition is characterized by an increase in the size and quantity of mound groups and open sites and a reduction of sheltered sites. A greater degree of permanence is also indicated by the increased quantity and variety of artifacts associated with the Effigy Mound tradition. The Bigelow site (47-Pt-29) is considered here as the *mound* type-site of the Middle Effigy Mound tradition as it was both extensively radiocarbon dated and excavated. I do not consider any of the mound, campsite/village, or rockshelter sites of the early phase as candidates for "type-sites" as the rockshelters are either not fully excavated, multi-component, or disturbed; the mound groups have not been fully excavated or dated; and the campsites or villages cannot be more fully excavated.

The Bigelow site lacked a contiguous village and the non-mound and sub-mound excavations indicated that limited camping was done by Effigy Mound peoples who constructed an ultimate total of 28 mounds. The mound forms consisted of turtle effigy, bear effigy, and bird effigy; linear mounds; and conical mounds. The mounds appear to have been added to the locality between A.D. 670 and A.D. 1120 while the campsite activity extended to A.D. 1370 ± 65 (WIS-187). With the exception of an Historic component at 47-Pt-29 (Lange, 1969), the non-mound, sub-mound, and mound artifacts had their individual cycles of use but the major period of contemporary utilization was during the Middle Effigy Mound period. The ceramic artifact types from this site include the Madison Ware types of Madison Cord Impressed, Madison Fabric Impressed, Madison Folded Lip, Madison Plain, Madison Punctated, Leland Cord-marked, Aztalan Collared, Hahn Cord Impressed, and Point Sauble Collared. The lithic and bone artifacts associated with the Effigy Mound component include Sanders Triangular, Triangular, and Corner Notched projectile points; drills; end scrapers; cores; worked flakes; pecked stones; polishing stones; and an antler tine flaker.

There may have been phases of occupancy at the Bigelow site where several mounds were constructed at the same time; however, neither phases nor a regular rate of mound construction, e.g., a mound every 25 years, could be ascertained with any certainty.

The site was known by Effigy Mound peoples for a half-millennium and they returned to camp briefly to construct conical, effigy, or linear mounds and to inter their dead as primary flexed burials or as secondary cremations. Cords and fabrics were used to decorate vessels and $s\genfrac{}{}{0pt}{}{z}{Z}$ cords appear to have been preferred by peoples using cords with both $s\genfrac{}{}{0pt}{}{z}{Z}$ and $z\genfrac{}{}{0pt}{}{s}{S}$ basic elements. The Bigelow site demonstrated a cyclic pattern which was both geographical and temporal, similar to the proposed "Central-Based Wandering" pattern (Meggers, 1956:138).

The large series of dates allowed for the ordering of ceramic and lithic types which had heretofore been relatively dated, associated with one date, or found only at one dated site. Madison Cord Impressed, Madison Fabric Impressed, Madison Plain, and Madison Punctated types appear to begin at the Bigelow site as early as A.D. 670. The Madison Folded Lip, Leland Cord-marked, Aztalan Collared, Hahn Cord Impressed, and Point Sauble Collared types are present at the Bigelow site by A.D. 810. Five of these Madison Ware types continued to A.D. 1120—Madison Fabric Impressed, Madison Plain, Madison Punctated, Leland Cord-marked, and Aztalan Collared, with the Aztalan Collared type absent by circa A.D. 1370. The lithic types of Sanders Triangular and Triangular are present as early as A.D. 670 with a corner notched form appearing at A.D. 990. Diagnostic lithic types are absent after A.D. 1120; however, drills and cores are present until A.D. 1370.

As the Bigelow site was the location of periodic camping for mound construction, the full range of the Effigy Mound material culture could not be expected to be present at all times or in equal numbers. This aspect also applies to the other mound groups to be discussed below. With the exception of Dane Incised and its variety Dane Incised variety fingernail impressed, the two Madison Plain varieties (jar and punctated), and Heins Creek Corded Stamped types which are absent from the Bigelow site, the remainder of the Madison Ware types are present at this mound group. The missing lithic types are Waubesa Contracting Stem, Madison Side Notched, Durst Stemmed, and Monona Stemmed points and the Kolterman Indented Base Knives. As each of the ceramic and lithic forms may have its own geographic and temporal range, these omissions are not of major significance. The view proposed here is that they are present at another mound, village, or rockshelter site dating from this time and that different bands of the Effigy Mound culture produced or used different cultural items. Each band may have had its own territory containing campsites, village sites, and mound locations which would be most amenable to the Central-Based Wandering community pattern concept and this pattern ultimately led to a more permanent center or a "Semi-Permanent Sedentary" village (Meggers, 1956:140-141).

The use of the Bigelow site as the mound type-site for the Middle Effigy Mound period (A.D. 700 to A.D. 1100) permits us to assess the other mound locations, to be presented for this period on the basis of their radiocarbon dates and/or material culture. The earliest dated mound site, other than the Bigelow site, is the Kolterman Mound Group which contained otter effigies, linear and conical mounds. Two otter effigy mounds were excavated. One yielded fragments of two Madison Cord Impressed vessels, two Triangular projectile points, and fragments of a cremation which dated at A.D. 776 ± 250 (M-398). The second otter effigy mound produced a primary burial (Wittry and Bruder, 1955; Wittry, 1956:133-134). At the Krisbaher-Llewellyn site (47-Wn-6) a panther effigy mound was excavated and it yielded ceramics similar to Dane Incised and the proposed Dane Incised variety fingernail impressed as well as Waubesa Contracting Stem and Triangular projectile points (Steinbring and Farvour, 1958:130-144). The Raisbeck Mound Group (Fig. 1) consisted of 38 conical, 14 linear, three oval, and 25 effigy (bird, canine, and problematical) mounds. Excavations of 20 of these mounds produced 80 individual primary burials; ceramics which can be placed in the types Madison Cord Impressed and Madison Plain; a rocked-dentate stamped sherd; elbow pipes; perforators and bone artifacts (Rowe, 1956:44-46). With the exception of the large number of burials, the material culture items from the Raisbeck and Kolterman Mound groups are similar to those from the Bigelow site while the artifacts from 47-Wn-6 seem more closely related to the Sanders site. Three new effigy forms are added by these sites—otter, panther, and canine—and the presence of a large number of burials is not uncommon for mounds dating from the Middle Effigy Mound period, for example, Clam Lake (47-Bt-1) and Spencer Lake (47-Bt-2).

At the Prawatschke Mound Group in Dodge County (Fig. 1), 10 burials, cord-marked (Madison Plain?) and incised (Dane Incised?), ceramics, a rolled copper bead, stemmed points, and a Triangular point were recovered. Although Niehoff (1956:87-94) considered this mound group as earlier than the Effigy Mound tradition, I see no reason to exclude it from the tradition. In the

Madison area, the Picnic Point Mound cluster consisted of two linear and five conical mounds and they yielded three burials, a Madison Side Notched point fragment, four Triangular points, scrapers, knives, a ground and polished axe or celt, a Middle Woodland rim sherd, Madison Cord Impressed and Aztalan Collared artifacts (Baerreis, 1966:118-124). The artifacts from this mound group and the nearby Frost Woods Mound Group (47-Da-3), which consisted of linear and conical mounds yielding a burial with a Triangular projectile point (Baerreis, 1954:47), suggest that they and the Prawatschke mounds were constructed by Effigy Mound peoples at circa A.D. 900 ± 100.

In northwestern Wisconsin two large conical mounds, the Clam Lake (47-Bt-1) mound and the Spencer Lake (47-Bt-2) mound, were excavated in 1935 and 1936. These mounds yielded 109 primary burials, 22 Triangular points, side notched points, scrapers, knives, a drill, three elbow pipes, sandstone abraders, wood fragments, birch bark, and beaver skins. Two ceramic types, Burnett Stamped conoidal and Clam River, wrapped-stamped globoid were proposed (McKern, 1963). A series of three Michigan radiocarbon dates (M-1581 to 1583) suggests a date of circa A.D. 500 for the Clam Lake mound while one Michigan date (M-1596) and four Wisconsin dates (WIS-180, 181, 183, 186) indicate that the mound was constructed between A.D. 750 to A.D. 1100. To further complicate matters, there is the suggestion that the preserved birch bark, beaver skins, and a charred wood fragment showing "chopping strokes of a steel axe" (McKern, 1963:69) indicate a proto-Historic or Historic age (1963:1, 61). I consider the Clam River Focus to have ceramics similar to the Minnesota Blackduck types and to the Madison Cord Impressed and Madison Plain types of the Effigy Mound tradition. The proposed types are difficult to assess as there are only a few specimens; however, further work in this poorly known area may produce additional examples. I would place the Clam Lake mound at circa A.D. 900 to A.D. 1100 with the Spencer Lake mound dating slightly later than the A.D. 1100 estimate. This assessment is a bit earlier than Griffin's date of A.D. 1200 (1964*a*:110) and more in line with the more recent radiocarbon dates from the site. The artifacts recovered seem to agree with the age estimate and not with the earlier range.

Excavations at two mound locations in Iowa have brought to light a slightly different set of problems. The Sny-Magill Mound Group and mounds from the Effigy Mounds National Monument of northeastern Iowa have produced evidence of mounds dating from the Early and the Middle Effigy Mound period. The Sny-Magill Mound Group of five effigies, six linears, and 85 conical mounds had limited excavations conducted in 1953. One conical mound, Mound 24, yielded vessel fragments with combinations of zoned rocker dentate stamping and cord impressions which were considered to be evidence of a blending of Hopewellian and Effigy Mound cultural influences (Beaubien, 1953*b*:60). Conical Mound 7 produced three Triangular projectile points and it would seem that Mound 24 dates from the Early Effigy Mound period while Mound 7 dates from the middle of the tradition. The problem of stratigraphy, associations, and multi-components at the Sny-Magill Mound Group needs to be more carefully examined as the picture is not as clear as we might wish. A further example of this situation was reported by Beaubien on his work within the National Monument. Bear effigy Mound 30 produced charcoal which was dated at A.D. 930 ± 300 (M-41) and conical Mound 55 which produced Hopewellian artifacts was dated at A.D. 900 ± 300 (M-40). The latter date is not accepted by Griffin (1952:369) while the former is within the range of the Effigy Mound tradition. Beaubien viewed these dates as giving evidence of cultural fusion (1953*b*:65), which is possible, but only at the time of the Harpers Ferry Valley mound (A.D. 220 ± 150; M-743) or at the time of bear effigy Mound 1 from the monument (A.D. 375 ± 100; I-441).

The final mound group to be considered here is the Nitschke Mound Group of Dodge County, Wisconsin. This mound group yielded artifacts similar to those reported from the other mound sites of the Middle Effigy Mound period as well as from the Sanders sites. McKern reported on both the Kletzien and Nitschke Mound Groups (1930). The Kletzien group consisted of 22 effigy (panther and deer), five linear, two oval, and four conical mounds in Sheboygan County (Fig. 1). Of these 33 mounds only seven were not excavated and the remaining 26 mounds yielded flexed, bundle, and cremated burials. An examination of the artifacts from the Kletzien Mound Group is disappointing in range and number as the very few artifacts at the Milwaukee Public Museum are Madison Ware types such as Madison Cord Impressed and Madison Plain. The Nitschke Mound Group of Dodge County (Fig. 1) consisted of 30 turtle, panther, canine, buffalo, deer, bird, and indeterminate effigy mounds and 32 mounds classed as oval, linear, or conical. Twenty-four of these mounds were not excavated and the remaining 38 mounds yielded 29 burials and a large quantity of artifacts. The ceramic types present at the Nitschke site appear to be Dane Incised, Dane Incised variety fingernail impressed, Madison Cord Impressed, Madison Fabric Impressed, Madison Folded Lip, Madison Plain, Madison Punctated, Aztalan Collared, Hahn Cord Impressed, and Point Sauble Collared. The bone artifacts associated with burials in the mounds at the Nitschke site are unique for Effigy Mound sites as they include harpoons, beamer scrapers, and polished and decorated awls (McKern, 1930:Pl. LXV). Only one date has been published for this most complex mound group, A.D. 1040 ± 55 (WIS-182), and it indicates a late placement in the Middle Effigy Mound period.

The mound sites from the Middle Effigy Mound period appear to belong to several classes as some are primarily burial locations (Raisbeck, Prawatschke, Picnic Point, Frost Woods, Clam Lake, Spencer Lake, Kletzien, and Nitschke) while other (Bigelow and some mounds from northeastern Iowa) do not have mounds yielding a significant number of burials. Linear, oval, and conical forms are present at most mound sites and the effigy forms include bear, bird, panther, otter, turtle, deer, canine, buffalo, and indeterminate shapes. Additions to the material culture list are elbow pipes, harpoons, bone beamer scrapers, sandstone abraders, and the full range of Madison Ware ceramics. Madison Side Notched, Waubesa Contracting Stem, and Triangular projectile points were also present at these mound sites and the full range of point forms may be increased by a re-examination of the Nitschke specimens.

The proposed village type site for the Middle Effigy Mound period is the Sanders site (47-Wp-26 and Wp-70) which clearly dates within the proposed temporal bracket (A.D. 700 to A.D. 1100). The Sanders site is a multi-functional site having effigy (panther, bird, and bear), conical, linear, and oval mounds and an associated village. The 12 excavated mounds, 63 features, and three houses at this partially excavated site are identified as belonging to the Effigy Mound tradition. A total of 45,213 artifacts was recovered and except for a small minority associated with a poorly represented Middle Woodland component, the majority are associated with Effigy Mound peoples who also had in their possession trade vessels from an emerging Oneota tradition. The Middle Woodland utilization is estimated to have occurred at circa A.D. 300 (WIS-218), with the Effigy Mound occupation placed between A.D. 700 and A.D. 1100. Between A.D. 670 and A.D. 860 (WIS-217 and 219) Oneota vessels were traded into the village and these non-Effigy Mound items were kept separate from the inclusive mound artifacts. The Middle Woodland component artifacts include Sister Creeks Punctated, Shorewood Cord Roughened, and Rocker Stamped ceramics. The Oneota trade vessels belong to two types—Grand River Trailed and Grand River Plain. The remaining ceramic and lithic types, type varieties, and tool categories represent the fullest range of material culture items associated with the Effigy Mound tradition and they form the core of this analysis and the "culture core" for our present site comparisons. The Madison Ware ceramics from the Sanders site include: Dane Incised, Dane Incised variety fingernail impressed, Madison Cord Impressed, Madison Fabric Impressed, Madison Folded Lip, Madison Plain, Madison Plain variety punctated, Madison Plain variety jar, Madison Puncated, Leland Cord-marked, Aztalan Collared, Hahn Cord Impressed, Point Sauble Collared, and Heins Creek Corded Stamped. The Heins Creek Corded Stamped type may be ultimately excluded from the Madison Ware category and an alternative proposal will be offered below. The lithic types associated with the Effigy Mound component at the Sanders site are: Waubesa Contracting Stem, Madison Side Notched, Durst Stemmed, Sanders Triangular, and Triangular projectile points. There is also a wide variety of lithic and copper tool categories from the Sanders site, as well as an elbow pipe, and they indicate a rich variety of material culture items in use during the Middle Effigy Mound period.

Cord and fabric analyses of the Sanders site ceramics indicated a high degree of cord heterogeneity and complexity with more than one cord being used on vessels. The fabrics utilized for decoration indicate that spaced weft-twining was preferred during this period and that a total of 55 fabrics could be reconstructed from an analysis of this ceramic attribute. All of the Effigy Mound material culture artifacts listed above date from the Middle Effigy Mound period and the dated examples do not reflect the full temporal range of each type recovered from the site. The total number and range of artifacts, mounds, and village features and houses suggest that the Sanders site was an important locality during the Middle Effigy Mound period; its more permanent aspects suggest that it was either a major center of a Central-Based Wandering community pattern or a more permanent center classifiable as a Semi-Permanent Sedentary village (Meggers, 1956). The range of cultural activity recorded for the Sanders site does not appear to be unique for this period as a careful re-examination and re-assessment of the complex Nitschke site of Dodge County may show it to have been an equally important permanent center. Both the Sanders and Nitschke sites may in turn be a part of a larger, more complex settlement pattern network of village/mound sites, camp/mound sites, campsites, rockshelter sites, and mound sites.

The degree of similarity between the Bigelow and Sanders sites can be measured according to the individual principal component analyses which can now be combined. The samples from 47-Pt-29 and 47-Wp-26 which totaled 539 specimens were subjected to a final principal component analysis. Table 45 shows that the first eigenvalue accounts for 35 percent of the total variance while the second brings the total to 60 percent. The results of Table 45 were then plotted according to two vectors as illustrated in the scattergram of Figure 63. This scattergram is somewhat different than those of Figures 30 and 62: more specimens in tighter clusters occur above the 115 line and between the 115 and 135 line. The specimens from both 47-Pt-29 and 47-Wp-26 are also re-clustered between the 135 and 160 line. One cannot simply read these clusters from top to bottom as less decoration in few locations with less cord or fabric impressions (top); more decorations in more locations with more cord or fabric impressions (middle); and most decoration in most locations with most cord or fabric impressions. The configurations of these five variables do not add up in this manner: we now have two vectors representing two new configurations which equal more than the sum of the five variables.

In order to measure the dispersion or variation in which these five ceramic variables were classified the data was subjected to a Multivariate Analysis of Variance program (Van de Geer, 1971; Senter, 1969; Sokal and Rohlf, 1969). Multivariate analysis deals with the simultaneous variation of two or more variables and, in this instance, a number of variables (5) have been measured for two samples.

TABLE 45

PRINCIPAL COMPONENT ANALYSIS: 47-Pt-29 AND 47-Wp-26 (539 Specimens)

Eigenvalues	1.76051	1.25270	0.88956	0.79830	0.29890
Cumulative Percentage of Eigenvalues	0.35210	0.60264	0.78055	0.94021	0.99999

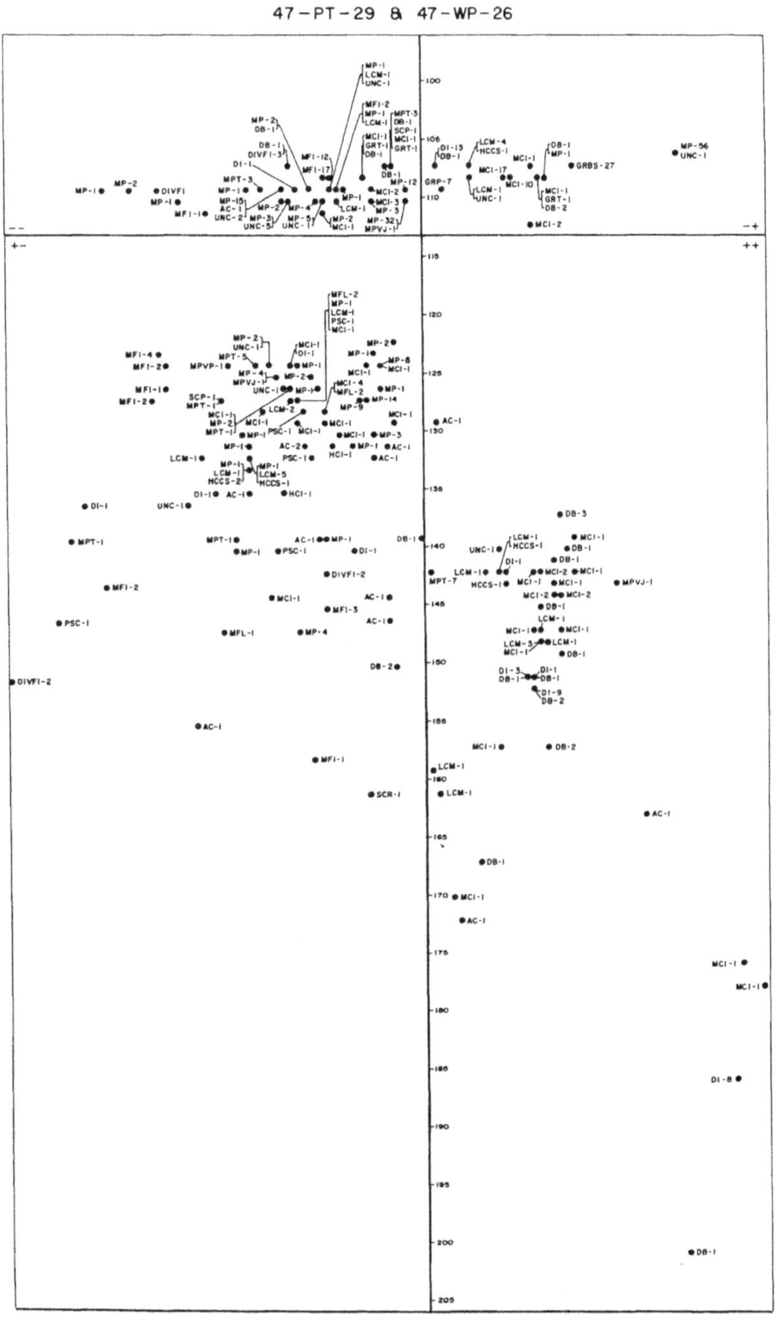

FIG. 63. Scattergram of principal component analysis of Bigelow and Sanders ceramics.

> The technique of principal axes is important in multivariate analysis, where instead of ellipses we encounter clouds of observations describing hyperellipsoids in a multidimensional space. To simplify the description of these clouds of points, we calculate principal axes through the hyperellipsoids . . . the eigenvalues, which represent the variance along the principal axes, are always maximized, so that as we take successive principal axes . . . we are successively removing the greatest, second greatest, and successively smaller sources of variation (Sokal and Rohlf, 1969:532).

Table 46 is the output from this program and two measurements have been taken. First, the program measures the total variance *within* each group and between several groups. Second, it measures the extent to which each annotation class (color vs. yellow which is an attribute) contributes to the separation of the two groups. Extensive discussion of multivariate analysis of

TABLE 46

MULTIVARIATE ANALYSIS OF VARIANCE: CERAMICS FROM 47-Pt-29 AND 47-Wp-26

47-Pt-29 (258 specimens)	Variable 1	Variable 2	Variable 3	Variable 4	Variable 5
Means	5.72	3.51	3.18	2.35	1.67
Standard Deviations	3.81	2.15	12.49	3.71	2.30
47-Wp-26 (281 specimens)					
Means	5.39	3.33	3.60	1.93	1.67
Standard Deviations	3.34	2.29	14.50	3.41	2.23
Means (Total Sample)	5.55	3.42	3.40	2.13	1.67
Standard Deviations (Total Sample)	3.57	2.22	13.58	3.56	2.26

Test for Equality of Dispersions: M = 32.332
F = 2.134

Univariate F-Ratios with One and Two Degrees of Freedom = 537

Variable	Among Means^2	Within Means^2	F-Ratio	ETA^2
1	14.60	12.77	1.14	0.0021
2	4.39	4.94	0.89	0.0017
3	24.50	184.39	0.13	0.0002
4	24.58	12.67	1.94	0.0036
5	0.00	5.12	0.00	0.0000

variance will be found in the authors cited above as will clarification concerning F-Ratios. For our purposes we will look at the ETA^2 column. If the ETA^2 were close to .1 it would indicate that the variables were not related. The farther away from .1 the more related or the less useful for distinguishing one from the other. Variables 3 and 5 are of a very low order, variables 1 and 2 are closely related, and variable 4 is the highest. In general, the program suggests that the two sites are similar.

The degree of site similarity can be seen in Table 47 where the two groups are again compared and if one centroid is positive and the other negative we can see that the degree of difference in a Multiple Group Discriminant Analysis Program is 0.008, or again that the sites are similar. The results of these three forms of analysis were based on only five multistate continuous variables. Two state or alternative variables (continuous or discontinuous) might yield similar or dissimilar results. In order to properly evaluate the full range of ceramic attributes a class and attribute list for ceramic analysis (Hurley and Wagner, 1972) has been devised and both Late Woodland and Oneota specimens (4,000) have been coded according to this more exhaustive system. The

TABLE 47

MULTIPLE GROUP DISCRIMINANT ANALYSIS

Wilks Lamda = 0.9911 Generalized Correlation Ratio, Eta^2 = 0.0089
F-Ratio for H2, Overall Discrimination = 0.95
Chi-Square Tests with Successive Roots Removed

Roots Removed	(Eta) Canonical R	(Eta^2) R^2	Eigenvalue	Chi-Sq.	N.D.F.	Lambda	% Trace
0	0.094	0.009	0.009	5	5	0.99	100.00

Factor Pattern for Discriminant Functions

Test 1 = 0.488
2 = 0.430
3 = 0.166
4 = 0.635
5 = 0.012

Communalities for One Discriminant Factor
1 = 0.238 2 = 0.185 3 = 0.028 4 = 0.403 5 = 0.000

Percentage of Trace R Accounted for by each Root 1.17086

Centroid for Group One in One Dimensional Discriminant Space 1 = 0.98

Centroid for Group Two in One Dimensional Discriminant Space 1 = -0.090

results of this research will be available in 1975. Until that time we can state that on the basis of the mounds, the material culture items, cord and fabric studies, radiocarbon assessments and statistical analysis of a limited ceramic sample that the sites appear to be related. This relationship is so extensive that it suggests they may belong to a band that occupied both the Bigelow and Sanders sites over a period of several hundred years.

Directly northeast of the Sanders site is the Heins Creek site (Fig. 1) which was actively occupied at the same time as the Sanders locality. Excavations at this single component fishing station (Mason, 1966:5) yielded 36 Triangular projectile points, knives, a drill, scrapers and bone harpoons, pins and/or needles. The ceramics recovered include Heins Creek Cord-marked, Heins Creek Corded Stamped, Heins Creek Cord-wrapped stick, Point Sauble Collared, Madison Cord Impressed, punctated, incised, and fabric impressed sherds. The proposed Heins Creek Complex is dated at A.D. 720 ± 150 (I-678) and the complex may represent an Effigy Mound fishing station or an undefined Late Woodland culture co-existing at the same time as the Effigy Mound culture. The Heins Creek ware was seen by Mason as genetically related to his Middle Woodland North Bay culture at the Mero site (1966:148-149). I would suggest that further excavations may demonstrate that the Heins Creek Complex was a separate and distinct northern Wisconsin Late Woodland culture. External relationships may be found with Salzer's post-Nakomis culture material from north-central Wisconsin and with the western Grand River Focus. If this assumption is proved correct then I would recommend the removal of Heins Creek Corded Stamped from the Madison Ware category and its assignment as a trade ware when found in an Effigy Mound context.

The evidence from the Heins Creek site appears to support the view that trade was occurring, as it also produced Point Sauble Collared, Madison Cord Impressed, incised (Dane Incised?), and fabric impressed (Madison Fabric Impressed?) ceramics. At the Third Annual Meeting of the Canadian Archaeological Association in Ottawa on March 14-16, 1970, Robert Salzer suggested that the Wisconsin floristic Tension Zone (Fig. 2) may have been a prehistoric culture tension zone separating the Middle Woodland Nakomis and North Bay cultures from the Havana and Waukesha manifestations of southern Wisconsin. This concept could be extended into Late Woodland times and I would suggest that at least for the northeastern portion of Wisconsin, the Heins Creek "culture" was also separated from the southern Effigy Mound tradition even though trade contacts were taking place.

Directly west of Heins Creek in Shawano (now also Menominee) and Oconto counties is the locus of the proposed Keshena culture which may invalidate the separate northern Late Woodland culture hypothesis presented above. These counties are north of the Tension Zone (Fig. 2) and they contained a large series of mound and habitation sites, with the mound forms consisting of conical, linear, and effigy shapes (Barrett and Skinner, 1932).

The major sites investigated yielded important data concerning both the Middle and Late phases of the Wisconsin Effigy Mound tradition. The Makimitas site, located northwest of Watasa Lake, appears to have been a major cremation and burial area—54 large pits were located and they contained large amounts of charcoal and cremated human bones. This site led Barrett and Skinner (1932:425) to conclude that

> . . . the Makimitas pits were formerly graves containing regular primary burials, but that after the dead had been interred for some time, these were opened and, except for the skulls, the bones which remained were burned in them. The skulls, and coarser fragments of the burned bones were then gathered up and carried off for secondary deposition in mounds.

The artifacts in association with the burial pits appear to belong to the Dane Incised, Madison Cord Impressed, Madison Fabric Impressed, Point Sauble Collared, Triangular, and Monona Stemmed types (*ibid.*:Pl. LXXVII).

The Watasa Lake Swamp site had a catfish-shaped mound and three conical mounds which yielded primary burials, cremations, and mound fill artifacts. These mounds were adjacent to campsites which yielded large quantities of faunal remains (*ibid.*:431). The illustrated artifacts include celts, drills, Triangular points, Madison Punctated, Madison Folded Lip, Madison Fabric Impressed, Madison Plain, Aztalan Collared, Point Sauble Collared, Grand River and Lake Winnebago foci ceramics (*ibid.*:Pl. LXXVIII-LXXX). The Kakwatch site consisted of a mound group with 13 conical, linear, and catfish mounds and a village with a large number of pits (*ibid.*:Fig. 37). Each of the investigated mounds yielded partly cremated and calcined bones in association with an unburned skull and possibly polished bear jaws (*ibid.*:441-451). One catfish mound, Mound No. 3, yielded two vessels, one containing a calvarium. The vessels appear to be of the types Heins Creek Corded Stamped and Madison Punctated (*ibid.*:Plates LXXXVI-LXXXVII); the latter example is quite similar to the vessel from Feature 1 of Mound 2 at 47-Wp-26 (Pl. 31). Artifacts from the Kakwatch village site were recovered from the surface and from the cache, refuse, and fire pits. One pit, No. 3, was a fire pit 2.5 feet deep which contained a vessel which looks as if it belongs in the type Aztalan Collared (*ibid.*:Fig. 44; Pl. LXXXIV, Figs. 1 and 2; Pl. LXXXV), while the majority of the recovered sherds were decorated with cord-wrapped stick impressions (*ibid.*:445). The non-ceramic artifacts consisted of serrated and non-serrated Triangular projectile points, a blade, celts, mortars, and hammerstones (*ibid.*:458-459).

The Pewisit Lake Mound Group consisted of 11 hemispherical, linear, and catfish mounds. Hemispherical Mound 2 yielded animal bones, chips, sherds, and a serrated Triangular projectile point and a burial (*ibid.*:460-463). The Nakuti's Berry Patch Mound Group contained 16 catfish, linear, and oblong mounds (*ibid.*:Fig. 49) which yielded primary burials and cremations; however, no artifacts are described or illustrated from this mound group. The final site to be considered from this area at this time is the La Belle Lake Mound Group which consisted of 18 catfish or oval mounds in two separate clusters (Mounds 1-12 and Mounds 13-18). These mounds contained cremated, primary and secondary bundle burials and, in one instance, an associated vessel (*ibid.*:Fig. 52). The artifacts from this mound group appear to belong to the Madison Ware types of Madison Cord Impressed, Madison Folded Lip, Madison Fabric Impressed, Aztalan Collared, and Point Sauble Collared. Triangular projectile points, blades, and celts were also recovered from this site.

The majority of the sites are presently within Menominee County with only the Pewisit Lake Mound Group and Nakuti's Berry Patch Mound Group in Oconto County. Both counties are north of the Wisconsin Tension Zone (Curtis, 1959) and the sites described by Barrett and Skinner represent the best evidence of Effigy Mound tradition camp, village, and mound localities in northeastern Wisconsin. Trade vessels would be expected to go beyond the Effigy Mound "territory" to such sites as Heins Creek, Mero, and the Sorg site (Fig. 1), but single component sites (with the Kakwatch mound having a trade Heins Creek Corded Stamped vessel) appear to have been the pattern described by Barrett and Skinner.

The Watasa Lake Swamp site is the single exception as it yielded Madison Ware types and Grand River and Lake Winnebago foci ceramics. This site may date within the Late Effigy Mound period (A.D. 1100 to A.D. 1642) as the majority of the Lake Winnebago dates are post-A.D. 1100 (Table 48). The Madison Ware types present at these mound, camp, and village sites include Dane Incised, Madison Cord Impressed, Madison Fabric Impressed, Madison Folded Lip, Madison Plain, Madison Punctated, Aztalan Collared, and Point Sauble Collared examples. The diagnostic lithic types included Monona Stemmed points and Triangular points, the latter category being in the majority. These sites were presented as a unit instead of according to the division utilized thus far of open versus mound or rockshelter sites as it seemed that the data would be distorted if the mounds were separated from the open sites. One remaining site extends the northern distribution of effigy-shaped mounds beyond the line drawn by Rowe (1956): the Koontz Farm Eagle Effigy Mound (*ibid.*:Fig. 58), and its campsite, are west of Menominee County in the Township of Gresham in Shawano County (Fig. 1); neither the mound nor the campsite was excavated. These sites could represent an intrusion or a "cultural peninsula" north of the accepted Effigy Mound tradition distribution or they could be the result of the interest and work of anthropologists. If the latter is the case, then detailed surveys between these sites and Wittry's Wakanda Park Mound Group (1959*b*), located in Dunn County (Fig. 1), may also extend the north central limits of the Effigy Mound tradition sites.

TABLE 48

RADIOCARBON DATES OF HOPEWELLIAN, EFFIGY MOUND, AND MISSISSIPPIAN MANIFESTATIONS IN THE EFFIGY MOUND REGION

Dates	Source	Site/Area
	Hopewellian	
B.C. 610 ± 70 (WIS-234)	Bender, Bryson, & Baerreis, 1968*a*	Schwert
B.C. 480 ± 70 (WIS-174)	Bender, Bryson, & Baerreis, 1967	Schwert
B.C. 200 ± 80 (WIS-163)	Bender, Bryson, & Baerreis, 1967	Silver Creek I
B.C. 130 ± 70 (WIS-231)	Bender, Bryson, & Baerreis, 1968*a*	Schwert
B.C. 90 ± 100 (M-1437)	Crane and Griffin, 1965	Price
B.C. 10 ± 90 (I-296)	Buckley, Trautman, & Willis, 1968	Iowa
A.D. 130 ± 55 (WIS-210)	Bender, Bryson, & Baerreis, 1968*a*	Millville

TABLE 48 (Continued)

Dates	Source	Site/Area
	Hopewellian (Continued)	
A.D. 160 ± 100 (I-888)	Mason, 1966:125	North Bay
A.D. 170 ± 75 (WIS-154)	Bender, Bryson, & Baerreis, 1967	47-Gt-1
A.D. 180 ± 65 (WIS-212)	Bender, Bryson, & Baerreis, 1968*a*	Millville
A.D. 190 ± 55 (WIS-211)	Bender, Bryson, & Baerreis, 1968*a*	Millville
A.D. 190 ± 65 (WIS-208)	Bender, Bryson, & Baerreis, 1968*a*	Millville
A.D. 210 ± 110 (I-295)	Buckley, Trautman, & Willis, 1968	Iowa
A.D. 220 ± 150 (M-743)	Bastian, 1962:60	Iowa
A.D. 290 ± 65 (WIS-218)	Hurley, 1970 House 3, Fill	Sanders
A.D. 300 ± 100 (M-1436)	Crane and Griffin, 1965	Price
A.D. 310 ± 80 (WIS-239)	Bender, Bryson, & Baerreis, 1968*a*	Millville
A.D. 340 ± 55 (WIS-237)	Bender, Bryson, & Baerreis, 1968*a*	Millville
A.D. 340 ± 65 (WIS-237)	Bender, Bryson, & Baerreis, 1968*a*	Second Lake
A.D. 350 ± 55 (WIS-335)	Bender, Bryson, & Baerreis, 1970	Gov. Dodge
A.D. 360 ± 60 (WIS-236)	Bender, Bryson, & Baerreis, 1968*a*	Second Lake
A.D. 370 ± 55 (WIS-214)	Bender, Bryson, & Baerreis, 1968*a*	Millville
A.D. 430 ± 70 (WIS-150)	Bender, Bryson, & Baerreis, 1967	47-Gt-1
A.D. 500 ± 60 (WIS-241)	Bender, Bryson, & Baerreis, 1968*a*	Schwert
A.D. 900 ± 300 (M-40)	Beaubien, 1953:65	Iowa
A.D. 1680 ± 55 (WIS-240)	Bender, Bryson, & Baerreis, 1968*a*	Second Lake
	Effigy Mound	
A.D. 320 ± 70	Bender, Bryson, & Baerreis, 1970	Mayland Cave
A.D. 360 ± 55	Bender, Bryson, & Baerreis, 1970	Mayland Cave
A.D. 375 ± 100 (1-441)	Bastian, 1962:60	Iowa
A.D. 490 ± 120 (M-1583)	Ritzenthaler, 1964:219	Clam River
A.D. 490 ± 150 (M-871)	Bastian, 1962:59	Beloit

TABLE 48 (Continued)

Dates	Source	Site/Area
	Effigy Mound (Continued)	
A.D. 530 ± 150 (M-1582)	Ritzenthaler, 1964:219	Clam River
A.D. 580 ± 110 (M-1581)	Ritzenthaler, 1964:219	Clam River
A.D. 625 ± 100 (I-412)	Bastian, 1962:60	Iowa
A.D. 670 ± 55 (WIS-197)	Hurley, 1970 Md.A, Fea. 26	Bigelow
A.D. 670 ± 75 (WIS-217)	Hurley, 1970 Houses 2 & 3, Fea. 30	Sanders
A.D. 700 ± 55 (WIS-182)	Bender, Bryson, & Baerreis, 1967	Utley
A.D. 720 ± 150 (I-678)	Mason, 1966:27-28	Heins Creek
A.D. 720 ± 55 (WIS-221)	Hurley, 1970 Md.23, Burial 2	Sanders
A.D. 720 ± 60 (WIS-233)	Hurley, 1970 Wp-70, House 1, Floor, Burial 1	Sanders
A.D. 750 ± 60 (WIS-183)	Ritzenthaler, 1964:219	Clam River
A.D. 760 ± 65 (WIS-181)	Ritzenthaler, 1964:219	Clam River
A.D. 770 ± 55 (WIS-223)	Hurley, 1970 House 3, Fea. 26	Sanders
A.D. 775 ± 55 (WIS-224)	Hurley, 1970 House 2	Sanders
A.D. 776 ± 250 (M-398)	Wittry, 1956:133-134	Kolterman
A.D. 800 ± 55 (WIS-202)	Hurley, 1970 Md.S, Burial 8	Bigelow
A.D. 810 ± 50 (WIS-200)	Hurley, 1970 Md.L, Fea. 13	Bigelow
A.D. 830 ± 65 (WIS-192)	Hurley, 1970 Md.4, Fea. 1	Bigelow
A.D. 860 ± 55 (WIS-219)	Hurley, 1970 Houses 2 and 3, Fea. 33	Sanders
A.D. 880 ± 70 (WIS-177)	Hurley, 1970 Md.3	Sanders
A.D. 880 ± 70 (WIS-171)	Hurley, 1970 Md.2, Fea. 1	Sanders
A.D. 890 ± 65 (WIS-180)	Ritzenthaler, 1964:219	Clam River
A.D. 890 ± 60 (WIS-206)	Hurley, 1970 Houses 2 and 3, Fea. 29	Sanders
A.D. 900 ± 50 (WIS-186)	Ritzenthaler, 1964:219	Clam River
A.D. 900 ± 70 (WIS-204)	Hurley, 1970 Md.17, Fea. 8	Sanders
A.D. 930 ± 300 (M-41)	Beaubien, 1953:65	Iowa

TABLE 48 (Continued)

Dates	Source	Site/Area
	Effigy Mound (Continued)	
A.D. 930 ± 70 (WIS-242)	Hurley, 1970 Md.B, Fea. 1	Bigelow
A.D. 930 ± 55 (WIS-203)	Hurley, 1970 House 2, Fea. 40	Sanders
A.D. 930 ± 60 (WIS-230)	Hurley, 1970 Wp-70, Fea. 2	Sanders
A.D. 940 ± 75 (WIS-235)	Hurley, 1970 Wp-70, Sq. S105W45, Level 4	Sanders
A.D. 940 ± 55 (WIS-357)	Bender, Bryson, & Baerreis, 1970	Mayland Cave
A.D. 960 ± 75 (WIS-238)	Hurley, 1970 Wp-70, Fea. 5	Sanders
A.D. 990 ± 60 (WIS-226)	Hurley, 1970 Md.R	Bigelow
A.D. 1010 ± 60 (WIS-207)	Hurley, 1970 Md.9, Fea. 1	Sanders
A.D. 1040 ± 55 (WIS-182)	Bender, Bryson, & Baerreis, 1967	Nitschke
A.D. 1060 ± 65 (WIS-232)	Hurley, 1970 Wp-70, Fea.	Sanders
A.D. 1100 ± 100 (M-1596)	Ritzenthaler, 1964:219	Clam River
A.D. 1120 ± 70 (WIS-168)	Hurley, 1970 Md.N, Fea. 3	Bigelow
A.D. 1120 ± 45 (WIS-273)	Bender, Bryson, & Baerreis, 1968*b*	Dietz
A.D. 1150 ± 200 (M-447)	Johnson, 1964:34-49	Minnesota
A.D. 1170 ± 50 (WIS-193)	Bender, Bryson, & Baerreis, 1967	Dietz
A.D. 1190 ± 60 (WIS-315)	Bender, Bryson, & Baerreis, 1969	Dietz
A.D. 1200 ± 200 (M-814)	Wittry, 1959*b*: 12	Wakanda
A.D. 1370 ± 65 (WIS-187)	Hurley, 1970 Area K, Fea. 6	Bigelow
A.D. 1520 ± 75 (I-413)	Bastian, 1962:60	Iowa
	Middle Mississippian	Aztalan
A.D. 750 ± 150 (M-1037)	Ritzenthaler, 1961:139	Aztalan
A.D. 1030 ± 55 (WIS-191)	Bender, Bryson, & Baerreis, 1967	Aztalan
A.D. 1100 ± 80 (WIS-68)	Baerreis and Bryson, 1965:207	Aztalan
A.D. 1130 ± 80 (WIS-63)	Baerreis and Bryson, 1965:207	Aztalan
A.D. 1130 ± 80 (WIS-73)	Baerreis and Bryson, 1965:207	Aztalan

TABLE 48 (Continued)

Dates	Source	Site/Area
	Middle Mississippian (Continued)	Aztalan
A.D. 1140 ± 60 (WIS-162)	Bender, Bryson, & Baerreis, 1967	Aztalan
A.D. 1220 ± 80 (WIS-74)	Baerreis and Bryson, 1965:297	Aztalan
A.D. 1370 ± 100 (M-1214)	Ritzenthaler, 1963; Hurley, 1964	Aztalan
A.D. 1630 ± 200 (M-642)	Ritzenthaler, 1960:68	Aztalan
	Upper Mississippian	Koshkonong Focus
A.D. 890 ± 80 (WIS-77)	Bender, Bryson, & Baerreis, 1966	Koshkonong Focus
A.D. 990 ± 250 (M-786)	Hall, 1958:174-175	Koshkonong Focus
A.D. 1020 ± 250 (M-785)	Hall, 1958:174-175	Koshkonong Focus
A.D. 1140 ± 50 (WIS-382)	Bender, Bryson, & Baerreis, 1970	Crescent Bay Hunt Club
A.D. 1150 ± 50 (WIS-348)	Bender, Bryson, & Baerreis, 1970	Crescent Bay Hunt Club
A.D. 1170 ± 50 (WIS-358)	Bender, Bryson, & Baerreis, 1970	Crescent Bay Hunt Club
A.D. 1190 ± 50 (WIS-346)	Bender, Bryson, & Baerreis, 1970	Crescent Bay Hunt Club
A.D. 1520 ± 250 (M-747)	Hall, 1958:174-175	Koshkonong Focus
	Upper Mississippian	Grand River Focus
A.D. 1130 ± 60 (WIS-194)	Bender, Bryson, & Baerreis, 1967	Pipe
A.D. 1200 ± 55 (WIS-277)	Bender, Bryson, & Baerreis, 1968*b*	Walker-Hooper
A.D. 1210 ± 50 (WIS-290)	Bender, Bryson, & Baerreis, 1969	Walker-Hooper
A.D. 1230 ± 55 (WIS-270)	Bender, Bryson, & Baerreis, 1968b	Walker-Hooper
A.D. 1240 ± 45 (WIS-268)	Bender, Bryson, & Baerreis, 1968*b*	Walker-Hooper
A.D. 1290 ± 50 (WIS-288)	Bender, Bryson, & Baerreis, 1969	Bornick
	Upper Mississippian	L. Winnebago Focus
A.D. 990 ± 70 (WIS-50)	Bender, Bryson, & Baerreis, 1966	L. Winnebago Focus
A.D. 1170 ± 80 (WIS-47)	Bender, Bryson, & Baerreis, 1966	L. Winnebago Focus
A.D. 1170 ± 80 (WIS-62)	Bender, Bryson, & Baerreis, 1966	L. Winnebago Focus

TABLE 48 (Continued)

Dates	Source	Site/Area
	Upper Mississippian (Continued)	
A.D. 1220 ± 65 (WIS-159)	Bender, Bryson, & Baerreis, 1967	L. Winnebago Focus
A.D. 1270 ± 80 (WIS-57)	Bender, Bryson, & Baerreis, 1966	L. Winnebago Focus
A.D. 1400 ± 70 (WIS-161)	Bender, Bryson, & Baerreis, 1967	L. Winnebago Focus
A.D. 1480 ± 60 (WIS-158)	Bender, Bryson, & Baerreis, 1967	L. Winnebago Focus
A.D. 1480 ± 70 (WIS-164)	Bender, Bryson, & Baerreis, 1967	L. Winnebago Focus
	Upper Mississippian	Orr Focus Iowa
A.D. 980 ± 95 (GX-1996)	McKusick, 1971	Grant Village, Iowa
A.D. 1005 ± 115 (GX-1995)	McKusick, 1971	Grant Village, Iowa
A.D. 1080 ± 180 (GX-1994)	McKusick, 1971	Grant Village, Iowa
A.D. 1290 ± 120 (GX-1998)	McKusick, 1971	Hartley Fort, Iowa
A.D. 1460 ± 85 (GX-1993)	McKusick, 1971	Lane Enclosure, Iowa
A.D. 1475 ± 95 (GX-1989)	McKusick, 1971	Lane Enclosure, Iowa
A.D. 1480 ± 120 (GX-2000)	McKusick, 1971	Hartley Fort, Iowa
	Upper Mississippian	Orr Focus Wisconsin
A.D. 1270 ± 55 (WIS-337)	Bender, Bryson, & Baerreis, 1970	Mayland Cave
A.D. 1420 ± 70 (WIS-61)	Bender, Bryson, & Baerreis, 1966	Midway
A.D. 1630 ± 60 (WIS-79)	Bender, Bryson, & Baerreis, 1966	Midway
	Upper Mississippian	Blue Earth Focus
A.D. 1060 ± 55 (WIS-434)	Bender, Bryson, & Baerreis, 1971	Bartrom Site Minnesota
A.D. 1100 ± 55 (WIS-423)	Bender, Bryson, & Baerreis, 1971	Bartrom Site Minnesota
A.D. 1340 ± 110 (M-1891)	Crane and Griffin, 1970 Oneota and Late Manitoba	Backland Mound
A.D. 1290 ± 100 (M-2071)	Crane and Griffin, 1970 Oneota	Summer Island
A.D. 1290 ± 100 (M-2072)	Crane and Griffin, 1970 Oneota	Summer Island

The Blackhawk village site (47-Da-5) in the Madison area was the type site for Madison Cord Impressed ceramics and Monona Stemmed projectile points (Baerreis, 1953*a*:10-15). Four Hopewellian sherds and Triangular projectile points were also recovered from this salvage excavation. At the time of publication Baerreis considered the new types as associated with the Effigy Mound culture and the Hopewellian sherds as trade items with the Effigy Mound culture dating from the Middle Woodland period (1953*a*:19). The Triangular points were considered to be associated with later Mississippian cultures. The points are now acceptable Effigy Mound material cultural items (Keslin, 1958:264-267) but the possibility that they date from Middle Woodland times (circa A.D. 300 to A.D. 500) has not as yet been demonstrated. The four Hopewellian sherds were in a site situation where additional controlled specimens would have made the context less questionable; however, the data presented for the Early Effigy Mound period suggest that Hopewellian and Effigy Mound culture contact was more than just an assumption.

Excavations in Dodge County at the Hahn (47-Dg-1 and 47-Dg-2) and Horicon (47-Dg-5) sites continued to provide evidence on Effigy Mound culture open sites. The Woodland component at 47-Dg-1 yielded four primary burials which lacked associated grave goods, although the burial pit yielded a Triangular projectile point and sherds identified as Dane Incised. Keslin (1958:203-205) considered the Dane Incised pottery from the burial pit fill as early Woodland in age and possibly not associated with the burials. The presence of a Triangular projectile point and the absence of any other cultural component suggest instead that this site was an Effigy Mound campsite and/or burial area dating from the Middle Effigy Mound period. The nearby Hahn Site 2 (47-Dg-2) was a campsite assigned to the Effigy Mound culture (Keslin, 1958:231) and it produced Monona Stemmed and Triangular projectile points, Madison Cord Impressed, the type specimens of Hahn Cord Impressed and of Madison Plain, Dane Incised, Aztalan Collared, and ceramics identified as belonging to both the Grand River and Orr foci (*ibid.*:217-231). The site assemblage now suggests an Effigy Mound campsite having the Madison Ware types of Dane Incised, Madison Cord Impressed, Madison Plain, Aztalan Collared, and Hahn Cord Impressed plus Monona Stemmed and Triangular projectile points. Keslin considered the Oneota examples as trade vessels and on the basis of the Aztalan Collared specimen and the Triangular points he viewed the site as having been occupied at A.D. 1200 to A.D. 1300 (*ibid.*:243-244; 266); however, I would place the site somewhat earlier on the basis of the Dane Incised ceramics.

Thirty miles northeast of 47-Dg-2 was the Horicon site (47-Dg-5). This campsite yielded Monona Stemmed and Triangular projectile points; Dane Incised, Madison Cord Impressed, Madison Plain, and Hahn Cord Impressed Madison Ware types, plus punctated and rocker stamped sherds. The Hopewellian rocker stamped sherds were thought to date the site at A.D. 1000 (Keslin, 1958:271), but this date is much too late and I would suggest a date of circa A.D. 500 if the context of the rocker stamped ceramics is with the Effigy Mound Madison Ware types. Keslin noted the presence of dentate stamped sherds at the Blackhawk (47-Da-5) and Horicon (47-Dg-5) sites and suggested that these associations had occurred far too often to be dismissed (*ibid.*:271). I agree with this view and also suggest that there were connections between the Hahn sites (47-Dg-1 and 47-Dg-2), the Horicon site (47-Dg-5), and the Nitschke site of Dodge County. These sites may extend from the Early Effigy Mound period into the Middle Effigy Mound period and the single date from the Nitschke site of 1040 ± 55 (WIS-182) may not date the full period of utilization. The occupation and re-occupation of sites over several hundred years have been demonstrated for the Effigy Mounds National Moument of Iowa, the Bigelow site (47-Pt-29), and the Sanders site (47-Wp-26 and Wp-70).

There is one additional site dating from the Middle Effigy Mound period which should be briefly considered here and that is the Mayland Cave site (47-Ia-38) located in Iowa County (Fig. 1) and recently excavated by Peter Storck, now of the Royal Ontario Museum at Toronto. The material from this site has undergone full analysis and Storck has recovered Madison Cord Impressed, Madison Plain, and Aztalan Collared ceramics which have been dated at A.D. 940 ± 55 (WIS-357), and Powel Plain and Grand River Trailed specimens which have been dated at A.D. 1270 ± 55 (WIS-337) (Storck, 1972). This is the only sheltered site dating from the Middle Effigy Mound period and it is restricted (as are the earlier rockshelter sites) to that area of Wisconsin which has the majority of cave and rockshelter locations. One date of A.D. 320 ± 70 (WIS-370) has been offered as possibly dating the beginning of the Late Woodland occupation. The date of A.D. 1270 ± 55 (WIS-337) agrees with the Grand River Focus dates listed in Table 48.

In this examination of the Middle Effigy Mound period (circa A.D. 700 to A.D. 1100) several sites—Sny-Magill, Prawatschke, and Hahn Site 2—were ordered according to their artifact content and it was suggested that this ordering could be shifted as more radiocarbon dates are recorded for the undated sites. The temporal placement of such types as Dane Incised, Leland Cord-marked, Aztalan Collared, Point Sauble Collared, Heins Creek Corded Stamped, Triangular, Sanders Triangular, Monona Stemmed, Madison Side Notched, Durst Stemmed, and Waubesa Contracting Stem is "secure" as they are now considered to be Effigy Mound cultural items. Such types as Durst Stemmed, Madison Side Notched, and Waubesa Contracting Stem may begin before or during Middle Woodland times while the cultural affiliation of others, for example, Burnett Stamped conoidal and Clam River wrapped-stamped globoid, is difficult to assess. As the Effigy Mound tradition developed, its cultural contacts with indigenous Middle Woodland cultures became more attenuated and Middle Mississippian and Upper Mississippian or Oneota (Koshkonong, Grand River, Lake Winnebago, and Orr foci) loomed in importance. In the examination of sites suggested as dating from the Middle Effigy Mound period there were sites which yielded diagnostic ceramic artifacts associated with the Wisconsin Oneota tradition. At the Sanders site the Grand River types of Grand River Trailed and Grand River Plain were found in an Effigy Mound village and they are considered to have been traded into the village between A.D. 670 and A.D. 860. The Watasa Lake Swamp site (Barrett and Skinner, 1932) yielded both Madison Ware ceramics and examples of Grand River and Lake Winnebago foci vessels. Hahn Site 2 also produced Oneota (Grand River and Orr foci) ceramics in association with Madison Ware types and these Oneota vessels were considered trade vessels (Keslin, 1958:243-244). Many other sites have yielded excellent evidence of Effigy Mound-Oneota contacts (Mero, Carcajou, Spike Hollow Rockshelter, and Mayland Cave) and the status of Effigy Mound-Oneota cultural relationships needs to be critically examined.

Gibbon (1972) has presented a hypothesis concerning the development of the Oneota Life-way in Wisconsin. His paper presented the most recent evaluation of Wisconsin Oneota with particular emphasis on the emerging Grand River Focus and its possible connections with the Effigy Mound culture. Gibbon's recent excavations and analysis of the Walker-Hooper and Bornick sites did not disclose the origins of early Oneota; however, Gibbon advocated the view that there was a transformation of the Effigy Mound tradition into the Oneota tradition between A.D. 900 and A.D. 1100. The Effigy Mound tradition would have formed the base of the emerging Oneota tradition through contact and acculturation of the Effigy Mound peoples. The basis of this metamorphosis pivoted on socioeconomic inferences and not on material culture; yet it is the former cultural facet which is the least known aspect of the Effigy Mound tradition.

The Effigy Mound peoples during the Middle Effigy Mound period were considered by Gibbon to have been hunters and gatherers who periodically visited sites to bury their dead and to construct their mounds. Central to Gibbon's hypothesis is the view that maize cultivation would have had a significant impact on these hunting and gathering peoples and would have altered their community size, food resources, social organization, and pottery manufacture and design attributes. The vagaries of seasonal food resources and the implied unstable subsistence pattern of hunters and gatherers would have made the Effigy Mound peoples, according to Gibbon's arguments, potential and ready-made converts to a new and a more secure subsistence base. The gradual shift to a more secure food supply would have led to a way of life which could have developed into the Oneota Life-way in Wisconsin. As the only documented and published evidence for maize cultivation at an Effigy Mound culture site is at the Dietz site (Dietz, et al., 1956), which is dated at circa A.D. 1100 to A.D. 1200 (see below), the impact of horticulture on the Effigy Mound tradition during A.D. 900 to A.D. 1100 must remain conjectural at best. In a manuscript on file at the University of Wisconsin (Hurley, 1963:1-21), I was able to demonstrate, through the use of primary ethnohistoric sources, that the economic subsistence pattern of the Mdewakanton Sioux from the historic period of 1642 to 1837 was one of hunting and gathering with a marked resistance to maize horticulture evident throughout this 200-year period. Their successful adjustment to forest, riverine, and swamp environments supported Caldwell's "primary forest efficiency" hypothesis (Caldwell, 1958). Dependence on undocumented maize horticulture to produce the proper Effigy Mound culture setting for the development of the Oneota tradition is untenable and I will depend here on the more reliable non-economic "culture core"—the ceramics—to evaluate both traditions.

Gibbon's proposed abrupt ceramic transition occurred either in the Wisconsin Oneota "heartland" (the area of the Sanders,

Walker-Hooper, and Bornick sites) or along the *Wisconsin* margins, i.e., at the Carcajou Point site. The only documented evidence is at the Mero site where there appears to have been a transition between the Mero I Complex and the later Mero II Complex (Mason, 1966:160-161). The dates on the Sanders Oneota specimens (A.D. 670 to A.D. 860) are much earlier than the believed occupation range for the Middle Mississippian-Effigy Mound site of Aztalan (Fig. 1) as the majority of the dates cluster between A.D. 1100 to A.D. 1300. This one source for early emerging Oneota is apparently too late for Gibbon; however, there are two earlier dates for Aztalan—A.D. 750 ± 150 (M-1037) and A.D. 1030 ± 55 (WIS-197) which might date the initial site-unit intrusions of Middle Mississippian peoples into the state. I have argued elsewhere (Hurley, 1964) that the full range of Aztalan dates should be considered in the reconstruction of the site's prehistory, while Baerreis and Bryson (1965) stressed that the major occupation of the site occurred during the 200-year period of A.D. 1100-1300. The early dates from Aztalan (M-1037 and WIS-197) do correspond to the early dates for the Cahokia area, and the cultural influences from Cahokia, dating from circa A.D. 800, may account *in part* for the Oneota development in Wisconsin. The early Cahokia and Aztalan dates do not pre-date the Sanders Oneota specimens (A.D. 670 to A.D. 860), which indicates that the Grand River Focus was already present in Wisconsin.

Gibbon has also argued that the area of the known Grand River, Koshkonong, and Lake Winnebago foci sites is similar to that occupied by Effigy Mound peoples and that this area was most favorable to the early Oneota horticulturists. The acculturation of the Effigy Mound peoples would have occurred during the subsequent intense competition for these favorable areas. I am perplexed by this prehistoric confrontation theory: if Oneota peoples were already developed when they came in contact with the Effigy Mound peoples, where and from whom did they develop? If Oneota developed out of Effigy Mound then was this an in situ adaptation; if so, how do we account for the continued existence of a viable Effigy Mound tradition?

As we have seen from the Sanders site, the 200 to 300 years of Oneota contact did not seem to have any major effect on the Effigy Mound component at this site. During the time when Gibbon considers the Effigy Mound tradition to have been attenuated (A.D. 900 to A.D. 1100) we find the most vigorous manifestation of the tradition, in a site yielding artifacts exhibiting a richness of types and decorations. The crux of Gibbon's hypothesis is that he did not excavate the earliest Grand River Focus sites and that he did not fully control the Effigy Mound data nor appreciate the extent of the Sanders site. Even with these gaps, his hypothesis must be tested against the evidence to be presented below for the Late Effigy Mound period.

LATE EFFIGY MOUND (A.D. 1100 TO A.D. 1642)

There is a series of Effigy Mound culture sites which are camp, village, or mound locations or sites which contained Effigy Mound artifacts and which date from the Late Effigy Mound period. One of the more important locations is the Mero site (Mason, 1966) of Door County (Fig. 1) which had a Middle Woodland component (North Bay culture) which is dated at A.D. 160 ± 100 (I-888) by Mason (1966:125). The North Bay culture is believed to be the predecessor of the Late Woodland Heins Creek component present at the Mero site. By extension from the Heins Creek site, Mason dates this component at A.D. 720 ± 150 placing it within the Middle Effigy Mound period rather than Late Effigy Mound. However, it is included here for reasons given below. The Heins Creek component yielded ceramic and lithic artifacts of the following categories: Heins Creek Cord-marked, Heins Creek Corded Stamped, Heins Creek Cord-wrapped Stick, Point Sauble Collared, Madison Cord Impressed, Madison Plain, Hahn Cord Impressed, fabric impressed sherds, and Triangular projectile points.

I have suggested in this chapter that Heins Creek wares may be representative of a separate northern Wisconsin Late Woodland culture which developed out of the North Bay culture or a previously unrecognized ware which can not be associated with the Effigy Mound tradition. Mason has suggested that Heins Creek wares antedate cord-impressed types and we have seen that this assumption is not valid for the region south of the Tension Zone. It may be that further work in northern Wisconsin will close the North Bay-Heins Creek chronological gap (A.D. 160 to A.D. 720), extending Heins Creek back to circa A.D. 400 to 500. If the Heins Creek site and the Heins Creek component at the Mero site represent a separate Late Woodland culture, then it was interacting with the Effigy Mound culture. My inspection of the Heins Creek ceramics leads me to favor this interpretation even though I have tentatively placed one of the ceramic types (Heins Creek Corded

Stamped) within the Madison Ware category. The Heins Creek radiocarbon date (I-678) is not sufficient (no single date is) to give the full temporal range of this proposed culture. The component at the Mero site may date later than the Heins Creek date indicates. The proposed Heins Creek culture did interact with the Effigy Mound tradition during the middle period of that tradition and it probably continued to do so during the late part of the tradition. Mason's excavations document a northeastern distribution of Madison Ware types and Triangular points which had only been hinted at in Freeman's report (1956) on the Point Sauble site. The status of the Heins Creek complex is critical to our understanding of what was to occur next at the Mero site.

The Mero I Complex yielded grit-tempered Oneota ceramics which were then replaced by shell-tempered Oneota ceramics of the Mero II Complex. Mason saw Mero I and II as sequential regional expressions of the Grand River Focus and dated the total Mero Complex at circa A.D. 1200 to A.D. 1400 (1966:186). This temporal estimate resulted from his summary view and statement that:

> The picture emerging . . . on the peninsula is one of replacement in the second of the two millennia A.D. of the resident Woodland cultures by others of Upper Mississippian (Oneota) affiliation . . . one wonders why, after approximately fifteen hunderd years of residence, the Woodland cultures on the peninsula were seemingly so suddenly and completely replaced by a Mississippian culture when there is no evidence, particularly locally, of a technologically superior adaptation to the environment on the part of newcomers (1966:193-194).

Mason wondered what happened to the resident Woodland cultures and I would suggest that the Mero I Complex holds the answer: it may not be an example of culture replacement, as suggested by Mason, nor acculturation, as Gibbon would advocate, but seemingly a sui generis in situ example of culture change of the Mero I into the later Mero II Complex. McKern noted (1945:163) that the Green Bay area appeared to have a separate and distinct Upper Mississippian manifestation and he suggested that it, along with the manifestation in the vicinity of Lake Koshkonong, might rate separate foci classifications. Instead of displacement or annihilation of the resident Woodland peoples and their culture could not the culture of the Late Woodland peoples (Heins Creek complex?) have evolved into the Mero I Complex? Mason has suggested that the Mero Complex should date sometime between A.D. 1200 and A.D. 1400 and I would suggest that both dates need to be supported by radiocarbon assessments.

If a northern Wisconsin locus for the Late Woodland base of the emerging Oneota tradition is to be proved correct, other sites similar to Mero need to be found and excavated. Recently David Brose (1968) has supplied us with a site somewhat like Mero, but the Backlund Mound Group is from Menominee County, Michigan. This mound group (20-Me-2) consisted of eight conical mounds, of which three were excavated and Brose considered the mound fill to have been derived from a nearby midden. Mound 4 yielded sherds, a celt fragment, a copper awl, and a Triangular projectile point (1968:37). Mound 8 had a sub-mound pit which was sterile and the mound fill yielded sherds and faunal remains. Mound 5 contained a cluster of limestone rocks and charcoal (Feature 2) and a small feature (Feature 1). Feature 1 yielded fragments of a child burial, an adult female primary burial; a worked deer bone; a copper point similar to Wittry's Group 1, type E (Wittry, 1957:214); sherds; and charcoal flecks. Feature 2 yielded a multiple secondary burial of 26 individuals, a skull of a Red-Tailed hawk, sherds, and charcoal. The mound fill produced two bi-polar cores, a Triangular point, and two end scrapers (*ibid.*:38-41). Brose considered the copper point as an accidental inclusion into the mound (*ibid.*:43) and sherds from Feature 1 were found to fit sherds from the other mounds and from surface collections.

Twelve vessels are represented by the sherds recovered and Brose groups them into the following categories: two Grand River Plain (six sherds); three Carcajou Plain (11 sherds); one Carcajou Plain, Grit-tempered variant (two sherds); one Carcajou Curvilinear (one sherd); two vessels similar to Heins Creek Corded Stamped (16 sherds); a Blackduck Brushed vessel (one sherd); and one vessel identified as either Manitoba Horizontal or Heins Creek Cord-wrapped Stick (two sherds) (*ibid.*:43-46). Brose considered these ceramics most related to the Mero Complex and to the Koshkonong Focus and their dates to fall between A.D. 1000-1300. The Oneota and Late Manitoba Focus ceramics were later dated at A.D. 1340 ± 110 (M-1891). The low conical mounds are considered as late in time (circa A.D. 1000 to A.D. 1300) and I would reject this view as conical mounds (with or without effigies) have been presented here in much earlier contexts.

The Backlund site was then considered to be temporally related to "early" Koskonong and Grand River foci: to the Keshena Culture where Brose considered mounds to be earlier because they lacked Oneota ceramics. Brose then postulated a two occupation sequence for the Keshena area on the basis of mounds versus villages (Effigy Mound versus Oneota). The Sanders site village and mounds were contemporary and yet the mounds lacked Oneota vessels so this view of the Keshena Culture may be in error. As the dates for some of the comparison sites are estimates, his age assignments are only broad temporal indicators (1968:48-49). Of importance is the northeastern location of a mound site in Menominee, Michigan with Triangular points; Heins Creek, Grand River, and Carcajou wares and examples of Manitoba Horizontal and Blackduck Brushed ceramics. As Brose stated, "the Bucklund site . . . did not yield any 'pure' Effigy Mound ceramics" (*ibid.*:48) and I would suggest that further investigations in northeastern Wisconsin and the upper peninsula of Michigan will yield further and earlier evidence of Heins Creek Complex—Oneota (Grand River Focus?) relationships. These relationships will be similar to the suggested culture in transition situation represented by the "Green Bay Focus" (Mero I and Mero II). Neither Gibbon, Brose, nor I will be able to resolve this complex problem without further excavations and radiocarbon dates on excavated components (Mero I and Mero II). However, the evidence suggests that the Late Effigy Mound period continued while Oneota was developing.

The next site in this period is the Dietz site (47-Da-12) where 16 pits were excavated and yielded hickory nuts, wood, wild plum seed, a section of a prehistoric corn cob, faunal material, Madison Cord Impressed and Aztalan Collared ceramics (Dietz et al., 1956:1-16). The Dietz site is the only Effigy Mound site in Wisconsin which has produced evidence of maize; the only other Effigy Mound locality with maize was Mound 6 of the Chapman site in Jo Daviess County, Illinois (Bennett, 1945:71). The Dietz site has been recently radiocarbon dated and it was occupied during the late Effigy Mound period, i.e., A.D. 1120 ± 45 (WIS-273), A.D. 1170 ± 50 (WIS-193), and A.D. 1190 ± 60 (WIS-315) (Bender, Bryson, and Baerreis, 1967, 1968*b*, 1969).

To the northwest at the Sorg site in Minnesota, Elden Johnson (1959) excavated a multi-component site consisting of the Middle Woodland Sorg Focus and a Late Woodland component designated as the Nininger Focus. The Nininger Focus component contained Nininger Cord-wrapped Stick Impressed and Madison Plain specimens which were dated at A.D. 1150 ± 200 (M-447). The Nininger Focus was considered by Johnson to be related to the Effigy Mound tradition of Wisconsin (1959:27).

The most important site dating from the Late Effigy Mound period is the Wisconsin site of Aztalan (47-Je-1). This complex village has been subjected to very extensive analysis (Barrett, 1933; Baerreis and Freeman, 1958; Wittry and Baerreis, 1958; Hurley, 1964; Schneider, 1964; Baerreis and Bryson, 1965) and its contribution to our understanding of the Effigy Mound tradition is considerable. The site appears to have been a stockaded village constructed by a group composed of Middle Mississippian peoples and Effigy Mound peoples. The Middle Mississippian ceramics and lithic artifacts include Madison Plain, Madison Cord Impressed, and Aztalan Collared ceramics. The range of dates for this village is from A.D. 750 to A.D. 1630 (Table 48) and I would reject the A.D. 1630 ± 200 (M-642) date as dating the Mississippian manifestation. Baerreis and Bryson consider the major occupation to have occurred at A.D. 1100 to A.D. 1300.

We have seen from the Bigelow and Sanders sites that these three Madison Ware types date prior to A.D. 1100 and that they are present in Effigy Mound culture contexts during the temporal range of the early Aztalan date, i.e., A.D. 750 ± 150 (M-1037). Directly to the east across the Crawfish River is a series of effigy and conical mounds and directly west of the village was (with some remaining) a long series of effigy and conical mounds. The points which can be made from the data derived from the Aztalan site are as follows: (1) Aztalan was being used prior to A.D. 1100 by both Effigy Mound and Middle Mississippian peoples; (2) Aztalan may represent a hybrid of two distinct cultures; however, the majority of the ceramic artifacts are Effigy Mound; (3) As a culture contact site there is some excellent evidence of trait borrowing and this type of contact situation is similar to the Type A1 form where:

> In an area of more or less homogeneous culture, Culture A, a different culture, Culture B, appears as one or more site-units. Subsequently, the two cultures remain identifiable over a long period of time, but a few types of artifacts and design features characteristic of each culture are found in sites of the other (Lathrap, 1956:9);

(4) If we were to follow Gibbon's hypothesis (1972) the Middle Mississippian peoples should have been in contact with Oneota peoples and not Effigy Mound peoples; (5) As the occupation of Aztalan extends to at least A.D. 1300, this date would be 200 years beyond the date proposed for the acculturation of the Effigy Mound peoples; and (6) Did the Effigy Mound peoples burn Aztalan and drive off the Middle Mississippians? Aztalan is not the only site in Wisconsin to have evidence of both Effigy Mound and

Middle Mississippian peoples—Hall (1967:179) mentioned the Hamilton-Brooks site in Green Lake County where Old Village wares and Aztalan Collared ceramics were excavated. In this same report Hall, like Gibbon, sees the Woodland peoples in the Mississippi Valley after A.D. 800 developing toward a Mississippian way of life (1967:180). If this is true, there should be *no* Effigy Mound culture sites after A.D. 1100 to A.D. 1200.

There are, however, several other open and mound sites which are suggested as dating from the Late Effigy Mound period. The James Island site (Fig. 1) was recently reported by Mason and this multi-component unstratified site yielded evidence of Middle Woodland, Late Woodland, and Oneota occupations. Thirty-six sherds representing 14 vessels have dentate stamping, rocked dentate, simple stab-and-drag, and incised over cord-marked or incised over plain decorations. The latter two decoration forms appear to be Dane Incised ceramics and I would remove them from the Middle Woodland component. The Late Woodland component yielded 3,481 sherds representing 61 Madison Ware vessels and the Oneota component was represented by 117 shell-tempered sherds belonging to three vessels. Fourteen Triangular points were assigned to the Late Woodland and/or the Oneota component (1968:67-70). The Late Woodland and Oneota components at this site have not been dated; they may date from either the Middle or Late Effigy Mound period and the site location may serve as an important link between the Sanders site and the Effigy Mound artifacts from the Door Peninsula.

Brose (1968:49) saw two occupations making up the Keshena Culture: a mound building Effigy Mound occupation and a later Oneota village site occupation. This cultural dichotomy proposed a mound versus village temporal division which I have suggested is not a valid division. There is, however, a later phase of occupation reported by Barrett and Skinner. The Big Eddy site (in the present Menominee County) is adjacent to the Big Eddy falls on the Wolf River (Barrett and Skinner, 1932:475-479). Excavations in this very rich fishing site midden yielded thousands of bone fragments, sherds, lithic and copper artifacts, plus historic Menominee artifacts. The deposit was no more than six inches deep and of the thousands of sherds recovered only a few are identified as shell-tempered Oneota examples. The ceramics illustrated for the Big Eddy site (1932:Pl. XCVI:7-15) appear to include Madison Fabric Impressed, Madison Punctuated, and Point Sauble Collared Madison Ware types as well as ceramics with incised and punctated designs which I would exclude from the Dane Incised or Madison Ware categories. These ceramics appear to be similar to Wittry's Type I pottery from the Bell site in Winnebago County (1963:21-25) which is considered to belong to the Fox Indian culture and to date from A.D. 1680 to A.D. 1730. The multi-component Big Eddy site appears to have been a favorite fishing location for the historic Menominee Indians and it was favored by the prehistoric inhabitants of the area. The illustrated lithic artifacts are quite diverse: there appear to be a Plainview point (1932:Pl. XCV, Spec. No. 300094); Fox River Valley Stemmed points (Ritzenthaler, 1967:21); Monona Stemmed; Waubesa Contracting Stem; and serrated Triangular points, plus drills and scrapers. This open site may date from any time during the Late Effigy Mound period but I would favor a post-A.D. 1200 time on the basis of the ceramics recovered.

The final sites from Menominee County to be considered here are the Five Islands Mound Group and the Five Islands village (Barrett and Skinner, 1932:484-491). The Five Islands Mound Group consisted of three catfish and five hemispherical mounds which yielded primary flexed and disarticulated burials. These mounds were associated with a series of village pits extending along the Wolf River for one-half mile. Sixteen or 18 pits were opened and two yielded Triangular points; the others contained flakes, charcoal, bone, and ceramic fragments. The typical sherds from the Five Islands site (1932:Pl. XCVI:1-6) appear to be Madison Fabric Impressed, Point Sauble Collared, and incised examples more similar to Wittry's Type 1 pottery (1963) than to the Dane Incised Madison Ware type.

It is interesting to note that during the Late Effigy Mound period a large number of sites (Mero, James Island, Big Eddy, and Five Islands) were centered in northeastern Wisconsin and that the remaining three sites to be presented are located in northwestern Wisconsin. In Dunn County at the Wakanda Park Mound Group (47-Dn-1) were 17 conical and oval mounds of which 14 were excavated. Outside of the burials recovered, these mounds yielded fragments of a clay burial mask, incised and punctated ceramics (Angelo Punctated; Hurley, 1966), Madison Cord Impressed, Madison Plain, and an intrusive Mississippian vessel plus an elk antler arm band and copper beads. Mound 16, which contained a Madison Cord Impressed rim sherd, was dated at A.D. 1200 ± 200 (M-814). The absence of effigy-shaped mounds was considered to be due to geographic location and/or temporal position (Wittry, 1959*b*:112). The site was considered as "... close to, if not within, the Effigy Mound culture ..." (1959*b*:112) and I see no reason now to exclude the site from the Effigy Mound tradition.

The Diamond Bluff Mound Group (Maxwell, 1950) contains conical, oval, and a panther mounds adjacent to an Oneota campsite. Excavated conical Mound 4 produced grit- and shell-tempered ceramics and fragments of a Middle Mississippian bowl and an Oneota jar for evidence of a late (A.D. 1200—A.D. 1400) date for the mound's construction. Panther Mound 26 contained a side notched point, a Triangular point, fragments of two Middle Mississippian jars, a small Oneota loop-handled jar, and a shell-tempered bowl fragment. Maxwell considered Mound 26 as a late manifestation of the Effigy Mound culture having Mississippian trade vessels, or that the Oneota culture began much earlier as there were combinations of Oneota and Middle Mississippian elements on the same vessel. I would offer the suggestions that this is a Late Effigy Mound culture site, that there was contact with both Oneota and Middle Mississippians, and that Mound 26 dates from A.D. 1200 to A.D. 1400.

The final Late Effigy Mound period site to be examined here is Indian Mounds Park at Rice Lake reported by Cooper (1959), where 19 round or oval mounds remained out of a total of 51 mounds (1959:1, 9). Cooper excavated a large "double round" mound from which 11 burials were removed and three pits. Burial Pit 1 of Mound 1 yielded eight individuals, worked flakes, an antler tine flaker, beaver teeth, mammal and animal bones, a stone knife, three Triangular projectile points, an elbow pipe, birch bark, sheet copper, twined cedar fabric, turtle shell fragments, a copper tinkler cone, a lead button, and a small steel spring (1959:17-24). The mound fill yielded side notched points, scrapers, a knife, a drill, and ceramics assigned to the type Madison Cord Impressed and to the Blackduck wares of Minnesota. The association of the historic artifacts with the burials was quite certain and Cooper concluded that the mound was constructed by the Dakota Sioux in the seventeenth century (1959:43-48). This mound could have been constructed by Late Effigy Mound peoples (elbow pipe, Triangular points, antler tine flaker, and Madison Cord Impressed) who occupied northwest Wisconsin during the seventeenth century. Movements of tribes from the east into Wisconsin (Swanton, 1952:250-259) created an increase in population density and culture contact situations in eastern Wisconsin while northwestern Wisconsin apparently remained unaffected well into the eighteeenth century (Hurley, 1963).

Throughout this assessment of the Effigy Mound tradition we have seen a culture with a generalized economic base centered around hunting, fishing, and gathering or a subsistence pattern which allowed for the exploitation of various resources. This generalized economic base with its near absence of maize horticulture should not be viewed as a weakness: it enabled the Effigy Mound peoples to readily adapt to changing local conditions or new areas and to be independent of one food resource. Wild rice, deer, buffalo, ducks, fish, limited beans and maize and other floral and faunal resources permitted the Dakota Sioux to adapt to the changing conditions during the early Historic period (Hurley, 1963). The lack of beans or extensive maize horticulture did not bring about the proposed demise of the Effigy Mound tradition.

The Effigy Mound tradition from circa A.D. 300 to A.D. 1642 interacted with many other cultures while retaining its own cultural identity. There were contacts with Hopewellian, North Bay, Nakomis, and Heins Creek cultures and the Waukesha, Green Bay (Mero I and Mero II), Grand River, Koshkonong, Lake Winnebago, Nininger, and Orr foci. The concept of the Effigy Mound tradition providing the metamorphic base for the emerging Oneota tradition cannot be demonstrated. I consider the Effigy Mound tradition as quite viable and not attenuated during the time proposed (A.D. 900 to A.D. 1100) for this transformation. Too little is known of northern Wisconsin to eliminate the possibility of earlier Oneota sites being found north of the Tension Zone as well as Late Effigy Mound culture sites.

The material culture associated with this tradition has allowed for an assessment of the growth and development of the Effigy Mound culture. Many facets of this culture tradition still need to be explored. The distribution of various effigy-shaped mounds (bird, panther, or bear) might indicate band territories. A very large number of Effigy Mound burials have been excavated and the majority of them reside unstudied in the Milwaukee Public Museum. Radiocarbon assessments need to be made on samples from excavated sites and some sites—Nitschke, Big Eddy, and Diamond Bluff—need to be re-investigated. The current research of Mason and Salzer in northern Wisconsin has indicated that this area was as extensively occupied as southern Wisconsin and yet both areas are still imperfectly known. The historic tribal end product of this 1,300 year tradition remains the major unresolved problem of the Effigy Mound tradition. Such anthropologists as Radin, McKern, Rowe, and Gibbon have offered their candidates and I will offer none. Until direct historic archaeology is conducted in all areas of northern Wisconsin, any suggestion offered here would lack the much needed scientific proof.

BIBLIOGRAPHY

Baerreis, David A.

1949 Some Comments on Trait Lists and the Hopewell Culture. The Wisconsin Archeologist, Vol. 30, No. 4, pp. 65-73.

1952 Pottery Type Descriptions. Paper presented at a conference of the Wisconsin Archaeological Survey held on the Madison Campus of the University of Wisconsin, November 15, 1952.

1953*a* The Blackhawk Village Site, (Da 5) Dane County, Wisconsin. Journal of the Iowa Archaeological Society, Vol. 2, No. 4, pp. 5-20.

1953*b* The Airport Village Site, Dane County. The Wisconsin Archeologist, Vol. 34, No. 3, pp. 149-164.

1954 Further Information on the Frost Woods Mound Group. The Wisconsin Archeologist, Vol. 35, No. 2, pp. 43-49.

1958 Review of Chandler W. Rowe's: The Effigy Mound Culture of Wisconsin. American Antiquity, Vol. 23, No. 3, pp. 320-321.

1963 Review of Roger B. Parsons': Indian Mounds of Northeast Iowa as Soil Genesis Benchmarks. The Wisconsin Archeologist, Vol. 44, No. 1, pp. 79-82.

1966 Early Salvage Excavations in the Madison Area, Dane County, Wisconsin. The Wisconsin Archeologist, Vol. 47, No. 3, pp. 101-131.

1968 Review of: Hopewell and Woodland Site Archaeology in Illinois. The Wisconsin Archeologist, Vol. 49, No. 3:138-146.

Baerreis, David A. and Reid A. Bryson

1965 Climatic Episodes and the Dating of the Mississippian Cultures. The Wisconsin Archeologist, Vol. 46, No. 4, pp. 203-220.

Baerreis, David A. and Joan E. Freeman

1958 Late Woodland Pottery in Wisconsin as Seen from Aztalan, The Wisconsin Archeologist, Vol. 39, No. 1, pp. 35-61.

Bakken, Charlotte T.

1950 Preliminary Investigations at the Outlet Site. The Wisconsin Archeologist, Vol. 31, No. 2, pp. 43-70.

Barrett, S. A.

1933 Ancient Aztalan. Bulletin of the Public Museum of the City of Milwaukee, Vol. XIII.

Barrett, S. A. and E. W. Hawkes

1919 The Kratz Creek Mound Group. Bulletin of the Public Museum of the City of Milwaukee, Vol. III, No. 1.

Barrett, S. A. and Alanson Skinner
1932 Certain Mounds and Village Sites of Shawano and Oconto Counties, Wisconsin. Bulletin of the Public Museum of the City of Milwaukee, Vol. X, No. 5.

Bastian, Tyler
1958 The Beliot College Mound Group—A Preliminary Report. The Wisconsin Archaeologist, Vol. 39, No. 3, pp. 155-173.
1962 Some Additional Data on the Beloit College Mound Group. The Wisconsin Archeologist, Vol. 43, No. 3, pp. 57-64.

Baum, B. R. and L. P. Lefbovitch
1972*a* A model for cultivar classification and identification with reference to oats (avena). I. Establishment of the groupings by taximetric methods. Canadian Journal of Botany, Vol. 50:121-130.
1972*b* A model for cultivar classification and identification with reference to oats (avena). II. A Probabilistic definition of cultivar groupings and their Bayesian identification. Canadian Journal of Botany, Vol. 50:131-138.

Beaubien, Paul L.
1953*a* Some Hopewellian Mounds at the Effigy Mounds National Moument, Iowa. The Wisconsin Archeologist, Vol. 34, No. 2, pp. 125-138.
1953*b* Cultural Variation within Two Woodland Mound Groups of Northeastern Iowa. American Antiquity, Vol. 19, No. 1, pp. 56-66.

Bender, Margaret M., Reid A. Bryson, and David A. Baerreis
1966 University of Wisconsin Radiocarbon Dates II. Radiocarbon, Vol. 8, pp. 522-533.
1967 University of Wisconsin Radiocarbon Dates III. Radiocarbon, Vol. 9, pp. 530-544.
1968*a* University of Wisconsin Radiocarbon Dates IV. Radiocarbon, Vol. 10, No. 1, pp. 161-168.
1968*b* University of Wisconsin Radiocarbon Dates V. Radiocarbon, Vol. 10, No. 2, pp. 473-478.
1969 University of Wisconsin Radiocarbon Dates VI. Radiocarbon, Vol. 11, No. 1, pp. 228-235.
1970 University of Wisconsin Radiocarbon Dates VII. Radiocarbon, Vol. 12, No. 1
1971 University of Wisconsin Radiocarbon Dates VIII. Radiocarbon, Vol. 13, No. 2.

Bennett, John W.
1945 Archaeological Explorations in Jo Daviess County, Illinois. The University of Chicago Press.
1952 The Prehistory of the Northern Mississippi Valley. *In*: Archaeology of Eastern United States, ed. James B. Griffin, University of Chicago Press, pp. 108-123.

Berger, K. C.
1960 The Vinylite Resin Method of Taking and Mounting Soil Profiles. Contribution from the Department of Soils, University of Wisconsin (Mimeo.).

Berger, K. C. and R. J. Muckenhirn
1945 Soil Profiles of Natural Appearance Mounted with Vinylite Resin. Proceedings of the Soil Science Society of America. Vol. 10, pp. 368-370.

Black, Robert F.
1964 The Physical Geography of Wisconsin. The 1964 Wisconsin Blue Book, pp. 171-177.

Blake, Bradley
1961 Portage County Site Report. The Wisconsin Archeologist, Vol. 42, No. 2, pp. 57-77.

Bonney, Rachel
1965 Evidence for Early Woodland Occupations in Southwestern Minnesota. The Minnesota Archaeologist, Vol. 27, No. 1, pp. 2-48.

Brose, David S.
1968 The Backlund Mound Group. The Wisconsin Archeologist, Vol. 49, No. 1, pp. 34-51.
1970 The Archaeology of Summer Island: Changing Settlement Systems in Northern Lake Michigan. Museum of Anthropology, University of Michigan, Anthropological Papers 41.

Brown, C. E.
1906 A Record of Wisconsin Antiquities. The Wisconsin Archeologist, Vol. 5, Nos. 3 and 4, pp. 289-429.

Bryson, Reid A. and Wayne M. Wendland
1967 Tentative Climatic Patterns for some Late Glacial and Post-Glacial Episodes in Central North America. *In*: Life, Land, and Water, ed. W. J. Mayer-Oakes. Proceedings of the 1966 Conference on Environmental Studies of the Glacial Lake Agassiz Region. University of Manitoba Press, pp. 271-298.

Buckley, James D., Milton A. Trautman, and Eric H. Willis
1968 Isotopes' Radiocarbon Measurements VI. Radiocarbon, Vol. 10, No. 2, pp. 246-294.

Butzer, Karl W.
1964 Environment and Archeology: An Introduction to Pleistocene Geography. Aldine Publishing Co.

Caldwell, Joseph R.
1958 Trend and Tradition in the Prehistory of the Eastern United States. Memoirs of the American Anthropological Association, No. 88.

Caldwell, Joseph R. and Robert L. Hall (editors)
1964 Hopewellian Studies. Illinois State Museum, Scientific Papers, Vol. 12, No. 3.

Clarke, David L.
1968 Analytical Archaeology. Methuen & Co. Ltd. London.

Coe, Michael D.
1961 La Victoria: An Early Site on the Pacific Coast of Guatemala. Papers of the Peabody Museum of Archaeology and Ethnology, Harvard University, Vol. LIII.

Cole, Fay-Cooper and Thorne Deuel
1937 Rediscovering Illinois. University of Chicago Press.

Collie, G. L. and R. H. Becker
1912 Researches in Wood and Portage Counties. The Wisconsin Archeologist, Vol. II, No. 2. pp. 39-65.

Cooper, Leland
1959 Indians Mounds Park, Archaeological Site, Rice Lake, Wisconsin. Science Bulletin No. 6 the Science Museum of the St. Paul Institute, St. Paul, Minnesota.

Cowgill, George L.
1968 Archaeological Applications of Factor, Cluster, and Proximity Analyses. American Antiquity, Vol. 33, No. 3: 367-375.

Crane, H. R. and J. B. Griffin
1958 University of Michigan Radiocarbon Dates II. Science, Vol. 127, No. 3306, pp. 1098-1105.
1961 University of Michigan Radiocarbon Dates VI. Radiocarbon, Vol. 3, pp. 105-125.
1965 University of Michigan Radiocarbon Dates X. Radiocarbon, Vol. 7, pp. 123-152.
1970 University of Michigan Radiocarbon Dates XIII. Radiocarbon, Vol. 12, No. 1: 161-180.

Cummings, Patricia and Michael Mitchell
1968 Incising and Trailing. MSS. on file in Department of Anthropology, University of Toronto, pp. 1-6.

Curtis, John T.
1959 The Vegetation of Wisconsin. An Ordination of Plant Communities. The University of Wisconsin Press.

Deetz, James
1962 A Non-typological Approach to the Analysis of Archaeological Materials. Paper read at the American Anthropological Association Meetings, Chicago, November 17.
1965 The Dynamics of Stylistic Change in Arikara Ceramics. University of Illinois Studies in Anthropology, No. 4.

Dietz, E. F., David A. Baerreis, Robert Nero and Hugh C. Cutler
1956 A Report on the Dietz Dite, Dane County, Wisconsin. The Wisconsin Archeologist, Vol. 37, No. 1, pp. 1-19.

Dixon, George I., Bradley A. Blake, and Patricia Scribner
1956 Bigelow-Hamilton Site "I." The Wisconsin Archeologist, Vol. 37, No. 3, pp. 65-72.

Douglass, John M.
1946 Textile Imprints on Wisconsin Indian Pottery. The Wisconsin Archeologist, Vol. 27, No. 3, pp. 71-80.

Dumond, D. E.
1963 A Practical Field Method for the Preservation of Soil Profiles from Archaeological Cuts. American Antiquity, Vol. 29, No. 1, pp. 116-118.

Durrenberger, E. Paul
1965 Anderson's Mill (41-TU-130): A Historic Site in Travis County Texas. Bulletin of the Texas Archeological Society, Vol. 36, pp. 1-69.

Emerson, J. Norman
1968 Understanding Iroquois Pottery in Ontario: A Rethinking. The Ontario Archaeological Society, Special Publication, pp. 1-32.

Emery, Irene
1952 Naming the Direction of the Twist in Yarn and Cordage. El Palacio, Vol. 59, No. 8, pp. 251-262.
1966 The Primary Structures of Fabrics. The Textile Museum, Washington, D.C.

Evans, Clifford
1955 A Ceramic Study of Virginia Archaeology. Bureau of American Ethnology, Bulletin 160, Washington, D.C.

Evans, G. Edward
1961 Ceramic Analysis of the Blackduck Ware and Its General Cultural Relationships. The Minnesota Academy of Science, Proceedings, Vol. 29, pp. 33-54.

Fitting, James E. (ed.)
1966 Edge Area Archaeology. The Michigan Archaeologist, Vol. 12, No. 4.

Ford, James A. and Clarence H. Webb
1956 Poverty Point, A Late Archaic Site in Louisiana. Anthropological Papers of the American Museum of Natural History, Vol. 46, Part 1.

Freeman, Joan E.
1956 An Analysis of the Point Sauble and Beaumier Farm Sites. Unpublished Masters Thesis. University of Wisconsin.
1969 The Millville Site, A Middle Woodland Village in Grant County, Wisconsin. The Wisconsin Archeologist, Vol. 50, No. 2, pp. 37-88.

Frye, J. C., H. B. Willman, and R. F. Black
1964 Outline of Glacial Geology of Illinois and Wisconsin. *In*: The Quaternary of the United States. A Review Volume for the VII Congress of the International Association For Quaternary Research, Princeton University Press, pp. 43-61.

Gibbon, Guy
1966 The Midway Village Site, an Intra-site Analysis. Unpublished Masters Thesis. University of Wisconsin.
1969 Cultural Dynamics and Development of Oneota Life-way in Wisconsin: An Hypothesis. A paper presented to the 34th Annual Meeting of the Society for American Archaeology, May 1-3.
1970*a* A Brief History of Oneota Research in Wisconsin. Wisconsin Magazine of History 53, No. 4, Madison: State Historical Society of Wisconsin.
1970*b* The Midway Village Site: An Orr Phase Oneota Site in the Upper Mississippi Valley. The Wisconsin Archeologist, Vol. 51, No. 3, September: 79-162.
1971 The Bornick Site: A Grand River Phase Site in Marquette County: The Wisconsin Archeologist, Vol. 52, No. 3, September: 85-137.
1972 Cultural Dynamics and the Development of the Oneota Life-Way in Wisconsin. American Antiquity, Vol. 37, No. 2; April: 156-185.

Gordon, Garland J.
1965 Excavation at Effigy Mounds National Moument. Newsletter, Iowa Archeological Society, No. 37, p. 1.

Griffin, James B.
1943 The Fort Ancient Aspect. University of Michigan Press. Ann Arbor. (Reprinted in 1966).
1952*b* Some Early and Middle Woodland Types in Illinois. *In:* Hopewellian Communities in Illinois ed. Thorne Deuel, Illinois State Museum, Scientific Papers, Vol. V, pp. 95-129.
1958 The Chronological Position of the Hopewellian Culture in the Eastern United States. Anthropological Papers, Museum of Anthropology, University of Michigan, No. 12.

1960*a* Climatic Change: A Contributory Cause of the Growth and Decline of Northern Hopewellian Culture. The Wisconsin Archeologist, Vol. 41, No. 2, pp. 21-33.

1960*b* An Hypothesis for the Prehistory of the Winnebago. *In*: Culture in History: Essays in Honor of Paul Radin, ed. Stanley Diamond. Columbia University Press, pp. 809-865.

1964*a* Review of William C. McKern's: The Clam River Focus. The Wisconsin Archeologist, Vol. 45, No. 2, pp. 104-111.

1964*b* The Northeast Woodlands Area. *In*: Prehistoric Man in the New World, ed. Jesse D. Jennings and Edward Norbeck. University of Chicago Press, pp. 223-258.

1965 Late Quaternary Prehistory in the Northeastern Woodlands. *In*: The Quarternary of the United States, ed. H. E. Wright, Jr. and David G. Frey, pp. 655-667.

1966 The Fort Ancient Aspect. University of Michigan, Museum of Anthropology, Anthropological Papers, No. 28.

Griffin, James B., (ed.)

1952*a* Archeology of Eastern United States. The University of Chicago Press, Chicago.

Haag, William G. and Clarence H. Webb

1953 Microblades at Poverty Point Sites. American Antiquity, Vol. 18, No. 3, pp. 245-248.

Hall, Robert L.

1950 A Style Analysis of Wisconsin Woodland Pottery. The Wisconsin Archeologist, Vol. 31, No. 1, pp. 1-42.

1958 Commentary on Carcajou Carbon 14 Dates: the Wisconsin Archeologist, Vol. 39, No. 3: 175-176.

1962 The Archeology of Carcajou Point: With an Interpretation of the Development of Oneota Culture in Wisconsin, 2 Vols. The University of Wisconsin Press.

1967 The Mississippian Heartland and its Plains Relationships. The Plains Anthropologist, Vol. 12, No. 36, pp. 175-183.

Harris, R. K., Inus Marie Harris, Jay C. Blaine, and Jerrylee Blaine

1965 A Preliminary Archaeological and Documentary Study of the Wormak Site, Lamor County, Texas. Bulletin of The Texas Archeological Society, Vol. 36, pp. 270-363.

Henning, Dale R.

1961 Oneota Ceramics in Iowa. Journal of the Iowa Archaeological Society, Vol. 11, No. 2, Iowa City.

1970 Development and Interrelationships of Oneota Culture in the Lower Missouri River Valley. The Missouri Archaeologist, Vol. 32, December: 1-180.

Holmes, W. H.

1884 Prehistoric Textile Fabrics of the United States. Bureau of American Ethnology, Vol. 3, pp. 393-425.

1886 Ancient Pottery of the Mississippi Valley. Bureau of American Ethnology, Fourth Annual Report, 1882-1883. Washington, D.C.

1888 A Study of the Textile Art in its Relation of the Development of Form and Ornament. Bureau of American Ethnology, Vol. 6, pp. 189-252.

1896 Prehistoric Textile Art of the Eastern United States. Bureau of American Ethnology, Vol. 13, pp. 3-46.

1903 Aboriginal Pottery of the Eastern United States. Bureau of American Ethnology, Twentieth Annual Report, 1898-1899, Accompanying Paper, pp. 1-237.

Horn, M. E.
1960 A Pedological Study of Red Clay Soils and their Parent Materials in Eastern Wisconsin. Ph.D. thesis on file, Department of Soils, University of Wisconsin, p. 238.

Hurley, William M.
1963 An Economic Interpretation of the Santee Sioux Occupation of Wisconsin. MSS. on file at the Department of Anthropology, University of Wisconsin, pp. 1-21.
1964 The Recent Aztalan Date. The Wisconsin Archeologist, Vol. 45, No. 3, pp. 139-142.
1966 The Silver Creek Sites (47-Mo-1 to Mo-5): A complex of five Woodland site locations in Monroe County, Wisconsin. M.S. thesis, University of Wisconsin, Madison.
1968*a* Cord Twist; A Patterned Decorative Ceramic Attribute: North American and Japanese Methodology. Paper presented for the symposium, Prehistoric Cultural Relations in Northern Eurasia and Northern North America, at the VIII International Congress of Anthropological and Ethnological Sciences, Tokyo, Japan.
1968*b* Kickapoo Whistle System: A Speech Surrogate. Plains Anthropologist, Vol. 13-41, pp. 242-247.
1970*a* The Wisconsin Effigy Mound Tradition. Paper Presented to the XXXV Annual Meeting of the Society for American Archaeology, Mexico City, May 1: 1-16.
1970*b* The Wisconsin Effigy Mound Tradition. Ph.D. Thesis, Department of Anthropology, University of Wisconsin, Madison: 1-1059.
1971 Rates of Soil Development at Two Wisconsin Effigy Mound Sites. Prehistoric Investigations, No. 3, University of Iowa Department of Publications, Iowa City: 66-79.
1972 A Proposed Ceramic Analysis Class and Attribute List for the Northeast. Presented to the Computer Archaeology Conference Waterloo, Ontario, April 29, 1972: 1-65.
Mss.A Culture Contact: Effigy Mound and Oneota: to be published by the Minnesota Historical Society.
Mss.B Coding and Cluster Analysis of Wisconsin Ceramics. Paper accepted for the IX International Congress of Anthropological and Ethnological Sciences, August-September, 1973, Chicago.
n.d. Excavations at Aztalan State Park. (Manuscript in preparation).

Hurley, William M. and Norman E. Wagner
1972 Ceramic Analysis: A Class and Attribute List for the Northeast. Anthropological Series No. 13, Dept. of Anthropology, University of Toronto, Toronto.

Ives, John C.
1962 Mill Creek Pottery. Journal of the Iowa Archeological Society, Vol. 11, No. 3, March.

James, William R.
1966 Some Aspects of Pollen Research in the Vicinity of Effigy Mounds National Monument, McGregor, Iowa. MSS. on file at the Effigy Mounds National Monument.

Jeske, John A.
1927 The Grand River Mound Group and Camp Site. Bulletin of the Public Museum of the City of Milwaukee, Vol. III, No. 2, pp. 139-214.

Johnson, Elden
1959 Spring Lake Archaeology: the Sorg Site. Science Bulletin No. 3, Part 3, the Science Museum of the St. Paul Institute, St. Paul, Minnesota.
1964 Twenty New Radiocarbon Dates from Minnesota Archeological Sites. Minnesota Archaeologist, Vol. 26, No. 2, pp. 34-49.

Johnson, Thorley
1949 The Armstrong Site, an Upper Mississippi Site at Pepin, Wisconsin, The Wisconsin Archeologist, Vol. 30, No. 4: 79-86.

Keslin, Richard O.
1958 A Preliminary Report of the Hahn and Horicon Sites, Dodge County, Wisconsin. The Wisconsin Archeologist, Vol. 39, No. 4, pp. 191-273.

Keyes, Charles R.
1927 Prehistoric Man in Iowa. The Palimpsest, Vol. 8, No. 6: 185-229.
1929 Some Methods and Results of the Iowa Archeological Survey. The Wisconsin Archeologist, N.S., Vol. 8: 135-143.

Knudson, Ruth A.
1967 Cambria Village Ceramics. Plains Anthropologist, Vol. 12, No. 37:247-299.

Koeppler, Paul
1961 The Pipe Site. The Wisconsin Archeologist, Vol. 42, No. 4, pp. 174-177.

Krieger, Alex
1944 The Typological Concept. American Antiquity, Vol. 9, No. 3: 271-288.

Lange, Frederick W.
1969 The Bigelow Site (47-Pt-29) Portage County, Wisconsin. The Wisconsin Archeologist, Vol. 50, No. 4, pp. 215-255.

Lapham, I. A.
1855 The Antiquities of Wisconsin, as Surveyed and Described. Smithsonian Contributions to Knowledge, Smithsonian Institution.

Lathrap, Donald W. (ed.)
1956 An Archaeological Classification of Culture Contact Situations. *In*: Seminars in Archaeology: 1955, ed. Robert Wauchope. Memoirs of the Society for American Archaeology, No. 11, pp. 3-30.

Lewis, T. H.
1890 Macalester College Contributions No. 6.

Lewis, Thomas M. N. and Madeline Kneberg
1946 Hiwassee Island. University of Tennessee Press, Knoxville, Tennessee.

Logan, Wilfred D.
1953 Archaeological Investigation of Spike Hollow Rock Shelter, Allamakee County Iowa. Journal of the Iowa Archeological Society, No. 2, Nos. 2 and 3, pp. 4-30.
1958 Analysis of Woodland Complexes in Northeastern Iowa. Ph.D. thesis, University of Michigan.

Loy, James D.
1968 A Comparative Style Analysis of Havana Series Pottery from two Illinois Valley Sites. *In*: Hopewell and Woodland Site Archaeology in Illinois. Bulletin 6, Illinois Archaeological Survey, University of Illinois, Urbana.

Lurie, Nancy Oestreich
1960 Winnebago Protohistory. *In*: Culture in History: Essays in Honor of Paul Radin, ed. Stanley Diamond. Columbia University Press, pp. 790-808.

McKusick, Marshall
1971*a* Oneota Longhouses. *In*: Prehistoric Investigations, ed. M. McKusick. Report No. 3, Office of the State Archaeologist, the University of Iowa, Iowa City: 86-93.
1971*b* The Grant Oneota Village. Report No. 4, Office of the State Archaeologist, The University of Iowa, Iowa City.

MacNeish, Richard S.
1958 An Introduction to the Archaeology of Southeast Manitoba. National Museum of Canada, Bulletin No. 157, Anthropological Series No. 44.

Maher, Robert F. and David A. Baerreis
1958 The Aztalan Lithic Complex. *In*: Aztalan: Exploration and Reconstruction, ed. Robert Ritzenthaler. The Wisconsin Archeologist, Vol. 39, No. 1, pp. 5-35.

Martin, Lawrence
1916 The Physical Geography of Wisconsin. Wisconsin Geological and Natural History Survey, Bulletin No. XXXVI, Educational Series No. 4.
1965 The Physical Geography of Wisconsin. University of Wisconsin Press, Madison.

Mason, Carol
1964 An Early Woodland Vessel from Wisconsin. The Wisconsin Archeologist, Vol. 45, No. 4, pp. 158-160.

Mason, Ronald J.
1966 Two Stratified Sites on the Door Peninsula of Wisconsin. Anthropological Papers, Museum of Anthropology, University of Michigan, No. 26, Ann Arbor.
1968 Fox Valley Archaeology: James Island Site. The Wisconsin Archeologist, Vol. 49, No. 2, pp. 57-75.

Maxwell, Moreau S.
1950 A Change in the Interpretation of Wisconsin's Prehistory. Wisconsin Magazine of History, Vol. 33, No. 4, Madison.

McKern, W. C.
1928 The Neale and McClaughry Mound Groups. Bulletin of the Public Museum of Milwaukee, Vol. III, No. 3.
1929*a* Regarding the Origin of Wisconsin Effigy Mounds. American Anthropologist, Vol. 31, No. 3, pp. 562-564.
1929*b* A Hopewell Type of Culture in Wisconsin. American Anthropologist, Vol. 31, No. 2, pp. 307-312.
1930 The Kletzien and Nitschke Mound Groups. Bulletin of the Public Museum of Milwaukee, Vol. III No. 4.
1931 A Wisconsin Variant of the Hopewell Culture. Bulletin of the Public Museum of Milwaukee, Vol. X, No. 2.
1935 Notes and News. American Antiquity, Vol. 1, No. 2, pp. 157-158.

1939 The Midwest Taxonomic as an Aid to Archaeological Study. American Antiquity, 4, No. 4: 301-13.

1942 The First Settlers of Wisconsin. Wisconsin Magazine of History, pp. 153-169.

1945 Preliminary Report of the Upper Mississippi Phase in Wisconsin. Milwaukee Public Museum Bulletin, Vol. 16, No. 3: 109-285.

1958 Comments on the Review of the Effigy Mound Culture in Wisconsin. American Antiquity, Vol. 24, No. 2, pp. 191-192.

1963 The Clam River Focus. Milwaukee Public Museum Publications in Anthropology No. 9, Milwaukee.

McKern, W. C. and R. E. Ritzenthaler

1949 Trait Lists of the Effigy Mound Aspect. The Wisconsin Archeologist, Vol. 30, No. 2, pp. 39-48.

McPherron, Alan

1967 The Juntunen Site and the Late Woodland Prehistory of the Upper Great Lakes Area. Anthropological Papers, No. 30, Museum of Anthropology, University of Michigan, Ann Arbor, Michigan.

Meggers, Betty J. (ed.)

1956 Functional and Evolutional Implications of Community Patterning. *In*: Seminars in Archaeology: 1955, ed. Robert Wauchope. Memoirs of the Society for American Archaeology, No. 11, pp. 129-157.

Miner, Horace

1936 The Importance of Textiles in the Archaeology of the Eastern United States. American Antiquity, Vol. 1, No. 3, pp. 181-192.

Movious, Hallam L. Jr., Nicholas C. David, Harvey M. Bricker, and R. Berle Clay

1968 The Analysis of Certain Major Classes of Upper Palaeolithic Tools. American School of Prehistoric Research, Peabody Museum, Harvard University, Bulletin No. 26.

Nash, Philleo

1933 The Excavation of the Ross Mound Group 1. Bulletin of the Public Museum of the City of Milwaukee, Vol. XVI, No. 1.

Nero, Robert

1948 Primary Flake Implements. The Wisconsin Archeologist, Vol. 29, No. 2, pp. 23-28.

Niehoff, Arthur

1956 The Prawatschke Mound Group, a Woodland Burial Complex. The Wisconsin Archaeologist, Vol. 37, No. 3, pp. 87-94.

Osborne, Douglas and Carolyn Osborne

1954 Twines and Terminologies. American Anthropologist, Vol. 56, pp. 1093-1101.

Parsons, Roger B.

1962 Indian Mounds of Northeast Iowa as Soil Genesis Benchmarks. Journal of the Iowa Archaeological Society, Vol. 12, No. 2.

Peske, G. Richard

1966 Oneota Settlement Patterns and Agricultural Patterns in Winnebago County. The Wisconsin Archeologist, Vol. 47, No. 4, pp. 188-195.

Porter, James Warren

1964 Thin Section Descriptions of some Shell Tempered Prehistoric Ceramics from the American Bottoms. Research Report No. 7, Southern Illinois University Museum Lithic Laboratory, pp. 1-26.

Quimby, George I.
1960 Indian Life in the Upper Great Lakes. University of Chicago Press.
1961 Cord Marking versus Fabric Impressing of Woodland Pottery. American Antiquity, Vol. 26, No. 3, pp. 426-428.

Rachlin, Carol
1955 The Rubber Mold Technique for the Study of Textile-Impressed Pottery. American Antiquity, Vol. 20, No. 4, pp. 394-396.

Radin, Paul
1911 Some Aspects of Winnebago Archaeology. American Anthropologist, Vol. 13, No. 4, pp. 517-538.
1923 The Winnebago Tribe. Bureau of American Ethnology 1915-1916 37th Annual Report, pp. 35-560.

Random House, Inc.
1966 The Random House Dictionary of the English Language. The Unabridged Edition. Random House.

Rao, C. Radhakrishna
1964 The Use and Interpretation of Principal Component Analysis in Applied Research. Sankhȳa: the Indian Journal of Statistics: Series A: 329-358.

Ritchie, William A.
1961 A Typology and Nomenclature for New York Projectile Points. New York State Museum and Science Service, Bulletin No. 384.

Ritzenthaler, Robert E.
1960 Radiocarbon Dates for Wisconsin. The Wisconsin Archeologist, Vol. 41, No. 3, pp. 65-69.
1961 Radiocarbon Dates for Aztalan. The Wisconsin Archeologist, Vol. 42, No. 3, p. 139.
1963*a* Another Radiocarbon Date for Aztalan. The Wisconsin Archeologist, Vol. 44, No. 3: 180.
1963*b* The Effigy Mound Builders in Wisconsin. Lore, No. 9, Milwaukee Public Museum.
1964 The Riddle of the Spencer Lake Horse Skull. The Wisconsin Archeologist, Vol. 45, No. 2, pp. 115-122.
1966 Radiocarbon Dates for the Clam River Focus. The Wisconsin Archeologist, Vol. 47, No. 4, pp. 219-220.
1967 A Guide to Wisconsin Indian Projectile Point Types. Popular Science Series II, Milwaukee Public Museum.

Rouse, Irving
1939 Prehistory in Haiti: A Study in Method. Taplinger (Human Relations Area). Reprinted, 1964.

Rowe, Chandler W.
1956 The Effigy Mound Culture of Wisconsin. Milwaukee Public Museum, Publications in Anthropology No. 3.

Salzer, Robert J.
1964 The Highsmith Site (Je-4): An Early, Middle, and Late Woodland Site in the Upper Rock River Drainage. Unpublished Masters Thesis. University of Wisconsin.
1967 Notes on Two Previously Undescribed Middle Woodland Assemblages in Wisconsin. MSS. presented to the Wisconsin Archaeological Survey, pp. 1-8.

Sanger, David
1968 The High River Microblade Industry, Alberta. Plains Anthropologist, Vol. 13, No. 41, pp. 190-208.

Schneider, Kathryn J. (ed.)
1964 Aztalan, Wisconsin Then and Now. The State Historical Society of Wisconsin, Madison, Vol. XI, No. 2, pp. 1-5.

Scully, Edward G.
1951 Some Central Mississippi Valley Projectile Point Types (Mimeo.). Museum of Anthropology, University of Michigan.

Senter, R. J.
1969 Analysis of Data. "Introductory Statistics for the Behaviorial Sciences" Scott, Foresman & Co., Glenview Illinois.

Setzler, Frank M.
1940 Archeological Perspectives in the Northern Mississippi Valley. *In:* Essays in Historical Anthropology of North America. Smithsonian Miscellaneous Collections, Vol. 100, pp. 253-290.

Shepard, Anna O.
1968 Ceramics for the Archaeologist. Carnegie Institution of Washington, Publication 609.

Smith, Carlyle S.
1960 Two 18th Century Reports on the Manufacture of Gunflints in France. *In*: Indian Trade Guns. Missouri Archaeologist, Vol. 22, pp. 40-49.

Smith, H. W., R. A. McGreery, and C. D. Moodie
1947 Collection and Preservation of Soil Profiles. Soil Science, Vol. 64, No. 1, pp. 61-69.
1952 Collection and Preservation of Soil Profiles: II. Soil Science, Vol. 73, No. 3, pp. 243-248.

Soil Survey Staff
1960 Soil Classification. A Comprehensive System, 7th Approximation. Soil Conservation Service, United States Department of Agriculture.

Sokal, Robert R. and F. James Rohlf
1969 Biometry. W. H. Freeman and Co., San Francisco.

Spaulding, Albert C.
1953 Statistical Techniques for the Discovery of Artifact Types. American Antiquity, Vol. 18, No. 4: 305-313.

Spencer, Robert F. et al.
1965 The Native Americans. Harper & Row, New York.

Steinbring, Jack and Franklin Farvour
1958 An Effigy Mound at Rush Lake. The Wisconsin Archeologist, Vol. 39, No. 2, pp. 130-144.

Storck, Peter L.
1972 The Archaeology of Mayland Cave. 2 Vols. Ph.D. thesis, University of Wisconsin. Madison.

Stout, A. B.
1911 Prehistoric Earthworks in Wisconsin. Ohio Archaeological and Historical Quarterly, Vol. XX, No. 1, pp. 1-31.

Straffin, Dean
1971 The Kingston Oneota Site. Report No. 2, Office of the State Archaeologist, University of Iowa, Iowa City.

Struever, Stuart
1965 Middle Woodland Culture History in the Great Lakes Riverine Area. American Antiquity, Vol. 31, No. 2, Part 1, pp. 211-223.

Swanton, John R.
1952 The Indian Tribes of North America. Smithsonian Institution, Bureau of American Ethnology, Bulletin 145.

Thomas, Cyrus
1894 Report on the Mound Explorations of the Bureau of Ethnology. Bureau of American Ethnology 1890-1891. 12th Annual Report

Van de Geer, John P.
1971 Introduction to Multivariate Analysis for the Social Sciences. W. H. Freeman and Company, San Francisco.

Wagner, Norman E.
1971*a* Computer Studies of Ontario Iroquois, Waterloo Lutheran University, Waterloo, Ontario.
1971*b* Coding and Clustering Pottery by Computer. Waterloo Lutheran University, Waterloo, Ontario.

Wedel, Mildred Mott
1938 The Relation of Historic Indian Tribes to Archaeological Manifestations in Iowa. Iowa Journal of History and Politics, 36, No. 3: 227-314, Iowa City.
1959 Oneota Sites on the Upper Iowa River. The Missouri Archaeologist, Vol. 21, Nos. 2-4, pp. 1-181.

West, George A.
1907 The Indian Authorship of Wisconsin Antiquities. The Wisconsin Archeologist, Old Series, Vol. 6, No. 4, pp. 169-256.

Whallon, Robert
1971 A Computer Program for Monothetic Subdivisive Classification in Archaeology. Technical Report No. 1, Museum of Anthropology, University of Michigan, Ann Arbor.
1972 A New Approach to Pottery Typology. American Antiquity, Vol. 37, No. 1, January: 13-33.

Whiteford, A. H.
1952 A Report of the Outlet Site on Lake Monona. The Wisconsin Archeologist, Vol. 30, No. 1, pp. 22-35.

Wilder, Charles G.
1951 Kincaid Textiles. *In*: Kincaid, A Prehistoric Illinois Metropolis. Fay-Cooper Cole, ed., University of Chicago Publications in Anthropology, Archaeological Series, III.

Willey, Gordon R.
1966 An Introduction to American Archaeology, Vol. I, North and Middle America. Prentice-Hall, Inc. Englewood Cliffs, New Jersey.

Wittry, Warren L.
1951 A Preliminary Study of the Old Copper Complex. The Wisconsin Archeologist, Vol. 32, No. 1, pp. 1-18
1956 Kolterman Mound 18 Radiocarbon Date. The Wisconsin Archeologist, Vol. 37, No. 4, pp. 133-134.
1959*a* The Raddatz Rockshelter, Sk5, Wisconsin. The Wisconsin Archeologist, Vol. 40, No. 2, pp. 33-69.
1959*b* The Wakanda Park Mound Group, Dn 1, Menomonie, Wisconsin. The Wisconsin Archeologist, Vol. 40, No. 3: 95-115.
1959*c* Archeological Studies of Four Wisconsin Rockshelters. The Wisconsin Archeologist, Vol. 40, No. 4, pp. 137-267.
1963 The Bell Site, Wn 9, an Early Historic Fox Village. The Wisconsin Archeologist, Vol. 44, No. 1, pp. 1-57.

Wittry, Warren L. and David A. Baerreis
1958 Domestic Houses at Aztalan. *In*: Aztalan: Exploration and Reconstruction, ed. Robert Ritzenthaler. The Wisconsin Archeologist, Vol. 39, No. 1, pp. 62-77.

Wittry, Warren L. and E. G. Bruder
1955 Salvage Operations at the Kolterman Mound Group, Dodge County. The Wisconsin Archeologist, Vol. 36, No. 1, pp. 3-12.

Wolff, Hans
1950 Comparative Siouan. International Journal of American Linguistics, Vol. 16; Baltimore.

Wood, W. Raymond
1967 An Interpretation of Mandan Culture History. Bureau of American Ethnology, Bulletin 198, Washington, D.C.

Woodward, Arthur
1960 Some Notes on Gun Flints. *In*: Indian Trade Guns. Missouri Archaeologist, Vol. 22, pp. 29-39.

Wray, Donald E. and Richard S. MacNeish
1961 The Hopewellian and Weaver Occupations of the Weaver Site, Fulton County, Illinois, ed. Warren L. Wittry. Illinois State Museum, Scientific Papers, Vol. VII, No. 2, pp. 1-71.

Wright, James V.
1966 The Pic River Site. Paper No. 3, National Museums of Canada, Bulletin No. 206.
1967 The Laurel Tradition and the Middle Woodland Period. National Museum of Canada, Bulletin 217.
1968 The Michipicoten Site, Ontario. Paper No. 1, National Museums of Canada, Bulletin 224.
1972 Ontario Prehistory "An Eleven-thousand-year Archaeological Outline" National Museums of Canada, National Museum of Man.

Yamanouchi, Sugao
1964 Nihon Genshi Bijutsu (Primitive Arts of Japan) 1, Jomon Pottery. Kodansha Publishing Co., Tokyo.

Plate 1. Mound B, Burial 7.

Plate 2. Mound A, section 1, north and east walls.

Plate 3. Mound R, Burial 1.

Plate 4. Madison Cord Impressed rim sherds: (a) Mound A, N410W5-3-1; (e) N45W30-3-1; (g) Mound R, N463E90-2-1; (h) Mound A, N405E5-4-1; Madison Folded Lip: (b) Mound L, N70W20-2-1; Madison Fabric Impressed: (c) Mound R, N458E93-1-1; (d) Mound L, N65W25-3-2; (f) Mound R, N473E90-2-1.

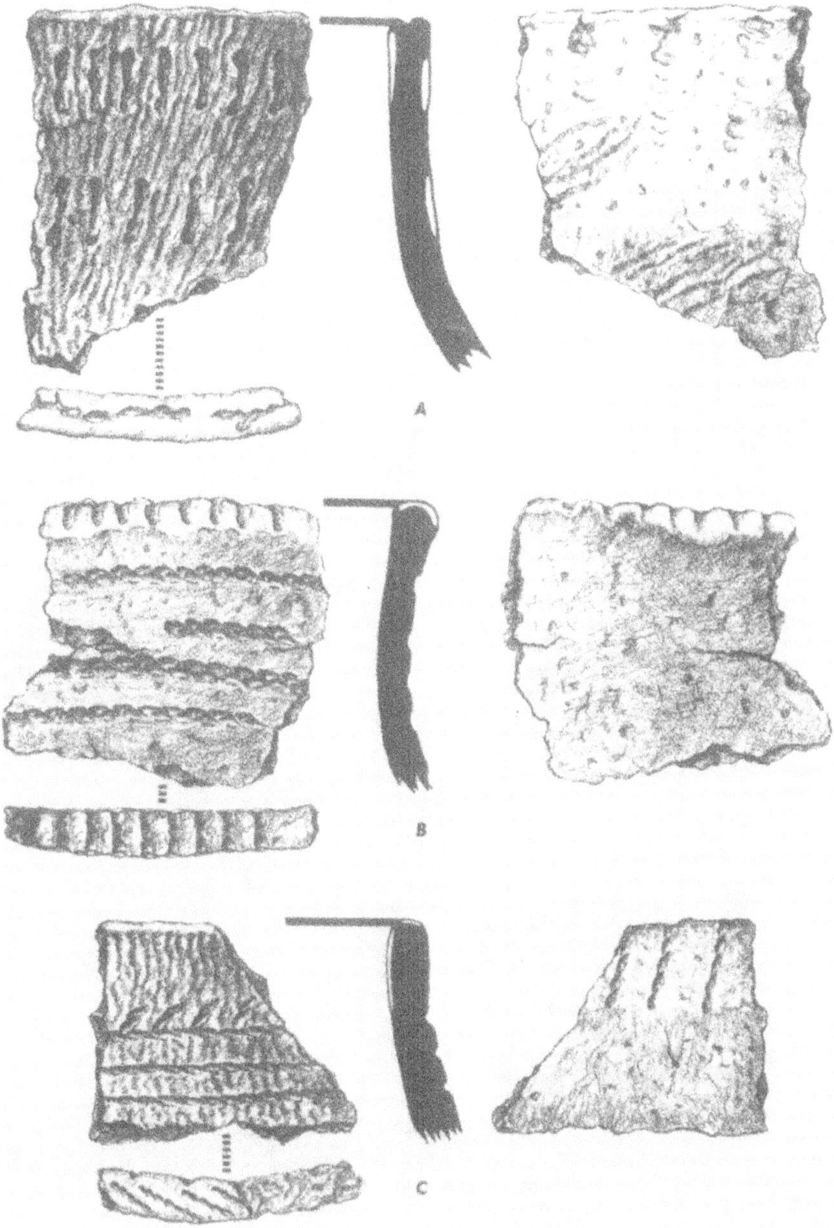

Plate 5. Madison Cord Impressed: (a) Mound A, N410W5-3-1; Madison Folded Lip: (b) Mound L, N70W20-2-1; Madison Fabric Impressed: (c) Mound R, N458E93-1-1 (artifacts approximately one-half natural size).

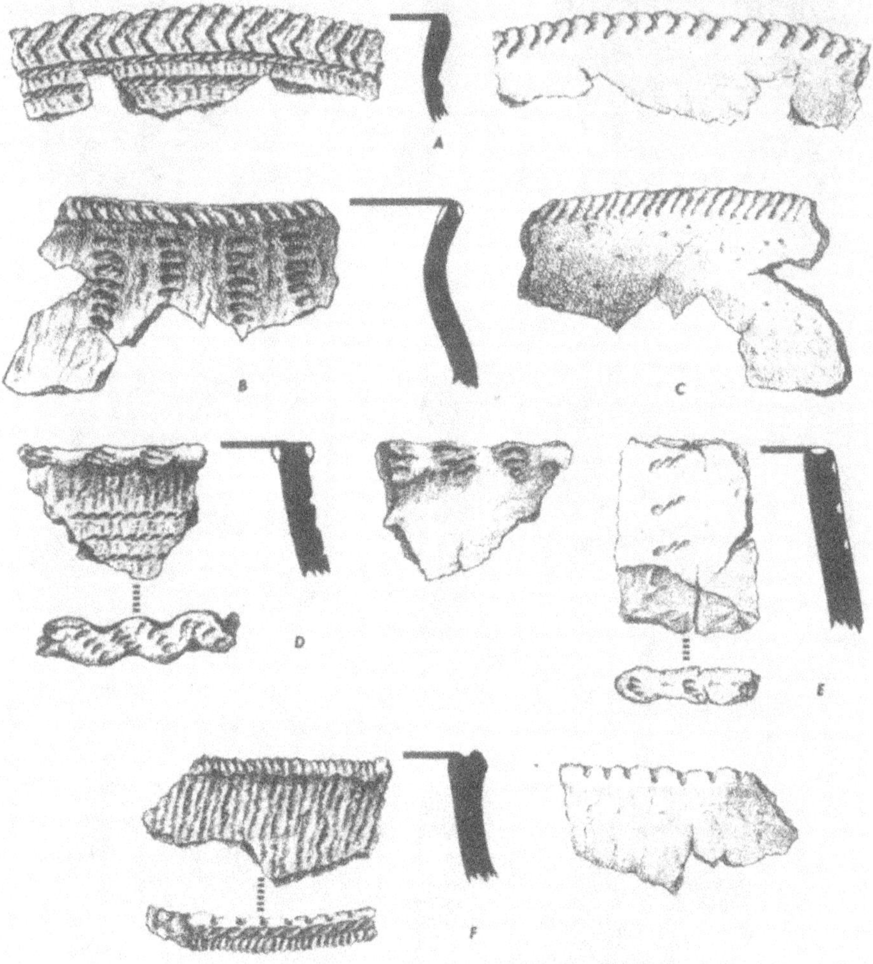

Plate 6. Madison Fabric Impressed: (a) Mound L, N65W25-3-2; (d) Mound R, N473E90-2-1; Madison Cord Impressed: (b)-(c), N45W30-2-1; (e) Mound R, N480E90-2-1 (artifacts approximately one-half natural size).

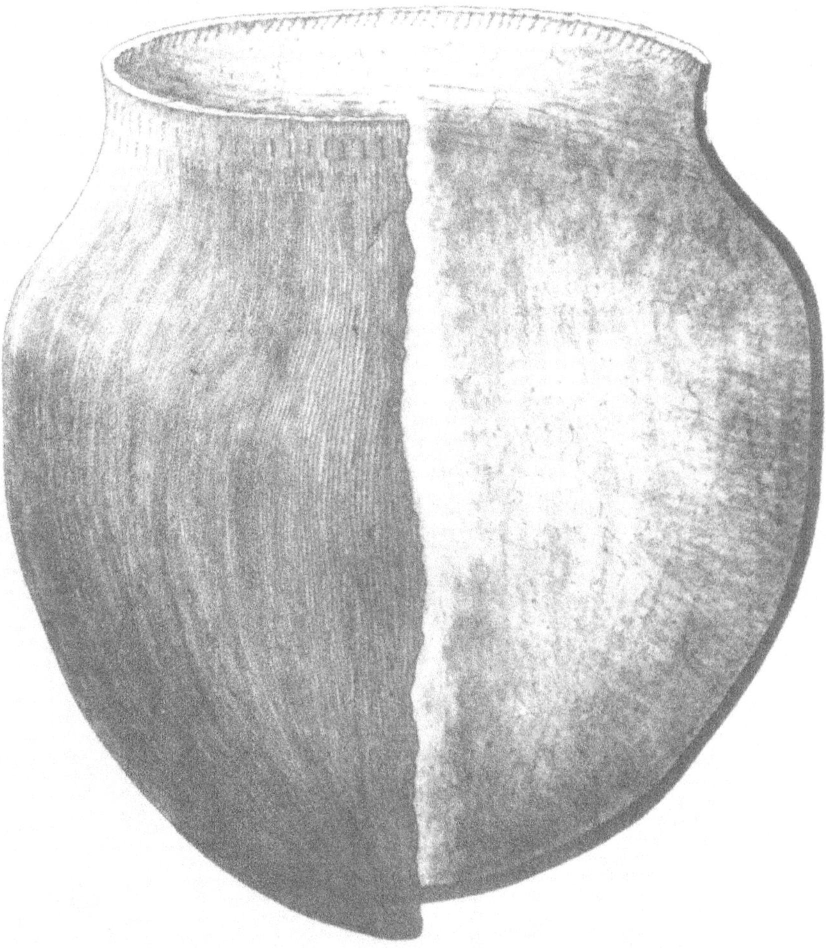

Plate 7. Reconstructed Madison Cord Impressed vessel (one-quarter natural size): Mound L, Feature 13. Vessel is 59 cm high, with an orifice of 38 cm, lip thickness of 8 mm and rim thickness of 7 mm.

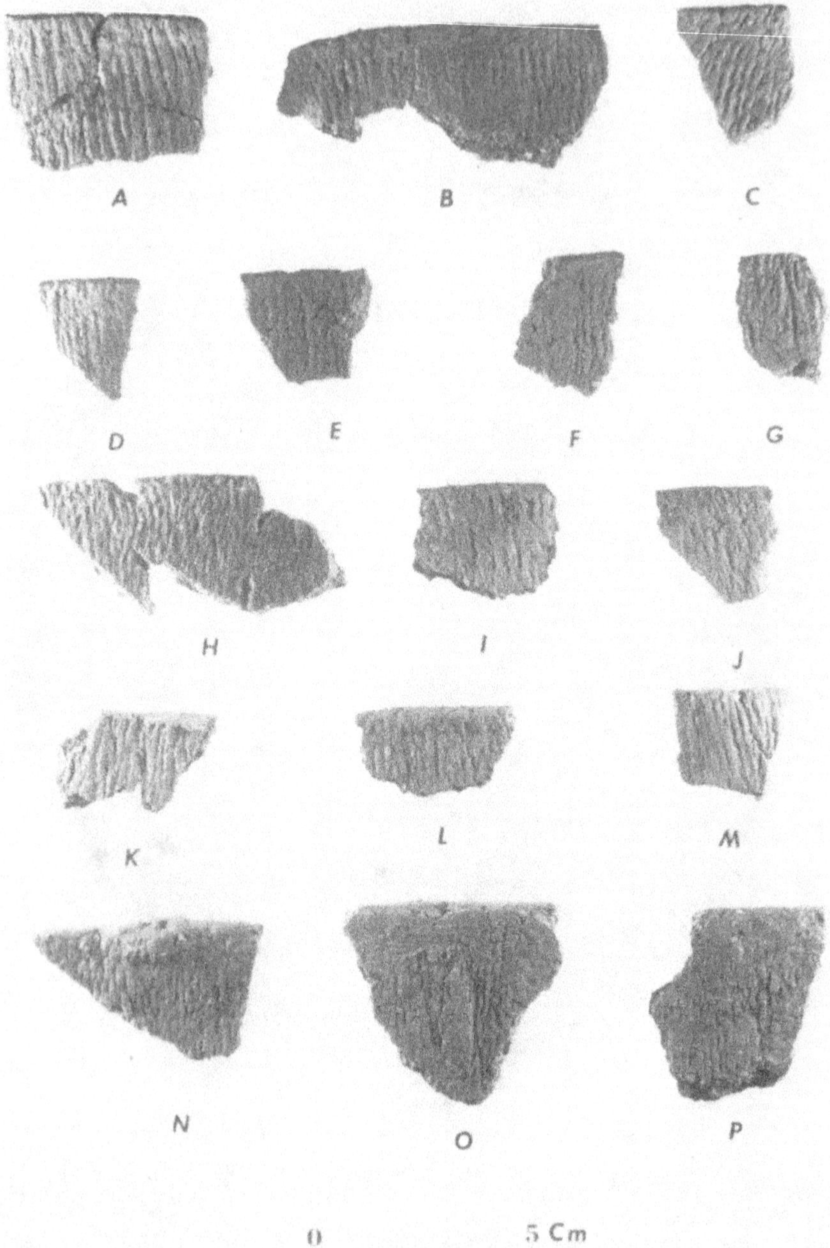

Plate 8. Madison Plain rim sherds: (a) Mound L, N65W20-2-3; (b) N195W30-3-1; (c) N50W25-2-11; (d) area K, N155W40-3-1; (e) Mound A, N410E0-3-1; (f) Mound B, N330W10-1-8; (g) Mound N, S67W5-1-1; (h) F-16-2; (i) Mound R, N480E90-2-1; (j) Mound R, N485E90-2-2; (k) Mound 1, N65W10-2-4; (l) Mound 9, N37W129-1-1; (m) Mound 13, S36W5-2-2; (n) Mound 13, BF-2; (o) Mound 13, BF-1; (p) Mound 13, S3E10-1-1.

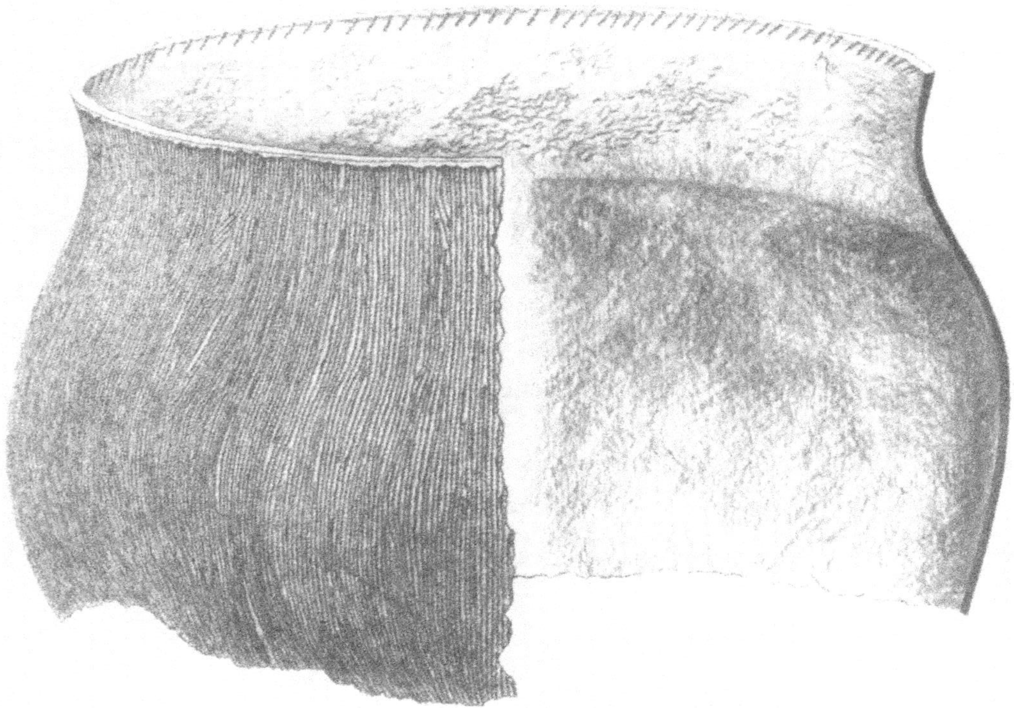

Plate 9. Reconstructed Madison Plain vessel (approximately one-quarter natural size): Mound R, Feature 16. Known height is 29.5 cm, with an orifice of 40 cm, lip thickness 6 mm, and rim thickness 5 mm.

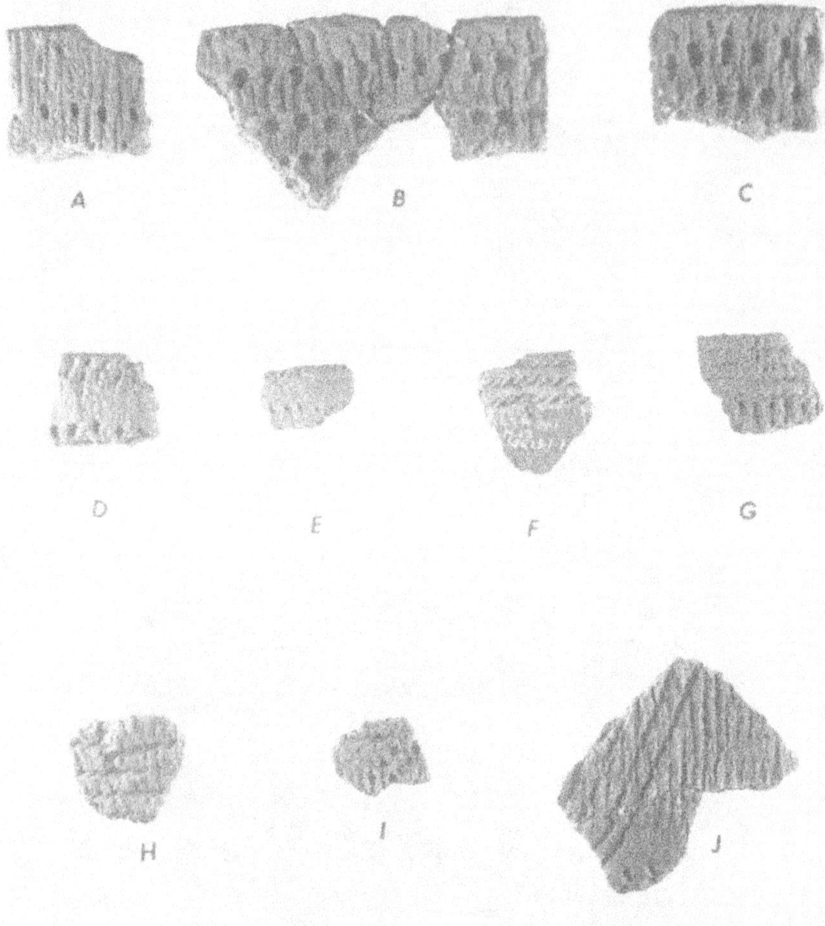

Plate 10. Madison Punctated rim sherds: (a) area K, N155W30-3-4; (e) Mound A, N405W5-3-2; Madison Fabric Impressed rim sherds: (b) N160W40-3-1; (c) N160W40-3-2, (d) Mound L, N65E16-3-1; body sherds: (g) Mound R, N470E90-2-3; (h) Mound R, N475E90-2-5; (j) Mound A, N405E5-4-3; Madison Cord Impressed rim sherds: (f) Mound 13, S8E25-1-1; body sherds: (i) Mound B, surface 1.

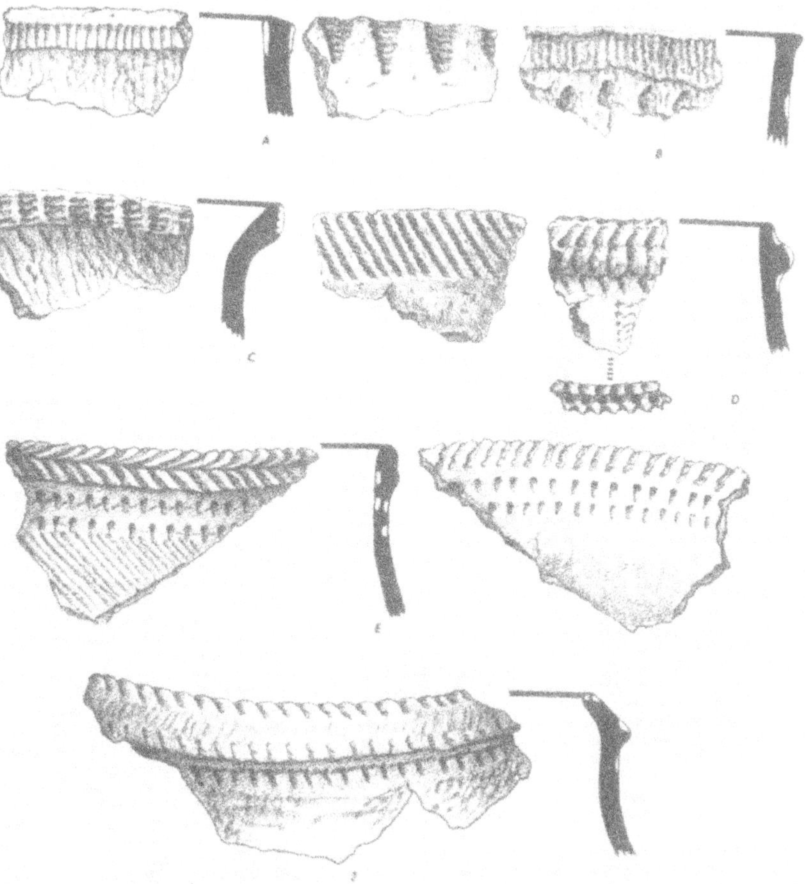

Plate 11. (a) Aztalan Collared, Mound M, S30W20-4-2; (b) Aztalan Collared, Mound N, S67W5-3-1; (c) Aztalan Collared, N160W10-2-1; (d) Hahn Cord Impressed, Mound L, N65W20-3-2; (e) Point Sauble Collared, Mound M, S30E25-3-14; (f) Point Sauble Collared, Mound L, N65W20-3-1 (artifacts approximately one-half natural size).

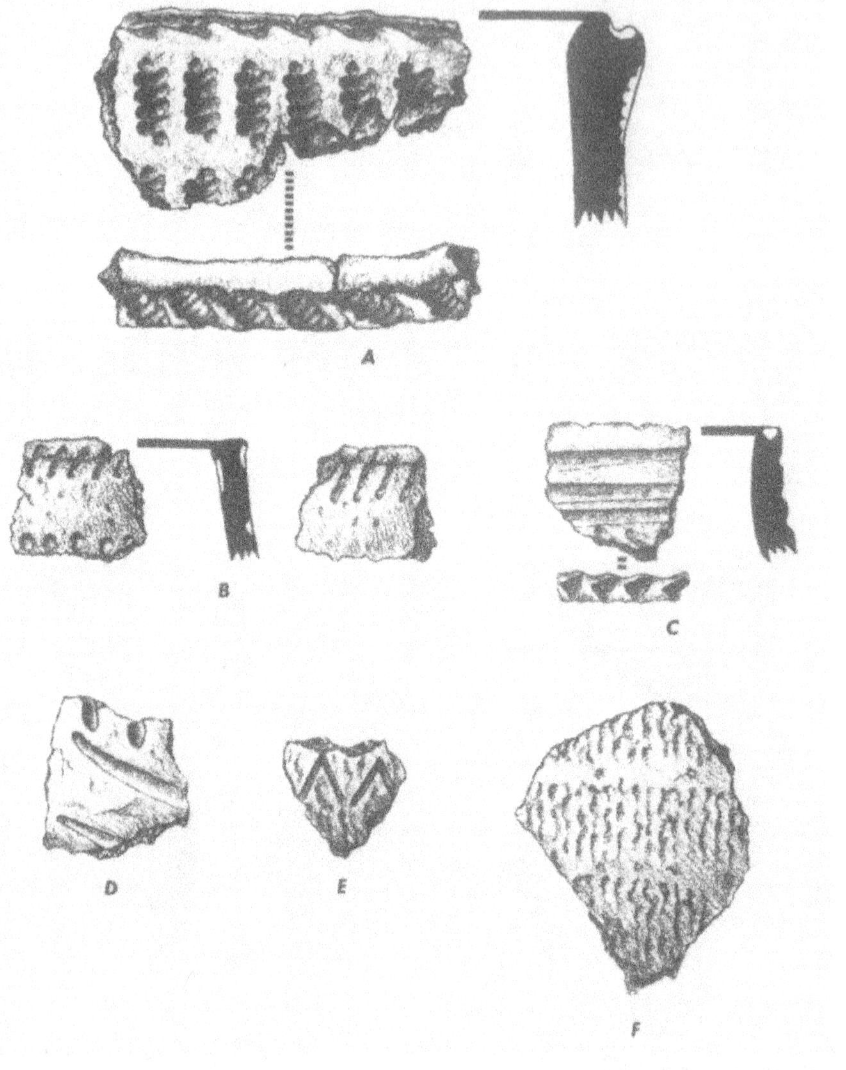

Plate 12. (a) Unclassified rim sherd: a, t.s.1-3-2 & 2-1; (b) Madison Fabric Impressed, Mound L, N65E16-3-1; (c) trailed rim sherd, N600E90-1-1; (d) trailed body sherd, area K, N160W35-2-4; (e) incised body sherd, Mound A, N405W5-3-7; (f) trailed body sherd, Mound R, N458E93-1-25 (artifacts approximately one-half natural size).

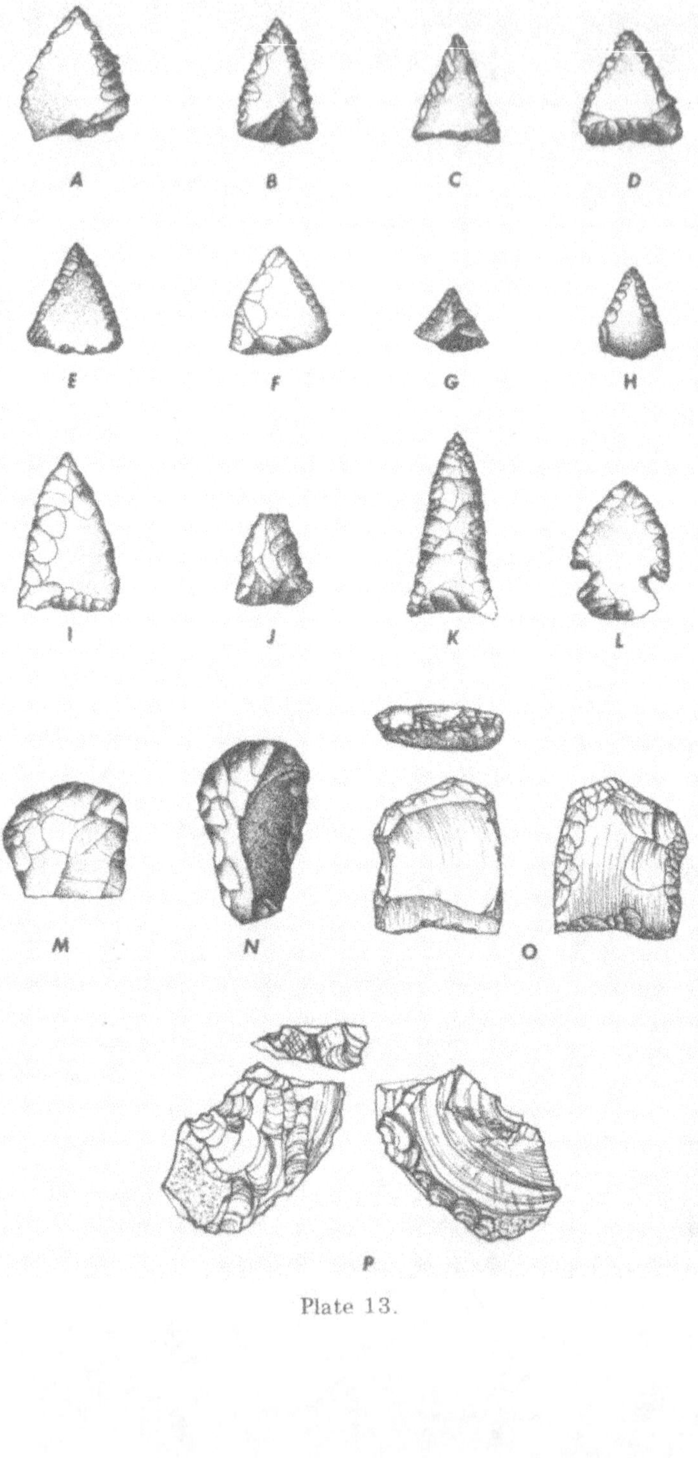

Plate 13.

Plate 13. (artifacts approximately one-half natural size)
(a) Sanders Triangular projectile point, quartizite, Mound M, S25W25-4-8.
(b) Triangular (A) projectile point, quartzite Mound R, N440W90-3-1.
(c) Sanders Triangular projectile point, quartzite, Mound A, N405W5-3-1.
(d) Sanders Triangular projectile point, quartzite, Mound B, N330W5-3-4.
(e) Sanders Triangular projectile point, quartzite, Mound S, N200W25-1-1.
(f) Sanders Triangular projectile point, quartzite, S20W5-1-1.
(g) Triangular (B) projectile point, quartzite, Mound A, N405W5, Burial 5.
(h) Sanders Triangular projectile point, quartzite, S50W45-2-1.
(i) Triangular (B) projectile point, quartzite, Mound A, N415E0-3-1.
(j) Triangular (B) projectile point, quartzite, Mound A, N405E0-2-1.
(k) Triangular (B) projectile point, quartzite, Mound B, N330W10-3-4.
(l) Corner Notched projectile point, quartzite, Mound R, N455E90-1-1.
(m) End scraper, quartzite, Mound R, N45E90-2-1.
(n) End scraper, quartzite, N195W30-1-1.
(o) Conventional gunflint, musket type, flint, N350E30-1-1.
(p) Blade core, chert, area K, N160W40-2-5.

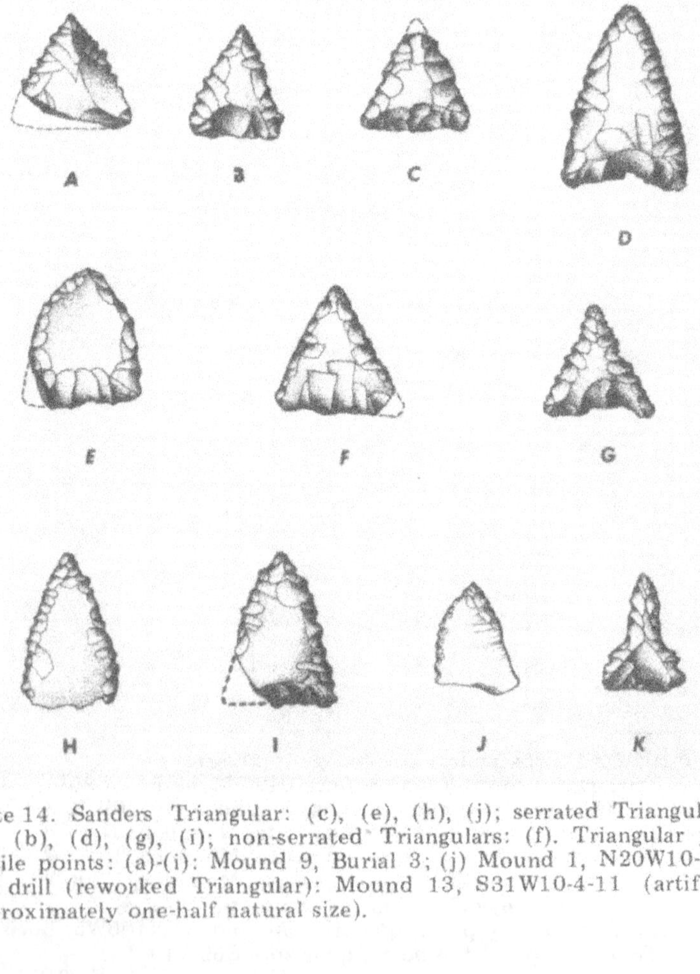

Plate 14. Sanders Triangular: (c), (e), (h), (j); serrated Triangulars: (a), (b), (d), (g), (i); non-serrated Triangulars: (f). Triangular projectile points: (a)-(i): Mound 9, Burial 3; (j) Mound 1, N20W10-2-2; (k) drill (reworked Triangular): Mound 13, S31W10-4-11 (artifacts approximately one-half natural size).

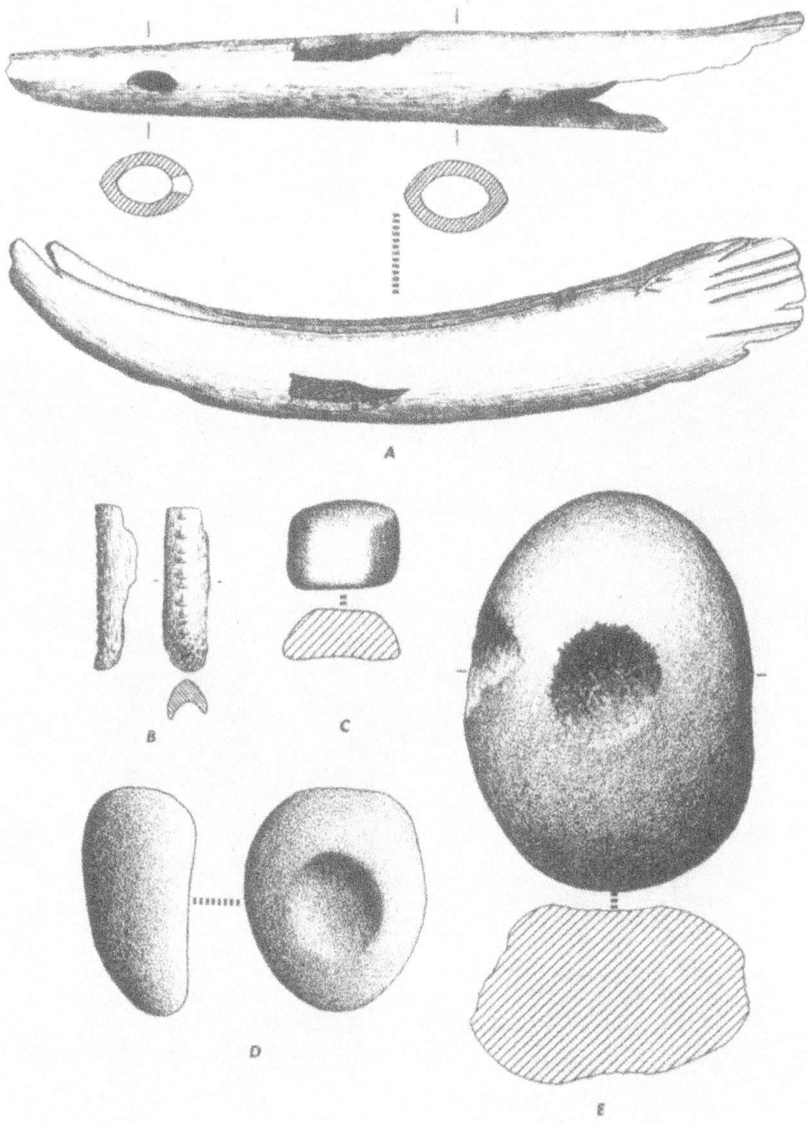

Plate 15. (a) Deer antler flaker, Mound A, N405W5 Burial 5-4; (b) cut bone, Mound A, N405W5, Burial 5-7; (c) polishing stone, S20W5-1-8; (d) pecked stone, Mound L, N45L5-5-3; (e) pecked hammerstone, Mound L, N65W20-3-56 (artifacts approximately one-half natural size).

Plate 16. Sister Creeks Punctated rim sherd: (a) 47-Wp-70, S110W50-2-1; body sherds: (b) S105E60-2-7; (c) F4-3; Rocker Stamped body sherd: (d) 47-Wp-26, S15W125-2-5; Dane Incised body sherds: (e) 47-Wp-70, S105W55-2-1; (f) S105W55-2-2; (g) S105W55-2-3; (h) S110W45-4-4; interior cord rolled body sherds: (i) 47-Wp-26, S945W400-2-32; (j) S835W405-2-101; interior brushed body sherd: (k) S960W405-2-43.

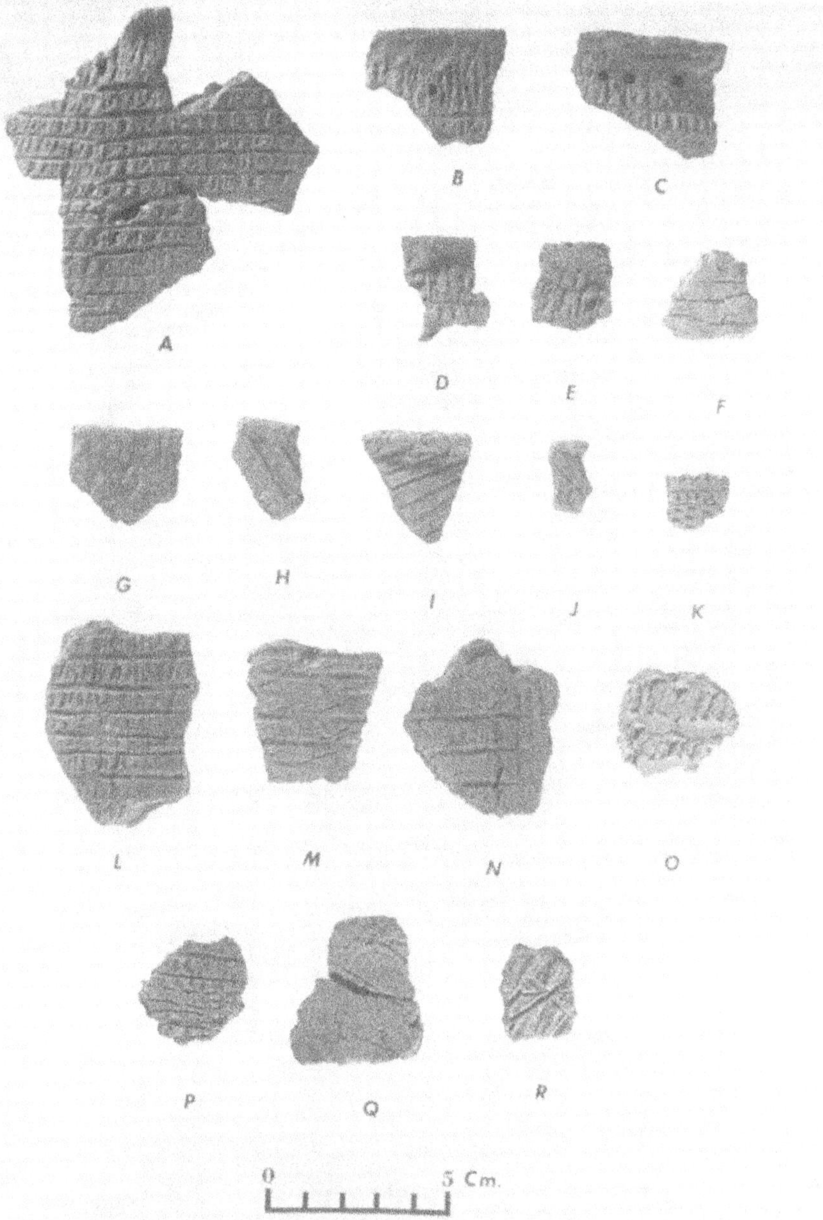

Plate 17. Dane Incised rim sherds: (a) 47-Wp-26, S935W410-2-8, S945W405-2-17, and features 16-17 and 18; (b) S940W405-2-99; (c) 47-Wp-70, S110W45-2-7; (d) 47-Wp-26, S945W400-2-2; (e) S945W410-2-18; (f) S995W400-2-14; (g) H1-6 floor; (h) S985W395-2-11; (i) F16-11; (j) H3-F-31; (k) 47-Wp-70, S115W50-3-42; body sherds: (l) 47-Wp-26, S940W410-2-151; (m) S980W405-2-4; (n) H2-F2-27; (o) S1010W380-3-8; (p) 47-Wp-70, S115W45-2-15; (q) 47-Wp-26, Mound 25, S1083W325-2-16 and 17; (r) 47-Wp-70, S105W50-2-2.

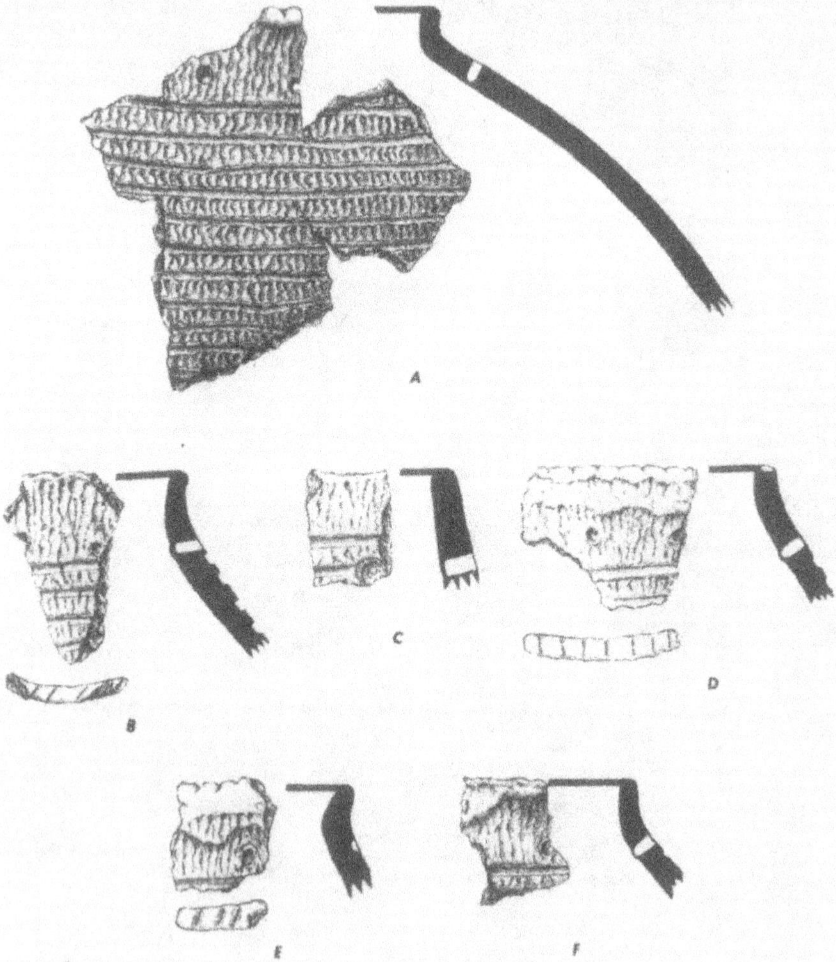

Plate 18. Dane Incised rim sherds: (a) 47-Wp-26, S935W410-2-8, S945W405-2-17, and feature 16-17 and 18; (b) S940W405-2-97; (c) S15W20-2-4; (d) S940W405-2-99; (e) S945W410-2-18; (f) S945W400-2-2 (artifacts approximately one-half natural size).

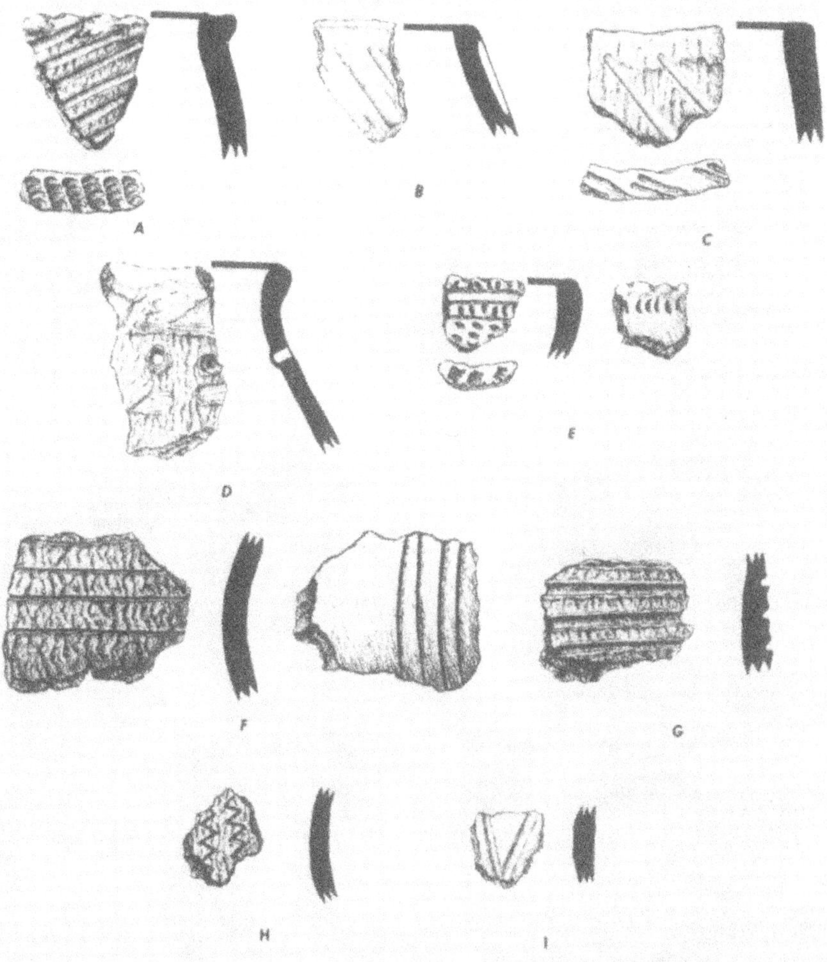

Plate 19. Dane Incised rim sherds: (a) 47-Wp-26, F16-11; (b) S985W395-2-11; (c) H1-6 floor; (d) S1000W390-2-3; (e) 47-Wp-70, S115W50-3-42; body sherds: (f) 47-Wp-26, F36-4; (g) Mound 28, S895W295-5-7; (h) S5W120-1-4; (i) Mound 12, S5W130-2-1 (artifacts approximately one-half natural size).

Plate 20. Shorewood Cord Roughened rim sherds: (a) 47-Wp-26, Mound 28, S985W295-4-14; (b) Mound 28, S895W295-5-1; Dane Incised, variety fingernail impressed rim sherds: (c) S955W405-2-1; (d) H2-feature 40-20; (e) S975W405-2-10; (f) Mound 1 (1965), N30W10-2-7; (g) Mound 1 (1965), N35W5-3-7; body sherds: (h) Mound 24, S830W180-3-25; (i) Mound 1 (1965), N30W10-2-3; (j) Feature 22-4; (k) Mound 28, S985W295-2-15; (l) 47-Wp-70, H1-F12-2; (m) H1, HF-4.

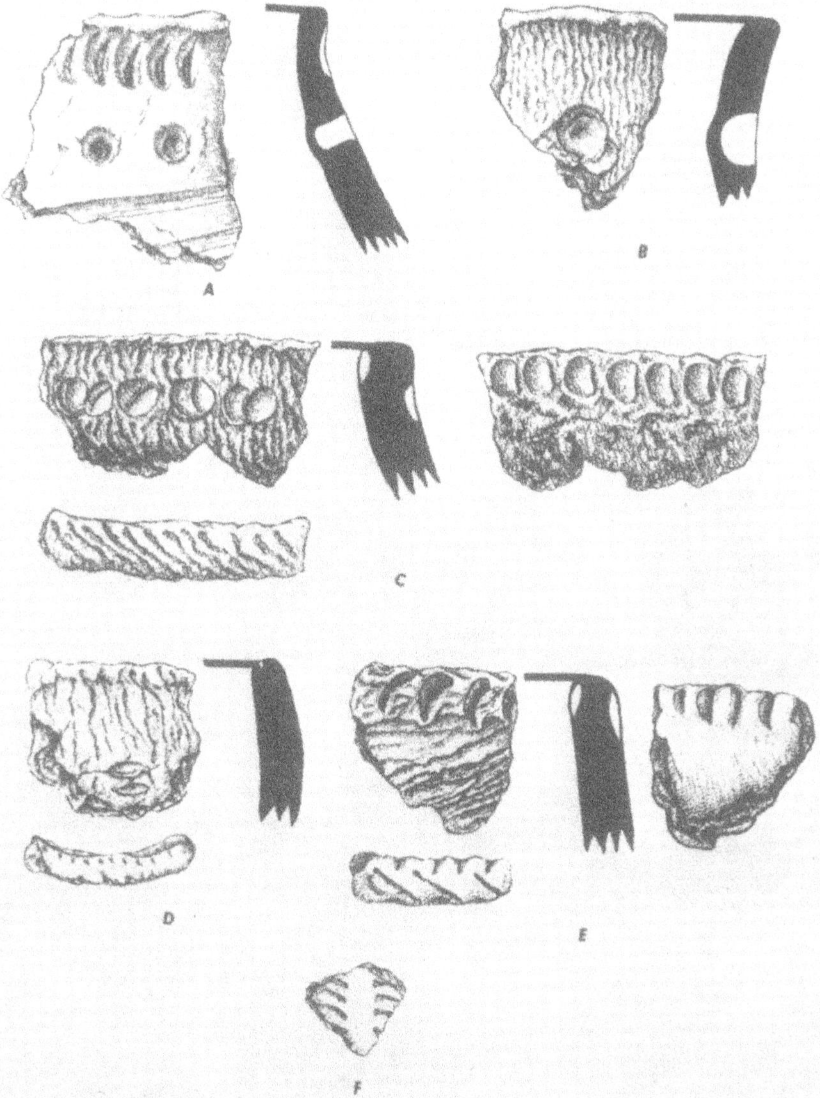

Plate 21. Dane Incised variety fingernail impressed rim sherds: (a) 47-Wp-26, S955W405-2-1; (c) H2-F40-20; (d) Mound 1, (1965), N30W10-2-7; (e) Mound 1 (1965), N35W5-3-7; (f) S955W405-2-2; Shorewood Cord Roughened rim sherd: (b) S950W405-2-3 (artifacts approximately one-half natural size).

Plate 22. Madison Cord Impressed rim sherds: (b) 47-Wp-26, S940W405-2-75/S945W410-2-23; (e) area 9, N0E140, feature 1-1; (f) S990W395-2-2; (j) H2-feature 40-17; Madison Fabric Impressed: (a) S870W415-2-2; (c) Mound 25, S1085W325-2-5; (d) area 9, N0E140-2-2; (g) Mound 28, S895W297.5-2-1; (h) Mound 25, S1088W325-5-2; (i) S935W400-2-6; (k) S995W400-2-9; (l) S930W395-1-25; (m) H2-feature 40-16; (n) 47-Wp-70, S115W50-3-40.

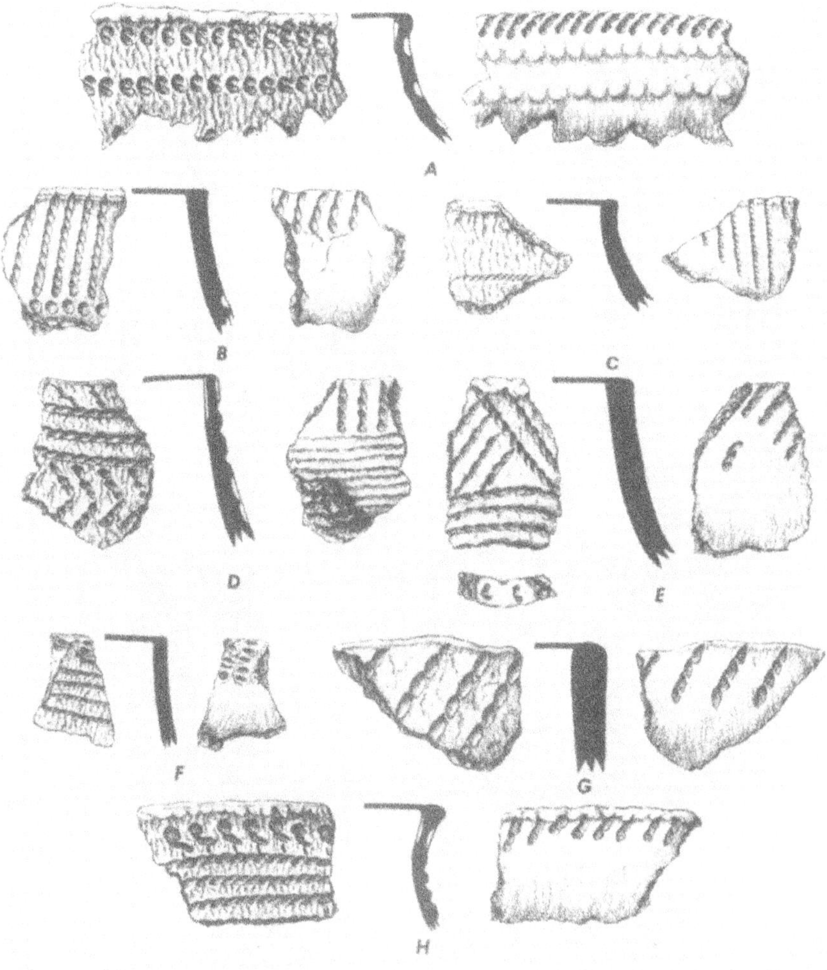

Plate 23. Madison Cord Impressed rim sherds: (b) 47-Wp-26, S860W410/15-2-117; (c) S890W400-2-1; (g) H2-feature 40-17; Madison Fabric Impressed: (a) Mound 4, S360W117-3-2; (d) Mound 28, S895W297.5-2-1; (e) Mound 25, S1088W325-5-2; (f) H3-HF1-18; (h) H2-Feature 40-16 (artifacts approximately one-half natural size).

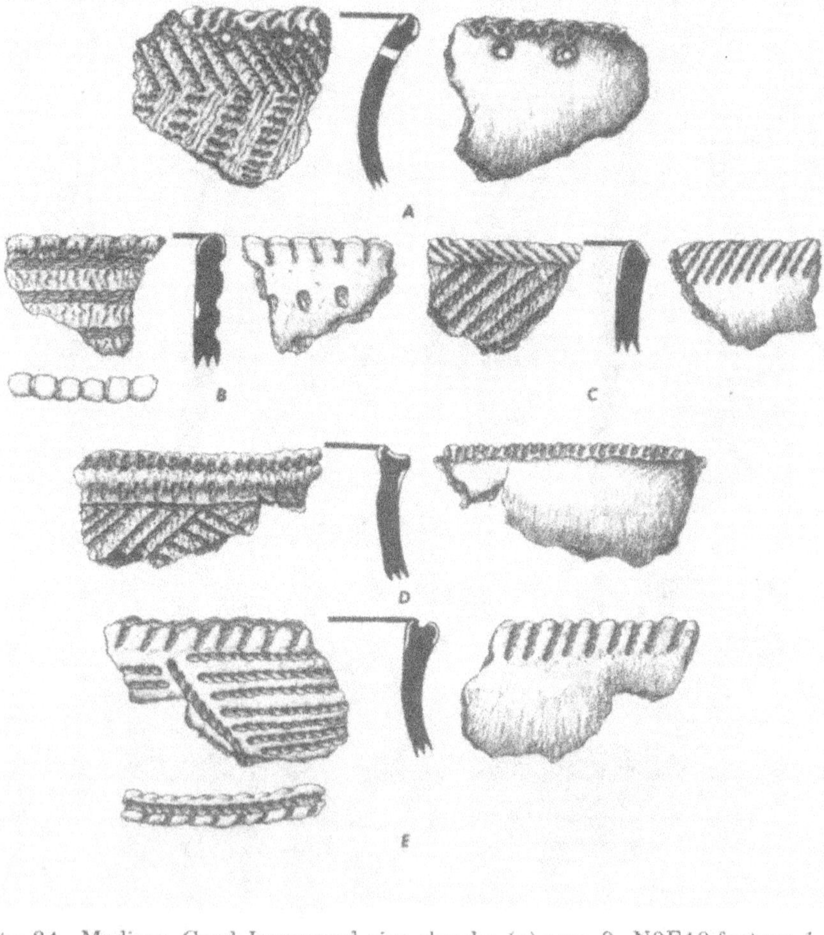

Plate 24. Madison Cord Impressed rim sherds: (a) area 9, N0E40-feature 1-1; (e) S940W405-2-75; Madison Fabric Impressed: (b) S930W395-1-25; (c) S935W400-2-6; (d) S870W415-2-2 (artifacts approximately one-half natural size.)

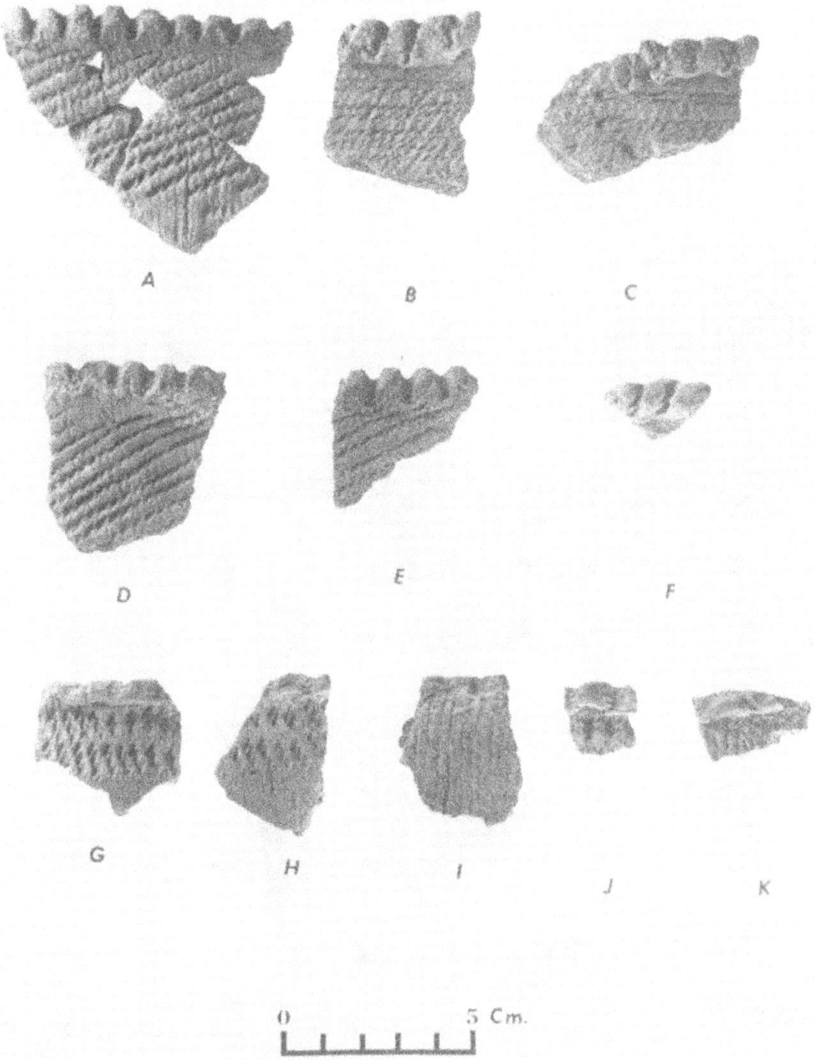

Plate 25. Madison Folded Lip rim sherds: (a) 47-Wp-26, S830W405-2-43; (b) S855W425-2-1; (c) H3-F-27; (d) S830W405-2-44; (e) S830W405-2-41; (f) S825W425-2-58; (g) S960W405-2-22; (h) S965W405-2-1; (i) F16-8; (j) S855W405-2-3; (k) S830W430-2-45.

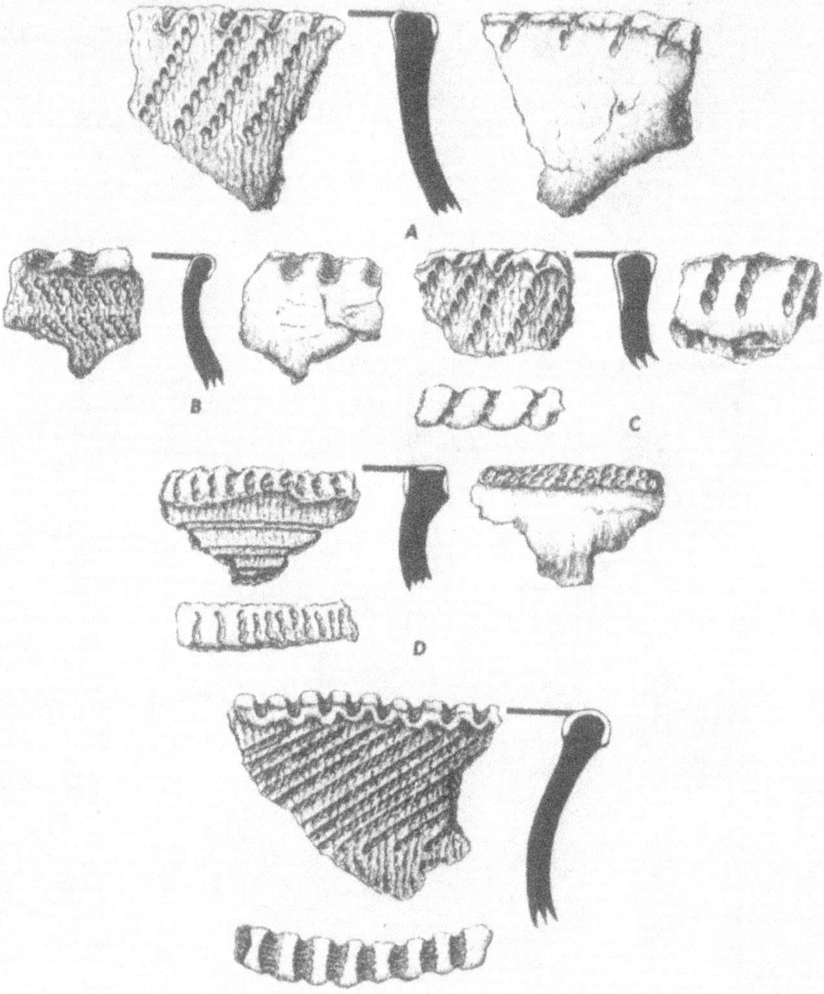

Plate 26. Madison Cord Impressed rim sherds: (a) S990W395-2-2; (c) Mound 1, N35W5-3-4; Madison Fabric Impressed: (d) area 9, N0E140-2-2; Madison Folded Lip: (b) S960W405-2-22; (e) S830W405-2-43 (artifacts approximately one-half natural size).

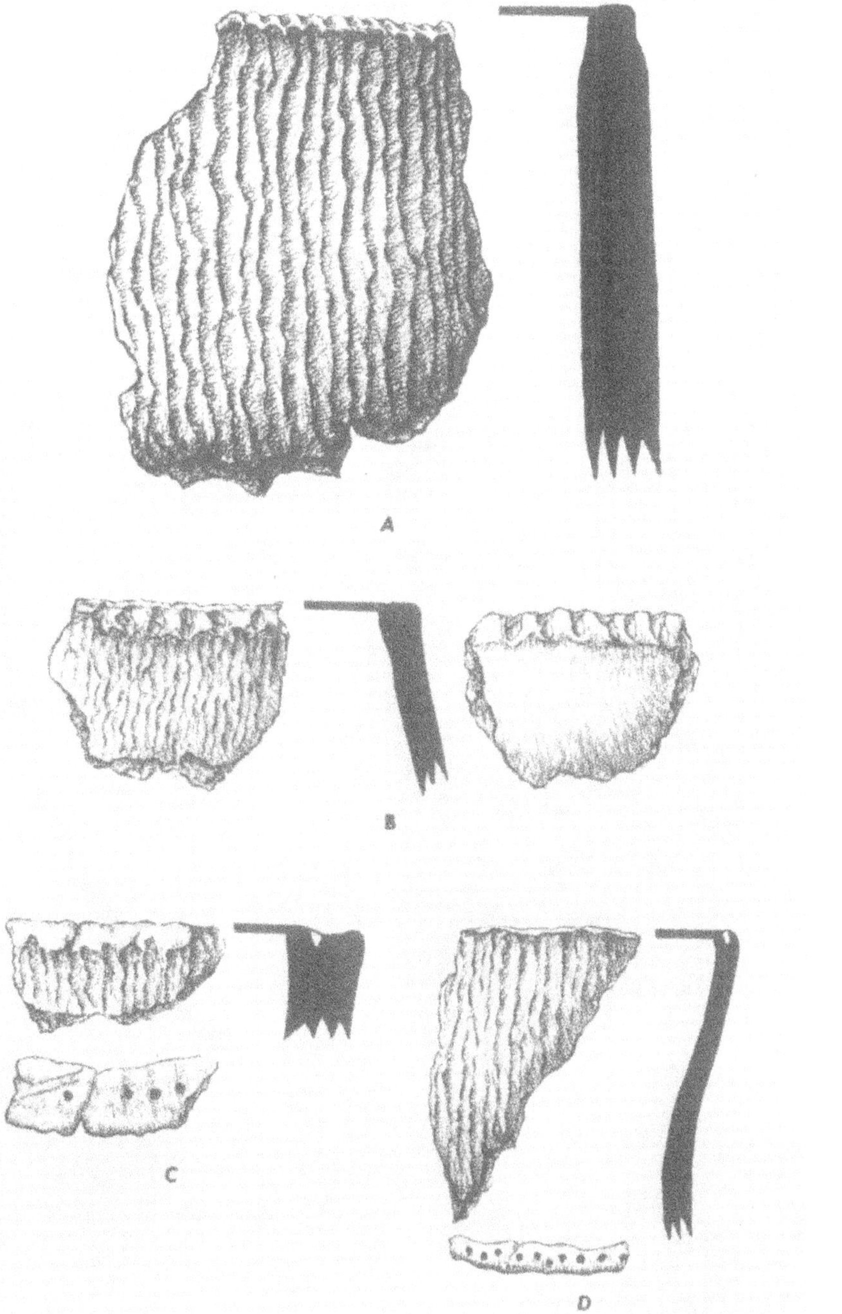

Plate 27. Madison Plain rim sherds: (a) 47-Wp-26, Mound 19, S640W207-1-3, 4 and 6; (b) S855W415-2-30; Madison Plain, variety punctated: (c) S835W405-2-100; (d) 47-Wp-70, S120W45-4-1 (artifacts approximately one-half natural size).

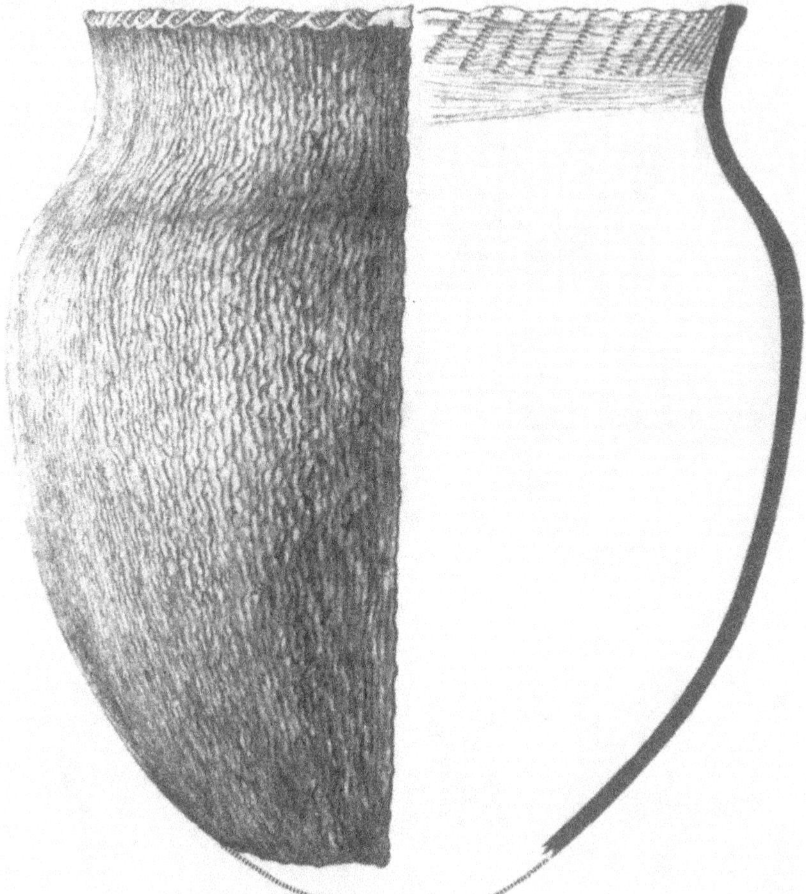

Plate 28. Reconstructed Madison Plain vessel (approximately one-half natural size) 47-Wp-26, S950W410-2, feature 50. Estimated height is 32 cm, orifice diameter is 28 cm, lip thickness is 9 mm, and rim thickness is 8 mm.

Plate 29. Madison Punctated rim sherds: (a) 47-Wp-26, S950W430-2-12; (b) S830W425-2-31; (c) H2-F2-24; (d) S830W425-2-30; (e) S865W405/410/415-2-174; (f) S955W410-2-6; (g) S945W425-2-4; (h) S860W410/415-2-117; (i) H3-F-32; (j) S955W410-2-21; (k) S970W405-2-26; body sherds: (l) S990W400-2-47; (m) Mound 24, S830-W180-3-6.

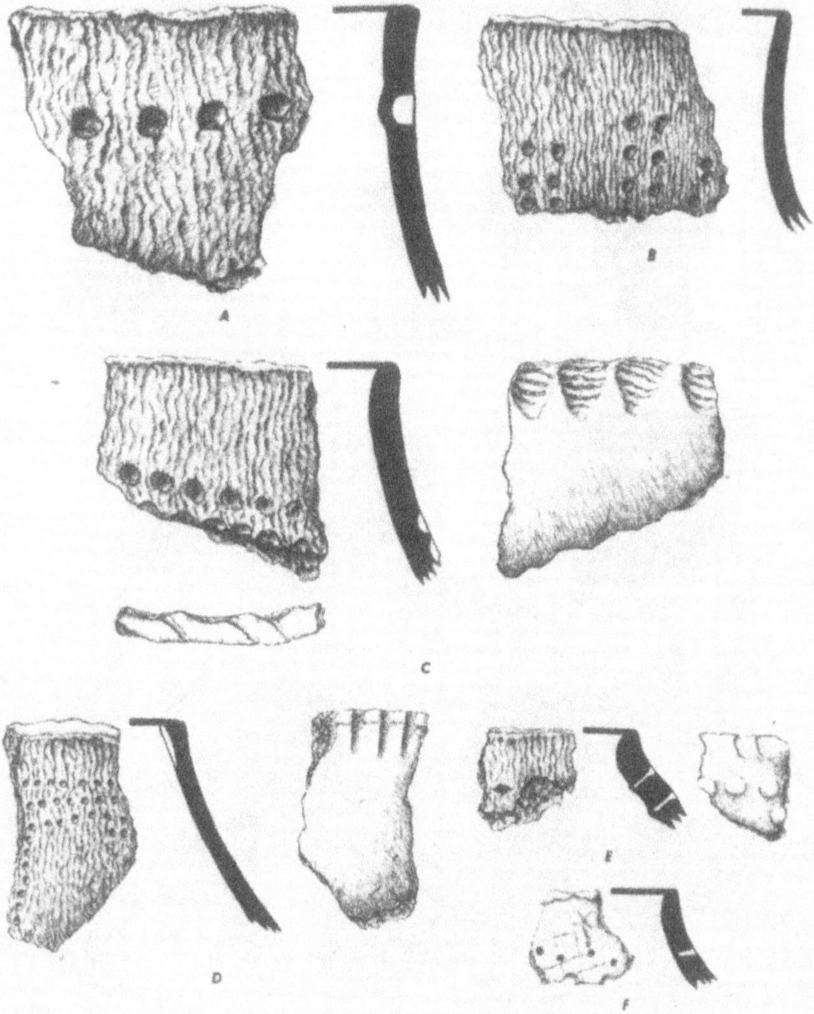

Plate 30. Shorewood Cord Roughened rim sherd: (a) 47-Wp-26, Mound 28, S895W425-4-14; Madison Punctated: (b) H3-F-32; (c) S950W430-2-12; (d) S830W425-2-30; (e) S955W410-2-6; (f) S860W400-2-54 (artifacts approximately one-half natural size).

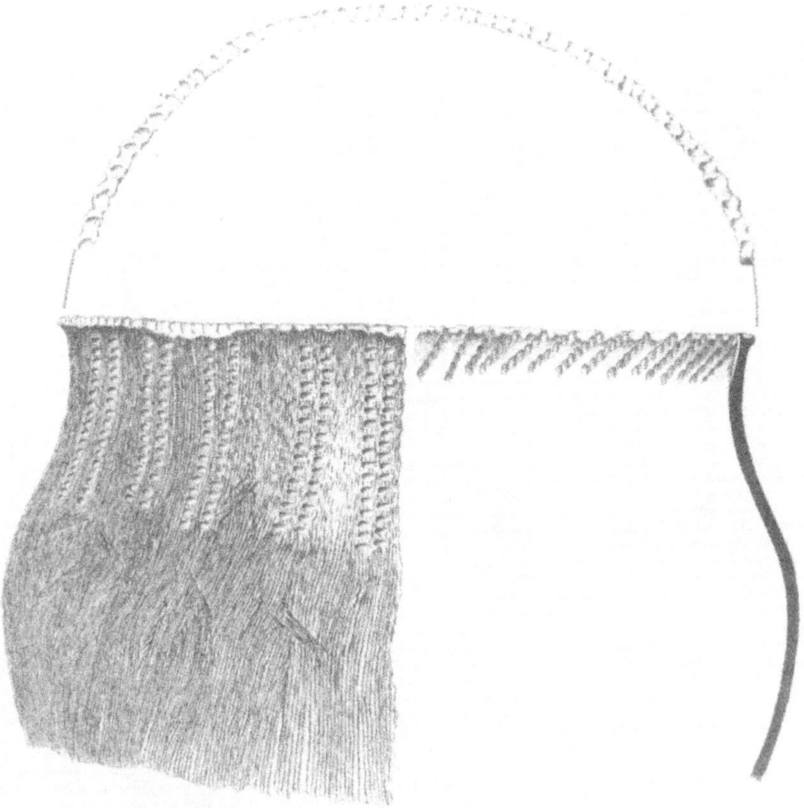

Plate 31. Madison Punctated vessel. Mound 2, feature 1. Partially reconstructed height is 28.1 cm, orifice diameter is 33 cm, lip thickness is 14 mm, and rim thickness is 7 mm.

Plate 32. Leland Cord-marked rim sherds: (a) 47-Wp-26, S860W410/415-2-107; (b) H2-PF-1-5; (c) H2-feature 40-13; (d) S855W415-2-113; (e) S855W415-2-126; (f) S835W405/410-feature 29-10; (g) S835W405-2-115; (h) S985W405-2-27; (i) S960W405-2-1; (j) S970W410-3-1; (k) S1000W390-2-1.

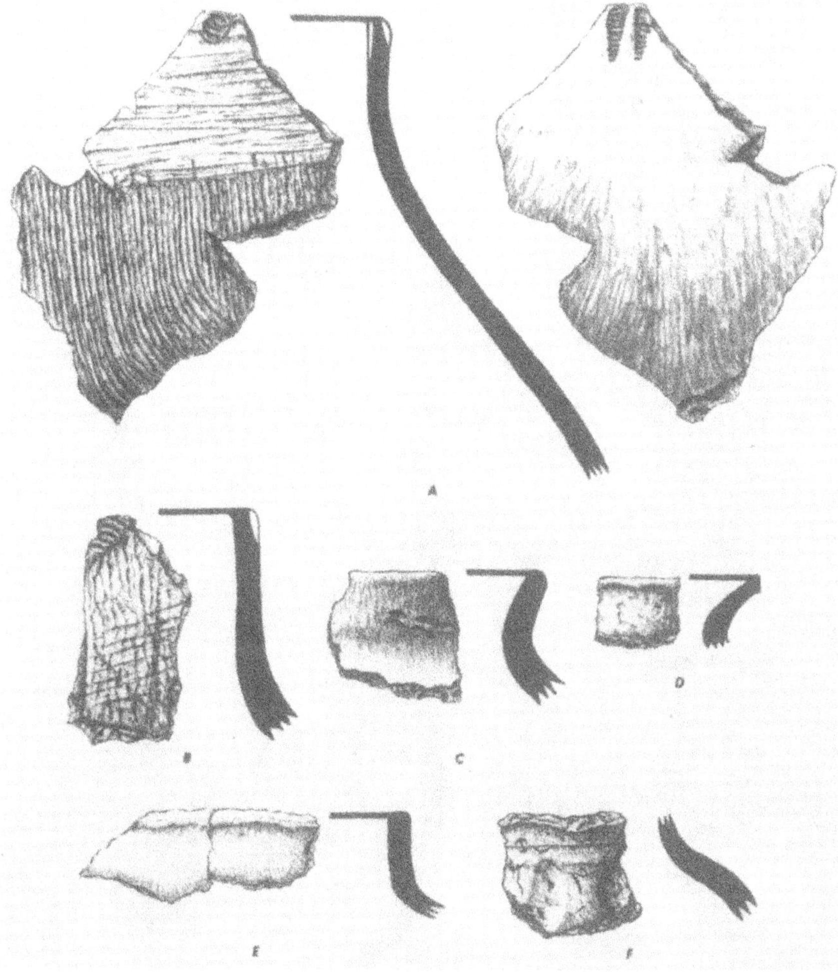

Plate 33. Leland Cord-marked rim sherds: (a) 47-Wp-26, S1000W390-2-1; (b) S985W405-2-27; Grand River Trailed: (c) S895W400-2-1; (f) S850W412-2-3; Grand River Plain: (d) S830W430-3-46; (e) S885W400-2-111 (artifacts approximately one-half natural size).

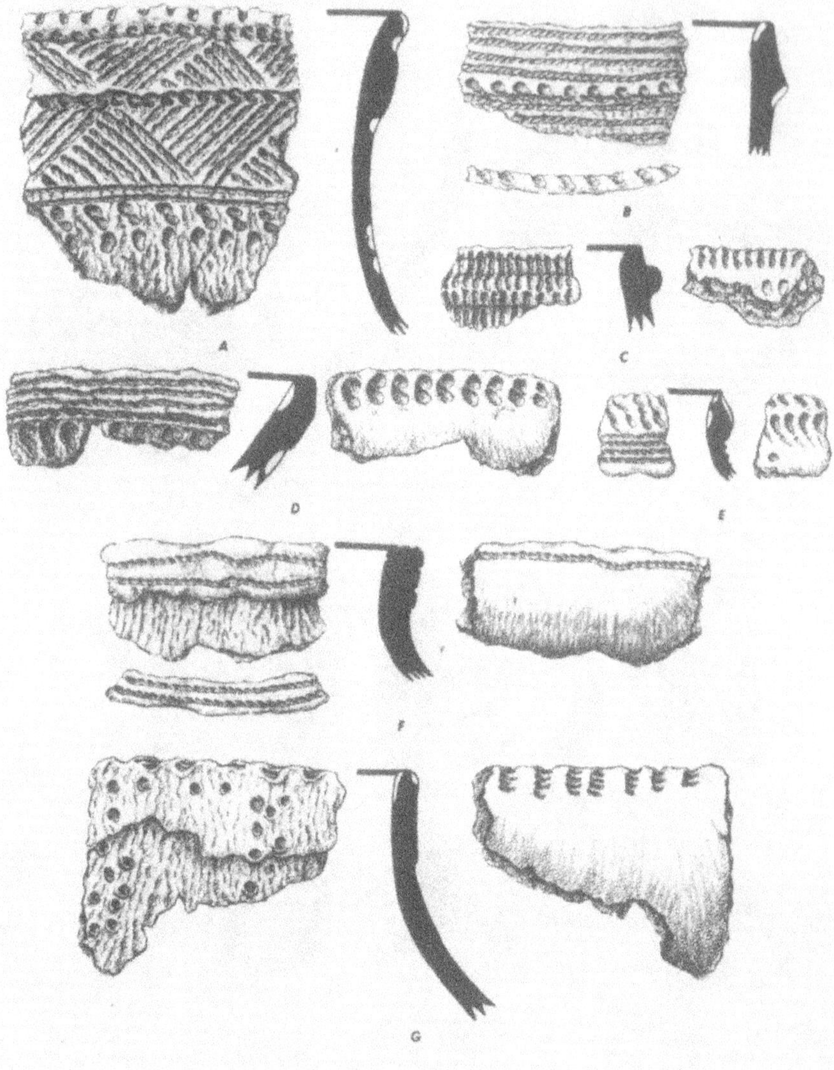

Plate 34. Aztalan Collared rim sherds: (f) 47-Wp-26, S885W415-2-109; (g) Mound 19, S640W212-3-1; Hahn Cord Impressed: (c) S885W400-2-107; Point Sauble Collared: (a) 47-Wp-70, F10-2 and 10, S115W45-2-5 and S115W50-3-1; (b) 47-Wp-26, S855W415-2-116; (d) S855W405-2-69; (e) S970W405-2-20 (artifacts approximately one-half natural size).

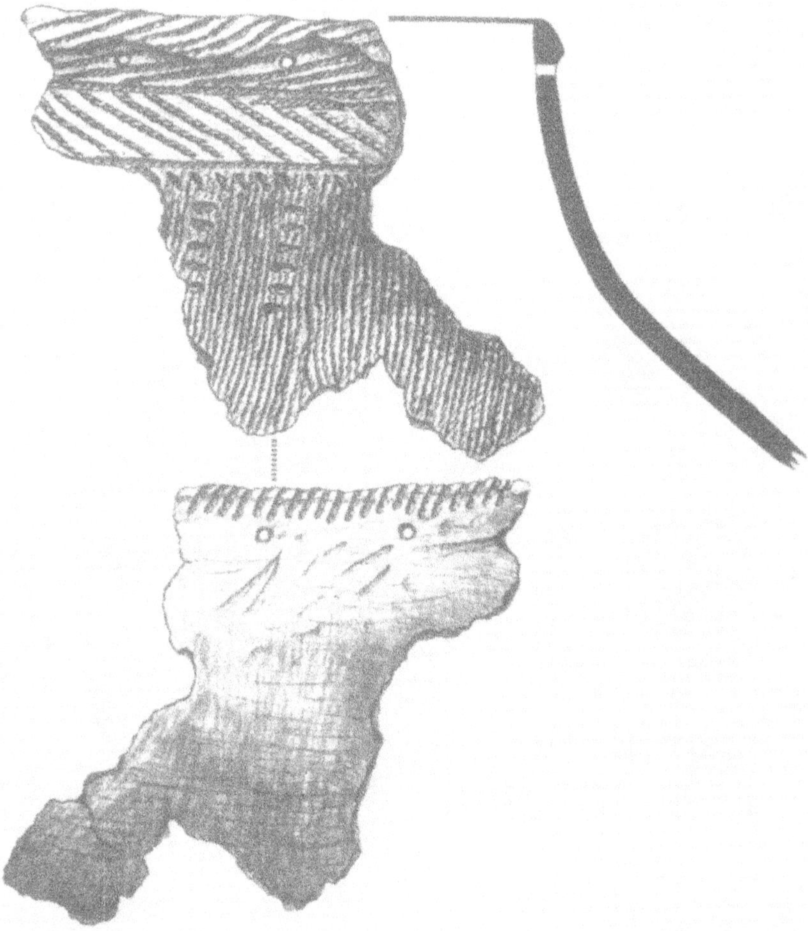

Plate 35. Point Sauble Collared rim sherd: 47-Wp-26, Mound 17, feature 6 (approximately one-half natural size).

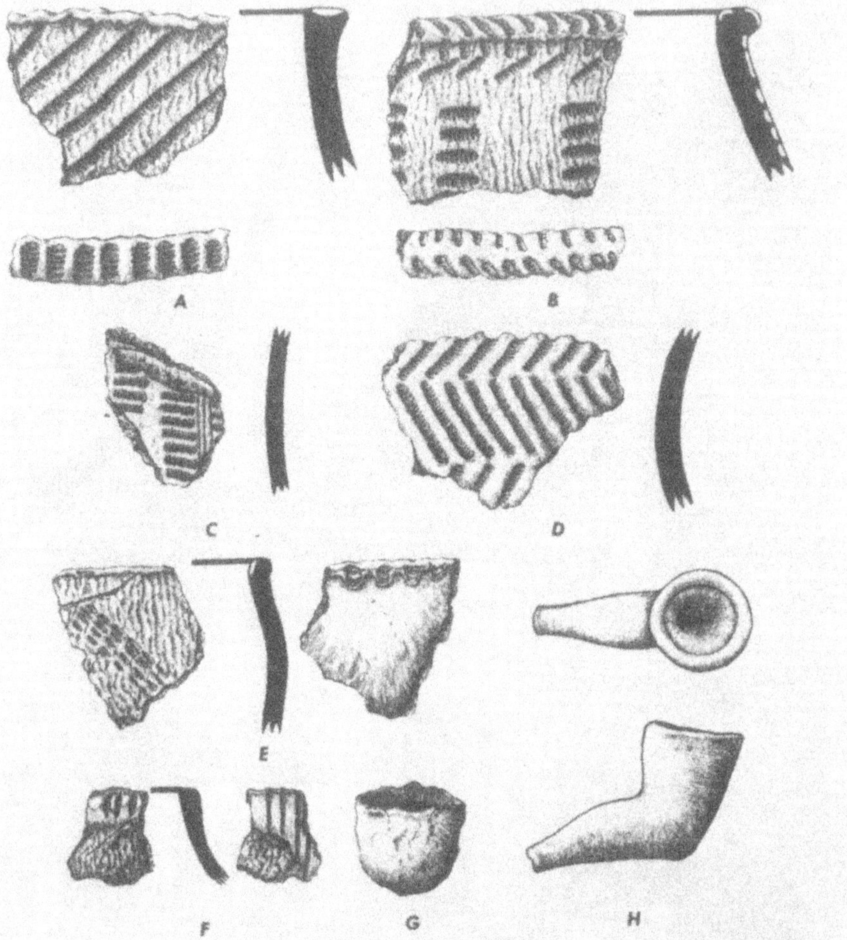

Plate 36. Heins Creek Corded Stamped rim sherds: (a) 47-Wp-70, S110W55-2-3; (b) S105W45-1-23; (e) 47-Wp-26, S865W425-2-7; body sherds: (c) S700W375-1-2; (d) N0E140-3-1; Leland Cord-marked rim sherd: (f) S860W410/415-2-107; child's pot: (g) 47-Wp-70, house floor, S120W55; elbow pipe: (h) 47-Wp-26, Mound 3, S430W170-2-12 (artifacts approximately one-half natural size).

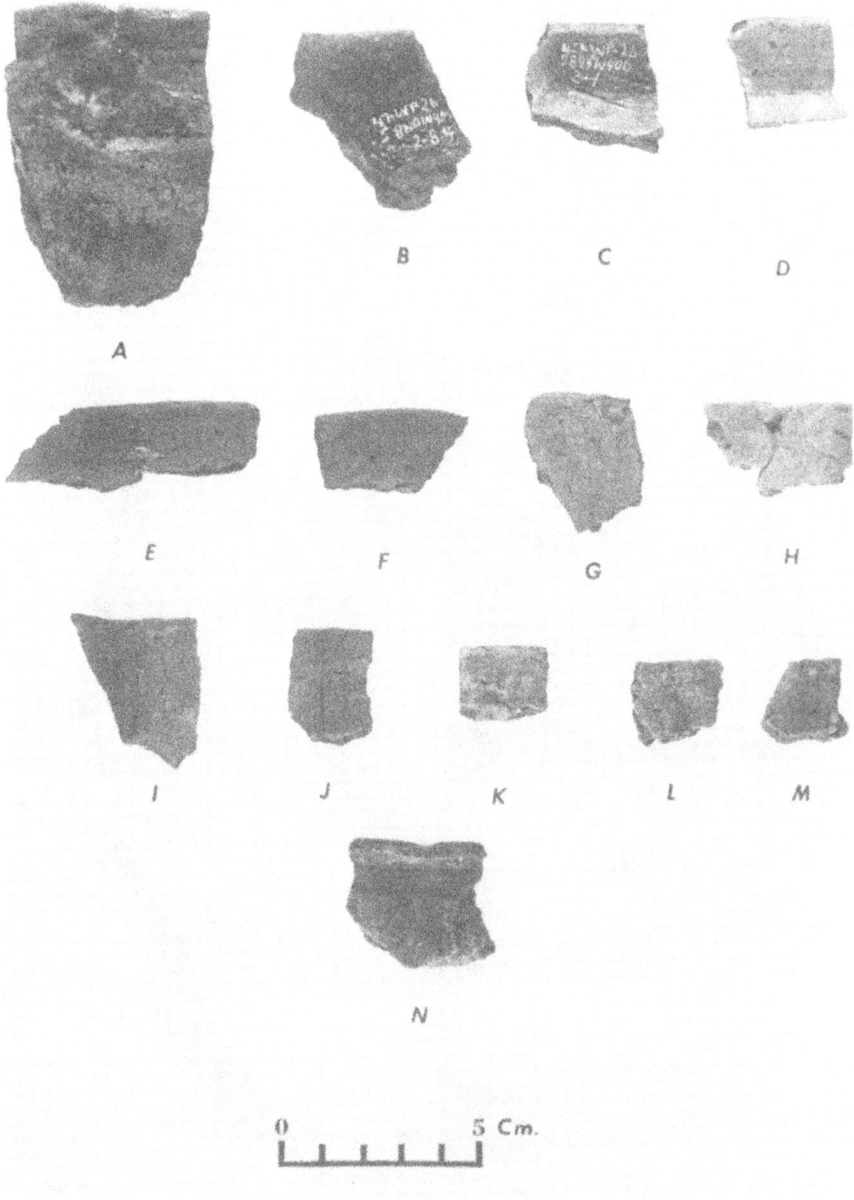

Plate 37. Grand River Trailed rim sherds: (c) 47-Wp-26, S895W400-2-1; (d) S860W405-2-83; (j) S865W405/415-2-118; body sherd: (n) S850W412-2-3; Grand River Plain: (a) S860W400-2-53; (b) S860W405-2-84; (e) S855W400-2-111; (f) S890W400-2-2; (g) S825W425-2-65; (h) S935W400-2-13; (i) H3-F46-2; (k) S830W430-2-46; (l) S885W400-2-113; (m) S850/855W420/425-1-2.

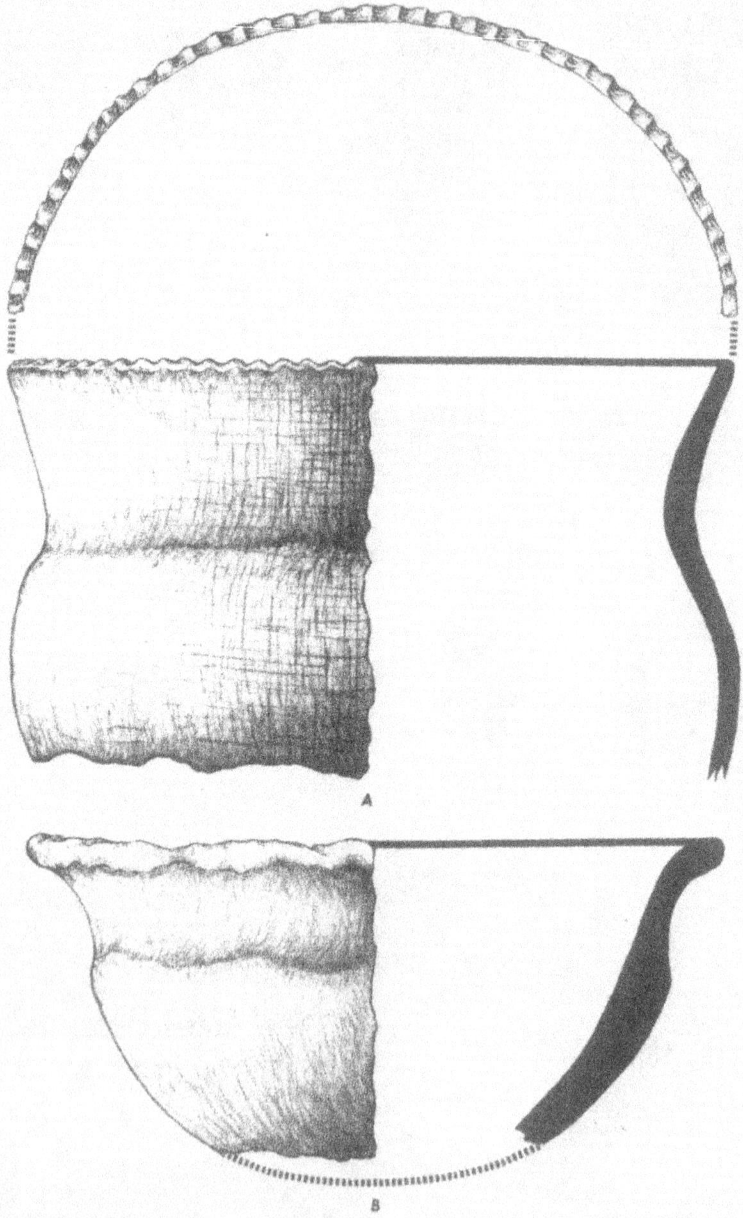

Plate 38. (a) Leland Cord-marked: 47-Wp-26, feature 17, partial reconstruction. Orifice diameter 18 cm, rim thickness: 7 mm, lip thickness: 4 mm, reconstructed portion: 9.4 cm high. (b) Grand River Plain: S860W400-2-53 and S860W405-2-84, partial reconstruction. Orifice diameter: 18 cm, rim thickness: 8 mm, lip thickness: 9 mm, reconstructed portion: 7.3. cm high.

A
B
C
D
0
5 Cm.

Plate 39.

(a) Side Notched projectile points: Madison Side Notched: 47-Wp-26, Mound 3, (1965) S25E10-3-1; Side Notched: S860W410/415-2-96; 47-Wp-70, S120W45-4-3; S120W50-3-2; S120W55-3-11; 47-Wp-26, S935W405-2-32.

(b) Side Notched projectile point (b2): 47-Wp-26, S870W410-2-23; Corner Notched projectile points: 47-Wp-26, S835W400-2-55; S995W395-2-1; 47-Wp-70, S120W50-2-5; 47-Wp-26, Mound 19, S640W207-5-1.

(c) Waubesa Contracting Stem projectile points: 47-Wp-26, Mound 1, S380W219-2-1; 47-Wp-26 (1965) N35W5-4-2; 47-Wp-70, S115W50-4-3; 47-Wp-26, S435W235-2-1; 47-Wp-70, S115W45-2-16.

(d) Waubesa Contracting Stem projectile points (d1-3, d5): 47-Wp-26, S1010W380-3-2; Mound 12, S5W140-3-2; S955W405-2-17; Mound 24, S830W175-1-1; Durst Stemmed projectile point (d4): 47-Wp-26, S940W415-2-2.

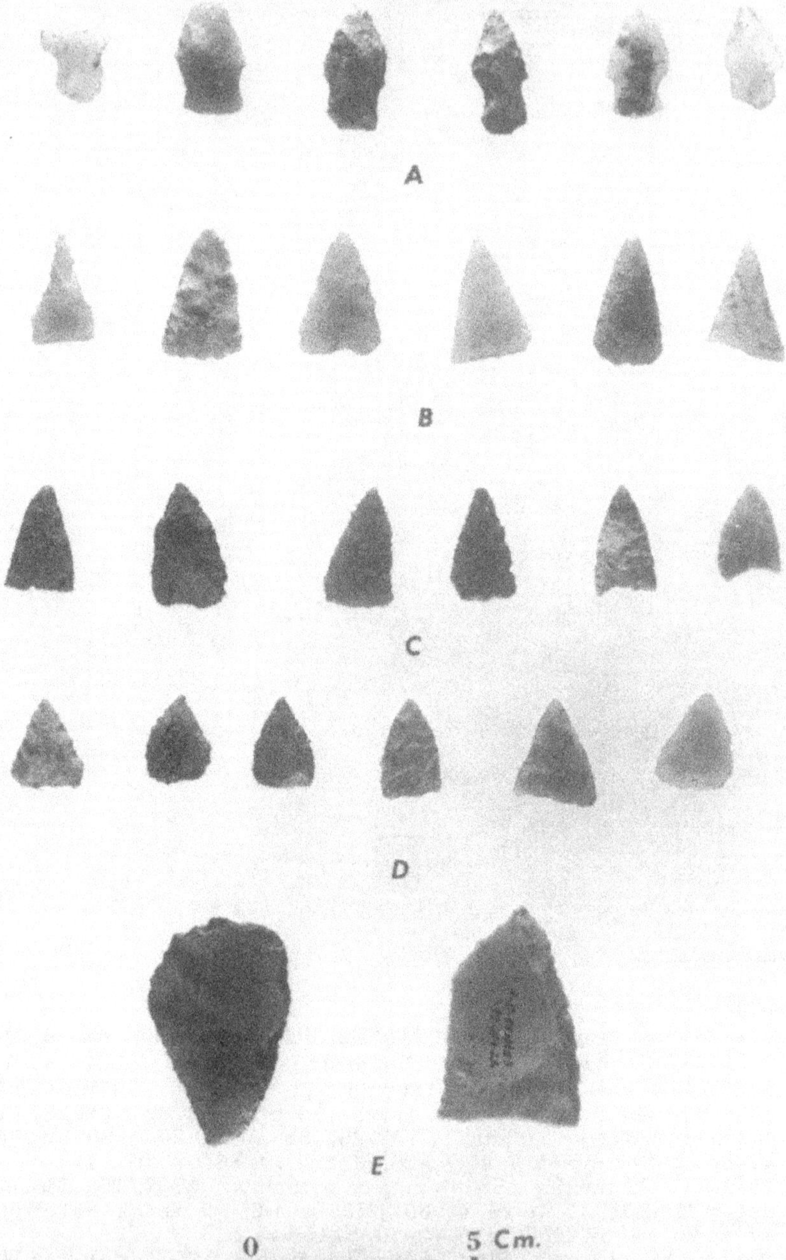
A
B
C
D
E
0
5 Cm.

Plate 40.

(a) Durst Stemmed projectile points: 47-Wp-26, F6-12; S855W415-2-106; S945W425-2-6; S890W400-2-10; S955W400-2-1; S865W425-2-14.

(b) Serrated Triangular projectile points (b1 and b6): 47-Wp-26, Mound 28, S895W297.5-3-1 and S835W405-2-99; Triangular projectile points (b2-5): 47-Wp-26, F34-2; S860W405/415-2-97; S990W395-2-13 and S865W405/410/415-2-163.

(c) Sanders Triangular projectile points (c2 and c6): 47-Wp-26, S835W410-2-52 and Mound 25, S1083W325-2-1. Serrated Triangular projectile points (c3-4): 47-Wp-26, S835W410-2-48 and Mound 3, S456W195-2-1. Triangular projectile points (c1 and c5): 47-Wp-26, S860W400-2-64 and S940W410-2-1.

(d) Sanders Triangular projectile points (d2-3): 47-Wp-26, Mound 25, S1083W325-2-2 and S870W410-2-24; Serrated Triangular projectile point (d6): 47-Wp-26, S990W400-2-14; Triangular projectile points (d1, d4 and d5): 47-Wp-26, Mound 3, S430W170-2-1; S950W4002-5; and S865W405/410/415-2-164.

(e) Scrapers: 47-Wp-26, S5W125-2-7 and 47-Wp-26, S5W120-2-1.

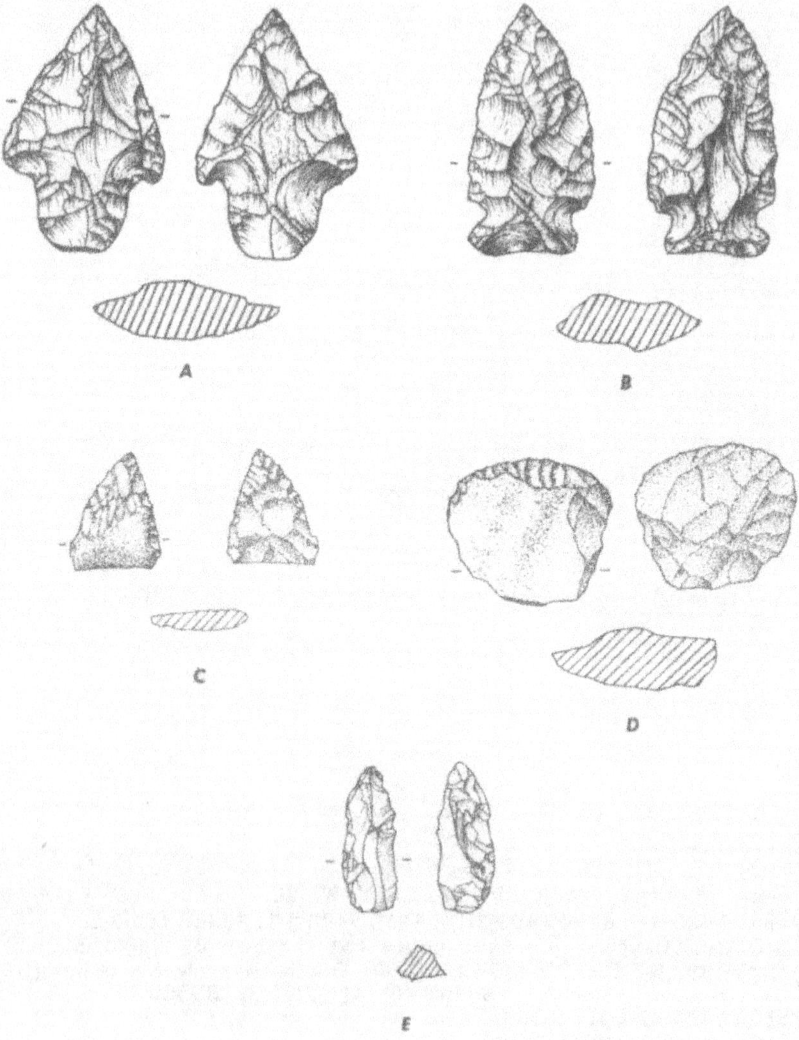

Plate 41. Waubesa Contracting Stem: (a) 47-Wp-26, Mound 1, (1965) N35W5-4-2; Madison Side Notched (b) 47-Wp-26 Mound 3, (1965) S25E10-3-1; Triangular (c) 47-Wp-26, Mound 1 N36W6.5-1-1; diminutive scraper (d) 47-Wp-26 Mound 3, (1965) S60E16-3-3; worked burin spall (e) 47-Wp-26, Mound 1, (1965) N30W10-2-11 (burin spall one-half larger than natural size).

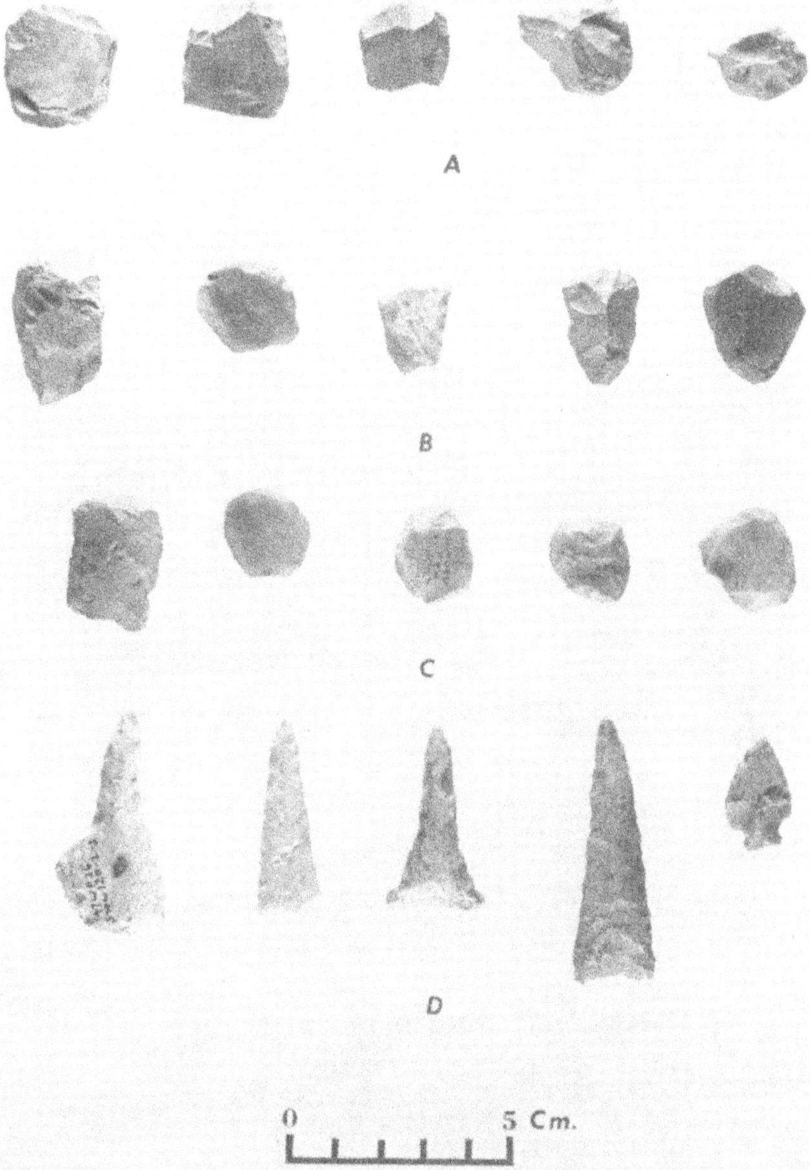

Plate 42. Diminutive scrapers: (a) 47-Wp-26, S860W410/415-2-94; Mound 12, S5W130-3-3; S940W435-2-9; area 9, N0E135-4-1; Mound 13, S35W155-2-1; (b) 47-Wp-26, S950W430-2-20; Mound 17, S535W207-5-2; area 9, N0E135-1-1; S5W120-2-4; S410W377-1-1; (c) 47-Wp-26, Mound 12, S5W135-2-1; S835W410-2-44; Mound 11, N20W125-2-3; S20W125-2-4; 47-Wp-70, S115W50-3-33; drills: (c) 47-Wp-26, S10W120-2-3; S940W435-2-10; H3, HF1-21; S995W410-2-2; graver: (d) 47-Wp-26, H3, F46.

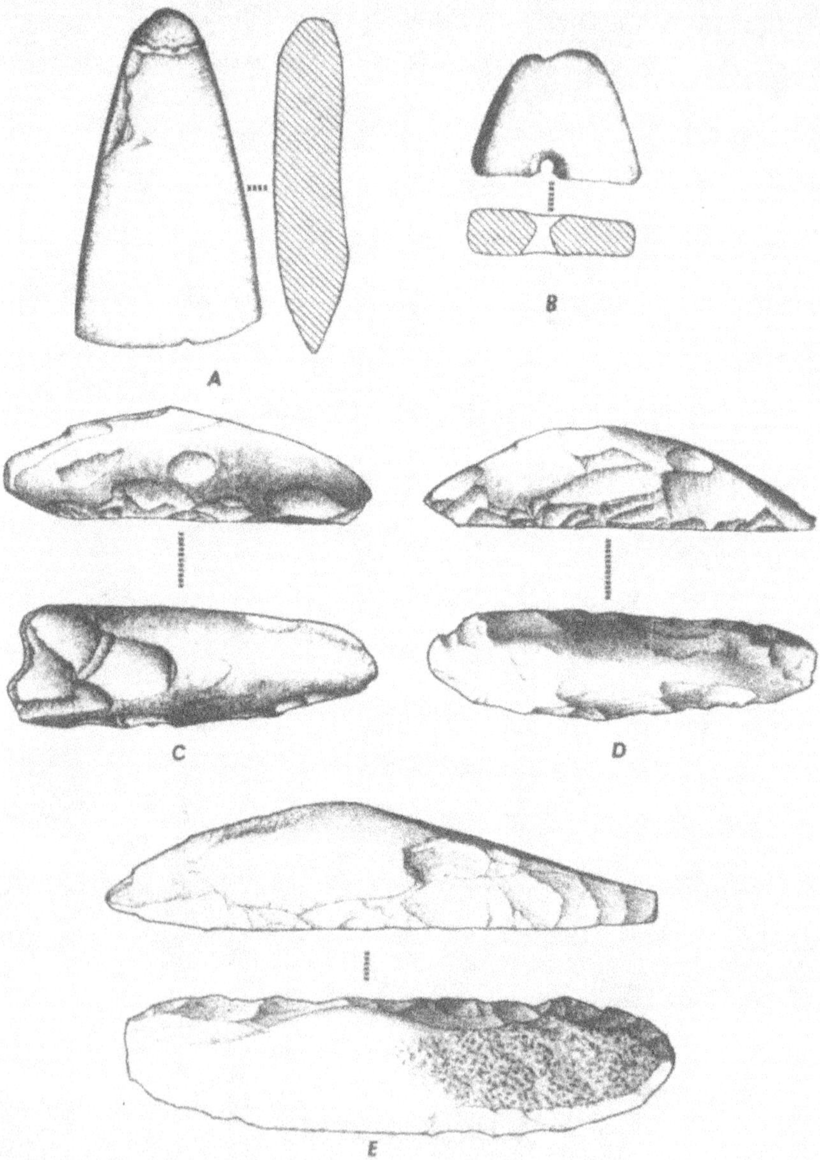

Plate 43. (a) Celt, 47-Wp-26, S241W287-2-1; (b) gorget, 47-Wp-26, S935W410-2-2; (c) adze, 47-Wp-26, Mound 17, S540W207-5-1; (d) adze, 47-Wp-70, S120W45-3-2; (e) adze, Sanders collection, 47-Wp-26-0 (artifacts approximately one-half natural size).

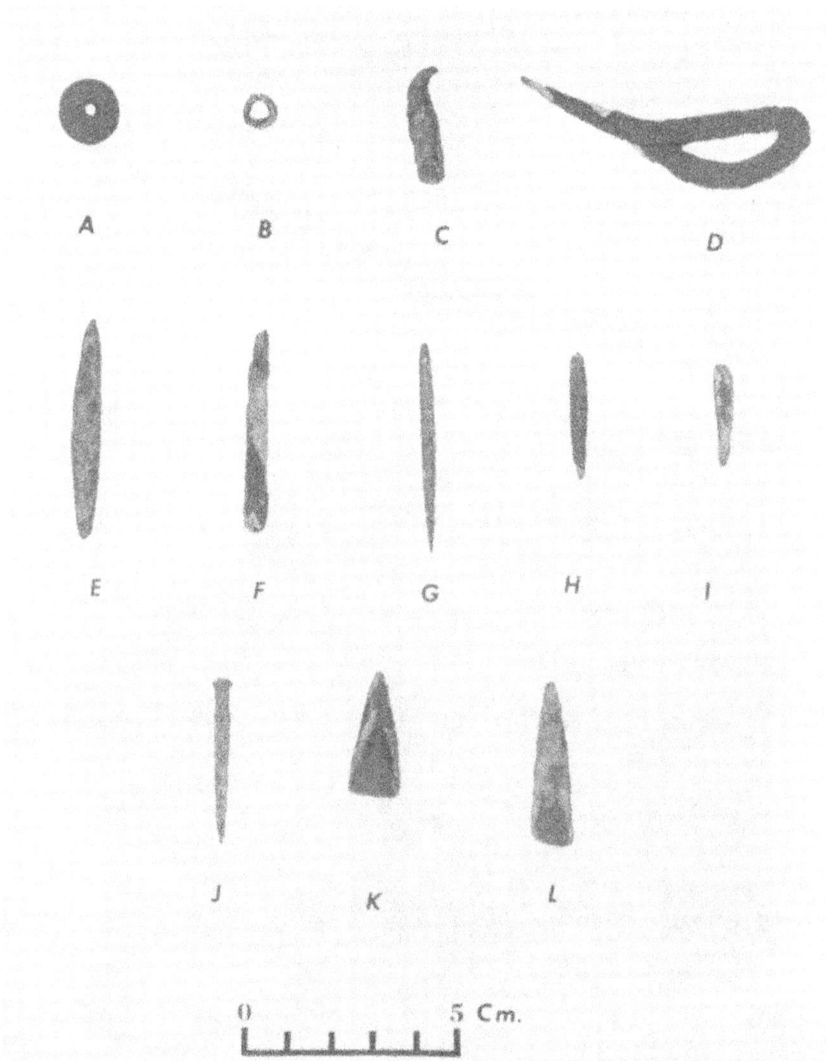

Plate 44. (a) Ceramic bead, 47-Wp-26, S860W420-2-2; (b) copper bead, 47-Wp-26, house 2, Fill-2; (c) copper pendant, 47-Wp-26, house 2, feature 40-3; (d) copper knife, 47-Wp-26, feature 18-1; (e)-(j) copper awls: 47-Wp-26, S830W430-2-1; feature 18-2; Mound 4, S355W112-2-6; 47-Wp-70, S120W45-4-1; S120W45-3-1; 47-Wp-26, feature 16-1; (k) copper conical point, 47-Wp-70, S110W55-2-1; (l) copper awl, 47-Wp-26, S850W400-feature 35-2-3.

Plate 45. Windrow Cord Impressed with its multiple stick cord-wrapped stick decoration at the lip and at the shoulder (above cord marking). 47-Mo-5, 0402-4-1.